Privilege and Prophecy

Privilege and Prophecy

Social Activism in the Post-War Episcopal Church

ROBERT TOBIN

Oxford University Press is a department of the University of Oxford. It furthers
the University's objective of excellence in research, scholarship, and education
by publishing worldwide. Oxford is a registered trade mark of Oxford University
Press in the UK and certain other countries.

Published in the United States of America by Oxford University Press
198 Madison Avenue, New York, NY 10016, United States of America.

© Oxford University Press 2022

All rights reserved. No part of this publication may be reproduced, stored in
a retrieval system, or transmitted, in any form or by any means, without the
prior permission in writing of Oxford University Press, or as expressly permitted
by law, by license, or under terms agreed with the appropriate reproduction
rights organization. Inquiries concerning reproduction outside the scope of the
above should be sent to the Rights Department, Oxford University Press, at the
address above.

You must not circulate this work in any other form
and you must impose this same condition on any acquirer.

Library of Congress Control Number: 2021925620

ISBN 978–0–19–090614–6

DOI: 10.1093/oso/9780190906146.001.0001

1 3 5 7 9 8 6 4 2

Printed by Sheridan Books, Inc., United States of America

For my parents,
faithful Episcopalians

Contents

Acknowledgments	ix
Abbreviations	xiii
1. An Establishment Church	1
2. All Sorts and Conditions (1945–1954)	10
3. Challenging the Church to Save It (1955–1959)	55
4. The New Breed Takes Charge (1959–1964)	89
5. Involvement Is Everything (1965–1967)	121
6. Passing Grace and Seized Microphones (1967–1969)	155
7. No Love without Justice (1970–1979)	200
8. A Prophetic Church?	247
Notes	253
Bibliography and Sources	327
Index	363

Acknowledgments

This book is the result of my effort to understand why the Episcopal Church in which I grew up felt so different from the one in which my parents had been raised a generation earlier. In trying to formulate at least a partial answer to this deceptively simple question, I have benefited from the help, enthusiasm, and insight of many people. Not least among these are my parents themselves, who have supported and encouraged me in this effort from the beginning. What follows is dedicated to them, both out of a deep personal gratitude and in recognition of the love and service they have rendered to the church throughout their lives. I also want to pay tribute to Gardiner Shattuck, Jr., whose own writings on the history of the Episcopal Church are exemplary and who has been unfailingly generous to me with his time and expertise. I am likewise indebted to my editor at Oxford University Press, Cynthia Read, who has kept faith with this project, even as I labored to complete it alongside full-time ministry and family life, and latterly, in the midst of a global pandemic.

For their readiness to share memories of certain individuals and important events, my thanks go to Douglas Carpenter, Michael Coburn, Philip Deloria, Lawrence Estey, Curtis Flowers, Frank Griswold, Janet Haugaard, Chris Hines, John Hooper, Pat Mathis, Barry Menuez, Anthony Morley, the late James Morton, Pamela Morton, Mary Nickerson, Muffy Paradise, John Rawlinson, Mimi Ayres Sanderson, Charlie Sumners, the late Arthur Walmsley, Albert Williams-Myers, Charles Willie, Sara Winter, and Lucila Woodard. Conversations and correspondence with these people have given me a more nuanced understanding of the priorities and assumptions that shaped Episcopal thinking during the post-war period.

In the course of my research, I was aided by many librarians, archivists, and historiographers. In particular, I am grateful to Mark Duffy and his staff at the Archives of the Episcopal Church, Wayne Kempton at the Diocese of New York, Diane Ney and Susan Stonesifer at Washington National Cathedral, and Christopher Pote and Joseph Thompson at Virginia Theological Seminary. These individuals were always eager to assist, as were

X ACKNOWLEDGMENTS

the reference librarians at the Episcopal Divinity School, the Seminary of the Southwest, and Virginia Theological Seminary.

More broadly, I am also grateful to the following archives and institutions for permission to cite unpublished materials in their collections: the Episcopal dioceses of Massachusetts, Minnesota, New York, Pennsylvania, Pittsburgh, Washington, and West Missouri; the Archives of the Episcopal Church, Austin; the Archives of the Cathedral of St. John the Divine, New York; the National Cathedral Archives, Washington; the Archives of Trinity Church Wall Street, New York; the John Hay Library, Brown University, Providence; the Butler Library, Columbia University, New York; the University Library, Cornell University, Ithaca; the University Archives, Harvard University, Cambridge; the Schlesinger Library, Radcliffe Institute for Advanced Study, Cambridge; the McWherter Library, University of Memphis; the Bentley Historical Library, University of Michigan, Ann Arbor; the University Libraries, Syracuse University; the Watkinson Library, Trinity College, Hartford; the Walter P. Reuther Library, Wayne State University, Detroit; the Divinity School Library, Yale University, New Haven; the Sherrill Library, formerly of the Episcopal Divinity School, Cambridge; the Christoph Keller, Jr. Library, General Theological Seminary, New York; the Archive of Women in Theological Scholarship and the Seminary Archives, Burke Library, Union Theological Seminary, New York; the African American Episcopal Historical Collection and Seminary Archives, Bishop Payne Library, Virginia Theological Seminary, Alexandria; and the Minnesota Historical Society, Minneapolis.

For additional copyright permissions, my thanks go to Sr. Helena, OSB (Ellen Barrett), Margarita Haugaard, Carter Heyward, Pamela Morton, Muffy Paradise, Diane Kennedy Pike, Nathan Pusey, Jr., Mimi Ayres Sanderson, Jim Wallis, Roberta Walmsley, William Weber, Sarah Willie-LeBreton, Sara Winter, and the Pauli Murray Foundation.

Most of the research for this book was undertaken during my tenure as chaplain and tutor at Oriel College Oxford. I am indebted to the Provost and Fellows of Oriel for an annual research grant and for a term of study leave in the spring of 2016. I am similarly indebted to the Board of Trustees of the African American Episcopal Historical Collection at Virginia Theological Seminary, from whom I received a generous research grant, and to the Bentley Library at the University Michigan at Ann Arbor for its award of a Bordin Gillette Research Fellowship. Alongside my thanks for such practical assistance, I am grateful to those who provided other forms of encouragement along the way: Susan Burnham, Richard Cheetham, Christopher

Chessun, Andrew Davey, Roy Foster, Cordelia and James Gelly, Isabel Gregory, Zachary Guiliano, Yvonne Horsfall Turner, the late Sam Hulsey, Tom Kennedy, John Kiddle, Cynthia Kittredge, Judith Maltby, Teresa Morgan, Alfred Moss, David Neaum, Nate Nickerson, Tom Poynor, Charles Stang, Tony and Pat Stoneburner, Moira Wallace, and Lauren Winner. Thanks likewise go to my fellow board members at the Historical Society of the Episcopal Church for stimulating conversation and useful feedback at our annual gatherings.

Lastly, I want to pay tribute to my wife, Olivia Horsfall Turner, who has accommodated this project in our lives for far longer than was reasonable to expect. For her infinite patience, keen editorial eye, and unwavering support, I am profoundly grateful.

Abbreviations

AAEHC	African American Episcopal Historical Collection, VTS
AEC	Archives of the Episcopal Church, Austin,
AEH	*Anglican and Episcopal History*
AFSA	Anglican Fellowship for Social Action
ATR	*Anglican Theological Review*
AWTS	Archive of Women in Theological Scholarship, UTS
BEDC	Black Economic Development Conference
BHL	Bentley Historical Library, University of Michigan, Ann Arbor
BIM	Boston Industrial Mission
CA	*Cathedral Age*
CALCAV	Clergy and Laymen Concerned About Vietnam
CLID	Church League for Industrial Democracy
CSR	Christian Social Relations
DioMass	Episcopal Diocese of Massachusetts
DioMinn	Episcopal Diocese of Minnesota
DioMo	Episcopal Diocese of Missouri
DioNY	Episcopal Diocese of New York
DioPenn	Episcopal Diocese of Pennsylvania
DioPitt	Episcopal Diocese of Pittsburgh
DioWash	Episcopal Diocese of Washington
DioWMo	Episcopal Diocese of West Missouri
DIM	Detroit Industrial Mission
ECF	Episcopal Church Foundation
ECW	Episcopal Church Women
EDS	Episcopal Divinity School, Cambridge, MA
EHPP	East Harlem Protestant Parish
ELSA	Episcopal League for Social Action
EPF	Episcopal Peace Fellowship
ESCRU	Episcopal Society for Cultural and Racial Unity
ETS	Episcopal Theological School, Cambridge, MA
ETSS	Episcopal Theological Seminary of the Southwest, Austin
EWC	Episcopal Women's Caucus
GCSP	General Convention Special Program
GTS	General Theological Seminary, New York
HMPEC	*Historical Magazine of the Protestant Episcopal Church*
IAF	Industrial Areas Foundation, Chicago

xiv ABBREVIATIONS

JAS	*Journal of Anglican Studies*
JUP	Joint Urban Program
LC	*Living Church*
MRI	Mutual Responsibility and Interdependence in the Body of Christ
NCAI	National Congress of American Indians
NCC	National Council of Churches
NCIM	National Committee for Industrial Mission
NYT	*New York Times*
OC	Operation Connection, Washington
PECUSA	Protestant Episcopal Church in the USA
SGC	Special General Convention II (1969)
SNCC	Student Nonviolent Coordinating Committee
SPIM	Society for the Promotion of Industrial Mission, Pittsburgh
TCH	Trinity College, Hartford
TCW	Trinity Church, Wall Street, New York
UBC	Urban Bishops Coalition
UBCL	Union of Black Clergy and Laymen
UBE	Union of Black Episcopalians
UML	University of Memphis Libraries, Memphis
UTC	Urban Training Center, Chicago
UTS	Union Theological Seminary, New York
VTS	Virginia Theological Seminary, Alexandria, VA
WNC	Washington National Cathedral
WP	*Washington Post*
WSU	Wayne State University, Detroit

1

An Establishment Church

Writing in the late 1920s about Christian denominations in the United States, the theologian H. Richard Niebuhr declared that "the Protestant Episcopal Church is still an English church."[1] This perception of the identity of the Anglican church in America has been common throughout much of the country's history. Notwithstanding its formal separation from the Church of England in 1789, many Americans have regarded the Episcopal Church as fundamentally alien, a kind of holdover from colonial times perpetuated under a different guise. Episcopalians themselves have often struggled to reconcile the values and sensibility of their ecclesiastical inheritance with the practical realities of being an independent church in a pluralistic setting.[2] At the heart of this inheritance lay the concept of "establishment," whereby a particular religious institution is legally integrated with and supported by the state and is expected to underpin the spiritual life of the nation as a whole.[3] In the English context, Elizabethan apologists such as John Jewel and Richard Hooker provided theological justifications for the established status of the Church of England, arguing that integration of church and state under the Crown ensured the health and well-being of Christian society.[4] Despite the turmoil that ensued in the following decades, the establishment principle emerged intact after the Act of Settlement in 1701, and whatever other differences they might have had, conforming churchmen were agreed on the essential rightness of their church order.[5] As befitted a Christian nation, England had at last achieved a constitutional framework under which its people might satisfy their political obligations in a manner pleasing to both God and king alike. The same also held true for the colonies across the Atlantic, at least through the first part of the eighteenth century.[6]

Admittedly, Anglicans were not alone in pursuing establishment in America: the Puritans had likewise instituted congregationalism as a form of state religion in parts of New England. But even in those colonies where the Church of England was not formally established, its unique relationship with the state conferred upon it a standing and influence out of all proportion to its size. Wherever they were, Anglican ministers assumed responsibility for

Privilege and Prophecy. Robert Tobin, Oxford University Press. © Oxford University Press 2022.
DOI: 10.1093/oso/9780190906146.003.0001

2 PRIVILEGE AND PROPHECY

the moral formation and pastoral care of their communities, whether their communities expected it or not.[7] And while it is evident that significant numbers of wealthy and privileged colonists conformed to the Established Church, it also claimed adherents from many other walks of life, among them farmers, fishermen, and tradesmen.[8] Thus, when the movement for independence began to spread in the 1760s, it was more than just a small elite who recognized it as both a political and religious act.[9] For those members of the Church of England who opted to remain in the new republic, the cultural and psychological adjustments required of them were acute. Clergy in particular had to adjust to an environment in which the exercise of spiritual leadership now depended on their powers of persuasion, rather than on the coercive power of the state.[10] Out of the ashes of revolutionary fervor and legal disestablishment, then, American Anglicans sought to create an independent, voluntary church that would still be faithful to their ecclesiastical and liturgical traditions. Chief among these, of course, was the episcopate. While central to Anglican claims to apostolicity, bishops nonetheless embodied what for many Americans were precisely the monarchical tendencies they had just fought to be rid of. The arrangement around which the Episcopal Church eventually coalesced in the 1780s—episcopal polity tempered by democratic constraints—appeared to be a suitably American answer to the English legacy. The child of Erastianism had emerged as but one denomination among many.[11]

Such an organizational settlement, however, did not automatically resolve deeper questions of Episcopal identity. As the Second Great Awakening dominated the country's religious life during the early decades of the nineteenth century, the Episcopal Church made limited public impact.[12] Institutional fragility and internal differences between its high and low church parties inhibited the church's ability to respond forcefully to its new environment.[13] Yet emboldened by the leadership of the third bishop of New York, John Henry Hobart, high churchmen in particular began to assert a clear alternative to the prevailing evangelical theology and culture. By the 1830s, American Anglicanism was once again making its presence felt, as its clergy gained in confidence and the number of converts from the other denominations started to swell.[14] For many, part of the attraction of the Episcopal Church was its rejection of the theological rigidity and moral intrusiveness of evangelicalism. But there was evidently a social attraction as well, as the formality and decorum of the church drew in those repelled by the coarser aspects of revivalism.[15] Up and down the East Coast and across the mission fields of the westward expansion, Episcopalianism appealed to the educated, the upwardly mobile, and the aesthetically sensitive.[16]

This growing popularity among particular segments of society confirmed suspicions among those who believed the church had never truly assimilated to its egalitarian setting.[17] What set Episcopalians apart from their compatriots, though, was more fundamental than matters of status and taste. As ingenious as the American adaptation of Anglican order and worship may have been, the order and worship remained rooted in the logic of their English origins, what Ephraim Radner has called the "integralist principle of forming one people according to one truth in one place for one purpose."[18] So, regardless of the practical concessions Episcopalians had made to religious pluralism, a deeply anti-pluralist impulse persisted among them. In this respect, an "establishmentarian" mindset remained long after formal disestablishment had occurred.[19] On the surface, at least, this mindset fit neatly with an unofficial religious establishment that had started to form around the Protestant denominations during the antebellum period. Despite (or perhaps even because of) the constitutional separation of church and state, these churches found themselves fulfilling a variety of important functions in American society. Through education, philanthropy, and a network of voluntary associations, together they exercised considerable influence in shaping the mores and character of the nation. In this way, a new "Protestant establishment" emerged and gradually filled the cultural vacuum left by the old colonial establishments.[20] Episcopalians embraced this new dispensation, even as they remained critically detached from it. This resulted in a paradoxical condition, whereby they operated simultaneously as "consummate insiders" and "elite outsiders."[21]

Fortifying the Episcopal Church's sense of otherness from the rest of American Protestantism was its improved relationship with the Church of England after the Civil War. Following the initial flurry of episcopal consecrations secured by the Americans in the 1780s, contact between the two churches had been limited.[22] But the Archbishop of Canterbury's decision to convene the first Lambeth Conference in 1867 assured Episcopalians that they were in fact part of a unique Christian tradition spanning the globe.[23] If this renewed connection bolstered the church's anglophile appeal at home, it also encouraged greater transatlantic communication among Anglican thinkers. One product of this exchange was the 1870 publication of *The Church-Idea: An Essay Towards Unity* by the Episcopal priest William Reed Huntington. In it, Huntington extolled the potential benefits of a

4   PRIVILEGE AND PROPHECY

"National Church" based on the core principles of Anglicanism. The purpose, he insisted, was not to recreate a legal establishment but to construct an ecumenical framework within which American Christians might come together to pursue a common mission.[24] While this proposal failed to gain serious traction among other denominations, it did provoke interest among Episcopalians, who regarded it as perfectly natural that their church should set the standard for such a venture.[25]

However much Huntington's ideas gratified the establishmentarian instincts of his co-religionists, they were born of a genuine desire to find a shared approach to the challenges of modern life. As members of a primarily urban denomination, he and other Episcopal activists were all too aware of the suffering brought about by the rapid expansion and industrialization of American cities. Here again they derived inspiration from what was happening in England, where Christian socialism had emerged in response to the same forces. Repelled by the greed and ruthlessness of competitive society and dismayed by the Church of England's failure to confront them, figures such as F. D. Maurice and John Ruskin promoted a vision of human cooperation rooted in the theology of the Incarnation.[26] With such precedents close to hand, Episcopalians took a leading role in developing the Social Gospel movement in the United States. Like its English equivalent, this movement emphasized social reform as foundational to Christian mission. Among its early proponents were two New York rectors, R. Heber Newton and Henry Codman Potter, both of whom were exposed to the realities of poverty and deprivation on the doorstep of their churches. Potter, who succeeded his uncle as bishop of New York in the 1880s, would become well known for his promotion of just labor practices.[27] Galvanized by Potter's leadership, in 1887 clerics James Huntington and W. D. P. Bliss formed the first Social Gospel organization, known as the Church Association for the Advancement of the Interests of Labor (CAIL). Certain of the church's responsibility to confront questions of labor and economics as part of its ministry in the world, CAIL became a fixture in industrial relations during the ensuing forty years of its existence.[28]

Few Episcopalians embraced the tenets of Christian socialism as fully as James Huntington and William Bliss. Even so, the Social Gospel made a lasting impression on the church's outlook and lent renewed vigor to its existing sense of responsibility for the well-being of the whole community. At the same time, by the close of the nineteenth century, Episcopalianism had become a byword for wealth and privilege. Although such a reputation did not reflect the mixed circumstances of the membership as a whole, the church's popularity among the upper classes confirmed its reputation for respectability.[29] Ambitious laity found the Episcopal Church to be a congenial environment in which to express their cultural dominance and sophistication.[30] Spurred on by their clergy, they also heeded the call of *noblesse oblige* by sponsoring an ever-expanding range of services to the poor and needy in city parishes. Yet rather than engender a greater sense of commonality, such charitable efforts often had the effect of reinforcing difference.[31] Indeed, the more the Episcopal Church gained in stature among the nation's elect, the less effective it became in securing the loyalties of those at the lower end the social and economic ladder.[32] Such a dynamic was to persist throughout the twentieth century and served to copper-fasten the church's exclusivist image. Even in those places where working-class Anglicans were to be found in sizable numbers, such as the mill towns of southern New England, their presence was regarded as increasingly anomalous, if not undesirable.[33] The relative narrowness of their class identity has proved a source of perennial ambivalence for Episcopalians, inspiring feelings of both pride and guilt, and helps explain their inarticulacy in addressing this feature of American life.[34]

By the start of the new century, then, certain traits and tendencies had converged within Episcopalianism to assure its standing as the religion of choice among America's ruling classes. The confidence of its establishmentarian worldview, the politeness and order of its worship, and the idealism of the Social Gospel all combined to generate a form of Christian faith agreeable to those in positions of power.[35] There was to be no better example of the church's prominence and ambition during this period than its decision to erect a neo-Gothic cathedral overlooking Washington, DC, as "a house of prayer for all people." This undertaking received the formal sanction of Congress in 1893, and both President Theodore Roosevelt and the Bishop of London addressed the crowd that gathered for the laying of the cornerstone in 1907.[36] While its character remained unabashedly Anglican, in the years to follow the cathedral became a natural setting for shared observances at turning points in the country's life.[37] The fact that a disproportionately large number of senior politicians and judges were themselves members of the Episcopal Church made this arrangement seem less peculiar than it might appear in retrospect. Not so readily noticed but equally revealing was the prevalence of Episcopalians in the upper echelons of the military. Episcopalianism set the religious tone at West Point during its first 150 years, such that nearly half the Army's generals were adherents between 1898 and 1940, a figure that

6   PRIVILEGE AND PROPHECY

still stood at 40% even after the Second World War. Similarly, over a quarter of midshipmen at the Annapolis naval academy between 1900 and 1920 were Episcopalian, an affiliation that rose to 42% among admirals by 1950. In addition to showing that many military officers came from Episcopal families, these figures indicate that a significant proportion also joined the denomination as part and parcel of their advancement in the ranks.[38] Here, as in other elite settings, the prestige of belonging to the Episcopal Church became self-perpetuating, as converts replenished its standing with their own success and eagerness to conform.

No Episcopalian in the twentieth century was to have a greater impact upon the United States than Franklin D. Roosevelt from 1932 to 1945. Notwithstanding his patrician background, the president had the common touch, instinctively empathizing with ordinary citizens amidst the hardships they endured.[39] Having been shaped by the muscular Christianity and service ethos of his headmaster, Endicott Peabody of Groton, Roosevelt possessed an engrained sense of both his right and obligation to improve society. Under the additional influence of his wife Eleanor and friends Frances Perkins and Harry Hopkins, he went on to express his Social Gospel values in the programs and legislation of the New Deal. Seen through the lens of his Episcopal formation, Roosevelt's mixture of old-school paternalism and progressive politics becomes more intelligible.[40] It also provides an important link between the Christian socialism of his youth and the liberal activism that would dominate the Episcopal Church after the war. If some of his co-religionists found the president's domestic policies too left wing, they largely shared his interventionist attitude toward the emerging conflict in Europe. Despite America's isolationism during the 1930s, Roosevelt and other anglophile Episcopalians naturally rallied to the British cause and made little secret of their preferences. Thus, when the United States finally entered the war in December 1941, members of the church took a leading role in the effort.[41]

Although American Protestantism had suffered a notable downturn during the 1920s and 1930s, this loss was easily forgotten during the resurgence it experienced after the Second World War.[42] Together, the mainline denominations enjoyed a substantial increase in membership and a corresponding structural expansion from the late 1940s to the early 1960s.[43] Buoyed up by this revival, the Protestant establishment reasserted itself as a tangible presence in national life. Church leaders were once again expected to stand as symbols and spokesmen for the aspirations of the American people.[44] Unsurprisingly, the Episcopal Church assumed a central place in this activity, while still managing to retain a clear sense of its Anglican distinctiveness.[45] To meet the needs of its burgeoning flock, the church now raised up clergy from a generation of men who had been shaped by the extraordinary events of the recent past. In keeping with denominational norms, most of them were educated WASPs reared in middle- and upper-middle-class homes, with a sprinkling from the white working class and a small but resolute band of African Americans.[46] Many had seen active service in the war and had internalized the military virtues of hierarchy, loyalty, and cohesion. As they entered ordained ministry, they shared with other veterans a spirit of masculine activism in tackling new challenges.[47] This conditioning served them well as they pursued the church's institutional development during the 1950s. Yet it was to take on a very different guise in the course of the 1960s, when a growing number of Episcopal priests lent their support to the civil rights and anti-war movements. Here social conscience and male assertiveness dovetailed, as clerics joined in marches, sit-ins, and other activities confronting the very establishment they represented.[48]

Of course, the upheavals that engulfed the Episcopal Church in the sixties were not unique but typified what Digby Baltzell has called "the most antiauthoritarian, anti-elitist and disestablishmentarian decade in American history."[49] With post-war prosperity had also come a crisis of meaning, as middle-class whites increasingly questioned the consumer lifestyle they had fought so hard to attain.[50] Longing for greater authenticity, they began to romanticize outsiders—both groups and individuals—whom they identified as untainted by materialism and social convention.[51] This impulse went hand in hand with a skepticism toward institutions in general, including the mainline denominations in which the affluent had commonly been reared. Such a stance was encouraged by certain religious leaders, who were quick to point out the shortcomings of their own churches. As guilt over past failings took root, self-recrimination became reflexive in liberal Protestant circles.[52] For Anglicans, this rejection of establishment norms was to prove particularly disruptive, forcing them to reconsider inherited ideas about their role in society and relationship to power. Setting aside the *noblesse oblige* of their fathers, some of them concluded it was now their Christian duty to relinquish privilege rather than to use it.[53]

Just how much post-war Episcopal progressives articulated a distinctive theological viewpoint, rather than simply parroting the sentiments of secular culture, has long been a source of debate.[54] Nonetheless, those who maintained a critical stance toward both church and state often regarded

8 PRIVILEGE AND PROPHECY

themselves as justified by biblical precedents. Looking back to the words and deeds of the great Hebrew prophets, they were inspired in their efforts to confront the injustice they saw all around them.[55] Invoking the prophetic tradition became a way for church activists to express their dissent within the Judeo-Christian framework, while also tapping into the countercultural sensibilities of the sixties.[56] What they failed to recognize was how fundamentally conservative their Old Testament role models actually were. These prophets had attacked the religious and political structures of their day in an effort to redeem rather than to destroy them, suffering all manner of opprobrium while championing their integrity and survival.[57] For liberal Episcopalians, however, prophecy served as a rationale for endorsing a variety of ideas and causes, some of a decidedly iconoclastic nature.[58] The frequency with which activists employed the concept in these years points to a crucial change taking place within the discourse of the Episcopal Church. Assuming the prophetic mantle became a means for progressives not so much to save the establishment as to dissociate themselves from it, even as it supplied them with a more culturally resonant way of asserting the church's relevance. Thus, by repudiating their own traditions, these empowered Christians sought to ensure their voices might still be heard in a post-establishment America.[59]

That mainline religion underwent a decline in vitality and influence during the latter part of the 1960s was undeniable.[60] By the mid-seventies, it was likewise evident that the Protestant establishment had begun to fall apart. While the reasons for this reversal were largely beyond their control, the oldline denominations experienced considerable discord while confronting their loss of position.[61] How each went about making sense of such changes and adapting to their impact is surely revealing of its essential identity and values.[62] Within Episcopalianism, this crisis was frequently construed as an internal battle over what the church's primary mission should be. The zeal with which many clergy had come to prioritize social action alienated conservative laypeople, who felt their leaders were too politicized and disengaged from the concerns of the membership, whereas for progressives, such activism was essential to making the church a more authentic and inclusive community.[63]

What follows is a study focused mainly on the liberal white men who dominated the Episcopal Church after the Second World War and ensured that social action became the defining feature of its domestic agenda.[64] Energetic, capable, and well-resourced, these leaders pursued a range of experimental ministries, learning programs, and policy reforms that would gradually shift the church's self-image from that of custodian of tradition to catalyst for change. To recognize certain priorities and attitudes they shared in common, however, is not to assume that their efforts were always coordinated or that no theological or cultural variation existed among them. Neither is it to take for granted the vital contributions that other Episcopalians likewise made to the church's development, often by directly challenging the prevailing assumptions of the national leadership. It is to suggest, however, that certain individuals, despite obvious geographical, generational, and social differences, converged to make questions of social justice central to the church's life and thought during this period.

Such efforts were often accompanied by telling ironies along the way. Not least among them was the readiness with which these liberals assumed their own establishmentarian status while lobbying so assiduously against the establishment itself. In a similar fashion, they routinely neglected their black, female, and working-class co-religionists, even as they espoused the causes of equality and liberation in the wider society. Still, whatever their shortcomings and contradictions, this generation of liberal leaders oversaw the transformation of Episcopal identity during the years 1945–1979. The church these men inherited was widely regarded as a bastion of WASP wealth and respectability; the one they eventually handed over was known for its commitment to progressive causes.[65] To acknowledge this fact is neither to absolve them of their failures nor to acquiesce in the whiggish tendency among Episcopalians to read their history as an unbroken march toward social and theological enlightenment.[66] But it is to insist that however much this shift was an accommodation to larger cultural forces, it also required a significant impetus from within, which is precisely what these men provided. In the process of doing so, they revealed some of the unique potential of the Episcopal Church, as well as some of its inherent dilemmas.

2

All Sorts and Conditions (1945–1954)

In April 1962, the retired bishop of Missouri, William Scarlett, was invited to conduct a seminar on the Social Gospel at the Episcopal Theological School in Cambridge, Massachusetts. "I have never thought there is a Social Gospel," Scarlett announced to the gathering. "There is only the Gospel, and it is indivisible. But out of the spiritual experience it offers men . . . there issues a social compulsion, a social compassion, which thrusts a man deep into the human problems of his day."[1] Scarlett was in fact deeply indebted to the Social Gospel movement but had long recognized its tendency to idealize human nature. In this he closely resembled his long-standing friend Reinhold Niebuhr. The two had first met as young men in the summer of 1923, when they joined a study tour of post-war Europe organized for ministers and academics. During the trip, they traveled together through the Ruhr valley, where they were shocked by evidence of atrocities committed against German civilians by occupying French soldiers.[2] In the face of such stark realities, they began to question the optimism of their liberal predecessors. The ease and simplicity with which these reformers had believed they could attain a just society appeared to the pair not only politically naïve but also theologically inadequate. In his 1932 book *Moral Man and Immoral Society*, Niebuhr upheld the goal of a just society but insisted its advocates must come to terms with the painful complexities of power while seeking to achieve moral ends.[3] The book struck a chord among Protestant progressives and provided the impetus for a new "Christian realism" capable of confronting the anxieties and deprivations of interwar life.[4] Sharing his friend's clear-eyed analysis of the human condition, Scarlett devoted his ministry to a brand of activism that constantly affirmed the relationship between personal faith and public witness. In Niebuhr's estimation, if there really was no such thing as the Social Gospel, it was because people like Scarlett had shown what a truly integrated Christian life should look like.[5]

Growing up in a middle-class Episcopal home in Columbus, Ohio, Scarlett (1883–1973) had assumed from an early age that social improvement was inherent in the church's mission. A close family friend and mentor was

Privilege and Prophecy. Robert Tobin, Oxford University Press. © Oxford University Press 2022.
DOI: 10.1093/oso/9780190906146.003.0002

ALL SORTS AND CONDITIONS 11

Washington Gladden, long-time pastor of Columbus's First Congregational Church and a nationally renowned figure in the Social Gospel movement. Looking back on Gladden's influence, Scarlett paid tribute to a fearless Christian leader who had "stirred the religious and social consciences of thousands of men and women all over this Land." After graduating from Harvard in 1905 and spending a year ranching in Nebraska, Scarlett entered Episcopal Theological School (ETS) to prepare for ordination. During his studies at the seminary he read Walter Rauschenbusch's *Christianity and the Social Crisis* (1907), which "came as a great light to many of us who were searching for relevance in Religion. . . . I know that this book helped to keep in the Christian Ministry a number of men who were beginning to wonder if it was the place for them, I among them."[6] Rauschenbusch's assertion of the continuing importance of Christianity in redressing society's ills reassured young liberals like Scarlett, who were struggling to find both spiritual meaning and social purpose in an increasingly secular world.[7] In the event, Scarlett was ordained to the priesthood in 1910 while serving his curacy at St. George's Church in New York. Just a year later he was called as dean of Trinity Cathedral in Phoenix, where he remained for eleven years until being appointed to the same post at Christ Church Cathedral in St. Louis.

It was during his tenure as dean of St. Louis in the 1920s that Scarlett gained a reputation for public advocacy and ecumenical outreach. He proved popular not only with Missouri Episcopalians but also among the city's Jewish and black communities, who saw him as their champion within the Protestant establishment.[8] When Bishop Frederick Johnson called for a coadjutor in 1929, Scarlett was the overwhelming choice and was consecrated in May 1930. Succeeding Johnson as diocesan bishop in 1932, he quickly demonstrated his activist approach by intervening in local labor disputes, using his position to gain access to both state and federal authorities.[9] At the same time, he also began to speak out across the diocese against racial segregation, which unsurprisingly alienated many of his co-religionists. Recalling some of the negative reactions he received during the first years of his episcopate, Scarlett observed that "those who were advocating the principle of Equality many years before the Supreme Court decisions made it respectable expected brickbats and were not disappointed. And from sources where one might least anticipate it, at times from those one regarded as friends." As a socially progressive bishop, Scarlett was quickly discovering that under the polite veneer of Episcopal respectability sometimes lay much more ruthless impulses. Notwithstanding his "realist" stance, he admitted that "it has

12   PRIVILEGE AND PROPHECY

always interested and shocked me to see how far a few so-called 'best' citizens [and] 'good' church people will go in the distortion of truth, when . . . their prejudices and selfish interests are challenged."[10]

Meanwhile, the new bishop displayed a certain ruthlessness of his own when recruiting clergy from across the country to serve in his diocese.[11] In the years to come, a significant number of future leaders of the Episcopal Church came under Scarlett's tutelage at the start of their ministries.[12] Prominent among them was future presiding bishop John E. Hines (1910–1997), who came from the small town of Seneca, South Carolina. The youngest child of a Presbyterian father and an Episcopalian mother, Hines was educated in the public schools. His father, the local doctor, dedicated himself to serving both white and black members of the community, an example of Christian integrity his son cited as essential to his own moral formation.[13] Under his mother's guidance, Hines was confirmed in the Episcopal Church and subsequently gained a scholarship to enroll at the University of the South in 1926. From there he went directly to Virginia Theological Seminary (VTS) in 1930 to train for ordained ministry. Virginia's low-church liberalism suited Hines, with its emphasis upon biblical exegesis and homiletical skill. Yet even as he flourished in his studies, occasional visits to nearby Washington reminded him of the destitution wrought by the nation's deepening economic crisis. When it came time to prepare a senior thesis, he chose to write on Archbishop William Temple, whose social vision of "engagement in God's name with the world" inspired him.[14] Competent, outgoing, and socially concerned, Hines was precisely the sort of clergyman Will Scarlett wanted in Missouri.

Hines arrived in St. Louis in September 1933 to serve his curacy under Karl Morgan Block, rector of the vibrant and affluent Church of St. Michael and St. George. A powerful preacher, Block would go on to serve as bishop of California in the 1940s and 1950s. Hines credited Block with showing him during these early days that "you could be an administrator and still have compassion, that you didn't have to be insulated from people just because you were administering some kind of institution or institutional setup." This insight became an article of faith for Hines throughout his ministerial career, and not only as a lesson in pastoral sensitivity but more broadly as an affirmation of the church as a valid agent of social reform. In Scarlett he identified what he considered "an authentic replication of the great prophetic tradition in Christianity," an activist bishop willing to engage the world's problems in their complexity and to work for fundamental, not merely cosmetic, change. Equally important, Hines recalled that Scarlett never undertook "the business of social change without its religious Gospel roots. . . . In fact, he was very articulate and very careful to connect them."[15] Occasional visits by Reinhold Niebuhr to the bishop's monthly clergy gatherings strengthened Hines's interest in the tough-minded, realist approach the two older men espoused, as did close study of Niebuhr's growing body of writings. As a result, Hines would eventually describe his own theological position as "Niebuhrian."[16]

Another promising young cleric to fall under Scarlett's spell during this time was Stephen F. Bayne, Jr., whom the bishop recruited to become rector of Trinity Church in St. Louis in 1934. Although himself more at home in the liberal evangelical tradition, Scarlett was eager to secure the best priest possible whose churchmanship suited the city's only Anglo-Catholic parish. A New Yorker by birth and upbringing, Bayne (1908–1974) came from a close-knit, middle-class Episcopal family and was educated at Trinity School on the Upper West Side. A brilliant student, he went to Amherst College at the age of sixteen and then on to General Theological Seminary (GTS) five years later. There he encountered a faculty grounded in Anglo-Catholic orthodoxy but committed to modern scholarship, a combination that would characterize Bayne's own theological position.[17] It was at General that he was also taught to regard the Episcopal Church as accountable not just to its own members but to society at large. "It is perhaps needless to point out that this quality of national responsibility is bred into all of us who are even the remotest children of the Church of England," he noted later. "Even in secularised America a 'parish' is still a geographical term, and when a man is instituted into a parish, he must accept the cure of souls for a whole community. But actually this is in large part a fiction, and we know it."[18] While Bayne accepted there was much about this ecclesiastical inheritance that might be unrealistic in practical terms, it continued to shape his vision of what Episcopalians should aspire to as members of the universal church.

Sharing this catholic approach to parochial ministry was his seminary classmate John Vernon Butler (1906–1983), a dedicated high churchman and fellow Amherst graduate, who remained close to Bayne for the rest of his life. Even when their respective careers separated them geographically, the two men maintained a steady correspondence that was often bantering in tone but serious about the nature and work of priesthood.[19] The year before Bayne and his wife moved to Missouri, Butler was called as rector of St. Peter's in Springfield, Massachusetts, having served a two-year curacy in New York. The young priest thrived at St. Peter's, an Anglo-Catholic parish that allowed him to give full liturgical expression to his tractarian

14 PRIVILEGE AND PROPHECY

principles.[20] At the same time, it was a community peopled by "an economic class ill able to cope with the hard times" of the Depression, such that Butler quickly found himself engaged in a whole range of social welfare activities. This work attracted the attention of his bishop, W. Appleton Lawrence, who later put Butler in charge of Christian Social Relations (CSR) for the Diocese of Western Massachusetts.[21] Confronted by widespread need, ritualists like Butler and Bayne regarded the sacramental life of the church as anything but escapist. Rather, it was the necessary spiritual basis on which to recognize the humanity of others and to frame a compassionate and informed response to their suffering.[22]

Whatever their theological orientation, clergy across America were challenged by the sheer scale of hardship they encountered all around them. In September 1935, President Roosevelt sent a "letter of inquiry" to over 121,000 ministers, soliciting their views on New Deal policies. The responses were predictably diverse, but the overwhelming majority commended the president for his efforts to help those in immediate, dire need. Tacit in this praise was an acknowledgment that the churches' traditional, voluntarist methods for managing communal well-being were no match for the systemic problems the country now faced.[23] Such an endorsement, however, did not necessarily mean a wider sympathy for the administration's political and economic philosophy, which many regarded as excessively interventionist. As a group, Episcopal clergy conformed to this pattern, and despite having one of their own laymen in the White House, were slightly more critical of the government than average.[24] If this posture was in certain respects contradictory, it was not new. Despite the notable involvement of Episcopalians in the Social Gospel movement for over half a century, most clergy and laity remained wary of its structural critiques of industrial society and preferred instead to focus on the amelioration of local conditions.[25]

Small though they might be in number, reform-minded Episcopalians were nonetheless becoming increasingly influential in shaping the social agenda of the national church.[26] Alongside Will Scarlett, another Episcopalian rooted in the Social Gospel and active throughout the interwar period was educator and activist Vida Dutton Scudder (1861–1954). Initially educated at the Boston Girls' Latin School and Smith College, Scudder did postgraduate study at Oxford before taking up a teaching post in literature at Wellesley College in 1887. Pushing against the constraints of her Brahmin background, she became deeply involved in the Christian Socialist movement and in promoting the rights of labor among the privileged circles of the

Boston intelligentsia and the Episcopal Church.[27] Scudder formally joined the Socialist Party in 1911, only to split with it over her support of American intervention in the First World War. She retained her commitment to radical politics but believed it was essential to create a united Christian left that could draw together socialists and liberals in defending civil liberties and pressing for industrial reform. Thus in 1919 she spearheaded the creation of the Church League for Industrial Democracy (CLID), which identified the conflict between capital and labor as its central concern without explicitly endorsing socialism. The Church League proved an effective platform for educating Episcopalians about economic realities and encouraging support within the church for workers' rights. Among its most immediate legacies was the work it did with Episcopal seminaries. In 1926, a "Students in Industry" project was set up, through which seminarians took industrial jobs during the summer vacation and spent weekends in conversation with union organizers, businessmen, and others about the relationship between church and workplace.[28] One student to take part in this program was Joseph Fletcher (1905–1991), a student at ETS who later returned there as a professor and became well known in the 1960s as an advocate of situation ethics.[29]

Working closely with Scudder before and after the Second World War was William B. Spofford, Sr. (1892–1972), a priest who became executive secretary of the Church League in 1924. A native of Claremont, New Hampshire, he took his B.S. degree from Trinity College Hartford in 1914, followed by preparation for ordination at Berkeley Divinity School in New Haven. After serving two years as a master at St. Paul's School in Concord, New Hampshire, in 1919 Spofford became rector of St. George's Church in Chicago. Soon after his arrival there, he was appointed editor of *The Witness* magazine, which had been founded by Bishop Irving P. Johnson of Colorado a few years before as an independent journal focused on the Episcopal Church's social mission. Spofford held the post for more than fifty years, running the magazine alongside parish assignments in New Jersey and Pennsylvania until 1948 and then full-time until his death in the early 1970s. Under his stewardship, *The Witness* served not only as a mouthpiece for the cause of industrial democracy but a rallying point for a whole range of progressive causes. It also became an occasional sparring partner of *The Living Church*, a national weekly with an Anglo-Catholic sensibility and more moderate social views. In criticizing both the Church League and *The Witness* for being too radical politically, *The Living Church* reflected the prevailing attitudes of Episcopalians

16 PRIVILEGE AND PROPHECY

generally.[30] Yet the leftist vision of Scudder, Spofford, and others was leaving its mark on the church's leaders, a disjunction that would prove a major source of tension in the decades to come.[31]

That such a disjunction was growing became obvious to Will Scarlett as he got to know the wider church community in the course of the 1930s. "When I first joined the House of Bishops," he later admitted, "I thought I would be getting into a very conservative group. Nothing could be further from the truth." At General Conventions, he noted, the bishops rarely failed to pass progressive resolutions on social issues, usually unanimously. By contrast, the House of Deputies, composed of priests and laymen, tended to be more circumspect about such matters, and these same resolutions often ran into strong opposition.[32] As a well-known advocate of liberal causes, Scarlett grew accustomed to navigating such resistance as he urged the church to engage with the vital concerns of the day. At the General Convention in 1940, he was appointed chair of a new joint commission mandated "to keep themselves informed regarding the work of the Archbishop of York"—a reference to recent English initiatives headed by Archbishop William Temple investigating forms of social reconstruction in the post-war world.[33] Joining Scarlett in this effort were fellow bishops Beverley Tucker of Ohio and Charles C. J. Carpenter of Alabama, both known to share his eagerness to bolster the church's role in public affairs. The commission's first report, entitled *A Better World for All Peoples* and written mainly by Scarlett, was presented to the General Convention in 1943.[34] Disseminated more widely in pamphlet form, it sought not just to acquaint Episcopalians with contemporary social thought in the Church of England, but in so doing, also to impress upon them the significance of their own responsibilities: "Nothing is more important than that the people of the Christian Church be acutely aware of the problems which lie ahead, and prepared to make their decisions on the basis of their Christian convictions."[35]

When the Second World War finally came to an end in the summer of 1945, most Americans were eager to get on with rebuilding their own lives. For Bishop Scarlett, though, to have won the war hardly meant winning the peace, and he continued to press Episcopalians to embrace their calling as agents of reconciliation in a broken world. Yet before they could hope to do so effectively, Christians must first recognize the war as a sign of their own failure, for there had been "within Christendom no unifying conception strongly enough held, widely enough held, to overcome the tensions and cleavages between men and nations."[36] If the churches had failed to counteract the forces of hate that gave rise to the war in the first place, then plainly the problem was not with the Gospel but with the way it had been practiced and preached. "[T]he technique of Christianity has failed," Scarlett declared in December 1945. "For the techniques on which Christianity has depended are sermons, services, rituals. And it has been found this is not enough." Instead, he reasoned, "we have to go farther today. I think we have to organize. I think we have to organize so as to bring our ultimate beliefs to bear on our practical political decisions if we are going to achieve what we as Christian people should achieve in this crisis of humanity."[37] Here Scarlett's Social Gospel impulses once again come to the fore, shorn of sentiment by years of economic depression and global conflict, but nonetheless dedicated to lending substance to religious piety through coordinated action. And out of a sense of repentance for past shortcomings must proceed a renewed sense of urgency among Christians in seeking to shape the post-war dispensation.[38]

Under the auspices of the Joint Commission on Social Reconstruction, in 1946 Scarlett oversaw the publication of *Christianity Takes a Stand*, a collection of essays addressing an array of current domestic and international problems. Among the contributors were prominent Episcopal laypeople Eleanor Roosevelt, Frances Perkins, Sumner Welles, Stringfellow Barr, and Eduard Heimann, along with seminary professor W. Russell Bowie and bishops Angus Dun and Edward L. Parsons. Scarlett unsurprisingly also included Reinhold Niebuhr, as well as the Nobel Prize–winning physicist Arthur H. Compton and philosopher of religion W. E. Hocking.[39] In the leading essay, Angus Dun (1892–1971), who had become bishop of Washington in 1944, echoed Scarlett's call to direct engagement with the economic, political, and cultural challenges besetting American society. "I do not see how anyone who could be taken seriously as an interpreter of the Christian faith and life would deny the Christian's responsibility for the patterns of social behavior," he wrote. Without denying the range and complexity of these challenges, Dun emphasizes that this duty is at once corporate and individual, such that each Christian "must be set upon his feet to labor as a reconciling, leavening influence in the place where he stands." At the same time, he acknowledges that "where we stand will determine where we enter the struggle. Some will be managers, some governors, some powerful, some having a humble place. We shall see things very differently, depending on where we stand. There are diversities of gifts, but one spirit." Dun identifies Christian discipleship as the unifying basis on which individuals should strive for an equality transcending race, class, and nation, even

18 PRIVILEGE AND PROPHECY

as he concedes that such distinctions persist among Christians themselves. Yet only a church prepared to honor variety within its own membership can hope to relate the Christian message to all sorts and conditions of people comprising the wider society.[40]

Christianity Takes a Stand was lauded within the Episcopal Church and more widely as an attempt to integrate Christian ethics with serious analysis of the changes facing the United States at war's end.[41] Of course, the fact that such changes were imminent was plain to many, well before the cessation of hostilities. Among these was Francis O. Ayres, Jr. (1908–1968), rector of St. John's Church in Waterbury, Connecticut. Ayres had grown up in Scarsdale, New York, and boarded at the Taft School in Connecticut before going on to study at Yale. Leaving the university after a few years, he then went to work as a banker in Manhattan, during which time he came under the influence of Horace Donegan (1900–1991), rector of St. James's Church, Madison Avenue. Donegan's advocacy on behalf of the city's poor and marginalized persuaded Ayres that priesthood was still a viable option for a young person wanting to improve society, and in 1936 he entered ETS to prepare for ordination.[42] Writing at Christmas 1944 to his parishioners on active duty, he warned that "the great danger is that when the war is over all of us will want to take a good long rest—too long a rest. This would be a tragedy, for there is much to do." Alluding to long-standing social divisions within their community, as well as to the damage done by the Depression, he insisted that "we have got to work hard, and work together, and work intelligently if we are going to make the changes which are necessary and . . . in keeping with our great democratic traditions."[43] Having entered a war to combat tyranny and injustice abroad, it seemed axiomatic that Americans should also be prepared to tackle them forcefully at home. In the meantime, Ayres impressed upon his readers just how important their current experiences would be to this future effort.

Even as he struck an encouraging tone, though, Ayres knew that many church people did not share his assumption that religion had a direct bearing on their actions in society. Someone who did was Gibson Winter (1916–2002), who had studied alongside Ayres at ETS after graduating from Harvard in 1938. After ordination, Winter had served as his friend's curate in Waterbury before eventually joining the war as a naval chaplain in 1944. More than 6,000 Protestant ministers volunteered as military chaplains during the Second World War; of these, nearly 500 were Episcopalian.[44] Serving aboard the *USS Cebu*, a repair ship based in the Pacific, Winter spent long hours talking and listening to members of the crew, many of whom had been raised in Christian homes. In doing so, however, Winter realized most of these men "had little or no sense of what Christianity was actually teaching," such that "they seemed to see no connection between their lives and the faith in which they had been raised."[45] Another naval chaplain to draw the same conclusion was Francis B. Sayre, Jr. (1915–2008), who served in the Pacific beginning in 1942. Recalling the many conversations he had with the men under his care, Sayre judged that "somehow the Church had failed to reach the great majority of our young men with any knowledge of her tradition, faith and practice."[46] This wartime realization of just how disconnected many laypeople felt from their own Christianity proved crucial in shaping the innovative ministries both priests undertook later on.

In the meantime, though, these chaplains had the much more immediate task of simply being present amidst the traumas of combat. For Sayre, this meant two years aboard the heavy cruiser *USS San Francisco*, a tenure from which he emerged with seven battle stars and which he considered "the finest ministry of my life."[47] The memories of what he witnessed during that time could still bring him to tears over fifty years later.[48] "The most difficult part of the experience was the funerals," he remembered. "[W]e'd be in fights back and forth with the big artillery, and we had people killed on the ship. Killed right when they were talking to me. . . . It was a crew that was susceptible to my ministry as a chaplain—they were out there, subject to being killed. It was hard, hard for everyone." For Sayre, the lesson was clear: "The Church belongs where people are."[49] This was no small recognition for a man who himself had been raised under highly privileged and often rarefied circumstances. The grandson of President Woodrow Wilson, he was born in the White House and educated privately in Massachusetts, Paris, and Switzerland. His father, Francis B. Sayre, Sr., was a Harvard law professor who served as assistant secretary of state under Franklin Roosevelt. When the teenaged Sayre made a social call on the president in 1933, it was reported by the *New York Times*.[50] After spending a year working on his family's vast ranch in Montana, Sayre enrolled at Williams College, where he began to take an active interest in Christianity. When he was elected vice president of the Williams College Christian Association in 1936, the event was again deemed newsworthy by the *Times*, as was his intention to train for the ministry after graduating the following year.[51] He proceeded to Union Theological Seminary and then to ETS before being ordained in the Diocese of Massachusetts and serving his curacy at Christ Church in Cambridge.[52]

20 PRIVILEGE AND PROPHECY

The war brought a patrician Episcopalian like Sayre into contact with a wider cross section of American society than he had ever encountered at home. The same was true for Paul Moore, Jr. (1919–2003), who was born into a family of extraordinary wealth and status. His grandfather was William Henry Moore, an attorney and financier who in the late nineteenth century had made a vast fortune through ventures in banking, railways, steel, and other industries. By his own account, Paul Moore enjoyed "a gilded childhood" on family estates in Morristown, New Jersey, and Palm Beach, Florida, both staffed by an array of servants. In keeping with family tradition, he was sent at the age of twelve to St. Paul's and then on to Yale in 1937. While at boarding school he underwent a personal conversion and became an increasingly committed Anglo-Catholic throughout his undergraduate years. Upon graduating in 1941, he enlisted in the US Marine Corps and was eventually deployed to the South Pacific as a platoon leader. He was seriously wounded in action during the Battle of Guadalcanal and was awarded both the Silver Star and Navy Cross. Recounting these events years later, Moore emphasized the liberating effect they had on his social outlook: "Finally I broke out of the sheltered world of privilege and met men from other places, men with other ways of thinking, speaking, and acting. I came to know and love them, and after a while we acted together as if we had grown up on the same block."[53] For Americans in general, the war did much to cut across class barriers and draw them closer together in a common purpose. For Episcopalians in particular, few of whom were as socially elite as Sayre and Moore but often from educated and well-heeled backgrounds, such exposure proved a crucial by-product of their wartime service.[54]

The contingency of mere survival was enough for Paul Moore to re-evaluate all his plans and expectations of the future. "A man who has been to war will never be the same," he wrote while stationed on Gaudalcanal, "for he has lost the virginity of living around the edges of life. . . . This is weariness and a new knowledge of what is necessary and what is not," releasing one from "the shapeless ambitions of a too cluttered livelihood."[55] He recalled later feeling that having come so close to death, "I was, in a sense, living on borrowed time, and that this was another good reason to give my life to the Lord, and it seemed that being a priest was the way."[56] Another combatant whose war experiences led him to ordained ministry was William A. Wendt (1920–2001), a native of Mitchell, South Dakota, who flew eighty missions over Germany as a fighter pilot. Joking that he decided to become a priest "so I would never be involved in anything like that again," Wendt went on to train at GTS and became well known for his ministry in urban parishes.[57] Although already ordained, Frank Sayre likewise returned home with a heightened sense of vocational purpose. Well before his discharge in 1946, he began to use his inherited celebrity to promote the idea of industrial chaplaincy in the press. Asserting that "the youth of today is spiritually hungry and groping," he argued that "Christianity must be made a vital force in the post-war world by placing it on a seven-day-a-week basis . . . and making it meet the needs of workers and their families."[58] He envisioned chaplains as a visible presence in the workplace in the same way they had been on battlefields and aboard ships. Seizing upon the spirit of the moment, he offered a challenge: "Religion went to war with men. Why can't it go to work with them?"[59]

Sayre was not the first person to ask this question or to suggest the possibility of placing clergy in industrial settings. As he began to explore the concept, he learned that E. R. (Ted) Wickham had initiated a mission among the workers and managers of the steel industry in Sheffield, England, while the Canadian priest Sidney W. Semple had begun full-time factory ministry in London, Ontario. Sayre also later cited the French worker-priest movement as a further stimulus to his thinking during this time.[60] Yet when he raised the idea of launching a similar initiative with his bishop, Henry Knox Sherrill of Massachusetts, the response was discouraging. "[T]his whole field of industrial chaplaincy is new to me and I doubt if it has been thoroughly tested out," he wrote to Sayre in December 1945. "There seem to be a number of complications; the relationship of the management, the freedom which you would have, the fact that most of the people would be living in communities where there are churches and parishes, all is somewhat perplexing to my mind in the practical working-out of such a plan. I should be inclined, if I were you, to take parish work."[61] Such skepticism prompted Sayre to identify more precisely what such a ministry might look like in practice and what function it should fulfill. In contrast to Bishop Sherrill's assumptions, the whole point was to provide a form of Christian ministry that was not bound by existing church structures or beholden to any specific group. To be employed by either company management or labor union would automatically compromise the chaplain's position as pastor to everyone. Instead, Sayre envisioned an industrial chaplain who, akin to a military chaplain, in "representing God . . . mediates between enlisted men and commanding authority." Anticipating that with demobilization might come renewed tensions between capital and labor, it was doubly important that industrial chaplains should be regarded not as partisans but as intermediaries

22   PRIVILEGE AND PROPHECY

amidst such conflict. At the same time, Sayre foresaw the difficulties such a role would bring with it. "Is impartiality on a religious level possible?" he wondered, concluding that any chaplain seeking to minister to all concerned would face the dilemma of "justice versus neutrality."[62]

Very quickly, then, it became apparent that any serious effort to bring the Christian faith into the workplace must entail engagement with the ethical complexities of economic life itself. To Sayre, the fact the church had so often stood aloof from these realities was one reason it had become marginal, if not irrelevant, to many working-class Americans.[63] He paid tribute to the advances made by organized labor in improving the material conditions under which workers functioned and hoped that "if the Union is the watchdog of the workers' physical well-being, a Chaplain, working with the Union, would look out for the spiritual welfare."[64] Even so, he did not romanticize the unions, later noting that their internal power struggles often hindered non-aligned chaplaincy as much as any attempted manipulation by management. In spite of these frustrations, Sayre remained convinced that the only lasting basis on which to sustain a factory ministry was to persuade labor and management to sponsor it jointly.[65] Having been released by Bishop Sherrill to seek opportunities beyond the Diocese of Massachusetts, he secured one year of sponsorship from Bishop Tucker of Ohio, with the understanding that the initiative would thereafter seek financial backing from both labor and management and would be interdenominational in its approach. It was on this basis that the bishop introduced and endorsed Sayre's scheme among the business community in Cleveland.[66]

Soon after making these plans, Sayre was invited to take part in a conference in May 1946 in New York sponsored by the Industrial Relations Division of the Federal Council of Churches.[67] Here he encountered Joseph Fletcher, who by this time was teaching ethics at ETS and had become a leading light in CLID.[68] In keeping with Sayre's own thinking, the conference consensus was that industrial chaplaincy ought to operate free from the conventions of the institutional church on the one hand and the interests of management on the other. Given the entrenchment of the mainline denominations in polite, middle-class society, these conventions and interests were all too easily conflated in the minds of employees and must be kept firmly apart. Even among progressive-minded clergy, though, there persisted a visceral tendency to correlate social class with religious respectability, leading the conference to warn that industrial chaplains must beware any tendency to assume "the

ALL SORTS AND CONDITIONS   23

religious inferiority of workers in comparison with the religious stature of the management."[69]

Yet the need to overcome traditional social distinctions and widen the church's mission among working-class Americans was not a task for industrial chaplains alone. G. Paul Musselman (1895–1987), a priest who had experience both as a union chaplain and columnist for a union newspaper, testified in *The Living Church* in 1949 that Episcopal clergy would find a warm reception among wage-earners if they were only more willing to extend themselves.[70] Elsewhere, the success of St. Andrew's Church in Flint, Michigan, in attracting union families from the local car industry was cited as evidence of what was possible for Episcopal parishes similarly located in industrial settings.[71] By far most concentrated effort to build up parish life among factory workers during these years took place in the Diocese of Pittsburgh, under the leadership of Bishop Austin Pardue (1899–1981). Raised in upstate New York, Pardue's vocation was shaped in part by his family's financial difficulties and the pastoral care he had received from the church during his childhood. He later remembered "what good guardians and normal he-men the Episcopalian rectors and choir masters had been and what real good they had done for boys whose families, like his, were in straitened circumstances."[72] Having done military service during the First World War, he completed his undergraduate degree at Hobart College, followed by seminary studies at Nashotah House and GTS. After ordination in 1925, he served parishes in Chicago, Minnesota, and Iowa before becoming dean of St. Paul's Cathedral in Buffalo in 1938. It was during his tenure in Buffalo that Pardue first became friendly with the union movement, often in the face of hostility from the local Protestant establishment.[73] Moving to Pittsburgh to be consecrated bishop in 1944, he continued to build close ties with the unions, particularly the United Steelworkers of America, who invited him to address their convention on a number of occasions. Respected as both a preacher and pastor, Pardue readily used his episcopal standing to foster working relationships between Pittsburgh's union leaders and business community.[74]

Accompanying Pardue in his move from New York to Pittsburgh was Joseph Wittkofski (1912–1976), a former Maryknoll Father who had been received into the Episcopal Church as a priest in 1943.[75] Taking charge of a mission church in the blue-collar community of Charleroi, Pennsylvania, Wittkofski built it into a bustling Anglo-Catholic parish with a strong outreach to lapsed Roman Catholics. Determined to assemble a cadre of priests

24 PRIVILEGE AND PROPHECY

who would follow Wittkofski's lead and revitalize the neglected Episcopal missions sprinkled across the industrial towns of the Mon Valley, the bishop required all postulants in his diocese to spend a year working in either a mill or factory. Walter Righter (1923–2011), a war veteran who later became bishop of Iowa, remembered that Pardue was emphatic about the need for middle-class Episcopalians "to gain an understanding of working-class culture" before they could undertake such ministry.[76] At the same time, it soon became clear to him and Wittkofski that the challenges in the Diocese of Pittsburgh were not unique and that a nationwide, cooperative strategy was needed. This realization led to the creation of the Society for the Promotion of Industrial Mission (SPIM) in November 1951, which the Diocesan Convention endorsed formally upon the bishop's request in 1952. Writing shortly after SPIM's founding, Wittkofski explained that it would strive to create a common approach to the problems of church extension across industrial dioceses, to raise awareness of this work throughout the Episcopal Church, and to provide support to clergy who, in undertaking industrial mission, were often underpaid and overlooked. He also emphasized that while the society was committed to good labor relations and security for workers, "SPIM has evangelism as its first object. The society was established to make the Episcopal Church and its mission relevant to industrial workers."[77] In contrast to the non-aligned, non-denominational approach of industrial chaplaincy, then, industrial mission was explicitly geared toward attracting and incorporating new Episcopalians into existing parish structures.

The undertakings of clergy like Sayre, Wittkofski, and others were spurred on by the revival in religious participation sweeping across the United States during these years. This period has been aptly referred to as a kind of "Indian summer" for mainline Protestantism after the frosty conditions it withstood during the Great Depression.[78] War-weary but increasingly prosperous, Americans flocked to the churches in search of meaning and structure for their lives. As the post-war baby boom gathered pace, they brought their growing families with them, such that Sunday schools and other church-sponsored activities once again began to enjoy a central place in the social life of many communities.[79] In response to this influx of both adults and children, the Episcopal Church characteristically turned to education as a means for providing spiritual formation and fostering identity. In 1946, the House of Bishops mandated the creation of a curriculum sponsored by the national church, which resulted two years later in a comprehensive parish education program known as the Seabury Series.[80] This included not just school materials for children, but also books for adults on Christian faith and practice known as the Church's Teaching Series. Later, various training opportunities for clergy and laity were introduced through the Parish Life Conferences, which sought to cultivate shared learning and reflection at the congregational level.[81] Both the Seabury Series and Parish Life Conferences were designed by a national staff eager to build a church membership at once socially engaged and institutionally loyal.[82] The same was true among those charged with developing chaplaincies at colleges and universities. Writing in the official church newspaper *Forth*, Roger Blanchard, the executive secretary of the National Division of College Work, argued that given the disproportionately large percentage of Episcopalians in higher education—as much as a tenth of the American total—it was crucial for the church to support campus ministry. Doing so helped keep young people connected to the church and gave them a context in which to explore the relationship between their spiritual and intellectual lives. Of this work with students, Blanchard concluded: "We believe it is the most important missionary job the Church has."[83]

Another educational area in the church demanding attention during this time was ordination training. The rapid expansion of the Episcopal Church after the war soon made evident a shortage of clergy, and even with large numbers of veterans coming forward to meet this lack, there were not enough seminary places available to accommodate them.[84] One Episcopal leader especially attuned to this problem was William Scarlett's protégé John Hines. Having served his curacy in St. Louis, Hines went on to incumbencies in Hannibal, Missouri, and Augusta, Georgia, before becoming rector of Christ Church, Houston, in early 1941. Highly regarded for his powerful preaching and outspoken advocacy of social justice in church and society, Hines was elected bishop coadjutor of the Diocese of Texas in 1945. The young bishop quickly set about bolstering the diocese's educational presence in this rapidly developing part of the country. In 1949, he broke ground for St. Stephen's Episcopal School on the outskirts of Austin, the first racially integrated boarding school in the South. Then, in response to the pressing need for more clergy across the region, in 1952 he established the Episcopal Theological Seminary of the Southwest (ETSS).[85] From the start, though, Hines was determined ETSS would be more than a mere stop-gap; rather, he wanted not only to train priests but also "to inculcate in priests who are being trained a sense of understanding of both the conflict between and the intersecting interests of the Christian faith and culture."[86] To that end, the

26 PRIVILEGE AND PROPHECY

seminary curriculum covered the traditional areas of theological study while also introducing students to fields such as sociology, political science, and economic philosophy. In keeping with his commitment to social equality, Hines also ensured that the seminary's admission policy explicitly rejected the exclusion of any student "on the basis of color or race."[87] Here again, the seeds were being sown through education for a very different Episcopal Church from the one that had come before.

While perhaps not as overtly daring as the venture in Austin, the existing seminaries were hardly intellectually moribund. ETS had long enjoyed a reputation for high-caliber but sometimes unorthodox faculty, to the extent that certain bishops would not allow their postulants to enroll there.[88] At Virginia, professors Albert Mollegen and Clifford Stanley became champions of the "crisis theology" that had crossed over from Europe. Their renowned lecture series, "Christianity and Modern Man," challenged a generation of seminarians to take a critical approach to the society in which they lived.[89] And while General Seminary in New York was still known for its traditional ethos, scholars such as Norman Pittenger and Cuthbert Simpson injected a liberal sensibility through their teaching.[90] In a very different setting, the same was true of the faculty at Sewanee, whose positive view of racial integration would lead to a major confrontation in the 1950s. Especially noteworthy in this respect was Robert McNair, who as professor of ethics and moral theology recognized that gentility hardly absolved southern Episcopalians of complicity in structural oppression.[91]

The sense of purpose and possibility that the influx of young veterans brought to the seminaries reflected their generation's instinctive faith in the value of institutions. As men who had grown up amidst depression and war, they were accustomed to strong leadership and collective effort as the basis for overcoming adversity.[92] In joining the ranks of the Episcopal clergy, they were thus already conditioned to function within hierarchical structures. The bishops who received them into the ministry expected no less. Roger Blanchard (1910–1998), who would succeed the patrician Henry Hobson as bishop of Southern Ohio in 1959, noted that while bishops such as Hobson, Will Scarlett, Beverley Tucker, Henry Sherrill, Appleton Lawrence, Malcolm Peabody, and Angus Dun were regarded as great liberals in their day, there was never any doubt about who was in charge. All were autocrats in their dioceses, but "this was not negative," insisted Blanchard. "We just assumed it was right and the way it ought to be, and these were great men."[93] This traditional deference to authority was a key ingredient in the church's organizational coherence during the post-war years, as indeed it was for American society as a whole. Within this essentially conservative context, these bishops could champion progressive causes in church and society without in the process jeopardizing the security of their own position. In this respect, they were often highly effective at operating within the established order but not always receptive to innovations that moved beyond it. Frank Sayre saw this tendency at work in Henry Sherrill's treatment of clergy who, like himself, pushed against the boundaries of conventional discipline and practice. Although a man with a broad vision for the church's role in society, Sherrill had little patience for individuals who did not conform. "Young man," he informed Sayre early in his ministry, "you have something to learn. You have to learn that the church is a whole lot bigger than you are."[94]

The election of Henry Knox Sherrill (1890–1980) as presiding bishop in the autumn of 1946 heralded a new phase in the institutional life of the Episcopal Church. During his eleven- year incumbency, he would oversee its transformation from a loose federation of dioceses into a self-consciously national body.[95] The National Council, which was created in 1919, had become the basis for increasing centralization of church affairs, and gradually the number of departments and programs began to proliferate.[96] Recognizing that the presiding bishop's executive tasks were becoming onerous, the General Convention of 1943 had mandated that the post should no longer be held in conjunction with diocesan responsibilities. Sherrill's predecessor, Henry St. George Tucker of Virginia, had duly resigned his see in 1944, but Sherrill was the first bishop to be elected to the office in its revised form.[97] He was well suited to take charge under these new conditions. A native of New York, he attended the Hotchkiss School and Yale before studying for ordination at the Episcopal Theological School. He served his curacy at Trinity Church in Boston and eventually returned there in 1923 as rector, while simultaneously teaching at both ETS and the Boston University School of Theology. Active in various civic and religious bodies, Sherrill soon distinguished himself as a capable administrator and fundraiser and in 1930 was elected bishop of Massachusetts. During these years he also become a trustee of Massachusetts General Hospital and a fellow of the Yale Corporation, organizations to which he remained devoted throughout his career.[98] For a consummate insider like Sherrill, running such institutions blended easily with his ministry in the church: all could be seen as sharing a commitment to human welfare and development.[99] By the time he became presiding bishop, he was thus widely regarded as a pillar of the liberal establishment who could

28   PRIVILEGE AND PROPHECY

bring both confidence and experience to the work of strengthening the church's structural presence.

The nationalization of the Episcopal Church did not take place in a cultural vacuum. A fascination with large-scale, "scientific" approaches to management and administration began to dominate various aspects of public life during the post-war period.[100] Like Americans engaged in business, government, and education, religious leaders in the mainline denominations became enamored of the ideal of organizational efficiency. Through central planning and professional expertise, they sought to maximize the church's effectiveness in mission and social work.[101] Yet not everyone greeted this stress on managerial rigor with enthusiasm. "We wonder whether the Protestant Episcopal Church in the U.S.A. isn't being well nigh organized to death," W. B. Spofford complained in *The Witness* in September 1948. "We are, presumably, bold to the point of rashness in suggesting that most of our national, diocesan and parish machinery is a hindrance rather than a help to the cultivation of the spiritual and moral life in individuals and groups on every level of our ecclesiastical fellowship."[102] If Spofford exaggerates here, he was not wrong to detect a shift in Episcopal self-perception as a result of such bureaucratizing impulses. Besides its implications for corporate decision-making, this emphasis on centralized authority also had an impact on Episcopalians at the local level. More and more, they began to regard their parish communities as extensions of a national institution that set the normative terms for identity and belonging.[103]

As presiding bishop, Henry Sherrill came to embody the Episcopal Church's prominence and prestige in American life. By the end of his tenure, he had molded the position so that, in the words of the *Episcopal Churchnews*, it united the roles of "pastor, business executive and Christian statesman."[104] Reflecting on his father's leadership style, Henry W. Sherrill characterized it as "monarchical," noting that "anything anybody said about the imperial presidency applies to the imperial bishop."[105] Moving easily among the nation's elite, Bishop Sherrill had no compunction about cultivating power in the interests of the church. An obvious case in point was his creation of the Episcopal Church Foundation (ECF) in 1949. Having noticed that wealthy Episcopalians gave generously of their time and money to Mass General Hospital and to Yale, Sherrill wondered how the same people might be more effectively engaged in the life of their denomination. He therefore envisioned the Foundation as a means not just for raising funds but also instilling in eminent laymen a sense of concern and responsibility for the church.[106] By the spring of 1950, he had assembled a formidable board of directors composed of businessmen from across the country to generate and disperse financial resources for special projects he identified.[107] The Foundation's success demonstrates Sherrill's personal standing among the powerful, as well as his incremental approach to effecting change. In contrast to many clergy a generation later, he was essentially sympathetic to such people and sought to conciliate rather than confront them in the name of social progress.[108]

Amidst the mounting tensions of the Cold War, Americans derived reassurance from religious figures like Sherrill, who simultaneously exuded an air of traditional authority and modern competence. Millions welcomed the idea of a unified American Protestantism that would uphold the nation's values at home and stand as a bulwark against godless communism abroad.[109] Under such conditions, ecumenical cooperation blossomed, and when the National Council of Churches (NCC) was formed in late 1950, Sherrill appeared the obvious choice to serve as its president.[110] "The Council marks a new and greater determination that the American way will increasingly be the Christian way," he predicted at the time of his election. "Together the Churches can move forward to the goal—a Christian America in a Christian world."[111] As these comments suggest, Sherrill and other mainline leaders regarded the NCC as a means by which to coordinate and promote their growing influence in the public sphere. In seeking to do so, they obviously believed the churches might convert the people of the United States. Yet as H. Richard Niebuhr observed in his 1951 book *Christ and Culture*, culturally integrated Protestants were less likely to succeed in transforming their society through Christ than they were in simply harmonizing one with the other. In the process, they fell prey to a variant of that "Culture-Protestantism" which Karl Barth had previously identified and condemned among liberal German Christians of the late nineteenth century.[112] For young American Protestants coming of age in this milieu, scholar James Griffiss later recalled, "it was very easy to confuse the norms of our white, middle-class culture with Christianity."[113] Whatever impact church spokesmen might hope to make upon the American conscience, then, their agenda was often constrained by the social and political conditions to which they had already consciously or unconsciously submitted.[114]

It would be wrong, however, to suggest that Henry Sherrill himself was altogether insensitive to this reality. Addressing the General Convention for the first time as presiding bishop in 1949, he had warned Episcopalians that "the Church as represented by us is too often a reflection not of the glory

30   PRIVILEGE AND PROPHECY

of God revealed in the face of Jesus Christ but a pale reflection of the contemporary society in which we happen to live."[115] Others detected a more general trend emerging in the 1950s whereby mainstream religious groups not only reflected society but endorsed a generic "culture-religion" in which Protestants, Catholics, and Jews all had a stake. Sociologist Will Herberg famously identified the "American Way of Life"—a synthesis of ideals and aspirations "that commends itself to the American as the right, the good, and the true"—as the quasi-spiritual basis for this pluralistic convergence. But, as Herberg also observed, what made this shared idealism workable was that really it was "a religiousness without religion, a religiousness with almost any kind of content or none, a way of sociability or 'belonging' rather than a way of reorienting life to God."[116] By acquiescing in this state of affairs, the churches may have retained a place in the evolving structures of national consensus, but in so doing compromised their distinctive purpose. Culture-Protestantism became harder and harder to distinguish from the "American Way of Life."[117]

One incisive critic of this phenomenon was Episcopal layman William Stringfellow (1928–1985), who went on to become a unique and challenging voice in the church throughout the 1960s and 1970s. Born in Rhode Island and raised in western Massachusetts, Stringfellow came from a working-class Episcopal family. He earned a scholarship to Bates College in Maine at the age of only fifteen and subsequently studied at the London School of Economics on a Rotary scholarship.[118] Fulfilling his military service in the early 1950s, he was stationed with the US Army in Germany, where he encountered a "superficial, sickly, false, proud pan-Protestantism" that passed for Christianity in the American forces. Writing to the authorities in 1952 to protest the inadequacy of ministry offered to soldiers, he explained that "so low is the denominator that one is unable to discover if there is really a difference between being a Christian and being a Kiwanian—since both try to live 'good' lives and do 'good' things for other people and recognize that, whatever else is claimed in Him, Christ was a very wise man and a very wonderful person."[119] Though hardly an opponent of ecumenical collaboration, Stringfellow pinpoints here how readily inculturated Protestantism could surrender to a banal, chauvinistic Americanism. Following this logic, a year later Stephen Bayne argued in *The Optional God* that the challenge faced by the contemporary church was not so much old-fashioned paganism as "paganism with Christian words and Christian values." Bayne, who after his time in St. Louis under Bishop Scarlett served a parish in Northampton, Massachusetts, and as chaplain at

Columbia University, had become bishop of Olympia in western Washington in 1947.[120] During this time he had emerged as an astute commentator on church and society, and like Stringfellow, began to suspect that the worldly forces the churches presumed to shape were in fact more often shaping them. "The optional God can be dispensed with inside a secularized Church quite as well as outside," he contended. "Certain linguistic problems are awkward, no doubt; but if you never preach on the doctrine of God, and use Him as an adjective as often as possible, even these are solved. The edges are blurred, and your chaplaincy to the secular world is secure."[121]

The particular form this temptation took for the Episcopal Church in the 1950s derived from its reputation, even among the mainline denominations, as the most affluent and genteel of communions. In a chapter entitled "The Long Road from Pentecostal to Episcopal," Vance Packard in his popular study of contemporary class behavior observed that status-conscious Americans often embraced Episcopalianism as an expression of their upward mobility.[122] In so doing, they perpetuated the church's position among the upper echelons of society, and not just in traditional strongholds along the East Coast and in the Deep South. John Hines, reflecting on his time as a bishop in the Southwest during the 1940s and 1950s, noted that despite their relatively small numbers, Episcopalians were disproportionately represented among the power elite of the region. He cited their dominance on educational boards, as presidents of colleges and banks, as senior partners in law firms and oil companies, and especially at the Texas Supreme Court, where at one stage they occupied six of nine seats.[123] Yet if such prominence was the source of pride to some, it was the cause of anxiety to others. Long-serving General Seminary professor Norman Pittenger (1905–1997) worried in the pages of the *Anglican Theological Review* that "the tremendous truth and significance of our Anglican witness will never make its right impact . . . unless the Episcopal Church becomes something other than the church to which the nicer, more refined, people like to go."[124] And while *The Witness* and *The Living Church* might part company on various matters, on this they were agreed: the Episcopal Church's snob appeal fundamentally undermined its theology and mission. As W. B. Spofford put it bluntly in one editorial, "to have social acceptance the hall mark of any group who call themselves Christians is a reversal of the gospel." He then speculated that "we do not talk seriously about this very often because such an obvious discrepancy between the teachings of Christ and our daily lives is an uncomfortable thing to contemplate."[125]

32 PRIVILEGE AND PROPHECY

In actuality, the Episcopal Church during this period was more demographically diverse than its upper-class WASP image allowed for. A 1952 survey commissioned by the National Council's Department of Christian Social Relations to assess clergy and laity views of the church's outreach programs also provided statistical data about their own social and economic condition. It reported that in comparison to other denominations, the Episcopal Church "attracts a membership which is modally of a higher class," but nonetheless "the average Episcopalian can scarcely be described as wealthy." In examining the relationship between class standing and church participation, the study noted that although lower-class members of the church were consistently more active, they remained less likely to attain leadership positions. On this basis, the authors opined that the church retained "a basically upper class orientation" that did not reflect some members' actual experience and which sometimes served to erect class barriers within the institution itself.[126] Despite persistent indications of elitism, church apologists preferred to dwell on signs of emerging diversity within the membership. Writing in the mid-1950s, historian George E. DeMille presented a list of "ethnic" names found on clergy rolls as proof that the Episcopal Church "is no longer a class Church, it is no longer a racial Church, but a Church that fairly represents all of the United States." As such, he added, "the Episcopal Church is a more truly Catholic body . . . than it was in 1900."[127] Quite apart from the question of whether the evidence cited could possibly support such a claim, it is telling that DeMille should be so eager to make it. For alongside thinkers such as Bayne, Stringfellow, and Pittenger, he plainly perceives here that unless Episcopalianism managed to shed its reputation for social exclusivism, its claim to represent the universal church would continue to ring hollow.

Such discrepancy between theological inheritance and cultural identity was by no means new. Episcopalians' perennial attraction to the national church ideal, that of constituting a normative form of Christianity to which the whole country might look for leadership, derived from their rootedness in Anglican notions of catholicity and establishment. On this basis, they felt obliged, insofar as possible, to serve and shape all aspects of American society. The growth that the Episcopal Church enjoyed as a result of the postwar religious boom lent fresh confidence to this particular sense of calling.[128] Yet what had long attracted many people to Episcopalianism and lent its ambitions a material basis was in fact its status as an elite entity. The notion that in order to fulfill its catholic mission the church must become more

ALL SORTS AND CONDITIONS   33

inclusive culturally and socioeconomically thus collided with its denominational appeal as the church of the powerful, the prosperous, and the well-born.[129] This tension was highlighted as a growing number of clergy began to question the church's complicity in the structural injustices of the status quo, thereby placing them in costly conflict with their own membership. "[W]hen the church calls for specific social change," observed the 1952 CSR survey, "it must face the fact that it will lose support among those who are living comfortably within existing conditions." At the same time, the report reasoned that "while church leaders with strong social consciences may justifiably resent being supported financially by hypocritical parishioners, the complete withdrawal of such finances could render the church wholly impotent."[130] For a church not just accustomed to exercising social influence but in many respects committed to doing so, the threat of such divergence had serious implications for all concerned.

Even as the Episcopal Church flourished, the standing of its priests often remained ambiguous. For much of the century, American Protestant ministers generally had experienced a crisis of function as they watched many of their traditional roles and responsibilities slowly appropriated by academics, social workers, government officials, and other specialists. The cultural prestige most clergymen enjoyed diminished as that of the newer professions increased, a trend clearly discernible in economic terms: the US Census Bureau reported in 1949 that during the previous decade, Protestant ministers had dropped from the highest 30% of salaried workers to the lowest 30%.[131] And even though Episcopal clergy were usually less subject to congregational caprice than those of other mainline denominations, they still tended to be among the worst paid, a state of affairs one commentator described as "a national scandal."[132] Suspecting that many Episcopalians perceived their ministers to be "a superficially pious caste unable to do more than frame and publish ambiguous resolutions," another concluded ruefully that "the clergy are politely tolerated, but seldom respected."[133] Likewise, Michael Allen, who became well known in the 1960s for his social activism at St. Mark's Church in-the-Bowery in Manhattan, records in his memoir the story of an old priest who had spent most of his ministry serving a wealthy "society" church. One day, as the rector and his curate stood looking at the portraits of their predecessors in the parish, he exclaimed: "Do you realize that those men there and you and I and every man who ever served this church have been lackeys, nothing but lackeys to lick the boots of the men who called us here to serve them?"[134] This outburst named a reality with

34   PRIVILEGE AND PROPHECY

which not a few Episcopal clergy were familiar, the feeling that they retained their moral authority only insofar as they did not exercise it, or at least not in ways that might challenge directly the worldly concerns of their people.

Given the nervous political climate of this period and the prevailing social orientation of Episcopal laypeople, it is unsurprising that priests with radical left-wing views in particular should encounter hostility. Generic appeals to Social Gospel values had long been tolerated from the pulpit, but overt expressions of sympathy for socialism was an area into which only a small number of clergy dared venture.[135] An obvious exception, of course, was the redoubtable W. B. Spofford, Sr., who alongside his roles as editor of *The Witness* and executive secretary of CLID was for many years also a trustee of the American Civil Liberties Union. Joining him in his advocacy work after the war was his son, W. B. Spofford, Jr. (1921–2013), who was ordained in 1945 and would later serve as bishop of Eastern Oregon in the 1970s. Together they ensured the survival of CLID, announcing in early 1948 that it was being renamed the Episcopal League for Social Action (ELSA), with W. B. Spofford, Jr., succeeding his father as executive secretary. In reforming the association, they hoped it would build upon the Church League's labor concerns and push more broadly for "racial, political and social democracy, even while recognizing that, in our interdependent industrial society, many of these are dependent on an honest extension of democracy to the economic field."[136] The Spoffords faced considerable criticism both inside and outside the church. In April 1947, the *Chicago Tribune* cited them by name as examples of American Protestant clergy whose views made them "unwitting propagandists" for communism.[137] Even liberal Episcopalians in accord with their general goals were sometimes concerned that they were going too far. Writing in 1950, the dean of Wilmington, J. Brooke Mosley (1915–1988), complained to Andrew van Dyke that "the Fletcher-Spofford-E.L.S.A. line always drops me off somewhere before they reach that Wonderland where every Russian prospect pleases." Convinced that the organization had lost its way as a Christian enterprise, Mosley resigned his membership and his place on its national committee.[138]

Some leftist clergymen, particularly those in parochial ministry, were subjected to more than just criticism for expressing their political ideas. One such was William M. Weber (1909–1992), an activist and frequent contributor to *The Witness*. A graduate of St. Stephen's (now Bard) College and General Seminary, Weber was ordained in 1935 and served in North Dakota before being called as rector of Trinity Church in Arlington, New Jersey, outside Newark. An enthusiastic organizer, in 1946 he founded an area "cell" of the Anglican Fellowship for Social Action, an initiative he had encountered in Montreal and which defined itself as a group "pledged to advocacy of Christian social principles." Among these was the assertion that "our present economic system frustrates brotherhood, as its appeal is primarily to self-interest, and its basis is competition; therefore this system is unchristian and immoral."[139] By his own account, Weber first encountered formal opposition from his vestry in 1947 when he "slammed the Taft-Hartley bill" from the pulpit. This bill, which passed into law over the veto of President Truman as the Labor Management Relations Act, was designed to restrict the activities of labor unions. As a result of this confrontation, Weber agreed not to voice his political views at church but reserved the right to "go my own way in my own life and on my own time."[140] This was where things stood when, on March 5, 1948, he joined a small demonstration outside the Newark bureau of the Immigration and Naturalization Service to protest against the detention of six alleged communists.[141] When Weber's name appeared in the news report of the incident, his vestry wrote immediately to the Bishop of Newark, Benjamin Washburn (1887–1966), charging that he had engaged in activities "we deem to be foreign to Episcopalian ministrations." They then declared that the only resolution possible was for either the rector or vestry to be removed.[142] Not long after, the bishop opted to move Weber out of the parish, promising to find him another post elsewhere.

The episode is illustrative of the triangular dynamic at work among bishop, priest, and people when conflicts arose over the nature of social witness. Under Episcopal polity, as Weber noted at the time, "the bishop is the ultimate arbiter and judge" in conflicts between a rector and congregation. Such an arrangement affirmed the Anglican principle of episcopal authority and in theory protected clergy from arbitrary dismissal and other forms of local intimidation. Yet in practice, Weber decided, "really stringent social action is outside the province of an Episcopal rector, until he has converted either his parish—at least a *voting* majority—or his bishop!"[143] Bishop Washburn, while sympathetic to his priest, was unwilling to antagonize the community, and Weber himself recognized that he had been naïve to think that he could engage so freely in political dissent without consequences.[144] The following year, a similar conflict erupted at Holy Trinity Church in Brooklyn, when both the long-serving rector, John Howard Melish, and his son and assistant minister, William Howard Melish, were removed from their posts by Bishop James DeWolfe of Long Island. DeWolfe acted in response to a petition from

36 PRIVILEGE AND PROPHECY

certain vestry members, who claimed that by chairing the National Council on American-Soviet Friendship, the younger Melish was engaged in "subversive" activities. In explaining his decision, the bishop argued that Melish's behavior had caused "doubt and confusion in the church" and added that "a priest in good standing in the church is necessarily representative of the church in his public actions." Rather than resolve matters, such assertions served only to complicate them, for there were parishioners on both sides of the debate and some who in response to the bishop's action sought the removal of the vestrymen who made the original complaint.[145] Under the circumstances, it appeared the bishop was not seeking so much to mediate the situation as take sides based on his own sentiments.[146]

There were, of course, Episcopalians in no way enamored of communism but nonetheless critical of the self-righteous and reactionary impulses beginning to characterize Cold War America. Serving as rector of St. Paul's Church in East Cleveland alongside his industrial mission work, Frank Sayre challenged his congregation to guard against the widespread tendency to conflate piety with patriotism. "The provincialism of our concept of God!" he exclaimed when preaching in May 1950. "We believe His will is practically identical with the Constitution and every other American institution." From a truly Christian point of view, however, he insisted that both capitalism and communism were human rebellions against divine love, and as such, Americans had nothing to feel morally superior about. "If anyone would find God in America," Sayre concluded, "it must first be as judge of ourselves."[147] In a similar fashion, William Scarlett continued to speak forcefully against social inequality in the United States, maintaining that so long as white Americans failed to address discrimination and violence against their own black compatriots, they could hardly expect to offer morally compelling leadership in the wider world.[148] As he approached the end of his tenure as bishop of Missouri, Scarlett also warned against the habit of silencing dissent in the name of domestic security. Addressing a gathering of students not long before retiring in 1952, he condemned the mendacity of communism but also castigated Americans who employed "the technique of the lie, the smear, the mean and unwarranted suggestion in our own land in these hysterical days when characters and careers are blighted by innuendo and implication. Whoever for any ends whatsoever makes use of the lie does a vast disservice to his country and is really an enemy of this Republic."[149] With the Red Scare tightening its grip on the nation, establishment liberals like Sayre and Scarlett began to worry that the very freedoms for which Americans had recently fought abroad were now in danger of being denied them at home.

This was already very much the case for African Americans, who, having served their country in wartime, found they were expected once again to assume second-class status upon their return. As with many of their white counterparts, though, young black Episcopalians were determined to build a different America through Christian activism. One example was David Harris, who wrote in his 1947 postulancy application that in seeking ordination in the Diocese of Washington, "I intend to demand and contest for equal opportunities to progress. There is a serious need for progressive leaders to overcome racial problems. The ministry can be a place for such leadership."[150] Another was John Burgess (1909–2003), who would later become the first African American in the history of the Episcopal Church to be elected a diocesan bishop. Burgess was a native of Michigan who proceeded directly from his undergraduate degree at Ann Arbor to study for the priesthood at ETS. Ordained in 1935, he served parishes in Michigan and Ohio before being appointed Episcopal chaplain at Howard University in 1946. It was in this capacity that early in 1948 he addressed a gathering of black Episcopalians, suggesting that even if tackling racial discrimination was primarily the responsibility of white Christians, "effective social action involves the Negro as well. . . . He cannot avoid entirely the responsibility for vigorous and sacrificial work in behalf of social justice by saying it is the white man's duty alone to achieve a change in the American scene." Crucially, Burgess urged his listeners to examine the particular reasons their church did not enjoy a broader appeal among their fellow African Americans. He argued that too often black Episcopalians took pride in attracting "the best people of our communities," a form of "caste feeling [that] can be traced to the defenses any middle class builds up when its permanence is not too sure." In pushing this assessment, Burgess conceded white congregations were just as guilty of fostering a "class church" but was adamant this must not be used as an excuse. "Too few of our Negro Churchmen are deeply involved in the affairs of their communities," he stated flatly. "In emphasizing class distinctions, the Negro congregation has imagined that it, like its white counterparts, is set apart from the common affairs of men." Amidst this critique, Burgess sounded a note of optimism when discussing the courage and intelligence of the young people he pastored at the university. "These men and women are interested in the presence and extent of discrimination in Church institutions and in parish life. They are interested in the Church's identification of itself with the

38 PRIVILEGE AND PROPHECY

underprivileged and mistreated." He concluded: "I take it that it is part of my job to encourage them in these interests."[151]

A contemporary of Burgess's who likewise became a mentor to a whole generation of black Episcopalians was Tollie L. Caution, Sr. (1902–1987). A native of Baltimore, he was educated at Lincoln University and the Philadelphia Divinity School before being ordained priest in 1930. He served parishes along the eastern seaboard until 1945, when he was appointed the church's secretary for Negro Work in New York. This was the first of a number of positions he held at the National Council that focused on advancing educational opportunities for African Americans and, more broadly, on promoting the Episcopal Church among minority groups.[152] In a church whose white leaders often spoke eloquently about racial equality but often proved timid in practice, Caution toiled to secure basic recognition and resources for black clergy.[153] He traveled constantly, visiting churches, schools and colleges, counseling and encouraging minority churchpeople and attending their conferences, conventions, and ordinations.[154] Over time, he emerged not only as an ambassador for the National Church but as a kind of symbol of black Episcopalianism itself.[155] Many priests later credited him as essential to their vocational development, among them Walter D. Dennis (1932–2003). A native of Washington, DC, Dennis trained as a lawyer at New York University before taking his M.Div. degree at GTS in 1956. He eventually became a residentiary canon at New York's St. John the Divine and then suffragan bishop of the diocese. Throughout his life, he regarded Caution as a surrogate father-figure who had seen him through the difficult early years of his training and ministry.[156]

Despite the discrimination black Episcopalians faced within their own church and the elitist attitude they in turn displayed within the African American community, the church retained the ability to attract thoughtful black Christians from other traditions. The lay theologian Verna Dozier (1917–2006), who had been raised in the Baptist tradition in Washington, DC, first came across Episcopalianism during her student career at Howard University in the 1930s. She recalled being fascinated by the Anglican ethos but also quickly perceived a disjunction between theory and practice, telling her new friends that "you Episcopalians write so well and live so poorly!" In keeping with John Burgess's analysis of a decade later, she noted that "there was a class barrier that corresponded to the religious and racial barrier: my classmates, for example, who were Episcopalians were always the fairest-skinned. They were always the ones whose parents had gone to college, and

ALL SORTS AND CONDITIONS   39

whose parents didn't have laboring jobs. Episcopalians were always a more privileged group, and they seemed a world apart from me." Yet for Dozier, these social impediments could not deter her from embracing the tradition's underlying appeal: "I entered the Episcopal Church through *liberty*," she affirmed. "I was drawn to the liberty of the Episcopal Church because they seemed to me to gather up all that I thought Christianity and the biblical story were all about."[157] In the decades to follow, Dozier would become a nationally respected Christian educator for the church, who, through teaching and preaching, invited Episcopalians into an ever-deepening relationship with scripture in daily life.

The young John T. Walker was likewise drawn to the Episcopal Church after encountering it while a student at Wayne State College in the mid-1940s.[158] Born in Georgia, Walker (1925–1989) grew up in Detroit as the great-grandson of an African Methodist Episcopal pastor whose nine sons had all become AME clergymen as well. Writing in the tense atmosphere of 1967 about these earlier days, he evoked "that long ago romantic age of war and post-war America . . . when youth and optimism were strong upon us [and] some far-reaching decisions were made." In his own case, not the least of these was the decision to become an Episcopalian, thereby apparently turning his back on his family's venerable history in the AME tradition. He wondered whether those "who served black people in black churches" would ever accept, let alone comprehend, his desire to join a primarily white denomination. Using the language of the sixties, he conceded in retrospect that "the Black Power men might say that I became a favorite son, a favored bit of tokenism. Face it[,] they might even say Uncle Tom."[159] But such an appraisal would entirely overlook the considerable personal cost Walker paid in making his contribution to a racially integrated Episcopal Church. This reality is well encapsulated in the story of his meeting with Bishop Richard Emrich of Michigan, who, despite Walker's reluctance, decided his young postulant was the obvious person to integrate Virginia Theological Seminary (VTS) in 1951. Having repeatedly observed Walker's extraordinary capacity to remain gracious in the face of racial enmity, Emrich said simply: "It has to be you, John."[160] This was just one of a succession of "firsts" Walker would undertake as an Episcopalian: after graduating in 1954, he returned to Detroit to become the first black rector of the integrated St. Mary's Church, and after that, he moved to New Hampshire to become the first black master at St. Paul's School.[161] And while not everyone at VTS was enthusiastic about civil rights during this period, Walker made important friendships there, not

40 PRIVILEGE AND PROPHECY

least with his classmate John Morris (1930–2010).[162] A white Southerner passionate about racial justice, Morris helped found the Episcopal Society for Cultural and Racial Unity (ESCRU) in 1959 and for seven years served as its executive director. In 1954, during their final year at Virginia, he and Walker collaborated on a term paper for their church history course, in which they examined the history of racial prejudice in the Episcopal Church and ways it might overcome this legacy in the future.[163]

One example cited by Walker and Morris of Episcopal action in a Northern context was a group ministry by then well established in Jersey City. Its roots lay in the convergence of three men at General Seminary shortly after the war. Having been discharged from the Marines in 1946, Paul Moore, along with his wife Jenny, moved to New York to pursue his battlefield calling to ordained ministry. "We charged into seminary brimming with enthusiasm for change," Jenny Moore recorded years afterward. "There was to be no compromise, and we were sure that with a little luck we could change the world."[164] Alongside his studies at General, Moore attended lectures by Reinhold Niebuhr and Paul Tillich at Union Seminary and Jacques Barzun at Columbia, and together he and Jenny also became regular guests at the Niebuhr apartment in Union Quad. In order to fulfill his fieldwork requirement, Moore was assigned to Christ Church, Poughkeepsie, under the supervision of the new rector, James Pike, and soon the Moores and Pikes became good friends. Looking back on the experience, Moore jokingly remarked that "we found weekends with the Pikes exhilarating, even if it took us most of the following week to recover."[165] James A. Pike (1913–1969) was already on his way to becoming one of the most exuberant and controversial figures in the post-war Episcopal Church.[166] Raised Roman Catholic in California, he first encountered Episcopalianism while a postgraduate at Yale in the mid-1930s and became increasingly drawn to it after moving to Washington, DC, to work as a lawyer for the federal government. The Episcopal Church appealed to Pike's social as well as intellectual sensibilities. He would later recall that in attending a service at the National Cathedral in the early 1940s, he saw that "it looked like a church ought to look," and his letters leave little doubt about the prestige he attributed to Episcopal membership.[167] At the same time, he celebrated Anglicanism for holding "the highest standards of intellectual honesty and freedom," standards which he would repeatedly test in the ensuing years.[168] By the end of 1944, Pike had secured ordination from Bishop Angus Dun, the first step in his energetic ascent of the church hierarchy.

Back in Manhattan, another dynamic personality to whom Paul and Jenny Moore were drawn was C. Kilmer Myers, an instructor in patristics at the seminary. Myers (1916–1981) was a native of Saratoga County in upstate New York, where he had grown up in the Dutch Reformed tradition in a middle-class family. While an undergraduate at Rutgers University he joined the Episcopal Church, and after attending seminary at Berkeley Divinity School was ordained priest in 1940. He continued his postgraduate studies at Yale until enrolling in the war effort in 1944 as a naval chaplain and was stationed in the Atlantic and Mediterranean. After leaving the Navy in 1946, he joined the faculty at General.[169] Not content to restrict his ministry to the seminary, however, in the summer of 1947 Myers volunteered to look after nearby St. Peter's Church, situated in one of the poorer parts of Chelsea. He brought to this work a notable urgency and rigor. "Kim was extreme," Jenny Moore observed. "He sensed drama in every encounter. . . . Personal comfort meant little to him, and he always thought of concepts like Welcome and Succor in the most absolute terms."[170] Myers's radical vision of social ministry proceeded directly from his commitment to Anglo-Catholic sacramentalism, augmented by recent exposure to the French worker-priest movement.[171] Carl Russell Sayers, a young seminarian who knew Myers during this time, remembered the older man's advice: "Carl, if you are a Catholic, you can be anything else you want to be in this world."[172] For Myers, the catholic tradition was essential not just to reforming the Episcopal Church but to redeeming the whole of American society.

A natural ally in this project, Paul Moore arranged to serve his summer placement alongside Myers at St. Peter's. Reporting to his sponsoring bishop, Charles K. Gilbert of New York, about his activities, Moore explained that their pastoral approach to the neighborhood had "entailed being *WITH* the people as much as possible—with them physically and also with them in friendship, sympathy and point of view."[173] Over thirty years later, Moore still regarded these months on the streets of Chelsea as a turning-point in his vocational formation. "I loved walking the sidewalks and climbing dark, smelly tenement stairs to knock on strange doors," he confessed. "It made me feel I was following in the footsteps of the great London priests of the turn of the century who had inspired me so long ago when I read about them at school." In imagining himself a successor to the Anglo-Catholic slum priests, Moore knew that he was reacting to a deep sense of guilt about his own privileged upbringing. Yet whatever mixed motives he may have brought to the effort, he insisted that "this ministry seemed real and made my prayers, the

42 PRIVILEGE AND PROPHECY

Communion Service, the Bible, and indeed Jesus Himself come alive in a way that the classes at the seminary and the beautiful Evensong in the chapel never had."[174] This urge to break down the barrier between institutional religion and the immediacies of the world was shared by Robert Pegram, a priest from an upper-class Southern family who taught alongside Myers at GTS.[175] Together, the three men, along with Jenny Moore, began to envision a shared ministry in precisely the sort of impoverished, inner-city neighborhood the Episcopal Church had begun to abandon as many of its members migrated to the suburbs. Behind them, these departing Episcopalians left beautiful old churches and a sense of abandonment among those who remained.[176] "It is rare for people who live in the suburbs to have a sense of responsibility to the city's inhabitants," Paul Moore subsequently pointed out. "There was once at least the concept of *noblesse oblige*[;] now we keep the *noblesse* and throw out the *oblige*. Those who kneel to worship the crucified Christ on the comfortable cushions of outlying Churches must somehow reach out to their brothers."[177]

In seeking to make their vision a reality, Kim Myers wrote to various bishops whose dioceses included large urban areas, offering the services of three clergy in a joint enterprise. Many expressed their enthusiasm for the idea, but only Bishop Washburn of Newark responded with a concrete proposal, offering the priests a ministry at Grace Church in the Van Vorst section of Jersey City. What made the plan viable was that Moore, Myers, and Pegram already had enough by way of personal resources to share just one salary among them. As soon as the academic year ended in June 1949, the two bachelors and the Moore family moved together into the rundown rectory in Jersey City. "It was an odd set-up," Jenny Moore acknowledged in her 1968 memoir, *The People on Second Street*. Four adults and a growing number of Moore children lived communally in a house that was also "fast becoming a community center," as the door of the rectory was open to all.[178] "God has certainly blessed the beginning of the work," Paul Moore wrote excitedly to Bishop Gilbert a few months after their arrival. "It is wonderful to be finally doing what I have been looking forward to for so long."[179] Yet adjusting to an environment so often characterized by degradation and want exacted a price from these privileged newcomers. Moore recalled that it was particularly hard returning to the neighborhood after a day off, citing an occasion when, having attended a beautiful ballet performance in New York, he and his wife came home to find a man passed out and covered in vomit on their front steps.[180] Jenny faced challenges of her own as a young mother trying to raise a family alongside the intense demands of their work. When she asked the Roman Catholic activist Dorothy Day how to manage the tension between Christian service and running an orderly household, the older woman replied brusquely: "Lower your standards."[181] Though they had sought out the poor in order to serve them, the group soon found that they were the ones being transformed by the experience.

The ministry of presence pursued by Myers, Pegram, and the Moores began to gain ground among the inhabitants, especially the many black children nearby.[182] The altar in the church and the kitchen table in the rectory became twin sites of welcome and gathering, and soon, in Jenny Moore's words, "imperfect, vulnerable to satire, a very fragile community did exist." Yet not everyone delighted in the clergy's inclusive approach to parish life; some of the aging white parishioners felt the church had been taken away from them, and many in the neighborhood were suspicious of the goings-on at Grace Church.[183] Just over a year after the team's arrival, area residents sent a petition to Bishop Washburn registering their concerns: "We believe that everyone should go to church to ask for the blessings of the Lord," they wrote, "but that is w[h]ere it should end and not have gangs ranging around and make it into a playground. At the Rectory there is music and dancing."[184] Despite such protests, the team persisted, believing their approach constituted the means of renewal not just for one parish, but for an entire church imprisoned by its own respectability. "The Episcopal Church as we had known it was not fitted to express to our people the passionate love of Christ," confessed Paul Moore a few years later, and "we, her ministers, [were] not fitted by experience or training to know and understand the touch which would open a heart, the kind of handshake which would be warmly returned." This they learned through daily solidarity with the people themselves. At the same time, Moore was sure that the Episcopal Church had something unique to offer in return. Not only did it have great financial resources to share, but "we are the only Church with the sacramental and liturgical resources of Catholicism together with the freedom and democracy of Protestantism, the power to heal and the freedom to fight the social illness of the big cities."[185] This is an important statement, invoking as it does a modern version of the Anglican *via media* as both a theological and practical solution to the pressing needs of urban America.

That such a solution was urgently required had of course become clear to other Episcopalians as well, and the Jersey City priests were not the only socially conscious clergy whom Bishop Washburn had recruited to tackle

44   PRIVILEGE AND PROPHECY

the challenges in his diocese. The unfortunate William Weber had been one; another was Arthur Lichtenberger, dean of Newark's Trinity Cathedral from 1941 to 1948. Lichtenberger (1900–1968), who went on to succeed Henry Sherrill as presiding bishop, grew up in Wisconsin and graduated from Kenyon College in 1923. He trained for the priesthood at ETS before teaching theology in China for two years and holding rectorships in Ohio and Massachusetts. Addressing an Episcopal gathering in Atlantic City in the spring of 1948, Dean Lichtenberger reminded his audience that the church's social outreach must not be "merely palliative, remedial, patching up a life here and there so that people may somehow keep going. It is to share, with all our inadequacies, in the work of redemption."[186] Like the Jersey City group, Lichtenberger saw that the church's pastoral concern for urban life must be accompanied by a critical and sustained appreciation of the socioeconomic forces that created and perpetuated suffering in the first place.[187] The same was also true for John B. Coburn, who followed Lichtenberger as dean of Newark from 1953 to 1957. A native of Danbury, Connecticut, Coburn (1914–2009) came from an old New England family. Both his parents had engaged in church social work before their marriage, his father as a priest and his mother as a deaconess, a precedent Coburn regarded as formative to his own vocational calling.[188] Educated at the Wooster School and Princeton, he went on to teach at Robert College, Istanbul, before undertaking ordination training at Union Seminary in the early 1940s. At Union, Coburn was drawn to the teaching of Reinhold Niebuhr, an influence discernible in his comment to Bishop Washburn in 1942 that "justice between power groups in society is just as much a concern of the Christian faith as love between individuals."[189] Here again, Coburn's sentiment reflects the sense among younger churchmen that to be meaningful, personal faith must promote a public witness unafraid to question the status quo.

The preference for a more involved, holistic approach to urban ministry began to take root in pockets across the Episcopal Church. Long-standing city missions in places such as Boston, New York, Philadelphia, and Detroit increasingly spoke of the need to address the conditions of poverty and inequality, rather than simply to provide charity.[190] And even as the Jersey City team was being feted as a standard-bearer for this new style of Episcopal outreach, its members were learning tough lessons about the difficulty of effecting lasting, substantive change.[191] Recounting his attempts to confront the oppressive power structures under which his parishioners lived, from exploitative landlords to corrupt police, Paul Moore recalled his disillusionment when the resistance of entrenched interests became clear to him. The first lesson for the faithful Christian activist, he concluded, was not to be defeated by "the morale-shattering disappointments which follow when dedicated persons, full of heart, work long and hard with great enthusiasm—and suddenly, nothing happens."[192] Such opposition to social change found outside the church was matched by the complacency and evasion frequently found within it. Jenny Moore, in visiting suburban parishes to talk about the team's work, struggled to break through the psychological walls that separated life in Jersey City from the life familiar to most white, middle-class Episcopalians. "I was never sure what I wanted of my audiences," she admitted later.

> They collected clothes, they sent money; some of them came over and looked around. But I wanted them to know that the gift of cast-off clothing is not enough, that tutoring one day a week is too brief a relationship. I wanted them to know that their values were not the only values; the mutual concern of city people—on the city streets where I lived—for one another, against the common hazards of eviction, hunger, and bloodshed, had taught me the meaning of the Christian gospel. . . . I told them that being "churchy" was very different from being Christian, but the words seemed to hang in the air and flutter away unconsumed. I should have asked for their hearts and guts.[193]

Out of the welter of emotions expressed here emerges a conviction that the Episcopal Church must undergo a collective conversion of sorts, a fundamental re-evaluation of the social terms of its Christian commitment. And the only way to achieve this transformation was deliberately to embrace the suffering and vulnerability that many of its members sought to keep at arm's length.

By the early 1950s, a growing number of idealistic Episcopal clergy were turning to inner-city ministry as a means of renewing the church's mission and witness. If their readiness to do so often derived from inherited Anglican notions of institutional responsibility and self-assertion, it was sustained by a commitment to sacramental community as the basis for human equality.[194] Beginning in the New York area and eventually spreading to other cities along the East Coast, the Urban Mission Priests movement became the platform for promoting social ministry premised on such Anglo-Catholic theological and liturgical sensibilities.[195] In voicing its aims and principles, the

46 PRIVILEGE AND PROPHECY

group emphasized "all *false barriers* of race, national origin, and economic status must be broken through, that all may be joined, one to the other, in Christian love."[196] Importantly, this vision of reconciliation remained closely bound up in the daily experience of the eucharist, for it was here that "the life of the Community is most truly represented[,] as each brings his offering of self and all find their wholeness in the sacrifice of Christ."[197] In welcoming all sorts and conditions into the church, though, there was no question that the mission priests were dedicated to making and molding Christians in their own particular tradition. Shortly before Myers, Pegram, and the Moores had moved to Jersey City, a group of students from Union Theological Seminary had established the East Harlem Protestant Parish (EHPP), a collection of storefront churches that would become centers of Christian social action in one of Manhattan's most deprived neighborhoods.[198] The founders of EHPP were in many ways natural allies of the Grace Church priests, and the two groups soon developed a friendly association. Yet an essential difference emerged when Donald Benedict of EHPP suggested they work together in developing a joint ministry free of denominational constraints. Scarcely concealing his displeasure, Kim Myers answered curtly: "Count me out. I'm in Jersey City to make all the Episcopalians I can."[199]

If Myers's response was blunt to the point of rudeness, it was not out of keeping with the skeptical attitude many Anglo-Catholics held toward other denominational groups. The 1946 General Convention had effectively shut down plans for organic union with the Presbyterian Church, largely as a result of vociferous opposition from high churchmen.[200] "We have a strange fear of cooperation with non-Episcopalians," observed Norman Pittenger in 1948. While Pittenger understood well enough the theological grounds for upholding Anglican catholicity, he was nonetheless frustrated by his co-religionists' defensiveness. "[W]e need not be afraid to work with all men of good-will, and especially with our Protestant brethren, in many fields of Christian interest and service, without committing ourselves to 'immediate reunion' or endangering our particular witness."[201] In fact, Anglo-Catholics were wary of cooperation not just with other denominations, but even with more protestant or evangelical members of their own church. Though the social upheavals of the 1960s would later eclipse them in importance, disagreements over churchmanship remained a primary source of tension among Episcopalians in the years after the Second World War. The House of Bishops became sufficiently concerned about the situation that in November 1947 it asked Bishop Sherrill to form a committee to find ways to improve internal relations.[202] At the same time, party rancor in the House of Deputies was tempered by the astute guidance of John Butler, who emerged during this period as floor leader of the catholic party at General Convention. After nearly a decade of ministry in Western Massachusetts, in 1942 Butler had become rector of St. Martin's Church in Providence, Rhode Island, followed six years later by a call to Trinity Church in Princeton, New Jersey.[203] During these years he gained a reputation for quiet but highly effective leadership, exemplified by his relationship with Charles Kean, his low-church counterpart in convention floor debates. Every night, Butler would stop by Kean's hotel room to divulge his strategy for the next day, and his friend would reciprocate. In this way, the two rivals worked behind the scenes to ensure that differences over churchmanship did not derail the larger purposes of the church. When Kean died in the mid-1960s, he surprised many by leaving strict instructions that Butler was to conduct his burial office.[204]

By the end of 1952, Kim Myers had left Jersey City in order to take charge of the Lower East Side Mission, comprising the Trinity Parish chapels of St. Christopher and St. Augustine.[205] Joining him in this ministry was Bill Wendt, who, after serving as a fighter pilot in the war, had prepared for ordination at General Seminary. Wendt would subsequently become a much-loved if controversial figure in the Diocese of Washington, where he was longtime rector of the inner-city parish of St. Stephen and the Incarnation.[206] Serving alongside him was Edward Chandler, another priest committed to a ministry of sacramental presence among the poor. Yet whatever their principled commitment to the disciplines of the church as the bedrock of their priesthood, these Anglo-Catholic activists did not always find it easy to defer to their superiors. In one telling exchange, Chandler protested to the rector of Trinity, John Heuss, about his failure to consult with the mission regarding financial decisions directly affecting their work. Having lodged his complaint, Chandler immediately conceded, "this is perhaps an example of the paradox of the position of the American Episcopalian who, as Episcopalian, gives hearty approval to the hierarchical principle but, as an American, is upset in practice by the principle of the decision from above."[207] Such a candid assessment of this paradox did not resolve it, though, as would become all too evident in the decades to follow. In the meantime, Robert Pegram and the Moores continued their ministry at Grace Church Van Vorst and in 1954 invited the newly ordained James Parks Morton (1930–2020) to replace Kim Myers on the staff.[208] Born in Houston and graduated from Exeter Academy and Harvard College, Morton prepared for the ministry at

48   PRIVILEGE AND PROPHECY

GTS. He was joined later in the year in Jersey City by his wife Pamela, who, like Jenny Moore, took an active role alongside the clergy in team activities and decision-making.[209]

However effective their efforts might be locally, it soon became clear to those engaged in industrial and urban mission that they needed a coordinated presence in the institutional processes of the Episcopal Church. In developing such a presence they found a ready advocate in Almon R. Pepper, director of the National Council's Department of Christian Social Relations. Pepper (1899–1973), was a native of Wisconsin educated at Kenyon College and Bexley Hall. He graduated from Nashotah House in 1924 and was ordained to the priesthood the same year. After stints in parish, hospital, and prison ministry in Ohio, Pepper moved to New York to study psychiatric social work at Columbia before taking up his post at the national church in 1936. By the late 1940s, he had begun hosting annual conferences on urban ministry at Seabury House in Connecticut, and out of these gatherings emerged the Episcopal Fellowship of Urban Workers, whose stated purpose was "to organize national training institutes and regional conferences" in an attempt to bring ministry techniques up to speed with rapidly changing industrial conditions. Along with the Society for the Promotion of Industrial Mission and the Urban Mission Priests group, the Fellowship formed the basis for an important new constituency in Episcopal affairs.[210] Persuasive figures such as Austin Pardue, Arthur Lichtenberger, Kim Myers, and Paul Moore worked together to get their concerns recognized by the General Convention of 1949, which in turn led to the creation of the Division of Urban Industrial Work by the General Convention of 1952.

Achieving this place in the organizational structures of the church was an important step, although the new division remained badly underfunded throughout the 1950s. As a result, Pepper and the division's executive secretary, Paul Musselman, had to secure private funding from the Lily Endowment to launch a network of training centers and conferences designed to "arouse the clergy and laity in all parts of the country to the immediate importance of ministering to city populations."[211] Yet besides budgeting concerns, Pepper and Musselman faced another challenge, that of juggling the contrasting agendas of those committed to "industrial mission" with those primarily interested in "urban mission." For the former, mission was about ministering to the longtime residents of areas that had become undesirable and depressed through close proximity to industrial plants; whereas for the latter, mission was about caring for those living in inner-city neighborhoods abandoned by the white bourgeoisie, usually poor black people who had migrated in large numbers from the rural South. Even though both approaches proceeded from a concern for the neglected and marginalized, inevitably they led to different conclusions about how and where the church ought to focus its resources.[212] Pepper and Musselman worked hard to accommodate these diverging priorities within the division's programming, while still championing the cause of social engagement across the wider church.[213] For despite the devotion of certain activists, the average member of the Episcopal Church too often remained disengaged from the problems of contemporary society. "The acceptance of social responsibility on the part of many Episcopalians is still weak," concluded Powel Mills Dawley in the Church's Teaching Series. "People need a keener awareness of the reality of human community, a more firmly grounded assurance of the meaningfulness of their lives in terms of brotherhood and vocation."[214]

Someone eager to promote such awareness both inside and outside the church was Frank Sayre, who since 1947 had combined his passion for industrial chaplaincy with parish ministry in East Cleveland, Ohio. Sayre's circumstances were to change dramatically early in 1951, however, when Bishop Angus Dun, an old family friend, invited him to become the fifth dean of Washington National Cathedral.[215] "I am feeling very terrified of the great responsibilities that lie ahead," he confessed to Will Scarlett shortly after his appointment.[216] For Sayre, the special opportunities that his birth and status conferred upon him had always come with a corresponding sense of duty. His wife Harriet, the daughter of a former commander of the Pacific Fleet, explained years later that "we were both brought up with a strong recognition of the fact that we certainly were privileged people and with privilege goes responsibility and obligation. And there was no question that was the job."[217] For his part, Bishop Dun saw that in order for the cathedral to realize its potential, it needed a leader with the confidence and vision to place it at the center of the nation's consciousness. In discussing what the job held in store, Sayre recalled Dun describing the cathedral "with its institutions and its friends and its great undeveloped power as being like a great organ which needed an organist. He challenged me to come and play this great instrument. It was the kind of call that no man could refuse."[218] Part of the challenge, of course, was that the "instrument" itself was far from finished, ensuring that building construction would be a constant preoccupation throughout the dean's twenty-seven-year tenure. Meanwhile, as the cathedral towers slowly rose over the Washington skyline, so did Sayre's reputation as a

50 PRIVILEGE AND PROPHECY

preacher and activist. In keeping with Bishop Dun's expectations, he proved fearless in providing moral commentary about the wide range of social and political controversies facing the country.[219]

Sayre had scarcely been installed as dean before he made plain his views on racial equality. With Dun's encouragement, in June 1951 he recruited John Burgess of Howard University to join the cathedral staff as its first black canon.[220] He would also routinely condemn segregation from the cathedral pulpit as a violation of Christian teaching.[221] Even so, he was pragmatic about operating within the constraints of the existing culture, as demonstrated by his handling of a dilemma that arose in 1952. As the cathedral's annual fundraising dinner drew near that spring, Sayre realized to his horror that the country club where it was scheduled to take place did not admit African Americans, meaning Canon Burgess and his wife would be barred from attending. Writing to Burgess, Sayre expressed "the almost agony that is in my heart over this" but wondered if it was wise to take a principled stand that could derail the event and sow division within the cathedral community.[222] Burgess's reply was gracious and equally pragmatic, agreeing that this battle was not one worth fighting. Instead, he sought to place the incident in the context of the church's theological and ecclesiological development. "It has always seemed to me that the appointment of a Negro to the Cathedral staff was done in a manner to show its reasonableness in light of scripture and catholicity," he wrote. "To use it as a red flag to inflame all the traditional prejudices of the community would accomplish nothing at all. . . . As we deal with each situation individually in the light of its own importance I am confident that our original objective will be best realized." Provided reconciliation was not confused with mere appeasement, Burgess remained hopeful the National Cathedral could serve as a beacon of racial progress, such that "time may prove that this is the great justification for the cathedral building itself."[223]

This episode is illustrative of the cautious approach Episcopalians took to racial matters after the war. Much remained unsaid, and attempts to press questions of equality in the church were often deflected in the name of seemliness. At the 1948 Convention of the Diocese of Texas, for example, delegates voted to maintain segregation at all social gatherings, citing "certain present limitations preventing an immediate consummation of the Christian Ideal in bi-racial matters."[224] Similarly revealing of the Episcopal mentality was the response Clifford Morehouse got when he tried to clarify the church's racial policies at the General Convention of 1949. Morehouse (1904–1977), then editor of *The Living Church* and later president of the House of Deputies, proposed a canon to make explicit the "equal rights and status" of every baptized member of the Episcopal Church, regardless of race, color or nationality. The relevant committee sidestepped his resolution on the grounds that it was simply unnecessary. (A canon very similar to the one mooted by Morehouse would be passed fifteen years later, by which time it became impossible to deny that certain Southern churches were refusing to admit black people and civil rights workers to Holy Communion.)[225] Yet nowhere during these years would the tension between Episcopal decorum and social responsibility become more evident than in the controversy engulfing Sewanee's School of Theology in 1952. When in June of that year the University of the South's Board of Trustees rejected a proposal to desegregate the seminary, the faculty objected strongly, threatening to resign en masse if the trustees did not reconsider their decision. In the face of this ultimatum the university administration remained unyielding, and in October the professors confirmed their intention to leave at the end of the academic year.[226]

Caught in the middle of the conflict between the administration and faculty was Duncan M. Gray, Jr. (1926–2016), son of the bishop of Mississippi and elected leader of the seminarians. Having studied engineering at Tulane and trained as a naval officer during the war, Gray worked in industry before enrolling at the School of Theology in 1950. What made his position as student president particularly challenging was the fact that he was also the nephew of Edward "Ned" McCrady, vice chancellor of the University. In voicing the seminarians' support for their teachers, Gray found himself very much on the other side of the argument from his uncle. This was only the first of many occasions on which Gray worked for social reform among people whom he loved and respected, despite painful disagreements. Unsurprisingly, however, this local, more relational aspect of the controversy was of little interest to outsiders, who often seized upon it for their own purposes. An obvious case in point was James Pike, by then dean of St. John the Divine in New York after a stint as chaplain at Columbia University. When Sewanee invited Pike to receive an honorary doctorate at the 1953 commencement, he quickly alerted the press that he could not accept "a doctorate in the white divinity" from a segregated institution.[227] As would be the case throughout his career, Pike managed to turn a matter of legitimate principle into an opportunity for self-promotion. Others critical of Sewanee proved more willing to admit that discrimination in the church existed outside the South. In an editorial in *The Witness*, W. B. Spofford affirmed his

52 PRIVILEGE AND PROPHECY

condemnation of the university's policy but reminded his fellow liberals that "we must go one step further and ask ourselves wherever we may live, if our consciences are clean; we who have built walls around Harlems and ghettos to protect our Episcopal suburbs from some of our Christian brethren."[228] In the event, the Board of Trustees met again in June and this time voted to open the School of Theology to African American applicants.

Duncan Gray's experience of advocating racial equality among his fellow Episcopalians at Sewanee proved valuable preparation for the challenges he faced upon returning to Mississippi to undertake ordained ministry.[229] In mid-May 1954, the US Supreme Court handed down its landmark decision, *Brown v. Board of Education*, which ruled unconstitutional all state laws mandating separate public schools for black and white students. In a unanimous decision, the court concluded "separate educational facilities are inherently unequal" and therefore should be integrated with "all deliberate speed." Predictably, the judgment unleashed furious opposition in the South, where gradualism remained the watchword in all matters pertaining to race.[230] Under these tense conditions, Gray prepared a document on behalf of the Diocesan Department of Christian Social Relations, in which he affirms integration on scriptural grounds. "Man, be he white or black, is made in the image of God," he reasons. "This is fundamental to the Biblical concept of the Fatherhood of God and the brotherhood of Man. Our attitude toward the Supreme Court's decision is, therefore, essentially a religious question, since it concerns what we really believe about God and His creation." Having laid down the theological grounds on which Episcopalians should embrace the court's ruling, Gray then attends to the pastoral realities. "The people who are really involved in this situation," he observes, "are those of us who live in small southern communities, whose children attend school, who meet our neighbors along the streets, and who, for the most part, worship God in His Church. It is we who have to search our hearts, pray for grace and wisdom, and learn to live within the Court's decision."[231] Committed as he is to the rightness of racial equality, Gray's tone here nonetheless reflects his compassion for those white Christians struggling to accept a new dispensation that will fundamentally alter their way of life. So, even though Gray is now justly celebrated as an exemplar of Southern progressivism during the civil rights period, to honor him as exceptional is in fact to misconstrue the very nature of his ministry and outlook. Rooted in the Anglican parochial tradition, he regarded his social witness as inextricably bound up in the people and place he had been called to serve.[232]

ALL SORTS AND CONDITIONS   53

The anxiety that some Americans felt regarding the *Brown* decision dovetailed all too easily with the Cold War hysteria that reached its height around the same time.[233] And while Episcopal leaders still struggled to find their collective voice regarding the racial situation, they proved robust in condemning the scare-mongering of Joseph McCarthy and his supporters. Frank Sayre led the way in early 1953, excoriating the senator and other redbaiters for presuming that "God and the nation are best served by the frightened and credulous collaborators of a servile brand of patriotism." For Sayre, the bully tactics such men employed revealed an essential hubris, a presumption of "omnipotence that pretends it can ferret out all sin and purify all else."[234] Following suit were bishops Arthur Lichtenberger of Missouri, Horace Donegan of New York, and Theodore Ludlow of Newark, who openly deplored the anti-communist investigations at their springtime diocesan conventions, as did the presiding bishop at the House of Bishops' meeting in November.[235] Sayre made headlines again by confronting the issue in March 1954, when he and James Pike used a pulpit exchange to launch a joint denunciation of McCarthy. Preaching at St. John the Divine, Sayre censured the American public as a whole, whom he blamed for fueling the senator's witch-hunt. "He would be nothing without the active support of what has been estimated to be at least one-third of our people," asserted the dean. "McCarthy is only the spokesman, but the guilt is as widespread as man's carelessness of God, his forgetfulness of the moral law."[236] In fact, McCarthy himself would soon fall from grace, but his campaign exposed a deep and abiding resentment at work among certain white Americans. Notwithstanding the benefits they enjoyed as citizens of the most powerful nation on earth, many harbored a visceral suspicion that liberal elites in the federal government, the universities, and the churches were undermining their values and interests.[237] This undercurrent of reaction and mistrust would serve as a perennial check on the progressive impulses of the mainline denominations as they navigated the upheavals of the years to come.[238]

That such impulses were gaining momentum in the Episcopal Church was clear. During the decade after the war, scattered efforts by idealistic, young priests to take ministry in new directions prompted them to question the very nature of the church's mission to modern America. For even as Episcopalianism prospered in the suburbs, its appeal among inner-city and industrial communities remained limited, constrained by its all-too-comfortable identification with the status quo. Having sought to broaden the terms of Christian outreach, these post-war clergy began to appraise church

54 PRIVILEGE AND PROPHECY

and society alike in increasingly prophetic terms, indicting them for their moral complacency and structural injustice. In doing so, they took up the mantle of veteran activists like Will Scarlett and Vida Dutton Scudder, who had gained their own inspiration from the great Social Gospel figures of the nineteenth century. Not long before his retirement as bishop of Missouri in 1950, Scarlett once more affirmed the need for prophets, people unafraid to risk opprobrium by witnessing to a radical vision of society. "Who will try to see the world as God sees it?" he asked. "Who will speak for human brotherhood, a brotherhood transcending divisions of race and class? Who will contend for the individual person and his dignity and his rights against the powerful who would crush him? Who will try to sense the direction in which the Kingdom of God lies and give mankind a push along that path?"[239] It was out of their growing conviction that they were called to fulfill this need that certain members of the Episcopal Church turned their efforts to this mission during the latter half of the 1950s.

3

Challenging the Church to Save It
(1955–1959)

Looking back on his experiences as a priest in Nebraska in the mid-1950s, Robert S. Ellwood described the atmosphere of the Episcopal Church during these years as the "institutional equivalent of family togetherness." Ellwood (b. 1933), who later became a professor of world religions at the University of Southern California, remembered Episcopal parish life as reassuringly staid, presided over by clergy who were expected to be "conventional, well-organized, businesslike men who knew the value of real estate and how to emcee a dinner."[1] Yet despite their reputation for social confidence in local communities, Episcopalians in many parts of the country remained comparatively thin on the ground. Particularly for those in rural dioceses, it was common to travel long distances for services, conferences, and social events that bolstered their sense of collective identity.[2] The greatest Episcopal gathering of all was of course the triennial General Convention, which in 1955 was scheduled to take place in Houston. Bishop Clinton Quin of Texas had secured the role of host only after considerable debate at the convention of 1952, where some delegates queried the appropriateness of holding their national forum in a racially segregated city.[3] In response, Quin worked hard to reassure his co-religionists that black churchmen would be shielded from discriminatory treatment during their visit.[4] As the time drew closer, though, black Episcopalians became more vocal in their objections. When prominent African American clergy such Thomas W. S. Logan, Richard Martin, and Tollie Caution gathered for a meeting of the Episcopal Church Workers in April 1954, they concluded that Texas was an unacceptable location for the convention, as "members of the Negro race will be subject not only to many inconveniences but danger of physical violence."[5] Responding to these protests, presiding bishop Henry Sherrill belatedly transferred the convention to Honolulu, an action that outraged Bishop Quin. "You had neither the moral nor the legal right to remove the General Convention from Houston," he told Sherrill. "But you will see our Texas loyalty to the Church just the

Privilege and Prophecy. Robert Tobin, Oxford University Press. © Oxford University Press 2022.
DOI: 10.1093/oso/9780190906146.003.0003

56   PRIVILEGE AND PROPHECY

same."[6] From behind the patina of familial unity there had emerged basic differences over how to accommodate the regional and racial diversity of the Episcopal family itself.

When the presiding bishop finally addressed General Convention in the autumn of 1955, he acknowledged that not all Episcopalians approached the church's corporate identity in the same way. "There have been many sincere men and women," he observed, "who feel that the Church as a Church should have little to do with events and problems which are not immediately ecclesiastical." For people such as these, it was up to individuals rather than the institution to intervene in the realm of public affairs. In contrast to this position, however, Sherrill insisted that Christians had a shared responsibility "to state great ethical and spiritual principles" in modern life. "At her best," he asserted, "in every age the Church has fulfilled a prophetic role."[7] In a speech delivered the following June at Princeton, James Pike pressed the point further, arguing that as ordained representatives of the Christian community, clergy were obliged to "speak in the name of Christ in judgment against the sins of society." At the same time, he claimed that "there is not one thing which the minister is called to do that his laymen are not called to do with him," such that they must likewise be ready to "share in the prophetic function of social criticism." If some church members felt that ministers pronounced too readily on political or social matters they did not properly understand, it was up to them as laypeople to add their expertise and experience to the church's prophetic ministry.[8] "No parson is wise enough on all aspects of history and of current events to speak infallibly on specific proposals or particular candidates," Pike conceded to another audience later that year. "But he should be able to recognize evil—corporate and entrenched—when he sees it, and thus perform the negative function of criticism. He also ought to be able to perceive and enunciate the general principles which would govern a right solution; and thus he fulfills a positive function."[9] Clergy and laity might honestly disagree sometimes about the best way to fulfill these "functions" of prophetic speech, but that such functions belonged to all Christians was beyond doubt.

Given the degree to which ordained ministry had become professionalized in mainline Protestantism, acknowledging laypeople had a calling and ministry of their own was a significant development of the post-war years. Someone who took seriously the need to foster lay activism in the church was Arthur E. Walmsley, who eventually served as bishop of Connecticut in the 1980s. Like William Stringfellow, Walmsley (1928–2017) came from a working-class New England background and was the first person in his family to enter higher education. Having completed his undergraduate degree at Trinity College, Hartford, he graduated from ETS in 1951 and was ordained deacon the same year. Alongside other promising young clerics such as W. Murray Kenney and James H. Clark, Walmsley became known as one of "Lichty's boys" after Arthur Lichtenberger recruited him to serve as priest-in-charge of Trinity Church in St. Louis.[10] Having flourished under the leadership of Stephen Bayne in the 1930s, this Anglo-Catholic parish now strained to adapt itself to the demographic changes of the inner city. The bishop assigned Walmsley to the job of galvanizing the congregation into change.[11] As part of this process, on one occasion he preached that Christian ministry was about what church members did Monday through Saturday, not just on Sunday mornings. Late that night he was woken up by a phone call from a member of his congregation. "[Y]our sermon has kept me awake," explained the man, who also happened to be the chairman of the Federal Reserve in St. Louis. "I do believe that my ministry is what I do as a banker. Will you tell me what in hell that means!" This *cri de coeur* led to a group of professionals meeting regularly with Walmsley to explore the nature of their vocation as lay Christians active in the world.[12] Reflecting on the challenges such people faced, Walmsley later observed that "the spectacle of the committed layman caught in a vast system of business or industry, struggling to translate the exhortation 'be good' into meaningful terms in an impersonal, mechanized, horribly interrelated mass may well be this generation's picture of the Christian martyr."[13] Even though church leaders paid lip service to the importance of empowering laypeople, few as yet seemed to grasp the complexity of the task.[14]

Priests for whom the ministry of the laity became a vital concern throughout this period were Gibson Winter and Francis Ayres. After completing his chaplaincy service in the war, Winter and his wife Blair had settled into a church in Foxboro, Massachusetts, while Fran and Florence "Sis" Ayres continued serving their congregation in Waterbury, Connecticut. Certain that the church had a key part to play in reforming society, it was not long before the two couples began confiding in each other their dissatisfaction with the banality and conservatism of parish life.[15] In particular, they lamented the continuing marginalization of laypeople, leading them to envision a lay training center patterned after European "centers of renewal" such as the Iona Community in Scotland, the Church and World Institute in Holland, and the German evangelical academies.[16] Having been his students at ETS before

58   PRIVILEGE AND PROPHECY

the war, in late 1947 Ayres and Winter contacted Bishop Richard Emrich of Michigan in hopes that he might support their plan.[17] As it happened, the diocese had only recently acquired a farm in Brighton, Michigan, which it planned to develop as a conference and retreat center. With the bishop's encouragement, this property was turned over to Ayres and Winter to initiate what became known as the Parishfield community. Introducing the project to readers of *The Witness* in October 1948, Ayres explained that it was based on the premise "that the Church is at present 'unequal to her task' and that if men of God are to 'rise up and make her great' something more than goodwill is needed—the power of the Holy Spirit working through new men and new channels." In particular, Parishfield was to be a place for laypeople "to go deeper into the knowledge and love of God," as well as "prepare them for specific jobs in their own parishes such as parish-callers, teachers, and Christian witnesses and prophets within their own vocations." In pursuing this program, he concluded, Parishfield would justify its name as a gathering place for those "working in the field of parish life seeking to strengthen the life of a particular parish or to find new ways by which the life of the Church can be reinvigorated."[18]

Recalling his occasional visits to Parishfield in the 1950s, Tony Stoneburner described the center as "a compromise between a very small college campus and a cluster of farm-buildings about an hour's drive from Ann Arbor and Detroit."[19] As soon as the couples and their families took up residence in the spring of 1949, they established a shared discipline of work and leisure, reading and discussion, reflection and worship. And though the community was to be self-consciously ecumenical throughout its existence, its liturgical sensibility remained rooted in the eucharistic theology of its Episcopal founders.[20] For Winter and Ayres, gathering everyone around a central altar for communion was the obvious sacramental expression of the renewed communal life they believed Parishfield should model and encourage.[21] Participants visiting the center for conferences and other activities were expected to partake fully in the daily routine, so that they could return to their parishes with an enhanced sense of responsibility for their own discipleship and witness.[22] Besides the inspiration derived from the lay centers of Europe, another formative influence on the Parishfield staff was the work of Dietrich Bonhoeffer, the German theologian and leader of the Confessing Church, executed by the Nazis in April 1945.[23] In his letters from prison prior to his death, Bonhoeffer had asked what it meant to express the Christian faith authentically in a "world come of age," no longer informed by the language and assumptions of traditional religion.[24] For people looking to recover a sense of organic community amidst the institutionalism of postwar American Protestantism, these writings provided an exciting new vocabulary. Reference to Bonhoeffer's life and thought became so pervasive at Parishfield that Jane Barney, who joined the staff in the late 1950s, later characterized him as "almost an invisible presence in the community."[25] Eager to engage with cutting-edge theological thought and then apply it to daily life, the Parishfield group came to regard itself as an outpost of human solidarity in an increasingly hostile and dehumanizing world.[26]

As part of his engagement with European trends in church renewal, Ayres began a correspondence with Hendrik Kraemer, a Dutch lay theologian and missiologist. Over the years, Kraemer would become a regular visitor, as would the French Protestant Suzanne de Diétrich, whom he introduced to the community in 1953. Like Kraemer, de Diétrich was a lay theologian and ecumenist, known for her innovative approach to Bible study at the Bossey Institute in Switzerland. And while Bible study was already a well-established habit at Parishfield, de Diétrich invigorated the process there, challenging participants to explore the immediate relevance of the texts to personal feelings and social concerns alike. Given the tendency of many Episcopalians to prioritize the *Book of Common Prayer* over the Bible, this emphasis upon shared discernment of the Word became one of the hallmarks of the Parishfield experience.[27] Mary White (1928–2007), who with her husband Hugh joined the staff in the early 1950s, confessed that despite being a longtime member of the Episcopal Church, it was only at Parishfield that she began to read scripture seriously: "I hadn't paid much attention to the Bible before then."[28] Like his wife, Hugh C. White, Jr. (1921–2001), was a native of Michigan. He studied at the University of Virginia before performing war service as an ambulance driver with the American Field Service in the Middle East.[29] Having prepared for ordination at VTS, he then returned to Michigan to serve as rector of St. Luke's Church in Ypsilanti, a town about thirty miles south of Brighton. In this post he had been preceded by another early friend of Parishfield, Robert L. DeWitt, who left St. Luke's in 1948 to become rector of the affluent Christ Church Cranbrook in Bloomfield Hills. Though born in Boston and educated at Amherst, DeWitt (1916–2003) was no stranger to Cranbrook, having served his curacy there from 1940 to 1944.[30] Attractive and urbane, he was a much-loved pastor to his wealthy parishioners, while at the same time proving a highly effective fundraiser on behalf of experimental ministries and outreach across the diocese.[31]

60 PRIVILEGE AND PROPHECY

Although critical of the conventionality of Episcopal life, the residents of Parishfield nonetheless continued to grapple with issues of wealth and status in their community. Discovering when they first came to the farm that there were clay tennis courts on the property, Ayres and Winter quickly dismantled them, judging tennis to be an excessively individualistic and elitist sport.[32] In fact, such gestures were a reaction to their own privileged background, and there were moments when the whole project seemed driven by an urge to dismantle the established hierarchies of this inheritance.[33] At the same time, the willingness to discuss candidly such matters as the Christian use of money became a distinctive part of Parishfield's ministry to visitors, many of whom came from suburban parishes where such questions tended to be addressed obliquely, if at all.[34] The effort to practice what they preached could sometimes lead the Parishfield families into conflict, as when Sis and Fran Ayres agreed to send their daughter Mimi away to boarding school rather than to the inferior public school in Brighton. This decision incensed Gibson Winter, who regarded it as a betrayal of their shared commitment to plain living, though in due course he and his wife felt obliged to make the same choice on behalf of their children, too.[35] The attempt by these upper-middle-class Episcopalians to cultivate a frugal Christian lifestyle often led, in Sara Winter's recollection, to "a strange mixture of simplicity and grandeur," epitomized by her mother's use of the family china and silverware for everyday meals.[36] And at least in the early years, part of this effort to live alternatively included recognizing women as equal contributors to the community, a point strongly emphasized in the teaching of Hendrik Kraemer and Suzanne de Diétrich. As was the case with the group ministry in Jersey City, the role that clergy wives at Parishfield took in planning and decision-making was unusual for the Episcopal Church at the time. But the idea that they might exercise a priestly ministry like that of their husbands was not as yet even a subject for conversation.[37]

The addition of Hugh and Mary White to the staff in 1952 marked the start of a new phase in the development of Parishfield and its mission. It also served to heighten some of the tensions about the way the community operated. For unlike the Ayres and Winters, the Whites had no income other than the small salary they received, an essential difference in circumstances never openly acknowledged. In recalling this dynamic, Mary White noted that "Hugh got really pissed about it and I felt unworthy," though she also remembered feeling it lent a certain irony to all the discussions about economic justice. Her misgivings were compounded when she learned that

CHALLENGING THE CHURCH TO SAVE IT   61

Ayres was actually paying salaries and operating expenses out of his own pocket, for she knew this arrangement made genuine equality in the group impossible.[38] As the daughter of a man who ran a gas station, White's sense of unworthiness proceeded from her self-identification as working class in an overwhelmingly middle-class environment. She concealed her background from the lawyers, doctors, and other professionals who made up the majority of Parishfield's visitors. "Once you get into the Episcopal Church," she later remarked, "there's sort of a class thing [at work], kind of a snobby [thing]." Even though Hugh White came from what his wife deemed "good stock," he tended to maintain a "belligerent, smart-ass attitude" about such distinctions, preferring to identify with working people. This affinity would play an important part in shaping his subsequent ministry.[39]

Two young Episcopalians for whom Parishfield proved formative during this period were Caroline and Mike Bloy.[40] Caroline Kuhn (1925–2011) first became acquainted with the center while serving as a church worker at the University of Michigan in Ann Arbor. Born into a distinguished New York family, Kuhn had attended the Chapin School in Manhattan before going on to the Bouvé School of Physical Education in Boston. Her future husband, Myron B. Bloy, Jr. (1926–1985), was a native of Detroit who served in the US Navy during 1944–1946 and then attended Kenyon College and the University of Connecticut. When he and Kuhn met in 1953, Bloy was teaching English at Ohio State and serving as an admissions officer at Kenyon. At Parishfield, the couple received training in "group dynamics," made popular by the Episcopal Church's Seabury Series in adult education. Like the Bible studies led by Suzanne de Diétrich, these sessions sought to impart a greater sense of religious agency among laypeople.[41] In retrospect, some Episcopalians identified the questioning, exploratory attitude of the Seabury courses as a kind of "seed-bed" for their activism during the 1960s and 1970s.[42] In the case of Mike Bloy, this exposure led to the decision to seek ordination, and in 1953 he enrolled at ETS. Yet in joining the priesthood, he was determined not to become the rector of a comfortable suburban parish, for this would be merely to perpetuate what he considered an already moribund institution.[43] Here the influence of Parishfield was once more apparent, for by the mid-1950s the staff itself was becoming skeptical that renewal of the church could take place within its existing structures. Again and again, they heard from laypeople who, having returned from Parishfield eager to undertake a life of Christian servanthood, found their home congregation a lonely and even resistant environment. As a result, those who were

62 PRIVILEGE AND PROPHECY

among the most committed to their faith increasingly turned away from the concerns of the church and instead focused their energies on the needs of the wider community.[44]

The conclusion that parish life was not in fact the best environment in which to pursue Christian renewal set the Parishfield community on a new trajectory, that of promoting what it called "frontier evangelism." Defined in staff working papers as "the proclamation of the gospel on the battle line between the Church and the world," this form of evangelism affirmed that "the only full witness to the Lordship of Christ is to witness to the possibility of life together under Christ." Such "life together"—the phrase is an obvious allusion to Dietrich Bonhoeffer's book by this title—required Christians to abandon the familiarity of their gathered congregations and to seek out God's unifying presence amidst the brokenness and confusion of modern American life.[45] In promoting this turn outward, the Parishfield community had, in Gibson Winter's words, begun to move "from indirect engagement with society *through the churches* to direct involvement in renewal within society *as the church.*" At the same time, he acknowledged that such a shift served as a kind of rebuke to the institutional church which the community had been created to serve.[46] Yet for Fran Ayres, such challenges were part of Parishfield's contribution to the reform that the church must undergo if it was serious about lay ministry on the one hand and society on the other. A genuine commitment to serving Christ in the world, he wrote, "will mean many changes for the church—changes in attitude, structure, procedure. Above all, it will mean a change in its willingness to take risks and to make sacrifices—new wine in new wineskins! All who love the church and appreciate what it has to give will work for change in all aspects of its life."[47]

A robust conversation partner for the community during its second phase was to be the theologian Paul M. van Buren (1924–1998). Grandson to an heiress and a bishop, van Buren was born in Virginia and educated at St. Paul's before volunteering in 1942 to serve in the US Coast Guard and then the Naval Air Force. At the end of the war he resumed his studies, graduating successively from Harvard College in 1948 and ETS in 1951. After ordination the same year, he and his wife Anne moved to Basel, where he undertook doctoral studies with Karl Barth. Although convinced of his calling to be a seminary professor, van Buren recognized the importance of ministering outside the academy before embarking on a teaching career. Writing from Switzerland about his plans for the future, he confided to his friend John Davis his need to "get out of the habit of theological jargon" and to learn

CHALLENGING THE CHURCH TO SAVE IT   63

to express Christian ideas "in words that a drunk can understand." Less facetiously, he admitted that "I have to learn how to instruct the parents of a child to be baptized, to teach catechumens the heart of the gospel. If I don't do this first, I stand in great danger of teaching theology as a subject to be 'learned' in order to pass exams." But if that were the only thing he could offer, "then all my work here and my ideas of what's wrong with the church and what to do about it will be in vain."[48] When he and Anne returned with their young family to the United States in 1954, he set about finding an urban parish where he and his friend Robert Gardner might attempt a shared ministry. In a letter to Bishop Emrich the same year, van Buren explained that they were looking for a church "where we can devote ourselves to a ministry of renewal with the people of the neighborhood in which the parish is located." This offer resulted in their appointment as part-time co-rectors of St. Thomas's Church in Detroit, as well as work as part-time staff members at the Episcopal City Mission.[49]

Not long after their arrival in Detroit, the van Burens got to know the staff of Parishfield, with whom they felt an immediate rapport. "They talked the same language we wanted to hear," Paul van Buren remembered, especially about the centrality of Bible study and the church's responsibility to society. He also shared their highly critical view of the religious status quo, coupled with their determination "to work from the inside of [it] instead of just turn[ing] the whole thing over."[50] Soon Paul and Anne van Buren became valued contributors to the Parishfield community. After two years of parish ministry at St. Thomas's and another year at the cathedral, in 1957 van Buren succeeded Hans Frei on the faculty at the Seminary of the Southwest in Texas. While his time in Michigan was comparatively brief, van Buren's experiences in inner-city Detroit and at Parishfield made a lasting impression, as became evident from the lectures in Christian dogmatics he delivered in Austin. In them, he is forthright in his indictment of the Episcopal Church and of American culture as a whole, particularly in regard to segregation.[51] To van Buren, the mainline denominations' complicity in racism was a natural result of Christianity occupying the position of a quasi-established religion in American life. Having assumed this role, the church in turn became the nation's conscience. The problem with this arrangement was it meant that the church "can raise many serious secondary questions, but it can never question the foundation of that of which it is the conscience. It means that Christianity, as the conscience of a culture or nation, belongs to that culture or nation, is committed to it, and can never be in fundamental

64 PRIVILEGE AND PROPHECY

opposition to it. It can reprove, correct, influence. It cannot, however, as religion and thus as the conscience of that culture or nation, be not of it." Importantly, Anglican establishmentarian sensibilities receive no quarter in this thoroughly Barthian analysis of the relationship of the church to the world. In clinging to the notion that it could reconcile culture to Christ, the Episcopal Church did no more than "baptize the world with a baptism that obligingly forgets that it is the sign of death."[52]

During the years the van Burens spent in Michigan, the Parishfield community had sought to lend substance to the idea of "frontier evangelism" by creating a program of "industrial work groups," intended to examine "what ways the Church can witness to her faith in and through the work life of her people."[53] By forming groups of people according to their employment and inviting them to spend weekends in the country, the staff hoped to prompt reflection about the interplay of work, values, and faith. Explicitly non-denominational and organized on the basis of personal contacts, the groups consisted of people ranging from senior executives and middle managers to rank-and-file union members and day laborers.[54] Yet getting blue-collar people to come to Parishfield proved difficult, for, as Mary White later explained, "it was too far away, they had so little time, and were not always comfortable sitting and just talking."[55] Out of these very practical constraints, a new initiative would emerge. The experiment with the industrial groups at Parishfield had persuaded Gibson Winter and Hugh White of the need for "full time responsible engagement" with people in the workplace.[56] Familiar with Frank Sayre's experiences as an industrial missioner in Cleveland after the war, in 1955 they traveled to Washington to discuss with him the possibility of doing similar work in Detroit.[57] Encouraged by the dean, they likewise secured the backing of Bishop Emrich, and by July 1956 the Detroit Industrial Mission (DIM) had been formally established with White as executive director, Sayre as chairman of the board, and Winter as the board secretary.[58] Meanwhile, the latter had accepted a teaching post at the University of Chicago Divinity School, so that in the summer both the Winter and White families ceased to be resident members of Parishfield.

Once based in the city, White discovered that connecting with working-class people continued to be a major challenge. In this realization he was not alone, as indicated by a series of regional conferences organized by Paul Musselman of the National Council.[59] At the gathering held in Wilkes-Barre in September 1956, for example, clergy working in industrial areas specifically cited their Episcopalianism as a hindrance to reaching manual laborers.

CHALLENGING THE CHURCH TO SAVE IT   65

"How are you going to convince them we're not the executive church," one priest asked, "when we *are* the executive church?" The group surmised that if the Episcopal Church was serious about developing a presence among such people, it needed to confront basic questions about its own social identity and attitudes.[60] As Musselman admitted a few years later, the church's history of aligning itself with established economic interests was a legacy that could not be immediately or easily overcome.[61] Yet Episcopal leaders were becoming increasingly vocal in disowning this reputation for elitism. Preaching at St. John the Divine in October 1956, James Pike lamented that the Episcopal Church was so widely known as a "class church," attended by only "the right sort of people." Such a notion was "theologically repugnant," he warned, concluding that the "church on earth is supposed to be an image of heaven. Some of us who have qualms about mixing with people will have a lot of adjusting to do."[62] Horace Donegan, who had succeeded Charles Gilbert as bishop of New York in 1950, made a similar point when articulating the diocese's attitude to the changing demographics of the city. The Episcopal Church was no longer just "an Anglo-Saxon Church," he emphasized; rather, "we are an American Church, created and designed to meet the needs of the American people, regardless of their national background, mother tongue, or color of skin."[63] Claims to being a catholic church with a mission to all classes must remain meaningless so long as Episcopalians tacitly clung to a sense of their inherent superiority.

Like Frank Sayre, another figure whose struggles with privilege drew him into the realm of industrial mission was Scott I. Paradise.[64] The son of a teacher at Phillips Academy Andover, Paradise (1929–2015) excelled at the school during the war years, where he remembered fellow Episcopalian and future president George H. W. Bush as captain of the baseball team. Following family tradition, Paradise then went on to study at Yale. But lurking beneath the surface of this successful student career lay an abiding discomfort with the injustices and inequalities of the world.[65] In college Paradise became fascinated by the history of the industrial revolution and the ongoing battle of the laboring classes to establish their rights. Having graduated from Yale in 1950, he spent the summer doing voluntary social work in London's East End before enrolling at ETS that autumn. Once at seminary he was further inspired by stories of slum priests in Britain and America and the worker-priest movement in France, which prompted him to spend another summer among the poor at a church in New York's Lower East Side.[66] As soon as he finished ETS and was ordained deacon in 1953, Paradise set off again for the United

66   PRIVILEGE AND PROPHECY

Kingdom, this time to join the Iona Community in Scotland. Established in 1938 by the Church of Scotland minister and social reformer George MacLeod, this innovative community was committed to "whole salvation rather than soul salvation," wherein the gospel became the basis for a holistic approach to the political and economic life of the country.[67] MacLeod welcomed the young American but felt he should be working alongside other Anglicans and therefore sent him to Canon Ted Wickham of the Sheffield Industrial Mission. Joining the mission in early 1954, Paradise quickly fell in love with his work as chaplain of Steel, Peech, and Tozer, a major steel producer in Rotherham, where he spent much of his time conversing with unchurched laborers.[68] Most of those whom he met considered the church irrelevant and hypocritical, but they also had an instinctive sense that Christ was on the side of the workers. "On one hand I found I was very challenged," Paradise remembered, "but on the other hand I found I could talk with these people. I began reading theology like it was a matter of life and death."[69] Having originally planned to stay in Sheffield for just a year, Paradise stayed for four.

As part of the inquiry into whether an industrial mission in Detroit was feasible, Gibson Winter had visited Sheffield in 1955 to consult with Ted Wickham, and during this trip he made the acquaintance of Scott Paradise.[70] This introduction eventually resulted in Paradise joining DIM as associate director in February 1957. A third person to join the staff was Robert Grindley, a retired industrial executive who had been working as a lay assistant at Christ Church Cranbrook. Grindley's involvement proceeded from the "associated parishes" dimension of DIM, something Bishop Emrich had insisted upon as part of his sponsorship of the project.[71] Christ Church was one of four suburban parishes where White and Paradise regularly preached and led discussion groups in hope of stimulating lay involvement in industrial mission.[72] Under Robert DeWitt's stewardship, Christ Church was also to be an important source of financial support to DIM during its first year.[73] At the same time, White proved to be a highly effective promoter of the mission, working closely with Frank Sayre to raise funds and make important contacts across the national church. This freed Paradise to devote himself to the "grassroots work" of spending time with people on the factory floors of the Detroit car companies.[74] Notwithstanding his experience as a missioner in England, gaining the trust of the workers was by no means easy. "I felt I was regarded as something like a lunatic wandering from a mental hospital," Paradise recorded. "I was treated gently and humored, lest I break out

CHALLENGING THE CHURCH TO SAVE IT   67

into some kind of bizarre behavior." In order to alleviate some of the discomfort caused by his presence, he even stopped wearing a clerical collar, but really it was simple persistence that won the day. Looking back on DIM's efforts, Paradise surmised that more important than anything said had been "our willingness to go to labor on its own ground, to listen carefully and learn about the real problems, and to offer personal friendship . . . out [of] the central concern of our faith."[75] This view was later confirmed by a union official who reported that despite being a clergyman, Paradise had "won total acceptance" among the membership and inspired many to ask what place work might actually have in the larger purpose of their lives.[76]

In Sheffield and Detroit alike, Paradise saw that although issues of economic disparity still demanded redress, industrial society now presented other, subtler challenges to humanity in general. "The great evil against which the prophets of our time must speak," he wrote in his journal, "is not that there are many down-trodden laborers but that we are all in danger of becoming happy robots."[77] He credited Ted Wickham with opening his eyes to the whole range of institutional structures beginning to dominate modern society, among them "the big manufacturing and distributing corporations, the labor unions, the advertising agencies, the mass media organizations, various social agencies, government departments and countless others." What all these entities had in common was not just their dehumanizing scale but the fact that they functioned with little or no reference to existing forms of community. "They cannot be tied down to a particular locality," observed Paradise. "They have their own interests, their own loyalties, their own ethos and atmosphere, their own set of rules."[78] Yet it was around these bureaucratic organizations that people were more and more forced to order their daily lives.[79] "Our new industrial society is raising up giants—or supermen— on the one hand, and crushing men, or making men feeble, on the other," Hugh White told an audience in November 1957. "Both the supermen and the crushed men in our industrial disorder are men of despair. There is a need amongst Christians to discover that their life as men is fulfilled in their creatureliness."[80] Faced with this reality, the church's task was at once pragmatic and theological: it must be prepared to adapt to this new environment, if only so that it might learn afresh how to convey the Christian message in relevant terms.[81]

Although he now taught at the seminary in Austin, Paul van Buren remained close to his Michigan friends and took an active part in helping DIM formulate its thinking.[82] He regularly emphasized the inadequacy of

68   PRIVILEGE AND PROPHECY

the parish as a place where contemporary laypeople could make connections between their work life and spiritual beliefs. In an address at the close of 1957 he pushed the point further, arguing that DIM "by its very existence raises the question as to whether the parish, a form of the life of the Church developed in and admirably suited to the structure of feudal society and the medieval village, is the best form for the Church today, and whether it is the proper agency through which Christ can best speak to the whole man."[83] Though they were less bold in questioning the very existence of the parish system, the DIM staff spoke often of the "psychological chasm" that had opened up between the domestic setting of religion and the corporate setting of modern business and industry. "The gulf between a man's job and all that is seen, done, talked, thought in the parish church is enormous," White told readers of *The Witness* in 1959.[84] Churches exacerbated the problem when they refused to acknowledge and honor the "secular" relationships that parishioners developed in the workplace, thereby fostering a sense of Christian identity that rarely transcended the confines of Sunday morning.[85] Reflecting on this difficulty from the perspective of a parish priest, Robert DeWitt admitted that "clergy need to be more informed on how their people make their living, the actual nature of the work they do, the decisions they have to make, the pressures under which they work. . . . Their picture of most people's work life is one hundred years or more out of date."[86] Though DIM might help parishes recognize the changes taking place in society, rescuing them from their own mounting irrelevance was hardly its primary concern. On this point Hugh White remained emphatic: the mission had been founded not to produce more pledge-paying Episcopalians but as a radical alternative to received modes of witness.[87]

Even with such a flexible remit, the job of engaging people about faith in the workplace presented formidable challenges. "To a frighteningly large degree," remarked Scott Paradise, "the traditional words and concepts used in the churches are simply meaningless when spoken in the context of modern industry." This being so, the immediate task of the missioner became "find[ing] ways of translating the essence of the Gospel into words and concepts that can break through to confront men once again with the Word of God."[88] Having listened to executives and laborers alike about the ethical dilemmas they faced, DIM concluded that nothing less than "a new moral theology" was needed, a way of talking about God's agency in a society where moral choices had become both more abstract in form and far-reaching in effect.[89] With such fundamental issues at stake, it was also obvious that

CHALLENGING THE CHURCH TO SAVE IT   69

denominational allegiances had to come second and Christians must function cooperatively in the industrial realm.[90] Speaking at the Seminary of the Southwest in 1959, White affirmed this ecumenical approach but insisted that it was only meaningful if embodied locally in daily life.[91] To that end, DIM expanded its staff the following year to include Robert Batchelder, a Congregationalist minister recently graduated from Yale, as well as James Campbell and Jesse Christman, two Presbyterian clergy with experience as assembly-line workers. This move toward the interdenominational went hand in hand with a move away from the Episcopal "associated parishes" model with which DIM had begun. As a result, the mission now devoted its energies to establishing a freestanding presence among the multiple interest groups that comprised industrial Detroit.[92]

While White and Paradise grappled with how to bring the Gospel message out of the churches and into the offices and factories of America, Gibson Winter was diagnosing the ways in which the church had become captive in the suburbs. It was unsurprising that the mainline denominations had been attracted to suburbia, for this was where many of their white, middle-class adherents had settled and started their families after the war.[93] With children and home life very much at their center, suburban communities proved highly amenable to the established patterns of parochial ministry. Along with the other major Protestant groups, the Episcopal Church found it could scarcely keep pace with the demand for new facilities and programming during the 1950s. But as Winter pointed out in his 1961 book *The Suburban Captivity of the Churches*, this success came at a price. For however much the mainline denominations had managed to draw upon the middle classes "as a pool of recruitment," the middle classes had in turn adapted congregational life to their need for "exclusive enclaves of social identity." Wittingly or not, the churches had once more allowed themselves to become havens of racial segregation and class privilege, thereby abdicating their Christian duty to promote an inclusive vision of humanity.[94] This damning analysis of the American religious scene resonated with clergy across the denominational spectrum, many of whom were all too familiar with the dynamic that Winter's "suburban jeremiad" had decried.[95] Paul Musselman, having spent much of the decade traveling the country in his work for the National Council, characterized the typical suburban minister as a "sort of a spiritual baby-sitter . . . proficient in the art of pandering to the immature preferences of the average, spiritually illiterate American." For Episcopal clergy in particular, he warned, the "greatest temptation is to accept the role of becoming

70 PRIVILEGE AND PROPHECY

stewards of good taste, genteel poise, and liturgical correctness, and at all costs to dodge controversial issues."[96]

The degree to which suburban parish life had become normative in the church's thinking did not, of course, go unnoticed by liberal activists. As important as ministry to middle-class families undoubtedly was, Episcopalians needed to remember that urban environments were full of people who did not readily conform to this model of domestic life.[97] In seeking to engage with the growing social diversity of American cities, the urban ministry movement continued to evolve throughout the 1950s. The Urban Priests Group, which had begun as a handful of parish priests attempting inner-city renewal along the East Coast, now spread westward to cities such as Cleveland, Indianapolis, Chicago, and Dallas.[98] At the same time, dioceses as disparate as Florida, Texas, and Los Angeles all instituted some form of program or structure for promoting urban mission.[99] And back in New York, Kim Myers continued his influential work at Trinity Parish's Lower East Side Mission, assisted by William Wendt and a half-dozen other priests, along with nuns from the Society of St. Margaret and a regular stream of student volunteers.[100] One of these volunteers was Grant Gallup, an ordinand from Seabury-Western Seminary in Illinois, who spent two summers on the mission staff. Besides the various activities they undertook with the children from the nearby housing projects, staff members shared in the clergy's routine of daily worship and shared meals. To a young man preparing for the priesthood, this life of Christian solidarity with the poor was exhilarating, for through it Gallup absorbed "the style and elements of liberation theology that were never then taught in classrooms." And while he conceded later that some might look back on the mission's approach as "romantic and unrealistic," Gallup celebrated Kim Myers as an exemplary Episcopalian, a figure who "inspired thousands of us, [and] gave us courage to confront oppression."[101]

Myers would provide his own account of the mission's work in the book *Light the Dark Streets*, published in 1957. In it, he evokes the deprivation and violence of the Lower East Side, most apparent in the gang culture of the neighborhood's teenagers. Having chosen to make young people the focus of his ministry, Myers recounts his efforts to gain a foothold among the rival factions and build up relationships of trust with their leaders. In one scene, he agrees to allow a local gang to use the church's youth center, but in doing so, he is unequivocal about his motives: "I told them quite frankly that our chief interest was not in them as a club, but that we were interested because of our long-range intention of bringing them individually into the church as active members." While he readily admits that many of the mission's programs could just as easily be provided by a community center or settlement house, Myers believes this religious motivation lends its work a unique character. "Perhaps because the Church—acting unashamedly *as* Church—does all this, our communal life seems to be different," he writes. "A dimension often new, and even unknown to the secular agency, is recognized—man is approached and understood as a total being. He is looked upon as a being rooted in history and yet as one whose destiny lies above and beyond history. He is a person and, therefore, of infinite value." Out of this conviction, Myers is emphatic about the necessity of raising up leaders from within impoverished communities, in contrast to secular agencies that assume outside professionals are needed to exercise authority. "This we believe is a fundamental heresy both from the Christian and the democratic point of view," he declares. Even when attempts at local empowerment seem inefficient and destined to produce only modest results, one must persist as an assertion of the dignity of all God's people.[102]

Myers's passionate concern for the poor and marginalized was inextricably linked to his high doctrine of the church. It was a connection he sought to elucidate in two short booklets prepared for the national church in 1958. In *Behold the Church*, written for the Youth Division of the Department of Christian Education, he begins with the premise that as the Body of Christ on earth, "the Church has a divine existence all its own. . . . The Church lives in holiness and righteousness because Christ lives." Once this truth has been grasped, it becomes obvious that the church is, by definition, an institution like no other: "We see it as one and unique. We view it as that holy Body which outlives civilizations and cultures. We never equate it with the passing nation or race." Having been equipped with this "catholic" understanding of the church, young Episcopalians must never mistake denominationalism for an adequate basis of religious identity. "Remember," Myers exclaims, "YOU ARE A MEMBER OF THE HOLY CATHOLIC CHURCH! Don't let anyone fuzz up your thinking by the weak doctrines of our weak American Christianity. . . . FIRST YOU ARE A CATHOLIC. Baptism made you so." To be baptized into the catholic church is to become part of "the New Race whose Head is the Lord Christ," a race in which skin color and economic status are irrelevant.[103] In *Baptized into the One Church*, Myers underscores the power of sacramental life to break down social barriers and transcend cultural norms. Not least, through the sacraments Episcopalians are reminded that "the acts of God are not affected by our subjective reactions," a liberating message in a society prone to conflate religion, patriotism, and good manners. Such a realization in turn frees catholic Christians to confront the pain and injustice of the world, knowing they are already citizens of heaven. "To live the life of the Church is the only life," he concludes. "Why did we try to find answers to life's problems somewhere else? Why did we struggle with problems of race and class and alien ideology before we understood and accepted the Good News of God in Jesus Christ?"[104] Firmly rooted in the language of Anglo-Catholic sacramentalism, Myers's writings envision the Episcopal Church as an instrument of radical social inclusion.

Of the clergy who pursued this vision through urban ministry in the 1950s, among the most acclaimed was James A. Gusweller. A native of New Jersey, Gusweller (1923–2009) had been a devout Episcopalian since boyhood. After service as a machine gunner in the war, he attended Carleton College in Minnesota, followed by seminary at GTS. His first post was in Keyport, New Jersey, where he and his young wife Suzie immediately instituted an "open rectory" policy.[105] In early 1956, the couple moved to Manhattan, where Gusweller became rector of the Church of St. Matthew and St. Timothy on West 84th Street. The situation was a familiar one, in which a formerly vibrant Episcopal parish had witnessed the decline of its neighborhood, so that most of the remaining congregation now lived elsewhere and only came back for Sunday services.[106] As a result, Gusweller began to focus his attention on the Puerto Ricans living in the surrounding tenements, inviting the young people off the streets and into the church. This influx of "colored" children alarmed the white congregants, one of whom wasted no time in complaining to the rector. When Gusweller responded by explaining that "this is the church of God" and thus all were welcome, she shot back: "Wasn't it the church of God when the other rector had it?"[107] The exchange captures more than just the antipathy of one elderly woman; it also bespeaks a more widespread hurt and confusion among Episcopalians who saw the church's attitudes changing in ways they did not comprehend. The panic at St. Matthew's gradually dissipated when, as a feature writer from *The New Yorker* wryly noted, "no one was mugged on his way to the altar rail to receive Communion." Even after overt tensions eased, though, fundamental cultural and economic differences between the old and new members persisted. Gusweller's attempts to engage the local community in parish affairs were hamstrung by the fact that control of the vestry stayed firmly in the hands of the middle-class whites. He did eventually succeed in raising sufficient funds to build a youth center

CHALLENGING THE CHURCH TO SAVE IT   73

next door to the church, which opened in 1962 and included a gymnasium, game room, showers, classrooms, library, and a nursery school. But the basic question of how to share power with the disenfranchised remained largely unresolved.[108]

As Gusweller got to know and love his Puerto Rican neighbors, he was appalled by the terrible conditions under which many of them lived. Before long, he became their advocate in combating exploitation by slumlords, often accompanying them in court. At the end of 1958, he presented the district attorney with charges that city inspectors, far from tackling such abuses, were in fact perpetuating them through their own corrupt practices. Gusweller's accusations made him the object of intense media scrutiny, and the strain of this experience bore heavily upon church and rectory alike.[109] Speaking in early December, Bishop Donegan publicly lauded his priest's efforts to expose the injustices suffered by poor people on the West Side, remarking that "it was quite proper for him to bring this matter to the attention of the public authorities who have the power to remedy the situation, and who will, I am sure, take appropriate action."[110] Certain abuses were in fact addressed as a result, though Gusweller had learned to expect others to take their place. Likewise, William Stringfellow, who served as Gusweller's legal counsel, commented that what impressed him most about the episode was "the enormity of the passion and perseverance which he and the people of his congregation and others had to sustain and suffer in order to achieve such a modest change."[111] As the Jersey City team had already discovered, there were decided limits to how much a single parish could hope to accomplish by way of reform in the face of entrenched interests.

After nearly a decade at Grace Church Van Vorst, in 1958 Paul and Jenny Moore left the East Coast for Indianapolis, where he had been called to serve as dean of Christ Church Cathedral. The bishop, John Craine, invited Moore to use his recent experience in urban mission to develop a program in which three inner-city Episcopal churches would work collectively to address the challenges they faced.[112] What was soon known as the "Indianapolis Plan" also became the springboard for a diocesan education initiative in which parishes were encouraged to study and discuss a range of contemporary social issues, ranging from traffic and highway construction to race, education, and welfare.[113] For Moore, this new role meant less time on the streets but more opportunities to try to influence those with power.[114] Yet in entering the world of policy and politics, he tried hard not to lose sight of what had motivated him in the first place: advocacy for the downtrodden in God's

74 PRIVILEGE AND PROPHECY

name. "The danger in knowing the workings of the power structure lies in misuse," he later reflected. "Cynical manipulation, alliance with less than moral sources of power, or unethical methods can cut the Church off from the source of ultimate power, God. As long as this is kept in mind, a Christian should not be afraid of the understanding and use of the power which exists as part of God's world around him."[115] The Episcopal Church was already known as a denomination with a privileged and well-connected membership; the question was to what end such advantages were to be used. By demonstrating the church's willingness to work alongside others for the common good, the Indianapolis Plan thus prompted a "gradual change in her *image* from a conservative, quiet, socially elite church to one deeply concerned with the problems of the total life of the city."[116]

Moore was not in Indianapolis long before he realized just what an outsider he was. With Bishop Craine's blessing, he had begun to press the matter of racial integration at the cathedral, only to face substantial resistance from the vestry. He was fortunate, however, in enjoying the support of the senior warden, Eli Lilly of the Lilly Pharmaceutical Company. Though Lilly was conservative politically and economically, as a devout Episcopalian he had a commitment to social progress, particularly in the area of civil rights. As the leading citizen of the city, he made it clear that Moore was not to be harassed, and he proceeded to give a million dollars to promote the church's urban mission plan. Notwithstanding such reassurances, Moore knew that resentment toward him persisted under the surface. One morning, while they stood together in the sacristy, one of the adult servers explained: "Father, you are good with poor people, you are at home with rich people, but you don't give a damn for the likes of us middle-class folks." In retrospect, Moore acknowledged the man had been "partly right" and that he and his wife had been guilty of "reverse snobbism against what we felt were the bourgeois values of Indianapolis."[117] Jenny Moore found the transition from Jersey City to Indiana particularly difficult. "At first I didn't know what to do with myself," she admitted. "Where before we had confronted directly the elemental needs of shelter, food, and clothing, and dealt with them on our doorstep or in our house, Paul now went through 'channels.' The results were good but the approach was different, and for a long time we felt ourselves in a no-man's land."[118] Ironically, their interest in cultivating social engagement among middle-class Episcopalians had led the Moores into precisely the kind of compartmentalized family and religious life they regarded as problematic. For if life in Jersey City had taught them nothing else, it was that Christianity could not be lived at a remove. "The Church must be immediately involved, face-to-face," Paul Moore reiterated in 1960. "The Church is the body of Christ reaching out and uniting herself to him in the suffering of his children. The Church cut off from union is not the Church."[119]

Initiatives such as the Indianapolis Plan reflected a growing recognition among Episcopalians that effective city ministry consisted of more than mission priests serving in blighted areas.[120] Both old downtown churches and new suburban churches had a role to play in the church's response to urbanization, as Morris Arnold reminded readers of *The Witness* in 1959. At the time he wrote, Morris F. "Ben" Arnold (1915–1992) was rector of Christ Church Cincinnati, having served as an army chaplain during the war and as a parish priest in Massachusetts before his call to southern Ohio in 1950. His experiences in Cincinnati had taught him that if the church were to flourish in urban settings, suburban and city parishes must cooperate in empowering laypeople who resided in one setting and worked in the other. Suburban churches' distance from the city hardly meant they were indifferent to what went on in it, as was sometimes too readily assumed.[121] Meanwhile, downtown churches, with their prestige and physical proximity to business and government, were clearly well placed to highlight issues such as poverty, housing, and unemployment.[122] In the effort to strengthen the Episcopal Church's involvement in these matters, in September 1959 Arnold and Moore gathered downtown rectors from across the country to found the Conference on Church and City, which soon became a powerful lobby in national church affairs.[123] While there may yet be disagreement about the best approach, there could be little doubt, as one commentator put it, that "the city is the great missionary challenge of the next decade."[124]

As white priests began to attract widespread attention for their work in urban settings during the 1950s, black Episcopal clergy felt their long-standing ministry in African American city churches had once again been overlooked.[125] Compounding this sense of grievance was the decision by some bishops to merge historically black congregations with their nearby white counterparts, in the hope of enforcing racial integration. The problem was that in practice the merger was always one way and led to the closure of black churches at precisely the moment when many whites were relocating to the suburbs. As a result, black Episcopal communities that had been built up over generations were destroyed and their members expected to fend for themselves in reluctant white congregations.[126] This disjunction between the church's affirmation of racial equality and its insensitive treatment of

76 PRIVILEGE AND PROPHECY

its own black membership would become a major sticking-point among Episcopalians during the course of the civil rights movement.[127] One black cleric who greeted the "new" enthusiasm for urban ministry with a degree of ironic detachment was John Howard Johnson, longtime rector of St. Martin's Church in Harlem. A native of New York, Johnson (1897–1995) had attended the city's public schools before taking degrees at Columbia and preparing for the priesthood at General and Union seminaries. After ordination he served for five years as his father's assistant at St. Cyprian's Church and in 1928 founded St. Martin's, which by the late 1940s had a congregation of more than 3,000.[128] Noting the church occupied an area of Harlem that had once been white and middle-class, Johnson observed that "a rather vague, new name has sprung up for these churches left by their original congregations. Politely and inoffensively they are referred to as Urban Churches. Apparently the title is understood and approved by those in the know. They are city churches but must not be confused with wealthy downtown parishes." Though he disdained the idea of the "black church" as a separate entity and actively endorsed integration whenever possible, Johnson believed that so long as neighborhoods remained segregated, so would churches.[129] Even those white Episcopalians prepared to welcome black co-religionists into their midst were a long way off from embracing black churches as viable equivalents to their own.

Another highly effective black priest working in Harlem during this period was M. Moran Weston. The son and grandson of Episcopal clergymen, Weston (1910–2002) grew up in North Carolina and graduated from St. Augustine's Junior College in Raleigh before going to New York in 1928 to continue his studies at Columbia. While working as a social worker in 1930s and 1940s, he studied theology at GTS and Union Seminary and was eventually ordained. In the mid-1940s he became active at St. Philip's Church in Harlem, where he cofounded Carver Federal Savings Bank, specifically in order help black homebuyers obtain mortgages. In late 1952 Weston was appointed executive secretary of the Division of Christian Citizenship in the Christian Social Relations (CSR) Department of the National Council, during which time he also completed a doctorate in social history at Columbia.[130] He returned to St. Philip's as rector in 1957, and over the next twenty-five years would oversee the funding and construction of housing developments, a community center, a nursing home, and treatment centers. Weston also served on the boards of various charitable organizations, notably that of the NAACP Legal Defense and Educational Fund, led by his friend and parishioner Thurgood Marshall.[131] When informed that he had been nominated to succeed Stephen Bayne as the bishop of Olympia in 1959, he politely refused, stating his ministry lay with the people of Harlem.[132] As priest, educator, and businessman, Weston became a leading citizen in Harlem, who, like John Johnson, exemplified the vital role often played by middle-class black Episcopalians in their communities.

After Weston's departure from the National Council, Arthur Walmsley from St. Louis was appointed his successor at the Division of Christian Citizenship, where he was assisted by Cornelius C. "Neil" Tarplee.[133] A native of Jacksonville, Florida, Tarplee (1911–1970) had attended the University of Virginia and VTS in the 1930s and then served as a parish priest and as a navy chaplain during the war.[134] In 1950, he accepted a call to St. Paul's Church in Lynchburg, where he remained until forced out by the vestry for his civil rights activities. This episode in turn led to his being hired by Weston at the start of 1957, in order to direct a new church program working to promote greater understanding among racial groups.[135] Known as "Bridge-Building in Areas of Racial Tension," the initiative was already underway when Walmsley took up his post the following year. With his personal background and recent experience of local conflict, Tarplee was especially well placed to encourage and counsel other white Southerners who faced hostility for their pro-integration views.[136] Often lonely in their challenge to the status quo, such progressively minded people quickly discovered the limits of support they could expect from the institutional church. "Most of the churches and related agencies do not seem to be realistically committed to anything much better than statements of general policy," Tarplee reported to the CSR Department in the spring of 1958. Moreover, well-meaning Northern activists, who were "highly aroused and effective in moments of acute crisis," had a habit of disappearing during "the long seasons of almost motionless deadlock" characteristic of much civil rights work. In concluding his assessment, Tarplee laid out the choice before the Episcopal Church in stark terms. "Either we seek peace and gain security at the cost of silence in regard to moral principles," he wrote, "or else witness clearly to the moral and religious principles involved and suffer the kind of persecution peculiar to our age—loss of membership, loss of popularity, loss of income—perhaps, in brief, to be set back a generation or two in the building of our ecclesiastical structure."[137]

When General Convention convened the following October in Miami Beach, a study document entitled *Report on Race Relations* formed the basis

78 PRIVILEGE AND PROPHECY

for debate about the church's evolving role in the racial situation. The report reiterated Tarplee's observations about the pressures and difficulties faced by advocates of racial equality, adding that the absence of authoritative church leadership tended to facilitate a "climate of timidity among moderate voices." At the same time, though, the report detected increasing defiance of the church's authority among laypeople, evidenced by "the disrespect and downright discourtesy publicly displayed to bishops and clergy speaking and acting in good faith" on social questions.[138] This rift between clergy and laity was demonstrated at the convention itself by sharp divisions within the House of Deputies over resolutions relating to civil rights, whereas the House of Bishops voted unanimously for a resolution put forward by John Hines calling on Christian leaders to reject "easy standards of local expediency" in their approach to racial matters.[139] Hines, who had succeeded Clinton Quin as diocesan bishop of Texas at the end of 1955, became well known across the national church during these years as both a vigorous proponent of racial justice and a critic of Episcopal complacency. Addressing a conference of the National Canterbury Association at Sewanee in November 1957, he informed the gathering that "all Christians stand condemned that the due process of law has blazed the trail for timid clergy and people alike."[140] Though the Episcopal Church was not uniquely culpable in this respect, its self-understanding as a shaper of culture could only serve to compound the sense of failure Hines here articulates.

That the church was now following where it ought to have been leading was a sentiment shared by J. V. Langmead Casserley, professor of dogmatics at General Seminary. "It ill-becomes the militant Church of God to run behind the secular authority giving vocal approval of principles, which, properly speaking, should first be enunciated and manifested by the Church," he said regarding desegregation in 1959. The best way to ensure the church lived up to its own teachings, Casserley argued, was "to raise up prophets from within, who will constantly prick her conscience and spur her on to proper and effective action." And while he acknowledged that not every member of the church was called to be such a person, "it is incumbent upon those of us who do not prophesy to lay the foundation upon which the prophets may walk."[141] This is an important series of statements, indicative of a shift underway in the thinking of certain Episcopalians about the church's identity in relation to the wider society. In it, there remains an inherited assumption that the Episcopal Church will be present and engaged in the public sphere as part of its establishmentarian mission. Yet there is also the more novel

CHALLENGING THE CHURCH TO SAVE IT   79

recognition that in order to fulfill this mission with integrity, the church must not merely tolerate critique and dissent from its prophetic voices but actively celebrate them. From these two premises would emerge the seemingly paradoxical conviction that the Episcopal Church could only justify its privileged position in the wider culture if it defined prophecy as normative within its own institutional life. Employing this logic in their approach to social activism would prove at once liberating and self-lacerating for Episcopalians in the years to come.[142]

An undeniably prophetic voice to issue from the Episcopal fold in the late 1950s was that of William Stringfellow. After completing his military service abroad, Stringfellow had enrolled at Harvard Law School, from which he graduated in the summer of 1956. He then moved to New York City, where he joined the Group Ministry of the East Harlem Protestant Parish (EHPP) as a legal advocate. Founded in 1948 by seminarians from Union Seminary, EHPP was an ecumenical ministry that had established a series of storefront churches as centers of community organizing and social service in one of Manhattan's poorest neighborhoods. Devoted as he became to Harlem and its inhabitants, Stringfellow's tenure at EHPP lasted only eighteen months, during which time he clashed repeatedly with other members of the ministry team.[143] Minutes of staff meetings from this period confirm that he could indeed be a contentious colleague.[144] For whatever its claims to the contrary, Stringfellow soon judged EHPP insufficiently radical and inclined to lapse into old-fashioned clericalism. Writing in 1957 to his former bishop, Appleton Lawrence of Western Massachusetts, he complained that "too much of the Parish's political witness has been directed by and identified with the clergy, rather than with the laity of our churches."[145] As an Episcopalian, Stringfellow recognized that the office of priesthood conferred upon individuals responsibility for preaching and teaching, dispensing the sacraments, and providing pastoral care, but beyond these specific duties he was prepared to make no further distinction between ordained and lay Christians.[146] While still a teenager, he had discerned that his own Christian calling was not to become a priest but to live out the Gospel through politics and practice of the law.[147] He lamented the fact that so few Americans expected their faith to connect with daily life but instead assumed "religion has only to do with religion," and not "all the awful, petty, terrific, sad, lusty, terrible, intriguing, trivial, fearful, ambiguous, momentous things of anybody's existence."[148] Yet it was ordinary laypeople, not the "professionalized"

80 PRIVILEGE AND PROPHECY

clergy, whom Stringfellow considered the church's primary evangelists, apologists, and prophets in the world.[149]

Although there was much about Stringfellow's life and thought that made him an unusual Episcopalian, his commitment to lay ministry proceeded from an essentially Anglican conception of the sacraments. As extensions of the Incarnation, baptism and eucharist for Stringfellow affirm Christ's claim upon the individual and the continuing action of divine grace through the life of the community. Together, these rites model and proclaim the full humanity God intends for all people.[150] But in contrast to someone like Kim Myers, Stringfellow is not interested in the church and its liturgies as an assertion of a separate holiness; rather, the chief purpose of worship is "to celebrate and proclaim God's presence and action outside the sanctuaries in the common life of the world." By this logic, what happens at the altar is "authenticated by the constant involvement of the people of the Church in the world's life and by the public witness of the Church in the world."[151] Worship for Stringfellow is therefore never an end in itself, but the basis on which the believer comes to frame all that he is and has as "sacraments of the gift of his own life." In this way, the false distinction between the spiritual and material is broken down, and Christians are free to intervene in the world, not as an assertion of moral standing but as a testimony to their own redemption through grace.[152] Flawed as the Episcopal Church may be, it was for this reason Stringfellow reckoned it unique among Protestant denominations in its capacity to express properly "the relation of sacrament to ethics."[153]

One of the major points of tension between Stringfellow and his colleagues in Harlem was his insistence on being a communicant at a local Episcopal church, instead of belonging to one of the EHPP congregations, none of which was Episcopal.[154] When he formally resigned from the staff in April 1958, he reiterated why the issue had held such great significance for him. "Nothing is more debilitating to the emergence of the Church in East Harlem than the ignorance within the group ministry about the reality of the Church elsewhere," he remarked. As dedicated as he was to the ecumenical ideal, he was frustrated by American Protestantism's solipsistic tendencies. Episcopalianism, on the other hand, conferred upon him a consciousness of the universal church across space and time: "It points to a sense of belonging to the Church, wherever I happen to be in the world," he explained. "It enables a concrete identification not only with Canterbury, so to speak, but also Colossae."[155] Not least, such a catholic understanding of the church enabled human beings to locate themselves correctly in the cosmic hierarchy.

CHALLENGING THE CHURCH TO SAVE IT   81

For as Stringfellow told the National Conference on Religion and Race in 1963, the abiding "heresy" of modern American religion was its egotistical assumption that "the whole drama of history takes place between God and humanity." Despite their much-vaunted attention to scripture, Protestants ignored what both the Bible and doctrine had long told them, that in fact "the drama of this history takes place amongst God and humanity and the principalities and powers."[156]

The biblical concept of "principalities and powers" occupies a central place in William Stringfellow's theology.[157] He readily concedes that for many people such language conjures up archaic visions of angels and demons, but insists principalities remain an objective reality in contemporary life. Taken together, principalities are all the images, institutions, and ideologies in the world that, due to their place in fallen creation, serve as objects of false worship for human beings. In rebelling against God and idolizing the principalities, human beings seek reassurances of vitality but in fact surrender to the demonic and worship death. They do this when they indulge in the cult of celebrity, when they valorize an organization, or when they glorify an abstraction.[158] Inasmuch as churches are social entities complicit in the divisions of the culture that surrounds them, they also function as principalities, rather than as "bastions of resistance to demonic power." That the Protestant denominational groups have proved such ready collaborators in schisms of class, race, and region leads Stringfellow to the damning conclusion that "in the apparent hierarchy of principalities, the American churches have more often than not been among the most menial, manipulated, and degraded vassals of the power of death."[159] In making this prophetic declaration, Stringfellow does not spare the Episcopal Church. Indeed, his engagement with biblical categories prompts him to challenge some long-standing tendencies in Anglican social thought. While sharing his tradition's incarnational focus, he rejects its propensity to interpret the Incarnation as the basis for an uncritical cooperation between church and society. As much as Christ entered creation to confirm divine love for humanity, he also came to name and destroy the structures of fallenness. Recognizing the Incarnation as both an affirmation of the world and a judgment upon it, Christians therefore must not perpetuate the established political and ecclesiastical orders but repudiate them.[160]

Such reasoning leads Stringfellow to suggest that the only way for the church to fulfill its mission against the principalities is to become the one institution willing to risk death so that the world might live. Since the beginning, he emphasizes, this has meant the church has been called to "a

82　PRIVILEGE AND PROPHECY

vocation of poverty as an *institution.*" Such a vocation, he goes on, means not just retreating from power and privilege, but actively expending all the church's material resources on the immediate needs of society. Contrary to conventional wisdom, then, this "disassociation from prerogative" is neither an abdication of responsibility nor withdrawal from the world, but a "profound engagement in the world as it is. It is the help which the Church freely and gladly offers in the midst of impending disaster."[161] When the institution empties itself in this way, its members are released from the burden of maintaining its reputation, wealth, and influence, and are in turn freed as individuals to relinquish whatever alienates them from God and other people.[162] For his own part, Stringfellow was in no doubt that his status as a white man was what Christianity prompted him to renounce, such that he privately stated in 1960: "William Stringfellow is a man who surrendered his race some time ago."[163] Preaching in a church in western Massachusetts the following year, he called upon his fellow Christians to undertake a similar process of self-abnegation. "Be suspicious of respectability," he counseled them. "Be suspicious, be *very* suspicious of success. Because if we look again at the ministry of Christ, the marks of that ministry are marks of collision between Christ and the world, marks of poverty, of sorrow, of betrayal, of rejection, of radical unpopularity." Christians who expected to avoid such marks in either their individual or corporate life were simply not being faithful to the Gospel. Yet it was evident that not only the Episcopal Church but most churches clung to the notion that without money, position, and access, they could not fulfill their ministry and mission. Whereas for Stringfellow, it was obvious that "just about the *opposite* is the case."[164]

This belief in the voluntary marginalization of the church grew out of Stringfellow's experience of living and working among the impoverished residents of Harlem. In his 1964 book *My People Is the Enemy*, he writes movingly of their struggle for dignity amidst degradation, and of his own attempts to know God through those whom he seeks to serve. He also records his dissatisfaction with the ministerial approach of EHPP, which he describes as prioritizing social betterment over Christian witness. It was, he suggests, as if the staff felt compelled to make the inhabitants more nearly like themselves—white, middle-class Protestants—before they would be ready to receive the Good News. But "the preaching and service of the Gospel do not depend upon any special social change," Stringfellow contends. The problem with EHPP lay not in its desire to assist the downtrodden, but in supposing that policies and programs were comparable to the transformative presence of Christ in the world.[165] An evident influence on Stringfellow's thought here is the French Protestant theologian Jacques Ellul, whose 1948 book *The Presence of the Kingdom* explores the tensions of Christian discipleship in technological society, a society in which believers are constantly tempted to "implement" their Christianity through technique rather than to embody it through grace. Out of this analysis, Ellul argues for the importance of developing a distinctly Christian "style of life," a way of being in the world but not of it.[166] For Stringfellow, cultivating this "style of life" in the ghetto was less about trying to save the poor than about recognizing the many ways God was already at work among them.[167] "It is essential to share life just as it is in a place like Harlem," he concludes. "It is the only way there is to honor the Incarnation."[168]

Identifying the other forms which a Christian "style of life" might take in modern America became a primary concern for Fran Ayres during the late 1950s. After the departure of the Winters and Whites from Parishfield in the summer of 1956, Ayres had invited the Mead and Barney families to become residential members of the community. This turnover signaled yet another phase in the project's development, and while the Meads' tenure proved relatively brief, the Barneys remained part of Parishfield until its demise a decade later. Roger Barney (1916–1978) was a Bostonian who had joined the Episcopal Church as an undergraduate at Dartmouth College. He then pursued his theological studies at Union Seminary, where he met Jane Lockwood (1914–2018), a native of Virginia who had attended Wellesley prior to moving to New York.[169] The couple married in 1941, the same year Barney was ordained to the priesthood. During the war he volunteered as a naval chaplain, eventually seeing action at the battle of Iwo Jima.[170] He then resumed parish ministry in New Hampshire and in 1950 became archdeacon and executive secretary of the diocese. In 1955 he contracted polio while on vacation and was left permanently disabled. After a lengthy stay in the hospital, he and his wife agreed to move their family to the center in Brighton. By the time they joined the community in 1957, Barney remembered, Ayres had become determined that the "compulsive and pietistic" mode Parishfield had adopted in its early years should be replaced by an approach less institutionally focused and more experimental.[171]

For William Stringfellow, Ellul's emphasis on "style of life" invited a radical and unmistakably Christian witness in the world, but one still very much rooted in the church. For Fran Ayres and other members of Parishfield, though, the concept lent itself instead to their understanding of Dietrich

84   PRIVILEGE AND PROPHECY

Bonhoeffer's idea of "religionless Christianity." Recalling the way in which they blended these ideas, Jane Barney explained that "style of life" was closely linked to Bonhoeffer's interest in "the secret discipline" as a way of framing Christian practice in a wholly secular context.[172] "[The] more and more difficult it was for people in our contemporary world to talk about our Christian belief," she summarized, "Christianity was a secret discipline, it was something that you dealt with inside yourself. You believed and you prayed but you couldn't be effective talking about it." This in turn they related to still another idea invoked by Bonhoeffer, that of "Christ incognito," which Barney defined as "Christ is in society, he's unseen and unknown but he's there, and you are to be Christ incognito in society."[173] To them, the most obvious example of this disguised style of Christian life was the worker-priest movement in France, where clergy labored in solidarity alongside factory workers and did not identify as priests but sought only to model their faith.[174] Nor were the Parishfield staff alone in making such connections. During a visit to East Berlin in the early 1960s, the theologian Harvey Cox encountered Christians debating the same concepts and drawn increasingly to abandon church structures in order to lead a genuinely Christian existence under communism.[175] As Parishfield became ever more outward-looking and conceptually expansive, it welcomed visits not just from Christian thinkers such as Hendrik Kraemer, Ted Wickham, and Joseph Fletcher, but also from secular intellectuals such as Will Herberg, Hannah Arendt, and Susan Sontag.[176]

Although it had always maintained its work was motivated by a desire to serve the church through renewal, Parishfield began to face concerns that its attitude and example were in fact prompting laypeople to abandon parochial life.[177] Roger Barney faced this question squarely in the community's monthly newsletter in April 1958. "Is Parishfield really against the parish?" he asked. "Let us begin by saying quite plainly that we believe in the parish. We are convinced that the local, geographical embodiment of the Church will always be necessary." At the same time, he insisted that "there can be no genuine renewal of parish life without corresponding renewal of the world. . . . Christians have not only a gathered life in the parish for worship and special activities but a scattered life in the world, in families and neighborhoods, at work and play and as citizens." To diagnose the ways in which parish participation often inhibited rather than encouraged this wider renewal effort did not equate to blanket condemnation of the parish itself.[178] By supporting laypeople who aspired to ministry beyond what the parish model could accommodate, Parishfield was simply trying to address a

CHALLENGING THE CHURCH TO SAVE IT   85

discernible need.[179] Despite these protestations, however, it was obvious that the Parishfield ethos was moving further and further afield from the mainstream of the Episcopal Church. Jane Barney later remembered Fran Ayres's contempt for traditional church culture and his pejorative use of the term "churchy" to refer to anyone or anything he deemed excessively invested in the organization. Unsurprisingly, few clergy in the diocese were sympathetic to Parishfield, and Barney admitted the staff made little attempt to bridge the gap during this period.[180] Even with the nearby Episcopal church in Brighton they had virtually no contact, and the only locals they got to know were those who took the initiative to visit the center.[181]

The aloofness Parishfield displayed toward the wider church led to tensions with Bishop Emrich, tensions which continued to deepen throughout the late 1950s and early 1960s. As someone who had facilitated the community's founding and supported it financially, Emrich was disturbed by what he considered the community's abandonment of its original purpose. He made this clear in his response to a promotional document prepared by Ayres in 1959. Writing in the margin of the draft text, the bishop instructed: "Add 'Church work' to 'work of the Church'. Need a strong experience of Church in order to go into the world. Also, self-preservation is the first (not greatest) responsibility of the Church—as of anybody. Have got to strengthen the structure." He went to urge that "Parishfield ought intellectually to present institutional ministry *with* ministry in world."[182] These comments leave little doubt as to the nature of the divergence. As bishop, Emrich recognized the experimental nature of Parishfield's ministry but expected it to uphold the essential legitimacy of the church. From the point of view of the staff, though, Emrich had become captive to his position, preoccupied, as Robert DeWitt put it, with "raising money and not offending people and not confusing the faithful."[183] And while relations continued to be cordial, plainly the close friendship between Ayres and Emrich had been damaged by these differences of principle.[184] Eventually, the bishop withdrew his formal support of Parishfield. In 1962 he agreed to secure an annual grant on its behalf from the National Council but refused to do so again the following year. "If your consciences lead you to attack the Church and the creeds," he wrote to Roger Barney, "I want you to follow your conscience. But I too have a conscience, and cannot give my approval to asking for Church money for that purpose. It would not be honorable."[185]

Nowhere were the conflicting demands of organizational responsibility versus ministerial innovation more keenly felt than in the church's

86 PRIVILEGE AND PROPHECY

seminaries. An obvious case in point was the Episcopal Theological Seminary of the Southwest. When Paul van Buren moved to Austin as a junior professor in 1957, he found what he later described as "a remarkably open and permissive ecclesiastical institution."[186] With the support of Bishop Hines, the dean, Gray M. Blandy, had not only built up a healthy student body but also assembled a faculty of cutting-edge scholars, among them philosopher William E. Poteat, church historian William A. Clebsch, and New Testament scholar Franklin W. Young. Having been invited to create an integrated curriculum that would prepare seminarians for ministry in modern society, the faculty provided their rationale for this "new program" in the course catalogue of 1958–1959. Among other things, they wrote, "it is the aim of the Seminary to lead students and faculty into an awareness of the judgement of irrelevance which contemporary culture has brought against the Church's life of thought, worship and action." Acknowledging this reality was only part of the task, however; it was also the seminary's function to encourage a penitent church that "may become a fit and open vessel for God's revelation of how He is relevantly to be known, worshipped, obeyed, and proclaimed by His people in this present age."[187] The culture's "judgement of irrelevance" was clearly one shared by the professors themselves, who constantly pushed the seminarians to explore their vocation in terms of the needs of the world around them.[188] Yet this pedagogical environment soon drew criticism from more conservative churchmen, including some of the bishops who decided whether or not their ordinands went to Austin for training. Claiming the students were not being adequately prepared to serve as parish priests, the bishops began to withhold their patronage. The result of this backlash was both a decline in applications and the departure of some of the seminary's leading faculty members.[189]

Another Episcopal seminary to gain a national reputation for liberal theology and social activism in the late 1950s was ETS in Cambridge.[190] This growing prominence was due in no small part to the leadership of John Coburn, who left his post at Newark Cathedral to become the seminary's dean in 1957. About the importance of training clergy he was adamant, to the extent that he refused the post of bishop coadjutor of Washington when elected against his wishes the following year.[191] In explaining his decision, Coburn cited his belief that the church was "on the threshold of a new era in theological education." So while quick to affirm the seminaries' role in maintaining among the clergy "high standards of learning and Godly life," he was certain they must also "recognize and accept responsibility for the preparation of men for the Ministry in ways that are relevant, wise and creative for the mission of the Church to the contemporary world."[192] Other prominent voices in the church began to strike the same chord. Nathan M. Pusey (1907–2001), a devout Episcopalian who became president of Harvard University in 1953, would take an active role in reforming seminary education during the coming decade. Writing in 1958, Pusey argued that more than ever, Americans required the presence of "the informed, compassionate, understanding scholar-minister," able to articulate the Gospel meaningfully amidst all their confusions and uncertainties. "The church is rousing itself," he predicted, "to provide such a ministry—an understanding ministry—in the new generation."[193] The comments of Coburn and Pusey alike reflect the optimism shared by many establishment progressives about the church's capacity to respond creatively to the challenges of the future.[194]

Eager as he was to raise up clergy to meet these challenges, John Coburn remained equally committed to the well-being and nurture of the wider Christian community. He demonstrated the strength of this conviction when James Pike was elected bishop of California and asked Coburn to preach at his consecration. (The two men had become friends during successive vacations in Wellfleet on Cape Cod, where they had been instrumental in setting up a summer chapel.)[195] At the service held in San Francisco's Grace Cathedral in May 1958, Coburn surprised many by the candor with which he delivered his charge to the new bishop.[196] Declaring to Pike that "you are a controversial person," he praised him for the zeal he always brought to fighting for principles of justice and equality. "This incarnational life for social issues is again part of your strength as a missionary," Coburn observed. But he also judged that such intensity had "caused some bloodshed and damage and separation not always necessary. Your stature as a Bishop will be determined in part as you engage in controversy as a last and not as a first resort." In assuming episcopal office, Pike must set aside his polemical urges and love for the spotlight in favor of the daily requirements of his fold. "You are now bound by the life of this Diocese," Coburn advised. "You can serve the Church only as you serve this clergy and people. The greatest sacrifice you can make for the sake of the Gospel and for the love of God will be to say No to all but a few of the calls that will come to you from beyond this place."[197] According to George Hadley, a priest present at the service, Pike listened patiently to his friend's charge without any discernible reaction. "Those of us who knew [Pike] personally were both amused and disturbed," Hadley later recounted. "Disturbed because the injunction sounded a good deal like sharp personal

88 PRIVILEGE AND PROPHECY

criticism[;] amused because we couldn't conceive of our friend avoiding controversy for any length of time anyway."[198]

Though Coburn's words were addressed specifically to Pike, they bespoke a larger concern with how to balance the prophetic and pastoral aspects of Christian ministry. During the latter half of the 1950s, the tension between the two had become increasingly apparent. On the one hand, the Episcopal Church was stronger than ever: membership numbers continued to grow, new churches were being built, and national and diocesan structures were expanding. At the same time, however, some held that for all its institutional vigor, the church was failing to address the social realities of modern life. Amidst their diverse settings, what united Parishfield, Detroit Industrial Mission, the Urban Priests Group, and other experimental ministries was the conviction that in order to remain relevant to society, the church must first reach beyond its traditional habits and assumptions. Rather than define ministry as something undertaken solely by clergy, the discipleship of laypeople needed to be recognized and encouraged. Rather than treat faith as something practiced discreetly in the domestic sphere, its meaning and application should be explored in the workplace. Rather than rely on suburban expansion as the basis for mission, a presence in the inner cities must be maintained and developed. In all these undertakings, there remained a fundamental confidence in the capacity of the Episcopal Church to renew itself. And out of such renewal, it was believed, not just a prosperous but a truly engaged church might yet emerge.

4

The New Breed Takes Charge (1959–1964)

Gathered for the General Convention in late 1958, the Episcopal House of Bishops issued a pastoral letter addressing the range of political, economic, and racial upheavals dominating the contemporary scene both at home and abroad. "An old order is vanishing," observed the bishops, "and a new order is struggling in pain to be born."[1] For Episcopalians, this transition was exemplified at the same convention by the election of Arthur Lichtenberger to replace Henry Knox Sherrill as presiding bishop. Perhaps more than any other individual, Sherrill had come to embody the benign authoritarianism of the post-war Protestant establishment.[2] Under his watchful gaze the Episcopal Church had prospered and consolidated; as liturgical scholar Massey Shepherd attested when Sherrill stepped down, "we are as a Church more at one with ourselves" than when he had taken up the role in 1947.[3] Even so, it had become evident that people were ready for a different type of leader, someone more accessible and consultative.[4] Having succeeded Will Scarlett as bishop of Missouri in 1950, Arthur Lichtenberger was a natural choice, loved and respected for his warmth, intelligence, and generosity of spirit.[5] Crucially, he also brought a more egalitarian approach to the affairs of the national church. "Lichty's style of leadership was the enabling style," John Hines recalled later. "He helped other people be and do the job they were responsible for. He was not one who had to make all the decisions and set all the policies," in obvious contrast to his predecessor.[6]

From the start of his tenure as presiding bishop, Lichtenberger made it clear that he expected Episcopalians to engage actively in the social challenges facing the American people. "The Church stands not on the outskirts but in the center of the town," he reminded the congregation at his installation service in January 1959. "We do not live in a world of worship and piety apart from the world we encounter in office or factory, at home or on the street. The gospel speaks to the totality of life."[7] Like his near contemporaries Stephen Bayne and John Butler, Lichtenberger's values had been shaped by the widespread poverty and unemployment he witnessed as a young priest during the Depression. Speaking up for the rights of labor and of minority groups

Privilege and Prophecy. Robert Tobin, Oxford University Press. © Oxford University Press 2022.
DOI: 10.1093/oso/9780190906146.003.0004

90 PRIVILEGE AND PROPHECY

would characterize every phase of his ministry thereafter.[8] But something that set Lichtenberger apart even from most liberal clergy of this generation was his sensitivity to the marginalization of women in both society and the church. Addressing an inter-seminary conference held at Nashotah House in Wisconsin in early 1960, he condemned the Episcopal Church for being "a segregated society" not just racially but also in terms of gender. He lamented that Episcopalianism's governance was still "that of an age-old masculine pattern," such that "women are not generally allowed to share fully with men in a complementary relationship." And while it was true such a state of affairs merely reflected the norms of the wider culture, this fact did not absolve Episcopalians from "the necessity of judging our corporate life in the light of the gospel."[9] As was to be the case throughout his years as presiding bishop, Lichtenberger demonstrated here a willingness to confront the shortcomings of his own community.[10]

Another of these shortcomings, as he knew all too well, was the Episcopal Church's abiding reputation for elitism and cliquishness. Speaking again in his native Wisconsin the same year, Lichtenberger enjoined Episcopalians to work harder at overcoming this reputation and making their parishes more welcoming to people in "mid-America."[11] This was easier said than done. Part of the problem, of course, was that no matter how often they decried this image, many Episcopalians were quietly proud of it and deeply invested in its perpetuation. Someone particularly attuned to this dynamic and its impact upon the church in the Midwest was Edward R. Welles, bishop of West Missouri. Welles (1907–1991), grandson of the nineteenth-century bishop of Wisconsin bearing the same name, had been educated at Princeton and Oxford in the 1920s. He was ordained in 1931 and went on to serve as a parish priest, boarding school chaplain, and cathedral dean in dioceses along the East Coast before becoming a bishop in 1950.[12] Addressing his diocesan convention in May 1961, Welles ruefully described the typical parish hall as "our Episcopal clubhouse," a good a summation as any of the exclusive social atmosphere that still pervaded many church communities.[13] Yet as had already been documented in 1952 by the national CSR Department survey, a significant number of post-war Episcopalians did not in fact conform economically or educationally to their popular stereotype as upper class.[14] When the official church newspaper *Forth* was relaunched as *The Episcopalian* in the spring of 1960, the editor eagerly pointed this out, reminding readers that "this generation of Episcopalians is just as likely to include a farmer as an industrialist, and list as many union members as lawyers."[15] Nonetheless, such

THE NEW BREED TAKES CHARGE 91

claims did little to erode the perception that Episcopalians generally saw themselves as socially superior, which in turn tended to discourage people of a humbler background from joining the church in great numbers.[16] Such a perception also sat uneasily alongside the leadership's growing outspokenness about social problems and the need for reform. The unhappy result, remarked one journalist, was the "double image" of a church that spoke eloquently of the need for equality and access but continued to neglect them within its own ranks.[17]

For Arthur Walmsley, though, striving for openness in the world and remaining a healthy church were inextricably linked. "Christian Social Relations is the New Evangelism," he proclaimed at the end of 1959. If Episcopalians were sincere about serving the wider community of which they were a part, they should expect to encounter people who did not conform to their existing membership. And if such outreach was to be genuine Christian witness and not simply a token gesture, they should also expect to be changed by the experience. "The parish seeking truly to evangelize people apart from 'our kind' faces a radical transformation of its organizational life," Walmsley wrote.[18] Still, even where Episcopalians were willing to take such a risk, it was not always immediately obvious how to break down certain barriers in practical terms. "How do insulated suburban congregations participate in a ministry to inner city gangs, different racial groups, and different social class levels?" asked Gibson Winter in 1961. It was one thing for "a few heroic individuals" to undertake such mission but plainly more complicated for Christians to do so collectively in a society as divided as the United States.[19] Edward Welles recognized this dilemma when delivering his annual diocesan address in the spring of 1963. "Most of us are simply not aware of the slums of our cities or of those who exist within them," he admitted, "for our usual travel pattern does not take us through those areas, and when they do we don't park our car, and go into one of the tenements and get involved in the drab, hopeless lives of the inhabitants." For the church to become more truly inclusive, Episcopalians must begin by overcoming their basic ignorance of other people's lives.[20]

Someone who made no secret of his impatience with Episcopal insularity was Stephen Bayne.[21] Throughout his episcopate, he admonished his co-religionists to spend less time being smugly self-conscious about their Episcopalianism and more time actually attending to God's diverse action all around them. Or, as he put it drily in 1953, they should indulge in "a little less giggling about our funny, broad ways, and a little more Gospel—a little

92 PRIVILEGE AND PROPHECY

less coziness in all being tolerant Episcopalians together among all those negroes, Roman Catholics, Communists, etc., and a little more attentiveness to the God who uses Assyrians quite as well as He does the Episcopalians."[22] After the 1958 Lambeth Conference created the position of executive officer of the Anglican Communion, Bayne resigned his see in Seattle and moved to London in 1959 to take up the post. During his five years in the role, he immersed himself in the task of getting to know every corner of the Anglican world, traveling as much as 150,000 miles a year. He listened carefully to the voices of local churches and sought to facilitate contact among the growing number of autonomous provinces. Even in a global communion, he was convinced that personal relationships remained the only basis for meaningful communication, built upon friendship, prayer, and shared enterprises.[23] Such ambassadorial efforts took place against the backdrop of rapid decolonization and the establishment of new nation-states among the peoples of Africa and Asia, a trend many American Christians had yet to acknowledge, let alone explore.[24] Bayne's tenure as executive officer culminated in the international Anglican Congress held at Toronto in the summer of 1963. The centerpiece of the gathering was the document "Mutual Responsibility and Interdependence in the Body of Christ" (MRI), which laid out his vision for an Anglican Communion predicated on genuine equality among the churches. In reframing their sense of Anglican belonging along the principles of MRI, Bayne hoped Episcopalians would develop a more reciprocal and generous worldview, both as Christians and as Americans.[25]

As Bayne worked to build up the structures of the Anglican Communion in London, those of the National Council flourished under Arthur Lichtenberger in New York. John Hines later described the sense of excitement in the national church during these years, as the presiding bishop encouraged his staff to debate and critique ideas and propose fresh policies.[26] Likewise, Kim Myers reported that under Lichtenberger's tutelage the Council had "changed so radically that even to visit its offices leads one to believe he is beholding a new church."[27] Not all Episcopalians were happy about such changes. Even before Lichtenberger had succeeded Henry Knox Sherrill, one disgruntled priest wrote to the *Living Church* charging that "the church is being taken out of the hands of its members, and being made the property of a small, clever, liberal clique who try to impose their partisan policies on everyone, and regard as disloyal anyone who won't agree with them."[28] In point of fact, many Episcopalians had only a tenuous grasp of the church's wider institutional framework, unable to make basic distinctions such as that between their own National Council and the National Council of Churches.[29] Despite (or perhaps because of) such confusions, the National Council became the favorite "whipping boy" of those church members who felt it did not accurately reflect their local concerns and values.[30] In some parts of the country, such mistrust of national religious leadership went hand in hand with a mistrust of national political leadership. Addressing his diocesan convention in 1961, Bishop George Quarterman of Northwest Texas warned against both these tendencies, reminding his people that authority in both church and state was distributed in accordance with constitutional processes.[31]

Throughout much of their history, Episcopalians' preference for diocesan and parochial autonomy had kept their central agencies relatively weak and underfunded.[32] The National Council did not even exist until 1919, and it was only after the traumas of the Depression and Second World War that it had been able to develop a full range of programs. After 1945, the infrequency of General Convention still tended to ensure a more reactive and ad hoc approach to policymaking, not least in the area of social relations.[33] Particularly as the racial crisis intensified in the late 1950s, however, some Episcopalians began to demand more immediate and authoritative engagement from the national church.[34] But the expectation that the National Council should provide a coordinated response to pressing social issues overlooked the fact that it was only empowered to do so with a clear mandate from General Convention.[35] The inherent tensions created by this arrangement were evidently felt by the Council's officers, as illustrated by an internal document Arthur Walmsley prepared for the CSR Department in November 1960. "It is recognized that the Department or its staff cannot presume to speak on social issues for the Episcopal Church and that the normal channel is the General Convention," he wrote. "It is also recognized that there are occasionally issues of great moment on which Churchmen have a right to expect the National Council to speak what it judges to be the Church's mind."[36] As the pace of events accelerated over the next few years, the department began to push for the right to speak and act on behalf of the church more freely. So long as they reflected the general will of their representative conventions and remained "answerable to such conventions for the actions they may take in times of stress," national and diocesan CSR departments alike should be able to coordinate the church's social witness at a rate commensurate with modern life. Otherwise Episcopalians were left between conventions "without voice or action at the level of the large

94 PRIVILEGE AND PROPHECY

nationwide, statewide, and citywide divisions," whereas "these are just the levels that call for the best statesmanship."[37]

The question of how much the National Council should be permitted to speak of its own volition was really part of the ongoing debate about the nature of the church's mission to society. For however obvious it might be to activists such as Paul Moore, Kim Myers, and William Stringfellow, many Episcopalians were still confused and skeptical about where social ministry fit into their Christian faith. Summarizing the discussion from one of the conferences he conducted on this topic, Arthur Walmsley reported that "much of the Church's social action is regarded as irrelevant, if not ludicrous, by the community, and by a large number of the Church's own people." The reason for this, participants explained, was "the unrelatedness of social pronouncements to the daily life of our people." Not for the first time, laypeople blamed the church for failing to provide clear teaching on how and why their religious practice should inform their decision-making as members of society.[38] Arthur Lichtenberger would corroborate these impressions in a speech he gave to the National Conference on Social Welfare in May 1962. Although few Episcopalians objected to the church engaging in traditional forms of social care, he observed, many became uneasy when it ventured into areas of social and political controversy, which they considered unrelated to spiritual matters. Yet to Lichtenberger, the distinction was a false one. "The Church in her concern for the welfare of people will necessarily be engaged in social education and social action," he reiterated. "We cannot prepare the way for the coming of grace simply by doing what we can to change the minds and hearts of individuals, and then hope for the best. Some of the obstacles and hindrances to the coming of grace are found in the political and social and economic structures of the nation. It is the responsibility of the Church, of Christian people to help remove those barriers."[39]

Clearly the most obvious barriers yet to be removed as the new decade began were those of racial discrimination and segregation. In late 1959, the Episcopal Society for Cultural and Racial Unity (ESCRU) was launched by John Morris, Neil Tarplee, and others, with the aim of defeating prejudice in both church and society.[40] Writing to Arthur Walmsley about the group's purpose, Tollie Caution's protégé Walter Dennis explained that ESCRU sought "to be more than just a barometer of opinion of Episcopalians on a given race issue. It must speak not so much *for* the Church as *to* the Church, pointing up areas of social tension and inequity which are only imperfectly recognized by the average churchman."[41] In challenging the status quo, members of ESCRU

THE NEW BREED TAKES CHARGE 95

made clear their readiness to employ the techniques of nonviolent protest against their own co-religionists.[42] The prospect of Episcopalians lining up on opposite sides of civil rights demonstrations led Walmsley and Caution to issue an advisory document in the spring of 1960, urging responsible behavior and mutual support among church members caught up in "crisis situations." Joining them in this effort was a small committee that included Tarplee, Dennis, and Kim Myers.[43] The evident commonality here and elsewhere between the church bureaucracy and the ESCRU leadership served to confirm suspicions that the national church was increasingly in the hands of social liberals. As Walmsley remembered later, a common joke among the activists themselves was that "ESCRU got people into jail, and I got them out."[44] By June 1961, Walmsley and Kenneth B. Clark, a prominent black Episcopalian and academic, were appealing to the presiding bishop to permit National Council staff to take part in the Freedom Rides that began the previous month. "We recognize the hazards involved in too close identification of the Church with secular movements or attachment to particular forms of social action," they wrote. At the same time, "we believe that history and the Gospel make it essential to identify with the goal of immediate desegregation of secular and church institutions."[45] Notwithstanding the discord that might ensue among Episcopalians as a result, the national church had to be willing to incarnate the principles it had so regularly and eloquently espoused.

This determination to confront Episcopalians with the realities of the civil rights struggle was at least part of the motivation for the "Prayer Pilgrimage" which ESCRU organized that fall. Following the pattern of other freedom rides, the "pilgrimage" was to be made by an inter-racial group of priests traveling by bus from New Orleans to Detroit, arriving in time for the General Convention taking place there in mid-September. In the event, only five of the twenty-eight pilgrims were black and almost all were from the North, prompting Kim Myers to withdraw from what he judged an unrepresentative group.[46] As devoted as he was to combatting racial oppression, Myers was quick to dissociate himself from anything suggesting that it was a uniquely Southern problem to which only outsiders held the key. Preaching in New York in May, he had lambasted Northern churchmen who spoke endlessly about human unity, even while "permitting a racial situation to build up which contains the seeds of bloody violence in the segregated ghettos of the great cities—including our own."[47] The "prayer pilgrims" encountered a very different form of Episcopal censure during their journey, when fifteen of them were arrested upon arrival in Jackson, Mississippi.[48] Appearing in

96 PRIVILEGE AND PROPHECY

court, they faced Judge James Spencer, an active layman who lectured them on Article 37 of the Articles of Religion, which enjoins Anglicans to give "respectful obedience to the Civil Authority." Having rebuked them from the bench, Spencer proceeded to hand down stiff sentences to the priests, most of whom were bailed on appeal.[49] When at last the group arrived in Detroit for the Convention, they received a warm welcome from the presiding bishop, who praised them in his opening address.[50] Lichtenberger also called on the church to repent of its institutional racism and to consider how to engage positively in a racist society without being defined by it.[51] This resulted in a resolution that affirmed the need for penitence and exhorted Episcopalians to engage in further prayer and study on the subject.[52] Such studiously vague declarations incensed William Spofford of *The Witness*, who expressed amazement at the church's failure to grasp the urgency of the moment. "Where is the Church in this period of change?" he demanded to know in early 1962. Aside from the heroic efforts of a select group of individuals, the Episcopal Church had yet to make a serious contribution to the most important social reform in modern American history.[53]

There were those fully committed to civil rights who nonetheless worried that amidst the mounting pressure to act, the theological reasons for doing so might get lost or be distorted. Among these was Peter M. Day (1914–1984), editor of the *Living Church*. In an editorial entitled "The Temptation to Relevance," Day voiced his unhappiness with the Episcopal Church's marginal place in the freedom struggle: "One is tempted to do something, to do anything, that would give the Church some relevance to this great social movement of our times," he wrote. Even so, Episcopalians must not yield to this temptation, lest they place human concerns ahead of divine antecedents. "Neither the Church nor the Lord of the Church is under any absolute compulsion to be relevant to the social issues of our times," Day reasoned. "The question is rather one of the relevance of our world and its social issues to God and His Kingdom."[54] Framing social activism in the proper theological context was likewise a concern for John Purnell, James Gusweller's curate at the Church of St. Matthew and St. Timothy in New York. Any such action undertaken by the church "must always be one side of a coin bearing on its other side the radical preaching of sin and redemption," he insisted. Thus for such efforts to be "genuinely redemptive" and not merely palliative, there should be no doubt they proceeded from Christians' readiness to suffer and witness in the name of Christ.[55] In raising these concerns, both men anticipated a problem that would vex not just the Episcopal Church but all the mainline denominations during the 1960s. The more preoccupied certain Protestants became with demonstrating their churches' relevance in the public realm, the more they began to define spiritual meaning in terms of practical contributions made to social and political progress. Yet in so doing, the religious conviction that had inspired them became ancillary to the causes they embraced. Eventually this reversal produced a new dynamic among Christian activists, one in which, to borrow Leonard Sweet's succinct phrase, "faith had become a kind of reward for good works."[56]

If some Episcopalians were anxious about the theological underpinnings for social activism, others were distressed by the negative impact such action was starting to have on relationships within the church. One such person was John M. Gessell, assistant professor in homiletics at the Sewanee School of Theology. A native of St. Paul, Minnesota, Gessell (1920–2009) had studied at Yale before being ordained in 1952 and serving parishes in southern Virginia and Massachusetts. After ESCRU held a series of sit-ins on the campus during the spring of 1962, Gessell criticized both the group and the national church for their failure to engage in dialogue with the university about how to address Sewanee's race problems. This seeming preference for confrontation over cooperation struck Gessell as a form of moral scapegoating, an attempt to blame one group of Episcopalians for a failure that properly belonged to the whole church. Moreover, it showed a disturbing lack of spiritual and emotional maturity to believe reconciliation was not inherent to all Christian action. On the contrary, any truly Christian solution to social conflict "must arise out of dialogue amongst the faithful, must always fall under the judgment of the Gospel, must be relevant to the actual situation and must provide the opportunities for faithful response," Gessell asserted. "It will neither be perfect nor will it afford the realization of absolute forms of justice. No one likes ambiguity but ambiguity can be excised only at the cost of life itself."[57]

This tension between immediate action and gradual reform was a recurring feature of the civil rights movement, one in which liberal white Southerners often found themselves caught in the middle. Whatever reproaches they might endure from their Northern co-religionists about the slow pace of change, Southern Episcopalians knew all too well the consequences of pressing for racial equality in their communities. Examples abounded of integrationist clergy who were driven from their pulpits or bullied into silence by resistant laypeople.[58] Reflecting on the best way for national denominations to support ministers contending with such pressures in local churches, Episcopal activist Anne Braden suggested monetary assistance was the most useful thing they could offer. "This would be about ten times more effective than a lot of pious statements about how segregation is a sin," she told a friend. "What Southern liberal church leaders need is something concrete to help *them* fight this battle."[59] The need to combine pragmatism with principle was borne out by the recent experiences of Duncan Gray, who for the past five years had served as rector of St. Peter's Church in Oxford, Mississippi. In the fall of 1962, Gray became embroiled in the violent confrontation at the University of Mississippi over the enrollment of James Meredith as its first black student. While pleading for calm among rioting students on the night of September 30, he had been mobbed and only narrowly escaped serious injury.[60] Gray's stand for integration during these tense times led to conflict with many of his own parishioners, some of whom left the church, while others withheld financial contributions. Faced with such challenges, he called upon his good friends Oscar Carr and Farley Salmon, prominent Episcopalians and much-loved Mississippians, to speak at the St. Peter's stewardship dinner that February. This intervention staved off insolvency, but the church would continue to lose money and members in the years to come.[61] Even as he fought to maintain the institutional integrity of the Episcopal Church, Gray was in no doubt about the ultimate meaning of the racial struggle. "My own state, my own community, my own church have known and felt the judgment of God," he attested. "It is not a pleasant experience. But every real encounter with God begins with His judgment upon us; and within each such encounter is always the potential for grace."[62]

While Duncan Gray saw God's redemptive purpose at work in the tumult of Mississippi, Frank Sayre looked for it in the affairs of the whole nation. Since becoming dean of the National Cathedral in the early 1950s, he had consistently spoken out against social injustice and emphasized Americans' collective responsibility for overcoming it.[63] In the wake of the Little Rock integration crisis of 1957, for example, he had accused his compatriots of "spiritual laziness" in their corporate failure to confront racism.[64] Sayre blamed the churches in particular for having failed to recognize their divine mandate in the battle over segregation. "We did not see the breadth of God's justice nor the wideness of His love in the public domain of a whole nation," he concluded on the tenth anniversary of the *Brown* decision. "Resurrection we shut up in churches, little expecting that it would blaze forth in the world, requiring profound and total transformation of the whole society."[65] Every Christian leader was called to preach the Gospel not just in terms of private morality, but as the basis for ethical living amidst the messiness of human power relations.[66] For Sayre, giving voice to the "public conscience" in this way was intrinsic to his Anglicanism. Speaking to fellow Episcopalians about their Church of England roots in 1961, he noted that "in our heritage, [there was] no division" between church and society, a premise that would have been "impossible except as a consequence of the Incarnation." The vocation of American Anglicans was to affirm this symbiosis in a pluralistic culture where formal religious establishment had no place. As an Episcopal leader ministering in the nation's capital, Sayre characterized his own approach to this challenge as a mixture of the prophetic, the pastoral, and the political. In telling the powerful what they did not always want to hear, he saw himself as a prophet; in remembering that the powerful were still people in need of grace and compassion, he tried to be a pastor. And by fulfilling these two functions equitably, he occasionally found himself called upon to exercise a political role as well, that of providing moral guidance to national leaders in moments of ambiguity or confusion.[67]

Of course, part of what made Sayre's public ministry in Washington effective was his undeniable status as a member of the national elite. He sat easily among the powerful and assumed his right to do so. In the course of his tenure as dean he served on a number of governmental commissions, notably the US Committee on Refugees, which President Eisenhower appointed him to lead in anticipation of the UN's World Refugee Year in 1959.[68] This and other activities brought him to the attention of John F. Kennedy, with whom he formed a lasting friendship. Kennedy regularly turned to Sayre for advice on how to address religious matters in public life, not least when his Roman Catholicism became a point of contention during the 1960 presidential election.[69] The dean's subsequent closeness to the Kennedy White House would lead the Saturday Evening Post to christen him "Chaplain to the New Frontier," an indication of his success in developing a power base for himself among the political establishment. This readiness to work with public officials led some critics to accuse him of personal ambition and an absence of objectivity.[70] Yet for Sayre, the point of building a national cathedral was not just to create a monument, but to engage in the practical business of shaping the national ethos.[71] To be squeamish or censorious about the realities involved was to his mind an abdication of Christian leadership.[72] In this respect, the cathedral under Sayre became a place where painful truths could be aired with dignity, and patriotism could be at once honored and critiqued.[73] Preaching on the Sunday after Kennedy's assassination in November 1963, he stirred

100 PRIVILEGE AND PROPHECY

controversy by suggesting the president's death was, in the first instance, an occasion for national penitence rather than for the assignment of individual guilt. "Blame not the man, nor the city, nor the region where the deed was done," he told his congregation. "But let us search our own hearts to see if pettiness or hostility or unworthy anger did not set the stage for the overt act."[74] It was a sign of Sayre's confidence in both the prophetic and pastoral aspects of his ministry that he felt able to offer such counsel at a moment of intense public grief.

Though he was equally invested in the church's social mission, a very different sort of person presided over the cathedral in New York during the first part of the 1960s. After James Pike left St. John the Divine to become bishop of California, John Butler was chosen to succeed him as dean. Butler accepted the post at the behest of Bishop Horace Donegan, whom he had known since the late 1920s when the latter served his curacy in Butler's hometown of Worcester, Massachusetts. Despite being well liked and well connected across the church, Butler had passed up a number of opportunities for higher office in the course of his ministry. He preferred to exert influence behind the scenes by promoting others, or as he put it, by taking on "the role of a Warwick."[75] Donegan turned to his old friend when it became clear that the cathedral needed a steadying hand after Pike's exciting but not always dependable leadership. In a *Newsweek* article reporting his appointment in January 1960, Butler acknowledged the importance of having "a courageous voice" at the cathedral, but also made plain his commitment to the disciplines of the church. "I'm not as vocal as Jim Pike," he remarked pointedly. "I'm a quieter man and remember that Donegan is my bishop."[76] In fact, Butler quickly set about putting his own stamp on things, such as attempting to recruit Walter Dennis as the cathedral's first black canon. The young priest instead accepted a call to start an inter-racial ministry in his native Virginia, but Butler eventually got his way when Dennis returned to New York and became a canon residentiary in 1965.[77] While not as fond of the limelight as either his counterpart in Washington or his predecessor in New York, Butler nonetheless proved highly effective at deploying the Episcopal Church's institutional standing to promote social progress.

Meanwhile, there were other clergy for whom challenging establishment norms would become the raison d'être of their public ministry during the 1960s. Among the best known of these was Malcolm Boyd, who regularly attracted media attention for his confrontational approach to Christian witness. Born in Buffalo, Boyd (1923–2015) grew up in Colorado and attended college in Arizona before going to California in the 1940s to work as a film producer. Called to the priesthood, he left Hollywood to attend the Church Divinity School of the Pacific in Berkeley and was ordained in 1954–1955. After additional study in Europe and at Union Seminary, he became rector of St. George's Church in Indianapolis, part of the urban church coalition set up by Paul Moore.[78] The close friendship Boyd developed with Moore during this collaboration proved a mainstay during the turbulent and peripatetic existence he led subsequently.[79] In 1959 he became the Episcopal chaplain at Colorado State University, where he sought to present questions of faith and meaning in terms relevant to the burgeoning youth culture. His "expresso nights," at which he gathered with students in bars and coffeehouses, led him into conflict with Bishop Joseph Minnis, who publicly scolded him for encouraging deviance among the young. The bishop wrote in the diocesan newspaper that "you can't think of yourself as a beloved Son of God and at the same time go around with matted hair, dirty bodies and black underwear," a statement which Boyd described as "absolute heresy."[80] Incensed by Minnis's conservatism, Boyd resigned in protest, but not before denouncing what he deemed the bishop's bourgeois hypocrisy. "There seem to be no problems when members of the clergy go into the Denver Country Club and have a cocktail and lunch," he commented. "There's really no difference that I can see, except that in a tavern you are contacting people of a lower class."[81]

After leaving Colorado State, Boyd stepped up his criticism of the church as a hindrance to authentic Christian living.[82] Having taken part in the ESCRU Prayer Pilgrimage in September 1961, he was appointed by Bishop Richard Emrich to serve as Episcopal chaplain at Wayne State University in Detroit. Alongside these duties he also became a popular speaker on college campuses around the country, believing, as he put it later, that "the church needs badly to get out on the road and engage in honest dialogue with the nation's students" about the evolving place of Christianity in modern society.[83] During Holy Week 1963 he accepted an invitation to mingle with college kids spending their spring break in Florida's Daytona Beach, though not all of them welcomed Boyd's presence. Some thought he was either a publicity hound or "some kind of phony," while one young person observed that he "never seemed to get very deeply into religion."[84] There was no doubt about Boyd's ability to provoke a response from the church hierarchy, however, as again became obvious when he produced a series of short plays focusing on the themes of religious and racial prejudice.[85] When Bishop Emrich condemned one of the plays for its use of "vulgarity and profanity,"

102   PRIVILEGE AND PROPHECY

Boyd quickly fought back through the papers, deploring what he called the bishop's "sensational, scathing" denunciation.[86] "If the church is to be open to the life of God's world for loving and blessing it," he asserted, "it must not pillory, harass, or attack those of us who work in experimental ways to achieve contact with men and women who have rejected Christianity or are indifferent to it."[87] The conflict once more resulted in the chaplain's resignation, and it began to seem the Episcopal Church had no place for this compelling and rebellious personality. Still, there were enough people within the institution who valued Boyd's troublesome presence, and led by Paul Moore, they set about cobbling together funds to make him a "chaplain-at-large," in order that he might devote himself full-time to writing, lecturing, and social activism.[88]

Like Malcolm Boyd, Michael Allen was a priest who appeared happiest when he was pushing against the status quo. Born in Paris to American parents, Allen (1927–2013) attended Harvard College and worked as a journalist for *Look* magazine during the early 1950s. He later credited James Pike with introducing him to a form of socially engaged Christianity he could commit to; after being baptized, he enrolled at ETS in preparation for the priesthood. Ordained in 1957, he served a curacy at Grace Church in lower Manhattan before being named rector of nearby St. Mark's Church in-the-Bowery in 1959. Under Allen's leadership, St. Mark's embraced the dynamic counterculture of the East Village, serving as a venue for art exhibitions, jazz concerts, poetry recitals, and underground film screenings. Bohemians began to regard St. Mark's as a gathering place, Allen later recounted, "because we had said loud and clear to the community around us, We are open to you. Come and ask." Meanwhile, the congregation increasingly reflected the diversity of the neighborhood—a blend of elderly ladies, black families, and young artists. In 1964, an actor called Ralph Cook started attending services at St. Mark's, and with Allen's encouragement, founded an avant-garde theater company at the church, Theatre Genesis. The first play Cook produced was *The Rock Garden*, written by aspiring playwright Sam Shepherd.[89] Charismatic and determined, Allen was convinced that the church's future lay in worldliness and showed little sympathy for those who questioned this vision.[90] A case in point was when he invited Cook to present Ernest Hemingway's short play *Today Is Friday* in place of the sermon at a Sunday service. When a member of the vestry objected to this plan, Allen suggested the man find another spiritual home rather than alienate the theater director.[91] Those who had long been insiders at St. Mark's discovered that they were now in fact outsiders.

As anti-establishment figures in the Episcopal Church, both Boyd and Allen often railed against the conditions that made their own position possible.[92] In so doing, they served to highlight what Robert Lee identified at the time as the general "organizational dilemma" of the mainline denominations. If the churches were to fulfill their original calling as missionary bodies, they required a certain level of institutional coherence to make such outreach possible. Yet their accumulated structures and habits served to inhibit the very experimentation on which modern mission depended. To Lee, resolution of the dilemma was virtually impossible and should instead be accepted as an inherent tension in organized religion.[93] Paul Moore echoed these sentiments in his 1964 book *The Church Reclaims the City*, in which he recognized the frustration some people felt with "the discrepancy between the changing world and the stubborn changelessness of the institution of the Church." Given the apparent shallowness and introversion of so many middle-class parishes, he appreciated why such people had come to regard the very concept of the parish as suspect. For all their shortcomings, though, Moore did not share the impulse to tear down the church's structures, noting that "reorganization does not eliminate sin." Even so, he conceded that those loyal to the parish system were perennially caught between creativity and conservation. "How much time is left for the leap into the radical new way," Moore asked, "while at the same time maintaining the old conventional way? How does one teach new concepts and old concepts simultaneously? How does one break the old trunk to graft in the new branch?"[94] In June 1962, he attended a conference on urban strategy alongside Kim Myers, James Morton, W. B. Spofford, Gibson Winter, and William Stringfellow, at which they discussed growing disenchantment with the institutional life of the Episcopal Church. "The problem is not one of *not* having institutions," the group surmised, "but rather redefining and rediscovering *what kind* of institutions we want and need to minister effectually to the mission as we now understand it." This in turn required Episcopalians to achieve a greater degree of clarity and consensus about their mission than they currently seemed to possess.[95]

Those pursuing experimental forms of ministry were already well acquainted with the friction between social criticism and organizational effectiveness. Writing about his experiences working for Detroit Industrial Mission, Scott Paradise recalled the constant struggle to chart "an even

104 PRIVILEGE AND PROPHECY

course between seduction by society as it is and exclusion from the sources of power—between employment as chaplains to the status quo and the position of impotent aliens on the fringe of society."[96] Diverging approaches to this challenge produced conflict among the DIM staff, particularly regarding the appropriate relationship they should have with industrial management. For Paradise, it was vital to cultivate friendly but detached relations with workers and managers alike, so that DIM might serve as a mediating presence between them. He became frustrated by his colleagues' apparent reluctance to engage in "shop floor work" among the laborers and their preference instead for time spent with mid-level executives.[97] Although many from the latter group were educated, middle-class churchmen like himself, Paradise struggled to connect with them, often finding them resistant to theological discussion.[98] In a confidential document he prepared in 1962 entitled "The Real Religion of the Manager," Paradise presented a theory as to why this might be. If these professionals appeared to place a high value on the church, he argued, it was mainly because they saw it endorsing socio-economic structures of which they were obvious beneficiaries. As such, "it would be inconceivable for them that they might be asked to choose between the God of Jesus Christ and the American Business System." Any attempt by the church to disrupt this equation would be met with hostility by the managers, for "they would see it as the clergy biting the hand that feeds them or else meddling in an area where they had neither competence [n]or right." If this hypothesis was correct, Paradise concluded, then the mainline denominations had been complicit in a "gigantic illusion," whereby a generation of managers had not just confused but conflated the Christian God with American capitalism.[99]

By his own admission, expressing such thoughts did little to improve Paradise's relations with other members of the DIM staff. He wrote in his journal that some had found his analysis "deeply antagonizing," asking "if I had enough appreciation of our System and if I was not bound by nineteenth century prejudices."[100] In fact, Paradise was motivated less by an impulse to attack industrial society than by an urge to formulate a "peculiarly Christian" response to it. Everyone at DIM agreed the starting place for this response was asserting Christ's presence in all spheres of life, including that of work.[101] Yet beyond this affirmation, Paradise worried the mission had shied away from specific theological claims out of a desire to make the Christian faith seem more relevant and appealing to industrial people.[102] He felt alone in his efforts "to discuss explicitly with laymen the fundamental truths of Christianity, in terms vivid enough to have life and meaning, . . . without unfaithfulness to their basic import." This insistence upon the continuing validity and utility of religious language placed him at odds with the ideas of Paul van Buren, who served as DIM's chief theological advisor.[103] Since moving to Austin, van Buren had become convinced that such language was unintelligible in the secular world that most people now inhabited.[104] Writing in the *Living Church* in 1961, he argued that it was a mistake to try "to describe today's fact in yesterday's terms and to apply the answers of yesterday to the questions of today." Under the circumstances, it was not surprising that "we make no sense to others, or even to ourselves, when we think, talk, and act in this anachronistic way."[105] Inspired by Dietrich Bonhoeffer's call for a "religionless Christianity," van Buren set about trying to write theology without any recourse to the traditional doctrine of God, pursuing instead an analytical technique compatible with the empiricism of the scientific age. The result of this effort was his book *The Secular Meaning of the Gospel*, which appeared in early 1963.[106]

Though by no means a religious conservative, Paradise was troubled by the practical implications of van Buren's thought. To begin with, he questioned what exactly Bonhoeffer had meant by the term "religionless Christianity" and doubted the German would have favored its use to justify widespread rejection of inherited Christian practices.[107] Moreover, he regarded van Buren's posture as fundamentally "defensive" in its approach to modern faith, summed up by the negative question, "How can a man believe in Christianity?" Whereas for Paradise, a more fruitful question was, "If a man believes, how should he seek to change society?" By framing the challenge positively, Christians could "take the offensive" while also taking seriously the demands and complexities of industrial life.[108] In their preoccupation with the secular as normative, both Parishfield and DIM seemed to him on the verge of ceasing to be Christian altogether. "Each expression of the Christian religion we tend to reject in turn," he wrote in his journal. "More and more we move away from theological orthodoxy. . . . What kind of Christianity do we have left?"[109] But it was evident that his colleagues in Brighton and Detroit were untroubled by this possibility. "We are secular men ourselves," Roger Barney announced in 1964. "If we are honest, we must admit that an expression like 'God's will' *is* unthinkable—literally."[110] Committed as he was to finding new ways of expressing Christian truth, Paradise was depressed rather than inspired by this attitude: "When we have ventured so far from traditional theology as this, why bother with the Bible and Biblical Theology at all?" There was also the pragmatic issue of whom exactly these arguments

106 PRIVILEGE AND PROPHECY

were intended to help. "It is possible that the secular world would be slightly bored by such a sophisticated theology," he remarked. "It is certain that the Church would reject it."[111]

Notwithstanding internal debates about its theological premises, DIM attracted national and even international attention. Ted Wickham praised it as "the most significant and serious piece of industrial work taking place in the USA," and a stream of visitors from across the globe came to observe its ministry in action.[112] These public relations efforts reached their apogee in September 1961, when over 600 bishops, priests, and laymen attending General Convention visited factories across Detroit to learn about the spiritual needs of the modern workplace.[113] Coordinating with the Joint Commission on the Church in Human Affairs, Hugh White and others hoped this exposure would build support for increased funding of industrial outreach.[114] But things did not turn out exactly as they planned. Since its inception in 1959, the Conference on Church and City had emerged as an influential group of rectors who prioritized the goals of urban mission over those of industrial mission. Dissatisfied with the performance of the Division of Urban Industrial Work, they lobbied the presiding bishop to initiate a full-scale review of urban programming for the 1962–1964 triennium. They did so with the support of Bishop Daniel Corrigan, who had recently joined the National Council staff as director of the Home Department. Born in Minnesota, Corrigan (1900–1994) had attended Nashotah House after naval service during the First World War. He spent over thirty years as a parish priest, becoming suffragan bishop of Colorado in 1958. An outspoken advocate of peace and human rights, Corrigan brought a new level of sophistication to the Episcopal Church's promotion of social mission. Unlike their rivals in the urban lobby, the industrial missioners had failed to keep abreast of the shifting power relations among the national staff. Thus, despite all their promotional activities at General Convention, they found themselves outmaneuvered in the budget appropriations process.[115] The result was a completely revised urban program, well funded and well staffed, with a mandate dictated by the Conference on Church and City.[116]

What soon became known as the "Joint Urban Program" embodied the style of activism taking root among mainline Protestant churches in the early 1960s. The confidence and optimism that post-war prosperity had conferred upon Americans was put to work against the social and economic inequalities persisting in spite of such affluence.[117] Any remaining doubts about the appropriateness of church involvement in public affairs were swept aside by a

THE NEW BREED TAKES CHARGE   107

"New Breed" of churchmen who now occupied key positions in their denominational structures. The interest of these leaders in addressing the causes of deprivation and not just alleviating its symptoms began to shape the national policies of their churches.[118] They eagerly drew upon the techniques of modern social analysis to determine how and where Christians should deploy their resources most effectively. "Church officials and social scientists are seeing more of each other," observed sociologist Guy E. Swanson at the 1961 General Convention. "Perhaps the social sciences can contribute to the churches' understanding of their vocation, of the special missions set for religious bodies by the texture of society in the United States."[119] The necessity of direct action was increasingly accompanied by an enthusiasm for research and policy development. Looking back on these years, Paul Moore recalled that in both the church and nation, "it was a time when *planning* was in vogue. We had many conferences on the techniques of planning, as if we could plan our way to utopia."[120] Symbolic of this faith in the power of organizational efficiency and coordinated effort was the opening of a new, multi-million-dollar Episcopal Church Center in midtown Manhattan in 1962.[121] In the course of the previous decade it had become obvious that the expanding staff and programs of the National Council had outgrown the old Church Mission House on Park Avenue, so that by 1960 the decision was made to build a new facility. Likewise emblematic of the times was the move to change the name of the National Council to "Executive Council" to reflect the expanding scope and importance of its administrative functions.[122]

It was under these conditions that James Morton was appointed coordinator of the Joint Urban Program (JUP) in early 1962. Morton, who had replaced Kim Myers on the clergy team at Grace Church Van Vorst in 1954, was a close friend and ally of Paul Moore, who came with the blessing of the Church and City group. The task of JUP, as Morton and his sponsors saw it, was to help the Episcopal Church adapt its mission and ministry to "an interdependent, power-centered, imbalanced urban society." Before presuming to minister to the poor and marginalized on a large scale, Episcopalians must familiarize themselves with the complex forces shaping metropolitan culture. To this end, Bishop Corrigan and Morton recruited urban planner Perry L. Norton to serve as JUP's chief consultant. A committed layman, Norton (1920–2009) was professor of planning at the Graduate School of Public Administration at New York University. He brought a strongly disciplined approach to social intervention that did not always sit well with co-religionists anxious to act quickly in the face of evident need.[123] Still, he

108   PRIVILEGE AND PROPHECY

insisted that it was precisely Christians' inability "to recognize the face of anxiety unless it is manifest in some familiar category of a clear and present deprivation" that so often undercut their attempts to help.[124] Seeking to inform Episcopal leaders about the realities of contemporary urban life, JUP organized a series of regional conferences in New York, Chicago, and San Francisco during the first part of 1963 and in Atlanta and Omaha the following year.[125] The gatherings revolved around workshops about a mythical metropolis called "Metabagdad," which Norton had devised to illustrate the kinds of political, industrial, and racial challenges typical of most American cities. Participants were then supplied with a series of imaginary maps, newspaper articles, and other documents and asked to compile a list of the city's problems and ways the Episcopal Church might address them.[126]

The response to the conferences was overwhelmingly positive and won over many who had been skeptical about their usefulness. However abstract the Metabagdad exercise may have been, it succeeded in educating Episcopalians about the interlocking power structures dominating urban society. In Paul Moore's estimation, this understanding played a key role in shaping the church's attitude to the upheavals that would subsequently overtake the country.[127] One leader for whom the experience proved vital was Bishop Hines, who chaired both the New York and Atlanta conferences. Addressing the latter gathering in February 1964, he spoke urgently about Christians' responsibility for society, warning that when it came to relating to the world, the church "must get with it or die."[128] Using the momentum generated by the conferences, JUP established an advisory committee in the spring of 1963 and a year later began publishing a quarterly journal called *Church in Metropolis*.[129] In the meantime, Bishop Corrigan recruited George H. "Jack" Woodard to the Home Department to serve as Morton's deputy.[130] Woodard had caught the attention of both men as a result of his urban mission efforts in Houston, where he had built a team ministry known as the Episcopal Covenant Parish. Born in Florida, Woodard (1926–2013) was raised in Texas and worked as an engineer before training for ordination at ETSS in the late 1950s. Inspired by the work and writings of the industrial missioners, his first call was to All Saints Church in Galena Park, a working-class area near Houston's petrochemical plants. There he soon established a reputation as a proponent of racial and economic equality, and in 1962 Bishop Hines appointed him chair of the diocesan department of metropolitan missions.[131] In this capacity he pushed for an Episcopal presence in all neighborhoods, "regardless of geographic category or sociological

THE NEW BREED TAKES CHARGE   109

classification," and denounced the unspoken assumption that the poor could be left in the hands of "fundamentalist or sectarian groups."[132] It was this passion for ministry cutting across social barriers that led to the team ministry project, which eventually comprised seven churches across the city.[133]

If the Metabagdad conferences were the centerpiece of JUP's first phase (later defined by Woodard as "Operation Wakeup"), the second phase revolved around what was known as the Urban Pilot Diocese Program.[134] This initiative was an attempt to put theory into practice by starting a series of inner-city mission projects sponsored by bishops across the nation. At the behest of John Seville Higgins of Rhode Island and Roger Blanchard of Southern Ohio, theirs became the first two "pilot dioceses" to participate.[135] When the JUP staff began working with dioceses to design local programs, though, it became obvious many Episcopalians still mistrusted approaches to "urban ministry" that did not prioritize the well-being of existing city churches.[136] Jack Woodard had already encountered this problem when setting up the Episcopal Covenant Parish in Houston. To propose forms of action that challenged the primacy of the parish unit was, in the words of Woodard's seminary professor Ruel Tyson, to defy "the entire theological-ideology of Anglicanism," grounded as it was in principles of parochial integrity and clerical hierarchy.[137] Yet for Woodard and others at JUP, it was time for ideology to yield to pragmatism and for the Episcopal Church to accept that inherited notions of ministry were ill-suited to the demands of modern America. They were also evidently debilitating to those expected to sustain them. "The present custom is to put a priest into a parish situation alone and isolated from other clergy," Woodard observed in 1964. "The demands on him to be a jack-of-all-trades in impossibly complex and abrasive situations eventually lower the effectiveness of his ministry, dampen his creativity, and cause many problems, including breakdown, with distressing frequency."[138] The more attentive Episcopalians became to the needs of the surrounding culture, the more they had to reckon with the insularity and conservatism of their own institutional life.

As part of its attempt to equip clergy for the new world they faced, JUP took a leading hand in establishing the Urban Training Center for Christian Mission (UTC), an inter-church initiative launched in mid-1963 "to deal with the problems of the church in metropolis." Despite his reservations about formal church union, Kim Myers readily embraced this kind of ecumenical cooperation and left his parish in Manhattan to accept the post of executive director.[139] The center was situated in Chicago in order to draw

110 PRIVILEGE AND PROPHECY

upon the expertise of several leading figures in urban activism, among them Gibson Winter, Don Benedict, and Saul Alinsky. In particular, the grassroots organizing techniques developed by Alinsky were to become central to JUP's thinking about the church's role in community development. Early in his career, Alinsky had grasped the importance of religious and civic bodies in effecting social change and in 1940 founded the Industrial Areas Foundation (IAF) to help such groups respond to oppression and injustice in their local communities.[140] Over the course of the next thirty years, he offered mainline progressives a framework for understanding and exercising their churches' place in the power structures of American life.[141] No one reflected the close association between IAF and the Episcopal Church during these years more clearly than layman D. Barry Menuez. Born in Ohio and raised in Chicago, Menuez (b. 1933) graduated from Kenyon College in 1955. Having fulfilled his military service in the Air Force, he entered Chicago Divinity School, where he studied ethics and sociology under Gibson Winter. He then went to work for Alinsky in early 1960, and following two years of training became director of IAF's Organization for the Southwest Communities, which sought to foster interracial harmony in southwest Chicago. After intensive lobbying from Jack Woodard, he eventually joined JUP in the spring of 1965, the start of a long and diverse career in the service of the national church.[142]

Meanwhile, Myers had assembled a dynamic staff for the new UTC, among them Archie Hargreaves, whom he had known in New York as one of the founders of the East Harlem Protestant Parish. Predicting that most of the white, middle-class clergy coming to the center would never have experienced "poverty and ostracism in their gut," Myers and Hargreaves decided students should spend the first week of every training course living on the streets of Chicago, fending for themselves with only minimal personal effects.[143] Myers admitted in *Church in Metropolis* that "the kind of participation in urban life envisaged by the Center is intense and somewhat brutal," but insisted this was the whole point of the exercise—to expose churchmen to the daily indignities that marginalized people faced in American cities.[144] Not least, the experience would teach them what it felt like to be "sitting on the *other side* of the professional desk," recipients rather than providers of charity and services. The practice of taking what became known as "The Plunge" soon spread across the country as other ecumenical urban training centers were opened in San Francisco, Omaha, Kansas City, Detroit, Washington, and New York.[145] Myers felt that undergoing this exercise was especially important for his own co-religionists, given, as he asserted elsewhere, "the radical acceptance of man by man, the human locking of hands and meeting of eyes is not the norm within our caste-conscious Episcopal Church."[146] Yet even before the first group of students arrived at UTC in the fall of 1964, Myers had resigned as director, having been elected suffragan bishop of Michigan the previous spring. James Morton was appointed his successor, with Jack Woodard taking the helm at JUP.[147] News of Myers's departure dismayed Gibson Winter, who considered him "a first-rate man" whose work in Chicago he judged "as about important as anything that is happening in the country." As such, Winter found it hard to fathom why Myers would leave UTC to take up "the relatively prosaic job of being a bishop."[148]

Perhaps due to his own disenchantment with the institutional church, Winter failed to appreciate the importance of episcopacy in Myers's theological vision. Though under no illusion about the church's self-serving tendency to align itself with conservative interests, Myers resisted the premise that it should compensate by becoming a purely radical institution. "Only the idealists think it is possible for the Church to become a movement for protest and attack only," he wrote in 1964. "A realistic view of the Church must admit its historical identification with the dominant structures of power and at the same time see within the historical Church the possibility of a ministry of protest." Such a view, according to Myers, depends on a catholic doctrine of the church, one capable of encompassing both identification and protest precisely because neither impinges upon its ultimate status as "the Ark of Salvation." Analogously, the bishop is "*the* sacramental person" who, in standing above the battle, "gives communion to both armies." A bishop who becomes identified exclusively with the rich and powerful or with the poor and disenfranchised cannot serve as the sacramental focus of Christian unity. It is necessary, therefore, for the bishop to have "one foot in the Conforming Church and the other (sometimes) in the Protesting Church," Myers concluded. "He ought to have both feet in the Catholic Church."[149] This was the theological basis on which Myers himself pursued social reform so passionately while affirming the disciplines of the church. The rector of Trinity Parish in New York, John Heuss, recognized this dynamic at work in Myers when he affirmed that "as an apostle to the poor, but always understanding and respected by the educated and successful, he will be a bishop to the whole diocese."[150]

Myers's call to Michigan was part of a series of episcopal elections that signaled a new wave of leadership in the Episcopal Church. In late 1962, John Burgess, who had served as archdeacon of Boston since 1956, was consecrated

112 PRIVILEGE AND PROPHECY

suffragan of Massachusetts, making him the first black Episcopal bishop to serve in an unsegregated capacity in a predominantly white diocese.[151] At the close of 1963, the dean of St. Louis, Ned C. Cole, Jr. (1917–2002), was elected coadjutor of central New York, placing another post-war progressive on the episcopal bench. Among the other candidates considered for this post were Ben Arnold, Robert Spears, and David Thornberry, all of whom became known as liberal voices in the House of Bishops during the 1970s.[152] A few months earlier, in mid-September, Paul Moore was elected suffragan bishop of Washington, to serve alongside William F. Creighton (1909–1987), who had succeeded Angus Dun as diocesan the previous year.[153] Recognizing that Moore had been elected in no small part because of his record of outreach and activism, Creighton placed him in charge of the diocese's efforts in this area.[154] "What better place, what better time to carry out a ministry of social action than Washington in the fall of 1963?" Moore reflected later. "A man of my generation was President, and many of my friends were at his side. The country was full of hope." Among his friends in the capital were luminaries such as McGeorge Bundy, Cyrus Vance, John Lindsay, and Ben Bradlee, and even President Kennedy took time to welcome the Moores to the White House.[155] From the start of his ministry, the new bishop was conscious of balancing his access to power with his concern for the powerless, of keeping one foot in the "Conforming Church" and the other in the "Protesting Church." Depending on the circumstances, he knew that joining a picket line was sometimes needed, while at other moments using his connections to see the mayor over a "two-martini lunch" was called for.[156] Whatever the cause, he was in no doubt that privileged Episcopalians needed to put themselves at the center of the great changes afoot in American life. "The Church [is] coming alive to a vocation as great as any since the Reformation," he promised the graduating class of St. Paul's School in June 1964. "Men, there is so very much to be done, and the doing of it is tremendously exciting."[157]

Moore had been in Washington less than a year when he was asked to preach at the installation service of another bishop who, like him, combined a genteel social background with a zeal for social progress. After a dozen years as rector of Christ Church Cranbrook, in 1960 Robert DeWitt had been elected suffragan bishop of Michigan with responsibility for urban work. From this post, in which Kim Myers succeeded him, DeWitt was elected coadjutor of Pennsylvania at the close of 1963.[158] Immediately upon taking office he signaled his commitment to racial equality by holding his installation at the Church of the Advocate, a majority black church in

North Philadelphia. The symbolism of this gesture was not lost on the local community, which had been wracked by race riots just two months earlier.[159] The rector of the church, Paul M. Washington, was to become one of Bishop DeWitt's close collaborators in the tumultuous years ahead. A native of Charleston, South Carolina, Washington (1921–2001) took his first degree from Lincoln University and then prepared for ordination at Philadelphia Divinity School. He was ordained priest in 1947 and following his curacy spent six years teaching at Cuttington College in Liberia. Returning to Philadelphia with his family, he served as vicar of St. Cyprian's Mission in Elmwood until his appointment as rector of the Advocate in 1962.[160] Over the course of his twenty-five-year tenure at the church, Washington would become known as the "conscience of Philadelphia," a tireless defender of the city's oppressed and excluded inhabitants.[161] Preaching from Washington's pulpit in October 1964, Paul Moore spoke bluntly to the people of the diocese, advising them that "in his special role as a symbol of the church, Bishop DeWitt will be called upon to set forth ideals no politician would dare utter; to speak the truth that no one wants to hear." Having embraced his leadership, they must be prepared not only to tolerate his prophetic word, but also to support attempts to enact it in their midst.[162]

The sense of urgency Robert DeWitt brought to the racial crisis was already widely shared by bishops across the Episcopal Church. Over the course of the spring and summer of 1963, leading figures such as James Pike, Horace Donegan, and Stephen Bayne had spoken out against gradualist approaches to social reform.[163] Most influential had been the Presiding Bishop's "Whitsuntide Message to the Church," in which Arthur Lichtenberger called upon all Episcopalians to work actively for civil rights. "Pleas of moderation or caution about timing on the part of white leaders are seen increasingly as an unwillingness to face the truths about the appalling injustice which more than a tenth of our citizens suffer daily," he wrote. "There is urgent need to demonstrate by specific actions what God has laid on us. Such actions must move, beyond expressions of corporate penitence for our failures, to an unmistakable identification of the Church, at all levels of its life, with those who are victims of oppression."[164] This high-profile pronouncement served to embolden not just Episcopal groups like ESCRU but galvanized activists across the mainline denominations.[165] On the Fourth of July, an ecumenical group of protestors tried to integrate the Gwynn Oak Amusement Park in suburban Baltimore, which resulted in the arrest of 283 people. Among the Episcopalians involved was Michael Allen of St. Mark's Church

114 PRIVILEGE AND PROPHECY

in-the-Bowery, who afterward claimed the incident showed that "the white middle class is finally becoming aware of the importance of this battle."[166]

Another Episcopalian arrested was Daniel Corrigan of the Home Department, whose presence incensed his fellow bishop Noble Powell of Maryland. A traditionalist on the cusp of retirement, Powell (1891–1968) was offended that Corrigan had entered his diocese in a public capacity without observing the usual etiquette of first asking permission.[167] This was an early example of what became a recurring tension in the months to come, as more and more bishops and priests crossed diocesan lines to join civil rights protests against the wishes of the local leadership. Fortunately this particular problem did not arise on the occasion of the March on Washington in August, as Bishop Creighton himself welcomed nearly a dozen fellow bishops among the 1,100 Episcopalians who traveled to the capital for the event.[168]

Almost as soon as it had taken place, the March was interpreted as a turning point among white, middle-class Christians, who now acknowledged in ever-greater numbers the need to achieve racial equality through legal and social reform.[169] For many, involvement in the freedom struggle was both a matter of personal conscience and an occasion to reassert the churches' role in the shaping of American society. This latter point was eloquently expressed by the bishop of Southern Ohio, Roger Blanchard, in a statement issued to his diocese at the close of October 1963. Blanchard (1910–1998) had grown up in Massachusetts and attended Boston University and ETS before his ordinations in 1936–1937. He went on to serve as a parish priest, as executive secretary of the national Division of College Work, and as dean of St. John's Cathedral in Jacksonville, Florida, where he was based when elected coadjutor of Southern Ohio in 1958. Addressing general concerns about the participation of Episcopal clergy in civil rights activities, Blanchard insisted that such involvement had "done much to redeem the Church's public image in the eyes of many of those who had begun to doubt the relevancy of the Church's life to the complex problems of the social order." Against the specific charge that the activism of individual clerics had misrepresented the views of their parishioners, the bishop ceded no ground, asserting that "priests of the church are not ordained in order to represent the opinions of local congregations: they are ordained in order to represent and to proclaim the Gospel of Christ. This Vocation is not to be qualified by the local opinions of any particular congregation." At the same time, Blanchard also issued a warning to those diocesan clergy participating in the protests, reminding them that by and large "their own property, their own livelihood,

THE NEW BREED TAKES CHARGE   115

their own 'social investment' is not threatened by the social change for which they demonstrate." He challenged them to join the struggle only after examining their motivations for doing so: "We must understand that much of the exhilaration we experience arises from our own sense of relief from the burden of guilt which we have borne for our prior silence and for our own careless avoidance of decisions . . . which we now cheerfully would impose upon others."[170]

Whether they had engaged in such careful self-reflection or not, the following summer Episcopalians joined with thousands of others from across the country to take part in the Mississippi Freedom Project. This initiative, spearheaded by the Student Nonviolent Coordinating Committee (SNCC), was designed to promote voter registration and political empowerment among African Americans. In cooperation with the project's organizers, the National Council of Churches set up a chaplaincy program to offer pastoral support to the young "freedom workers" operating under often hostile conditions. Not least, it was hoped that the presence of clergy might discourage violent behavior by segregationists. By the end of June, over 275 ministers from various denominations had signed up, usually promising to spend between ten days and two weeks in Mississippi.[171] Among the Episcopal clergy to volunteer was William Weber, who sixteen years earlier had been driven from his church in New Jersey for alleged communist sympathies. Since then Weber had pursued parish ministry in Littleton, New Hampshire, and latterly, in Derby, Connecticut. In updating his parishioners about his activities in the South, Weber explained that he was "not engaged in demonstrations but rather ministering to the college students who have answered God's call to aid the oppressed."[172] Another Episcopal cleric to take part was Paul Moore, who spent the last week of his vacation in Mississippi out of a desire "to make some small personal contribution" to the collective undertaking.[173] Writing in *The Witness* afterward, he paid tribute to the extraordinary courage of both black and white Southerners struggling to change their communities. He also proudly reported that many non-Episcopalians had assured him that of all religious groups in Mississippi, "our Church had the best record" on race issues.[174] A Presbyterian minister whom William Weber met in Tupelo corroborated this view, citing the number of priests "forced out for racial honesty" as evidence of the church's progressive leanings. At the same time, he observed that most Episcopal clergy had almost no contact with poor whites, "who except on voting are treated worse than Negroes in many counties."[175] However necessary their intervention in

116   PRIVILEGE AND PROPHECY

the racial struggle might prove to be, few Northern activists could pretend to grasp the complex interplay of Southern class, race, and religion during their brief forays into the region.[176]

Dislike of these Northern activists was not limited to those white Southerners who opposed integration.[177] Paul Moore later admitted that the behavior of many visiting clergy had been "very self-righteous and arrogant, pretentious, and patronizing" toward their fellow Episcopalians. "Those of us who went to Mississippi felt certain that we were doing the right thing, that we were part of a historic movement of liberation," he wrote. "You were either for us or against us. You were either a good guy or a bad guy."[178] Such Manichaean distinctions did little to comfort or encourage Southern liberals, who were already under intense pressure for advocating reform. Moore recalled an evening he and a few colleagues spent with the journalist W. Hodding Carter III (b. 1935), whose father was a renowned integrationist newspaper editor in Greenville.[179] Far from welcoming his co-religionists as comrades-in-arms, Carter attacked them, questioning their assumptions and motives for coming to Mississippi. "The atmosphere was not very nice," Moore remembered, concluding that "even the liberals were somewhat ambivalent about our being there."[180] This tension assumed an institutional form in the autumn of 1964, when an initiative known as the Delta Ministry was launched under the auspices of the National Council of Churches, with Moore as chairman. As its name indicated, the project sought to deliver relief services and political empowerment in the Mississippi Delta, where poverty, illiteracy, and isolation were rife among African Americans.[181] In promoting the Ministry's work, Moore stressed the duty of Christians to support immediate action. "God is working through the movement, and it would be blasphemy of the Church to stand outside of it," he wrote. "Every day that goes by it is one more day of hunger, one more day of degradation, one more day of fear and violence thrust upon the Negro, and one more day of anxiety, hatred and fear for the white."[182] Even if they shared these sentiments, local white churchmen nonetheless resented outsiders who presumed to solve their problems without any regard for the efforts they themselves were already making.

A prominent Episcopalian skeptical of the Ministry was Moore's fellow bishop, John Maury Allin. A native of Arkansas, Allin (1921–1998) had attended Sewanee as both an undergraduate and seminarian before his ordinations in 1944–1945. He went on to serve variously as a parish priest, college chaplain, and headmaster until being elected coadjutor of

THE NEW BREED TAKES CHARGE 117

Mississippi in 1961. After the turmoil of Freedom Summer, he helped found the Committee of Concern, an ecumenical and interracial alliance seeking to rebuild dozens of black churches fire-bombed by white supremacists.[183] Although Northern activists dismissed the Committee for operating within the existing power structure, Allin's involvement confirmed his local reputation as a liberal on racial matters.[184] At the same time, he criticized the Delta Ministry for failing to work cooperatively with white Mississippians and for condemning those who did not immediately subscribe to its program.[185] Looking back on his relationship with the National Council of Churches (NCC) during this period, Allin noted that "there was a tendency to interpret any such resistance as being 'opposed to'. . . We were supposed to be docile about this business. But that was the predicament we were in. Suspicion was a child of the confusion of those days."[186] Challenging the terms under which the NCC operated did not just place Allin at odds with Paul Moore; it also raised again the larger question of diocesan versus national authority.[187] In presenting the report of the Joint Commission of Ecumenical Relations in October, John Coburn noted that membership in the NCC had resulted in the Episcopal Church sponsoring civil rights activities in places where not all Episcopalians welcomed them.[188] Alluding specifically to the Delta Ministry, the report acknowledged that the church's relationship to the project was "not only about deciding whether to approve its purposes in the abstract, but also respecting the principle of diocesan autonomy. We cannot do through the NCC what we could not do through our own national agencies. Thus, any financial participation by the Episcopal Church in such a project would be contingent upon its successfully meeting any objections made by local leadership."[189] Armed with this recommendation, in December Allin pushed through an Executive Council resolution stipulating that whenever national church funds were deployed for civil rights projects, Episcopal priests must receive permission from local bishops to participate. On this basis he was able to stop outside clergy from engaging in the Delta Ministry.[190]

As the church debated matters of episcopal jurisdiction, Frank Sayre worried about the state of American political leadership. Preaching at Washington Cathedral in mid-September, he sparked controversy by asserting that voters faced "a sterile choice" in the upcoming presidential election.[191] Without mentioning Barry Goldwater or Lyndon Johnson by name, it was clear whom Sayre meant when he referred on the one hand to "a man of dangerous ignorance and devastating uncertainty" and on the other to "a man whose public house is splendid in its every appearance but whose

118 PRIVILEGE AND PROPHECY

private lack of ethic must inevitably introduce termites at the very foundation." That Goldwater was an Episcopalian and Johnson frequently accompanied his Episcopalian wife at cathedral services did little to soften the dean's
damning appraisal. When all was said and done, he reckoned, "the electorate
of this mighty Nation is left homeless by such a pair of nominees."[192] Sayre
admitted to being surprised by the uproar his comments provoked but was
nonetheless unrepentant, pointing out that most of the private correspondence he received had been supportive.[193] Both the Cathedral chapter and
Bishop Creighton upheld the dean's right to pronounce on political matters
from the pulpit, even if they did not share the views he expressed.[194] Among
the others who praised Sayre for his stand was Scott Paradise of DIM. "There
are times in a man's life when he must speak or lose his integrity," Paradise
wrote. "In doing so you abandoned the role of statesman and chaplain to
the Establishment and became a prophet.... I hold my head higher because
someone who has so much to lose spoke the truth."[195] Intended as a tribute
to Sayre's personal example, these remarks capture a more general trend discernible among Episcopal leaders. For, even as they remained embedded in
the established order, collectively they displayed a growing awareness that
this order was not responding adequately to the needs of society. As a result, the dominant tone of their pronouncements was increasingly critical
of institutions, including their own. "We aren't serving Christ at all," Sayre
complained to a fellow churchman during the fallout from his sermon.
"We're irrelevant, petty and mushy sentimental—and the country knows it
too."[196]

In his opening address to General Convention in St. Louis the following
month, Arthur Lichtenberger conceded that clergy dissatisfaction with the
institutional church was growing.[197] This was in marked contrast to the laity,
who, in the words of one survey, appeared "relatively uncritically satisfied
with the status quo" of Episcopal life.[198] This divergence became painfully
evident at convention time, when lay members of the House of Deputies
often blocked progressive resolutions favored by the House of Bishops and
their clerical counterparts.[199] In his study of the church's social policy during
the twentieth century, Moran Weston speculated that the large number of
Southern dioceses guaranteed a conservative majority among lay deputies,
one that did not accurately reflect the sentiments of the wider church membership.[200] Whatever their reasons, laymen repeatedly took advantage of
the convention structure to slow down the pace of change in the Episcopal
Church on certain critical issues.[201]

THE NEW BREED TAKES CHARGE   119

Not the least of these was admitting women into their own ranks, something lay deputies refused to do at every convention from 1952 to 1961.[202] When they once again voted against it in St. Louis, the presiding bishop took the unusual step of rebuking them publicly in joint session.[203] Watching this process closely was Cynthia Wedel, a highly respected educator in the church. Born in Michigan, Wedel (1908–1986) earned two degrees from Northwestern before becoming the National Council's director of youth work in 1935. She relocated to Washington when her husband, Theodore Wedel (1892–1970), was appointed to the staff of the College of Preachers during the war. There, alongside her many church activities, Wedel earned a doctorate in psychology and lectured at American University during the late 1950s.[204] Moderate in tone but unyielding on matters of principle, she appealed to common sense when explaining why the lay deputies had erred by their refusal. "In our day of growing emphasis on freedom and on sharing in decision making," she wrote, "many people question the wisdom of withholding from half of the church's membership a vote in regard to how their money is spent, a voice in the choice of the presiding bishop, an opportunity to share in formulating the position of the church in regard to family life, missionary outreach, or social issues."[205] To exclude women from the councils of the church was not only unjust but ultimately self-defeating.

Another area in which laymen defied the wishes of the ordained leadership at the 1964 convention was civil disobedience. A resolution adopted by the bishops recognizing the right of persons "for reasons of conscience and after prayerful consideration, to disobey laws and social customs that are in basic conflict with the concept of human dignity" was overwhelmingly passed by the clerical deputies but rejected by the lay order.[206] Thurgood Marshall, parishioner of St. Philip's in Harlem and member of the New York delegation, was so disgusted by what he called the "conservative and obstructionist tactics" used to defeat the resolution that he quit the convention in protest.[207] The Anglo-Catholic *American Church News* characterized the vote as an "outrageous usurpation by the laity of the teaching function of the Church," as well as an overt repudiation of the African American struggle for equality.[208] In addressing his colleagues at the convention's end, the president of the House of Deputies, Clifford Morehouse, ruefully acknowledged that "in this hard year, we have somehow shrunk from making decisions we know we must make. We seemed to want to hide under a haystack."[209] One Episcopal layman hardly known for avoiding contention was William Stringfellow, who caused a furor by circulating a "Statement of Conscience"

120 PRIVILEGE AND PROPHECY

that charged Barry Goldwater with a "transparent exploitation of racism" in his bid for the presidency.[210] By accident or design, Stringfellow's launching the declaration at the convention resulted in widespread confusion as to whether it represented the official position of the Episcopal Church.[211] While officials were quick to clarify that the document did not constitute church policy, almost 800 clergy and laity signed their names to it, among them Bishops Pike, Myers, and Moore.[212] Summarizing the 1964 proceedings in *The Witness*, W. B. Spofford noted that while some judged it "the most cantankerous and argumentative General Convention in a generation," others saw it as a turning point "which may well usher in a new era in Church vitality." Though the actions of convention did not yet confirm it, Spofford himself felt sure the Episcopal Church was finally on the move.[213]

When Arthur Lichtenberger announced that he would retire after St. Louis due to ill health, it was widely assumed the House of Bishops would elect Stephen Bayne to succeed him. Erudite and urbane, Bayne had recently won plaudits for his organization of the Anglican Congress in Toronto the previous year. It therefore came as a great surprise when John Hines of Texas was instead chosen as the new presiding bishop. As a low-church Southerner, Hines was not widely regarded among the East Coast establishment. Yet his friendly and unassuming manner endeared him to many on the episcopal bench, who often found him personally more accessible than Bayne.[214] It was also evident that geography played a part, for despite Hines's record as a social liberal, the Southern bishops supported him in the hope that he would be more sympathetic to their travails over race.[215] In believing this, they were deluded. For despite their differences of churchmanship and style, Hines fully shared Lichtenberger's prophetic impulses.[216] Addressing the Metabagdad conference in New York the previous year, he had offered a glimpse of these when evoking the functions of a modern-day prophet. Such a person, Hines told his audience, "stands uneasily in the permissive society of his day, a part of it and critical of it. . . . To a nation of the politically self-satisfied, he points to possible threats from north and south. When people want to sleep, he blows a trumpet. When they want to build a wall to surround their isolation, he points them to the world outside. When they seek sanctuary in liturgy, he thunders a sermon at them."[217] With such a portrayal, Hines might well have been describing himself.

5

Involvement Is Everything (1965–1967)

Not long after his election as presiding bishop of the Episcopal Church, John Hines received a letter of congratulation from Frank Sayre of the National Cathedral. In it, the dean encouraged Hines to make regular use of the cathedral on the grounds that "it is the kind of setting where religious leadership can sometimes better be exercised than through administrative procedure or the public press."[1] If this comment bespeaks Sayre's eagerness to raise the profile of the cathedral, it also displays an appreciation for the ways the office of presiding bishop had evolved in recent times. For just as the functions and influence of the national church continued to expand during the post-war period, so did the stature of the presiding bishop as chief pastor, preacher, and spokesman. As such, the role was large and diffuse enough that each incumbent could shape it according to his own particular gifts and priorities.[2] While he had not expected to be chosen for the task, Hines lost no time in assessing the terms under which he began his work. Speaking at a press conference prior to his installation service in January 1965, he admitted that "it is now or never for the church. In times of real social crisis, the church, historically, has been weighed in the balance and found wanting—and that includes myself."[3] A theological conservative with a liberal social outlook, his investiture sermon proclaimed his confidence in the power of Christians to effect change in the world. Having acknowledged that "the Church is caught up today in the throes of a world-wide convulsion," he declared that "the Church as an agent of God's reconciling love cannot sit out the revolution as an observer, nor should it."[4] Episcopalians were put on notice that their new presiding bishop planned to lead them into the very heart of social and economic change.[5]

Hines's record as bishop of Texas demonstrated his faith in the Episcopal Church as a progressive force in society. His tireless efforts at building up the organizational structures of the church testified to his faith in the established order. Yet amidst such labors he also displayed a readiness to risk the stability of that order in the name of social justice.[6] This willingness had become evident by the early 1960s, when his steady push for the integration of

Privilege and Prophecy. Robert Tobin, Oxford University Press. © Oxford University Press 2022.
DOI: 10.1093/oso/9780190906146.003.0005

122 PRIVILEGE AND PROPHECY

diocesan facilities polarized Texas Episcopalians.[7] Notwithstanding the pain that this and other conflicts might engender, Hines never doubted it was the vocation of Christians to confront such difficulties corporately. "When the love of God in Christ Jesus makes its moral demands," he later remarked, "it makes them in terms of the institutions and relationships of a given time and in a given place."[8] Thus in a period when some had begun to question the institutional church as the basis for authentic Christianity, Hines affirmed his status as "an institution man."[9] Such enthusiasm for the organization did not translate into a preoccupation with management, however; as presiding bishop, he routinely delegated administration in order to focus on the more pastoral and visionary aspects of his office. According to Stephen Bayne, who joined the national staff to run the Overseas Department, Hines traveled extensively during the first eighteen months of his tenure, to ensure that "everybody in the Church knows and trusts him. He's been leaning over backward to get acquainted personally with all sections of the Church."[10] During this initial phase the presiding bishop sought not only to share his vision for the future, but also to discover what Episcopalians expected of their national leadership. But it soon became clear that even among the bishops, there was no consensus on this point.[11] In sharing his first impressions of the post, Hines observed that "the Church puts a huge amount of responsibility on it, without having ever defined a commensurate amount of authority in it. I go on the basis that I do have the authority needed, and try to exercise it with restraint and what wisdom I can summon."[12]

The extent of the presiding bishop's authority and the proper use of it were to prove defining issues of John Hines's incumbency. They proceeded from an existing debate about the relationship between national and diocesan jurisdictions, a tension that mirrored the one between federal and state levels of American government. Due to their experience of outside groups undertaking civil rights work in their dioceses, Southern bishops had become anxious to protect the "Episcopal Principle," by which they asserted the primacy of local autonomy over external intervention.[13] It was on this basis that John Allin of Mississippi had secured a ruling from the Executive Council stipulating that whenever national church funds were deployed for civil rights projects, Episcopal clergy must receive permission from resident bishops to participate. The measure, adopted "amid some confusion" at the last council meeting chaired by the ailing Arthur Lichtenberger, was immediately contested by Paul Moore and other activists, who recognized it as an attempt to thwart the Delta Ministry and other NCC initiatives.[14] Writing to the new presiding bishop in early February 1965, William Stringfellow argued that the policy was uncanonical and "restricts the exercise of the rights of citizenship of clergy."[15] Other protests flooded in, especially from students and faculty members at the seminaries. When the Executive Council convened later the same month, both the CSR and Home Departments spoke in favor of rescinding the decision, while Bishop Moore warned that maintaining the policy would jeopardize the Episcopal Church's place in the freedom movement. Despite Bishop Allin's insistence that the original ruling had been in harmony with the episcopal polity of the church, the council reversed itself with the support of Presiding Bishop Hines.[16] In a matter as fundamental as racial equality, it was obvious to him that ecclesiastical prerogative must yield to moral urgency. Clergy must be empowered to join the struggle for civil rights regardless of the sentiments and wishes of local Episcopalians.

Another Southerner soon to part ways with Hines over jurisdictional matters was Charles C. J. Carpenter of Alabama. Like Noble Powell, Carpenter (1899–1969) was a bishop of the old school, whose episcopate had extended into a time he found increasingly difficult to comprehend.[17] Born into a clerical family in Georgia, he was educated at Lawrenceville and Princeton, an academic career briefly interrupted by service in the US Army at the close of the First World War. Carpenter went on to prepare for ordination at VTS and then returned to his home state in 1926 to take up parish ministry. Twelve years later he was elected bishop of the Diocese of Alabama, which prospered under his charismatic and dedicated leadership during the 1940s and 1950s.[18] When Hines joined him on the episcopal bench in 1945, the two men developed a warm friendship, holding in common an evangelical sensibility and a passion for public affairs. They also shared the view that the presiding bishop should not seek to overrule his fellow bishops, as they believed Henry Sherrill had done when he removed the General Convention from Houston to Honolulu in 1955. It therefore came as an unhappy surprise to Carpenter that once Hines in turn became presiding bishop, he proved so ready to sanction interference in the affairs of individual dioceses.[19] This became evident during the Selma-to-Montgomery marches, which the Southern Christian Leadership Conference (SCLC) initiated in March 1965 to promote voting rights. Americans were appalled by television footage of the first attempted march on March 7, when Alabama state troopers set upon peaceful demonstrators with nightsticks, leaving scores of them bloody and injured on the Edmund Pettus Bridge.[20] After Martin Luther King, Jr., issued a nationwide appeal, Episcopal and other religious leaders started traveling to

124 PRIVILEGE AND PROPHECY

Selma to lend their support. Having been telegrammed by Bishop Creighton that forty priests from Washington were planning to participate in the second march on March 9, Carpenter pleaded with his colleague to intervene: "I hope you will do what you can to discourage your clergy from breaking the law and deliberately causing trouble by their law-breaking."[21] But the spirit of the moment was against him. Without informing his old friend in advance, even John Hines had flown from New York to take part in the campaign.[22]

Prior to the events of 1965, Bishop Carpenter was already known nationally as a symbol of the gradualist approach to the racial crisis. Along with seven other prominent Birmingham clergymen, he had criticized Martin Luther King in the spring of 1963 for employing civil disobedience in the city's battle over integration. King replied by addressing the ministers in his "Letter from Birmingham Jail," charging that their pleas for moderation in the face of injustice were more detrimental to the cause than overt opposition from segregationists. The letter was widely circulated and soon became one of the defining texts of the movement. And while none of those named in it fared well from the experience, Carpenter was singled out for ridicule as an establishment figure incapable of taking a clear stand on the question of race.[23] Alabama Episcopalians saw their leader differently, mindful of his persistence in fostering mutuality and respect amidst the entrenched racism of Southern life. They remembered that in the dark days following the church bombing that killed four young African American girls, only Carpenter had possessed sufficient standing among Birmingham's black and white communities to keep the lines of communication open between them.[24] Notwithstanding such efforts at local reconciliation, the bishop's gradualism was perceived as obstruction when he called upon his co-religionists to stay away from the Selma marches. "I cannot be responsible for some Episcopalians from other parts of the country who have their homework so well organized that they can spend time telling us what to do in Alabama," he complained in the *Living Church*. "I hope that they will soon go home and let us get on with the progress we are trying to make in this part of the country for which we feel a special responsibility."[25]

What Carpenter failed to grasp was that the influx of visiting churchmen into Selma was about more than hurrying the pace of change in Alabama. As journalistic commentators soon perceived, the campaign had become an opportunity for religious progressives not just to support racial equality but to model a whole new style of Christian witness in the public realm. No longer would the mainline denominations be dismissed as standing on the sidelines and blessing the status quo. "The American Negro, in his travail, is causing the rebirth of the white church," pronounced Kim Myers in *Newsweek*.[26] When Jack Woodard arrived in Selma for the final march on March 25, it seemed as though every Episcopal activist he knew was already there. Yet however inspiring he found this show of Christian solidarity and however fervent his commitment to social justice, Woodard felt obliged to sound a cautionary note. "We must not make participation in street demonstrations a test of discipleship," he warned. "The Freedom Movement of these particular years of this particular nation is deeply Christian, but it is not the whole Gospel nor is participation in it the whole mission of the Church."[27] Others shared the concern that enthusiasm for protest among liberal churchmen should not become the ground for moral arrogance or theological presumption. Preaching at the National Cathedral shortly after returning from Selma, Frank Sayre reminded his listeners that "there is but little more righteousness among those who march in civil rights demonstrations than among those who scornfully stay home, for neither are they immune to the awful cowardice of relying for salvation upon themselves."[28] Looking back on his own experiences in Alabama, Sayre's fellow dean John Butler remembered fearing the possibility of violence while marching. But he also believed that demonstrating publicly in the South had required less personal courage than confronting the genteel racism of his parishioners while a rector in Princeton, New Jersey.[29]

Not all Northerners who joined the civil rights struggle possessed Butler's moral honesty or capacity for self-analysis. One of the concerns raised by field staff during Freedom Summer had been the tendency of white volunteers to idealize the Southern blacks they had come to help, ascribing to them spiritual qualities that had been lost in the modernity of the wider culture.[30] In fact, such romanticism was really just another form of white privilege, rather than an antidote to the racial supremacy the activists abhorred. For as middle-class idealists, these people had the ability to indulge a fantasy in which they became united with the oppressed and in the process found a worthy outlet for their feelings of estrangement and need for redemption. In seeking to resolve their own identity crisis, though, liberal whites often failed to engage meaningfully with African Americans as autonomous human beings.[31] Closely attuned to such ironies was William Stringfellow, who insisted that the "real recalcitrants" in the struggle were not Southern segregationists but those "respectable, sane, sincere, benevolent, earnest folk" who vocally championed the cause of racial equality. "They do not despise or

126 PRIVILEGE AND PROPHECY

hate Negroes," he noted, "but they also do not know that paternalism and condescension are forms of alienation as much as enmity."[32] Charging that religious and secular progressives alike were more preoccupied with salving their consciences than effecting radical social change, Stringfellow castigated both church and state for showing only "a dilettante concern" for the marginalized.[33] Such a paternalistic tendency was especially reprehensible among churchmen, he later noted, for even as they acknowledged feelings of guilt about the racism of the past, they quietly clung to a sense of racial superiority in the present.[34]

One young Episcopalian inspired by Stringfellow's outspoken faith was the seminarian Jonathan M. Daniels.[35] A native of Keene, New Hampshire, Daniels (1939–1965) attended local schools before enrolling at Virginia Military Institute, from which he graduated as valedictorian. Raised Congregationalist, he joined the Episcopal Church while pursuing graduate study at Harvard and began preparing for ordination at ETS in the fall of 1963. Like many students, he had answered the call to join the Selma marches, but he also felt compelled to remain afterward in order to register black voters, tutor children, and help integrate the local Episcopal church. In outlining his decision to stay in Alabama, Daniels explained, "I could not stand by in benevolent dispassion any longer without compromising everything I know and love and value."[36] At the same time, it did not take him long to realize that a need to overcome self-righteousness was "the price that a Yankee Christian had better be prepared to pay if he goes to Alabama."[37] As Daniels worked to make theological sense of his activities, Stringfellow encouraged him to consider how they might inform his eventual ministry in the North. "Maybe this present experience is your baptism for the witness to be made back in Cambridge," he suggested. "You must surely confront the ETS people with the facts you have suffered."[38]

The impact of Daniels's witness would ultimately extend far beyond the walls of his seminary. In mid-August, he joined an integrated group picketing whites-only businesses in the town of Fort Deposit, south of Montgomery. Having been arrested and jailed for six days in the county seat of Hayneville, the group was released from custody on August 20. As Daniels and three others waited outside a local shop for a ride back to Selma, they were confronted by Tom Coleman, an unpaid special deputy. When Coleman aimed his shotgun at the seventeen-year-old black activist Ruby Sales, Daniels pushed her aside and in so doing received the impact of the fired gun. He was killed instantly. This outrage was compounded when an all-white jury subsequently acquitted Coleman at trial on the grounds of self-defense.[39] In the meantime, a funeral for Daniels took place in New Hampshire on August 24, followed the next day by a memorial service in St. John's Chapel at ETS. Addressing members of the seminary community, Dean John Coburn reflected on what God might be saying to the church through this terrible event. To begin with, he saw it as a divine reminder that "every social issue is a moral issue," such that it was impossible for any Christian to claim neutrality. More than this, Daniels's sacrifice confirmed that the church was called to take a leadership role in the struggle, something it could only accomplish when "individual Christians continue to be actively engaged and are willing if necessary to die for Christ's sake."[40] The murder had a profound and lasting effect on Coburn, who thereafter became far more attuned to the complexity of America's social problems.[41] It also showed him and other Episcopalians what martyrdom looked like up close. "It took a long time to realize [Jon] was a martyr," he confessed later. "He was just a typical, questioning, struggling student, trying to make sense out of the issues, conflicts and injustices of our society."[42] Yet with time, Daniels came to be revered in the wider church as a Christian martyr who gave his life in the cause of human dignity.[43]

Paradoxically, the flowering of clerical support for civil rights at Selma came at a moment when mainline Protestantism was losing its authority and prestige in national life. Though church leaders' activism may have exacerbated resentment in certain quarters, a much broader combination of issues contributed to this trend, among them theological insecurity, social disruption, and demographic change. Whatever the precise combination of factors, clearly the religio-cultural consensus of the 1950s had started to crumble: between 1965 and 1975, the major denominational groups would experience a 10 percent decline in adult membership and a 30 percent decline in baptisms.[44] Some Episcopalians were more alert to this reality than others. One close observer of the trend was Charles P. Price (1920–1999), minister of Harvard's Memorial Church and preacher to the University. Born in Pittsburgh, Price had himself graduated from Harvard in 1941 before joining the Navy during the Second World War. He went on to study for the priesthood at Virginia and then served parishes in Pennsylvania and New York until 1956, when he returned to VTS to teach systematic theology. Having taken his doctorate from Union Seminary in 1962, he was recruited by President Nathan Pusey to Harvard the following year.[45] Throughout his tenure in Cambridge, Price's sermons were marked by a refusal to gloss over

128 PRIVILEGE AND PROPHECY

the uncertainties and ambiguities of Christian life in modern society.[46] "The churches are beginning to lose their position of moral leadership," he stated flatly in the spring of 1964. "There is still politeness, sometimes excessive respect, often wistfulness. But any real ability to influence the thought and behavior of people as a whole seems to me to be drying up."[47] Addressing Harvard Divinity School's graduating class a year later, Price repeated his diagnosis, yet also counseled his listeners not to lose heart. Rather than giving in to nostalgia—"O for grandfather's day, when things were really Christian"—they must instead take inspiration from the church's long record of adapting to shifting cultural sensibilities.[48]

The Protestant establishment's waning fortunes were linked to the wider assault on liberal institutions that proved such a feature of national life during the second half of the 1960s. It was during these pivotal years that New Dealers and other traditional progressives were opposed by proponents of the "New Left," who rejected their faith in the possibility of creating a just order by means of existing political structures.[49] Despite the promise held out by civil rights legislation and the Great Society, such people pointed to persistent racial and economic inequalities that the "moderate middle" running the country had been unable or unwilling to address. On this basis, they concluded that a truly equal society could only be achieved through a radical alteration of the system.[50] While this attack on the established order obviously threatened the values of many Americans, it posed a particular challenge to Episcopalians. For underlying their commitment to liberal reform lay not just an adherence to constitutional democracy, but also a distinctly Anglican notion of social harmony. From this heritage came a vision of society as an organic whole, coextensive with the sacramental body of the church and governed in accordance with the mandates of Christian love. Thus conditioned to regard the church as the spiritual basis for social stability, Episcopalians tended to be suspicious of civil disorder, let alone more serious forms of institutional rupture.[51] Sensitive to this reality, in 1966 John Coburn urged his co-religionists to consider the possibility of protest as a legitimate means for ensuring, rather than merely disrupting, the health of the body politic. Reflecting on the ways they might participate in the public realm, he suggested it was just as reasonable to do so by joining "in picket lines, in civil disobedience, in strikes" as "by working patiently within the structures set by the state." These seemingly opposite approaches were both valid, Coburn concluded, because "there is meant to be a struggle for power in which men are involved [so] that a more just social order may emerge."[52]

Someone who proved adept at operating both within and without the establishment in the struggle for human equality was Paul Moore. After becoming suffragan bishop of Washington in 1964, he had recognized that it was his vocation, as he wrote later, "to be a steward of power, to use my office to empower those who were too weak to achieve the modest goals of economic and political justice."[53] Moore immersed himself in city politics, routinely drawing attention to the needs of the poor living in the nation's capital. In the process, he built up a good reputation among Washington's black community, particularly through his work as co-chair of the Coalition of Conscience, a loose alliance of clergy and civil rights leaders.[54] He gained further prominence by supporting of the "Free DC" movement, which emerged in early 1966 under the direction of local SNCC representative Marion Barry. Described in the *Washington Post* as "a free-swinging band of home-rule militants," the group spearheaded a boycott campaign against businesses refusing to support the District of Columbia's bid for self-government.[55] Washington Episcopalians were divided in their reaction to the bishop's activism. Though some admired his outspokenness, others believed he was betraying the interests of his own people.[56] In March 1966, a group of lay leaders met to discuss the appropriateness of what they called Moore's "extra-curricular activities."[57] Later in the year, the vestry of All Souls' Church voted to halve their diocesan financial contribution in protest against the suffragan's public involvements.[58] Met with such disapproval, Moore was unrepentant. "If we really care, as Jesus cared," he insisted, "we'll use all of our ingenuity, all of the political and economic power we can mobilize, to deal with problems . . . which require a social rather than an individual approach."[59]

Differences between mainline clergy and laity over the church's place in society were hardly new, of course, but by the mid-1960s the depth of these tensions was impossible to ignore. Even though most Episcopal laypeople traditionally stood to the right of their ministers politically, they had tolerated their liberal preaching and policy statements.[60] Yet as more and more clerics began to press for systemic reform, lay discord became palpable.[61] To Gibson Winter, such animus was to be expected: the community organizing in which church leaders were increasingly engaged cut across the class interests and racial prejudices of their white, middle-class membership. Rather than enter into fruitless debates with conservatives about the legitimacy of political participation, though, he called on activists to develop and promote the Christian rationale for what they were already doing. "The

130 PRIVILEGE AND PROPHECY

churches have a servant role to fulfill," he asserted. "Not leading but encouraging community organization where possible. They also have a prophetic role to play—not letting community organization settle for token reprisals but pushing on to a new political and cultural vision."[62] Winter's pairing of servanthood with prophecy in this context is indicative of an important evolution underway in the social and theological outlook of mainline progressives. For taken together, these concepts reflect a growing consciousness among them of the need to reform society without presuming in the process to dominate it. So while the church must undoubtedly continue to speak in the world, it must assuredly do so for the world's sake and not its own.

The linking of servanthood to prophecy became pivotal in the activist language of the Episcopal Church during this period. One spokesman to explore their relationship was Reinhart B. Gutmann, executive secretary of the national division of Community Services. Originally from Germany, Gutmann (1916–2006) was ordained in England in 1941–1942 and served his curacy in London. He moved to the United States during the war, and after becoming vicar of St. Stephen's Church in Milwaukee in 1945, he established a city mission known as Neighborhood House. In the early 1960s, he was recruited to work for the National Council under Arthur Lichtenberger. Addressing the Wisconsin Welfare Council in 1966, Gutmann suggested that the connection between service and prophecy derived from the living example of Christ's own ministry. "Because He is servant of all, He dares to be a Prophet—to offer critical and sharp judgment upon society and to point towards the world of justice and fulfillment." In the same way, contemporary Christians must recognize that true service to the world sometimes brought an obligation to speak out against it. Whatever marginalization they might endure as a result was part of the sacrificial nature of radical servanthood. Yet in championing Christians' prophetic role in a technological society, Gutmann admitted that principles and expertise were two different things. "The Church corporately possesses no special competence in the arena of politics or economics," he conceded. Even so, this did not obviate its responsibility "to bring to bear moral and ethical judgment on social or political issues." Thus, authentic Christian prophecy was characterized not by claims to worldly authority, but rather by a readiness to contest such authority whenever it impaired human flourishing. "The Church committed to the essential quality of men is bidden to identify with the poor and downtrodden so that they may be given power for achievement of justice," Gutmann argued. "As the Church takes a radically critical view of society, it is committed to be itself an agent for change."

Christians seeking to serve the world must be prepared to protest against its oppressions, and in speaking out must also be willing to act in self-denying ways that empower the oppressed.[63]

If the notion of prophetic servanthood challenged Episcopalians to reimagine their mission to society, it also prompted concerns about the identity of existing social ministries within the institution. While on study leave at ETS in 1966, Gutmann's colleague Arthur Walmsley sought to evaluate the current status of professional "social action people" in relation to the church they were employed to serve.[64] By "social action people" he meant all CSR and other staff at national, diocesan, and local levels whose job it was "to 'worry' about how the Church relates to the social issues of the day." Like other commentators, Walmsley realized that the proliferation of such people within church structures alienated some of his co-religionists, who deemed them unrepresentative of the larger community.[65] Reflecting on his experience as a member of the national staff, he wondered how sustainable it was to employ people within the church bureaucracy "to act as radical critics of the social order" and to develop social action programs on the basis of their critique. The problem lay not just in the objections of others; many of the "social action people" themselves were deeply ambivalent about their situation. For they understood that like other components of the established order, the church was an agent of institutional power, and as such, any judgment they might make against the power structure necessarily extended to the church as well. The imperative to confront the vested interests of the organization that employed them naturally raised questions about credibility and independence. More broadly, Walmsley queried just how free such church-sponsored activists were to dissent from the governing assumptions of liberal reformist politics. Citing the mainline churches' support of Lyndon Johnson's "War on Poverty," he concluded that "we share the same social optimism which motivates our political leadership. Whether this ideology is adequate for the problems of the era into which we are moving is another question."[66]

As Episcopal progressives began to doubt the adequacy of liberal reform in the face of revolutionary social change, they found in the prophetic stance a timely resource. On the one hand, it provided a religious basis on which to engage the anti-establishment sentiment pervading the wider culture. On the other, it supplied a biblical vocabulary for justifying more experimental forms of social ministry within the church. Chief among these were types of outreach intended not just to comfort but empower the poor and oppressed. The Joint Urban Program (JUP) remained the national church's

132 PRIVILEGE AND PROPHECY

primary means for promoting the principle of empowerment during these years. Discussing JUP's pilot diocese program in 1966, Bishop Hines granted that the initiative was not the only way for Episcopalians to serve their communities, but praised it as "a major effort at renewal and experimentation through which new methodologies and procedures can be communicated to the whole Church."[67] In fact, the success of the program varied considerably, depending on the enthusiasm and understanding of the local leadership. Reporting to Bishop Hines after a nationwide evaluation, JUP director Jack Woodard singled out Missouri as the most creative of the pilot dioceses, in marked contrast to others.[68] This was due in no small part to the exertions of Anthony Morley, whom Bishop George Cadigan had appointed diocesan director of Research and Planning in 1965. Morley (b. 1930), who grew up as a Quaker in Washington and Philadelphia, attended Haverford College as an undergraduate. He became an Episcopalian in 1951, and after a Fulbright year in Vienna, prepared for ordination at ETS and undertook doctoral studies at General. In 1958, he succeeded Arthur Walmsley as rector of Trinity Church in St. Louis, which by then had become a thoroughly integrated parish. Having demonstrated a commitment to pushing urban mission in new directions, Morley emerged as the obvious person to coordinate the pilot operation.[69]

In a lecture he delivered at ETS in 1966, Morley offered a candid assessment of the ways Episcopal inner-city ministry had evolved over the past two decades. Alluding to the model of ministry exemplified by men such as Paul Moore, Kim Myers, and James Gusweller, he characterized the post-war years as a time when there was a "charismatic heroic urban slum priest at the head of things, radiating prodigious energy, exercising apparent public influence, acting as a lodestone for the ever-necessary money, placarding the Incarnation, and pricking the conscience of the Church at large." Such figures had been crucial in generating a sense of hope and excitement among Episcopalians about the church's continuing relevance in the cities. Yet their efforts had also shown that such personalized ministry was inadequate to the needs it had helped to expose. "You can't run tutoring programs or housing clinics on an expiatory messiah complex," Morley remarked wryly. It was not just that the tasks were too large and complex to be accomplished by individual clergy; the tasks themselves were no longer the same. In the 1950s, the challenge had been to save the old inner-city churches from extinction by reaching out to the newer, impoverished populations that surrounded them. This goal had been met in many instances, as the Episcopal Church learned repeatable techniques for ensuring a parochial presence in a range of neighborhoods. Having thus reasserted its institutional presence in the city, Morley argued that the church must focus less on its own survival and more on the well-being of the wider urban community."[70] Empowerment programs thus became the basis for a modern form of mission, which, to borrow a phrase much in vogue at the time, brought together city dwellers in a sense of mutual responsibility and interdependence.

One obvious way to lend substance to this vision was for Episcopalians themselves to coordinate their efforts across parochial and diocesan dividing lines. Inspired by the holistic approach of the Metabagdad conferences, Morley and his St. Louis colleagues sought to make common cause with their co-religionists across the Mississippi River in East St. Louis. Even though the two cities were in different states and different dioceses, it seemed obvious that the socioeconomic challenges they faced should be tackled together, rather than separately. Confident that the Episcopal Church was capable of transcending "the balkanizing boundaries of history and tradition," Morley championed "an across-the-river mind-set for planning, proposing, deciding and getting down to work" on community empowerment projects. Meanwhile, he also promoted the decidedly non-urban activities of the Missouri Delta Ecumenical Ministry, which priest William D. Chapman had started in response to the rural poverty endemic in the southeastern region of the state. A born organizer, Chapman (1925–1999) persuaded small landholders to form a cooperative specializing in the production and marketing of okra as a cash crop, thereby earning the ministry the nickname "Episcopal Okra." A third major initiative under the auspices of the pilot program was the Ecumenical Campus Ministry, which focused on the diverse social needs of students and staff based at commuter colleges in city settings. Looking back on such efforts during these years in Missouri, Morley recalled his sense of exhilaration as he and others worked to broaden the church's ideas about social outreach.[71]

Predictably, Episcopalians were especially drawn to education as a means of cultivating empowerment among the disenfranchised. But to do so effectively would require curricula attuned to the cultural sensibilities of inner-city minority groups, rather than employing existing educational materials produced for white congregations in the suburbs. Recognizing this need, in 1963 JUP recruited Lester McManis of the Christian Education Department to design a new program, whose content and methodology specifically addressed this requirement.[72] The result was the 1966 publication of the

134   PRIVILEGE AND PROPHECY

Handbook on Christian Education in the Inner City, which was assembled with input from various urban parishes, among them Grace Church in Jersey City, the Church of the Advocate in Philadelphia, St. Philip's in Harlem, and St. Stephen and the Incarnation in Washington. Introducing the handbook, McManis (1910–2002) stressed that Christian education should encourage self-worth among inner-city people caught in a culture of dependency. Contrary to its age-old reputation for mollifying the poor through handouts and promises of eternal reward, the church must instead help them reclaim their sense of dignity and agency in the present moment.[73] There were other, albeit modest, signs that the progressive emphasis on empowerment was taking root in the wider church. In a statement from their meeting in October 1966, the House of Bishops reaffirmed their support for the War on Poverty but registered concern that the program's beneficiaries were not being adequately consulted in its planning and execution. To include poor people in these processes was both an obvious opportunity to increase self-determination, as well as an obvious way to foster a "society of inter-dependence."[74] In a characteristically Anglican move, the bishops thus based their call for political inclusion not only on a principle of justice, but also out of a pragmatic desire to maintain social harmony.

Among the most incisive Episcopal voices espousing empowerment in the 1960s was that of African American priest and scholar Nathan Wright, Jr. Born in Shreveport and raised in Cincinnati, Wright (1923–2005) came from a family that put a premium on education. He was deployed in the Army Medical Administrative Corps during the Second World War, after which he completed his undergraduate studies at the University of Cincinnati, the first of six degrees he would earn. Following studies at ETS, he was ordained in 1950 and spent the next two decades in a range of ministries along the East Coast. From 1964 to 1969 he served as executive director of the Department of Urban Work in the Diocese of Newark, during which time he became closely associated with the Black Power movement.[75] Writing in *The Witness* in the spring of 1966, Wright offered a stringent analysis of the "Christ the Servant" theology gaining popularity in the Episcopal Church. Whatever might be valid about the vision of the church as the Body of Christ serving the world, he noted, too often in practice it remained "a kind of stoically-conceived *noblesse oblige*." If Episcopalians were sincere in their dedication to empowerment, they must be prepared to forgo the moral satisfaction of good deeds in favor of less gratifying but more meaningful changes to the social fabric. "We're never called—in terms of end purpose or goal—to make things better, but to make things right," Wright insisted. Outreach to the slums "may fulfill our felt need to serve but not fulfill the need for furtherance of growth into self-sufficiency on the part of those whom we would serve."[76] In taking seriously the latter goal, the church must be ready to embrace an understanding of race and power that would transform its own identity in turn. "For far too long our churches have shared in the colonialist mind," Wright wrote in 1967. "They have seen white clergy fit to minister to urban minorities but have not built an equitable two-way street for professionally qualified Negroes to minister to the white majority." For churchmen to endorse empowerment without expecting it to affect their internal relations was to misconstrue the premise from the outset. This conviction led Wright to warn that "we cannot be agents of change unless we are willing to be changed ourselves."[77]

As a senior cleric in the Diocese of New York, John Butler was quietly determined to lend substance to this notion. Having lost his wife unexpectedly in early 1966, he decided to leave the cathedral uptown and spend the final years of his ministry as rector of Trinity Parish. This move from dean to rector hardly constituted a diminution of responsibilities, however, as the mother church and its network of chapels across the city comprised almost 5,000 souls and a staff of twenty-five clergy.[78] And though he had always loved Trinity and counted many friends there, Butler believed that both the tone and structure of the parish required significant changes. In particular, he saw the chapel system as deeply paternalistic, such that the local worshipping communities had never developed indigenous leadership. He asked Bishop Donegan to use his sermon at Butler's service of institution to underscore the necessity of overhauling this system, so that the chapels might gain greater autonomy and move toward independence. The bishop obliged, congratulating the assembly on choosing someone so well suited to guide them through the important days to come.[79] Not everyone was pleased by what they heard; one warden refused to stay for lunch after the service, while another announced that "he did not wish to be a partner in the dissolution of the empire, à la Winston Churchill." Having already decided that he would limit his tenure at Trinity to five years, Butler set about diversifying the activities and programs of the parish, deliberately seeking to shed the image of Trinity as "a symbol of The Establishment in the Wall Street area."[80] He also oversaw the eventual creation of the "One Peppercorne Report," which set out an agenda of new priorities in the areas of administration, stewardship, outreach, and service. Crucially, the report included a plan for making all but one of the chapels independent, a decolonization of sorts that would enable them to become more truly integrated with their neighborhoods.[81]

While most progressive Episcopalians continued to draw upon the language and logic of the institution in seeking to make the church more responsive to contemporary society, others concluded that the institutional heritage itself was the problem. For some time, academic theologians had been debating the capacity of received teachings and norms to convey the Christian message meaningfully to an increasingly secular world.[82] But it was the intervention of two Anglican bishops that lodged these ideas in the public consciousness. In England, Bishop John A. T. Robinson had caused a sensation with the 1963 publication of his volume *Honest to God*, which drew upon the thinking of Dietrich Bonhoeffer, Rudolf Bultmann, and Paul Tillich.[83] In terms of impact, the American equivalent was James Pike's *A Time for Christian Candor*, which appeared the following year.[84] Like *Honest to God*, the book struck a chord with those churchgoers who, in Robert Bruce Mullin's phrase, felt they were "dying of spiritual thirst in a salt sea of religiosity."[85] According to Pike, the trouble was that too often Christians failed to encounter the real Gospel "because they are bogged down by too many doctrines, mores, precepts, customs, symbols and other traditions, with no sense of differentiation between the relative essentiality and nonessentiality of the respective items." If all these unhelpful accretions could only be shed, he suggested, then people would be free to experience an authentic faith.[86] Yet despite the breezy certainty of the diagnosis, it remained unclear how the crucial distinction between "essentials" and "non-essentials" was to be made. Charles Price of Harvard criticized Pike for depicting the procedure as a simple one, "like taking a product out of its packaging, or a treasure out of its earthen vessel." The reality was evidently much more complicated, and it was presumptuous to treat the task as a matter of common sense.[87] Moreover, as one of Pike's fellow bishops observed, even if the words and images of Christian orthodoxy might seem foreign to some, "to discard them is usually to jeopardize the doctrine they describe."[88]

These caveats meant little to those for whom secularity was not so much a fact to be reckoned with as an opportunity to be embraced. Arguing that traditional notions of the sacred had become meaningless in Western culture, Paul van Buren, along with fellow Episcopalians William Hamilton and Thomas Altizer, became known as the "death of God" theologians in the popular press.[89] Given, as van Buren wrote in the *Christian Century* in 1965, that Christian theology "has operated with a monistic cosmology and metaphysics which seems to have little or no relationship to our culture and its way of seeing how things are in this society," it was necessary not just to reform the church's discourse and apparatus, but to replace them entirely.[90] The result must be that "religionless Christianity" Bonhoeffer had spoken of two decades earlier, a distinctive way of being in the world that still placed Christians in the vanguard of the search for meaning.[91] Sharing in this combination of anti-institutional fervor and commitment to relevance was Gibson Winter, whose 1963 *Metropolis as the New Creation* in many ways anticipated Harvey Cox's bestselling book of two years later, *The Secular City*.[92] Together, Winter and Cox looked upon the secular urban centers of America as liberated spaces, blessedly free of institutional captivity. "The Church exists in the churches but she also exists in unacknowledged form among men and women who are committed to metropolis but not to religious organization," Winter wrote. Under these circumstances, a radical dissociation with the Christian past became possible, an essential prerequisite to building authentic spiritual community under the secular dispensation.[93]

Similarly eager to cast aside what they deemed the church's bankrupt inheritance were advocates of the "new morality," who made their case in the form of situation ethics. In arguing that reliance upon abstract moral codes must yield to contextual decision-making, situationists posited an ethical framework commensurate with the anti-establishment tenor of the times. The most prominent among them, Joseph Fletcher of ETS, stressed that situation ethics was a "non-system," whereby Christians must evaluate each moral choice according to what was most loving, and by so doing would determine the correct course of action. Or, as he summarized: "What is, in the light of what love demands, shows what ought to be."[94] As was generally the case with the "New Theology" of the 1960s, situationism counted among its proponents a disproportionately large number of Episcopalians. Whether this was due to their enmeshment in the wider trends of liberal Protestantism or proceeded from a specifically Anglican source is difficult to say. Certainly the tradition's emphasis on intellectual freedom and its instinctive preference for the pragmatic over the systematic would have emboldened those disposed to embrace theological innovation.[95] Yet there were other Episcopal thinkers alarmed by their colleagues' willingness to repudiate tradition and structure as part of their bid for relevance.[96] One of these was John Booty, professor of church history at Virginia Seminary. A native of Detroit, Booty (1925–2013) studied at Wayne State University and VTS before serving his curacy and pursuing a doctorate at Princeton. Though he shared the radical

138 PRIVILEGE AND PROPHECY

theologians' critique of the church as social actor, he detected in their attitude a culpably naïve view of humanity. "Like most Americans, they are not avid students of history," Booty observed. "Over and over again in history the optimists have been torn apart by violence, tragedy, human hatred. There is no warrant for us to believe that the industrial society which we have been building is any other than the Frankenstein which devours our lives."[97] Even those Christians who did not share Booty's level of skepticism might wonder at the new theologians' apparent disregard for the reality of sin in the world.

Given its long-standing association with figures such as Paul van Buren and Gibson Winter, the Parishfield community in Michigan was predictably enthusiastic about these theological developments. "We in this Community travel light," staff member Roger Barney affirmed at the end of 1965. "We are convinced that radical theology goes inseparably with the secular approach to life to which we are committed."[98] Early in the new year the community received a visit from theologian William Hamilton, who according to Barney praised them as "the only radically experimental or exploratory group of church people to have recognized the necessary connection between 'radical mission' and radical theology."[99] The mid-1960s were to be a period of sustained reflection at Parishfield about what its mission should be. In 1962, clergyman James B. Guinan (1918–1992) had been invited to join the staff, not least because of his civil rights activism and devotion to social justice. Passionate, funny, and adventurous, he brought a renewed sense of possibility to the community at a time when its rural setting felt isolated from the ferment of metropolitan society. With the help of Guinan's connections, Parishfield began to develop a presence in Detroit while still maintaining its established presence and routine in Brighton.[100] By the summer of 1965, though, the focus of their concern had shifted to Detroit to the extent that the staff decided to relocate there full-time.[101] If church renewal was still Parishfield's calling, surely this meant getting middle-class suburbanites involved in the city, rather than bringing them to the country to talk about it.[102]

The Ayres, Barneys, and Guinans defined their ministry in Detroit as that of "involved observers." Be it through community organizing, the freedom movement, or political action, they now sought ways to become "genuinely involved without becoming captive to any confined point of view or to any particular institution." So even when pursuing "religionless Christianity" in the secular realm, they sought to maintain the same critical distance Parishfield had always kept from the conventional church.[103] Having repudiated accountability on so many fronts, however, it was unclear exactly for whom Parishfield presumed to speak. The staff continued to attend Episcopal services but devoted considerable energy to articulating why the traditional structures had no future as the basis for mission and ministry in the metropolis.[104] Thus, when Jack Woodard of JUP invited them to serve as consultants during a review of the Home Department's strategy and goals, their attitude was largely negative.[105] "Jack and co. are obviously trying to do what can be done to breathe life back into the obsolescent institution," Roger Barney remarked dismissively in a memo. His wife Jane was similarly pessimistic. "The local parish or congregation does not, and by its nature cannot, function as a base for carrying on programs of social change," she declared without elaboration.[106] Perhaps inevitably, Parishfield's relations with Richard Emrich continued to deteriorate during this period, something Fran Ayres acknowledged when writing to the bishop in the spring of 1966. Even while conceding that "a serious communication problem" had developed between them, Ayres clung to a vision of Parishfield as "the ones within the institution who are commissioned to be the hair shirt, the burr under the saddle."[107] In fact, this was an increasingly self-appointed role, given how assiduously the group had distanced itself from the mainstream of the church. Amidst its eagerness to be relevant to secular society, Parishfield underestimated just how much it had depended on the institution when making all its anti-institutional pronouncements.

As Parishfield set its sights on Detroit, Scott Paradise was in the process of leaving it behind. Having witnessed the daily reality and impact of industrial life, he was becoming progressively more critical of the political and economic values on which it was based.[108] This led to deepening conflict with other members of the DIM staff, who did not share his readiness to question the liberal consensus.[109] An opportunity to interrogate industry through the lens of Christian social justice arrived when Paradise was asked to found the Boston Industrial Mission (BIM) in early 1965.[110] The move brought with it a new set of challenges: whereas in Detroit he had ministered among the laborers and executives of the car companies, in Boston he would be working with scientists and engineers engaged in research and development. Ministry informed by the everyday tensions of the workplace was replaced by dialogue about the long-term impact of technology on the created order.[111] In particular, Paradise sought to foreground the moral implications of technological advancement in the areas of wealth disparity, environmental degradation, and weapons production. Far from assuaging his fears about the future, his work at BIM confirmed his belief in the need "to radically reconstruct society

140 PRIVILEGE AND PROPHECY

on the basis of justice and sustainability." It also highlighted how rapidly interconnected the world was becoming. To argue for comprehensive changes in the economic and social relationships of the United States was tantamount to accepting the need for them across the planet. Gone were the days, Paradise concluded, when industry could act without regard for the needs of people everywhere.[112]

Such a global perspective was discernible among Episcopalians in other contexts as well. Their expanding role in the Anglican Communion reflected both the optimism and responsibility they felt as Christian citizens of a superpower. Actively promoting such internationalism was the priest and church official Daisuke Kitagawa (1910–1970). Traveling from his native Japan in 1937 to study at GTS, Kitagawa remained in the United States after his ordination to serve mission churches in the Diocese of Olympia. Alongside thousands of other Japanese Americans, he was interned during the war, acting as priest-in-charge for Episcopalians at the Tule Lake Relocation Center in Newell, California. This experience solidified his commitment to the universal church as transcending ethnic differences in all cultures.[113] After the war he continued ministry among displaced Japanese Americans and then worked for the World Council of Churches before becoming executive secretary of the division of Domestic Mission in 1962. During this period Kitagawa was outspoken in his support for the black freedom struggle but warned against treating it as unique. "The tensions among racial and ethnic groups now being experienced in this country are not peculiarly an American phenomenon but part and parcel of a world-wide phenomenon," he noted.[114] In keeping with this fact, Western churchmen must be prepared to confront their complicity in the suffering of oppressed peoples throughout the world.[115] It was in an effort to do so that the Episcopal International Peace Advisory Committee prepared a paper about the Vietnamese conflict in late 1965. Noting that American Christians generally "fail to realize how deep is the rift between them and their brethren in Asia," the committee called on Episcopalians to imagine what American involvement in Vietnam must look like from others' point of view. At the very least, they should not be surprised if Asian Christians "regard with abhorrence the silence of the Church when, in the conduct of the war, we kill the very people we are trying to save."[116]

Yet despite their confidence in speaking out critically on domestic issues, many liberal churchmen remained uncertain when addressing matters of foreign policy. A case in point was Charles Price, who in preaching at Harvard in May 1965 confessed to feeling ambivalent about US interventions abroad. On the one hand, he instinctively believed America had a duty to promote dignity and freedom beyond its borders. On the other, he wished that it were possible "to be more clearly on the side of popular and national sentiment instead of the feudal oligarchies and military coalitions which we seem to support so regularly."[117] In a sermon at the National Cathedral on New Year's Day 1966, Frank Sayre sounded a similar note of dissatisfaction. "It seems to be an unhappy fact that it is not only our enemies but our allies as well, not to mention a host of our own American citizens, who are sadly confused about what all our troops and our diplomats are about in the world today," he remarked ruefully.[118] Even to acknowledge such worries was not easy for clergy whose experience of the Second World War had instilled in them a powerful sense of America's unique moral standing among the nations. They also shared with many of their generation a reluctance to question the judgment of their leaders.[119] For Paul Moore, such deference sprang not just from military training but the fact that some of the administration's leading policymakers were old friends. He had grown up with McGeorge Bundy and had gone to Yale alongside Cyrus Vance, both proponents of the expanding war effort in Vietnam. "These were people whom I knew, whom I trusted, and who had been exposed to the same values I had," Moore later recalled. With time, however, he came to believe that American involvement was not "clear enough in purpose to warrant the kind of slaughter that was going on," such that by 1966 he felt obliged to oppose the war publicly.[120] The gradual move by men like Sayre and Moore from acquiescence to condemnation was indicative of a wider pattern to emerge among Episcopal clergy in the months to follow.[121]

Unsurprisingly, opposition to the war was most prevalent among middle-class young people and soon became a key ingredient in the counterculture dominating college campuses. The suspicious attitude with which students increasingly approached all structures of authority did not exempt the churches, which they regarded as both reactionary and hypocritical. As W. B. Spofford of *The Witness* observed, "youth sees the absurd anomaly of the most conservative men in our society supporting the institution which was founded by men who turned the world upside down."[122] And even though many chaplains embraced the challenge of making religion more relevant and responsive to the modern campus, few could pretend that their efforts matched the radical experimentation going on around them.[123] Alongside his fellow Episcopalian Charles Price, President Nathan Pusey of Harvard spoke candidly about the changes transforming both the university and

142   PRIVILEGE AND PROPHECY

wider society. In his baccalaureate address to the Class of 1965, for example, he contrasted his own generation of Harvard students with those about to graduate. While wary of what he deemed the self-righteous tendencies of the present student body, he praised them for having a more developed sense of corporate ethics than his cohort once did, as well as for their readiness to associate with the poor and oppressed.[124] Two years later, though, Pusey was more critical of the excesses of student discontent. Dismissing as childish the view that "our society is so rotten there is nothing redeemable in it," he also derided the constant use of the term "the Establishment" as intellectually lazy: "how much failure to look and think and appraise is papered-over by those who bandy about this cliché!" He conceded that older people had much to repent of in their conduct of affairs but rejected the tactics of demonization as futile. Faced with upheaval at home and abroad, what was needed from citizens of all ages was not "impatient, petulant complaint, but the creative, constructive force of a mature realism [e]stablished in courage and in hope."[125]

Yet, as he seems to have realized, Pusey's appeals for inter-generational cooperation were fundamentally out of step with the tenor of the times. An Episcopal figure appealing much more readily to the counterculture was Bishop James Pike, whose charismatic personality, freethinking attitude, and defiance of ecclesiastical niceties made him popular among the young.[126] He was decidedly less so among his fellow bishops, some of whom were scandalized by his radical social and theological pronouncements.[127] Added to this were Pike's evident lack of collegiality and insatiable desire for media attention, which confirmed the belief among certain conservatives that he was unfit for episcopal office.[128] Both Arthur Lichtenberger and John Hines tried hard to avert a confrontation, but repeated threats to bring heresy charges against Pike led to a showdown in October 1966 at the House of Bishops' meeting at Wheeling, West Virginia.[129] Hoping to avoid a formal heresy trial, Bishop Hines appointed a committee led by retired bishop Angus Dun, which was charged with summarizing the issues at hand and outlining how the House might proceed.[130] After considerable debate, a majority accepted the report's recommendation of a formal censure, a compromise Pike promptly sought to derail by demanding just the sort of formal investigation the House wished to avoid. The gathering thus ended in a state of some confusion as to what result had been achieved.[131] Writing afterward to congratulate Bishop Dun on his role in forestalling a crisis, William Wolf of ETS nonetheless reported that many seminary students felt Pike had been treated unfairly, with the result that they now regarded him as an "instant martyr."[132] Dun replied that Pike himself had done much to exacerbate the situation, not least by spending more time with the press than in dialogue with other bishops. "The isolation of Jim from real 'I-Thou' relations is central to the tragedy and pathos of the whole situation," Dun wrote. "He is not surrounded by a body of heartless men, but in the main by a body of very sad and frustrated brethren."[133]

Regardless of whether they shared all his views, the treatment accorded to Pike at Wheeling assumed a wider significance among progressive bishops.[134] Some of them, such as Robert DeWitt, Paul Moore, and Daniel Corrigan, spoke out forcefully against the Dun report, which they considered unjust and vindictive. Led by William Creighton of Washington, these dissidents later joined with almost twenty others in issuing a "minority statement" repudiating the majority position.[135] They believed that by focusing on Pike's personal integrity, their colleagues had in fact sidestepped larger questions about the church's evolving social and theological responsibilities.[136] What his opponents rejected as compulsive self-aggrandizement, his allies therefore welcomed as a form of much-needed prophetic leadership. But Pike's own long-standing confidant Darby Betts concluded that his friend's experience showed it was impossible to be a bishop and a prophet at the same time. "You cannot be a basic critic of the Church and a basic defender of the Church," Betts reasoned. "No one man can do that. And if you *are* a bishop[,] any criticism you may have of the Church has got to be subordinated to your obligation to defend the Church." When it became obvious that Pike's impulse to criticize the institution outweighed his willingness to defend it, Betts believed his position became untenable.[137] Still, long after the Pike affair had ceased to dominate the headlines, the episode left its mark on the way many Episcopal bishops conceived the nature and purpose of their office. As much as they were to be teachers, pastors, and symbols of unity, they now began to see themselves as disturbers of the status quo, called to challenge their people to overcome reactionary tendencies and embrace new trends. There were others, however, who saw in Pike's legacy a worrying indifference to episcopal collegiality and a slavish concern with cultural relevance. Thus, in ways that long outlasted his own troubled ministry as a bishop, James Pike managed to influence the terms under which thinking about episcopacy proceeded thereafter.[138]

Shortly before the events at Wheeling, Michigan suffragan Kim Myers was called to succeed Pike as diocesan bishop of California. On the surface,

144   PRIVILEGE AND PROPHECY

his election appeared to replace one liberal for another, with Myers emerging as the compromise candidate at a moment of uncertainty and distress among Californian Episcopalians.[139] In fact, the two men had fundamentally different perceptions of the church and their role within it. While Pike's social progressivism went hand in hand with his readiness to dissect inherited Christian thinking, Myers regarded his own as the fruit of creedal orthodoxy and church tradition.[140] Preaching at his enthronement, Myers implicitly criticized his predecessor's reliance on personal charisma and public exposure as tools of leadership, emphasizing instead the objective authority of the episcopal office. "The bishop is a sacramental person who serves, who humbles himself, as he is given grace," he told the assembly at Grace Cathedral in early 1967. It was only by submitting to the apostolic inheritance that a bishop could in turn ensure the church remained truly catholic, responsive to and inclusive of the whole community. "A view of the Church which is less than this," Myers asserted, "has no place in an urbanized world made small by the human technologies through which God chooses to move and act in this century." By such logic he celebrated the church's catholicity not merely for its own sake but as a means for framing contemporary social realities.[141] His belief in the encompassing power of episcopacy soon became evident in Myers's conduct as bishop of California. Though a rather shy and unassuming man by nature, he felt obliged to inhabit the role of the "prince-bishop" in public, a resolute figure embodying the church's sacramental discipline. In this way he often projected what some found to be a rigid and authoritarian manner even while advocating liberal social positions.[142]

Myers's support for ministry among the Bay Area's hippies proved a case in point. When San Francisco's Haight-Ashbury district emerged as a center of hippie culture in 1966, the local Episcopal rector, Leon Harris (1906–1985), opened up the facilities of All Saints' Church to the young people pouring into the neighborhood. Before long, the church hosted a full-time counseling center, a medical clinic, a legal aid center, as well as a dispensary where food, clothing, and advice on housing and employment were provided. Despite the fact that Harris had presided over All Saints since 1949, his willingness to embrace the counterculture met with fierce opposition from members of the congregation, who threatened to withhold their pledges if he continued to use the church's resources for hippie outreach.[143] Harris was undeterred, reminding parishioners that "in the Episcopal Church the Rector is the authority, and he does not have to ask permission" when deciding "who shall use the property and who shall not." More to the point, he argued, the church did not exist "to make its members comfortable, to protect them from the realities of the world outside or to be an insulation against awareness of cries for help and understanding and love which come from those outside [its] walls."[144] Unsurprisingly, this readiness to use the church's hierarchical structures in the service of social outreach and inclusion met with approval from the new bishop, who praised Harris publicly: "I am delighted—more than I can say adequately—with the relevant involvement of All Saints' Parish in the Haight-Ashbury community," Myers wrote in March. "I heartily endorse your efforts as a priest of the Church to minister to the youth of the neighborhood."[145] Despite the loss of income and membership the parish suffered as a result of his activities, Harris was likewise portrayed in the national press as offering exemplary Christian leadership in a time of growing social unrest.[146]

While many Episcopalians had witnessed the racial crisis from something of a distance, the rebellion among American youth was often taking place in their own homes. The majority of the "flower children" now congregating in cities and university towns were the products of white, middle-class families, whose conventional lifestyle they were eager to reject.[147] Recalling his interactions with young people gathered around St. Mark's Church-in-the-Bowery in New York, Michael Allen attributed their alienation to "parents who found them basically a bother as they climbed up the ladder of social success or traveled the martini circuit. They sent their children away to boarding school or just sent them into the bedroom to be ignored. And so they had to build a world for themselves." For Allen, what compounded the pathos of their situation was the hippies' naïveté in the face of urban realities, as exemplified by the murder of Linda Fitzpatrick.[148] The teenaged daughter of a wealthy Episcopal family from Connecticut, Fitzpatrick ran away in the summer of 1967 to join the counterculture scene in Greenwich Village, only to be found dead ten weeks later. Insisting that Linda had been "a nice, outgoing, happy girl," Mrs. Fitzpatrick expressed baffled anguish that her daughter had met such a violent end: "If anything's changed, it's changed awfully fast," she told the *New York Times*.[149] In contrast to Michael Allen's portrait of parents too busy or indifferent to attend to young people's needs, Episcopalians in Washington, DC, started the National Society for the Parents of Flower Children, a group dedicated to helping families reconnect with their estranged sons and daughters. In practical terms, the society sought to establish a national communications network to help parents locate missing adolescents and ensure that they had adequate food, money, and

146 PRIVILEGE AND PROPHECY

clothing. The group also became a forum where affluent professionals tried to make sense of the psychological chasm that had opened up between them and their children. Though "educated, active, and ambitious in the approved sense," explained one participant, "we suffer from frustration and the sense of failure and shame."[150] Having lived through the lean years of depression and war, such people struggled to grasp their children's disdain for the security and comfort they had worked so hard to provide.[151]

If white Episcopalians found their values and assumptions challenged by the hippie culture of these years, the Black Power movement likewise prompted a crisis among their black co-religionists. For generations, upwardly mobile African Americans had been drawn to the Episcopal Church and other mainline denominations, despite frequently being excluded from their white congregations. As a result, the "black bourgeoisie" built up their own congregations in cities across the nation, such as St. Philip's in Harlem, St. Luke's in Washington, St. Matthew's in Detroit, and St. Edmund's in Chicago, among others. In drawing together the prosperous and respectable, these churches formed part of the parallel culture which African American elites constructed to insulate themselves from both lower-class blacks and the effects of discrimination.[152] Out of this environment emerged a generation of younger, educated African Americans critical of their elders' assimilationist approach to a racist society. Instead, they embraced Black Power, with its critique of integration as the basis for civil rights and its focus upon the institutional nature of oppression. The movement also found support among certain clergy, who under the auspices of the National Committee of Negro Churchmen issued a declaration in July 1966 justifying its principles. "We must be reconciled to ourselves as persons and to ourselves as an historical group," claimed the statement, which appeared in the *New York Times*. "This means we must find our way to a new self image in which we can feel a normal sense of pride in self, including our variety of skin color and the manifold textures of our hair. As long as we are filled with hatred for ourselves we will be unable to respect others."[153] By championing group solidarity among all African Americans, proponents of Black Power rejected the class distinctions on which the elite based their sense of otherness. For rather than validating their superiority, such aloofness appeared merely to confirm their own racial self-loathing.[154]

Unsurprisingly, the younger generation's enthusiasm for Black Power became a source of tension among the middle-class families comprising most black Episcopal congregations. Such stress was readily apparent to Arthur

B. Williams, who served on the clergy staff at Grace Church in Detroit. Born and raised in Providence, Rhode Island, Williams (b. 1935) attended the local public schools and continued his studies at Brown University. Upon graduating in 1957 he joined the Navy, after which he prepared for ministry at GTS. He was ordained in 1964–1965 and then served parishes around Providence before being called to Grace Church in 1968. Reflecting on the eagerness with which young black Episcopalians sought to distance themselves from the values and sensibilities of their parents, Williams recalled that "some of the biggest Afros around were on the heads of the young people in my youth group and among the acolytes."[155] Meanwhile, activist clergy like Williams had also begun to draw on the concept of Black Power to challenge the treatment of their people in the wider church. Neither fully accepted into the structures of the denomination nor regarded as authentic members of the black community, African American Episcopalians had been routinely treated as "neither fish nor fowl" by their white co-religionists.[156] Even with the advent of the civil rights movement, many continued to feel patronized and excluded by a church whose pronouncements were often badly out of step with its practices.[157] Frustration with this state of affairs led members of ESCRU to stage an all-night vigil at Episcopal headquarters in November 1966, protesting the church's complicity in racial discrimination. The event culminated in Kim Myers placing a list of charges on the desk of the absent presiding bishop, on which he scribbled at the top: "Dear John: love, Kim."[158]

Yet the days when a demonstration against institutional racism could be headed by a white bishop were rapidly coming to an end. Having led the fight for racial unity in the Episcopal Church, ESCRU now found itself divided over the role of Black Power in its midst. John Morris, the white Southerner who had served as its executive director since early 1960, recognized why Black Power had arisen but rejected it as incompatible with the organization's theological and social premises. By the end of 1966 he was under mounting pressure not only from black members but also from Northern whites, notably Malcolm "Mike" Peabody, president of ESCRU's board of directors. Disagreements over the group's evolving mission resulted in Morris taking a six-month leave of absence, from which he would not return. Alarmed by Black Power's separatist tendencies, he castigated Peabody and others who endorsed it as "compulsively guilty, sick white liberals" and further charged that too often in the church, "*White Guilt* approached *White Masochism*."[159] Notwithstanding such warnings, ESCRU and other civil rights groups continued to fragment in these years, as white activists came to doubt the

148   PRIVILEGE AND PROPHECY

legitimacy of their participation.[160] Before its eventual demise in 1970, ESCRU's black leadership renounced its pro-integration stance in favor of dividing the membership into racial caucuses. One longtime supporter, the white priest and educator John Snow, recounted the grief this policy occasioned among both blacks and whites when it was implemented by the ESCRU chapter in Boston. Snow later came to regret the support he gave the decision, not least because he believed it had "let white people off the hook" in the name of black empowerment.[161]

Even as they demanded recognition of their distinctive identity, black Episcopalians simultaneously pressed for greater opportunities within the church. In February 1967, a group of African American clergy issued a public declaration to the House of Bishops and Executive Council, protesting their failure to hire more minorities onto the national staff. The document noted that despite a considerable increase in the number of senior posts at church headquarters since the war, only two out of thirty appointments had gone to black Episcopalians, and as yet none had been made at the level of department head. Under the circumstances, the statement concluded, it was impossible not to suspect "a subtle and well-nigh systematic exclusion of laity and clergy who are Negroes from the heart of the Church's life."[162] Their protest prompted Bishop Hines to invite the clerics to meet with him and other bishops in mid-April 1967. The delegation was led by Quentin E. Primo, rector of St. Matthew's Church in Wilmington. Born in Georgia, Primo (1913–1998) was the son of an Anglican priest from British Guiana. After high school in North Carolina, he took two degrees from Lincoln University and then graduated with a B.D. from Bishop Payne Divinity School in 1941. During the next two decades he gained extensive parochial experience in Florida, North Carolina, and New York before accepting the call to Delaware in 1963. In Wilmington he soon gained a reputation as an effective community leader, establishing a nursery school, a tutoring program, and a job-training center. His leadership qualities would eventually lead to his election as suffragan of Chicago in 1972. In the meantime, however, it was clear to Primo and his colleagues that the bishops could do much more to promote black priests to posts of diocesan and national responsibility. When Bishop Burrill of Chicago counseled patience and suggested it was the laity rather than the bishops responsible for the slow pace of change, he was contradicted not just by the delegation but by Bishop Burgess as well.[163] Meeting with members of the group for a second time in June, Bishop Hines promised to resume the conversation after the upcoming General Convention. Yet, as was the case with many church initiatives of that moment, this dialogue soon got lost amidst the dramatic events to follow.[164]

While by no means opposed to African American self-assertion, one black Episcopalian who continued to champion integration during this period was John T. Walker. Having spent most of his adult life breaking down racial barriers in the church, in 1966 Walker was recruited by Frank Sayre to become canon for urban outreach at the National Cathedral. Alongside his efforts to connect with Washington's black community, the new canon encouraged Episcopalians to take seriously the risks and rewards of embracing social change. Speaking at the cathedral in early 1967, he stressed that "whenever the Church becomes involved, it becomes vulnerable. It might lose its income if it speaks the truth too loudly and boldly. It might lose its life if it doesn't." Even amidst such trials, Christians must carry on the task of reconciliation without in the process mistaking God's power for their own.[165] Walker knew personally just how much humility and fortitude were required in the bridging of social divisions. Reflecting the same year on the growing popularity of black separatism, he nonetheless defined himself as one called to pursue "the lonely life of trying to live in both worlds." So while there were moments when he did not fit easily into either the white or black community, he clung to a vision of the church as fully integrated, reasoning that someday "a remnant of believers will be necessary when the two worlds begin to merge." However far off this reality might yet be, it was incumbent upon Episcopalians as both Christians and Americans to resist "choosing up sides."[166]

Another black Episcopalian to keep faith with racial integration in these difficult times was the layman Charles V. Willie. The grandson of a former slave, Willie (b. 1927) was born and raised in Texas before enrolling at Atlanta's Morehouse College, where he became class president. After graduating in 1948, Willie specialized in the field of sociology, earning a master's degree from Atlanta University and a doctorate from Syracuse University. He taught at Syracuse from 1950 to 1974, during which time he joined the Episcopal Church and became actively involved in its affairs. Recognized for his sociological expertise, in 1963 he was appointed to the Joint Urban Advisory Committee, followed five years later by election to the Executive Council. In his service to the church, Willie gained a reputation for complicating received wisdom with generosity and compassion. Writing in 1967, for example, he challenged Episcopalians not to assume ethical behavior was simply a matter "of trying to put ourselves in the other person's shoes." After

150 PRIVILEGE AND PROPHECY

all, he pointed out, "the other person may not have any shoes at all, and if he has shoes they may not fit us. And if they pinch our toes, they may not hurt us the same way they hurt the other person. So let's find out from others what they think and how they feel and stop projecting our thoughts and feelings upon them."[167] This refusal to objectify others or bypass communication was fundamental to Willie's conception of a racially healthy society. As was the case for John Walker, though, his commitment to interdependence often rendered him a "marginal man," a figure destined to operate on the borderlands of established identities. Willie later recalled the hostility he faced when he and his white wife together attended the black caucus meeting at an Episcopal conference where he was speaking. Soon afterwards, an anonymous sign appeared in the lecture hall announcing that "DR WILLIE IS AN OREO COOKIE"—a slur suggesting that while he might be black on the outside, Willie was actually white on the inside. Though many at the gathering were outraged on his behalf, Willie chose to use the incident as an opportunity to explore the pain, confusion, and anger that racism had engendered in black and white people alike.[168]

Still, there was no denying that with the spread of Black Power, increasing numbers of white liberals were withdrawing from civil rights activities and focusing their attentions on Vietnam instead.[169] In contrast to the question of racial equality, however, the war did not unite all progressive churchmen in a common stance. While leading figures like Paul Moore and Frank Sayre had already concluded that involvement in Southeast Asia was wrong and said so publicly, others remained circumspect. This was evident at a press conference that John Hines and Kim Myers held in conjunction with the latter's installation as bishop of California in January 1967. In broaching the subject of Vietnam, Myers criticized the Johnson administration for misinterpreting what was really at stake. "It is a problem of some nations having things and other nations not having things," he stated flatly. "The fundamental problem of the world is *non*-ideological; it has to do with food, clothing, and shelter. . . . We ought to give top priority to questions such as balancing trade [and] sharing technological knowledge, rather than the continuing issue of containing Marxism." Bishop Hines was less sure and sought to distance himself from Myers's comments. "I still believe that there is sufficient room for ideological differences not to write them off as being unreal or unjustified," he said. "Frankly I wish I knew more about this." While plainly troubled by the conflict, he proved wary of questioning the underlying logic of US involvement.[170] In a similar fashion, Charles Price of Harvard lamented the moral ambiguities of the war but persisted in defending the mandates of national loyalty. Preaching at the Memorial Church in the spring of that year, he acknowledged military service was an imminent reality for those about to graduate. As to whether it was legitimate to resist the draft, Price confessed that "I have a lot of sympathy with men whose consciences will not allow them to go. But to be quite honest, I can't raise my conscience to that pitch of sensitivity. I believe that the state has a right to ask military service of its citizens." Not facing the possibility of combat himself, he was anxious not to press simplistic judgments upon those who did. Nonetheless, having reflected on the role of the state in the maintenance of the common good, he felt obliged to "come down on the side of obedience to a law despite some serious reservations."[171]

A social progressive who shared this reluctance to condemn government policy was the bishop of Rochester, George W. Barrett. Born in Iowa, Barrett (1908–2000) was raised in Pasadena and studied at UCLA before preparing for ordination at ETS in the early 1930s. From this time until his consecration thirty years later, he gained extensive parochial experience and taught pastoral studies at General Seminary. In the summer of 1967, Barrett was invited to join a fact-finding mission to Vietnam organized by Robert S. Bilheimer, director of international affairs for the National Council of Churches. Alongside prominent figures from the Presbyterian and Methodist churches, Barrett was chosen by Bilheimer to represent the Episcopal Church because he enjoyed a reputation for reasonableness and objectivity. In the event, Bilheimer was to be disappointed by the bishop's apparent passivity during the month they spent together.[172] Yet as his journal from the trip reveals, Barrett was well aware of the divergent attitudes and expectations that members of the delegation brought to the experience. As the group struggled to compose a joint statement at the end of the mission, he speculated on the ways each participant revealed his "denominational ethos" in the process. In his own eagerness to avoid acrimony and maintain respect for the military authorities, Barrett conceded that "my Anglican establishmentarian background sometimes shows."[173] The instinctive urge to treat church and state as symbiotic is further discernible in a letter he wrote to General William C. Westmoreland, commander of US forces in Vietnam. In thanking his fellow Episcopalian for having taken time to meet with the NCC delegation, Barrett assured Westmoreland that "as a Bishop of the Episcopal Church, [I am] very glad indeed that a Churchman like yourself is representing our country under such crucial and difficult circumstances."[174]

152   PRIVILEGE AND PROPHECY

Having been shaped by the moral clarity of the Second World War, middle-aged liberals like Barrett found it difficult to conceive of a conflict in which America was regarded as the villain rather than the savior.[175]

As Episcopal leaders became ever more preoccupied with racial and generational tensions at home and an ethically contested war abroad, there were those who felt the church's basic functions were being neglected. One of these was the priest Tom Turney Edwards, who worried that in keeping with the anti-institutional fervor of the times, "the very concept of the parish is being called into question." Speaking alongside Arthur Walmsley and Anthony Morley at ETS in 1966, Edwards (1921–2013) sought not to condemn social engagement so much as warn against rejecting parochial life while pursuing it. "Why is it necessary to denigrate the parish and discredit it in order to build up these other types of ministry?" Edwards wondered. "All of a sudden we hear people talking as if the parish was in some way disreputable, as if it had betrayed the Church, as if it were somehow the actual cause of the troubles that beset us on every hand." Rather than treat the church's mission as a zero-sum game, Edwards encouraged his listeners to see the parish as a perennial source of "Christian nurture and slow growth"—essential ingredients to the church's capacity to witness creatively in the world.[176] Edwards's fellow priest Earl H. Brill echoed this sentiment in the pages of the *Christian Century* the following year. A native of Pennsylvania, Brill (1925–2001) graduated from the University of Pennsylvania in 1951 and five years later from Philadelphia Divinity School. After three years in parish ministry he devoted the remainder of his career to college chaplaincy and church education. Writing as Episcopal chaplain of American University in the spring of 1967, Brill admitted to being irked by "the ranks of stolid burghers who make up so many of our congregations: good, clean Christian folk who want to be reassured that the world is in order and who see the Christian life in terms of conventional goodness." Despite his frustrations, though, Brill was quick to acknowledge just how crucial such people were to the life of the church. Not only were they already paying the salaries of "us avant-garde types," but they were also the ones raising "good, honest, God-fearing kids who grow up to be wild and woolly avant-garde theologians." Like Edwards, Brill questioned whether the church's home-grown critics had anything to replace the structures and sensibilities that once had nourished them but now they so readily dismissed.[177]

Taking this critique of anti-institutionalism even further was Carroll E. Simcox of the *Living Church*. Born and educated in North Dakota, Simcox

(1912–2002) served mainly in parish ministry until succeeding Peter Day as editor of the paper in 1964. During his thirteen years in the post, he would regularly offer a dissenting viewpoint from what he considered the diet of liberal pieties emanating from the Episcopal leadership. Writing in April 1967, for example, Simcox chastised progressives for their eagerness to define as prophetic the range of harsh indictments leveled against the church from various quarters. The issue was not that the institution was somehow above criticism, but rather that the concept of prophecy was being treated as normative and in direct opposition to the concept of priesthood. Behind this false dichotomy, Simcox charged, rested the assumption that anyone promoting social change was a prophet, while priests were mere defenders of a reactionary status quo. In rejecting this logic, Simcox argued he was not repudiating the prophetic office so much as insisting on its correct place within the life of the church. "It is the proper business of the prophet to proclaim God's truth and righteousness to God's people who have forgotten it," he wrote. "But his function is not fundamental; it is corrective, hence occasional." By contrast, the function of the priest was "absolutely fundamental to the very life and being of the people of God" and therefore a prerequisite to any prophetic action that might arise. Rightly construed, then, the relationship was symbiotic, not adversarial. "There is never a Samuel without an Eli before him," Simcox concluded. "Where there is no priestly ministry and teaching, there is no prophetic passion for a better world wherein dwelleth righteousness."[178] Yet in a culture where being an outsider had become a sign of integrity and of solidarity with the oppressed, such pleas for mutuality and proportion were bound to fall on deaf ears.[179] For certain progressive Christians, prophecy could no longer be just one expression of their faith among many; it must become its default setting.

In this increasingly polarized atmosphere, Fran Ayres concluded that the time had come to disband the Parishfield community. A formal announcement was issued at the beginning of 1967 that operations would cease the following June.[180] According to Jane Barney, this decision rested solely with Ayres: because he had been the community's driving force financially and spiritually for nearly twenty years, Parishfield's fortunes were inextricably linked to his own.[181] And while it was evident Episcopalians had adopted many of Parishfield's ideas along the way, he believed its particular brand of experimentation no longer influenced the institution as it had previously.[182] This led Ayres to claim shortly before his death in 1968 that he had been "disowned" by the church. At the same time, he saw this estrangement as having taken place against the backdrop of a much wider crisis in American society, whereby "the middle ground was disappearing as a viable position. . . . One had to be radical or admit that one was a conservative. After thirty years of comfortable, self-indulgent, middle-class liberalism[,] this was a shaking of the foundations." For someone who had built both his ministry and politics on the premise of renewing institutional life from within, such extremes left Ayres feeling stranded. Even though he rejected calls for an "across-the-board revolution," he held out little hope that incremental reform would ever accomplish the kind of changes the country required. Not least, the poor would continue to be poor, for "the present system will leave me in affluence and them in desperate need for as long as I live and for considerable time beyond that." Still, having recently accepted a call to become Episcopal chaplain at MIT in Cambridge, he was determined to remain a part of the struggle for social betterment. "In looking for and finding some place where I can work, I hope to discover possibilities for students to work in the same way," he wrote. "The important thing is to get involved oneself— in order to be human."[183]

When John Hines became presiding bishop in early 1965, he proclaimed the responsibility of Christians to engage directly with the many changes taking place in society. He did so at a moment when the Episcopal Church had reached the apogee of its institutional power and exuded confidence in its ability to influence the direction of the wider culture. Yet there were already signs that the socio-religious consensus on which such confidence rested was beginning to fragment. As anti-establishment feeling spread across the country and among young and minority Americans in particular, some Episcopalians began to regard their church as being more part of the problem than the solution.[184] And while there were those, like Fran Ayres, who found this situation untenable, Bishop Hines and others retained their faith in the institution's capacity to serve as an agent of reconciliation and empowerment. Their commitment to this idea proved at once transformative and profoundly divisive in the course of the next few years.

6

Passing Grace and Seized Microphones
(1967–1969)

While the summer of 1967 was touted as the "summer of love" by flower children, it proved something very different for the poor black inhabitants of American cities. During June and July, over 150 race riots erupted in urban neighborhoods across the nation. Among the most violent and destructive of these was the week-long rioting that took place in Newark, which left twenty-six dead and hundreds more injured.[1] It was in the wake of such turmoil that Nathan Wright, director of urban work for the Diocese of Newark, convened the National Conference on Black Power on July 20–23. Although the conference did not have official sponsorship from the Episcopal Church, Bishop Leland Stark allowed Wright to hold it on diocesan premises, a decision that unsettled some white Episcopalians. Responding to these concerns, Stark wrote to his clergy prior to the gathering, both to reassure them as well as to encourage a more sympathetic understanding of Wright's efforts. "If *Black Power* is a disturbing term, then I think that we who are white should remind ourselves that we have often exercised *White Power*," he counseled. "While I personally should have been happier with a term other than Black Power, I respect the decision of the conferees to use it, and I hope that the Conference will succeed in redeeming the term."[2] The rage and disorder that engulfed the city immediately thereafter served to justify Stark's conciliatory approach and lent urgency to the conference proceedings.[3] In the event, over 1,000 delegates joined together to discuss issues ranging from the creation of black national holidays to the possibility of dividing the United States into two separate countries, one black and one white. Notwithstanding his radical views, Wright himself was generally perceived as more reasonable and constructive than other proponents of Black Power.[4] So while the *Living Church* dismissed SNCC chairman H. Rap Brown as "a hate-monger and provoker of strife," it depicted Wright as an American Christian championing the principle of self-determination.[5]

Privilege and Prophecy. Robert Tobin, Oxford University Press. © Oxford University Press 2022.
DOI: 10.1093/oso/9780190906146.003.0006

156 PRIVILEGE AND PROPHECY

This particular contrast was prompted by Brown's appearance at a rally on July 27 at the Church of St. Stephen and the Incarnation in Washington, DC. He had just been released on bail after being charged with inciting a riot in Cambridge, Maryland, earlier the same week. Speaking from the pulpit of St. Stephen's, Brown proclaimed to the assembly that a "shoot and loot" tactic was the best way to cure racial injustice.[6] William Wendt, rector of the church since 1960, faced considerable criticism for hosting an event at which an advocate of race war was the featured speaker. Bishop Moore quickly came to the priest's defense, arguing that it had been much better to hold the rally indoors, rather than on the streets of an already tense city.[7] Other community leaders joined Moore in backing Wendt's action, not only for its pragmatism but also as an acknowledgment of the widespread discord of which Brown was a symptom.[8] The editors of the *Washington Post* added their support, condemning Brown's incendiary rhetoric but praising Wendt and his parishioners for their "commitment to the idea that freedom of speech must embrace freedom for the thoughts we hate." The *Post* also shared Moore's view that the situation would have been more volatile without Wendt's intervention.[9] Episcopal clergy across the country similarly joined in the work of restoring calm to neighborhoods caught up in rioting and helping those affected by it. In Milwaukee, for example, William Miles and Lee Benefee took a leading role in these efforts, as did Robert Potts in Detroit, and Moran Weston in Harlem.[10]

Meanwhile, John Hines returned home early from a World Council of Churches meeting in Crete to ascertain how the national church might respond to the urban crisis. As part of this process, he arranged visits to riottorn neighborhoods in New York and Detroit in order to hear firsthand about living conditions in these places.[11] When touring the Bedford-Stuyvesant section of Brooklyn he was accompanied by Leon Modeste, a black layman who had grown up there and was now employed in the CSR department at Episcopal Church Center.[12] A cradle Episcopalian, Modeste (1926–2017) attended the public schools in Brooklyn prior to receiving his undergraduate degree from Long Island University in 1950. Opting for a career in social work, he went on to earn a master's degree from Columbia in 1953 and then spent the next dozen years in local agencies until being recruited by Reinhart Guttmann to work for the Executive Council.[13] Despite his relatively junior position in the church up to this point, Modeste would emerge as a key figure in the new dispensation about to unfold.[14] At the same time, established figures like Art Walmsley and Jack Woodard sought to impress upon

PASSING GRACE AND SEIZED MICROPHONES   157

the presiding bishop the urgency of the moment. In a memo dated August 8, Woodard and his JUP colleagues asserted that "the Church has a unique responsibility for interpreting the apocalyptic nature of the present crisis and proclaiming moral imperative. This should be done immediately with all power available and using every possible network of communication." Supporting groups such as the Urban Coalition, Urban America, and the Inter-Religious Foundation for Community Organization was one obvious means for doing this, but so was encouraging "ghetto groupings seeking to develop a power base for the poor."[15] Yet in meeting with inner-city leaders about how to pursue the latter objective, Hines encountered skepticism about the Episcopal Church's commitment to systemic change. To show it was serious, the church must be prepared not only to affirm the principle of Black Power but "wield its own economic power to guarantee social, political, and economic justice for Blacks . . . with the local people controlling the decision-making process." Having thrown down the gauntlet in this way, the group concluded: "The rest is up to you."[16]

In response to this challenge, Bishop Hines appointed a special task force to devise plans for a radical outreach program in time for General Convention, due to take place the following month in Seattle. The task force was led by the African American lawyer and civil rights activist William H. Booth, an Episcopal layman who would eventually sit on New York's State Supreme Court. After serving in the Air Force during the war, Booth (1922–2006) completed his undergraduate studies at Queens College and then earned both JD and LLM degrees from New York University. A Republican, in 1966 he was appointed chairman of New York City's Human Rights Commission by Mayor John V. Lindsay, a post he would hold until 1969.[17] In the short time it was given to fulfill its remit, the task force recommended that the national church create a new staff unit under black leadership, which would foster empowerment among the ghetto poor without reference to existing diocesan and parochial structures.[18] In justifying this approach to the Executive Council, the presiding bishop emphasized Episcopalians' complicity in the conditions that had led to the violence of the summer. "We in the Church are part of the problem," he asserted. "The sickness of society is our sickness. Our brokenness is expressed in fears for our own survival, in protection of our institutional status, in our insularity from the suffering and hostility of human beings." If the Episcopal Church really wanted to take part in the healing of American society, it must be willing to give away not only money but also control. "The most costly demand of all," Hines reasoned, "is that

158   PRIVILEGE AND PROPHECY

we surrender pride in our own plans and programs and go to the poor, the alienated and the outcast, making ourselves and our resources available to them in ways that they themselves see as helpful."[19] As an immediate gesture in this direction, he sought permission to move $221,000 from other departmental budgets to put toward inner-city projects during the remainder of the year. Though a few Council members objected that this constituted a "panic response" and would unfairly deprive other programs of much-needed funding, the majority supported the change alongside their approval of the larger plan.[20]

The address that Bishop Hines delivered at the opening of General Convention a few days later was to be a turning-point in the life of the Episcopal Church. In asking the bishops and deputies to endorse what became known as the General Convention Special Program (GCSP), he brought to bear all the confidence and determination of establishmentarian religion in the promotion of an anti-establishment cause. Through a major restructuring of its budget and personnel, he believed the national church could model the kind of institutional commitment needed to confront the urban crisis.[21] The initiative was necessary precisely because Episcopalians had neglected their duty to prioritize the poor and disenfranchised. Combining repentance for the past with hope for the future, Hines thus presented the program as an opportunity for the church to "take its place humbly and boldly alongside of, and in support of, the dispossessed and oppressed peoples of this country." It would do this in part by supplying funding to community groups "involved in the betterment of depressed urban areas, and under the control of those who are largely both black and poor, that their power for self-determination may be increased and their dignity restored." Specifically, he asked the Convention and the Women of the Church to allocate $3 million a year during the coming triennium to finance the plan.[22] Even as he requested such a formidable sum, Hines insisted that distributing money through a national program was not sufficient. Just as important was a "sensitive and sacrificial response" by Episcopalians at the local level, who must be ready to engage personally with the suffering of their neighbors. Such engagement was intrinsic to Hines's vision of a more generous and outward-looking church, a church capable of giving of itself without pre-conditions or designated outcomes. And while he hoped other churches would join the effort, he held that Episcopalians must press on regardless, "for it may be that we are in 'a moment of passing grace' given to us by God, that may never again re-occur—and in which we are given together the opportunity to act."[23]

Unsurprisingly, this dramatic call for action dominated the convention's proceedings. A committee comprising four bishops, four clerical deputies, four lay deputies, and four Triennial delegates was immediately convened to produce a response to Bishop Hines's address.[24] In their reply, entitled "An Open Letter to the Presiding Bishop," the group sought to draw out the theological and practical implications of his plan. They began by acknowledging that the church had been challenged to undertake both external actions and internal changes, which in turn were inseparable from each other. "Three-million dollars from us alone will not radically change the ghetto," the committee observed. "The question is: can the giving of it, and the understanding of the necessity for giving it, change our Church? If it helps, but not seriously alters, the ghetto, and cheaply assuages, yet not radically renews, our Church, then we would do better to go back to 'business as usual,' and forget the three-million dollars altogether." Having thus accepted the premise that the church's own spiritual health was intimately tied to the fate of the disempowered in American life, the group agreed that a faithful response was to "budget some of our money for others to spend on priorities they themselves have set." Whatever the sum, the committee recognized that this willingness to provide financial assistance to the ghetto poor with 'no strings attached' was the principle on which the entire proposal hinged. For not only did it serve to affirm the dignity and equality of the marginalized, it also constituted a necessary renunciation of power on the part of socially privileged Christians. Given the realities of "inter-group power-relationships" in contemporary society, it was evident that "the 'have-nots' must share in the power of the 'haves' before common community can be open to either."

While it endorsed the presiding bishop's bid for a national grants program, the "Open Letter" echoed his assertion that giving away money was not enough. Episcopalians must also be prepared to take a hard look at their own social attitudes and behaviors. Quite apart from its pronouncements, just how inclusive was the church in practice? Here the committee pointed specifically to the vexed issue of minority recruitment to the ministry, and by extension, the dearth of black people in positions of church leadership. At the same time, it queried Episcopalians' efforts to reach out personally to the poor in their local communities. With such a high proportion of civic and business leaders within its ranks, the church still possessed considerable potential for influencing political and economic life at diocesan and parochial levels. The committee therefore called upon dioceses to develop programs for "enlisting, supporting, and offering direct, individual, lay-involvement

160 PRIVILEGE AND PROPHECY

in renewal of the community." Among other things, Episcopalians should be encouraged to express their Christian values by investing in low-cost housing, mortgage provision, and job stimulation in ghetto areas, as well as by offering their technical and professional expertise to groups dedicated to self-empowerment. In offering these examples of how laypeople might engage directly in the social crisis, the group concluded by once more emphasizing the value of action over words. It mandated the presiding bishop and Executive Council to create structures for monitoring the church's progress "toward the goals of external action and internal change" he had outlined."[25] Yet determining how success should be measured and by whom would become matters of serious contention in the months ahead.

It remained to be seen whether the wider convention would approve the plan. As one of the authors of the "Open Letter," Kim Myers favored the "no strings attached" approach to grant-giving but worried this stipulation might derail the whole project.[26] One bishop to voice opposition on this basis was George Murray of Alabama, who wondered what he should tell people back home "when they ask me if this is the proper thing to do with money they put in the collection plate on Sunday morning." More typical, though, was the reaction of Edward Welles of West Missouri, who spoke in favor of the program while also predicting the church would likely "lose members and money" in the process.[27] This readiness to forge ahead characterized the mood of the Seattle convention as a whole, in marked contrast to the obstructionism on display three years earlier in St. Louis. More than one commentator observed that the urban crisis had prompted Episcopalians to set aside long-standing internal disputes and come together around a shared sense of social responsibility.[28] Crucial to moving forward was the cooperation of the Committee on Program and Budget, which swiftly rewrote the entire triennium program in order to accommodate the new proposal. In presenting its revisions, the committee sounded a note of proud defiance that Episcopalians were capable of such responsiveness: "The very fact that we are able to change and adapt and adjust to new situations," the committee asserted, "confounds those who criticize the Church as rigid, inflexible, and dying."[29] In the event, both houses voted to approve the revised budget by decisive majorities, allocating $2 million a year for initiatives related to the urban crisis, of which $500,000 per annum would take the form of "no strings attached" grants.[30] Crucially, the Episcopal Church Women likewise voted to contribute $2.26 million over the course of the coming triennium, thereby ensuring that the presiding bishop's request for $9 million in total would be met.[31]

No sooner had GCSP been approved than questions arose about how it should be implemented. Among those championing the "no strings attached" idea was Charles Willie, who saw it not just as a mechanism for distributing grants, but as the starting-point for all Christian social relations. He therefore encouraged Episcopalians to resist the urge to second-guess the priorities and preferences of those they presumed to help. "This was the old way which smacked of colonialism," he wrote, whereas now the church had an opportunity to share its power, rather than merely impose it. "This approach to the ghetto is respectful," Willie concluded, "and holds promise for a productive future and a new kind of involvement by the Church in the world."[32] Nathan Wright also endorsed the program but called on the convention to recognize the empowerment work black clergy were already doing in poor neighborhoods. Not to give these priests a key role in GCSP, he warned, would only confirm "the insolence and paternalism" they had long endured at the hands of their white co-religionists.[33] Also pressing for direct church engagement was Carroll Simcox of the *Living Church*, albeit for a different reason. Declaring that the initiative was "*Christ's* mission and ministry," Simcox argued that "those who receive it should be left in no doubt as to whence cometh their help," such that only "faithful Christians" should administer the program in local communities.[34] Despite their divergent views about the type of involvement Episcopalians should expect to have in it, what these and other supporters shared in common was a view of GCSP as a form of Christian mission. None seems to have anticipated how quickly even this basic premise would be challenged in the name of anti-establishment activism.[35]

In keeping with the same spirit of cooperation that made GCSP possible was the election of John Coburn as president of the House of Deputies. Urbane and clubbable, Coburn was a popular figure who managed to remain on friendly terms with many whose views he did not share.[36] So, although he was generally regarded as a "low churchman," he drew support in Seattle from many "high church" delegates attracted to his conciliatory manner and gentle progressivism.[37] Like John Hines, with whom he formed a close working relationship in the years to come, Coburn was, in his own estimation, a man "all about institutions." While voices around him clamored for immediate change, he retained his faith in institutional structures as the best means for achieving lasting reform. As such, he was an instinctively establishmentarian figure, who nonetheless worked to advance the causes of equality in both church and society.[38] His management of convention business would reflect

162 PRIVILEGE AND PROPHECY

his methodical approach and fondness for order, earning him the sobriquet "calm Coburn, always in control."[39] During a nine-year term that included some of the most divisive moments in the history of the Episcopal Church, he thus presided over the House of Deputies with an even-handedness that commanded almost universal respect.[40]

As Episcopalians focused on empowering those outside their ranks, some were still struggling to be recognized themselves. Since the early 1950s, successive conventions had rejected calls to include women in the House of Deputies, a resistance increasingly at odds with the church's perception of itself as enlightened and forward-looking. As one priest writing in *The Witness* noted, the Episcopal commitment to civil rights and other social causes "has not always been paralleled by a matching compassion for the Church's own members."[41] Shortly before General Convention assembled in Seattle, educator Cynthia Wedel again made the case for allowing women delegates, highlighting not only the injustice of the current arrangement but its shortsightedness. "The task of the church in the world today is a staggering one," she observed. "It needs the best talents of every member if it is to meet the demands placed upon it. The woman power of the church is a reservoir of great ability and dedication which must not be squandered on the trivial."[42] Evidently this message finally got through to the House of Deputies, who approved by "resounding voice vote" the necessary changes permitting women to join them at forthcoming conventions.[43] In the meantime, the House of Bishops also urged the inclusion of more young people in the church's decision-making bodies, recognizing that it was crucial to hear their views about such matters as the war in Vietnam.[44] The refusal of lay deputies to pass resolutions critical of American foreign policy instead merely confirmed the view the church was out of touch with a generation fighting a war in which it did not believe.[45] It also demonstrated, not for the first time, that it was laymen and not clergy who were more cautious about placing the institution on the front line of social action and critique.

If enthusiasm for GCSP distracted attention from questions of internal representation, it likewise tended to overshadow efforts to think strategically about the church's long-term mission and ministry.[46] One of the major issues facing the 1967 convention was that of clergy training and deployment. Having long suffered from a shortage of priests, the Episcopal Church had labored since the Second World War to redress the balance. These efforts had proved so successful, however, that by the mid-1960s there was a surplus, and many bishops openly worried about how to find posts for all the men graduating from seminary.[47] There were rumblings, too, about whether existing models of theological education prepared clergy adequately for the realities of the modern parish.[48] In order to take a comprehensive look at these challenges, a Special Committee to Study Theological Education was formed under the leadership of President Nathan Pusey of Harvard. This resulted in a report entitled *Ministry for Tomorrow*, which the chairman formally presented to the delegates at Seattle. Pusey was blunt in his assessment. "Our church is falling short both in what it should and might be doing to help individuals cope with the perplexities and difficulties which confront them in these times," he asserted. "It fails at these points because the parishes are less strong, less well guided, and less well informed than they should be."[49] In order to compensate for these deficiencies, the report emphasized the importance of training priests as versatile generalists, able to function as effective administrators as well as good pastors. At the same time, it acknowledged that as more and more Episcopalians attained higher degrees, clergy must be academically prepared to contend with the theological concerns of their parishioners. To help educators address these diverse requirements, Pusey and his committee recommended the formation of a Board for Theological Education, which would encourage greater accountability and coordination among Episcopal seminaries.[50]

Sharing the Pusey Report's concern with how the church should respond to the cultural demands of contemporary life was the so-called Advisory Committee, which John Hines asked Stephen Bayne to convene at the beginning of 1967. While clearly prompted by the discord surrounding James Pike at the bishops' meeting in Wheeling the previous year, Bishop Bayne was emphatic that the committee's inquiries transcended individual personalities.[51] Rather, in taking up the presiding bishop's mandate, the group sought to assess more broadly what the church's role should be in "encouraging theological discussion and social criticism" among Episcopalians and society at large. In the process, the committee sought to mark out the obligations of those engaged in such activities and to ascertain what applicability the concept of heresy might have for the present day. The resulting report was presented to Bishop Hines in time for the Seattle convention and was published with supplementary essays under the title *Theological Freedom and Social Responsibility*.[52] Predictably, the committee's remark that "heresy trials are anachronistic" became the focus of media attention, though in fact the document as a whole assumed a more nuanced position than this phrase alone might suggest.[53] In assessing the dynamic between free inquiry

164   PRIVILEGE AND PROPHECY

and ecclesiastical discipline, the report affirmed "the right of every man to choose what he will believe without any kind of coercion whatever," while also positing that "if an individual finds himself unable, in good conscience, to identify with the living tradition of the Church, . . . he should as a matter of personal integrity voluntarily remove himself from any position in which he may be taken to be an official spokesman for the whole community." In a tacit appeal to Anglican reasonableness, the committee did not so much deny the reality of heresy as cast doubt on its utility as a conceptual tool for resolving differences among contemporary Christians.[54]

Accompanying the report were "advisory papers" intended to explore and illuminate the matters at hand. Theologians John Macquarrie, J. V. Langmead Casserley, John Knox, Eric Mascall, and Arthur Vogel all made contributions, as did the Jesuit ecumenist John Courtney Murray and the Episcopal lay-woman Theodora Sorg. The collection was rounded out by statements from four bishops: John Robinson, James Pike, Paul Moore, and Albert Stuart. Among the most insightful essays is one by New Testament scholar John Knox (1901–1990), who had recently joined the Seminary of the Southwest after twenty-three years of teaching at Union Seminary in New York. For Knox, no agreement among Episcopalians about their role in society will be possible unless they grant the "existential a priori" of the church as a God-given entity with a unique identity and way of life. "The Church has its own peculiar way of being relevant to the orders (and disorders) of the world," he argues.

> It may not take this way, but there is no other way for it to take and still be relevant *as the Church*. The fuller realizing of the Church's own true nature and the fuller discharging of its own true mission in the world are really one thing. For the Church is by definition a fellowship in the love of God, and its mission is to be the constantly growing sphere of a constantly deepening reconciliation. Here is the distinctively Christian ground for the abhorring of all injustice, cruelty, and neglect, whether among individuals or within the structures of our social, economic, and political existence.

In being truly itself, the church will engage actively with the needs of the world. And while it does so, Knox sees no reason why Christians should not to cooperate with secularists sharing their commitment to a just and compassionate society. What they must not do, however, is mistake common cause for shared motivation. "The Church's *grounds* for action will be its own," he

PASSING GRACE AND SEIZED MICROPHONES   165

declares, "and these grounds will affect the quality of the action itself." The problem with the current generation of radical theologians is not their challenge to traditional values but their abandonment of the essential otherness of Christian identity. As a result, they have voluntarily positioned themselves outside the "existential reality" of the church.[55]

For James Pike, of course, insisting upon this separate reality was simply a form of escapism. It seemed obvious to him that more and more laypeople found the church's conceptual framework irrelevant to their experience, and any wall between the sacred and secular was rapidly crumbling. If Episcopal leaders wanted to contribute meaningfully to the betterment of society, they must start by engaging honestly with their own loss of authority and the growing disaffection among their membership.[56] In the months prior to General Convention, some of Pike's allies hoped the appearance of *Theological Freedom and Social Responsibility* might provide a fresh opportunity to resume the debate begun at Wheeling.[57] But as with many other questions facing the Episcopal Church in the autumn of 1967, interest in the fate of Bishop Pike was quickly overtaken the sense of urgency surrounding GCSP.[58] Thereafter Pike continued to move further and further away from the institutional church, culminating in his decision to leave it formally in the spring of 1969. He did so in a characteristically public fashion, announcing in the pages of *Look* magazine that he was now joining "the ever-swelling ranks of the *Church alumni*."[59] Less than five months later he would die of exposure in the Judean desert, where he and his wife Diane had traveled as part of an investigation into the historical Jesus. Having entered the wilderness without maps and supplies, Pike, in the words of one commentator, met his end "with the drama of a religious media hero, but sadly, like the anti-hero in a Lost Generation novel, looking for God in the wrong places."[60]

The endorsement that GCSP received at Seattle was undoubtedly a vote of confidence in the personal leadership of John Hines. At the same time, it signaled the growing power and prestige of the national church, a trend underway since the 1950s that reached its apotheosis during these years.[61] Many regarded this centralization of authority as a positive step in adapting the Episcopal Church to the demands of modern life.[62] But there were others who detected a gap opening up between national decision-makers and the grassroots, as the former appeared increasingly out of touch with the sensibilities of the latter.[63] With some justification, they worried that the support given to GCSP at the convention would not meet with a corresponding

166   PRIVILEGE AND PROPHECY

enthusiasm in the church at large.[64] Nonetheless, the presiding bishop and his staff took immediate steps to implement the new program, among them the appointment of Leon Modeste as director.[65] On the face of it, Modeste was a logical choice: a young black Episcopalian already employed by the national church and experienced in both social work and community development.[66] By putting him in charge, though, Hines effectively sidelined the black clergy, who despite their race were not considered sufficiently attuned to the "poverty-stricken ghetto class" the program was designed to help.[67] Apart from the insensitivity of this decision to existing racial politics within the church, it underscored a paradox at the heart of Hines's attitude and approach. For despite his assertion that GCSP could only flourish through active local participation, he showed few signs of trusting Episcopalians as a whole to join in its development. Almost from the start, it appeared empowerment was to be a top-down affair.[68]

The determination of Bishop Hines and others to use GCSP to shake up the institutional status quo was exemplified by their treatment of Tollie Caution. For over twenty years, Caution had been a mainstay of the Home Department and served as an unofficial spokesman for black Episcopalians at the national church level. As plans for the new initiative took shape, he therefore impressed upon his superiors the discontent many African American clergy felt at their evident exclusion.[69] But only a few weeks later, Caution himself was to be ousted by Hines and Home Department head Daniel Corrigan, who demanded his immediate retirement at the close of 1967. His humiliation was complete when Bishop Corrigan even presented him with the letter of resignation that he was expected to sign.[70] Caution submitted on the condition that his employment was extended until the end of June 1968, so that he might conclude his work at the Executive Council "in such a manner as to maintain a degree of personal dignity and integrity."[71] When news of Caution's termination became public, letters of protest from black churchmen flooded into Corrigan's office.[72] Besides objecting to the shabby treatment of their champion, they stressed why Caution was in fact pivotal to GCSP's success. "It was Tollie's endorsement that persuaded many Negro churchmen to accept the sincerity of the objectives of the Presiding Bishop's program," wrote the chaplain of Howard University, Albion Farrell. Citing the "unrest, rejection, and militancy" rife among young African Americans, Farrell explained that "we need the Tollie Cautions[,] who have both the ear of the people and the ear of the power figures within the Church to interpret each to the other."[73]

The decision to fire Caution confirmed for African American clergy just how little their efforts were either valued or understood by the white leadership. Writing to Corrigan, Bishop John Burgess of Massachusetts affirmed his commitment to GCSP but emphasized that it was no replacement for the ministry these clergy already provided in black neighborhoods. He was particularly incensed that even though Caution had done more than anyone to encourage this ministry, he was now openly patronized by young white colleagues who regarded him as old-fashioned and out of date.[74] Attentive to the dynamics of race and class at work in the situation was sociologist Charles R. Lawrence, who had become active in the national church as a consultant for the Joint Urban Program. The son of teachers, Lawrence (1915–1986) grew up in Mississippi before earning degrees from Morehouse College, Atlanta University, and Columbia. He taught sociology at New York's Brooklyn College until 1976, when he retired to become the first black president of the House of Deputies.[75] In spelling out for Bishop Corrigan the implications of Caution's dismissal, Lawrence saw black Episcopalians being used as a foil in the church's newest bid for cultural relevance. For like most of their co-religionists, African American clergy and congregations were either middle-class or aspired to be so. Yet it was precisely for this reason that they were not considered "real" black people, the poor and marginalized with whom the church sought to demonstrate its solidarity. The result, as Lawrence perceptively noted, was that the black churchman was often treated with contempt by his white liberal counterpart, "for the former, being more middle-class than Negro, stands as a judgment on the latter, who is more middle-class than either liberal or radical." The leadership was mistaken if it thought that bypassing middle-class blacks would help secure credibility among ghetto-dwellers or Black Power advocates. On the contrary, doing so would merely confirm the image of a white church interested in pursuing racial equality on its own terms.[76]

With the start of the new year, discord over Caution's fate unleashed what Walter Dennis described as "a tense internecine struggle" between black clergy and the national church.[77] On January 5, a group of priests hastily assembled in Washington to discuss the possibility of a collective response. One of the meeting's conveners was Austin R. Cooper (1933–2001), a Miami native who had studied at St. Augustine's College and then trained for the ministry at Seabury-Western in Illinois. Ordained in 1960–1961, Cooper went on to serve parishes in Florida, New York, and Texas before becoming rector of St. Philip's Church in Jacksonville in 1966. In addressing the group,

168   PRIVILEGE AND PROPHECY

Cooper urged the creation of a new association of black priests, which would lobby for improved opportunities and greater recognition in the church.[78] At a second gathering held a month later at St. Philip's Church in Harlem, he and sixteen others voted to establish the Union of Black Clergy and Laymen of the Episcopal Church (UBCL).[79] While Caution's dismissal had undoubtedly served as a catalyst for this move, the founding of UBCL bespoke deep and long-held resentments at work within the black Episcopal community.[80] Despite this sign of trouble to come, Hines and Corrigan pressed on with their reorganization at church headquarters, authorizing Modeste to assemble his own team to run GCSP.[81] Eager that the new program should be credible among the poor and marginalized, Modeste recruited associates whom he believed would communicate effectively with these constituencies. Few of them, however, displayed much interest in organized religion or sought to hide their suspicion of the churchmen paying their salaries.[82] What Hines and Corrigan claimed was a necessary streamlining of operations was in fact beginning to look more like a *kulturkampf*.[83]

Convinced that black Episcopalians were too bourgeois to engage meaningfully in empowerment work, Modeste and his staff gave funding priority to secular groups over programs initiated by inner-city parishes.[84] Observing this trend was Richard B. Martin, who had recently been consecrated suffragan bishop of Long Island. Ordained in 1943, Martin (1913–2012) had attended Allen University in South Carolina before continuing his studies at Bishop Payne Divinity School, the University of the South, and Union Seminary. He served in parish ministry until his appointment as archdeacon of Brooklyn in 1964, followed by his episcopal election at the close of 1966. Describing the tensions between local clergy and GCSP staff during this time, Martin recalled the bitterness many black priests felt as they "watched entrepreneurial projects mushroom in their respective neighborhoods with substantial funding from GCSP while their parishes struggled to survive."[85] Under the circumstances, some began to question what, if anything, was distinctly Christian about the whole undertaking. Perhaps the most egregious example of the staff's contempt for the church was its refusal to fund St. Philip's Community Center, one of the many projects undertaken by Moran Weston in Harlem. Having worked as a social worker in the 1930s and 1940s and on the staff of the national CSR Department in the 1950s, Weston had come to personify Episcopal outreach since taking over St. Philip's in 1957. Failing to cooperate with activists like Weston was a fatal error, for instead of creating much-needed allies for GCSP, it only added to the growing number of detractors.[86]

Notwithstanding the sentiments of his staff, Modeste quickly realized it was essential to the program's future that Episcopalians should grasp what was being done in their name.[87] To that end, he traveled extensively in the years to come, addressing parish groups, diocesan conventions, and other gatherings.[88] He was later joined in these efforts by Barry Menuez, who had transferred from JUP to become the only white member of the GCSP staff. Menuez characterized their efforts as an attempt "to interpret for Episcopalians the self-interest of the church in supporting this kind of work."[89] Even so, communication between New York and the wider church proved a major stumbling-block throughout the program's existence.[90]

Besides black clergy, certain bishops likewise expressed unhappiness about the way GCSP was being implemented. In keeping with the "no strings attached" approach to empowerment, General Convention had stipulated that bishops should be consulted about GCSP-sponsored projects in their dioceses but have no control over their funding. John Hines felt such an arrangement was particularly important in the South, where black-led initiatives were most likely to encounter resistance.[91] Unsurprisingly, disagreement soon arose over what constituted adequate consultation during the grant-making process.[92] Behind this debate lay the persistent question of how much authority the national church should seek to claim for itself.[93] Bypassing the "Episcopal Principle" of local autonomy in pursuit of GCSP's aims, Hines proved his willingness to take full advantage of his centralized powers.[94] Yet for John Allin of Mississippi, Hines's pronouncements about the need for concerted prophetic action could not justify the lack of transparency characterizing the program's administration. "There was no accountability and there wasn't supposed to be," Allin later charged. "In the haste to move forward, management went out the window."[95] Even bishops strongly committed to GCSP, such as Kim Myers, would eventually question the apparent arbitrariness of the grant-making process and the failure to provide basic information about decisions. Having heard secondhand that community projects he supported were refused funding without any explanation, Myers gently remonstrated with Modeste: "If grant proposals have been rejected, I would appreciate being notified, and in each case, knowing the specific reasons why the organization does not meet the established criteria for receiving GCSP funds."[96] It was difficult to see how sympathetic bishops

170 PRIVILEGE AND PROPHECY

could promote the program if they were unaware of what it was doing in their own backyard.

For Modeste, though, this concern with accountability revealed how little Episcopalians grasped the social differences between themselves and the people they wished to help. "Orderly disciplined process is a prized value among the middle and upper-class white leaders of the nation," he asserted, whereas "to ghetto activist groups, the emphasis on orderly process is irrelevant. The prize value in the ghetto is getting the job done, the babies fed, the mothers clothed and housed, the community organized. . . . The orderly procedures of the Episcopal Church are of very little interest."[97] Seen through this lens, administrative niceties became just another means by which privileged whites sought to maintain control in the face of black advancement. By resisting this pressure, GCSP staff members saw themselves as acting in solidarity with the ghetto and taking a stand against the "institutional racism and white suprem[ac]ist ideology" of the church.[98] Predictably, such defiance led to a tense working environment at Episcopal Church Center, as well as strained relations with members of the Executive Council.[99] Even with the unswerving support of Bishop Hines, the strain of trying to do "a black thing in a white place" began to take its toll on Modeste personally. "A lot of the time I feel pretty alone," he later admitted in an interview with the *Episcopalian*. "I have to figure out how much a white board can take and not jeopardize my own integrity. It's hard to keep the lid on. Sometimes it blows."[100] Writing in the spring of 1969, Charles Willie praised Modeste for performing under such trying circumstances, but encouraged him not to define administration as a racial issue. This strategy only led to name-calling and diverted time and energy away from the primary business of aiding the poor. Instead of accusing GCSP's opponents of racism, Willie concluded, the best rebuttal was "to painstakingly show that procedures were followed" and thereby leave such people to reveal their own prejudices.[101]

Among those who shared Modeste's readiness to challenge Episcopal sensibilities was the young priest David M. Gracie. Born in Detroit, Gracie (1933–2001) took his undergraduate degree from Wayne State University and prepared for ordination at ETS. He was ordained in 1961–1962 and spent five years serving parishes in Michigan before Robert DeWitt invited him to become "Urban Missioner to Areas of Tension" in the Diocese of Pennsylvania.[102] Not long after his arrival in Philadelphia in 1967, Gracie sparked controversy over his engagement in anti-war activities. As was the case in the nation as a whole, Episcopalians remained deeply divided over

American involvement in Vietnam, such that General Convention had been unable to produce any official statement on the matter.[103] When Gracie publicly encouraged young men to burn their draft cards at a demonstration in mid-October, local churchmen were scandalized and demanded his immediate resignation.[104] Even those opposed to the war urged Bishop DeWitt to dismiss him, warning that Gracie's inflammatory rhetoric could undermine lay support for GCSP and other social initiatives.[105] But to Edward Lee, Episcopal chaplain at Temple University, such cautious thinking was precisely part of the problem. Preaching at an anti-war eucharist in late November, he argued that it was perfectly reasonable for co-religionists to be divided over the war. For to contend publicly in this way demonstrated that Episcopalians were more concerned with the needs of the world than with "ecclesiastical self-preservation." Moreover, Lee suggested, such open disagreement presented an opportunity "to end once and for all the cultic role of hired holy man which the Church has played for so long in this country, whereby we give some kind of predictable spiritual sanction to so much of the prevailing national goals and aspirations." This comment once more exemplifies the eagerness of progressive churchmen to repudiate establishmentarian religion in favor of a more overtly 'prophetic' form of social witness. Having done so, they were in turn persuaded that "civil disobedience, non-violently understood and penalties accepted, becomes a patriotic act."[106]

David Gracie was by no means the only Episcopal priest undertaking provocative actions against the war. Around the same time as the demonstration in Philadelphia, Robert Morrison, who had succeeded Gracie as rector of St. Joseph's Church in Detroit, announced that he had offered "sanctuary" to seventeen young men wishing to avoid military service.[107] Supporting Morrison in this advocacy was the group Clergy and Laymen Concerned About Vietnam (CALCAV), an ecumenical coalition founded in 1965 with a significant number of Episcopalians in its ranks.[108] By the following summer, the principle of sanctuary had generated sufficient interest that the Diocese of New York felt obliged to issue guidance to parishes, clarifying the concept's lack of legal standing and offering advice on how best to negotiate with police.[109] Morrison's support of draft resisters in Michigan put him on a collision course with Bishop Emrich, who condemned his behavior and rejected sanctuary as "a euphemism that cloaks a clear illegality."[110] For an activist bishop like Kim Myers, however, formulating a Christian response to draft resistance was not so straightforward. Toward the close of 1967, the San Francisco chapter of CALCAV sought his permission to hold a service in

172 PRIVILEGE AND PROPHECY

Grace Cathedral at which draft cards were to be burned. Though personally opposed to American policy, Myers refused the request, worried that doing so would imply law-breaking was "the only possible or legitimate Christian response to the moral dilemma of the war in Vietnam." Rather than endorse such a radical approach, he believed the church must instead "espouse the middle way between the two unacceptable extremes in the present social polarization."[111] For those who had come to associate Kim Myers with the cutting-edge of Episcopal social witness, this was a disappointingly moderate position for him to adopt. Yet as he subsequently admitted, becoming a diocesan bishop had forced him to consider the dynamic between his prophetic impulses and his responsibility to ensure the health and stability of the diocese.[112] Given the evident lack of consensus among Episcopalians regarding Vietnam, he therefore felt compelled to set aside his own views and assume a stance more inclusive of the church as a whole.

Back in Philadelphia, Bishop DeWitt responded to the uproar over David Gracie's activities in Philadelphia by defending the principle of civil disobedience in a pastoral letter to his clergy. He affirmed Gracie's right as an individual to join in peaceful demonstrations but conceded it was wrong for a diocesan official to encourage others to break the law. "I personally respect Father Gracie's integrity and understand what he is doing," wrote DeWitt, though he emphasized that such behavior did not reflect official policy on either Vietnam or civil disobedience. Such distinctions would do nothing to mollify those who were already unhappy with the bishop's leadership before Gracie's arrival. In this respect, as DeWitt himself put it, the present conflict was just another iteration of a continuing problem, that of the church's "awkward stance in reference to its new and specialized ministries."[113] Since coming to Pennsylvania in 1964, he had made such ministries a priority, taking a prominent stand on racial equality and community empowerment.[114] When later asked why those who objected to his activism had elected him bishop in the first place, DeWitt replied gently: "Well, I guess they just didn't know enough about me." In fact, this misunderstanding bespoke a basic difference between the bishop and many in his flock regarding the nature of his office. "The church [is] meant to be prophetic," DeWitt insisted. "What many, both inside and outside the church, don't seem to realize is that a bishop is not meant to represent his *people*, but to represent God *to* his people."[115] Some who felt their bishop had been doing neither formed the organization Episcopal Renaissance in 1967 to save the church from "the spiritual treason" they believed he had been spreading instead.[116]

PASSING GRACE AND SEIZED MICROPHONES   173

Another group, calling itself the Committee for the Preservation of Episcopal Principles, likewise emerged specifically as a reaction against David Gracie. The Committee would eventually persuade the Diocesan Convention to cut funding for DeWitt's most controversial social programs, despite the support these enjoyed among inner-city parishes.[117]

Working alongside Gracie in "specialized ministries" was James E. P. Woodruff, whom the bishop appointed associate director of diocesan communications in the fall of 1967. Born in Trinidad, Woodruff (1936–2002) was raised in the United States from the age of two. Having taken his first degree from SUNY Buffalo, he graduated from Seabury-Western in 1960. After ordination he was called to Nashville, where he served as vicar of St. Anselm's Church and chaplain to the nearby black institutions of higher learning: Fisk University, Tennessee State University, and Meharry Medical School. Active in civil rights, Woodruff went on to embrace Black Power and sponsored a "liberation school" at St. Anselm's, designed to empower black children but which police instead claimed taught them "hatred for the white man."[118] When the bishop of Tennessee ordered the school's closure, Woodruff accepted Robert DeWitt's offer to come to Philadelphia, where he was put in charge of outreach to the black community.[119] Describing the nature of his new task, Woodruff explained that "I am a priest in a church which is trying hard to stop being a white church," and his contribution to this process was to show inner-city people that "Christianity can be black."[120] Yet like Gracie, Woodruff soon became a bogeyman to certain conservatives, threatened by his militant language and aggressive tactics. One local paper captured their feelings when it dismissed Woodruff as someone who "preaches 'hate Whitey,' promises bloodshed, and slurs everything that is American, including Abraham Lincoln." And he did all these things, readers were reminded, "under the cloak of the Episcopal Church."[121]

In the face of mounting opposition, Bishop DeWitt felt obliged to convene a committee in early 1968 to assess the impact of the urban mission program for which the two priests were responsible. Under the leadership of prominent Philadelphian Stanhope S. Browne, the group produced a report in November 1968 that acknowledged the disruption caused by Gracie and Woodruff's activities. As a result of them, "more traditionally-minded members of the Diocesan family . . . have felt alienated from their church and their Bishop," observed the committee. "They have seen a source of comfort become a source of sorrow and even shame . . . [and have] been told that their deepest assumptions about their church and their society are at best

174 PRIVILEGE AND PROPHECY

mistaken and at worst immoral." Here was a remarkably candid assessment of the way in which liberal activism had begun to intrude upon Episcopal identity at a fundamental level. But having recognized the sense of loss and disorientation many churchmen were experiencing, the committee did not doubt that this was a price worth paying. "Our denomination has been the most successful in breaking out of its old white, middle-class shell," the report boasted, and consequently it was the only church "able to bridge the widening polarization between whites and blacks." Woodruff received particular praise for his work in raising the profile of the Episcopal Church in the inner city. And while it examined closely the allegations made against Gracie regarding his role in draft resistance, the committee recommended that both men should continue in their respective ministries. However stressful the upheavals taking place in society might be, it was futile to blame or silence those trying to engage with them positively. "It is not possible ever again to return to the tranquil Diocese of an earlier time," the report concluded. As such, Episcopalians must learn to embrace the present changes as signs of new life in their midst.[122]

This was, of course, much easier said than done. By the spring of 1968, the United States appeared more divided than at any other time since the Civil War. The optimism and reformist zeal of the early 1960s had yielded to confrontation and calls for revolutionary social change. Even Martin Luther King, revered by liberals for his conciliatory approach to racial equality, now spoke urgently about economic injustice and the need for a redistribution of wealth.[123] In seeking to press the issue, King initiated the Poor People's Campaign, which would culminate in a mass gathering in the nation's capital.[124] Concerns about this plan prompted Frank Sayre and others to invite King to visit the District, so that they might learn firsthand what to expect in the coming weeks. As a result, he addressed a congregation of a thousand in the National Cathedral on the Sunday just before his assassination.[125] Reflecting later on why King had seen the campaign as necessary, Bishop John Burgess suggested that "this is not basically a racial thing at all. It is a class thing. . . . So far as the power structure of America is concerned, the worst thing that could happen would be for black poor and white poor and Spanish-speaking poor to get together. . . . But this is the one thing that the power structure is not going to tolerate."[126] King's murder just days after his visit seemed to confirm Burgess's analysis. Yet as riots raged across the country in response, what Nicholas von Hoffmann termed the "process of canonization" was already underway. On April 5, Dean Sayre led a memorial

PASSING GRACE AND SEIZED MICROPHONES   175

service at the cathedral attended by over 4,000 people, among them the president, the vice president, the justices of the Supreme Court, and many other dignitaries and officials. Writing in the *Washington Post*, von Hoffmann highlighted the irony of the situation, whereby "the troublesome, revolutionary, religious leader" had been transformed into an "object of national piety." He further questioned the appropriateness of holding the service in a setting whose grandeur and pretension so obviously "ran counter to [King's] life."[127]

Meanwhile, Paul Moore joined in a very different kind of occasion across town at the Church of St. Stephen and the Incarnation, where rector William Wendt conducted a midnight requiem mass in one of Washington's most volatile neighborhoods.[128] It so happened that Moore had just started a three-month leave of absence from his duties as suffragan bishop, in order to direct a new inter-faith venture called Operation Connection (OC). Designed as an "eight-month crash program," Operation Connection was an attempt, in Moore's words, "to help mobilize and release the resources of the community toward economic power by the poor, especially the black poor."[129] By pursuing this goal, OC sought to make good on a principle endorsed by General Convention but largely neglected by GCSP, that of local churches taking an active part in the empowerment process. While no stranger to working alongside secular organizations in tackling social problems, Moore himself remained adamant that people of faith had a unique role and must not compromise or conceal their spiritual identity.[130] Before such people could be effective, however, they must come to terms with the full scale and nature of the racial problems besetting American cities. Encouraging them to do this was OC's first objective. The next step was to bring white churchmen and business leaders into direct contact with black activists. Once the OC staff determined the agenda of the latter, Moore explained, "we would present it to the white leadership, get the groups together, and leave them to work things out."[131] In pursuing this strategy, the bishop recruited his good friend Robert S. Potter (1920–1988), a corporate lawyer who later served as chancellor for the Diocese of New York.[132] Potter's expertise in the worlds of law and industry were to be invaluable in forwarding the program's aims. After his time at OC had come to an end, he confessed to a colleague that the work there had been the most rewarding of his life, and he would have gladly carried on with it. Asked why he had not stayed, he said it was because he knew the reason he had been able to contribute in the first place was because "I had a foot in the system."[133] To withdraw from that system would have been to

176 PRIVILEGE AND PROPHECY

forfeit the very thing Potter could lend to the cause of empowerment: his own access to power.

That Episcopal leaders had become preoccupied with the needs of African American ghettos did not escape the notice of those committed to other causes. One such person was Father Joseph Wittkofski, who had converted from Roman Catholicism during the war and served under Bishop Pardue in the Diocese of Pittsburgh ever since. Having devoted himself to ministry among blue-collar Episcopalians in the Mon Valley for twenty-five years, Wittkofski was distressed that the demands of black militants seemed to be dictating the shape of the church's social witness. White working-class people in industrial towns increasingly struggled with the same poverty, unemployment, and social deprivation that afflicted their black urban counterparts, but this fact seemed to make little impression on the wider church.[134] At the 1968 Diocesan Convention in Pittsburgh, Wittkofski reminded delegates that four times as many people lived in sub-standard housing outside the metropolitan area as within it. As such, he introduced a resolution mandating that any diocesan funds put toward improved housing in the inner city should be matched by equal expenditure on housing projects outside Pittsburgh. To Wittkofski, this resolution was an obvious and much-needed corrective to an uneven approach to Christian outreach. Its rejection by the convention served only to confirm his suspicion that race had come not just to dominate but also to distort Episcopal thinking.[135]

Someone else highly critical of the terms under which the church was pursuing its social mission during these years was layman Vine Deloria, Jr. The son and grandson of Native American clergymen in South Dakota, Deloria (1933–2005) attended Episcopal boarding schools in Minnesota and Connecticut before serving in the Marines from 1954 to 1956. He went on to take a science degree from Iowa State University, followed by a master's degree in theology from Augustana Theological Seminary in Illinois. But rather than pursue ordination, in 1964 Deloria accepted a three-year term as director of the National Congress of American Indians (NCAI), an organization devoted to protecting the rights of indigenous tribal governments and combating cultural repression on the reservations.[136] After completing his tenure at NCAI, in 1968 he was elected to the Executive Council of the national church, in addition to serving on GCSP's Screening and Review Committee.[137] This involvement in Episcopal affairs was to prove a deeply disillusioning experience.[138] In attempting to work with Leon Modeste and his staff, Deloria found them angry that GCSP should be extended to other minority groups like his own. He was particularly frustrated with John Hines, whom he considered at the time to be "a prisoner of militant rhetoric who could not distinguish either issues or personalities." Instead, it appeared that Hines and other whites spent most of their time simply reacting to "the uncontrolled emotions" that had been allowed to take over Episcopal Church Center.[139] Deloria's efforts to bolster the church's commitment to Native American ministry was a case in point. Having presented the Executive Council with proposals for strengthening indigenous Episcopal leadership, he was then charged with establishing a National Committee on Indian Work.[140] It did not take long, however, before he found this initiative derailed by members of the national staff, who judged it a threat to the church's focus on the inner city.[141]

Deloria's view that GCSP had fallen prey to separatist tendencies found corroboration elsewhere. When the Cardozo Heights Economic Development Center in Washington applied for project funding in the summer of 1968, its board members were shocked by the behavior of GCSP representatives during their site visit. One wrote to grants administrator Charles Glenn afterward, voicing disgust that the field appraisers had actively promoted "separation of the black community from 'cracker.'" She further charged that the appraisers had attacked the Center's program not on its merits but purely because one of its nine board members happened to be white. As an overwhelmingly black organization seeking to empower the local black community, the Center concluded that it would not accept money from GCSP due to "your attempt to further separate societies within our country. . . . We pity your ignorance, but our Board does not wish to become associated with it in any manner whatsoever."[142] Edward Winckley, a priest in Tacoma, Washington, was similarly distressed that his church's daycare was refused support on the grounds that white Episcopalians had helped to organize it. And this was so, he reported, despite the fact that 90 percent of the children attending the daycare were black, its teachers were black, and its board president and vice president were black. Given this commitment to African American self-determination, Winckley found it difficult to grasp why their funding application had been rejected outright.[143] Perhaps more predictable were the objections raised by Bishop George Murray of Alabama, who had been skeptical of GCSP from its inception. Based on the grants given in his diocese, Murray questioned why preference was so often given to "black militant organizations who want nothing to do with the white community" in favor of those working inter-racially and in which local Episcopalians might

178   PRIVILEGE AND PROPHECY

be involved. Under the circumstances, Leon Modeste's claim that GCSP was willing to assist both types of groups struck Murray as disingenuous.[144]

In response to such criticism, John Hines remained unswervingly loyal to Modeste and his team. To start second-guessing them, he believed, would lead all too easily to the old patterns of white dominance.[145] Instead, he appealed to the church to keep faith with GCSP as a gesture of service and self-giving in a time of deep uncertainty.[146] A few months later, he reiterated the point when discussing the hostility that the program had faced during its first year of operations. What really bothered people about GCSP, Hines argued, was less its use of money than the challenge it posed to "our omnipresent, if skillfully camouflaged, sense of superiority." In this respect, the program gave Episcopalians an important opportunity not just to empower others but also undergo a process of spiritual surrender themselves.[147] As Charles Willie saw it, such a process was essential if privileged Christians were to play a genuine role in the renewal of society. Yet the Episcopal Church "has not worked well with both the meek and the mighty," he noted. "It has taught the meek and the lowly to be courageous but not fulfilled its responsibility to the powerful and strong by teaching them to be humble. We cannot resolve the human relations revolution until both the meek and the mighty learn their lessons, and learn their lessons well."[148] For Bishop Burgess, the first step in developing such humility was for the powerful to take seriously what the powerless were saying. Speaking at Brown University in June 1968, Burgess observed that "it is not easy to be quiet and listen when we have been accustomed to making the final decisions on how other people who are beholden to us must act. It is not easy to have them speak directly to us about their needs and aspirations, when we usually depend upon interpreters and flunkies who say what we like to hear."[149] If they truly wished to take part in healing the nation, Episcopalians must be willing to defer more readily to the judgments of others, even when those judgments cut across their most cherished assumptions.[150]

While few churchmen were prepared to contradict such ideas openly, they made their feelings known by withholding financial support from the institution. By the beginning of 1969, the national church faced a major deficit in funds for the first time in living memory, with 10 of 87 continental dioceses having failed to pay their pledge the previous year. In discussing the news, Bishop Bayne surmised that a combination of factors had led to this situation, not least basic differences over who and what the Episcopal Church was for. He admitted that more than ever, it was necessary for leaders

PASSING GRACE AND SEIZED MICROPHONES   179

to confront the "lack of understanding, lack of communication, lack of trust, which are hurting diocesan as well as national budgets."[151] For his part, the presiding bishop stayed upbeat. Addressing the Executive Council in February, he conceded that the shortfall was unfortunate but insisted that no adjustment to programs was required.[152] Others were not so sanguine. In a memo circulated among Council members the following month, Bishop David E. Richards cautioned his colleagues against mistaking their own priorities with those of the church as a whole. The budget problems they faced would only worsen, he predicted, as long as Episcopalians felt they were being taken for granted by the leadership.[153] Writing to John Hines in late March, Richards repeated his concern that GCSP would not survive if more effort were not put into conciliating the grassroots. "Church pledges cannot be expended as if they were Government tax funds," Richards pointed out. "Taxpayers do not need the same quality and quantity of effective interpretation as pledge givers need."[154] Richards's warnings were echoed by Carroll Simcox of the *Living Church*. "Many Episcopalians will no longer support a program or policy simply because their leaders in convention have set it up," Simcox wrote in an editorial. For the national church to regain credibility among local communities, he argued, it must once again focus on activities discernibly Christian to those paying the bills.[155]

That the hierarchy had failed to produce a compelling theological case for social action troubled opponents and supporters alike. It was as if such explication were considered a luxury amidst the crises of the moment.[156] "We are being sold short by a religion whose only jargon is derived from sociological and educational sources," charged Walter Witte of St. Stephen's Church in St. Louis. The white rector of a majority black parish, Witte was passionately committed to the struggle for racial equality. At the same time, he was adamant that this devotion to social justice should proceed from theology, and not the other way around. "When we borrow the jargon and imitate the methods of other disciplines or, indeed, of the government, we surrender our unique role as Church," Witte warned.[157] As one of the highest-ranking officers of the church, Stephen Bayne had reached the same conclusion. Though he had worked tirelessly alongside John Hines in promoting GCSP, Bayne was distressed by the lack of attention paid to articulating its Christian rationale. So while he remained confident that the church was moving in the right direction, he worried that too often it was for the wrong reasons.[158] That Episcopalians disagreed about the church's role in society was nothing new, he wrote to a friend in late 1968. The issue was that amidst

180 PRIVILEGE AND PROPHECY

such disagreements, no common theological ground had been maintained "where differences of opinion and differences of emphasis and differences of technique can find a new unity in a common obedience, which overrides the differences among individuals." Without this shared framework, social and political justifications for GCSP were ultimately irrelevant, and "we shall have nothing left to us but misunderstanding and suspicion and lack of confidence."[159]

As the decade of the 1960s drew to a close, it became evident that the Episcopal Church was experiencing not just a diminishment of funds, but also of people. From a high-water mark of 3.64 million in 1966, church membership started to decline both as a percentage of the overall population and in absolute terms. Such a drop-off was by no means unique; all the mainline denominations had begun to suffer a comparable loss in numbers.[160] Early commentators saw this as evidence that laypeople were alienated by their leaders' preference for social action over traditional concerns such as evangelism and pastoral care.[161] Subsequent analysis, though, has revealed this explanation to be incorrect. The downward trend was already underway before the intense social activism of 1960s became a feature. And as disgruntled as some laypeople undoubtedly were with the social and political involvements of their clergy, this did not in fact lead to a widespread withdrawal of the established membership. Instead, the fall was due to a failure of the mainline to replenish itself with new members. Many of the educated and affluent young people who had been raised in these denominations simply proved unwilling to replace their parents in the pews.[162] For as with so much else about the established order, they saw the church of their childhood as part of the problem with, rather than part of the solution to, what was wrong in the world.[163]

Blind confrontation between rebellious youth and their reactionary elders has long been a trope in the narrative about the 1960s. Yet liberal Episcopal leaders, like their counterparts across the mainline denominations, often proved eager to interpret the repudiations of the young as a sign of renewed divine activity. Speaking at Philadelphia Divinity School in May 1968, for example, Paul Moore enjoined his audience to embrace "the chaos of our day, and see the revolution as it is, a source of revelation for a deeper understanding of man as he is made in the image of God. . . . Young men and women are asserting their freedom. . . . This is a movement of the *Spirit*."[164] Likewise, in a Lenten address in early 1969, Robert DeWitt acknowledged that while few young people could be regarded as "deeply Christian," neither should they be dismissed as merely "long-haired and wrong-headed."

Instead, he insisted, "let us recognize that God is doing something in our midst, let us consider it carefully, and see what we can learn from it. What we can learn about them. Perhaps what we can learn about ourselves."[165] Others took youthful critiques of the church just as seriously but detected in them new forms of hubris and alienation. Delivering the Kellogg Lectures at ETS later the same year, John Snow spoke sympathetically of the younger generation's refusal "to carry on their backs what they are convinced is a thousand years of bad history," but he worried that in disavowing Christian history altogether, they were embracing a vision of the past "devoid of any redemptive force."[166] William Stringfellow detected a similar irony at work in young radicals' rejection of conventional religion. In its determination to throw off the shackles of bourgeois moralism, the youth movement had, in his view, succeeded in producing merely another brand of conformity, one "more rigid, inverted and bereft of social conscience than that against which it complains with such disillusionment, imagination and poignancy."[167]

Meanwhile, even the young men preparing for ordination in the Episcopal seminaries betrayed a distaste for the institution they were preparing to lead. Writing in the *Christian Century*, Norman Pittenger of GTS commented that "the first thing that strikes one about the modern theological student is the degree to which he *hates* the church."[168] Speaking in New York in early 1968, Dean John Coburn of ETS confirmed this judgment. While still eager to explore the riches of Christian spirituality, Coburn reported, his students were for the most part "suspicious and not impressed with what a divided, withdrawn and weak church has accomplished."[169] They were particularly scathing about the failure of the Episcopal Church to provide clear leadership regarding the war in Vietnam, which was plainly the central issue of their generation.[170] Compounding their sense of guilt and irrelevance was the fact that as future ministers, they themselves were automatically exempted from the draft. In an effort to ease the tensions resulting from this situation, Coburn and his fellow deans proposed that seminarians be required to undertake some form of alternative service for a period of two years. This could be done by joining the Peace Corps, Vista, the American Friends Service Committee, the International Voluntary Service, or any other agency "whose purpose is to serve mankind and alleviate human suffering." This provision, the deans hoped, would enable their students to identify "more fully with the generation they are called to serve and to share the anguish as well as the satisfaction of wrestling with the central issues of society."[171] In soliciting episcopal support for their plan, the deans were to be disappointed. A resolution

182   PRIVILEGE AND PROPHECY

commending the proposal to the House of Bishops on an informal basis was voted down at their autumn meeting.[172]

Although the idea of alternative service for seminarians failed to gain traction among the bishops, it did prompt John Coburn to initiate a dramatic change in his own life. In a letter to the ETS community in June, he announced that he had resigned his position as dean in order to teach high school dropouts in Harlem. Having so often challenged his students to engage more directly with the struggles of the world, Coburn felt it was time now to lead by example, or as he put it, "to practice (for once) what I preach." Furthermore, the move was a deliberate attempt on his part to live out the GCSP principle of personal involvement in the reconciliation of society. "This concern to establish person-to-person relationships seems to me to be one of the distinctive Christian contributions that the Church can make," he concluded.[173] Teaching ninth-grade English for the Urban League's Harlem Street Academy was to be a deeply humbling experience for Coburn. "I do not understand why the place hasn't blown sky-high long ago," he confessed afterward. "It's a great mystery of the human spirit that no matter what the odds against it, it always presses on to create and affirm and strengthen— not to destroy. And I consider that a miracle." While reluctant to comment further on what he had witnessed in the inner city, Coburn was sure most Episcopalians still failed to grasp the reality of deprivation in American life. So even as he acknowledged the token nature of his recent efforts, he remained adamant that seminarians should not be ordained without first undergoing "face to face participation in human suffering."[174]

After surprising friends and colleagues by spending the school year in Harlem, Coburn surprised them again by agreeing to serve as rector of St. James's Church on Madison Avenue. As one of the wealthiest and most prestigious Episcopal churches in New York, St. James's was a far cry from the ghetto neighborhoods where Coburn had just been teaching.[175] But he went there on the condition that the parish would join him in deploying its considerable resources in the service of urban outreach.[176] In this respect, he saw his ministry among the elites of St. James's as a natural progression from the one he had recently attempted among marginalized youths further uptown.[177] Following a similar trajectory during this period was Arthur Walmsley, who resigned his post as assistant director of the national CSR Department in the summer of 1968. Writing to Bishop Hines about his decision, Walmsley explained that after ten years of pushing hard for civil rights and racial empowerment, he felt it was time to reconnect with the "white grassroots" of the church. To that end, he had accepted a one-year posting as priest-in-charge of Grace Church in the college town of Amherst, Massachusetts. At a time when so many of his fellow activists had come to doubt the church's relevance to society, Walmsley wanted to find out what contribution "a largely white, generally affluent community [can] make in coming to terms with racism in our national life and arrogance in our national manner."[178] Working within the constraints of their tribe, however, was something younger priests often appeared loathe to do. In an interview he gave while attending the Lambeth Conference in England, Bishop Austin Pardue of Pittsburgh praised the eagerness of younger clergy to engage directly problems of race and poverty. Nonetheless, such activity was only part of the work that needed to be done. "If you go only to the slums alone and do not convert the mass of people back in the parishes to an open-mindedness on social issues, then you still have your problems all over again," he noted. "The young hot bloods want to do nothing but condemn the racial prejudice on the part of the whites rather than convert them, but it takes some patience and some time."[179]

Yet by the spring of 1969, patience and time had evidently come to an end. The appearance of the Black Manifesto in late April put paid to any lingering hopes that the cooperative spirit of the civil rights years might be revived.[180] Spearheaded by SNCC activist James Forman under the auspices of the Black Economic Development Conference (BEDC), the Manifesto called on white churches and synagogues to pay $500 million in reparations for their complicity in the oppression of African Americans. This money would be used for a variety of purposes, among them the creation of a black university and land bank, as well as black-run publishing houses and television networks.[181] As part of a series of planned confrontations with religious institutions, Forman presented himself at Episcopal Church Center on May 2 to make the demand for reparations in person. With John Hines out of the country, Bishops Stephen Bayne and Brooke Mosley received Forman and agreed to conduct a joint press conference with him. During the discussion, they conceded that the Episcopal Church was racist and that the Manifesto's call for compensation was just. Even so, they insisted that the national church could not deliver what Forman wanted. "You're not wrong in asking," Mosley explained, "you're asking the wrong people." Both were emphatic that BEDC's radical tactics would only be counterproductive in the long run.[182]

In the wake of Forman's visit, a group of Executive Council members attempted to formulate a more considered response to the Manifesto, which the Council as a whole then discussed at its June meeting. The debate over

184 PRIVILEGE AND PROPHECY

this interim document revealed there was considerable disagreement about the way forward, prompting the Council to appoint a special committee to "explore new and sacrificial ways" that Episcopalians might engage with the continuing racial crisis.[183] Lending impetus to this effort was the forthcoming Special General Convention II, scheduled to take place at the University of Notre Dame during the first week of September. So much business had remained unfinished at the close of the triennial conference at Seattle that the presiding bishop was instructed to call a special meeting of the same convention during the summer of 1969.[184] With an eye toward producing a report in time for the gathering at South Bend, John Coburn was placed in charge of a group including familiar figures such as Stephen Bayne, Clifford Morehouse, and Charles Willie. As a black layman who rejected separatism but was staunchly committed to GCSP, Willie was to play a vital role in conciliating the divergent attitudes at work.[185] Leon Modeste, on the other hand, was becoming more and more contentious in his public pronouncements and approach.[186] Reporting to the Council at the same June gathering, he provocatively suggested that if GCSP was about empowering the poor, it was also about disempowering the church's own membership. The two were inextricably linked, he reasoned, given how many Episcopalians enjoyed positions of prominence in the established order. It was naïve to think that the marginalized could secure greater political and economic power without disrupting status quo interests. "If influential and respected members of our Church do not become acutely uneasy about the changes taking place in their communities," Modeste argued, "then there is substantial reason to doubt whether the staff of the Special Program is doing what the Council and the Presiding Bishop have directed it to do."[187] By framing the program's work in such zero-sum terms, it was clear Modeste and his staff had abandoned any pretense of working collaboratively with local communities.

The demands placed upon the church by the Black Manifesto served as something of litmus test for Episcopal leaders, underscoring the sharp differences present among them. In Detroit, Bishop Richard Emrich dismissed out of hand the notion that his diocese should pay $10 million as its share in reparations.[188] Once considered a champion of progressive causes, Emrich had grown increasingly conservative in his social and political views.[189] By the late 1960s, he openly railed against the existence of anti-establishment attitudes in the church and American life generally.[190] When local proponents of the Manifesto demanded $100,000 from the affluent parish of Christ Church Cranbrook, the bishop did not conceal his opposition, and soon the battle lines were drawn within the diocesan community.[191] In late June, eight white Episcopal women occupied Emrich's office to protest his refusal to meet with BEDC representatives, announcing they would remain until he engaged in "good faith bargaining" on behalf of the church. "It's their office, they can stay as long as they like," he said of the group, which was led by Belle Hargreaves, head of the Episcopal Churchwomen and member of the diocesan executive board.[192] In an editorial a few days later, the *Detroit News* evinced little sympathy for the women or their motives. "For whites so guilt-ridden that flagellation feels good, there may be no other way to salvation but surrender to the angriest black man in sight," the paper declared. "That judgment is their prerogative for themselves. Others are entitled to seek reconciliation in more constructive ways."[193] Though Bishop Emrich agreed to meet informally with BEDC, he was adamant that doing so did not constitute negotiation on behalf of the diocese.[194]

The response of Robert DeWitt in Philadelphia could not have been more different from that of Emrich in Detroit. As BEDC spokesmen continued the practice of interrupting church services to present their reparation demands to white congregations, DeWitt issued guidelines on how best to respond. He encouraged clergy to accommodate the protests and do what they could to keep their parishioners "cool" amidst the tensions of the moment. He further counseled against involving police unless absolutely necessary.[195] Meanwhile, Paul Washington of the Church of the Advocate arranged an introduction between DeWitt and local BEDC leader Muhammad Kenyatta, whose arguments cemented the bishop's support for the Manifesto.[196] On July 10, DeWitt invited Kenyatta to present the Manifesto to the diocesan council, in hope of securing affirmation of BEDC's program and a pledge of financial support for its work in Philadelphia. The council's hostile reaction to Kenyatta incensed Washington, who, as the group's only African American member, walked out of the meeting in disgust. Despite what he considered the extraordinary eloquence of Kenyatta's presentation, he angrily charged that "it happened all over again for the 20 millionth time[:] the process of negation, dehumanization, invalidation, reductions, and destruction." Bishop DeWitt likewise characterized the council's behavior as "little short of disastrous," because in rejecting Kenyatta, he believed it had also rejected the Union of Black Clergy and Laymen, which had already publicly endorsed the BEDC agenda. Writing to the council about the meeting afterward, he asked: "If you were a black clergyman, what would you have heard? I feel very strongly that what you would have heard was a highly placed church

186 PRIVILEGE AND PROPHECY

body making expressions which were custodial in intent, defensive in spirit, critical in word; and that no discernible trace of understanding or sympathy with the fundamental issue appeared."[197]

DeWitt's analysis speaks to why so many of his black co-religionists supported the Manifesto, even when they did not necessarily share its philosophy. The reason was simple, as Walter Dennis later explained in a sermon at the Cathedral of St. John the Divine in New York. African American Episcopalians refused to disown the language and tactics employed by BEDC militants because these had "made the church listen when generations of polite and reasonable requests, years of non-violent language and non-violent leadership[,] had brought no deep response from the nation and from the majority of churchmen."[198] Approached from this angle, the Manifesto became a valuable tool for black leaders looking to shake up the racial complacency within the Episcopal Church. But there was another reason why moderates were reluctant to criticize radical spokesmen like Forman and Kenyatta. To do so was to risk being branded a "Tom" by other black people and "bourgeois" by liberal whites, fear of which ensured a semblance of racial solidarity where it might not really exist. "The high rhetoric of the late sixties," Dennis concluded, "made it impossible for we blacks to criticize one another."[199] Lastly, and particularly for black Episcopalians of the younger generation, embracing this discourse became a means of mitigating their class and religious differences from the rest of the African American community, a status their parents had worked hard to maintain but which many of the children were now eager to reject.[200]

One black Episcopalian who openly rejected the Manifesto was Pauli Murray, surely one of the most brilliant and versatile Christian activists of her generation. Born in Baltimore and raised in North Carolina, Murray (1910–1985) was the product of an old Episcopal family.[201] At sixteen she left the South to enroll at New York's Hunter College, from which she eventually earned her BA while working a variety of jobs to survive. Having been denied graduate admission to the University of North Carolina on racial grounds, Murray determined to combat segregation as a civil rights lawyer and undertook legal studies at Howard University in 1941. She became active in the NAACP and organized some of the earliest sit-in campaigns to desegregate lunch counters. Despite graduating at the top of her class at Howard, Murray was then prevented from enrolling at Harvard Law School because of her gender, a formative experience in her development as a feminist. She continued her studies at the University of California at Berkeley instead, after which she practiced law in New York and won praise from Thurgood Marshall for her 1951 book, *States' Laws on Race and Color*. Following a brief stint teaching in Ghana, from 1961 to 1963 she served as legal advisor to the Presidential Commission on the Status of Women and subsequently helped found the National Organization of Women. In 1965, she became the first African American to take a Doctor of Juridical Science degree from Yale, and in 1968 she joined the faculty at Brandeis University, earning tenure there in 1971.[202] Not long after her arrival at Brandeis, Murray encountered a group of black male students who sought to disrupt her classes and intimidate their white peers. Reflecting on this dynamic, she observed that "privileged groups voluntarily pursuing change on behalf of those who seek the instant realization of opportunities long denied are sometimes as vulnerable to attack as downright racial bigots. . . . In the agony of breaking free from the bondage of untouchability, its victims flailed at friends and enemies alike."[203]

As someone who had devoted her life to fighting discrimination, Murray understood perfectly well where such anger came from. But she refused to condone what she deemed the shallow thinking and self-defeating behavior of BEDC and other militant groups. This became clear in August 1969, when the assistant priest at St. Mark's Church-in-the-Bowery, David Garcia, circulated the Manifesto to the "Black and Brown oppressed" of the parish and invited them to discuss "the possibility of forming a Caucus of Black communicants."[204] Murray had been associated with St. Mark's since the 1950s and had been active in the parish since returning to New York in 1966. Her reply to Garcia, which she copied to rector Michael Allen and presiding bishop John Hines, resolutely upheld the principle of racial interdependence. "As the victims of three hundred and fifty years of separatism and exclusiveness, *Negro Christians should be the last to foster separatism*," declared Murray. She then proceeded to heap contempt on the Black Manifesto, dismissing it as "a hodge-podge of revolutionary quasi-Marxist language which, when boiled down and coupled with [the] demand for 'reparations' is a classic example of 'begging by coercion.'" To Murray, such bombast and bullying hardly constituted a Christian approach to the struggle for racial freedom. Especially in a small parish like St. Mark's, forming a Black Caucus could only result in the "ultimate destruction" of the church, a process she had no intention of endorsing. "The whole Black Caucus Movement has in it the seeds of racism," she stated flatly. "It has the potential of being un-Christian, un-brotherly, un-sisterly, and un-lovely. If Black is really beautiful, as the slogan says, it is high time that the slogan-bearers act in a beautiful

188 PRIVILEGE AND PROPHECY

manner."[205] However important it was for Episcopalians to honor social diversity in their midst, Murray never ceased to believe in the church as a place where, by definition, such distinctions were secondary.[206]

This negative reaction to Garcia's proposal evidently surprised Michael Allen, who instinctively supported the creation of a Black Caucus at St. Mark's. Over the course of the previous decade, he had devoted himself to turning the parish into a gathering-place for the neighborhood's eclectic mix of inhabitants. He had also made it a center of experimental worship, not least by introducing the unique "St. Mark's Liturgy" in 1967, which sought to integrate contemporary cultural sensibilities into the Sunday service.[207] In keeping with this spirit of innovation, in 1968–1969 he welcomed the Christian rock band Mind Garage to play its "Electric Mass" at St. Mark's as an accompaniment to the eucharist.[208] For Allen, the appearance of a Black Caucus was simply another opportunity to embrace the *zeitgeist* and welcome those who felt excluded or let down by the mainstream church. Writing to Murray, he reasoned that just as artists and hippies had been included at St. Mark's without compromising their distinctive identity, so black people should also be able to participate in parish life without having to defer to WASP sensibilities.[209] Murray's reply was tart. "I was born into the middle class," she announced, "and I have no quarrel with those human values which coincide with middle class values. I happen to like all the fol-de-rol of the Church rituals in their most elaborate cultural sense. . . . I do *not* like rock and roll as a steady diet; I do *not* like profanity, or dirty hair; and I do not like exclusion in any form." Ironically, Allen's progressive commitment to pluralism led him to think more readily in terms of groups than individuals, which in turn produced the erroneous assumption that the Manifesto reflected the views of all black people. On this point, Murray quickly set her rector straight. "Black Unity is a myth just like White Unity," she chided him. "*Justice, equality and fraternity* are the values which bind us all who believe in them, and you are my 'soul brother' to the extent that we share these values. A Black person who does *not* share them is *not* my soul brother. Do I make myself clear?"[210]

As parish and diocesan leaders grappled with the local impact of the Black Manifesto, the Coburn committee worked to develop the church's formal response in time for the upcoming convention at South Bend. In addition to the Executive Council members already appointed to the group, four representatives from UBCL were invited to join in the consultations. The committee's final report opened by affirming GCSP as the basis on which the

Episcopal Church should continue its efforts at racial empowerment. At the same time, it lamented that so many had come to regard the grants program as the church's only intervention in the process of reconciliation, "as though 'they' over there in New York were doing the whole thing." This view ignored the myriad ways Episcopalians across the country had sought, through both ecclesiastical and secular means, to heal social divisions in their midst. "Person-to-person involvement on the local level has been lost sight of," alleged the committee. "Its rediscovery will determine whether the Episcopal Church will ever... make any kind of significant contribution to the national crisis." Here John Coburn's concern with the centrality of direct action left a discernible imprint on the report's language. Likewise, the UBCL representatives made their own presence felt in the assertion that "the black people best qualified to speak to the Episcopal Church are black Episcopalians," such that support for them and their work should be a "Number 1 priority" going forward. Yet having reasserted the institutional identity of GCSP in this way, the committee was careful not to foreclose the possibility that the church might continue to support secular groups whose goals it broadly shared. Thus, in what could only be a reference to BEDC, the report concluded that although "it is not always necessary that we agree with the philosophy of such groups, it is necessary that we agree with their programs."[211]

When the Executive Council met in South Bend to receive the Coburn report prior to the Special General Convention II, it remained divided about the best way to respond to the Manifesto. Eventually it passed a resolution crafted by John Coburn and Charles Willie, stipulating that if BEDC wished to apply for "seed money" from the church "to fulfill its promise of being an expression of the principle of self-determination," then it must do so through the existing procedures of the GCSP grants program.[212] In an article later published in *The Episcopalian*, Willie offered his own rationale for this comparatively moderate approach. The difficulty with the Black Manifesto, he argued, was that in it "the prophetic and the preposterous are all balled and bound together. It isn't easy to sort out one from the other." Under such circumstances, it was tempting "to take the easy way out and uncritically accept the whole ball, or reject the whole bundle." Despite such confusion, it was important to understand that the real issue was not finally money, but recognition. "The Black Manifesto is an awkward cry from blacks to be included rather than excluded from the mainstream of American life," insisted Willie. "Woe be unto the Church should it mistakenly interpret the call and merely pay off blacks to stay where they are."[213] In seeking to be more inclusive itself,

190   PRIVILEGE AND PROPHECY

the Council voted to add six new members to its ranks, two of whom must be between the ages of eighteen and thirty, and four of whom must be ethnic minorities.[214] This move to diversify the Council dovetailed with a separate proposal to broaden participation in the upcoming convention. As the body charged with planning the Special Convention, the Advisory Committee on Agenda had already recommended that in addition to bishops and deputies, each diocese should send a representative from three groups: women, ethnic minorities, and youth. These special representatives would be permitted to sit in joint sessions and take part in discussions but would have no voting power in legislative sessions. Also, their admission could only take place if both the "constitutional houses" first approved the proposal at the start of convention business.[215]

In the event, bishops and deputies alike lent their overwhelming support to the plan when the Special Convention convened on August 31. Of 107 dioceses, only five had refused on principle to send special representatives to Notre Dame.[216] Reporting on this development, the *New York Times* observed how eager the Episcopal Church evidently was to "erase a popular conception that it was controlled largely by wealthy, white Anglo-Saxons."[217] In his opening sermon, John Hines spoke candidly about the ways their identity continued to inhibit Episcopalians' connection with others. "It is so difficult for most of us in this white-dominated, upper-middle-class, fairly well-educated, fairly well-heeled Episcopal Church to put ourselves in the place of a people whose skin is darker than ours," he declared. "When they seek what is justly theirs, sometimes with a militancy and a stridency that offends our middle-class values, we learn to our discomfort that our commitment to Christian love of our neighbor is almost purely cerebral. All too often we discover that we do not love black people in the flesh." Having championed the presence of the special representatives, Hines now portrayed the Special Convention as a chance to break down personal barriers and tackle the prejudices on which they were built. On the one hand, he challenged his fellow whites "to seek a more comprehensive justice than that which our whiteness is inclined to try to dictate," while on the other, he appealed to blacks "not to settle for a self-determination which, though it may rightfully enhance the beauty of their racial integrity, separates them from their brothers in Christ."[218] Yet if Hines's sermon confirmed his unswerving faith in the church's capacity to model social reconciliation, it also suggested a startling lack of realism about the level of estrangement at work among black and white Episcopalians alike.[219]

Many of the African American delegates attending the Special General Convention made it plain they were not in a conciliatory mood. Speaking on their behalf, UBCL president Frederick B. Williams announced upon arrival that "we are here, perhaps for the last time, to assist the church in doing what must be done."[220] Few could have predicted the dramatic form that such "assistance" would shortly take. Encouraged by Paul Washington and others, BEDC leader Muhammad Kenyatta had traveled from Philadelphia to South Bend to confront Episcopalians directly with the call for reparations.[221] During the opening plenary session on the night of August 31, a dashiki-clad Kenyatta mounted the dais and seized the microphone from a lay deputy in the midst of a report on clergy deployment. As more than 1,000 people looked on, the presiding bishop reflexively intervened, and a brief tussle ensued. After an exchange with the black activists assembled around the stage, Hines asked for a show of hands from the assembly as to whether Kenyatta should be permitted to speak. Shouts of "throw them out" and "you asked for it, Johnnie" issued from the crowd, but a majority favored hearing what Kenyatta had to say.[222] Demanding the Episcopal Church "and all other white establishments get about the business of eliminating racism and implementing anti-racist education," Kenyatta called on the convention to make an immediate "donation" of $200,000 to BEDC. "We must drastically disorganize the church and put it back together in a new way," he concluded.[223] Having already introduced Kenyatta, Paul Washington was invited by Bishop Hines to address the assembly again. Washington took this opportunity to call on his fellow African Americans to walk out of the hall. "White people cannot set the agenda for this church," he asserted. "Black people must set the agenda for this church and for this nation. And since you refuse to deal with our agenda, I have no choice but to call upon all blacks to leave this convention." Enough of them did so that Hines and Coburn felt compelled to revise the order of business for the next day, so that the demand for $200,000 could be discussed without delay.[224]

The crisis precipitated by the microphone incident continued to unfold over the course of the next few days. At a hastily organized hearing on the morning of September 1, black deputies challenged the view that funding requests related to the Black Manifesto should go through the existing procedures of the General Convention Special Program. To begin with, UBCL spokesman Joseph Pelham pointed out, BEDC was making a demand and not a request, and reparations should not be confused with grants. Despite the vocal support it received from certain deputies and bishops, others expressed

192 PRIVILEGE AND PROPHECY

uneasiness about BEDC's ideology and what exactly the $200,000 in question would be used for. In speaking out against the proposal, clerical deputy Gerald McAllister of West Texas condemned what he saw as the "Marxist, anti-Christian, anti-Semitic, and anti-Democratic" aspects of the Manifesto from which it derived.[225] The diocesan bishop of Arkansas, Robert Brown (1910–1994), expressed his opposition in more nuanced terms. Although he had "listened desperately for the voice of Christ" in the arguments made on behalf of BEDC, he still felt unable to accept "a clenched fist as the ultimate arbiter of church problems."[226] At a second session held on the evening of September 2, tensions mounted once more as the House of Deputies voted to shelve the proposal. This decision was quickly reversed, however, after a passionate intervention by the young priest Junius F. Carter.[227] A native of Maryland, Carter (1927–2001) had served in the Navy during the Second World War and studied at St. Augustine's College in Raleigh. He prepared for ordination at Philadelphia Divinity School and began his ministry in New Jersey before becoming rector of Holy Cross Church in Pittsburgh, where he soon earned a reputation for creative social action.[228] Faced with the deputies' decision to refuse BEDC immediate funds, Carter reacted with anger and frustration: "I'm sick of you," he shouted at his white co-religionists. "You don't trust me, you don't trust black priests, and you don't trust black people."[229]

For many delegates, this outburst helped to clarify what was actually at stake in the debate. Notwithstanding their continuing disapproval of the Black Manifesto, they now understood that the demand for funds was in fact a test of their capacity to trust the advice of their own black clergy and lay leaders.[230] Thus, in response to the protestations of Carter and others, the deputies voted that $200,000 should go from voluntary sources to the moderate National Committee of Black Churchmen, with the tacit understanding that this money would make its way to BEDC in due course. This compromise plan was affirmed by the House of Bishops the following day.[231] As with the deputies, the bishops had come to recognize the symbolic value of this action as a means of honoring the wisdom and insight of black Episcopalians, even in the face of conservative reaction.[232] Thus, in addressing his diocese the following month, George Barrett of Rochester conceded the bishops' support was controversial, but emphasized the importance of not second-guessing the judgment of the African American delegates. "They may have been wrong, for no one is infallible," Barrett acknowledged. "But we had no doubt of their integrity, nor that they understood the needs and mood of the black people of this country far more than the rest of us—for the most part privileged white people—did or do."[233] As Charles Willie had predicted even before the Special Convention got started, the cultural politics of the moment made it impossible for Episcopalians to engage meaningfully with the question of racial equality without also entertaining the radical demands of the Manifesto. This dynamic led one commentator to summarize the scene as one where "the love and trust which the liberals rightly urged was inextricably bound up with those immoderate attacks on the existing structures which the conservatives found intolerable."[234] Predictably, the compromise action pleased neither the militants nor their opponents, with both sides accusing the Convention of moral cowardice.[235]

As important as they were in setting the tone at South Bend, clergy such as Washington and Carter were not the only voices to influence the conversation about race. Lay deputy Oscar C. Carr, Jr., likewise roused the Convention when sharing his experiences as a white Mississippian coming to terms with the realities of racism. A cradle Episcopalian and scion of an old planter family, Carr (1923–1977) had been educated at Cornell and the US Naval Academy. After three years' active duty at sea, he returned to his hometown of Clarksdale, where he took up management of the family farm and chairmanship of the local bank. He also assumed a prominent role in his local church, serving on the parish vestry and eventually joining the Diocesan Standing Committee. Amidst all this activity, Carr had become, in his own estimation, "a full-fledged member of the 'Southern way of life'—living in a racially segregated society, thinking little of it. Half-naked black children on porches of tenant shacks on our own plantation . . . blended into the landscape like native cypress trees against the Southern sunset. In spite of travel and a good education, I really didn't have a world view. The 'closed society' was working so well, I didn't even know it was closed!" Yet when faced with the demands of the civil rights movement, Carr realized that "I had never really learned to think for myself," and over the next several years he evolved into a different man, actively seeking to uncover "who I was, what I believed, and how I would 'live out' that belief."[236] This process of self-discovery led him to embrace the activism of both the national church and Democratic politics, and in 1968 he served as co-chair of Robert Kennedy's presidential campaign in Mississippi.[237]

Carr's address at the Convention was one of four that John Coburn had organized on the topic of "Race and the Mission of the Church." Commenting later on the enthusiastic response he got—his speech received a lengthy

194   PRIVILEGE AND PROPHECY

standing ovation—Carr quipped that "I really don't know why, unless I said in 'personal witness style' what conservatives were willing to go along with and what liberals wanted to hear."[238] What seems to have resonated with many who heard him was Carr's candor and humility in describing the ways race pervaded just about every aspect of his life. Notwithstanding his evident devotion to civil rights, he refused to dissociate himself from the unrepentant racist whom he so often counted as a neighbor or colleague. "Perhaps I have been too close to this man in the deer camps, at Ole Miss football weekends, in the plantation office, at the country store," he mused. "If I had not lived with him in an atmosphere of suspicion, distrust, ignorance, misinformation, and nefarious political leadership, surely my heart would break less when I see him fomenting mob violence in front of his schoolhouse or his church house." As sympathetic as he was to those who wanted the Episcopal Church to act more decisively on matters of racial justice, Carr cautioned against imposing solutions on local communities not ready to embrace them. "It is difficult to have an effective program which is *objectively* right when the people to whom the Church looks to carry out the program are not *subjectively* convinced it is right," he reasoned. Here one detects a critique of the whole approach taken by the national church to the racial crisis. For like Stephen Bayne, Carr increasingly saw Episcopalians' failure of leadership in this area not as a matter of competence but of conviction. No amount of grant money or sociological research could finally make up for an absence of theological understanding in the parishes. And this was something that would neither develop overnight nor take root of its own volition. It required a concerted effort at improved communication at all levels of church life, for as Carr concluded, "a climate of trust develops when participants sense they are not being manipulated toward some unknown destination."[239] Given the warm reception that followed his remarks, it was evident Carr's plea for greater mutuality had struck a chord.

Quite apart from the moments of drama and conflict, the mere presence of young people, women, and minorities on the convention floor set this gathering apart from its predecessors. Their participation fundamentally altered the mood of the sessions and forced deputies to reconsider what an Episcopalian might sound and look like. Reflecting on this aspect of the proceedings, John Krumm of New York judged it nothing short of "miraculous" that the special representatives "were taken seriously despite their clothes and manners. They were listened to and they made an impact. A few angry shouts were directed at them, but the great mass of deputies seemed glad for the signs of vitality and promise they brought with them."[240] Even before the convention drew to a close, there was a palpable sense that something unique in the history of the church had taken place.[241] Long pent-up grievances about race, war, and social authority had at last been given a public hearing, and by acknowledging the sheer range of views in its midst, the assembly had achieved a form of catharsis.[242] "Everything was different after that," recalled Lucila Woodard. "You could talk about the Episcopal Church in terms of before South Bend and after South Bend."[243] But if some hailed the birth of a new dispensation, one in which the church's diversity was not only recognized but celebrated, others wondered how the church could remain unified amidst such divergence. This was a major challenge produced by the convention, argued William Lea in the pages of *The Episcopalian*, warning that "this holding of radically different positions can be maintained within one family only if there is great tolerance and great humility on the part of everyone."[244] The problem was that the events of South Bend had demonstrated all too clearly the benefits of an adversarial approach. So, precisely at a moment when they needed to rediscover a shared sense of purpose, Episcopalians were increasingly drawn to confrontation as a means of shaping the church's decision-making process.[245]

The claim that the Special Convention had fundamentally transformed the Episcopal Church was greeted with skepticism by Pauli Murray—not because she questioned its importance as part of the struggle for recognition by black people, but because she detected no corresponding sense of urgency about the condition of women. Such a failure she attributed to the "blindness, lack of imagination, and lack of experience" characterizing the mindset of the white men still in charge of the church.[246] Speaking out about gender discrimination was of course nothing new for Murray. In 1966, she had written to the vestry of St. Mark's Church-in-the-Bowery, questioning why no women took a role in leading worship and demanding that the situation should be addressed.[247] When she also voiced her own sense of calling to the priesthood, even the self-consciously progressive members of St. Mark's were astonished; it had simply never occurred to them such a thing might be possible.[248] Her belief in the church's essential conservatism about gender was confirmed when a laywoman was again refused her seat in the House of Deputies at South Bend, despite being elected to replace a layman unable to attend.[249] Given such recalcitrance, Murray marveled at the arrogance of expecting women to contribute to the $200,000 special fund, when they themselves were still being accorded second-class status.[250] Corresponding

196 PRIVILEGE AND PROPHECY

with Betty Bone Schiess in late October, she suggested that "what happened at Notre Dame was primarily an accommodation of white males to black males, . . . with an underlying and implicit determination to continue to exclude females from any meaningful sharing of power."[251] This analysis, which Murray circulated widely after the convention, elicited an irritated response from fellow black Episcopalian John Burgess. Although Bishop Burgess agreed that women had been denied opportunities to which they were entitled, he rejected the idea that the church had merely caved in to pressure or bought its way out of an awkward situation. "I feel very strongly," Burgess wrote to Murray, "that if you had been at South Bend and experienced the great spiritual confrontation that the deputies and bishops underwent during those days of agony and real struggle, you would agree that the Episcopal Church experienced one of its finest hours."[252]

Still, the question of whether or not the convention's $200,000 special fund constituted a form of reparations could not be set aside so easily. On September 6, the *New York Times* published an editorial criticizing the Episcopal Church for appearing to legitimize the financial demands made by the Black Manifesto. That it had done so indirectly by giving to a third party merely sidestepped the fundamental issue. "Where does this concept of reparations end?" the editorial asked. "Everyone, in and out of the religious establishment, owes it to the country and to himself to do racial justice now; but there is neither wealth nor wisdom enough in the world to compensate in money for all the wrongs of history."[253] Stung by this rebuke, John Hines and John Coburn responded with a letter that appeared in the *Times* on September 11. They denied the premise that Episcopalians had endorsed the concept of reparations, insisting the fund would be distributed in accordance with criteria already set out by GCSP. In this way, the church had ensured that the focus of its mission "was upon present and future attitudes and actions rather than upon the acknowledgement of a right to compensation for injuries in the past."[254] John Coburn later sought to elaborate on this point, arguing that the catalyst for the convention's gesture had not been reparations but repentance—a recognition of how much there was still to do in building "a new life together" across the racial divide.[255] Defenders of the special fund were quick to point out the ways in which such distinctions had been misrepresented or caricatured in the media.[256] But the fact remained that within the church itself, there were many who simply did not agree with what had taken place at South Bend.[257] By October, parishes across the country began withholding a percentage of their diocesan giving in direct protest against the Special Convention's actions.[258]

Conversely, there was a handful of parishes in which the convention inspired more radical action at the local level. Despite the opposition of Pauli Murray and with active encouragement from the clergy, a "Black and Brown Caucus" was formed at St Mark's Church-in-the-Bowery. A few weeks after the Notre Dame gathering, the group made itself known to the wider congregation by interrupting a Sunday service and presenting a list of demands. Among these was that the Caucus should immediately be given $30,000 for its exclusive use and four guaranteed places on the Vestry. Referring to the modern liturgy currently in use at St. Mark's, the Caucus also called upon the congregation to "cease and desist this WASP service, conceived solely by whites to help themselves over their middle class hang ups." By contrast, and to reflect better their own sensibilities, the Caucus stipulated that whenever the peace was shared at the eucharist, worshippers should be reminded that "there can be no peace without freedom." Likewise, the dismissal at the end of each service henceforth should always be: "Power to the people!"[259] Having presented their demands to rector Michael Allen, the group then staged a walk-out, inviting all those in solidarity with them to do the same. The majority of those present joined in, including Allen and the presiding priest, thereby abandoning those in the congregation who chose to remain.[260] In a less dramatic fashion but with the same belief in minority empowerment, a "Committee of Blacks" was established at Christ Church in Cambridge, Massachusetts, during the latter half of 1969. With the encouragement of rector Murray Kenney, a corresponding "Committee of Whites" was created in order to raise $100,000, which would then be offered to the Committee of Blacks to distribute as they saw fit.[261] To Kenney, it was essential that white people learned to extend to black people the same level of trust they routinely placed in one another.[262] Thus at both St. Mark's and Christ Church, the Black Manifesto prompted a larger conversation about the nature of authority and status within the parish community as a whole.

Employing disruptive tactics was hardly the exclusive purview of those espousing Black Power. Although their efforts were largely overshadowed by the reparations debate, Episcopalians opposed to the Vietnam War had likewise made a dramatic intervention at the Special Convention. On September 2, at a reporting session on peace work, Bishop Kim Myers and CALCAV leader Richard Fernandez interrupted the proceedings by escorting two military servicemen onto the platform. They explained that the young men had

198 PRIVILEGE AND PROPHECY

been refused conscientious objector status by their superiors, and having gone AWOL, were now appealing to the convention for sanctuary. Aided by members of the Episcopal Peace Fellowship (EPF), Myers and Fernandez then staged an altar call of sorts, inviting deputies to join them on the dais "to give the men their pastoral support." About half of those present came forward.[263] Superficially at least, this mixed response reflected the ambivalence among Episcopalians and other mainline Protestants about the legitimacy of the war. By the close of the decade, most clergy opposed American involvement in Southeast Asia, but a majority of laypeople only followed suit a few years later.[264] This lack of consensus was evident when Frank Sayre allowed a peace service to take place at the National Cathedral on November 14 as part of the "Moratorium to End the War in Vietnam" demonstrations.[265] Over 5,000 people attended the event, but thousands more wrote to Sayre afterward, objecting that the cathedral had been used for this purpose.[266] More controversial still was the "Mass for Peace," which EPF had organized the previous day at the Pentagon. Almost 200 people gathered for a eucharist presided over by Bishops Edward Crowther and Daniel Corrigan, with Malcolm Boyd preaching. About halfway through the service, federal police stepped in and arrested the entire group for creating a "loud and unusual noise." As suffragan bishop of Washington, Paul Moore hastily intervened to ensure that those taken to jail had the necessary funds to post bail.[267] While he shared their anti-war stance, Moore had not participated in the service, explaining later that "I didn't think that the mass should be used as an instrument for social action."[268]

Moore's comment is indicative of his struggle to maintain some kind of theological coherence amidst the upheaval of the times. Though he continued to champion a traditional sacramentalism, he was increasingly skeptical of the church's ability to respond meaningfully to the seismic changes taking place around it. "We in the Church are tied in canonical knots, separated by Gothic walls, stifled by seventeenth-century language and medieval thought forms," he charged.[269] Preaching at General Seminary in October, he went further, insisting it was futile to speak in "measured Anglican phrases of the beauty and the power of Christ" to young people who were now in the thrall of the counterculture. Instead, he encouraged seminarians to focus on the power of personal experience over creedal orthodoxy: "Would it not be better to affirm the spiritual reality of what they do without first requiring intellectual assent to our categories, to somehow allow Christ to be there with them unknown and then at a most delicately appropriate time to help them recognize Him[?]"[270] How such epiphanies were to be facilitated Moore did not say. What is striking nonetheless is his readiness here—at least rhetorically—to relegate Christian doctrine to a matter of secondary importance in a bid for popular relevance. As was to prove the case so often in his career, the bishop was treading a fine line between defending the institutional church and attacking it.

Of course, part of what made Moore's edgier pronouncements compelling was his undoubted status as a member of the WASP establishment. It was this combination of patrician background and progressive politics that made John Butler of Trinity Parish certain that Moore was destined to succeed Horace Donegan as bishop of New York. Thus, even before Donegan had formally called for the election of a coadjutor, Butler was busy making plans for his friend's candidacy.[271] Moore himself later acknowledged that with all his "old school-tie friends" among the laity, his high church credentials among Anglo-Catholic clergy, and his record of civil rights activism alongside blacks, he had the necessary appeal to capture a range of constituencies.[272] Orchestrated by Butler and other supporters, the process that unfolded in the course of 1969 was, in Jenny Moore's words, one of "rumors and genteel yet intensely political non-campaigning in Paul's behalf."[273] When the election finally took place in mid-December, he was elected on the second ballot by an overwhelming majority.[274] Speaking after the result was announced, however, Moore was keen to reassure those who might still doubt his commitment to the institutional structures he was called to uphold. So rather than pronounce on the need for further social action, he instead focused on the importance of life in the parish church, for it was here, he insisted, that "the battles are being fought concerning the gut issues of the day—racism, peace, family life, even sex education."[275] Having already detected a shift in the climate of both church and society, Moore was signaling his readiness to lead his diocese through the more introspective period of the 1970s.

7
No Love without Justice (1970–1979)

Few would now claim that the political, social, and cultural phenomenon known as the sixties ended promptly on New Year's Day 1970. Many of the conflicts and controversies that had so animated the previous two years remained urgent and showed little sign of dissipating. Arguably it was not until the withdrawal of the United States from Vietnam and the crisis over Watergate in 1973 that this tumultuous time finally drew to a close.[1] Even so, with the arrival of a new decade there was a palpable sense that the mood was changing, in the country at large and the Episcopal Church in particular. Addressing the Executive Council in February, Presiding Bishop John Hines recognized that Episcopalians were experiencing "a period of deep tension." The reasons for this, he argued, were various, ranging from "distrust of the national leadership, to disagreement over the nature of Christian mission, to confusion over theological bases for commitment, to the financial pressures of inflation, to loss of nerve, to 'battle fatigue.' "[2] Others had also begun to notice a deepening malaise among their co-religionists. "So few churches do much more than try to survive," lamented Jack Woodard in a sermon. "We seem to have lost our nerve somehow."[3] As they grappled with the complexity of America's problems and their own increasingly marginal role in confronting them, the mainline denominations were beset by disillusionment and self-doubt.[4] For lay theologian William Stringfellow, the defeatism taking root among liberal Protestants was symptomatic of an "idolatry of death," one underpinned by a "fascination of whites with their own guilt. . . . It is a monstrous self-hate which is suicidal in principle—a literal, cowardly, compulsive and pathological worship of death."[5] Seen through the lens of Stringfellow's apocalyptic vision, the churches' depressed state was a sign not just of institutional failure but profound spiritual crisis.

Without denying the Episcopal Church had entered a dry season, Charlie Price of Harvard had little time for pessimism. "What else in heaven's name do you expect?" he asked a gathering at the Episcopal Theological School in May. "Our troubles might even be the sign that we are doing our priestly ministry in this world."[6] John Coburn likewise sought to frame the signs of

Privilege and Prophecy. Robert Tobin, Oxford University Press. © Oxford University Press 2022.
DOI: 10.1093/oso/9780190906146.003.0007

exhaustion as an opportunity for renewal. "We clearly have got to go through some kind of refining process if we are to recapture the integrity that we ought to have for the authentic Gospel," he wrote to a friend.[7] Yet there was also a growing sense that such renewal depended on a willingness to return to first principles, as though Episcopalians had lost their way while trying to engineer social change. Having taken stock of all the programs and initiatives of recent years, Frank Sayre conceded that "perhaps the church's peculiar 'thing' now may be the humble job of just being what it is—a symbol and sign of the Lord, a reminder to men that [there] is another dimension of life beyond our making."[8] In a similar vein, Arthur Walmsley, once such a pivotal figure in promoting Episcopal social engagement, welcomed the "measure of humility" he detected in more recent forays into the public sphere. Amidst their eagerness to transform society, Walmsley admitted, church activists like himself had been so enamored of their own solutions that they sometimes "forgot the quality of human relationships and our sensitivity to people's major needs should be the decisive factor."[9] Instinctively, then, even those who remained committed to the church's agenda felt an urge to reclaim the basic Christian values that had prompted their efforts in the first place.

Under these conditions, criticism of John Hines and the General Convention Special Program continued to mount, with some conservatives calling upon the presiding bishop to resign. Speaking in Houston in early 1970, Hines jokingly compared his personal situation to that of Lyndon Johnson during the president's final months in the White House.[10] But it was no longer just opponents who were voicing concerns about the direction GCSP was taking. One clergyman wrote to Director Leon Modeste in February affirming his support for the program but wondering if too often "we are doing the wrong things for the right reasons."[11] Prominent GCSP advocates John Coburn and Charles Willie worried privately that Modeste and his staff were undermining confidence in the program with their confrontational attitude and provocative actions.[12] Not the least of these was their readiness to fund organizations that had a reputation for advocating violence, such as the Malcolm X Liberation University in North Carolina and the Alianza Federal de Mercedes [Federal Land Grant Alliance] in New Mexico.[13] Appearing on the Dick Cavett talk show later in the year, Bishop Hines defended such grants, explaining that "when you help people who are on the desperate cutting-edge of life, then you help people whose condition borders on the violent." And while he was adamant that the church did not condone such behavior, he insisted that it "understands how this is

202 PRIVILEGE AND PROPHECY

a possibility for people who are themselves oppressed and depressed by society."[14] The problem, of course, was that such distinctions were actually lost upon most Episcopalians. Instead, they simply felt estranged from what was being done in their name, as national officials appeared not just aloof but paranoid in their defense of GCSP.[15]

Meanwhile, Paul Moore was installed as bishop coadjutor of New York in a service at the Cathedral of St. John the Divine on May 9.[16] In certain respects, it was an occasion that hearkened back to days now fast receding, when the investiture of an Episcopal bishop still symbolized stability and coherence in the established order. This sense was underlined by the presence of the mayor of New York, John Lindsay, an old friend of Moore's who had been his contemporary at both St. Paul's and Yale. Themselves upper-crust Episcopalians, Lindsay and his wife Mary had hosted a dinner dance in honor of the Moores at Gracie Mansion the previous evening.[17] Speaking at the service, Bishop Donegan sought to emphasize the personal and institutional continuity Moore's election represented. "He is yet another in the great tradition," he told the congregation of 2,000. "It seems almost unnatural that I should welcome him because in so many ways it seems he has always been here. He stands for everything to which this Diocese is committed."[18] Despite such assurances, however, the tragic events of the past week cast a shadow over the proceedings. On April 30, President Richard Nixon had announced the deployment of US troops into Cambodia, which triggered renewed protests across the country. During a demonstration held at Kent State University on May 4, four students were shot dead by the Ohio National Guard, sparking further protests and the temporary closure of over 200 college and university campuses.[19] Following his sermon, Bishop Donegan led a moment of silence for those killed in Cambodia and at Kent State, while Suffragan Stuart Wetmore delivered a statement from all three bishops calling for a halt to the invasion, "which has undercut the chances for serious negotiations on disarmament and the settlement of the Indochina war."[20]

President Nixon's controversial Vietnam policy exacerbated some of the deep antipathies already pulling the nation apart. The day before Paul Moore's installation service, construction workers had attacked a student peace march in lower Manhattan, leaving seventy people injured. The rector of Trinity Wall Street, John Butler, twice had to order the church's gates closed during what the *New York Times* described as "a wild noontime melee," as the helmeted workers tore down a Red Cross banner from the church railings and then also attempted to remove the flag of the Episcopal

Church. "I suppose they thought it was a Vietcong flag," commented an exasperated Butler.[21] As deplorable as the workers' behavior surely was, it served as a timely reminder that Americans were divided not just by age and race, but by class as well. And nowhere was this division more apparent than among young people. While middle-class students railed against traditional values and protested the war, their working-class contemporaries were more likely to treat religion and patriotism as bastions of stability in a fractured world.[22] As a result, they had little sympathy for the rebellion of their more privileged counterparts, who seemed so ready to take for granted opportunities to which they could only aspire.[23] Preoccupied with bringing down the establishment, the children of mainline Protestantism appeared largely indifferent to the conservative resurgence underway among this "silent majority" in their midst.[24]

The degree to which educated young people had become hostile to their society was a source of bafflement and irritation even to the most well-disposed of their elders. Austin Warren, a distinguished literary critic and long-time professor of English, confessed in 1972 that "I try hard to sympathize with the young; but they seem to me so unlovely, so intolerant, so opinionated, so ungenerous. I find them inimical to any culture save their own limited and provincial sub- and counter-culture, and arrogant in their ignorance of history."[25] Similarly, Warren's fellow Episcopalian Nathan Pusey found himself increasingly at odds with the student body at Harvard, whose belligerence and dogmatism he struggled to comprehend. This estrangement came to a head in April 1969, when Pusey called in state police to eject a group of 300 protestors who had occupied the university's main administrative building.[26] Widely criticized for his decision to handle the situation with force, in February 1970 Pusey announced his intention to retire as president the following year.[27] Before going, though, he fired a parting shot at the students in his last Baccalaureate Address: "We talk about love while behaving in a thoroughly unlovely manner," he told the Class of 1971. "Some march and chant, smash windows, steal and misrepresent, burn automobiles and buildings.... Some do this daily, almost hourly, and yet talk about beauty in life and profess concern for justice and loveliness and peace! It is hard to discern in all this just who is kidding whom, but surely something is sadly mixed up."[28] Another prominent figure to retire early from his post during these years was Bishop Richard Emrich of Michigan. After twenty-seven years at the helm, he had become disillusioned by what he considered the excesses of the age.[29] Like Nathan Pusey, Emrich had once been hailed as a

204 PRIVILEGE AND PROPHECY

great liberal but was now branded a reactionary by those who had little interest in his past accomplishments.[30]

Still another pillar of the Episcopal establishment to step back from public life at this time was Stephen Bayne. For five years, he had served as the presiding bishop's chief lieutenant, a loyal and eloquent defender of his progressive agenda. Yet in the wake of the Special General Convention, it had become clear to Bayne that the church was headed for still more, not less, confrontation. He had had enough. In December 1969, he informed the Executive Council of his intention to resign as first vice president and deputy for program, effective the end of June 1970.[31] Though many interpreted his departure as a judgment on John Hines's controversial leadership, Bayne insisted this was not the case. That there should be disagreement within the Episcopal Church about its identity and mission was not the problem for him so much as the paucity of theological reflection accompanying these debates. Thus, amidst all the turmoil of South Bend, what had disappointed him most was the convention's rejection of a proposed Advisory Council on the Church's Teaching, an initiative he hoped would promote a more informed discourse. Writing to Ivol Curtis in light of this defeat, Bayne reiterated his view that the gravest deficiency facing Episcopalians "is our inability across the board to come to grips with our history theologically, and find the new and deeper level of obedience in mission which we lack." After leaving Episcopal Church Center, he joined the faculty of General Seminary, devoting his final working years to teaching and serving, in his words, as a "link between the Church that is and that which was."[32]

In doing what he could to bridge the generational divide, Bayne recognized that the repudiation of history was indicative of the larger authority crisis in American life. Somehow, the church had to find new ways to inspire reverence for its heritage at a time when familiar concepts such as discipline and obedience had become anathema. "Discipline too easily sounds like conformity," he conceded, "and obedience awakens unhappy echoes of repression and authoritarianism. We rightly distrust and resent authoritarianism, without reflecting deeply enough on the fact that the sting of authoritarianism is precisely that it does not reflect authority but merely coercive power. It is a substitute for authority." The challenge, as Bayne had already noted in the 1967 report *Theological Freedom and Social Responsibility*, was to develop new forms of decision-making that upheld the church's essential authority while in some way accommodating modern sensibilities.[33] With traditional notions of leadership now widely under attack, however, it was by no means certain how mainline churches would achieve and enforce consensus in the future.[34] The problem was especially acute for Episcopalians, who had always relied upon their hierarchy to not just govern the institution but collectively embody the principles of order and unity as well.[35] Such assumptions were fast disappearing, as Bishop Robert Brown of Arkansas acknowledged prior to his retirement. "Our revolutionary world has destroyed every sentimental image a bishop may have about himself," he observed in his final diocesan address.[36] Kim Myers corroborated this view a few years later in the pages of *Newsweek*. "It used to be that as a bishop you knew what your role was," but recently that role had become much more ambiguous and contested. "People today want someone to direct them, but not authority figures."[37] With the decline of inherited forms of social deference, bishops could no longer assume that their position alone guaranteed their flocks would follow wherever they led.

When General Convention convened again in the fall of 1970 in Houston, Episcopal leaders were manifestly struggling to hold together a divided church. In a pastoral letter entitled "A Call for Unity," the House of Bishops pleaded for greater forbearance on all sides. "Christ is crucified anew every time a liberal churchman sees in his conservative brother nothing but a fool," they wrote. "And Christ is crucified every time a conservative churchman sees a communist agent or a dupe in his liberal brother."[38] It was inevitable, though, that differences over GCSP would dominate the proceedings, as debate over its future was no longer just about minority empowerment but the integrity of the church itself. As such, more than a few delegates arrived in Texas ready for a fight.[39] "This program is killing the Episcopal Church," warned a deputy from Tennessee, claiming it had lost all support among his people.[40] By contrast, the Union of Black Clergy and Laymen proclaimed its readiness to defend GCSP against "conservative, reactionary dioceses," lest the institution forfeit its remaining credibility among people of color.[41] In his opening address on October 11, Bishop Hines admitted the program had polarized the church but maintained this was a price worth paying. Calling on Episcopalians to become "ministers of radical change," he therefore reaffirmed his commitment to GCSP and its administration.[42] Yet for all his compelling oratory, it was not obvious how much longer the presiding bishop could shield the program from the intense criticism both he and it were facing.[43]

In the event, the Houston convention agreed to renew GCSP for a second triennium, but only under certain conditions and with a reduced budget. The

206 PRIVILEGE AND PROPHECY

power of the Screening and Review Committee to recommend grants over the objections of local bishops had been a source of friction and complaint since the program started, as had the refusal of GCSP staff to disclose details of funding applications and field appraisals. The House of Deputies now sought to reform the process, mandating that bishops must be given advance notice of possible grants made in their jurisdiction, as well as provided with all relevant documentation. If a bishop chose to protest against the funding of a particular project, this objection could only be overridden by a majority of the full Executive Council.[44] Not least, it was hoped such constraints would prevent further support of groups believed to advocate violence, a recent practice many deputies were determined to end.[45] Advocates claimed that the new rules would preserve the principle of "no-strings-attached" empowerment, while at the same time preserving the rights of diocesan authority.[46] Backed by the black caucus, members of the GCSP staff reacted angrily, accusing the plan's sponsors of turning the Episcopal Church into "a chaplaincy to the oppressors."[47] Their fears were compounded when it emerged that the newly elected Executive Council would be of a decidedly more conservative bent, especially among the bishops. The notable exceptions to this trend were Oscar Carr, who had made such an impression at South Bend, and Charles Willie, who had been elected vice president of the House of Deputies.[48] GCSP may have survived for a further three years, but only just.[49]

What John Hines, Leon Modeste, and others could no longer afford to ignore was the fundamental mistrust characterizing relations between the national and local levels of the church. Reflecting on this problem in the wake of the General Convention, William Lea of *The Episcopalian* called for the creation of a new communications program, which would work to rebuild relationships and encourage congregations to express their priorities and values. "At present, staff make too many policy decisions which laymen are simply unwilling to follow," Lea argued. "Our leadership can inspire great movements, but leadership cannot force them, nor manipulate them."[50] In practical terms, the rift was most evident in the continuing decline in financial giving: by the close of 1970, over half of all dioceses had failed to meet their national quota.[51] What Bishop Hines termed members' "pocket-book rebellion" was plainly a protest against GCSP, though its negative impact was to be much more widespread.[52] With a projected budgetary shortfall of $2 million for 1971, Executive Vice President Roger Blanchard announced that Episcopal Church Center would reduce its staff by one-half during the first part of the new year, resulting in the loss of 100 employees.[53] Deep cuts were also made to funding for foreign missions, campus ministry, and a host of other initiatives with no immediate connection to empowerment.[54] At the same time, a gift of $750,000 from the Diocese of Rochester enabled the creation of a new Office of Development, charged with renewing support for the full range of national programs.[55] Celebrated for his ability to get along with churchpeople of all kinds, Oscar Carr was appointed director of the venture, prompting him to introduce himself thereafter as a "Mississippi cotton farmer, known sinner, and temporary church bureaucrat."[56]

The concern over money, however, had ceased to be just a matter of how much and also become an issue of what kind. One product of the social movements of the past decade was a growing structural critique of American capitalism that challenged Episcopalians to interrogate the sources of their own institutional wealth. Commenting on this process, William Stringfellow noted that "for generations, as it accumulated property and multiplied investments, the Episcopal Church refused to recognize the social and political import of such holdings," but now questions were being asked about "how far the Church has been supporting and profiting from weapons production, racism, ecological waste, redundant technology."[57] Following this line of inquiry, in early 1969 John Hines began pushing for divestment from apartheid South Africa, a proposal that met with immediate opposition from conservatives.[58] Undeterred, in early 1971 he called upon General Motors, in which the church was a substantial investor, to cease its operations in South Africa.[59] To drive home the point, Hines personally attended the annual GM shareholders' meeting to put forward a resolution to the same effect. Although the resolution was defeated, the episode signaled an important development in Episcopal thinking about the nature and extent of Christian social witness. In response, the Executive Council established a Committee on Social Responsibility in Investments to monitor the church's decision-making and to coordinate future lobbying efforts.[60] Over time, the Committee could point to a number of successes in influencing the policies of major corporate entities, among them Philips Petroleum, Polaroid Corporation, and Chase Manhattan Bank.[61] Nonetheless, this success highlighted a basic paradox that could not be easily overcome. The reason the Episcopal Church was in a position to apply pressure on these companies was because it benefited from the economic system permitting their problematic behavior in the first place.[62]

Someone well acquainted with pursuing reform from within was John Walker, who in the spring of 1971 was chosen to succeed Paul Moore as

208 PRIVILEGE AND PROPHECY

suffragan bishop of Washington.[63] Walker's elevation made him the third African American to join the current House of Bishops, alongside diocesan John Burgess of Massachusetts and suffragan Richard B. Martin of Long Island. Almost as soon as Moore's election in New York had been announced, a campaign was launched to ensure that a black priest would replace him in Washington.[64] Overriding claims of reverse discrimination, the 1970 Diocesan Convention formally endorsed this aspiration, leading all but two white candidates to withdraw their names from consideration.[65] Walker was duly consecrated by Bishop Hines in the National Cathedral on June 29, with Bishop José Antonio Ramos of Costa Rica preaching.[66] In his charge, Ramos enjoined his friend to stand at "the forefront of the forces of liberation" overcoming the oppression that the "white, western, so-called Christian West has sown throughout the world."[67] Yet as some of his supporters were soon to discover, Walker's approach to changing society—in contrast to that of his predecessor—had little to do with making bold gestures or grabbing headlines. "I'm not interested in statements," he told an interviewer a few years later. "I'm interested in hard work. Blasting this group or that one isn't social action; that's an ego trip and I'm not on an ego trip."[68] For Walker, true and lasting reform came about mainly through conversion, rather than confrontation. To that end, he worked quietly but assiduously to promote contact and cooperation between Washington's wealthy, white elite and its impoverished black majority.[69] "We must know the poor and not content ourselves with social theories and pious illusions," he counseled. "Know the poor and you begin to know the darkness of our collective existence as a society. Know the poor and you begin to understand that the Church itself is poor before God."[70]

Even as Episcopalians continued to agonize over the nature of their responsibilities in the realms of race and class, the future of women within the institution was likewise becoming an urgent matter. Since its inception, the Episcopal Church had functioned on the basis of gender segregation, with nearly all positions of leadership reserved for men.[71] But alongside this male hierarchy had also developed a kind of female "parallel church," consisting of various guilds and organizations that played an essential role in the church's ministry and mission.[72] It was only with increasing professional opportunities for women and the advent of second-wave feminism during the 1960s that this arrangement was called into question.[73] Slowly the doors of the seminaries began to open, with ETS admitting women in 1958, followed by VTS in 1961 and the Seminary of the Southwest and Church Divinity School of the Pacific a few years later.[74] In 1966, a committee of bishops studying the possibility of women in ordained ministry concluded the burden of proof was on those who opposed it, for to do so was "to hold that the whole trend of modern culture is wrong in its attitude toward the place of women in society."[75] Having supported the civil rights movement for African Americans, a growing number of Episcopal women began asking why they, too, should not enjoy full recognition within their own community.[76] This comparison between racial and gender equality resonated powerfully with progressives, who already felt self-conscious about the caution with which the Episcopal Church tended to embrace social change.[77] The decision of the 1970 General Convention to admit women to the diaconate but withhold access to the priesthood and episcopate therefore struck them as precisely the kind of gradualist approach to be eschewed.[78]

An organized campaign to secure women's ordination at the next General Convention took shape during the final months of 1971. A prime mover in this effort was Suzanne R. Hiatt (1936–2002), who had graduated from Radcliffe in 1958 and earned her M.Div. from ETS six years later. Having trained as a social worker at Boston University, she coordinated urban welfare projects in Philadelphia before joining the diocesan staff of Bishop DeWitt in 1970.[79] It became clear to Hiatt and other activists that despite the support of individual bishops, the episcopal bench as a whole remained tentative about next steps. This suspicion was confirmed when, at a special meeting in October 1971, the House of Bishops rejected a formal call to endorse women's ordination and instead referred the matter for further study.[80] A week later, at a conference on church work taking place at Virginia Seminary, the Episcopal Women's Caucus (EWC) was formed in direct response to this refusal. In an open letter to the Presiding Bishop, the newly constituted Caucus stated that "we decline to participate in further betrayal of ourselves and our sisters. . . . We call upon all women seriously to consider their own predicament in the church and make no peace with oppression."[81] Eager to avoid a conflict between the activists and the hierarchy, Robert DeWitt recognized that he and other bishops in favor of women's ordination must take a more active role in promoting it. Not least, he felt a pastoral responsibility to those, like Hiatt, whom he had ordained to the diaconate but to whom he could offer no such path to the priesthood.[82]

On the other side of the debate was Kim Myers of California, whose Anglo-Catholic traditionalism led him to speak out against the possibility of female priests. In a paper presented to the bishops' meeting in October, Myers cited a number of reasons why priestly ministry should remain available only to

210 PRIVILEGE AND PROPHECY

men. First and foremost, he argued, "a priest is a 'God symbol' whether he likes it or not," and throughout scripture God is represented with masculine imagery. So, even though the divine nature is by definition beyond gender, nonetheless "the male image about God pertains to the divine initiative in creation. Initiative is, in itself, a male rather than a female attribute." By the same logic, he reasoned, it is the maternal receptivity of the Blessed Virgin Mary, not the masculine assertiveness of Christ, that offers a paradigm for the ministry of women. Aside from these considerations, Myers also worried about the impact female priests would have on ecumenical relations with the Roman and Orthodox churches.[83] Unsurprisingly, the bishop's paper incensed pro-ordination activists, who dismissed his ideas as a jumble of unreconstructed patriarchy.[84] But it was left to William Wolf, longtime professor of theology at ETS, to identify a more specific problem. Given Anglicans' devotion to the historic threefold order, whereby deacons, priests, and bishops are held to constitute the ordained ministry in its totality, why had Myers not objected with similar zeal to the admission of women to the diaconate? "Just as priests are the commissioned agents of Christ and share His priesthood, so deacons are commissioned agents of Christ and share His diaconate," observed Wolf. "Plainly if women cannot represent the male Christ in His priesthood, they cannot by the bishop's argument represent His diaconate either." Yet even as he made this point, Wolf acknowledged that it was emotion, rather than reason, that would dictate the terms of the emerging debate.[85]

While the battle lines over women's ordination were being drawn within the church, the conflict in Southeast Asia continued to confuse and divide the nation at large. The court martial of Lieutenant William Calley in early 1971 for the My Lai Massacre underscored the profound discomfort many people felt about the war and its conduct.[86] "The conviction of the young man has touched the raw nerve," Frank Sayre asserted in the *New York Times* after the trial. "It is a moment of paroxysm in the nation's conscience." Though he was certain Calley must be held accountable for his individual actions, the dean also called upon Americans to take responsibility for what was being done in their name.[87] Writing in the pages of the same paper a few weeks later, Paul Moore assumed an even more stringent tone, criticizing his fellow Christians for failing to speak out boldly against policies they claimed to oppose.[88] Moore himself attracted controversy when he permitted the People's Coalition for Peace and Justice to hold an anti-war fundraising event in the Cathedral of St. John the Divine in early December. Drawing nearly 5,000 people, the gathering featured well-known figures such as Norman Mailer,

Tennessee Williams, Gloria Steinem, and Charles Mingus. Organizer Dotson Rader later explained how important it had been to secure Bishop Moore's support, for it had not only guaranteed a large venue but lent "much needed respectability" to both the event and the Coalition.[89] Perhaps inevitably, some Episcopalians criticized Moore for allowing the Cathedral to be used in this way. The bishop, however, was unrepentant, countering that "to worship the God Jesus is blasphemy unless we join hands with everyone who is working for peace."[90]

By the time he formally succeeded Horace Donegan as bishop of New York in May 1972, there was no doubt Moore would continue to deploy the stature and resources of the diocese on behalf of progressive causes.[91] Notwithstanding a propensity to make fashionably countercultural statements, he retained his faith in the inherited church structures, insisting that by them "we can wield some weight on behalf of those whose lives are the offscouring of a busy America. These are tools for the work of loving. . . . It is in this time and place and with these tools that we are set down to do our work."[92] And while he conceded such activism was bound to put pressure on his parish clergy, Moore remained adamant that as bishop he had a responsibility to broach difficult topics. "The more controversial the action," he reasoned, "the more emotionally involved people become, and therefore, the more open they are to hearing the rationale behind the action as well as the issues spoken to."[93] If this remark reflects Moore's commitment to the principle of episcopal leadership, it also bespeaks an underlying confidence in his own powers of persuasion. At a time when many church leaders had become self-conscious and uncertain about their relationship to power, he continued to draw upon his place in the WASP elite to challenge conservative attitudes. This was evident when a group of wealthy New Yorkers complained about his decision to appoint an African American to the board of an Episcopal mission society. Having listened to their arguments about why doing so would be socially inappropriate, Moore finally had enough. "Don't give me any more stuff about Groton and Princeton," he snapped. "St. Paul's and Yale tell me different."[94] The ability to address even the most powerful as his equals had long been one of Moore's advantages as a liberal clergyman. But in the context of the church as a whole, it had started to feel like the vestige of a former time.

For as the 1970s took hold, it became apparent that the Protestant establishment which Moore personified had in fact begun to splinter.[95] Within the Episcopal Church, the networks of class, wealth, and education that had once secured its place in the upper echelons of American society and bound together its clergy and laity now ceased to command the same levels of loyalty from either.[96] In the eyes of William Stringfellow, such change was a liberation, for it signaled a belated end to the "Constantinian Accommodation"—his term for Christianity's movement from persecuted sect to the dominant religion of the Roman Empire in the fourth century. Ever since, he declared, the Western Church had maintained a "vested interest in the established order," exemplified by the way the Episcopal Church was now "culpably identified with the institutional status quo in culture and society, in economics and politics, in warfare and imperialism, in racism and sexism." Only by relinquishing their association with these forms of dominance could Episcopalians hope to reclaim the integrity of an apostolic witness.[97] While Stringfellow regarded the Protestant establishment's disintegration as an unqualified good for both church and society, others were not so sure. Writing in *Newsweek*, veteran journalist Stewart Alsop worried that however arrogant the old WASP elite sometimes may have been, no one of comparable ability and coherence had emerged to take their place.[98] Meanwhile, State Department official Stephen R. Lyne wondered why, when Americans desperately needed a "new national synthesis of values," Episcopal leaders proved so ineffectual in contributing to this process.[99] Increasingly inclined to view temporal power and moral authority as mutually exclusive, they appeared ashamed of their links to the former while diffident about asserting the latter.[100] Above all, they gave off the impression of being embarrassed by their own constituency.[101]

Renewing and strengthening communication among the different levels of the church was a priority for Oscar Carr when he took over the national Office of Development in early 1971.[102] To that end, he recruited a team of over a hundred bishops, priests, deacons, and laypeople to gather opinion from across the dioceses during the autumn of 1972. A summary of the group's findings, entitled "What We Learned from What You Said," was published the following spring.[103] Predictably, the exercise revealed that even though many Episcopalians still affirmed the principle "of helping people to help themselves," they had become highly dissatisfied with the administration of GCSP and its hold over the national agenda. In focusing so assiduously upon social action, their leaders had neglected the equally important areas of spiritual development, education, and evangelism. The point was not to swing from one extreme to another, they felt, but to treat these realms as "interrelated, each dependent upon and growing out of the other." In this respect, religious empowerment of individuals and congregations within the church was just as important as social and economic empowerment of groups outside of it. Those surveyed were especially critical of the sharp cuts that had been made to Christian education programs and higher education chaplaincy in the push to fund GCSP. Recognizing the seismic changes in youth culture during the past decade, they were emphatic that more should be done "to assimilate and hold young people in the life of the church."[104] Here again, it felt like a false distinction between nurture and reform had been imposed, one that was damaging the church's own future.

Over the course of the next several years, Carr traveled the country extensively, engaging Episcopalians in the question of how to rediscover a shared sense of identity and purpose. Along the way, he displayed a talent for expressing unsettling ideas in sympathetic terms, combining a humorous tone with an underlying seriousness about the church's mission. Reflecting the desire of his co-religionists for a more holistic approach to Christian life, he acknowledged that social action was not the only criterion for gauging authentic discipleship. "I want to make it perfectly clear that I do not view the Church as having to justify its existence by being the superstar of the problem solvers," he told one gathering. "Salvation and solution are two entirely different words."[105] At the same time, he refused to downplay the moral demands of Christianity. Preaching before a congregation in Monroe, Louisiana, he raised the issue of integrated neighborhoods to illustrate the point. If he and other Southern liberals were truly committed to human equality, they needed to be honest about the personal sacrifices involved. "To decide that you are going to be involved in fair housing and sell your home to a black in an all-white suburb," Carr maintained, "means that you are going to be unable to help your white neighbors[,] who consider you a traitor to the white middle class."[106] With similar candor, he pushed Episcopalians to ask why, with the wealthiest membership of any denomination in America, they still ranked forty-fourth among church groups in per capita giving.[107] In an address to the Episcopal Churchwomen of New York, he claimed that communicants in their diocese enjoyed a combined income of approximately $1 billion annually. He further explained that if these same people were on welfare benefits instead and then gave 10% of their income, the receipts would still be five times what was actually received in 1971.[108] As much as Episcopalians were inclined to blame the national leadership for the church's problems, Carr persistently challenged them to look for solutions closer to home.[109]

214　PRIVILEGE AND PROPHECY

Meanwhile, John Hines surprised everyone by announcing his intention to step down as presiding bishop in May 1974, well over two years before the completion of his term in office. After nearly three decades as a bishop, he cited exhaustion as the chief reason for his decision.[110] When the House of Bishops met in New Orleans at the end of October 1972, he thanked his colleagues for "the patience with which you have regarded my idiosyncrasies, and the restraint with which you have tempered my excesses"—a passing acknowledgement of the upheaval that had so often distinguished his tenure.[111] Whether Hines was retiring early due to fatigue or because of his growing unpopularity soon became a source of debate.[112] Another critical development in New Orleans was the bishops' decision, based on the recommendation of the committee appointed the previous year, to endorse the principle of women's ordination to the priesthood and episcopate. By a vote of 74 to 61, the House mandated that a formal resolution amending the canons should be put to the General Convention in 1973.[113] Asked why he had voted in favor of this change, Bishop Emrich of Michigan explained that even though "much nonsense is talked by some women's liberation groups, a far greater nonsense is talked by arrogant men. People should be treated as individuals, and we ought to stop our sweeping statements about women as we ought to stop them about race."[114] In a similar vein, Bishop McNairy of Minnesota affirmed the ordination of women theologically but rejected any effort to justify it on the grounds of feminism.[115] Yet this desire to frame the issue separately from the wider women's movement underscored a fundamental difference between the bishops and the activists championing the cause. For the latter, secular ideas about gender equality were not merely incidental to their outlook; they were in fact central to it.[116]

Despite his decision to leave office, John Hines remained a staunch defender of GCSP in the months to follow. A new round of controversy beset the program in mid-December, when Bishop Wilburn C. Campbell of West Virginia resigned from the Screening and Review Committee, citing various "personal, emotional frustrations" he had experienced while fulfilling his role. Enumerating these to the Executive Council, he characterized the attitude of the committee as one of basic hostility to the church, such that "there have been moments when I felt that I was meeting about Black Muslims and not Christianity." The bishop went on to criticize the program staff's lack of organization, its bias for and against certain types of grant application, and its disregard for financial accountability. All this led him to conclude that the Screening and Review Committee served as little more than a "rubber stamp" for a decision-making process impossible to pin down. None of these complaints was new, but Campbell's episcopal standing made his charges difficult to ignore. Hines's response to his colleague was telling. Bypassing the issues raised, he argued that the real problem lay not so much with the administration of GCSP as with privileged white people unaccustomed to minorities in positions of leadership. As such, he believed that instead of questioning staff members, church authorities should seek to learn from them, remarking that "I am not always sure that as bishops we either understand this accurately or respond to it in a mature fashion."[117] For Hines at least, GCSP had evolved into a highly personal form of spiritual catharsis.[118] The conflicts it provoked were therefore to be embraced as intrinsic to its function.

What this episode finally reveals is the degree to which the presiding bishop had come to share in the anti-institutional assumptions of the GCSP staff.[119] When concerns about the program again featured at the Executive Council meeting in February, he continued to deflect the criticism, preferring to focus on what he branded the "conviction-fatigue" of the wider church.[120] This readiness to reproach the membership, rather than concede any limitations in the program itself, bespoke a tension at the heart of Hines's leadership. The Episcopal Church he had been elected to preside over a decade earlier was buoyant and well-resourced, and it was precisely because of this that he was able to initiate GCSP in the first place. In the years that followed, however, Hines increasingly used the program as a tool for challenging establishmentarian structures and values, even as he continued to rely upon the institution to advance his agenda. When the erosion of these same structures and values eventually led to a diminishment in the power of the national church, he refused to accept that his own policies had invited this result.[121] Instead, he simply concluded that his co-religionists had proved unequal to his prophetic vision of the church as an agent of transformation.[122] While this judgment undoubtedly applied to some, it willfully overlooked many Episcopalians who had sought to contribute to the empowerment program and were not only rebuffed but insulted while doing so.[123]

News of Bishop Hines's forthcoming retirement was accompanied by two other events in late 1972 which compounded the feeling that progressivism was now in retreat. The first was the passing of W. B. Spofford, Sr., who as editor of *The Witness* had provided a platform for liberal opinion in the church for over fifty years. Publication of the magazine ceased abruptly with his death, and it was unclear whether or when it might resume

216   PRIVILEGE AND PROPHECY

under new leadership.[124] Shortly thereafter, Robert DeWitt dismayed some and delighted others by announcing his intention to step down as bishop of Pennsylvania in June 1974 at the age of only fifty-six. He denied succumbing to the oft-repeated calls for his resignation, although he admitted his unpopularity among conservatives had begun to inhibit the causes he sought to advance.[125] Still, as with Bishop Hines, it was clear the decision to retire did not mean DeWitt was giving up. During the first half of 1973, the two men invited a group of activists to Seabury House in Connecticut for a series of consultations about the future of Christian social witness.[126] Nicknamed the "Seabury Caucus," the assembly included figures such as Jane Barney, David Garcia, David Gracie, Robert Potter, William Stringfellow, and Hugh White. From these conversations emerged an initiative known as "Church and Society," which Bishop DeWitt hoped might fulfill "something like the purpose of the Church League for Industrial Democracy of a generation ago."[127] He reasoned that just as CLID had educated Episcopalians about economic injustice in the 1920s and 1930s, so Church and Society should confront them in the present with those "structural problems in our society which go deeper than merely ameliorative efforts can reach."[128] Along the way, he believed "a new and progressive leadership network" could be fostered, one which would set the course for Episcopal outreach and mission in the years to come.[129]

DeWitt was not unique in recognizing that the liberal wing of the church must adapt itself to the post-sixties dispensation. With the 1973 General Convention taking place in Louisville in the autumn, groups such as the Union of Black Episcopalians, the Church and City Conference, and Episcopal Peace Fellowship joined together in forming Coalition E, an alliance designed to push progressive causes at the national level.[130] This strategy was to bear fruit in the elections for Executive Council, with Coalition E candidates winning seven of the thirteen available seats.[131] Such a demonstration of solidarity, however, could do little to counteract the mood of reaction that was to dominate the proceedings as a whole.[132] Anticipating this shift, John Hines used his opening address to strike a defiant note, calling upon delegates not to abandon their commitment to the poor and marginalized. "The pressure of the powerful, whose privilege is challenged by articulate spokesmen for the deprived minorities, may be causing the timid and self-serving to beat a 'strategic retreat,'" he warned. Rather than take refuge in the comfortable and familiar, though, Episcopalians must be willing to surrender their place among "the carriage-trade clientele of our society" and instead become "a witnessing community of unquestioned integrity." If the institution continued to suffer diminution as a result, then so be it.[133] Yet even as he spoke these words, Hines and his supporters knew that the GCSP approach to empowerment was at its end.[134] In the preceding months, they had drawn up plans for a replacement entity called Community Action and Development, in the hope of salvaging elements of the program in a more conventional form. Among other things, this new agency would oversee the work of four separate ethnic ministries or "desks," all of which were to be placed on an equal footing.[135] In deliberate contrast to GCSP, this revised structure would also be administered directly by the Executive Council, a provision essential to its acceptance by the 1973 Convention.[136]

The final repudiation of John Hines's vision came with the election of John Maury Allin to succeed him as presiding bishop. As bishop of Mississippi, Allin had actively opposed the national church's involvement in local struggles over civil rights and later became a vocal critic of GCSP as well. In so doing, he clashed repeatedly with figures such as John Coburn and Paul Moore, making no secret of his belief that leadership of the church was unfairly dominated by East Coast liberals.[137] Standing in the election alongside Robert Spears of Rochester, Christoph Keller of Arkansas, John Burt of Ohio, and Kim Myers of California, Allin emerged as the candidate for conservative Episcopalians from the South and Midwest who felt their priorities had been neglected.[138] Nonetheless, his selection by the House of Bishops ran into unprecedented resistance from the House of Deputies, whose members engaged in a three-hour debate before voting their assent by a narrow margin.[139] As a Southerner with a preference for traditional models of evangelism and pastoral care, it was perhaps inevitable Allin should face suspicion among those committed to the Hines model of activism.[140] Openly acknowledging their fears, he sought to reassure opponents in his acceptance speech. "Let it be understood, in my most Southern accent," he proclaimed, "that I consider the mission of the Church to include the dignity of people and empowering of those who are depressed, oppressed, and deprived."[141] But he also made it clear, as he would repeatedly in the years to come, that the distinction between service to those within the church and those outside it was to him largely a false one. "We need to nurture our people if they are to reach out in mission with renewed strength," he insisted. "Self-determination, yes, by all means—for all people, including the people in our pews."[142]

In his bid to heal a divided church, Bishop Allin encountered his first major task almost immediately. Just hours after his confirmation, the House

218 PRIVILEGE AND PROPHECY

of Deputies rejected the House of Bishops' resolution approving the ordination of women to the priesthood and episcopate.[143] The verdict stunned members of the EWC, who had come to Louisville cautiously optimistic about the outcome. Carter Heyward, who alongside Sue Hiatt had emerged as one of the primary figures of the movement, recalled her shock when the result was announced: "I felt nauseated, sick, and immobile, as my eyes gazed out upon the arena of deputies who had torn us apart as surely as if they had been lions and we, those early Christians whom no one would believe." A cradle Episcopalian from North Carolina, Heyward (b. 1945) had attended Randolph-Macon College in Virginia before earning an M.A. in Comparative Religion from Columbia and an M.Div. degree from Union Theological Seminary. During her studies at Union she was admitted to the postulancy under Bishop Moore, which in turn led to her ordination as a deacon in June 1973.[144] Amidst their grief and anger at what had taken place, Heyward, Hiatt, and other EWC activists issued a public statement addressed to the Convention, questioning the legitimacy of the canonical process itself: "We have in common with you and with each other a basic humanity, established by Christ, in which vocational response to God . . . is *not* a 'debatable option,'" they wrote. "It is not, in fact, something a House of Deputies or of Bishops can ultimately legislate." The women affirmed their determination to carry on the struggle and called upon others to join them.[145] In retrospect, some of them realized there had been fundamental flaws in their Louisville strategy: the movement was too concentrated in the Northeast, and not enough had been done to foster relations with groups such as the Episcopal Church Women (ECW). They concluded that such problems must be addressed if a positive result were to be secured in 1976. Meanwhile, however, others began to talk seriously of pursuing ordination without bothering to wait for the approval of General Convention.[146]

Church progressives did little to conceal their contempt for the new presiding bishop. No sooner had the convention ended than his fellow Mississippian Charles Granville Hamilton attacked John Allin in the pages of *The Churchman*, dismissing him as "a retreaded Southern Baptist [who] has never been accused of having religion."[147] Allin was to suffer an even more direct assault when meeting with the leadership of UBCL, who subjected him to the tactic of "mau-mauing," defined by Edward Rodman as "the art of verbal abuse taken to the brink of physical confrontation." In recalling the incident, Rodman reports that Allin "endured this indignity with aplomb," though why a group of Christians should deliberately accord anyone such treatment he does not say.[148] A particularly vocal critic of the presiding bishop in the years following would be John Shelby Spong, who was elected bishop coadjutor of Newark in 1976. A native of North Carolina, Spong (1931–2021) attended local public schools in Charlotte before graduating Phi Beta Kappa from Chapel Hill in 1952. He proceeded directly to VTS, where he earned his M.Div. degree in 1955. He then served parishes in North Carolina for a decade until relocating to the Diocese of Virginia, first as rector of St. John's Lynchburg and latterly of St. Paul's Richmond. Inspired by the theological writings of John A. T. Robinson and the liberationist discourses of the sixties and seventies, Spong continued to move further and further away from doctrinal Christianity in the course of his ministry.[149] An ardent admirer of John Hines, he condemned Bishop Allin as "a man who replaced creative vision with an unthinking reaction wrapped in the language of a dishonest and threadbare piety."[150] In the face of such personal animus, it was difficult to see how anyone could hope to reconcile the polarized body the Episcopal Church had become.

Of course, liberals were right to suspect that John Allin possessed not just a different set of priorities from his predecessor but a whole different conception of leadership. Despite, or perhaps even because of, the conflict and confusion they experienced during his tenure, many felt John Hines had shown that the presiding bishop could indeed serve as a modern prophet, empowering his people to embrace new forms of faith and witness.[151] Bishop Allin, on the other hand, was adamant in rejecting this model of ministry, not only in practice but also on principle. "My understanding of the New Testament and my experience of Christian mission is that God chooses prophets, [and] none of them wanted to be," he explained later. "One of the confusions we have is in terms of electing an administrator as over against God choosing a prophet. . . . We have great difficulty when you have a bishop who decides he's going to be a prophet." He did not question the right of figures such as Hines, James Pike, or Paul Moore to deliver a prophetic message, but he doubted the responsibility of doing so while running the national church or overseeing a large diocese. To Allin, bishops should first and foremost strive to be figures of unity, rather than sources of contention. Moreover, he marveled at the apparent lack of irony among those who assumed the prophetic mantle, even as they continued to occupy positions of privilege in both church and society.[152] Fueling this analysis was an abiding resentment about the way Southern Episcopalians had been treated by their Northern counterparts during the civil rights movement. Allin allowed some

220 PRIVILEGE AND PROPHECY

of this bitterness to show when paying tribute to his home state of Mississippi during his installation service in June 1974: "It is a mysterious and lovely land and the Lord is there as He is in Minnesota, Massachusetts, Montana and Maine," he declared. "Oh yes, we are populated by the same sort of human beings with whom God has populated the rest of the world. That's why we so frequently can have our problems identified." If being prophetic meant focusing on the shortcomings of others and disrupting the church in the process, the new presiding bishop wanted no part of it.[153]

By contrast, people who felt the Episcopal Church required not less but still more disruption were those spearheading the campaign for women's ordination to the priesthood. Galvanized by their disappointment in Louisville the previous month, a group of deacons assembled in late November to discuss strategy with their bishops and other senior clergy sympathetic to their cause. The meeting ultimately broke down over the question of whether the bishops were prepared to ordain the women without prior consent from General Convention. When the bishops baulked at this prospect, the deacons walked out.[154] In early December, two of the deacons, Carter Heyward and Carol Anderson, met again with Bishop Moore, accompanied by John Coburn, to state their intention to present themselves "as a witness" at the priestly ordinations about to take place at St. John the Divine. Recounting this exchange, Heyward highlights the sense of mutual incomprehension at work between the women and the men: "Carol and I continued to speak of justice, human rights, and being female in the Church. . . . And the two male priests—both bright, sensitive, earnest clergymen with longstanding commitments to justice and human rights—stared at us as if we were speaking a foreign language." She goes on to explain that only when they spoke of their cause explicitly in terms of "God" did Moore and Coburn "register any signs of comprehension"—perhaps not so strange or surprising a reaction as Heyward intimates. When the women did indeed come forward and kneel before the bishop during the service a few days later, he was visibly moved but still refrained from ordaining them. Even though she knew at the time Moore "meant us no harm, no injustice, no 'personal' rejection," Heyward still concludes that "as a bishop of the Church, he had dealt us as real a blow as if he had flailed us with his crozier."[155] It was left to Pauli Murray to reflect on the situation in less emotive terms. Writing to Bishop Moore the following day, she acknowledged that "we are still caught in a cruel dilemma. What if the next step is not within the customary framework of canonical procedure? . . . I pray that somehow we will all be led to find a way."[156]

NO LOVE WITHOUT JUSTICE   221

Alongside the question of who should be entrusted with leading worship in the Episcopal Church was the question of what form this worship should take in the modern age. The historic importance of the *Book of Common Prayer* in the emergence and development of Anglican identity is difficult to overstate.[157] When they separated from the Church of England in 1789, American Episcopalians quickly promulgated their own version of the book, which, with minor changes in 1892 and 1928, remained normative well into the post-war period.[158] By the 1960s, however, the impact of the ecumenical and liturgical movements prompted a more ambitious program of revision, and in 1967, General Convention approved new liturgies for trial use.[159] This initiative led to over a decade of consultation, during which congregations across the country were invited to respond to a succession of experimental rites. While this approach helped ensure the eventual acceptance of a new prayer book, it also provided a platform for a small but vocal minority adamantly opposed to reform of any kind.[160] In the face of such resistance, church leaders sought to reassure the anxious, encouraging them to embrace the process as an exercise in managed change.[161] Still, the prospect of losing the 1928 text was deeply unsettling to many, for whom it represented continuity and order, especially at a time when so much else seemed uncertain.[162] In addition to the personal consolations that the old book provided, advocates pointed to the unifying role it had played among Episcopalians across divisions of class, race, and region. They doubted that whatever might replace it could ever elicit the same level of loyalty and respect.[163]

As plans for a contemporary *Book of Common Prayer* gathered pace during the early 1970s, it became clear just how much the enterprise depended on parish clergy to promote the modern services in a positive manner. This was by no means a given, as many priests themselves had been profoundly shaped by the language and sensibilities of the inherited rites. Frank Griswold, who later served as presiding bishop from 1998 to 2006, recalls how difficult some older clergy found letting go of the traditional liturgy: "they had so identified themselves with those rhythms, with those patterns of speech, that they felt lost—they didn't know who they were any longer with this new order and these new words." In churches where the rector made plain his resentment, the laypeople would frequently adopt a negative attitude as well. On the other hand, if a priest was in favor of the revisions but failed to accommodate his people's grief or became impatient with their slowness to adapt, they were again likely to feel frustrated and angry.[164] Charles Price, who became one of the chief architects of the whole project, was highly sensitive to the pastoral

222 PRIVILEGE AND PROPHECY

issues at stake. Having left Harvard in 1972 to resume teaching at VTS, Price impressed upon seminarians the importance of affording parishioners the necessary time and space to adjust to the changes being introduced.[165] John Snow of ETS also supported a new prayer book while still empathizing with those who found the transition traumatic. "For some Episcopalians, the change was like having a limb amputated and replaced by a viable artificial limb," he recalled. "One is grateful for the new, but it doesn't exactly replace the old; one forgets that the old was amputated for good reason. It had lost its function. One remembers it as perfectly one's own, and one feels the loss painfully as one limps along on the new, trying to get used to it."[166]

The prayer book eventually ratified by General Convention in 1979 tried to mollify conservatives by including traditional language versions of the Daily Office, Eucharist, and Collects, alongside the range of modern liturgies.[167] Citing the ideal of Anglican comprehensiveness, Bishop Coleman McGhee commended this solution to his people in Michigan, assuring them that "the Prayer Book is not being abandoned by the Episcopal Church, nor is it being embalmed. It is being expanded and enriched to be a worthy vehicle of the common worship of all of us."[168] Duncan Gray, who had succeeded John Allin as bishop of Mississippi, likewise promoted the new book, though he privately regretted what he considered its downplaying of human sinfulness.[169] Others detected this shift as well, noting that penitential themes were now counter-balanced in the modern rites by an emphasis on praise and thanksgiving.[170] Another, even more obvious change was the incorporation of Anglo-Catholic sacramental practices into the mainstream of church life. The Eucharist was now expected to replace Morning Prayer as the primary form of Sunday worship, and the use of incense, personal confession, and other "high church" practices were presented as standard features of Episcopal worship.[171] While some bemoaned these allowances as a betrayal of their Reformation heritage, Bishop Burgess of Massachusetts was determined to keep the whole business in perspective. Preaching at his cathedral in Boston, he wondered aloud why those so exercised about liturgical reform were "not equally upset about the Church's failure to minister to the needs of people who are in desperate want in our society. It is blasphemous that we should be upset because a word in the Lord's Prayer has been changed and are not upset because little children live in rat-infested tenements."[172] If Burgess exaggerated here for effect, he nonetheless gave voice to a growing concern that the church was turning in on itself and thereby failing in its wider mission.[173] Although he did not disagree, Charles Price remained adamant that "we must get these in-house matters behind us. To the extent that our life is invested in them, we must lose that life."[174] Merely to ignore such issues or disparage their importance was in fact to invite a whole other set of problems.

Nowhere were the perils of discounting the church's internal life more evident than in the area of ministry to students and young people. Having devoted considerable time and resources to building up a network of college chaplaincies after the Second World War, the Episcopal Church increasingly neglected this work in the course of the late 1960s and early 1970s.[175] To some degree this was true of all the mainline denominations, as they looked for new ways of relating to the counterculture and anti-establishment sensibilities now prevalent in America.[176] But with the advent of GCSP, Episcopal leaders in particular embraced a dramatic recalibration of priorities, and their focus on empowerment permanently altered the standing of campus ministry and education programs in the life of the church.[177] Partly this was a matter of money: by 1974, national youth and college work programs had suffered massive cuts to budget and personnel.[178] At a more fundamental level, though, the shift suggested that cultivating Episcopal identity among the young was simply no longer regarded as of primary importance.[179] Chaplains and educators were not slow to point out the self-defeating logic of this attitude. For good or for ill, university campuses had become the place where the language and values of the nation's future leaders were shaped. It was therefore essential that the church should retain a strong voice and visible presence in this setting.[180] More specifically, college chaplaincies remained crucial to the formation and nurture of the church's own future leaders, lay and ordained. To treat such ministry as a self-indulgent habit that Episcopalians could no longer afford was, as one veteran chaplain later put it, "metaphorically cutting off the nose to spite the face."[181]

While most Americans in the summer of 1974 were preoccupied with the Watergate scandal and the downfall of Richard Nixon, the Episcopal Church was undergoing a major authority crisis all its own. In the second week of July, retired bishops Daniel Corrigan, Robert DeWitt, and Edward Welles issued a public letter, announcing their intention to ordain "some several women deacons" to the priesthood on Monday, July 29. In pursuing this course, they acknowledged their defiance of General Convention but noted that the majority of bishops and deputies were actually in favor of women's ordination. Yet it was neither church politics nor even pastoral concern that had brought them to this point, the three men explained. Rather, it was their sense of being

224 PRIVILEGE AND PROPHECY

compelled by the Holy Spirit, and in this regard, their action should be taken as "an act of solidarity with those in whatever institution, in whatever part of the world, of whatever stratum of society, who in their search for freedom, for liberation, for dignity, are moved by that same Spirit . . . to walk in newness of life."[182] Here a logic of emancipation, born of their social activism in the sixties, was now being applied by the bishops against their own church as an agent of spiritual bondage. In the process, they managed to antagonize opponents and allies alike. The most prominent among the former was the presiding bishop himself, who received no warning of their plans, which he learned of only by reading the *New York Times*.[183] Similarly caught off guard was Paul Moore, who felt not only personally deceived but convinced this approach would harm the cause he and others had been pushing through official channels.[184] Another key supporter to oppose the action was Ned Cole of Central New York. Even as he reiterated his commitment to women in ministry, Bishop Cole emphasized that non-canonical ordinations would undermine not just episcopal authority but that of the "entire corporate body of the church."[185]

As news spread about what was being planned, others echoed the view that the primary issue was not the legitimacy of women's ordination but the flouting of the church's procedures for collective decision-making.[186] Given that the proposed ordinations were to take place in Philadelphia, the problem was by no means an abstract one for Lyman Ogilby, who had succeeded Robert DeWitt as bishop of Pennsylvania the previous January. Ogilby (1922–1990) was the scion of a distinguished Episcopal family.[187] Educated at the Loomis School and Hamilton College, he joined the Navy during the Second World War before enrolling at ETS in 1946. Following his graduation, he was ordained priest in 1950 and went on to serve as a missionary bishop, first in the Philippines and then in South Dakota. In 1971, he accepted DeWitt's invitation to become assistant bishop of Pennsylvania and was duly elected coadjutor of the diocese two years later. Although he shared his predecessor's progressive agenda, Ogilby was by nature a more conciliatory figure.[188] Writing formally to his clergy on July 19 to summarize what was happening, he struck a moderate note, stating, "I am persuaded that this projected ordination will be theologically *valid*, though *irregular* in terms of the current ecclesiastical polity and structures of the Episcopal Church."[189] John Burgess of Massachusetts commiserated with Ogilby about the difficulties of his situation but disagreed that the women's priesting could be judged theologically valid. "Within the Anglican tradition we have insisted that the bishop does not act alone in ordinations but acts as representative of the total life of the Church," reasoned Burgess. Thus, he continued, when a bishop fulfills this function, he does so not unilaterally but with the assent of priests and laypeople elected to the Standing Committee of his diocese. "These two orders have a fundamental right in sharing in the determination of who will comprise the presbyterial order and the bishop has no right to determine by himself who the priests of the Church shall be." For Burgess, adhering to this process was not simply a matter of rules, but a statement about the nature of Christian community. In this respect, it was indeed a question of what did and did not constitute legitimate theology.[190]

Moreover, John Walker detected a paradox in the bishops' claim that their action would help free the church from its repressive tendencies. By proceeding without reference to the established forms of consultation, they would, in his view, be doing precisely the opposite, claiming for themselves a kind of "monarchical power or kingly authority."[191] As black bishops committed to the ordination of women, both Burgess and Walker were adamant about the importance of following the correct procedures to achieve the desired outcome. So, while they recognized certain parallels between the women's struggle for equality and their own as African Americans, they did not believe the deacons had reached the stage where extreme measures were justified. "I have always been convinced that sometimes we must force change by breaking the law," wrote Bishop Walker in mid-July, "but only after all legal means to redress grievances have been exhausted. I hardly think that the first legislative attempt and failure constitutes an exhaustion of all legal means."[192] Other black Episcopalians had arrived at the opposite conclusion. Notable among them was Paul Washington, who agreed to host the forthcoming service at the Church of the Advocate, his predominantly black parish in north Philadelphia. Having turned the Advocate into a center of Black Power during the sixties, Washington saw it as the obvious setting for another oppressed group to express its defiance of church and society.[193] Sharing Washington's stance was lay leader Charles Willie, who had spoken out forcefully about the continuities between the civil rights and feminist movements.[194] Still, when it became known that Willie intended to preach at the ordination service, a number of black clergy counseled him "not to get mixed up in that white women's mess." Convinced that "harm to some is harm to all," Willie countered that rather than discourage him, these clerics should instead be coming to Philadelphia to support the deacons.[195] Even before the ordinations had taken place, they revealed a diversity of opinion

226 PRIVILEGE AND PROPHECY

among black Episcopalians that most of their white co-religionists scarcely bothered to consider.[196]

Whether the campaign for women's ordination should be regarded as analogous to the black struggle for equality remained a bone of contention in the months and years to come. Yet for those who gathered at the Church of the Advocate on July 29, the parallel was self-evident and profound. "As blacks refused to participate in their own oppression by going to the back of the bus in 1955 in Montgomery," proclaimed Charles Willie in his sermon, so "women are refusing to cooperate in their own oppression by remaining on the periphery of full participation in the church in 1974 in Philadelphia."[197] Eleven women deacons received the laying on of hands from Bishops Corrigan, DeWitt, and Welles, who were joined by Bishop José Ramos of Costa Rica and dozens of priests.[198] As the *Living Church* was quick to point out, none of the deacons had secured approval from her bishop or standing committee to take part.[199] For the women themselves, at least, this had plainly ceased to matter. In different ways, nearly all of them believed theirs was a prophetic act, by which they sought not just recognition of their personal calling but the transformation of the whole ecclesial order.[200] For Carter Heyward, the battle to exercise sacramental leadership in the Episcopal Church put her in solidarity with oppressed people everywhere. This was because the church, like other parts of society, "renders women and non-white men, together with the poor of the world, less than fully adult human beings," thereby preventing them from "shaping our own lives (theologies, liturgies, politics, too)."[201] But not everyone accepted the premise that middle-class white women should be located so readily among the ranks of the outcast and marginalized. Whatever injustices they may have endured, the deacons ordained in Philadelphia still enjoyed privileges and protections that America bestowed upon all those of their race and class.[202] Under the circumstances, the claim of a shared condition confirmed for some African Americans that their own struggle had been not only eclipsed but appropriated.[203]

As soon as he learned that the ordinations had gone ahead, John Allin immediately convened an emergency meeting of the House of Bishops in Chicago on August 14–15. William Stringfellow later remarked that having summoned his colleagues in this way, the presiding bishop then had nothing to offer them other than his own hysteria.[204] In fairness, nearly all the bishops arrived at the gathering upset by what had happened, either because they opposed women's ordination or because they supported it and now felt put in a defensive position.[205] Allin made it clear from the outset that the purpose of the conference was not to debate the merits of either viewpoint but to address "the internal question of episcopal responsibility to constitution and canons." There followed two days of intense discussion about the relationship between the demands of the gospel and every bishop's commitment to uphold order and discipline. In an effort to move beyond the polarity pitting law against liberation, Bishop Arthur Vogel of West Missouri sought to reframe the issue, asking whether bishops who bypassed the wider church could be said to have achieved a meaningful outcome in doing so. Or, as he put it, "can those who fracture community admit to the community by the very act of fracture?" Judging they could not, he was prepared to honor what they had done "as an act of outreach and concern, but not as an ordination, because the ingredients of ordination simply were not present." The most emotional responses came from those, like Paul Moore and Ned Cole, who wanted to ordain their own deacons and thus felt betrayed by the bishops who had. "I asked you not to ordain them," Cole cried out in anguish. "That which I would love to have done and could not, you did—and I asked you not to do it."[206] Robert DeWitt, speaking on behalf of the dissidents, repeated that theirs had been "an act of obedience to the Spirit," but he also apologized, somewhat unconvincingly, for any offense their behavior had caused other members of the House.[207]

Meanwhile, it did not go unnoticed that the women themselves were entirely excluded from the conversation. It was not for lack of trying on their part: nine of them had traveled to Chicago for the proceedings but were then forced to stand in a group behind the press tables, as no seating was offered and their presence was pointedly ignored.[208] To William Stringfellow, the bishops had behaved "as if these persons did not exist," a response that exposed a pathology at the heart of their leadership. In moments such as this, he wrote, "sexism becomes conspicuous not only in the oppression and humiliation of its victims, but also in the dehumanization and anxiety of its practitioners."[209] While they did not perceive their error in quite such dramatic terms, a number of bishops conceded they had, in the words of Bennett Sims, displayed a "cold failure to reach out pastorally" to the individuals involved.[210] Charles Willie, who likewise had not been invited to the meeting but came anyway, lobbied for the women to have a chance to speak. Approaching John Burgess and Paul Moore during a break, Willie warned them that if the women were not included in the debate, the situation would only deteriorate further. He was discouraged that even as Burgess pledged

228 PRIVILEGE AND PROPHECY

his support for the cause, he refused to intercede and seemed annoyed by the women's presence.[211] That some of the bishops were as vexed by the situation's unseemliness as by its substance appeared confirmed by a remark from Stuart Wetmore of New York, who quipped that the ordinations had damaged the credibility of the House of Bishops, "which many look to as the best club in the country." Though made in a jocular vein, Wetmore's remark drew censure from John Allin, who commented that "if that's true, then there is a real need for renewal among us."[212]

When the conference ended with a vote declaring the ordinations invalid, Charles Willie was outraged. Prompted by the assembled media to comment, he accused the House of Bishops of outright sexism: "If you think the women ordained in Philadelphia are unlearned, we can send them to seminary. If you think they are not holy enough, we can teach them to pray. But if you dismiss them from the priesthood because they are female, they can do nothing because God Almighty made them that way."[213] Paul Moore, who witnessed the incident, was startled by Willie's vehemence. "All the resentment he must have harbored for years was flowing out in angry rhetoric," Moore wrote later. "For a Harvard professor, he sounded less than academic."[214] This dismissive attitude further antagonized Willie, who remembered how enthusiastic Moore had previously been about having him, a black layman, as part of the national leadership. Once he began to speak out forcefully about women's ordination, though, Moore's support quickly evaporated.[215] Believing his position had become untenable, Willie publicly resigned his post as vice president of the House of Deputies in a sermon he delivered soon after the Chicago meeting. He justified his decision on the basis that for Christians, "concern for personhood always takes precedence over concern for procedures," a view he deemed at odds with the current approach of the bishops.[216] Preaching again at Christ Church Cambridge in early 1975, he returned to the question of how Episcopalians might determine whether or not "the canons and customs of the church are out of harmony with the will of God." However complex the question might appear, Willie claimed that the criterion for answering it was simple. "Does the law or tradition, including church law and tradition, enhance personhood?" he asked. "If it does, it is loving and just. If not, it is evil and demonic."[217] By this logic, anyone prepared to defend the corporate processes of the Episcopal Church in this context was serving, wittingly or unwittingly, as an agent of human oppression.

Following the Chicago ruling, the "Philadelphia Eleven" were formally admonished by their respective bishops not to exercise any kind of priestly ministry.[218] Despite this injunction, members of the group made it plain that they now intended to function as priests. Speaking on their behalf, Carter Heyward announced that the women "do not accept the House of Bishops' 'opinion' of their ordination. They question the authority of the House to interpret its 'opinion' as a ruling which is either legislatively, theologically, or morally binding."[219] She made the point explicit by publicly celebrating the eucharist with Alison Cheek and Jeannette Picard at the interdenominational Riverside Church in Manhattan on October 27.[220] Such defiance placed Heyward's own bishop, Paul Moore, in precisely the role he wished to avoid, that of enforcing the church's rules against those whose cause he supported.[221] Writing in the *New York Times* in late November, he reaffirmed his commitment to women's ordination but insisted on securing General Convention's approval before taking further action.[222] This was the stance adopted by most liberal bishops, who, like Moore, then found themselves in the unhappy and unfamiliar position of being portrayed as reactionaries.[223] Despite his efforts to maintain contact with her during the ensuing months, Moore's relationship with Heyward gradually deteriorated to the point that she would only communicate with him through lawyers.[224] "It's become apparent to those of us who were ordained in Philadelphia that our bishops cannot bear to fathom *the depth of the alienation* we are experiencing," she explained. "If you could, you would not hesitate to 'regularize' us and ordain others."[225] To more dispassionate observers, however, it was obvious that the argument between the Philadelphia Eleven and the bishops had already reached an impasse.[226]

One Episcopal leader who remained unmoved by the demand for immediate, "prophetic" action was John Burgess of Massachusetts. Thus, when Carter Heyward and Sue Hiatt joined the faculty of the Episcopal Divinity School in Cambridge in early 1975, he turned down their request to be admitted to his diocese as priests.[227] Seeking to force the bishop's hand, the two women accepted an invitation from the Church of the Messiah in Woods Hole to preside at a eucharist during the coming summer. In response, Burgess issued a "godly admonition" to the leadership of the parish, enjoining them not to carry out their plans. "Surely in these times the Church faces many problems that will require our corporate witness," he reasoned. "To flout constituted authority, and distort one area of our ecclesiastical life, is to make impotent our efforts to speak to the world on issues that have wider significance throughout our society."[228] This plea for perspective fell on deaf ears, though, and Heyward and Hiatt duly celebrated Holy

230 PRIVILEGE AND PROPHECY

Communion at Woods Hole on Sunday, July 20. The next day, Burgess issued a stern letter reprimanding the rector and congregation for their disobedience.[229] In doing so, he was quick to disabuse them of any notion that their action was equivalent to those which African Americans had taken in their struggle for civil rights in the fifties and sixties. "The NAACP and the Rev. Martin Luther King were not interested in breaking the law," he wrote. "They were concerned that the law of the land be upheld." As such, it was presumptuous, not to say insulting, to equate the violence and humiliation African Americans had endured for generations to Heyward and Hiatt's recent experience of "a diocese of friends, who through education, prayer and canonical procedures" were working to regularize their ordination in just over a year's time. "This diocese deserves better treatment than what it has gotten from you," concluded the bishop tartly. "The cause of women's ordination certainly deserves better strategy."[230]

Even before Heyward and Hiatt had settled at EDS, Alison Cheek began exercising her priestly ministry at the Church of St. Stephen and the Incarnation in Washington, DC. Born and raised in Australia, Cheek (1927–2019) moved to the United States in the 1950s when her husband, an economist, went to work for the World Bank. While raising a young family in the Virginia suburbs, she began taking classes at VTS, eventually earning a Bachelor of Divinity degree. During this period Cheek experienced a call to ordained ministry and was admitted to the diaconate in early 1972. As one of the eleven irregularly ordained in Philadelphia, she was then invited by the rector of St. Stephen's, William Wendt, to serve as an assistant priest in his parish. Against the stated wishes of diocesan William Creighton, Wendt invited Cheek to celebrate the eucharist at St. Stephen's on November 10, 1974, making her the first woman to do so at an Episcopal altar.[231] Wendt's defiance prompted eighteen priests in the diocese to initiate formal proceedings against him, resulting in an ecclesiastical trial that began in late April 1975. Leading Wendt's defense team was William Stringfellow, who welcomed the trial as an opportunity to cross-examine John Allin about the House of Bishops' decision to repudiate the Philadelphia ordinations.[232] Allin's repeated failures to heed the court's subpoenas resulted in a stern memorandum from the five judges and some embarrassing press coverage, but little else.[233] Of greater significance was the way the judges themselves finally voted: the three male priests on the panel found Wendt guilty of disobeying his bishop, while the two laypeople, a man and a woman, opted to acquit him.[234] Writing to Stringfellow afterward, Pauli Murray embraced this split verdict, certain it could only help the cause of women's priesthood with further publicity.[235] What it might also suggest about essential differences between clergy and laity over church order, however, she did not address.

Like Paul Moore, Bishop Creighton endorsed the women's cause but believed the matter must be settled canonically. In the meantime, he chose not to ordain anyone—male or female—until the issue had been resolved by General Convention. He acknowledged this was not a positive solution, but at least it guaranteed that everyone in the church suffered through the process together.[236] The compromise did not last long. On July 28, Creighton received a letter from the retired bishop of Rochester, George W. Barrett, announcing his plan to ordain more women to the priesthood in the Diocese of Washington. "No one has a right to be ordained," Barrett conceded, "but everyone has a right not to be denied ordination on the ground of the sex to which she belongs." Creighton responded by withholding his consent and reiterating that no one in his diocese was currently being ordained priest.[237] Ignoring both Creighton and John Allin, Bishop Barrett proceeded to ordain Lee McGee, Alison Palmer, Elizabeth Rosenberg, and Diane Tickell to the priesthood at St. Stephen and the Incarnation on September 7.[238] At its autumn gathering a few weeks later, the House of Bishops voted to "decry" Barrett's action but otherwise seemed at a loss about what to do next.[239] This confusion exposed, not for the first time, how deeply alien many of the bishops found the behavior of the women and their supporters. Shaped by the hierarchical assumptions of their own upbringing and formation, even the most progressive among them assumed that the church's structures must ultimately be respected. The notion that these structures could be bypassed while claiming the very authority they provided seemed to invite chaos and a loss of all accountability. In this respect, the bishops' shared response revealed as much about their cultural conditioning as it did about the theology of the church. But something similar could also be said about those seeking to challenge the status quo. Having adopted a discourse heavily reliant upon secular ideals of personal fulfillment, these activists proved just as indebted to their social milieu and just as rigid in their judgments.[240] As a result, neither the bishops nor the activists were capable of employing a vocabulary meaningful to the other.[241]

As one of the bishops to participate in the Philadelphia ordinations, Robert DeWitt had already shown his readiness to confront gender inequality in the Episcopal Church. In the years to follow, he devoted himself to identifying more generally its complicity in patterns of social oppression. Having saved

232 PRIVILEGE AND PROPHECY

The Witness magazine from extinction following the death of W. B. Spofford, he shortly became its editor, thereby turning it into a mouthpiece for his Church and Society initiative.[242] Together, the paper and network became the means by which DeWitt sought to alert his co-religionists to the systemic injustices underpinning society.[243] He did so by offering them a "radical analysis" of their own church, one which "calls upon an institution to see itself as it is. In the case of an institution with a long establishment tradition, it involves facing that fact and seeing the liabilities which attach to it."[244] Not the least of these was the moral price the Episcopal Church had always paid for its privileged position in American life. Even now, DeWitt charged, it continued as "chaplain-in-residence to the established order, unable to be other than vaguely uneasy about the human suffering caused by the burgeoning industrial machines and corporate business structures."[245] To encourage those with a more disruptive approach to the church's role, DeWitt published *Struggling with the System, Probing Alternatives*, a "study/action guide" aimed at helping them "in their struggle to understand the nature of oppression and to explore ways out of it."[246] Written with the assistance of his old friend and colleague Hugh White, DeWitt used the guide to educate readers about the long history of progressive social action in their church. "Learning of this tradition," he wrote, "can help concerned Episcopalians today overcome feelings of isolation by introducing them to others who have stood where they stand against injustice and worked as they do for a more humane society." While these words were undoubtedly intended to reassure, they also tacitly recognized that such efforts had always been, and would likely remain, a minority pursuit.[247]

That said, DeWitt was hardly alone in trying to reframe the church's mission in light of systemic realities. Scott Paradise and his colleagues at the Boston Industrial Mission (BIM) had been doing so for nearly a decade, highlighting the material and spiritual impact of technology upon both individuals and communities.[248] In particular, Paradise's associate, Norman Faramelli, proved an astute commentator on the consequences of consumerism, not just in America but around the globe. A native of Pennsylvania, Faramelli (b. 1932) had studied chemical engineering at Bucknell University before earning his M.Div. at Philadelphia Divinity School in 1960. After ordination, he proceeded to a doctorate in religious studies at Temple University and in 1971 published *Technethics: Christian Mission in an Age of Technology*. Here Faramelli identifies a dilemma for Western Christians trying to tackle the inequalities of modern life: the tools of industrial culture at their disposal are in fact a major source of the problems they wish to solve.[249] Paradise echoed this view in a speech he delivered about the history of industrial mission in 1973. "In the balmy days following World War II we thought we could look ahead to a golden age of universal affluence brought on by world-wide industrialization," he noted, but instead "we have entered a period of unprecedented crisis. . . . To the threats of war, famine, social disintegration, and crushing poverty have been added dire warnings of ecological disaster."[250] The premise he and other industrial missioners began with—that Christian social values and technological progress were not only compatible but mutually beneficial—had been shown up as fundamentally wrong. Having devoted twenty years to the cause, Paradise had now arrived at the opposite position, concluding that for the church "to affirm or even acquiesce in the values of industrial culture is to betray its vocation." Even so, he conceded that in taking a more "subversive" stance toward industrial change, the church must still find ways of communicating meaningfully with the powerful people driving it.[251] To that end, BIM would devote considerable effort to building relationships with the technology companies that had begun to spring up along Boston's Route 128 in the course of the 1970s.[252]

How the church could serve as a pastoral and spiritual presence in society while actively challenging its oppressions had long been a matter of debate among mainline Protestants. The issue came to prominence once again in the spring of 1975, when a statement entitled "An Appeal for Theological Affirmation" appeared in the pages of *Worldview* magazine. It stemmed from a gathering of theologians and religious leaders that the editors of *Worldview*, Peter Berger and Richard John Neuhaus, had brought together a few months earlier at Hartford Seminary Foundation in Connecticut. In convening the group, Neuhaus and Berger hoped to formulate a collective response to tendencies in contemporary Christian thought which they considered "pervasive, false, and debilitating." On this basis, the conference identified thirteen "themes" they saw undermining the church's authentic work and witness. In light of the ongoing turmoil within the Episcopal Church, "Theme 9" was particularly germane: "Institutions and historical traditions are oppressive and inimical to our being truly human; liberation from them is required for authentic existence and authentic religion." In rejecting this premise, the group did not dispute that institutions could often be oppressive, but defended their necessity, arguing that "the modern pursuit of liberation from all social and historical restraints is finally dehumanizing." Likewise, in contesting "Theme 10," that "the world must set the agenda for the Church,"

234　PRIVILEGE AND PROPHECY

they upheld the church's role in social betterment, as well as the probability that its mission would often coincide with movements in the secular realm. But they were adamant that "the norms for the Church's activity derive from its own perception of God's will for the world," not the will of the world itself. As with the statement as a whole, these sentiments bespeak an urge not to repudiate modern life so much as to reassert a distinctly Christian approach to it.[253]

Perhaps unsurprisingly, many activist Episcopalians interpreted the "Hartford Appeal" as a reactionary document. In its call for spiritual renewal and theological rigor, they detected a bid to downgrade social concern in favor of personal piety.[254] (The great exception was Kim Myers of California, who, along with his colleague John Weaver, was one of only two Episcopalians to sign the Appeal.) In seeking to provide an alternative perspective on the nature of Christian responsibility, Scott Paradise and Norman Faramelli assembled a twenty-one-member task force under the auspices of BIM to develop a statement of their own. The result was the "Boston Affirmations," which, after widespread consultation, appeared in January 1976. As its title suggests, the text was framed by its authors as a series of positive assertions, rather than as a critique of other viewpoints.[255] Nonetheless, they made plain their unhappiness with the current state of affairs, noting that "we see struggles in every arena of human life, but in too many parts of the church and theology we find retreat from these struggles." Faced with this apparent lack of engagement, they invoked traditional theological concepts (creation and fall, covenant and prophecy) to affirm God's continuing activity through people and movements in the present-day world. On this basis, they detected "the transforming reality of God's reign" in efforts to overcome racial and sexual discrimination, to secure dignity for the poor and the vulnerable, to ensure equal treatment before the law, and all other such efforts intended to draw human beings into bonds of peaceful coexistence. And because of this belief, they affirmed their refusal to "stand with those secular cynics and religious spiritualizers who see in such witnesses no theology, no eschatological urgency, and no Godly promise or judgment."[256]

In the press, the "Hartford Appeal" and the "Boston Affirmations" were portrayed as offering diametrically opposed views of the relationship between spirituality and activism. Yet despite clear differences in language and emphasis, the declarations were in fact saying many of the same things.[257] Reflecting on the episode later, Scott Paradise conceded that neither text had suggested Christians "must spend our lives either on our knees or on the picket line." Even so, he remained critical of the Hartford group's apparent refusal to look for signs of divine initiative in secular events.[258] For his part, Richard Neuhaus continued to resist what he judged the Bostonians' preoccupation with reform as the primary meaning and expression of Christian discipleship.[259] Still others felt they had been down this road before and that the Hartford-Boston debate was, at least for Episcopalians, simply the newest iteration of an argument going on since the Second World War. Recalling the sociological portrait of the Episcopal Church from the early 1950s entitled *To Comfort or to Challenge*, Urban T. Holmes noted the parallels between the current debate and the issues that had exercised church people a quarter of a century earlier. Then, as now, Holmes observed, there was disagreement about what constituted the church's primary mission: was it mainly to provide nurture and consolation to its members, or to equip and embolden them to right the wrongs of the world? If Episcopalians since the 1960s had become more alert to their complicity in such wrongs, this recognition came at the price of making them less confident about the church's ability to redress them. What was needed going forward, Holmes concluded, was "a dialectical theology [that] would not allow a spiritual life to lapse into pietism any more than it would permit a concern for justice and human rights to become a mere secular program."[260]

The feeling that Christians had lost their public voice was felt acutely by Paul Moore, who saw around him a society in dire need of leadership and encouragement.[261] Frustrated that "our church is often so sick and gloomy," Moore resolved that as bishop of New York he must find concrete ways to express faith in the future, not just of his diocese but the city at large.[262] To this end, he decided to resume construction of the Cathedral of St. John the Divine, which Horace Donegan had halted in 1967 in response to the urban crisis.[263] Assisting Moore in this task was to be his old friend James Morton, whom he appointed as the cathedral's first dean since the departure of John Butler in 1966.[264] In addition to his professional role, Morton became a close personal confidant to Moore following the death of his wife Jenny in the fall of 1973.[265] Not everyone was gratified by the presence of the new dean. Walter Dennis, who had been a canon at St. John's since 1965, resented what he deemed Morton's patronizing manner and racial presumption. "He knew more about black folks than they knew about themselves," Dennis charged, adding: "beware of white liberals who love poor black folks and hate middle class blacks."[266] Besides such internal tensions, though, Morton and Moore also faced tough questions from civic groups about their plan

236   PRIVILEGE AND PROPHECY

to spend millions of dollars on a neo-gothic building in a poor neighbor-hood.[267] For Morton, this was justified by the cathedral's potential to serve not only as a sanctuary for worship but as a place where "the cultural, eco-nomic and human needs" of the whole community would be addressed.[268] More immediately, the project was to be a source of training for young people from nearby Harlem, recruited to learn the dying art of stone-cutting from a master mason imported from England. At its peak, the stoneyard had over fifty apprentices, most of them ethnic minorities. Thus, after a major fund-raising campaign, serious work on the building finally resumed in the au-tumn of 1982.[269]

Adding to the symbolic importance of this work was the fact that by the mid-1970s, New York was in deep trouble. Crime, arson, and unem-ployment had risen precipitously, and by late 1975 the city itself was on the verge of bankruptcy.[270] When President Gerald Ford refused to pro-vide a federal bail-out, Paul Moore was incensed. "I am ashamed," he said in response to Ford's hardline approach, "that one who is a member of our Episcopal Church and calls himself Christian dares to preach fiscal mo-rality when his heart is cold to compassion."[271] He was equally bitter toward the corporations and industries that had started leaving the city, thereby compounding its problems rather than helping to solve them.[272] In a con-troversial sermon delivered at the Cathedral on Easter Sunday 1976, Moore excoriated members of the business community for their withdrawal, who sensed "like rats, that the ship is sinking." By placing self-preservation ahead of social responsibility, political and economic leaders alike had failed to grasp that "the struggle for the city's survival is the struggle for the soul of America, for here is being played out what may be the preview of the disin-tegration of industrialist society." Yet by defying conventional wisdom and staying in the city, executives had an opportunity to "be part of the city's resurrection and our own," Moore declared, "for courage is as contagious as fear, hope as contagious as despair." In drawing his remarks to a close, the bishop returned to the theme of Easter, calling upon all New Yorkers to "be part of the rising, not the dying."[273] The sermon provoked consternation among some Episcopalians, who felt the bishop's remarks were inappro-priate to the occasion. But others rejoiced that he had confronted head-on the realities of the present moment and had provided the kind of moral leadership so lacking in other quarters.[274] "There is no movement to grab hold of," Moore explained afterward. "We have to generate the movement." In the years to come, he and other religious dignitaries continued to speak out about the ways in which the city failed to meet the needs of the most vulnerable members of the population.[275]

While Paul Moore and James Morton labored to renew the life and ministry of the cathedral in New York, Frank Sayre faced a very different set of challenges at the cathedral in Washington. In recent years he had accelerated its building program in anticipation of the 1976 bicentennial celebrations, when the completed nave and west rose window were to be dedicated in the presence of President Ford, Queen Elizabeth II, and the Archbishop of Canterbury.[276] By the end of 1975, though, Sayre was prepared to question whether the assumptions that had inspired construction of a national cathedral in the first place were still valid. In his annual report, the dean observed that "the church at large is less steady, less sure; she knows not how such eloquent loveliness as our cathedral might serve her. She hardly knows what to make of the State itself."[277] He was already convinced that the Episcopal Church's declining prestige had begun to erode his own standing and influence among the Washington elite. At one point he wrote to Katharine Graham, publisher of the *Washington Post*, to complain about the dearth of press coverage that he and other church spokesmen were now receiving. "There *are* events and people on the contemporary religious scene which are constructive and creatively relevant to a society," contended Sayre, "but these are either ignored by your paper, or else sequestered, and I would even add degraded, by being relegated to the paid ad section on Friday's back page."[278] For a man whose pronouncements were once routinely reported on the front page, this was indeed a fall from grace. The summer celebrations of 1976 were scarcely ended when the dean also had to face up to the cathedral's perilous financial state. Due to massive overspending on building works, the deficit had reached $760,000 for the year, in addition to an overall debt of $11 million. In an attempt to gain some control over the situation, the cathedral chapter imposed stringent economies, cutting staff and programs in the process.[279] With so much about Episcopal life already fragile and contested, such a move represented not only a return to fiscal restraint but a recognition of the shifting priorities of the wider church.

As Episcopalians prepared for their General Convention in September, it was obvious that the issue of women's ordination would predominate. In an open letter to the House of Bishops, Carter Heyward threw down the gauntlet, determined that none of them should be confused about what was at stake. "'Love' without justice is not love at all," she asserted. "We have known that we must insist upon justice in the world, which includes, of

238   PRIVILEGE AND PROPHECY

course, justice in the church."[280] In a similar vein, Bishops Barrett, Corrigan, and DeWitt called upon their colleagues to regularize the ordinations already performed, not as an act of canonical housekeeping but as a bid for a fairer society. So while they acknowledged that "most of us involved in these ordination events are white, middle to upper class, American, and economically privileged," they nonetheless believed that "each of us must discover the ways in which we can best deal with our culture and alleviate its injustices."[281] When the bishops gathered in Minneapolis for the convention, a majority of them initially supported the view that the women should submit to a second, "conditional" ordination. The next day, however, this position was reversed, and the house instead endorsed the idea of employing some alternative rite that would simply formalize the women's existing status.[282] If this concession appeared to some like a victory for justice, to others it merely showed the bishops' eagerness, as one commentator put it, to move beyond "the second-rate serialized melodrama we have become in the eyes of the world at large."[283] What remained painfully absent on all sides was any sustained engagement with the theological content of the decisions being made.[284]

Whatever the bishops might think, the legal ordination of women to the priesthood and episcopate still depended on the House of Deputies voting to amend the canons. As presiding officer, John Coburn was adamant that the tenor of these deliberations should be dignified and respectful. (Overseeing this process was to be one of his last major acts as president, since the previous year he had been elected bishop coadjutor of Massachusetts and was to be consecrated in Boston a few weeks later.[285]) When it came time for the deputies to vote, Coburn mandated that everyone should observe a five-minute silence. He was equally emphatic that once the result was announced, no public reaction of any kind would be permitted, either positive or negative.[286] In the event, the measure passed convincingly among both lay and clerical deputies.[287] Recalling the episode, Paul Moore credited Coburn with his skillful management of a tense situation. "I don't know if anybody else could have chaired that convention to a conclusion in the way John did," he remarked. "He is an ultimate politician and reconciler."[288] Coburn's diplomatic skills would be required again soon enough. For alongside the jubilation, a significant group of Episcopalians were manifestly unreconciled to what had taken place.[289] And such people were to be found not just in local congregations, but at the diocesan and even national levels of leadership.[290]

The new canon permitting women's priesthood and episcopacy came into effect on January 1, 1977. Pauli Murray was ordained by Bishop Creighton in Washington National Cathedral a week later, making her the first African American woman to be priested in the Episcopal Church.[291] For Murray, this occurrence heralded nothing short of a new phase in the evolution of human society. Speaking a month later in North Carolina, she excitedly told her listeners that women's ordination marked "the visible beginning of the Second American Revolution—a revolution marked by . . . the reconciliation of groups of Americans now alienated from one another by reason of race, color, religion, gender, age, sex preference, political and theological differences, economic and social status, and other man-made barriers."[292] If Murray's claims here seem more than a little exaggerated, they serve as a reminder of how intensely she had struggled to reconcile aspects of her own identity. She confessed to Moran Weston at one point that "I have been almost been torn asunder over the past ten years because I cannot make a priority between race and sex."[293] Writing in the *Anglican Theological Review* in early 1978, she voiced again her hope that despite the evident tensions between them, blacks and feminists in the church might yet discover a sense of shared purpose. The reason this had not happened already, Murray believed, was because both had "a tendency to identify one's own group exclusively with ultimate righteousness and divine election as an instrument of judgment." Given such an exclusive conception of their identity and calling, it was unsurprising the two groups had failed to develop a common language for the "universal liberation and reconciliation which lies at the heart of the Christian gospel."[294] It would be left to Murray and other black Episcopal women to try to draw these constituencies closer together without in the process demeaning the position of either.[295]

As if to lend credence to Pauli Murray's contention that 1977 marked the start of a different era, on January 10, Paul Moore ordained Ellen M. Barrett to the priesthood in Manhattan. What made his act exceptional was not Barrett's gender but the fact that she was, in the words of the *New York Times*, an "avowed lesbian."[296] Born into an Episcopal family in 1946, Barrett was raised and educated in Virginia. At the age of nineteen she converted to Roman Catholicism but eventually returned to the Episcopal Church in 1972, by which time she had moved to New York to pursue graduate study in history. She enrolled at General Seminary shortly thereafter and earned an M.Div. with honors three years later. Meanwhile, she had also taken a prominent role in Integrity, a solidarity group for gay Episcopalians founded by Louie Crew in 1974.[297] Conscious of her activism, Moore asked Barrett prior to her diaconal ordination in 1975 "not [to] discuss your private life openly

240 PRIVILEGE AND PROPHECY

at this time," as he feared doing so "would tilt the whole thing."[298] Now, as he ordained her to the priesthood, he remained personally supportive but continued to stress publicly that Barrett's homosexuality was incidental. Amidst the outcry that ensued, the bishop and standing committee issued a statement declaring that neither this nor any ordination in the diocese had been approved "out of concern for an oppressed minority group," not least because "no ordination decision can be generalized without regard to the vocation of the individual ordained."[299] The idea that her sexuality was irrelevant would be contradicted by Barrett herself when she told *Time* magazine that her lesbian relationship "is what feeds the strength and compassion I bring to the ministry."[300] Though annoyed by this indiscretion, for the most part the bishop was philosophical about the difficulties to come. "This leaves me out in left field for the hundred and thirteenth time," he joked to Barrett. "C'est la vie!"[301] In light of posthumous revelations about Moore's own sexuality, there is undoubtedly an added poignancy to these words.[302]

As expected, when the House of Bishops assembled in Port St. Lucie, Florida, in October for their autumn conference, they subjected Moore to a barrage of criticism.[303] One colleague accused him of displaying "an aristocratic disdain" for other dioceses, an obvious reference to his patrician background. Despite their displeasure, the bishops ultimately chose not to censure Moore, thanks to the advocacy and persuasion of John Coburn.[304] It also helped that some interpreted his action in the context of a bigger conversation underway about how to manage dissent. In his opening address, John Allin had announced that because he felt unable to accept women's priesthood, he was prepared to resign as presiding bishop. Having refused this offer, the house went on to adopt "A Statement of Conscience," which asserted that no bishop should be punished for refusing to support the ordination of women.[305] Predictably, liberal activists were outraged by what they considered the bishops' double standard: those in their midst who had defied the General Convention before 1976 had been rebuked and penalized, while those who wished to defy it now would be honored and protected.[306] With characteristic intensity, William Stringfellow castigated the bishops for "naming prejudice or eccentricity or retribution as conscience and then exonerating defiance of the law of the church on the pretext of so-called conscience."[307] Others wondered what the "conscience clause" revealed more generally about the current state of leadership in the Episcopal Church. Arthur Walmsley, who by this time was rector of St. Paul's parish in New Haven and would be elected coadjutor of Connecticut two years later, considered the solution to be a damning indictment. "It is ironic," he wrote in *The Witness*, "that a church which designates itself by the label 'episcopal' has in a radical way lost the office of bishop as either meaningful symbol of unity or effective center of authority." While few could wish for a return to heresy trials and other coercive sanctions, Walmsley warned that if the bishops could not even enforce a modicum of conformity among themselves, the church was indeed in very serious trouble.[308]

In summarizing what had taken place at Port St. Lucie, one journalist quipped that "the Episcopal Church has earned some sort of dubious prize for the amount of punishment it can inflict on itself and still survive."[309] As the 1970s wore on, there was no denying that the internal battles waged by Episcopalians had damaged their trust in each other and the structures they shared.[310] On the other hand, the openness with which they now pursued their differences bespoke a more transparent culture than in the past, when key decisions were made by a small and homogenous elite. Laypeople in particular expected their leaders to be less prescriptive and more collaborative in style and demanded a larger role in defining the church's priorities.[311] When clergy claimed that such changes were eroding their authority as ministers of the gospel, Charlie Price of VTS was quick to correct them. "Authority is to be sharply distinguished from power," he argued. "When the leadership of the church bemoans the loss of authority, they are often talking about the loss of power to effect their own will. The gospel itself never lacks authority."[312] Though he employed a different vocabulary, Robert DeWitt shared Price's logic. If people had become less deferential toward their priests and bishops, it was not because they had become less committed Christians, but simply because these leaders had failed to earn their respect. "Established authority is valid only insofar as it expresses and firms up the truth of justice," DeWitt reasoned. "This is the proper role of authority—or else it becomes romantic, or whimsical, or at worst, tyrannical."[313] Gone were the days, it seemed, when clergy could invoke an authority based purely on respect and affection for the institution.[314]

Having been elected bishop coadjutor of Washington in June 1976, John Walker was keenly aware of the ways the church's standing had changed, both among its members and in society at large. With Frank Sayre intending to retire as dean of Washington Cathedral in early 1978, Walker decided it was time to recalibrate its mission and leadership in line with current realities.[315] Prior to his installation as diocesan in September 1977, Walker therefore announced his intention not to appoint a new dean but to take over the

242   PRIVILEGE AND PROPHECY

position himself. Under this plan, the executive officer of the diocese, Charles Perry, would serve as provost of the cathedral and have responsibility for day-to-day operations, while Walker would function as its "chief liturgist and spokesman."[316] Convinced that "the national stature and the national role of the cathedral tended to downplay its role in the diocese," the bishop hoped this new arrangement would redress the balance and make the cathedral more responsive to the needs of the local community.[317] Frank Sayre did not conceal his unhappiness with Walker's decision. Writing to the cathedral chapter in October, he questioned the wisdom of trying to run such a big operation on a part-time basis. Moreover, he worried that by becoming dean, Walker would necessarily limit the cathedral's appeal to non-Episcopalians by virtue of his other office. "Washington Cathedral has a life unique to itself," Sayre declared, "not one to be defined in terms of a single Diocese, nor even of the National Episcopal Church."[318] Although he knew the times were changing, Sayre could not help but regard Walker's localist vision as a repudiation of all he stood for, whereas to Walker, Sayre embodied a dying order whose establishment pretensions were no longer merely a burden but a positive hindrance to progress.[319] Such pretensions had also left him an $11 million debt to pay, money he would have much preferred to have for empowering the poor and marginalized.[320]

In days gone by, bishops had readily cultivated the wealthy and powerful to advance the institutional goals of the Episcopal Church. It was in seeking not only to generate funds but also to instill a sense of responsibility among such people that Henry Knox Sherrill had created the Episcopal Church Foundation (ECF) in 1949. Especially during the tenure of John Hines, however, ECF's work among the affluent had declined, perhaps a sign of his own mounting discomfort with this aspect of the church's ministry.[321] John Allin, on the other hand, suffered no such misgivings and set about rebuilding relations with a traditional constituency that felt increasingly unwanted and unloved.[322] At the 1976 General Convention he launched a $100 million fundraising campaign called Venture in Mission (VIM), designed to renew a sense of common purpose among Episcopalians regardless of class, race, or region. In studied contrast to the dynamics created by GCSP, Allin likewise promoted VIM as a chance to foster respect and cooperation between national and local levels of the church. So, even if funds were raised by VIM staff, people on the ground would retain significant control over what kind of mission programs would receive funding.[323] Despite the presiding bishop's upbeat presentation, liberals were immediately skeptical of VIM, which they

NO LOVE WITHOUT JUSTICE   243

saw as little more than a ploy to shore up the church's support among suburban whites.[324] John Walker and Paul Moore were particularly mistrustful, feeling that once again John Allin had failed to take seriously the pressing and complex needs of city life.[325] Determined to draw attention to such needs in the VIM process, they launched the Urban Bishops Coalition (UBC) with sixteen of their colleagues.[326] In a statement issued at Minneapolis, the group endorsed VIM but demanded that 50 percent of its monies should be earmarked for urban projects. The bishops hoped that by taking this approach, the Episcopal Church might yet "break out of the kind of structures that seem to speak primarily to an upper middle-class clientele."[327]

Besides working together to gain some control over Venture in Mission, the bishops in the newly formed coalition recognized a need to be better informed about the cities they were called to serve. As UBC grew (it would eventually boast 55 members), it was decided to hold a series of consultations in urban centers across the country, so that people could testify directly to their experiences and concerns.[328] Veteran organizer Hugh White was appointed to direct the project, while activists Ed Rodman and Byron Rushing were recruited to liaise with local churches and community groups. Their efforts would result in public hearings taking place during the second half of 1977 in Seattle, Chicago, Newark, Washington, and Birmingham, as well as Colon, Panama. A second event in Washington would later be held to focus specifically on national issues.[329] Once this process was completed, UBC commissioned the dean of the Rochester Center for Theological Studies, Joseph A. Pelham, to write a report summarizing the gathered testimony and interpreting its meaning. In doing so, Pelham issued a hard-hitting challenge to what John Walker had elsewhere referred to as Episcopalians' "Lady Bountiful" approach to the urban poor.[330] For it was evident from the hearings that what people in the cities desired most from the church was not more money but a ministry of presence, a willingness to be alongside them in their struggles and to provide leadership in local affairs.[331] "We must decide to be *present* in a new way consistent with the principal of *incarnation*," advised Pelham. "This means quite literally to visit prisons, spend time in unemployment offices, experience what it means to live on a welfare subsistence budget for a certain number of weeks—so that the taste, touch, feel and smell of poverty and oppression can take on reality." Only through such direct engagement, he believed, could the Episcopal Church hope to develop a genuinely catholic understanding of its mission, in which it regarded "blacks, the poor, the working class, Hispanics, ethnic groups, gays and all the other

244   PRIVILEGE AND PROPHECY

present inhabitants [of the cities] as its own." In fact, there was much about this that readily conformed to traditional notions of responsibility for the geographical parish. Where it departed from this model was Pelham's added insistence that solidarity with the poor could only ever be genuine once the church had severed its links with the rich and powerful.[332]

Writing for the updated version of the Church's Teaching Series in 1979, Earl Brill echoed Joseph Pelham's diagnosis. Despite its claims to catholicity, Brill wrote, the Episcopal Church "is still predominantly Anglo-Saxon in its orientation and will continue to be so until it has brought its various racial and ethnic groups into the mainstream of its corporate life."[333] In an effort to revitalize the urban parishes in his diocese, John Spong of Newark embarked upon a policy of "indigenization," whereby churches sought to prioritize the needs and sensibilities of their immediate neighborhood. "When the WASPs leave, the Episcopal Church has no function," Spong reasoned. "Our Church has to become indigenous to its community and the people who live there, or it has no hope of survival."[334] What this dichotomy between poor minorities and wealthy WASPs overlooked yet again was the anomalous position of black Episcopalians. Few of Pelham's African American co-religionists shared his Manichaean approach to inclusion. Given that most black Episcopalians were "either upwardly mobile or solidly middle-class," Robert Hood thought it was pointless to pretend they had the same problems as those struggling in the inner cities. Instead of making false claims, they "ought to be liberating themselves to use the talents associated with the middle-class and which they also possess for service and ministry on behalf of the black poor and underclasses."[335] Don Taylor, who later served as bishop of the Virgin Islands, shared Hood's more nuanced approach. "Our future as Black Episcopalians lies not in abandonment of the Establishment," Taylor averred. "Rather, we need to close our ranks, dismiss our individual jealousies, and muster our own spiritual resources to redeem this church."[336] Unburdened by the self-lacerating guilt increasingly prevalent among liberal whites, black leaders remained committed to transforming the institution from within.[337] They were also pragmatic about the demographic realities. By the 1970s, African Americans continued to make up only 3% of the church's national membership, with a total of 250 clergy.[338] Whatever might be the case in the future, the "typical Episcopalian" at the end of the decade was still undeniably a WASP.[339]

In certain respects, the Episcopal Church's approach to urban mission appeared to be back where it started thirty years earlier, when Kim Myers,

Paul Moore, and Robert Pegram began their ministry at Grace Church in Jersey City. Of course, both the Episcopal Church and American society had changed radically along the way, but what had remained was a simple call to be present among those in need. As much as any Episcopal leader in modern times, Kim Myers had sought not only to answer this call personally but to dramatize it within the framework of the church's existing structures. Along the way, he had perplexed many, combining an Anglo-Catholic conservatism with a radical social vision.[340] If the former meant he was less likely to favor certain types of innovation, it also meant he retained a genuine humility in the face of the church's corporate wisdom. This enabled him to reverse his position on women's ordination to the priesthood, which having formerly opposed, he went on publicly to embrace.[341] In a similar fashion, he also came to support ordaining the openly gay, concluding that any baptized Christian must possess the potential to exercise sacramental leadership.[342] Still, as progressive as Myers undoubtedly was, he never lost sight of his primary calling to preserve the institution he loved. Shortly before his retirement in 1979, he was criticized by some of his priests for not having been more prophetic during his tenure as bishop of California. In response, Myers explained that every time he did something controversial, he knew some people in the diocese would take offense and withhold funds from their parish churches. Yet as the bishop, he was also ever-mindful of his obligation to look after his flock, not least the clergy. "I became responsible for the food on your tables, for your rent, for your health care, and for the survival of your congregations," he told them. "I decided it was immoral for me to make pronouncements and for you to suffer. I was protecting you and your families."[343] While some insisted there was no love in the church without justice, Myers was adamant that such justice would be fruitless if love for the church itself got lost along the way.

By the time Episcopalians convened in Denver for the 1979 General Convention, it was evident that a high price had been paid for the innovations of the past ten years. Although many greeted the regularization of women's priesthood and the introduction of a new prayer book as signs of progress, others regarded them as a betrayal of their precious Anglican heritage. But just as serious as the specific issues was the apparent breakdown of consensus among the bishops themselves about the nature of collegiality amidst controversy and change.[344] From the irregular ordinations of Philadelphia and Washington, to the priesting of Ellen Barrett in New York, to John Allin's offer to resign at Port St. Lucie, what emerged was a church no longer able or willing to work out its differences quietly behind closed doors.[345] In a pastoral letter issued after the Denver convention entitled "Toward Tomorrow," the bishops asserted that "social stability lies in granting one another dignity and value and a responsible share in the human enterprise of a world grown far too small for strife."[346] Whether the Episcopal Church managed to practice what it preached here to the rest of society would, of course, prove critical to its own future as a viable Christian presence in American life.

8

A Prophetic Church?

In February 1978, William Stringfellow published an article in *The Witness* entitled "The Embarrassment of Being Episcopalian." Recalling an earlier period in his life, during which he could "muster enthusiasm about the affiliation," Stringfellow cited Arthur Lichtenberger, James Pike, Parishfield, and the Urban Priests Group as exemplifying a time when the Episcopal Church "became a presence in American society—at once practical and sacramental—free of conformity or worldly compromise." He concluded that it was only nostalgia for these bygone days, coupled with a kind of tribal loyalty, that now prevented him from abandoning the church altogether.[1] By the close of the 1970s, Stringfellow was by no means alone among Episcopal progressives in idealizing the recent past, as well as expressing dismay with the present. It had become evident that a traditionalist resurgence was underway, one in which zeal for social activism had yielded to an emphasis on personal piety.[2] Reflecting on this change, Scott Paradise saw it as a direct response to the "psychic hangover" inflicted by the sixties upon all the mainline churches, leaving them with a "monstrous headache" to overcome.[3] As much as they might disapprove of this retreat from public engagement, though, liberal activists had a major dilemma of their own to contend with. Over the course of the previous decade and a half, a skepticism toward mainstream American aspirations and values had taken root among them. By the time Ronald Reagan was elected president in 1980, it was clear they were fundamentally out of step with the dominant civic culture, which not long before they had presumed to shape and lead.[4] If the Episcopal Church had failed to live up to the hopes of its progressives, arguably these same progressives had failed to adapt to the changing sensibilities of the nation at large.[5]

The struggle to reconcile their establishment heritage with the social idealism of the 1960s would preoccupy Episcopalians for years to come. While the church's loss of influence and declining membership were undeniable facts, how best to respond to them became a source of ongoing debate.[6] For some Episcopal leaders, especially those whose ministries had been shaped by the halcyon days of the 1950s, these changes were an

Privilege and Prophecy. Robert Tobin, Oxford University Press. © Oxford University Press 2022.
DOI: 10.1093/oso/9780190906146.003.0008

248   PRIVILEGE AND PROPHECY

aberration, surmountable by renewing the church's institutional structures and reasserting its establishmentarian norms.[7] It was people such as these to whom the sociologist Peter Berger was evidently referring when he joked that even though Puerto Ricans, Jews, and Episcopalians each made up two percent of the American population, "guess which group does not think of itself as a minority?"[8] For others, though, such an approach ignored the ways in which Episcopalianism had undergone a paradigm shift. Loss of belief in the church's elite standing came not only from the outside, but also from within. Growing numbers of clergy and laypeople began to express shame rather than pride in their white, European, and patriarchal roots. Yet doing so did not produce among them a corresponding clarity about what a post-establishment mission to society should look like.[9] During the past forty years, Episcopalians have instead been consumed by internal questions regarding the nature of equality and access to leadership among different groups within their ranks. In the process, they have not lost the urge to shape American life so much as turned it upon themselves with ever greater intensity. The result, as one commentator astutely observed, has been an "introversion of the national church ideal."[10] In this way, and even though it long ago ceased to exercise a meaningful hold over the wealthy and powerful, the Episcopal Church has retained an inflated sense of its own importance.[11]

By extolling the virtues of communal diversity and inclusion, however, Episcopalians did not succeed in making their church more attractive to a younger generation.[12] Having had their worldview radically altered by the sixties, liberal Episcopal leaders at century's end appeared unable to move beyond the pieties and paradigms of that earlier time.[13] And notwithstanding the theological premises that initially fired their activism, it became increasingly difficult to distinguish the social vision of these leaders from the secular identity politics of the eighties and nineties.[14] Such an elision was perhaps inevitable in a church that had come to identify the ethics of liberation as the essence of the Gospel: it was no longer obvious what specifically Christian demands were being placed upon adherents. In consequence, the drift from religion into secularity would prove relatively painless for many who had been raised within the Episcopal fold.[15] Meanwhile, this conciliatory posture did little to help the church regain its social footing in post-establishment America.[16] Confounded by their marginal status, Episcopal and other mainline leaders looked for ways to justify it, invoking the familiar concept of prophetic opposition to rationalize their changing fortunes. If they could no longer be leaders of the culture, then they must become its chief critics. In this way, irrelevance was to be embraced as a mark of integrity, the natural condition of the morally superior.[17] Addressing a clergy conference in 1987, Scott Paradise attempted to chart the stages of this evolution:

> In the 1950s we believed that conflicts between groups could be resolved by reasonable people meeting together for dialogue and negotiation. In the 1960s that belief gave way to the conviction that desirable social change could only come through the confrontation of power with power. Those who wanted change in the 1970s had less power, but at least they felt they could speak the truth to power. But the powerful were not listening. In the 1980s the only thing left to do was to confront power with weakness.[18]

Out of such weakness, progressive Episcopalians began to tell themselves a different story about who they were. From that point on, they would no longer seek to be an establishment church, but instead a prophetic one.[19]

Of course, the idea that not just individuals but the church as a whole might operate prophetically was not new. Preaching on Easter Day in 1984, John Hines looked back to the General Conventions of 1967 and 1969 to argue for the continuing importance of what he called "Institutional Prophecy." By this logic, the church's legislative and bureaucratic structures should be treated not primarily as tools for self-preservation but as a means for constantly challenging the status quo.[20] Still, the problem that once bedeviled Hines's own efforts had not gone away: many Episcopal laypeople simply did not share what they considered the left-wing tendencies of their bishops and other representatives.[21] "There is no possible way the Executive Council can enunciate views on public topics which will in all cases have the support of all Episcopalians," insisted the *Living Church* in 1978.[22] This divergence between a progressive leadership and a more conservative laity appeared to be confirmed by voting patterns in presidential elections. In 1980, 69 percent of Episcopalians voted for Ronald Reagan, while 60 percent did so again in 1984. By contrast, their clergy had begun to sound more and more like "McGovern-Mondale Democrats."[23] Under the circumstances, it is hardly surprising that some should dismiss the notion of a "prophetic church" as mere theological window-dressing for a set of predetermined social and political positions.[24] The fact that proponents of the idea never seemed to consider that prophecy might originate from other than a liberal source served only to confirm this suspicion.[25]

250 PRIVILEGE AND PROPHECY

Whatever their attitude to such matters, one thing Episcopalians still had in common at the turn of the twenty-first century was a reputation for being elite.[26] And while many of them felt embarrassed about it, such a reputation remained largely justified: the average church-member was still an educated, middle- to upper-middle-class WASP residing in a well-heeled neighborhood.[27] This persistent demographic reality has inevitably colored the church's subsequent claims to be a prophetic and inclusive community. For despite its efforts to confront racism, sexism, and homophobia in its midst, the Episcopal Church has consistently overlooked the complexities of class.[28] Not least, there has been a failure to appreciate the inherent privilege in the prophetic claim itself, which presumes the right to critique institutional structures precisely because of one's assured place within them. Far from making their church more accessible to working-class people, liberal Episcopalians' readiness to question traditional social values has only reinforced the denomination's elitist image in new ways.[29] A similar irony attends the Episcopal preoccupation with the concept of inclusivity. While efforts to make the church more open and welcoming have undoubtedly been sincere, they have rested on the assumption that the newly included will conform to the church's existing cultural norms. Thus, for all their emphasis on inclusion, Episcopalians have shown little interest in relinquishing control of the process or, indeed, in making room for those who might deviate from their brand of middle-class liberalism.[30]

If the Episcopal Church has failed to broaden its socioeconomic range, it has enjoyed greater success in promoting the diversity already to be found within its ranks. Over the past thirty years, considerable effort has gone into honoring the place and perspective of ethnic minorities, women, and homosexuals in the church's life. Yet attempts to address specific forms of discrimination have inadvertently created conflict among the marginalized groups themselves. Black Episcopalians in particular have resented the ways in which they believe their struggle for recognition has been eclipsed, first by the demands of middle-class white women, and latterly, by those of white gay men.[31] The fact that many of them have long stood among the nation's black elite has not lessened the feeling that they must defend a uniquely vulnerable position among their co-religionists.[32] Whatever initial benefits it may have offered, then, the church's concern with group identity politics has not lent it a shared sense of renewed purpose, but rather has codified a series of internal rivalries. Observing this dynamic in 1993, Jack Woodard chastised black and women clergy alike for what he considered their growing sense of entitlement. "What is disturbing is the failure of most black clergy to move beyond defensive, separatist thinking based on expecting to receive some kind of favored status because of their race," Woodard wrote. "What is also disturbing is women clergy continuing to act and think they are going to receive special consideration because of their gender." Citing his own long career of serving in deprived parishes, Woodard enjoined his fellow priests, regardless of background, to renew their "downwardly mobile commitment to love and serve Christ's world and people, at whatever cost."[33]

Like that of his mentor John Hines, though, what Woodard's vision of Christian witness took for granted was an institutional coherence that no longer existed. Like so many Episcopal activists of his generation, Woodard had been shaped by the church during its most stable and confident period. The risk-taking and experimentation that he and others so often championed thus relied upon an organization robust enough to absorb their effects. In this respect, they felt able to operate as anti-establishment figures because they had every reason to believe the establishment would always be there. When William Stringfellow died in 1985, Malcolm Boyd praised him as "a rebel within the establishment, which is the toughest place to play such a game."[34] But arguably the exact opposite was the case: men like Stringfellow and Boyd actually enjoyed considerable latitude within the structures for which they so routinely professed contempt.[35] Even the legacy of mainstream figures such as Paul Moore and Francis Sayre must be viewed, at least in part, through this lens. Delivering his last sermon as bishop of New York in 1989, Moore urged his listeners, not for the first time, to "liberate your thinking from the dusty metaphysics of the past to a new dynamic of the Gospel." In saying this, however, he failed to acknowledge his indebtedness to the theology and traditions he now disparaged, or the degree to which his ordained ministry had depended on their survival.[36] Similarly, Francis Sayre would look back proudly on his record as the "firebrand" dean of Washington Cathedral, without seeming to grasp how contingent his position had been upon the power and prestige of the wider church.[37] Once that power and prestige began to fade, bold gestures by Episcopal churchmen would appear superfluous, not to say futile.[38]

What remains today is a denomination at cross purposes with itself. Since the Second World War, the Episcopal Church has become progressively more attuned to questions of social justice and human equality, and in the process, has undergone a crisis of conscience about its role within the dominant culture. And while clearly its loss of hegemonic status was prompted by

252   PRIVILEGE AND PROPHECY

larger, external forces, many within the church have greeted this shift as a liberation.[39] Even so, the result has not been a dramatic change in the church's composition, so much as an entrenchment of guilt and confusion among its aging membership.[40] This is because concepts such as prophetic action and radical inclusion have not in themselves produced a unifying framework comparable to the establishment model of old.[41] Instead, they have fed off that model's lingering fruits, such that notions of progress remain paradoxically rooted in an unwanted past. Before Episcopalianism can hope to develop a genuinely new ethos and mission, then, it must take seriously the ways in which its ecclesiology remains bound up in establishmentarian logic.[42] Doing so will enable the church to make informed decisions about what is being repudiated not just socially but theologically.[43] If inherited authority structures continue to be diluted in the name of personal autonomy and congregational empowerment, the church must be prepared to recognize what is being lost as well as gained. In other words, it needs to be capable of explaining what remains distinctively episcopal about the Episcopal Church, and on what grounds it will claim a catholic identity for itself in the future.[44] It must decide which parts of its heritage are worth fighting for and why. By seeking to answer this question, today's church may yet discover it has more in common with preceding generations than it ever thought possible.

Notes

Chapter 1

1. H. Richard Niebuhr, *The Social Sources of Denominationalism* (1929; New York: Meridian Books, 1957), 108.
2. David Hein and Gardiner Shattuck, Jr., *The Episcopalians* (Westport, CT: Praeger, 2204), ix–xi, 51–60; Charles P. Price, *The Anglican Tradition: What Is it? Can It Last?* (Cincinnati: Forward Movement, 1980), 18–19.
3. E. R. Norman, *The Conscience of the State in North America* (Cambridge: Cambridge UP, 1968), 20.
4. Paul Dominiak, "Moses the Magistrate: The Mosaic Theological Imaginaries of John Jewel and Richard Hooker in Elizabethan Apologetics," in *Defending the Faith: John Jewel and the Elizabethan Church*, ed. Angela Ranson et al. (University Park: Pennsylvania State UP, 2018), 161–82.
5. John Walsh and Stephen Taylor, "The Church and Anglicanism in the 'Long' Eighteenth Century," in *The Church of England c. 1689–c. 1833: From Toleration to Tractarianism*, ed. John Walsh et al. (Cambridge: Cambridge UP, 1993), 58.
6. Rowan Strong, *Anglicanism and the British Empire, c. 1700–1850* (Oxford: Oxford UP, 2007), 117.
7. Jon Butler, *Awash in a Sea of Faith: Christianizing the American People* (Cambridge, MA: Harvard UP, 1990), 166–9.
8. Patricia U. Bonomi, *Under the Cope of Heaven: Religion, Society, and Politics in Colonial America* (New York: Oxford UP, 1986), 92–3.
9. J. C. D. Clark, *English Society 1660–1832: Religion, Ideology and Politics during the Ancien Regime*, 2nd ed. (Cambridge: Cambridge UP, 2000), 389.
10. Nancy L. Rhoden, *Revolutionary Anglicanism: The Colonial Church of England Clergy during the American Revolution* (New York: New York UP, 1999), 146–7; Sydney E. Mead, *The Lively Experiment: The Shaping of Christianity in America* (1963; New York: Harper and Row, 1976), 63.
11. Frederick V. Mills, *Bishops by Ballot: An Eighteenth-Century Ecclesiastical Revolution* (New York: Oxford UP, 1978), 302–7; John F. Woolverton, *Colonial Anglicanism in North America* (Detroit: Wayne State UP, 1984), 237.
12. Nathan O. Hatch, *The Democratization of American Christianity* (New Haven, CT: Yale UP, 1989), 59–61.
13. Robert W. Prichard, *A History of the Episcopal Church*, 3rd ed. (Harrisburg, PA: Morehouse, 2014), 157–63.
14. Robert Bruce Mullin, *Episcopal Vision/American Reality: High Church Theology and Social Thought in Evangelical America* (New Haven, CT: Yale UP, 1986), 104–5.

254 NOTES

15. E. Digby Baltzell, *Philadelphia Gentlemen: The Making of a National Upper Class* (Glencoe, IL: Free Press, 1958), 226, 236; Daniel Walker Howe, "Protestantism, Voluntarism, and Personal Identity in Antebellum America," in *New Directions in American Religious History*, ed. Harry S. Stout and D. G. Hart (New York: Oxford UP, 1997), 217.

16. David L. Holmes, "The Anglican Tradition in Colonial Virginia," in *Perspectives on American Religion and Culture*, ed. Peter W. Williams (Malden, MA: Blackwell, 1999), 67.

17. Richard E. Wentz, *Religion in the New World: The Shaping of Religious Traditions in the United States* (Minneapolis, MN: Fortress Press, 1990), 83, 96.

18. Ephraim Radner, "The Theological Accoutrements of Anti-Pluralism: The Confused Fate of American Episcopalianism," *JAS* 2.1 (June 2004): 31, 33–4.

19. Matthew Grimley, "The State, Nationalism, and Anglican Identities," in *The Oxford History of Anglicanism, Volume IV: Global Western Anglicanism, c. 1910–present*, ed. Jeremy Morris (Oxford: Oxford UP, 2017), 118–19.

20. Martin E. Marty, "Living with Establishment and Disestablishment in Nineteenth-Century Anglo-America," *Journal of Church and State* 18.1 (Winter 1976): 73–6; Robert T. Handy, *A Christian America: Protestant Hopes and Historical Realities*, 2nd ed. (Oxford: Oxford UP, 1984), 32–3, 38.

21. Robert Bruce Mullin, "Trends in the Study of the History of the Episcopal Church," *AEH* 72.2 (June 2003): 153–4.

22. Philip H. E. Thomas, "Unity and Concord: An Early Anglican 'Communion,'" *JAS* 2.1 (June 2004): 20.

23. Prichard, *History of the Episcopal Church*, 199–203. In convening the Lambeth Conference, Archbishop Charles Longley laid the groundwork for what is now known as the Anglican Communion. Held every ten years, the Conference brings together bishops from across the world to address shared theological and social concerns and renew the bonds of unity among the Anglican family of churches.

24. William Reed Huntington, *The Church-Idea: An Essay Towards Unity* (1870; Harrisburg, PA: Morehouse, 2002), 101–15.

25. Frank E. Sugeno, "The Establishmentarian Ideal and the Mission of the Episcopal Church," *HMPEC* 53.4 (Dec 1984): 291; Paul T. Phillips, "The Concept of a National Church in Late Nineteenth-Century England and America," *Journal of Religious History* 14.1 (June 1986): 29–31.

26. Cheryl Walsh, "The Incarnation and the Christian Socialist Conscience in the Victorian Church of England," *British Studies* 34.3 (July 1995): 354–60; Paul T. Phillips, *A Kingdom on Earth: Anglo-American Social Christianity, 1880–1940* (University Park: Pennsylvania State UP, 1996), 3–15, 167–70.

27. Michael Bourgeois, *All Things Human: Henry Codman Potter and the Social Gospel in the Episcopal Church* (Urbana: University of Illinois Press, 2004), 161–8.

28. Bernard Kent Markwell, *The Anglican Left: Radical Social Reformers in the Church of England and the Protestant Episcopal Church, 1846–1954* (Brooklyn, NY: Carlson, 1991), 107–10; Ronald C. White, Jr., and C. Howard Hopkins, *The*

Social Gospel: Religion and Reform in Changing America (Philadelphia: Temple UP, 1976), 70–2.

29. Peter W. Williams, *Religion, Art, and Money: Episcopalians and American Culture from the Civil War to the Great Depression* (Chapel Hill: University of North Carolina Press, 2016), 16, 215.

30. Peter W. Williams, "The Gospel of Wealth and the Gospel of Art: Episcopalians and Cultural Philanthropy from the Gilded Age to the Depression," *AEH* 75.2 (June 2006): 219–20.

31. John L. Kater, Jr., "Whose Church Is It Anyway? Anglican 'Catholicity' Re-examined," *ATR* 76.1 (Winter 1994): 59–60; Phillips, *A Kingdom on Earth*, 70–1; Bourgeois, *All Things Human*, 81.

32. David L. Holmes, *A Brief History of the Episcopal Church* (Harrisburg, PA: Trinity Press International, 1993), 177; Stephen R. Higley, *Privilege, Power, and Place: The Geography of the American Upper Class* (Lanham, MD: Rowman & Littlefield, 1995), 26.

33. *Witness*, Oct 2001: 10–11; interview with Arthur E. Walmsley, Jan 6, 2014 (Concord, NH).

34. Dwight J. Zscheile, *People of the Way: Renewing Episcopal Identity* (Harrisburg, PA: Morehouse, 2012), 63; E. Digby Baltzell, *Judgment and Sensibility: Religion and Stratification*, ed. Howard G. Schneiderman (New Brunswick, NJ: Transaction, 1994), 103.

35. Thomas F. Rzeznik, "'Representatives of All That Is Noble': The Rise of the Episcopal Establishment in Early-Twentieth-Century Philadelphia," *Religion and American Culture* 19.1 (Winter 2009): 69–70, 76–7.

36. *WP*, Sept 29, 1907: 1.

37. Ian T. Douglas., *Fling Out the Banner!: The National Church Ideal and the Foreign Mission of the Episcopal Church* (New York: Church Hymnal Corporation, 1996), 89–90.

38. Michael Snape, *God and Uncle Sam: Religion and America's Armed Forces in World War II* (Woodbridge, Suffolk: Boydell Press, 2015), 158–9, 162–3; Morris Janowitz, *The Professional Soldier: A Social and Political Portrait*, rev. ed. (New York: Free Press, 1971), 98–100.

39. H. W. Brands, *Traitor to His Class: The Privileged Life and Radical Presidency of Franklin Delano Roosevelt* (New York: Doubleday, 2008), 818.

40. John F. Woolverton with James D. Bratt, *A Christian and a Democrat: A Religious Biography of Franklin D. Roosevelt* (Grand Rapids, MI: Eerdmans, 2019), 31, 34–8, 48–51; Merin Gustafson and Jerry Rosenberg, "The Faith of Franklin Roosevelt," *Presidential Studies Quarterly* 19.3 (Summer 1989): 564–6.

41. Ray H. Abrams, *Preachers Present Arms: The Role of the American Churches and Clergy in World War I and II, with Some Observations on the War in Vietnam* (1969; Eugene, OR: Wipf and Stock, 2009), 31; Michael Snape, "War and Peace," in *The Oxford History of Anglicanism, Volume IV: Global Western Anglicanism, c. 1910–present*, ed. Jeremy Morris (Oxford: Oxford UP, 2017), 229–30.

256 NOTES

42. Robert T. Handy, "The American Religious Depression, 1925–35," *Church History* 29.1 (Mar 1960): 3–16; Martin E. Marty, *Righteous Empire: The Protestant Experience in America* (New York: Dial Press, 1970), 256–7.

43. Known as the "Seven Sisters" of American Protestantism, the denominations comprising the mid-century mainline were the Congregational Church, Episcopal Church, Evangelical Lutheran Church, Presbyterian Church USA, United Methodist Church, American Baptist Convention, and Disciples of Christ. Jason S. Lantzer, *Mainline Christianity: The Past and Future of America's Majority Faith* (New York: New York UP, 2012), 1.

44. William R. Hutchison, "Discovering America," in *Between the Times: The Travail of the Protestant Establishment in America, 1900–1960*, ed. William R. Hutchison (Cambridge: Cambridge UP, 1989), 306.

45. Elesha J. Coffmann, The *Christian Century and the Rise of the Protestant Mainline* (New York: Oxford UP, 2013), 221.

46. *LC*, Jan 13, 1946: 10–11; Jan 26, 1947: 10ff. *Witness*, Apr 17, 1947: 5–6; Dec 11, 1947: 10–12; Jan 29, 1948: 9–11.

47. Robert A. Nye, "Western Masculinities in War and Peace," *American Historical Review* 112.2 (Apr 2007): 423, 435; Robert D. Dean, *Imperial Brotherhood: Gender and the Making of Cold War Foreign Policy* (Amherst: University of Massachusetts Press, 2001), 37–62.

48. Leonard I. Sweet, "The Modernization of Protestant Religion in America," in *Altered Landscapes: Christianity in America, 1935–85*, ed. David W. Lotz et al. (Grand Rapids, MI: Eerdmans, 1989), 32–3. Evoking the image of minister as social warrior is the title of a 1964 volume edited by Malcolm Boyd: *On the Battle Lines: A Manifesto for Our Times by 27 Militant Clergymen* (New York: Morehouse-Barlow, 1964).

49. Baltzell, *Judgment and Sensibility*, 156.

50. James Hudnut-Beumler, *Looking for God in the Suburbs: The Religion of the American Dream and Its Critics, 1945–1965* (New Brunswick, NJ: Rutgers UP, 1994), 85–6.

51. Doug Rossinow, *The Politics of Authenticity: Liberalism, Christianity, and the New Left in America* (New York: Columbia UP, 1998), 2–6; Grace Elizabeth Hale, *A Nation of Outsiders: How the White Middle Class Fell in Love with Rebellion in Postwar America* (New York: Oxford UP, 2011), 1–7.

52. David A. Hollinger, *After Cloven Tongues of Fire: Protestant Liberalism in Modern American History* (Princeton, NJ: Princeton UP, 2013), 23.

53. Donald MacKinnon, *The Stripping of the Altars* (London: Collins/Fontana, 1969), 34.

54. James E. Griffiss, "A Hope for Theology in the Episcopal Church," in *A New Conversation: Essays on the Future of Theology and the Episcopal Church*, ed. Robert Boak Slocum (New York: Church Publishing, 1999), 203.

55. Brevard S. Childs, *Biblical Theology in Crisis* (Philadelphia: Westminster Press, 1970), 94, 100.

56. Walter Harrelson, "The Hebrew Bible and Modern Culture," in *The Hebrew Bible and Its Modern Interpreters*, ed. Douglas A. Knight and Gene M. Tucker (Philadelphia: Fortress Press, 1985), 492.

NOTES   257

57. W. Sibley Towner, "On Calling People 'Prophets' in 1970," *Interpretation* 24.4 (1970): 504, 508.
58. Urban T. Holmes, III, "Once Again: To Comfort or To Challenge?," in *Realities and Visions: The Church's Mission Today*, ed. Furman C. Stough and Urban T. Holmes, III (New York: Seabury Press, 1976), 178; Walter Brueggemann, *The Prophetic Imagination*, 2nd ed. (Minneapolis: Fortress Press, 2001), 3.
59. Paul Peachey, "Radicalization of the Religious Idiom and the Social Dislocation of the Clergy," *ATR* 55.3 (July 1973): 282, 288; William R. Hutchison, *Religious Pluralism in America: The Contentious History of a Founding Ideal* (New Haven, CT: Yale UP, 2003), 168.
60. Wade Clark Roof and William McKinney, *American Mainline Religion: Its Changing Shape and Future* (New Brunswick, NJ: Rutgers UP, 1987), 36.
61. Jackson W. Carroll and Wade Clark Roof, "Introduction," in *Beyond Establishment: Protestant Identity in a Post-Protestant Age*, ed. Jackson W. Carroll and Wade Clark Roof (Louisville, KY: Westminster/John Knox Press, 1993), 11–13.
62. For a study of the social experiences of the Presbyterian Church during the same period, see James K. Wellman, Jr., *The Gold Coast Church and Ghetto: Christ and Culture in Mainline Protestantism* (Urbana: University of Illinois Press, 1999).
63. William Sachs and Thomas Holland, *Restoring the Ties That Bind: The Grassroots Transformation of the Episcopal Church* (New York: Church Publishing, 2003), 87, 166–7.
64. Richard Kew and Roger J. White, *New Millennium, New Church: Trends Shaping the Episcopal Church for the 21st Century* (Cambridge, MA: Cowley Publications, 1992), 29–30.
65. Mathew L. Sheep, "Meaning, Discourse, and Design Thinking: Organizational Becoming in the Episcopal Church," in *What We Shall Become: The Future and Structure of the Episcopal Church*, ed. Winnie Varghese (New York: Church Publishing, 2013), 51; *NYT*, Mar 25, 1989: 29–30; *Christianity Today*, May 2008: 20.
66. William H. Katerberg, *Modernity and the Dilemma of North American Anglican Identities 1880–1950* (Montreal and Kingston: McGill-Queen's University Press, 2001), 136; Gillis J. Harp, "The Strange Death of Evangelical Episcopalianism," *AEH* 74.2 (June 2005): 185.

Chapter 2

1. AEC, 107.5.4 (Scarlett Papers): William Scarlett, "The Social Gospel" (1962), 1.
2. Richard Wrightman Fox, *Reinhold Niebuhr: A Biography* (1985; Ithaca, NY: Cornell UP, 1996), 77–80.
3. Larry Rasmussen, "Morality and Power," in *Reinhold Niebuhr, Theologian of Public Life: Selected Writings*, ed. Larry Rasmussen (London: Collins, 1988), 45–6.
4. A. James Reichley, *Religion in American Public Life* (Washington, DC: Brookings Institution, 1985), 226–8. For an overview of Christian realism, see Robin W. Lovin, *Reinhold Niebuhr and Christian Realism* (Cambridge: Cambridge UP, 1995), 1–32.

258 NOTES

5. AEC, 107.7.1/2 (Scarlett Papers): Reinhold Niebuhr, "Foreword," in William Scarlett, "A Parson's Tale" (c. 1963), n.p.

6. AEC, 107.5.4 (Scarlett Papers): Scarlett, "The Social Gospel," 2. For a broader analysis of the Social Gospel's influence on this generation, see William McGuire King, "An Enthusiasm for Humanity: The Social Emphasis in Religion and Its Accommodation in Protestant Theology," in *Religion and Twentieth-Century American Intellectual Life*, ed. Michael J. Lacey (New York: Cambridge UP, 1989), 49–77.

7. William R. Hutchison, "Cultural Strain and Protestant Liberalism," *American Historical Review* 76.2 (Apr 1971): 404–5.

8. Charles F. Rehkopf, "The Episcopate of William Scarlett," *Bulletin of the Missouri Historical Society* 20 (1964): 194.

9. AEC, 107.9.12 (Scarlett Papers): Records of the Social Justice Commission, 1932–53.

10. AEC, 107.7.1/2 (Scarlett Papers): William Scarlett, "A Parson's Tale" (c. 1963), 230, 235.

11. AEC, 107.10.24 (Scarlett Papers): Reinhold Niebuhr, untitled address (1950), 4.

12. *Christianity and Crisis*, Mar 1, 1948: 20. Among the many clergy who considered Scarlett their mentor were the article's author, Professor Clifford Stanley, as well as Dean Sidney Sweet and future bishops Bradford Hastings, Ned Cole, John Burt, and Roger Blanchard. John H. Burt, "Humbly and Boldly," in *Anniversary Booklet: A Tribute to John Elbridge Hines on the Fiftieth Anniversary of His Ordination to the Priesthood, October 1984* (1984), ed. John Shelby Spong, n.p; Columbia (Oral History): "Reminiscences of Roger Wilson Blanchard" (1982), 1.7–8.

13. *Episcopalian*, Oct 1966: 46.

14. Kenneth Kesselus, *John E. Hines: Granite on Fire* (Austin, TX: Episcopal Theological Seminary of the Southwest, 1995), 1–54; Patrick Gahan, *An Interview with The Right Reverend John E. Hines* (n.p: 1993): 18, 24.

15. Columbia (Oral History): "Reminiscences of John E. Hines" (1986), 1.48, 1.66. See also *Churchman*, Mar 19, 1932: 14–15.

16. Kesselus, *Granite on Fire*, 63.

17. John Booty, *An American Apostle: The Life of Stephen Fielding Bayne, Jr.* (Valley Forge, PA: Trinity Press International, 1997), 1–12.

18. Stephen F. Bayne, "Establishment: Responsibility and Privilege," *Anglican World*, Jan/Feb 1963: 49.

19. Butler Private Papers: Warren H. Turner to Janet Haugaard, Jan 17, 1984.

20. Janet Haugaard, email to author, Nov 5, 2014.

21. Butler Private Papers: John V. Butler, "My Life and Times at Trinity and Before" (1972), 4–5, 9.

22. Booty, *American Apostle*, 15–16; Janet Haugaard, email to author, July 30, 2013.

23. Alison Collis Greene, "The End of 'The Protestant Era'?" *Church History* 80.3 (Sept 2011): 602–3, 607–8.

24. Monroe Billington and Cal Clark, "The Episcopal Clergy and the New Deal: Clerical Responses to Franklin D. Roosevelt's Letter of Inquiry, September 1935," *HMPEC* 52.3 (Sept 1983): 296–7; Monroe Billington and Cal Clark, "Clergy Reaction to the New Deal: A Comparative Study," *Historian* 48.4 (Aug 1986): 524.

NOTES 259

25. David Hein, *Noble Powell and the Episcopal Establishment in the Twentieth Century* (Urbana: University of Illinois Press, 2001), 111.

26. William McGuire King, "The Reform Establishment and the Ambiguities of Influence," in *Between the Times: The Travail of the Protestant Establishment in America, 1900–1960*, ed. William R. Hutchison (Cambridge: Cambridge UP, 1989), 122–5.

27. Markwell, *Anglican Left*, 140, 169, 243–4; Christopher H. Evans, *The Social Gospel in American Religion: A History* (New York: NYU Press, 2017), 99–101.

28. Gordon Gatehouse, "The Church League for Industrial Democracy," in *Struggling with the System, Probing Alternatives: A Study/Action Guide*, ed. Robert L. DeWitt (Ambler, PA: Episcopal Church Publishing, 1976), 38–9.

29. EDS, FLE 1/4 (Fletcher Papers): Joseph M. Fletcher, unpublished anecdotes (mid-1980s), 29–30.

30. Robert Moats Miller, "The Social Attitudes of the American Episcopal Church during Two Decades, 1919–1939," *HMPEC* 25.2 (June 1956): 191–2.

31. Robert Booth Fowler, *Unconventional Partners: Religion and Liberal Culture in the United States* (Grand Rapids, MI: Eerdmans, 1989), 84–5; Eric P. Kaufmann, *The Rise and Fall of Anglo America* (Cambridge, MA: Harvard UP, 2004), 135–9.

32. AEC, 107.7.1/2 (Scarlett Papers): Scarlett, "A Parson's Tale," 128–9.

33. Preliminary Commission on Social Reconstruction, *A Better World for All Peoples* (Cincinnati: Forward Movement, 1943), 2.

34. AEC, 107.8.11 (Scarlett Papers): Joint Commission on Social Reconstruction, 1931–58.

35. Preliminary Commission, *A Better World*, 3. The report makes specific reference to the Malvern Conference of 1941, which took place shortly after the commission's formation: see William Temple et al., *Malvern, 1941: The Life of the Church and the Order of Society, Being the Proceedings of the Archbishop of York's Conference* (London: Longmans, 1941). The octogenarian Vida Scudder also praised the work of the Malvern Conference, which she called "a climax in the gradual awakening of the Christian social conscience." At the same time, she regretted that "we haven't had many radical statements from high ecclesiastical officials in this country. We can't match Archbishop Temple." Vida Dutton Scudder, "Anglican Thought on Property," in *Christianity and Property*, ed. Joseph F. Fletcher (Philadelphia: Westminster Press, 1947), 144–5, 149.

36. AEC, 107.3.13 (Scarlett Papers): William Scarlett, "The New Crusade" (1945), 1.

37. AEC, 107.5.8 (Scarlett Papers): William Scarlett, untitled sermon (1945), 4, 10.

38. AEC, 107.3.12 (Scarlett Papers): William Scarlett, "The Church" (1946), 1.

39. William Scarlett, "Introduction," in *Christianity Takes a Stand: An Approach to the Issues of Today*, ed. William Scarlett (New York: Penguin, 1946), 1–8.

40. Angus Dun, "The Social Responsibility of the Christian and of the Church," in *Christianity Takes a Stand: An Approach to the Issues of Today*, ed. William Scarlett (New York: Penguin, 1946), 17–19. Dun's essay had already appeared the previous year: *ATR* 27.4 (Oct 1945): 219–27.

41. Howard H. Hassinger, untitled review of *Christianity Takes a Stand*, ed. William Scarlett, *ATR* 29.2 (Apr 1947): 114. The Commission published a second volume in

260   NOTES

1949 focusing on the challenges presented by communism: see William Scarlett (ed.), *The Christian Demand for Social Justice* (New York: New American Library, 1949).

42. Mimi Ayres Sanderson, interview with author, London, Apr 14, 2015.

43. Ayres Private Papers: Francis O. Ayres to parishioners on active service (1944), 2.

44. E. Brooks Holifield, *God's Ambassadors: A History of the Christian Clergy in America* (Grand Rapids, MI: Eerdmans, 2007), 237; Prichard, *A History*, 280.

45. Sara C. Winter, *Religious Journey, Secular Road: An Account of the Parishfield Community, 1949–1967* (n.p: c. 2002): 1.18–20.

46. Francis B. Sayre, Jr., "Industrial Chaplaincy," *Parsons* 6.5 (May 1951): 1.

47. *NYT*, May 22, 1959: 9. A notable collection of future Episcopal leaders served as chaplains during the war, among them Morris F. Arnold, Scott Field Bailey, Stephen F. Bayne, John H. Burt, John B. Coburn, William F. Creighton, C. Kilmer Myers, Edward McNair, Lauriston L. Scaife, Albert R. Stuart, and John J. Weaver. See Roy John Honeywell, *Chaplains of the United States Army* (Washington, DC: Department of the Army, 1958); and Clifford M. Drury, *The History of the Chaplain Corps, United States Navy, 1939–49* (Washington, DC: Government Printing Office, 1984).

48. WNC, 163.5.1 (Oral History Project): Interview with Francis B. Sayre, Jr. (2000), 67.

49. Mason Lecky, "I wasn't big enough to be the conscience of the nation—but I tried to be," *St Alban's Bulletin*, Summer 2002: 11.

50. *NYT*, June 8, 1933: 6.

51. *NYT*, Mar 10, 1936: 24; *NYT*, Mar 23, 1936: 8.

52. *NYT*, May 22, 1959: 9; *Saturday Evening Post*, Sept 21, 1963: 70.

53. Paul Moore, Jr., *Presences: A Bishop's Life in the City* (Cambridge, MA: Cowley Publications, 1997), 7–77.

54. Richard Polenberg, *One Nation Divisible: Class, Race, and Ethnicity in the United States since 1938* (New York: Viking Press, 1980), 65, 69. See also Bennett J. Sims, *The Time of My Life: A Spiritual Pilgrimage Grounded in Hope* (Hendersonville, NC: Institute for Servant Leadership, 2006), 77; and Tony Stoneburner, *Making Waves: The Life and Work of Mike Bloy (The Rev. Myron B. Bloy, Jr.), 1926–1985* (Minneapolis, MN: Limekiln Press, 2015), 115–16.

55. AEC, 2003.01.8 (Moore Papers): Paul Moore, "War Diary-Letters 1942" (1940s), 31.

56. Paul Moore, Jr., "The Making of a Marine on Guadalcanal," in *The Pacific War Remembered: An Oral History Collection*, ed. John T. Mason, Jr. (Annapolis, MD: Naval Institute Press, 1986), 136.

57. *Los Angeles Times*, July 14, 2001: B13.

58. *Atlanta Constitution*, Nov 2, 1944: 4.

59. *Cleveland Plain Dealer*, Mar 25, 1945: 7; *Akron Beacon Journal*, Aug 18, 1946: 4B.

60. Columbia (Oral History): "Reminiscences of Francis B. Sayre, Jr." (1983). 12–13.

61. WNC, 18004.13.1 (Sayre Papers): Henry Knox Sherrill to Francis B. Sayre, Jr., Dec 12, 1945.

62. WNC, 18003.2.7 (Sayre Papers): Francis B. Sayre, Jr., "Industrial Chaplaincy: A General Outline" (c. 1945), 1–3.

63. *Army and Navy Chaplain*, Jan–Feb 1946: 13. Employing a similar logic, the Church League for Industrial Democracy also promoted industrial chaplaincy after the war,

so that the Gospel could be brought to "unchurched people who are not reached through the usual parish channels." *Program of the Church League for Industrial Democracy* (1946): n.p.

64. WNC, 18003.2.7 (Sayre Papers): Francis B. Sayre, Jr., "Something New: An Industrial Chaplain" (c. 1946), 1.

65. WNC, 18003.2.8 (Sayre Papers): Francis B. Sayre, Jr., "Extract from a letter on Industrial Chaplaincies" (1948), 1.

66. *Witness* 28 Mar 1946: 3–4; WNC, 18003.2.7 (Sayre Papers): Beverley D. Tucker to Robert F. Black, Apr 9, 1946.

67. WNC 18003.2.7 (Sayre Papers): Cameron P. Hall and Seward Hiltner to Francis B. Sayre, Jr., Apr 24, 1946.

68. WNC 18003.2.7 (Sayre Papers): Joseph Fletcher, "Industrial Chaplains: A Memorandum" (1946).

69. WNC, 18003.2.8 (Sayre Papers): Summary of Conference on Industrial Chaplaincy, May 1946 (1956), 3.

70. *LC*, Sept 4, 1949: 14. See also *Witness*, Nov 29, 1956: 3; and *Forth*, Dec 1956: 11.

71. *Forth*, Oct 1949: 12–13.

72. *The Bulletin*, Mar 29, 1945: 9ff.

73. *Witness*, Dec 28, 1950: 3–4.

74. DioPitt, 1.51 (Pardue Papers): Austin Pardue, "The Church has to go where the danger is .." (1968), 1–3a.

75. Wittkofski provides an account of his movement from Roman Catholicism to Episcopalianism in *Modern Canterbury Pilgrims*, ed. James Pike (New York: Morehouse-Gorham, 1956), 114–25.

76. Jeremy Bonner, *Called Out of Darkness into Marvelous Light: A History of the Episcopal Diocese of Pittsburgh, 1750–2006* (Eugene, OR: Wipf and Stock, 2009), 189, 203–6.

77. *Witness*, Jan 10, 1952: 3–4.

78. Hein, *Noble Powell*, 4. In 1956, church membership in the United States reached a record high, with over 60% of Americans claiming some type of formal religious affiliation. This was up from 36% in 1930, 49% in 1940, and 57% in 1950. *Witness*, Sept 20, 1956: 3. For an analysis in the Episcopal context, see Prichard, *A History*, 291–3.

79. David A. Roozen, Jackson W. Carroll, and Wade Clark Roof, "Fifty Years of Religious Change in the United States," in *The Post-War Generation and Establishment Religion: Cross-Cultural Perspectives*, ed. Wade Clark et al. (Boulder, CO: Westview Press, 1995), 60–1.

80. For a review of the new curriculum, see John M. Gessell, *Grace and Obedience: Theological Essays in Criticism* (Sewanee, TN: Proctor's Hall Press, 2002), 55–9.

81. Randolph Crump Miller, "Theology and Christian Education," *ATR* 38.2 (Apr 1956): 125. See also John Booty, *The Episcopal Church in Crisis* (Cambridge, MA: Cowley Publications, 1988), 27–9.

82. John H. Snow, *The Gospel in a Broken World* (Philadelphia: United Church Press, 1972), 26–7.

83. *Forth*, July–Aug 1950: 7ff. See also *Witness*, Apr 17, 1947: 5.

262   NOTES

84. Gray M. Blandy and Lawrence L. Brown, *The Story of the First Twenty-five Years of the Episcopal Seminary of the Southwest* (Austin, TX: ESSW, 1976), 1–3.

85. Kesselus, *Granite on Fire*, 122–6, 142–8.

86. Columbia (Oral History): "Reminiscences of John E. Hines" (1986), 2.155.

87. William A. Clebsch, "The Founding of the Episcopal Theological Seminary of the Southwest," *HMPEC* 27.3 (Sept 1958): 247–50.

88. Matthew Peter Cadwell, *A History of Episcopal Divinity School: In Celebration of Its Twenty-fifth Anniversary* (Cambridge, MA: Episcopal Divinity School, 2000), 6; Robert L. DeWitt, "One Pilgrim's Progress," Kellogg Lecture, Episcopal Divinity School, 1985, http://research.eds.edu/content.php?pid=279893&sid=2839425, accessed Apr 1, 2017 (site discontinued).

89. Robert W. Prichard, "Virginia Seminary since World War II," *VTS Journal* 37.1 (June 1985): 33, 36; Sachs and Holland, *Restoring the Ties*, 165.

90. AEC, 2003.095.1 (Barrett Papers): James Elliott Lindsley et al., *An Anecdotal History of the General Theological Seminary, 1947–1957* (1996), 57; Powel Mills Dawley, *The Story of the General Theological Seminary: A Sesquicentennial History, 1817–1967* (New York: Oxford UP, 1969), 321–3, 336–42.

91. Will D. Campbell, *And Also with You: Duncan Gray and the American Dilemma* (Franklin, TN: Providence House, 1997), 71–2.

92. Kew, *New Millennium*, 135–6.

93. Columbia (Oral History): "Reminiscences of Roger Wilson Blanchard" (1982), 1.8, 1.11; Pat Mathis, interview with author, Palm Beach, FL, Dec 14, 2013.

94. Columbia (Oral History): "Reminiscences of Francis B. Sayre, Jr." (1983), 5–6, 14–15.

95. Columbia (Oral History): "Reminiscences of Arthur E. Walmsley" (1984), 1.10–11. See also David E. Sumner, *The Episcopal Church's History, 1945–1985* (Wilton, CT: Morehouse, 1987), 4–5.

96. William Joseph Barnds, "A Study of the Development of the Office of Presiding Bishop of the American Episcopal Church, 1794–1944," *HMPEC* 27.4 (Dec 1958): 284–5.

97. *NYT*, Sept 18, 1946: 22; *Witness*, Dec 12, 1946: 3.

98. Henry Knox Sherrill, *Among Friends: An Autobiography* (Boston: Little Brown, 1962), 135–42, 274–5.

99. Columbia (Oral History): "Reminiscences of John Bowen Coburn" (1984), 1–25.

100. Benjamin E. Zeller, "American Postwar 'Big Religion': Reconceptualizing Twentieth-Century American Religion Using Big Science as a Model," *Church History* 80.2 (June 2011): 330–1.

101. James H. Moorhead, "Presbyterians and the Mystique of Organizational Efficiency, 1870–1936," in *Reimagining Denominationalism: Interpretative Essays*, ed. Robert Bruce Mullin and Russell E. Richey (New York: Oxford UP, 1994), 24–5.

102. *Witness*, Sept 23, 1948: 11.

103. Sachs and Holland, *Restoring the Ties*, 157.

104. *Episcopal Churchnews*, Aug 18, 1957: 25; Roland Foster, *The Role of the Presiding Bishop* (Cincinnati: Forward Movement, 1982), 59.

NOTES 263

105. Columbia (Oral History): "Reminiscences of Henry W. Sherrill" (1982), 38–9. In a similar vein, Sherrill's friend Liston Pope would later describe him as a "prince of the church." *NYT*, Nov 4, 1962: BR9.

106. Columbia (Oral History): "Reminiscences of Henry S. Noble" (1983), 1.3–4.

107. Apart from Sherrill, all members of the ECF board were laymen, among them George Whitney (J. P. Morgan), Harry M. Addinsell (First Boston Corp.), Prescott S. Bush (Brown Bros. and Harriman), William Crocker (Crocker First National Bank), Edmond duPont (DuPont and Co.), and Harvey S. Firestone (Firestone Tire and Rubber). *Witness*, Apr 27, 1950: 3–4.

108. Columbia (Oral History): "Reminiscences of Frederic C. Lawrence" (1982), 1.11–12.

109. Coffmann, *Christian Century*, 147; Kaufmann, *Anglo America*, 139.

110. *Witness*, Dec 7, 1950: 3–4.

111. Thomas C. Reeves, *The Empty Church: The Suicide of Liberal Christianity* (New York: Free Press, 1996), qtd. 45.

112. H. Richard Niebuhr, *Christ and Culture* (1951; New York: Harper and Row, 1975), 83–4. See also George Rupp, *Culture Protestantism: German Liberal Theology at the Turn of the Twentieth Century* (Missoula, MT: AAR Studies in Religion/Scholars Press, 1977), 9–14.

113. James E. Griffiss, *The Anglican Vision* (Cambridge, MA: Cowley Publications, 1997), 11.

114. King, "The Reform Establishment," 134–5; James H. Smyllie, "Church Growth and Decline in Historical Perspective: Protestant Quest for Identity, Leadership, and Meaning," in *Understanding Church Growth and Decline, 1950–78*, ed. Dean R. Hoge and David A. Roozen (New York, 1979), 77.

115. *NYT*, Sept 27, 1949: 29; *Witness*, Oct 13, 1949: 12.

116. Will Herberg, *Protestant, Catholic, Jew: An Essay in American Religious Sociology* (1955; Chicago: University of Chicago Press, 1983), 72–5, 260–3. See also Mark Silk, *Spiritual Politics: Religion and America since World War II* (New York: Simon and Schuster, 1988), 18–20.

117. Later, in 1960, Joseph Fletcher argued that "Protestant America is as obsolete as the sidewheel showboat, the cigar store Indian, and the Fourth-of-July oration. I can see a time coming, if present forces go on working, when every form of Biblical religion, of prophetic faith, whether Christian or Jewish, will be obsolete. Pious Americanism, the new Shinto, will have taken over." *Witness*, Nov 17, 1960: 9.

118. William Stringfellow, *My People Is the Enemy: An Autobiographical Polemic* (1964; Eugene, OR: Wipf & Stock, 2005), 37; Andrew W. McThenia, Jr., "Introduction: How This Celebration Began," in *Radical Christian and Exemplary Lawyer: Honoring William Stringfellow*, ed. Andrew W. McThenia, Jr. (Grand Rapids, MI: Eerdmans, 1995), 13–14.

119. Cornell, 4438.1 (Stringfellow Papers): William Stringfellow, "Comments on the Christian Ministry to Servicemen" (1952), 8.

120. Booty, *American Apostle*, 28–54.

121. Stephen F. Bayne, Jr., *The Optional God* (1953; Wilton, CT: Morehouse-Barlow, 1980), 9, 21.

264 NOTES

122. Vance Packard, *The Status Seekers: An Exploration of Class Behavior in America* (New York: D. McKay, 1959), 197–201. In keeping with this observation, sociologist Peter Berger observed that "in America one faces the somewhat strange fact that a person's religious affiliation immediately gives one an idea of that person's social status." Peter Berger, *The Noise of Solemn Assemblies: Christian Commitment and the Religious Establishment in America* (Garden City, NY: Doubleday, 1961), 75.

123. Columbia (Oral History): "Reminiscences of John E. Hines" (1986), 2.230–1.

124. W. Norman Pittenger, "Contemporary Anglicanism and the Challenge of Our Time," *ATR* 30.1 (Jan 1948): 12–13.

125. *Witness*, Dec 11, 1952: 9; *LC*, Jan 13, 1946: 9.

126. An analysis of the survey results was not published until fifteen years later: Charles Y. Glock et al., *To Comfort and to Challenge: A Dilemma of the Contemporary Church* (Berkeley: University of California Press, 1967) vii–ix, 81–3.

127. George E. DeMille, *The Episcopal Church since 1900: A Brief History* (New York: Morehouse-Gorham, 1955), 208.

128. Douglas, *Fling Out the Banner!*, 222–3.

129. Snow, *Gospel in a Broken World*, 24.

130. Glock, *To Comfort and to Challenge*, 172, 203, 208.

131. Edwin S. Gaustad, "The Pulpit and the Pews," in *Between the Times: The Travail of the Protestant Establishment in America, 1900–1960*, ed. William R. Hutchison (Cambridge: Cambridge UP, 1989), 28–32; Bonner, *Called Out of Darkness*, 200.

132. Walter H. Stowe, "'The Episcopal Church since 1900': A Review of Canon DeMille's History," *HMPEC* 24.4 (Dec 1955): 417.

133. *LC*, Jan 20, 1946: 9.

134. Michael Allen, *This Time, This Place* (Indianapolis, IN: Bobbs-Merrill, 1971), 55.

135. Phillips, *Kingdom on Earth*, 207, 232.

136. *Witness*, Jan 29, 1948: 5–6.

137. *Chicago Daily Tribune*, Apr 7, 1947: 3. At the same time, *The Living Church* continued to take issue with the editorial standpoint of *The Witness*. It noted in response to one *Witness* article that it "has tried to tell us what is good about Russia and Communism. By implication, it has indicated what is bad about the United States and American foreign policy. Now will it give us the other side of the picture and tell us what, in its opinion, is good about America?" *LC*, May 22, 1949: 14.

138. TCH, Series III: Fol: ELSA (Weber Papers): J. Brooke Mosley to Andrew van Dyke, Nov 20, 1950.

139. TCH, Series III: Fol: AFSA Correspondence (Weber Papers): William M. Weber to J. Raymond Hall, May 30, 1946; *Anglican Fellowship for Social Action* (1948).

140. TCH, Series II: Fol: Arlington (Weber Papers): William M. Weber to "Dad," Apr 7, 1948.

141. *Newark Evening News*, Mar 6, 1948: 3.

142. TCH, Series II: Fol: Arlington (Weber Papers): Wardens and Vestry of Trinity Church, Arlington, NJ, to Benjamin M. Washburn, Mar 10, 1948.

143. TCH, Series II: Fol: Arlington (Weber Papers): William M. Weber to "Dad," Apr 7, 1948.

NOTES 265

144. TCH, Series II: Fol: Arlington (Weber Papers): William M. Weber to "Father Smyth," Mar 16, 1948.

145. *New York Herald Tribune*, Mar 3, 1949: 1ff.

146. As time went on, DeWolfe made no secret of his political proclivities. In 1953, he called upon church officials "to clean their own houses of subversive clergy," boasting that "97 per cent of the clergymen with whom he came in contact in his diocese were loyal." The bishop did not explain how he arrived at this precise figure. *NYT*, July 15, 1953: 16.

147. WNC, 18002.5.1 (Sayre Papers): Francis B. Sayre, Jr., "Christian Outlook on Capitalism" (1950), 2; "Christian Outlook on Communism" (1950), 1.

148. *NYT*, Oct 3, 1949: 15. For an examination of perceptions of American racism and the country's role as a leader on the international stage, see Mary L. Dudziak, *Cold War Civil Rights: Race and the Image of American Democracy* (new ed.; Princeton, NJ: Princeton UP, 2011).

149. AEC, 107.5.6 (Scarlett Papers): William Scarlett, "One World—Under God" (1952), 3–4.

150. AAEHC, 25.1.11 (Harris Papers): David Harris, "Autobiography" (1947), 3.

151. *Witness*, Jan 29, 1948: 9–10.

152. This aspect of Caution's work is sometimes forgotten today. See AAEHC, A19: Series 3.11.1,2 and Series X2, Boxes 1–4 (Dennis Personal Papers): Correspondence and documents relating to conferences on church participation among various ethnic minorities, organized by Caution and Walter D. Dennis (late 1950s).

153. GTS, C25.22.33 (Caution Papers): Tollie L. Caution, "Decade of Progress" (1951), 1. See also Tollie L. Caution, "The Protestant Episcopal Church: Policies and Rationale upon Which Support of the Negro Colleges Is Predicated," *Journal of Negro Education* 29 (1960): 274–83.

154. GTS, C25.22.33 (Caution Papers): Tollie L. Caution, "Significant Facts in the Church's Work among Negroes" (1954), 23–4.

155. GTS, C25.31.43 (Caution Papers): Kenneth Hughes to Daniel Corrigan, Jan 17, 1968.

156. AAEHC, A19: Series 2.1 (Dennis Personal Papers): Walter D. Dennis, "A Spiritual Pilgrimage—some reflections on the 40s, 50s, 60s and 70s and a prospectus on the 80s and 90s" (late 1970s), 4–5.

157. Verna Dozier, *Confronted by God: The Essential Verna Dozier*, ed. Cynthia L. Shattuck and Fredrica Harris Thompsett (New York: Seabury Books, 2006), 29–30.

158. VTS, M182.63.28 (Walker Papers): John T. Walker, untitled lecture at VTS (1984), 6–7.

159. DioWash, 7.1.1 (Walker Papers): John T. Walker, "At the Bottom of the Well, or Lonely American" (1967), 8.

160. VTS, M182.63.28 (Walker Papers): John T. Walker, lecture at VTS: 9–11. See also Robert Harrison, *Transformed by the Love of God: John Walker, A Man for the 21st Century* (Cincinnati, OH: Forward Movement, 2004), 32–3.

161. *Forth*, Apr 1956: 17.

162. John Booty, *Mission and Ministry: A History of the Virginia Theological Seminary* (Harrisburg, PA: Morehouse, 1995), 280–1.

266 NOTES

163. VTS, M182.11 (Walker Papers): John B. Morris and John T. Walker, "The Separation of God's People: The Problem of Racial Prejudice in the Episcopal Church" (1954).

164. Jenny Moore, *The People on Second Street* (New York: William Morrow, 1968), 30.

165. Paul Moore, *Presences*, 98.

166. See David M. Robertson, *A Passionate Pilgrim: A Biography of Bishop James A. Pike* (New York: Vintage, 2006). For an acute if damning assessment of Pike, see also Joan Didion, "James Pike, American," in *The White Album* (1979; New York, 1990), 51–8.

167. *Time*, Nov 11, 1966: 58; William Stringfellow and Anthony Towne, *The Death and Life of Bishop Pike: An Utterly Candid Biography of America's Most Controversial Clergyman* (1976; Eugene, OR: Wipf and Stock, 2007), qtd 262.

168. Syracuse, Box 1 (Pike Papers): James A. Pike to W. J. Kropp, Oct 28, 1943. See also James Pike (ed.), *Modern Canterbury Pilgrims* (New York: Morehouse-Gorham, 1956), 307–17.

169. Dawley, *General Theological Seminary*, 341.

170. Jenny Moore, *Second Street*, 101.

171. *Life*, Sept 13, 1968: 54. The worker-priest movement began in France during the Second World War. Recognizing that the Roman Catholic Church had lost contact with large swathes of the urban working classes, the movement sent young clergy to live and labor alongside factory workers, in the hope of making a fresh Christian witness among them. See Gregor Siefer, *The Church and Industrial Society: A Survey of the Worker-Priest Movement and Its Implications for the Christian Mission* (London: Darton, Longman and Todd, 1964), 18–82. For a contemporary report of the controversies aroused by the worker-priests' activities, see Robert F. Byrnes, "The French Priest-Workers," *Foreign Affairs* 33.2 (Jan 1955): 327–31.

172. DioNY, 100.23 (Moore Papers): Carl Russell Sayers, "Eucharist for a Man and a Cause" (1981), 1.

173. DioNY, 50: Fol: Moore, Paul, Jr. (Donegan Papers): Paul Moore to Charles K. Gilbert, Sept 18, 1947.

174. Paul Moore, Jr., *Take a Bishop like Me* (New York: Harper and Row, 1979), 7.

175. *Life*, Sept 13, 1968: 54.

176. *WP*, Sept 8, 1968: G25.

177. AEC, 2003.01.25 (Moore Papers): Paul Moore, "A City Parish" (c. 1966), 13.

178. Jenny Moore, *Second Street*, 37–8, 101–4.

179. DioNY, 50: Fol: Moore, Paul, Jr. (Donegan Papers): Paul Moore to Charles K. Gilbert, Aug 18, 1949.

180. Paul Moore, *Presences*, 116.

181. Honor Moore, *The Bishop's Daughter: A Memoir* (New York: W. W. Norton, 2008), 100–1.

182. This outreach was to have a particular impact on Albert Williams and his three brothers, who first became involved in Grace Church through its summer camps. Albert went on to be baptized and confirmed in the Episcopal Church and was later adopted by Kim Myers. Albert J. Williams-Myers, email to author, June 9, 2017.

183. Jenny Moore, *Second Street*, 46, 112, 137.

NOTES 267

184. AEC, 2003.01.24 (Moore Papers): Residents of neighborhood of Grace Church, Second and Erie Streets, Jersey City, to Benjamin Washburn, Aug 7, 1950.

185. AEC, 2003.01.24 (Moore Papers): Paul Moore, GTS Alumni Day address (1953), 4, 15.

186. *Witness*, May 6, 1948: 9.

187. AEC, 43.6 (Lichtenberger Papers): Arthur Lichtenberger, "Inaugural Sermon, GTS" (1948), 10.

188. John B. Coburn, *Twentieth-Century Spiritual Letters: An Introduction to Contemporary Prayer* (Philadelphia: Westminster, 1967), 48–9

189. Milton McC. Gatch, "John Bowen Coburn, 1914–2009," *AEH* 79.4 (Dec 2010): 332.

190. E.g., *Forth*, Feb 1949: 20ff.; *Witness*, Jan 24, 1952: 3–4; *Witness*, Apr 17, 1952: 3–4.

191. *Forth*, June 1951: 13ff; *LC*, Jun 10, 1951: 7–9.

192. Paul Moore, "And Suddenly Nothing Happens," in *On the Battle Lines: A Manifesto for Our Times by 27 Militant Clergymen*, ed. Malcolm Boyd (New York: Morehouse-Barlow, 1964), 70–1.

193. Jenny Moore, *Second Street*, 195.

194. Gardiner H. Shattuck, Jr., *Episcopalians and Race: Civil War to Civil Rights* (Lexington: UP of Kentucky, 2000), 90–1.

195. Paul Moore, Jr., "The Church's Mission, I," in *Viewpoints: Some Aspects of Anglican Thinking*, ed. John B. Coburn and W. Norman Pittenger (Greenwich, CT: Seabury Press, 1959), 234–5.

196. AEC, 32.15.1 (Home Department Records): Urban Work—Beginning of Program, History: Unsigned, "Statement of Aims and Principles of Urban Mission Priests" (early 1950s), 1–2.

197. AEC, 32.15.1 (Home Department Records): Urban Work—Beginning of Program, History: Unsigned, "The New York Urban Priests' Group" (early 1950s), 1.

198. For an account of EHPP's genesis and development, see Bruce Kenrick, *Come Out the Wilderness* (New York: Harper and Row, 1962).

199. G. H. Jack Woodard, *The Episcopal Church's Struggle to Light the Dark Streets: Urban Ministry, 1948 to 1994* (n.p: 1994), 43–4.

200. Hein and Shattuck, *The Episcopalians*, 114–15; Katerberg, *North American Anglican Identities*, 129–31.

201. Pittenger, "Contemporary Anglicanism," 12–13.

202. The resulting "Committee of Nine" was made up of Bishops Stephen Bayne of Olympia, Angus Dun of Washington, John Hines of Texas, Austin Pardue of Pittsburgh, Beverley Tucker of Ohio, Thomas Carruthers of South Carolina, Wallace Conkling of Chicago, Walter Gray of Connecticut, and Benjamin Ivins of Milwaukee. DioWash, 6.4.2 (Creighton Papers): House of Bishops, Report of the "Committee of Nine" (1949), 2.

203. Butler Private Papers: Butler, "My Life and Times," 11–16.

204. Butler Private Papers: Warren H. Turner to Ruth Butler, Sept 27, 1983.

205. *LC*, Oct 3, 1954: 20–2.

206. *Washingtonian* July 1968: 37ff.

207. TCW, 44.20 (Heuss Papers): Edward Chandler to John Heuss, Dec 15, 1952.

268 NOTES

208. Morton Private Papers: James Parks Morton, "The Third Day: Jersey City" (c. 2014), 6–7.

209. James and Pamela Morton, interview with author, New York, Dec 17, 2014. Albert Williams-Myers likewise recalls the important role Jenny Moore and other women had in coordinating the ministry's programs. Albert J. Williams-Myers, email to author, June 9, 2017.

210. M. Moran Weston, *Episcopalians at Work in the World: A Study of Social Education and Community Action in the Protestant Episcopal Church in the United States of America 1949–1951* (New York: National Council, 1952), 19–20.

211. AEC, 211.1.1 (JUP Records): Almon R. Pepper and G. Paul Musselman, "Five Year Urban-Industrial Church Work Experimentation and Demonstration Progress Report" (1954), 5.

212. Woodard, *Episcopal Church's Struggle*, 55–6.

213. E.g., *Forth*, Feb 1954: 20ff; *Witness*, May 27, 1954: 3–4; *Witness*, Nov 29, 1956: 4–5.

214. Powel Mills Dawley, *The Episcopal Church and Its Work* (Greenwich, CT: Seabury, 1955), 235–6. See also *Episcopal Churchnews*, Oct 5, 1952: 4.

215. *WP*, Jan 22, 1951: 1; Unsigned, "The Revd Francis B. Sayre, Jr. Elected as Fifth Dean of Washington Cathedral," *CA* 26.1 (Spring 1951): 2.

216. AEC, 107.7.11 (Scarlett Papers): Francis B. Sayre, Jr. to William Scarlett, Feb 6, 1951.

217. WNC (Oral History Project): Interview with Francis B. Sayre, Jr. (2000), 69.

218. WNC, 18002.1.1 (Sayre Papers): Francis B. Sayre, Jr., address delivered at Annual Bishop's Dinner (1952), 7.

219. Margaret Shannon, "God's Emissary: The Prophetic Voice of a Cathedral Dean," *CA* (Winter 2008): 8–10. For a more critical assessment of Frank Sayre's leadership, see Frederick Quinn, *A House of Prayer for All People: A History of Washington National Cathedral* (New York: Morehouse Publishing, 2014), 120–30.

220. *WP*, June 22, 1951: 18.

221. *WP*, Oct 26, 1953: 9; *WP*, Oct 28, 1957: B1.

222. WNC, 18004.2.7 (Sayre Papers): Francis B. Sayre, Jr. to John M. Burgess, Apr 14, 1952.

223. WNC, 18004.2.7 (Sayre Papers): John M. Burgess to Francis B. Sayre, Jr., Apr 23, 1952.

224. *Witness*, Feb 12, 1948: 5.

225. Robert E. Hood, *Social Teachings in the Episcopal Church: A Source Book* (Danbury, CT: Morehouse, 1990), 114.

226. The trajectory of this episode is traced in Araminta Stone Johnston, *And One Was a Priest: The Life and Times of Duncan M. Gray Jr.* (Jackson: UP of Mississippi, 2011), 97–118.

227. *NYT*, Feb 13, 1953: 23. See also Shattuck, *Episcopalians and Race*, 48–9.

228. *Witness*, Feb 26, 1953: 6.

229. Duncan M. Gray, Jr., "Sewanee: There and Back Again," *Sewanee Theological Review* 46.2 (Easter 2003): 221.

230. See James T. Patterson, *Brown v. Board of Education: A Civil Rights Milestone and Its Troubled Legacy* (New York: Oxford UP, 2001), 46–69.

NOTES 269

231. Diocese of Mississippi Department of CSR, *The Church Considers the Supreme Court Decision* (Jackson: Diocese of Mississippi, 1954), 3, 7.

232. Donald Cunnigen, "Working for Racial Integration: The Civil Rights Activism of Bishop Duncan Montgomery Gray of Mississippi," *AEH* 67.4 (Dec 1998): 482, 498; Campbell, *And Also with You*, 141, 159.

233. The perceived linkage between racial integration and communist infiltration retained its salience well into the 1960s: see Jeff Woods, *Black Struggle, Red Scare: Segregation and Anti-Communism in the South, 1948-1968* (Baton Rouge: Louisiana State UP, 2004).

234. *NYT*, Feb 23, 1953: 14; *Witness*, Mar 12, 1953: 13–14.

235. *Witness*, May 21, 1953: 3–4; *Witness*, May 28, 1953: 6; *NYT*, Nov 11, 1953: 21.

236. *NYT*, Mar 22, 1954: 21; *Episcopal Churchnews*, Apr 18, 1954: 34–6.

237. E. Digby Baltzell, *The Protestant Establishment: Aristocracy and Caste in America* (1964; New Haven, CT: Yale UP, 1987), 287. For a contemporary analysis of this phenomenon, see Richard Hofstadter's 1954 essay "The Pseudo-Conservative Revolt," in his book *The Paranoid Style in American Politics* (1965; New York: Vintage Books, 2008), 41–65.

238. Phillips, *Kingdom on Earth*, 286.

239. AEC, 107.3.12 (Scarlett Papers): William Scarlett, "The Christian Ministry" (c. 1949), 9.

Chapter 3

1. Robert S. Ellwood, *The Fifties Spiritual Marketplace: American Religion in a Decade of Conflict* (New Brunswick, NJ: Rutgers UP, 1997), 4–5.

2. Pat Mathis, interview with author, Palm Beach, FL, Dec 10, 2013; Douglas Carpenter, email to author, Sept 20, 2014.

3. *LC*, Sept 28, 1952: 7.

4. Shattuck, *Episcopalians and Race*, 41–2.

5. *LC*, May 16, 1954: 6.

6. Alan Lake Chidsey, *The Bishop: A Portrait of the Right Reverend Clinton S. Quin* (Houston, TX: Gulf Publishing, 1966), 226.

7. *Witness*, Sept 22, 1955: 9.

8. Syracuse, Box 102 (Pike Papers): James A. Pike, Address at Princeton Theological Seminary (1956), 1.

9. Syracuse, Box 101 (Pike Papers): James A. Pike, "The Scope and Price of Prophecy" (1956), 1.

10. Columbia (Oral History): "Reminiscences of Warren Turner" (1984), 1.61.

11. Arthur E. Walmsley, interview with author, Concord, NH, Jan 6, 2014.

12. Walmsley Private Papers: Arthur E. Walmsley, "Second Meditation: Looking Ahead" (2012), 3.

13. *Witness*, Dec 10, 1959: 7, 9.

270 NOTES

14. Arthur E. Walmsley, "The Mission of the Church in the New Era," in *The Church in a Society of Abundance*, ed. Arthur E. Walmsley (New York: Seabury Press, 1963), 71.

15. BHL (Sara C. Winter Oral History Collection): Interview with Gibson Winter (1994–1995).

16. Francis O. Ayres, *The Ministry of the Laity: A Biblical Exposition* (Philadelphia: Westminster Press, 1962), 15; BHL, Box 1, Fol: Parishfield Histories (Parishfield Records): *This Is Parishfield* (early 1950s), n.p.

17. Sara C. Winter, Parishfield Oral Histories (1994–1995): Transcript of Bob DeWitt Interview—Tape One, 19–20.

18. *Witness*, Oct 7, 1948: 3–4.

19. Stoneburner, *Making Waves*, 6.

20. BHL (Sara C. Winter Oral History Collection): Interview with Paul M. van Buren (1994–1995).

21. Sara C. Winter, Parishfield Oral Histories: Transcript of Tony Stoneburner Interview (1994–1995), 9–11, 34.

22. *Christian Century*, June 14, 1967: 776–7.

23. The definitive biography of Bonhoeffer remains that by his friend and student Eberhard Bethge: see *Dietrich Bonhoeffer: Theologian, Christian, Man for His Times: A Biography* (rev. ed.; Minneapolis: Fortress Press, 2000).

24. The phrase appears in Bonhoeffer's letter to Eberhard Bethge dated June 8, 1944: Dietrich Bonhoeffer, *Letters and Papers from Prison*, trans. Reginald H. Fuller (new ed.; New York: Touchstone Books, 1997), 326.

25. Winter, *Religious Journey*, 2.3–4.

26. Sara C. Winter, Parishfield Oral Histories (1994–1995): Transcript of Mary White Interview—Tape One, 11.

27. Winter, *Religious Journey*, 2.4–5, 3.

28. Sara C. Winter, Parishfield Oral Histories (1994–1995): Transcript of Mary White Interview—Tape One, 1.

29. BHL, Box 8, Fol: Parishfield, Hugh White Correspondence, 1963–1971 (Barney Papers): Hugh White to NIM Board of Directors, Sept 1971, 1–2.

30. The elegant Christ Church was consecrated in 1928 as part of the Cranbrook Educational Community, an initiative of the philanthropist George Gough Booth. Williams, *Religion, Art, and Money*, 197–200.

31. WSU, 131.1.2 (DIM Records): Hugh C. White to Almus M. Thorp, Feb 20, 1958; John Hooper, interview with author, Blue Hill, ME, July 28, 2015.

32. Winter, *Religious Journey*, 1.9.

33. Mimi Ayres Sanderson, interview with author, London, Apr 14, 2015.

34. Sara C. Winter, Parishfield Oral Histories (1994–1995): Transcript of Tony Stoneburner Interview, 19, 24–5.

35. Mimi Ayres Sanderson, interview with author, London, Apr 14, 2015.

36. Sara Winter, interview with author, New York, Dec 20, 2014.

37. The one female member of staff with a formally recognized ministry was Olive M. Robinson, a deaconess who joined Parishfield in the early 1950s. Winter, *Religious Journey*, 1.14–16.

38. BHL (Sara C. Winter Oral History Collection): Interview with Paul M. van Buren (1994–1995); Sara C. Winter, Parishfield Oral Histories (1994–1995): Transcript of Mary White Interview—Tape Two, 37–8, 40–2.

39. Sara C. Winter, Parishfield Oral Histories (1994–1995): Transcript of Mary White Interview—Tape Two, 17, 36–7.

40. Nancy M. Malone, "Dedication to Mike Bloy, Broker of the Kingdom," *Journal of Law and Religion* 4.1 (1986): 6.

41. *LC*, Aug 7, 1955: 14; *Witness*, Dec 4, 1959: 8.

42. Snow, *Gospel in a Broken World*, 27–9; John Rawlinson, email to author, Sept 6, 2013.

43. Upon his graduation from ETS, Mike and Caroline Bloy returned to Detroit, where he served for two years at St. Paul's Cathedral before becoming the first full-time Episcopal chaplain at the Massachusetts Institute of Technology in 1958. *LC*, Sept 21, 1958: 10.

44. *Ann Arbor News*, July 5, 1957: 9.

45. AEC, 2003.01.26 (Moore Papers): Unsigned, "Parishfield: Working Paper on Frontier Evangelism No. 1" (1955), 2; Unsigned, "Parishfield: Working Paper on Frontier Evangelism No. 2" (1955), 6. Published in Germany in 1939, *Life Together* is a meditation on Christian community informed by Bonhoeffer's experience of teaching at the Confessing Church's underground seminary at Finkenwalde. See Dietrich Bonhoeffer, *Life Together*, trans. John W. Doberstein (New York: Harper, 1954).

46. *Christian Century*, June 14, 1967: 777–8.

47. Ayres, *Ministry of the Laity*, 132.

48. Ellen T. Charry, "Introduction," in Paul M. van Buren, *The Austin Dogmatics, 1957–1958*, ed. Ellen T. Charry (Eugene, OR: Cascade Books, 2012), qtd. xix.

49. Winter, *Religious Journey*, 2.8.

50. BHL (Sara C. Winter Oral History Collection): Interview with Paul M. van Buren (1994–1995).

51. Charry, "Introduction," xxi–xxii.

52. Paul M. van Buren, *The Austin Dogmatics, 1957–1958*, ed. Ellen T. Charry (Eugene, OR: Cascade Books, 2012), 303.

53. *Sword and Shield*, Mar 1955: 4.

54. BHL (Sara C. Winter Oral History Collection): Interview with Paul M. van Buren (1994–1995).

55. Sara C. Winter, Parishfield Oral Histories (1994–1995): Transcript of Mary White Interview—Tape Two, 19.

56. *Witness*, Aug 20, 1959: 8.

57. WSU, 131.2.1.25.22 (DIM Records): Hugh C. White to Francis M. Sayre, Jr., May 17, 1965.

58. WSU, 131.1.1 (DIM Records): Unsigned, "Detroit Industrial Mission" (1957), 1.

59. AEC, 85.13.40 (CSR Records): Urban Industrial Church Work: Conferences, 1953–1957.

60. *Forth*, Dec 1956: 10, 28–9. See also Kevin M. Schutz, *Tri-Faith America: How Catholics and Jews Held Postwar America to Its Protestant Promise* (Oxford: Oxford UP, 2011), 103.

272 NOTES

61. Division of Urban Industrial Church Work, *Report of the Joint Commission to Survey the Missionary Problems in Industrial Areas* (New York: National Council of PECUSA, 1958), 9.

62. *NYT*, Oct 15, 1956: 30.

63. *Witness*, Jan 29, 1959: 3–4.

64. Muffy Paradise, interview with author, Bedford, MA, Jan 6, 2015.

65. Paradise Private Papers: Interview with Scott Paradise by Charles Weiner: Session 1, Apr 29, 1992, 2–6.

66. Paradise Private Papers: Scott I. Paradise, "Paradise Saga" (2007): n.p.

67. Scott Paradise, *To Speak with Power: Sermons*, ed. Peter Paradise (2003): 18; Ron Ferguson, *George MacLeod: Founder of the Iona Community* (London: Collins, 1990), 199.

68. Paul Bagshaw, *The Church beyond the Church: Sheffield Industrial Mission, 1944–1994* (Sheffield: Industrial Mission in South Yorkshire, 1994), 18–20.

69. Paradise Private Papers: Interview with Scott Paradise by Charles Weiner: Session 1, Apr 29, 1992, 12, 14.

70. In the years to come, Wickham became a regular source of advice and encouragement to the DIM staff and visited Michigan on a number of occasions: see WSU, 131.1.3 (DIM Records): Correspondence of Hugh C. White and Edward "Ted" Wickham, 1957–1958.

71. WSU, 131.2.1.9.43 (DIM Records): Institute on the Church in Corporate Society, "A Study of the Detroit Industrial Mission" (c. 1961), 14.

72. Scott I. Paradise, *Detroit Industrial Mission: A Personal Narrative* (New York: Harper and Row, 1968) xv–xvi, 98.

73. WSU, 131.1.1 (DIM Records): Hugh C. White to Robert L. DeWitt, Sept 20, 1957.

74. Paradise Private Papers: Interview with Scott Paradise by Charles Weiner: Session 2, Part 1, May 21, 1992: 23; WSU, 131.1.2 (DIM Records): Correspondence of Hugh C. White and Francis B. Sayre, Jr., 1957–1958.

75. Paradise, *Detroit Industrial Mission*, 9, 13, 56.

76. WSU, 131.1.1 (DIM Records): Francis B. Sayre, Jr. to Scott I. Paradise, Oct 31, 1959.

77. WSU, 131.2.1.9.42 (DIM Records): Scott I. Paradise Journal Selections: "Toward a Christian Industrial Theology"—"New Directions for Prophecy" (late 1950s/early 1960s), 1.

78. Paradise Private Papers: Scott I. Paradise, "A Tale of Two Cities" (late 1950s), 3; WNC, 18003.2.9 (Sayre Papers): Scott I. Paradise, "The Mission of the Church to Industrial Society" (1959), 2–3.

79. Wickham and Paradise were by no means unique in identifying the underside of technocratic culture. In 1956, sociologist William H. Whyte published *The Organization Man*, which portrayed the type of person in Western society specially conditioned to excel in bureaucracies: William H. Whyte, *The Organization Man* (New York: Simon & Schuster, 1956).

80. BHL, Box 2, Fol: Programs—DIM (Parishfield Records): Hugh C. White, "Christianity and Work" (1958), 1.

NOTES 273

81. E. R. Wickham, *Church and People in an Industrial City* (London: Lutterworth Press, 1957), 239.
82. WSU, 131.2.2.29.11 (DIM Records): Correspondence of Hugh C. White and Paul M. van Buren, 1957–1965.
83. WSU, 131.1.1 (DIM Records): Paul M. van Buren, "Address, December 30th, 1957" (1958), 1, 4.
84. *Witness*, Aug 20, 1959: 9; Scott I. Paradise, "Christian Mission and the Technician Mentality in America," in *Christians in a Technological Era*, ed. Hugh C. White, Jr. (New York: Seabury, 1964), 135.
85. Hugh C. White, Jr., "The Basic Task of the Church," *Pastoral Psychology* 10.5 (June 1959): 29–30.
86. WSU, 131.1.1 (DIM Records): Robert L. DeWitt to Hugh C. White, June 10, 1958.
87. *Witness*, May 1, 1958: 4–5.
88. Scott I. Paradise, "A New Concept of Mission for Our Industrial Age," *CA* 36.3 (Fall 1961): 37. Though he characterizes the DIM staff as "unusually bright, perceptive, and sensitive observers of working-class religious culture," Matthew Pehl has recently argued that "their basic analysis of working-class religiosity suffered from the restrictions of their own racial, religious, gender, and class assumptions." Matthew Pehl, "Discovering Working-Class Religion in a 1950s Auto Plant," in *The Pew and the Picket Line: Christianity and the American Working Class*, ed. Christopher D. Cantwell et al. (Urbana: University of Illinois Press, 2016), 103.
89. WSU, 131.2.1.9.43 (DIM Records): "A Study of the Detroit Industrial Mission," 8.
90. WNC, 18003.2.9 (Sayre Papers): Paradise, "The Mission of the Church to Industrial Society," 5.
91. WSU, 131.2.1.25.43 (DIM Records): Hugh C. White and E. L. Cushman, "Advent Series of Church and World Lectures, Episcopal Theological Seminary of the Southwest, Austin" (1959), 14.
92. Paradise, *Detroit Industrial Mission*, xvi.
93. In 1950, a quarter of all Americans lived in suburbs; by 1960, that number had increased to a third. Kevin M. Kruse and Thomas J. Sugrue, "Introduction: The New Suburban History," in *The New Suburban History*, ed. Kevin M. Kruse and Thomas J. Sugrue (Chicago: University of Chicago Press, 2006), 1.
94. Gibson Winter, *The Suburban Captivity of the Churches: An Analysis of Protestant Responsibility in the Expanding Metropolis* (Garden City, NY: Doubleday, 1961), 35, 76–7, 103.
95. Hudnut-Beumler, *Looking for God*, 85–6. For an overview of Winter's thought, see Gary Dorrien, *Social Ethics in the Making: Interpreting an American Tradition* (Malden, MA: Wiley-Blackwell, 2008), 549–63.
96. G. Paul Musselman, *The Church on the Urban Frontier* (Greenwich, CT: Seabury Press, 1960), 131. Robert MacGill charged Winter and other critics of the suburban church with alarmism: "The nature and unity of the Catholic Body of Christ have been threatened time and again by cultural infiltration," he wrote. "It will take more than the fire of a few million backyard barbecues to prevail against it now." *LC*, Oct 7, 1962, 12–13.

274 NOTES

97. *Witness*, March 31, 1960: 9; *Witness*, Mar 22, 1962: 7.

98. *Forth*, Sept 1955: 8–9; AEC, 2003.01.24 (Moore Papers): Paul Moore, "Mission of the Church" (1958), 13.

99. AEC, 2003.01.26 (Moore Papers): Earl L. Conner to Paul Moore, Mar 31, 1959.

100. Albert J. Williams-Myers, email to author, June 9, 2017.

101. Grant Gallup, untitled sermon, May 29, 2005, http://rci.rutgers.edu/~lcrew/homil ygrits04_05/msg00052.html, accessed Apr 1, 2017 (site discontinued).

102. C. Kilmer Myers, *Light the Dark Streets* (Greenwich, CT: Seabury Press, 1957), 18, 24, 122, 137.

103. C. Kilmer Myers, *Behold the Church* (New York: Seabury Press, 1958), 5, 13, 24, 44.

104. C. Kilmer Myers, *Baptized into the One Church* (New York: Seabury Press, 1958), 7, 16, 20.

105. John Ehle, *Shepherd of the Streets: The Story of the Reverend James A. Gusweller and His Crusade on the New York West Side* (New York: William Sloane, 1960), 9–13.

106. Robert Rice, "Profiles: Church—I," *New Yorker*, Aug 1, 1964: 41, 59.

107. Ehle, *Shepherd of the Streets*, 63.

108. Robert Rice, "Profiles: Church—II," *New Yorker*, Aug 8, 1964: 45, 47–8, 50.

109. Ehle, *Shepherd of the Streets*, 77, 88, 196–7.

110. DioNY, 8.25 (Donegan Papers): Horace W. B. Donegan, press release with excerpts of sermon (1958), 2.

111. Stringfellow, *My People*, 21–2.

112. Musselman, *Church on the Urban Frontier*, 40–1.

113. Etan Diamond, *Souls of the City: Religion and the Search for Community in Postwar America* (Bloomington: University of Indiana Press, 2003), 126–7.

114. *Newsweek*, Mar 29, 1965: 77.

115. Paul Moore, "Suddenly Nothing Happens," 68, 70.

116. Paul Moore, Jr., *The Church Reclaims the City* (New York: Seabury Press, 1964), 150.

117. Paul Moore, *Presences*, 139–42, 150–2.

118. Jenny Moore, *Second Street*, 211–12.

119. *Witness*, March 31, 1960: 9.

120. *Forth*, May 1958: 11–12; AEC, 2003.01.28 (Moore Papers): G. Paul Musselman to Paul Moore, Aug 12, 1958.

121. *Witness*, May 21, 1959: 7–8.

122. DioMass, 1.A.12.1, Fol: Urban Strategy (Burgess Papers): James R. Whittemore, "Metropolitan Planning and Strategy—An Urgent Need" (1963), 13–14.

123. Besides Arnold and Moore, other leading figures in the Conference were Kim Myers, John Heuss, Kurt Junker, Julian Bartlett, and later, Moran Weston, Jesse Anderson Sr., Van Samuel Bird, St. Julian Simpkins, and Nathan Wright. Norman Faramelli et al., "Seeking to Hear and to Heed in the Cities: Urban Ministry in the Postwar Episcopal Church," in *Churches, Cities, and Human Community: Urban Ministry in the United States 1945–1985*, ed. Clifford J. Green (Grand Rapids, MI: Eerdmans, 1996), 104.

124. *Episcopalian*, Nov 1962: 30.

125. Shattuck, *Episcopalians and Race*, 96.

NOTES   275

126. VTS, M182.63.28 (Walker Papers): John T. Walker, untitled lecture at VTS (1984), 17–18. Writing about his ministry in Lynchburg, Virginia, in the late 1960s, Douglas Carpenter recalls the resentment felt by members of the local black parish when informed by the well-meaning white bishop that their church would be closed in the name of integration. Douglas Carpenter, *A Casserole for a Horse and Other Food for Thought* (Birmingham, AL: Mercy Seat Press, 2005), 32.

127. Opinion Research Corporation, *The Episcopal Church Today as Seen by Clergymen and Laymen: A Survey for the Episcopal Church Foundation* (Princeton, NJ: Opinion Research Corporation, 1964), 32.

128. *NYT*, May 25, 1995: B16.

129. *Witness*, Apr 30, 1959: 7.

130. AEC, 85.3.21 (CSR Records): Tollie L. Caution, "A Decade of Progress in Negro Work, 1941–1951" (1952). Weston's 1954 doctoral dissertation formed the basis of his invaluable *Social Policy of the Episcopal Church in the Twentieth Century* (New York: Seabury Press, 1964).

131. *NYT*, May 22, 2002: B7.

132. Columbia, 1326.7.52 (Weston Papers): Harold S. Shefelman to M. Moran Weston, May 29, 1959; M. Moran Weston to Harold S. Shefelman, June 6, 1959.

133. Arthur E. Walmsley, interview with author, Concord, NH, Jan 6, 2014.

134. *Spirit of Jefferson Advocate*, Feb 23, 1950: 1.

135. *LC*, Dec 30, 1956: 8.

136. Arthur E. Walmsley, interview with author, Concord, NH, Jan 6, 2014.

137. AEC, 107.11.22 (Scarlett Papers): Cornelius C. Tarplee, "Report of the Intergroup Education Project," 1–2, 9–10.

138. Warren A. Schaller, "Appendix: Social Policy of the Episcopal Church, 1951–1963," in M. Moran Weston, *Social Policy of the Episcopal Church in the Twentieth Century* (rev. ed.; New York: Seabury Press, 1964), A26–7.

139. After prolonged debate, the deputies eventually voted in favor of certain resolutions. *Witness*, Oct 30, 1958: 3.

140. *Witness*, Nov 19, 1957: 5.

141. *Witness*, Feb 19, 1959: 9.

142. In its report to the 1958 General Convention, the Joint Commission on Social Reconstruction asserted that "it is a function of the Church to speak prophetically." Schaller, "Appendix," A35–6. See also *LC*, Aug 24, 1958: 6–7.

143. Kenrick, *Come Out the Wilderness*, 142–4.

144. At one meeting, a fellow member of the Group Ministry became so incensed by Stringfellow's provocations that she exclaimed: "You ought to see a psychiatrist. What you say is so full of hatred." UTS, Box 10: Group Ministry–1957 (EHPP Papers): EHPP Staff Minutes, "Fall Retreat, September 1–4, 1957," 5.

145. Cornell, 4438.3 (Stringfellow Papers): William Stringfellow to W. Appleton Lawrence, Aug 26, 1957.

146. Cornell, 4438.3 (Stringfellow Papers): William Stringfellow to John Casteel, May 8, 1958.

276 NOTES

147. Cornell, 4438.8 (Stringfellow Papers): W. Appleton Lawrence to William Stringfellow, Oct 23, 1964.

148. Cornell, 4438.6 (Stringfellow Papers): "The Churches of Protestantism and the Secret of Christian Unity" (1962), 7; Cornell, 4438.6 (Stringfellow Papers): William Stringfellow to "My dear friends," Aug 27, 1962.

149. William Stringfellow, *A Private and Public Faith* (1962; Eugene, OR: Wipf & Stock, 1999), 38–55.

150. Wendy Dackson, "William Stringfellow's Sacramental Vision," *JAS* 2.2 (Oct 2004): 76–9.

151. Though Myers would undoubtedly reject the idea of sacraments requiring any form of external validation, he obviously shared Stringfellow's belief in the inherent link between sacramental identity and social activism. William Stringfellow, *Dissenter in a Great Society: A Christian View of America in Crisis* (1966; Eugene, OR: Wipf and Stock, 2005), 159–60.

152. William Stringfellow, *Free in Obedience* (1964; Eugene, OR: Wipf & Stock, 2006), 39.

153. Cornell, 4438.4 (Stringfellow Papers): William Stringfellow to "Richard," Jan 19, 1960.

154. Cornell, 4438.3 (Stringfellow Papers): William Stringfellow to "The Group Ministry," May 14, 1957.

155. Cornell, 4438.3 (Stringfellow Papers): William Stringfellow to "The Group Ministry," Apr 2, 1958.

156. Bill Wylie-Kellermann, "Not Vice Versa. Reading the Powers Biblically: Stringfellow, Hermeneutics, and the Principalities," *ATR* 81.4 (Fall 1999): qtd. 672.

157. E.g., Romans 8.38; Ephesians 6.12; Colossians 1.16.

158. Stringfellow, *Free in Obedience*, 49–73.

159. William Stringfellow, *An Ethic for Christians and Other Aliens in a Strange Land* (1973; Eugene, OR: Wipf and Stock, 2004), 121.

160. James E. Griffiss, "A Reluctant Anglican Prophet," in *Prophet of Justice, Prophet of Life: Essays on William Stringfellow*, ed. Robert Boak Slocum (New York: Church Publishing Corporation, 1997), 52–3.

161. William Stringfellow, *Instead of Death* (2nd ed., 1976; Eugene, OR: Wipf & Stock, 2004), 84–5.

162. Stringfellow, *A Private and Public Faith*, 78.

163. Cornell, 4438.4 (Stringfellow Papers): William Stringfellow, "Surrender as Solution in the Racial Crisis" (1960).

164. Cornell, 4438.6 (Stringfellow Papers): William Stringfellow, "The Ministry of the Church" (1961), 3.

165. Stringfellow, *My People*, 86–7, 99. See also Stringfellow, *A Private and Public Faith*, 69.

166. Jacques Ellul, *The Presence of the Kingdom*, trans. Olive Wyon (1951; Colorado Springs, CO: Helmers and Howard, 1989), 9–13, 65–6, 119–24. Stringfellow provided the introduction to the first American edition of the book, published by Seabury Press in 1967.

NOTES   277

167. Cornell, 4438.3 (Stringfellow Papers): William Stringfellow to "The Group Ministry," Apr 2, 1958.

168. Stringfellow, *My People*, 44.

169. Jason Wyman, "Nonagenarians: Still Exceptional," *Union Now: Magazine of Union Theological Seminary*, Fall 2014: 27.

170. BHL, Box 3, Fol: Navy, Iwo Jima, Diary, Etc.—1945–1956 (Barney Papers): Diary transcriptions (1945).

171. BHL, Box 1, Fol: Background—Parishfield Histories (Parishfield Records): Roger Barney to Sister Mary Louis Gordon, Apr 2, 1971.

172. Bonhoeffer first mentioned "religionless Christianity" and "the secret discipline" in his letter to Eberhard Bethge dated April 30, 1944: Bonhoeffer, *Letters and Papers*, 280–1.

173. Mimi Ayres Sanderson, Untitled Parishfield Memoir, n.p. Bonhoeffer's thoughts about "Christ incognito" are found in the lectures he delivered at the University of Berlin in 1933: see *Christ the Center*, trans. Edwin H. Robertson (New York: Harper and Row, 1978), 109ff.

174. Winter, *Religious Journey*, 3.4.

175. Harvey Cox, *The Seduction of the Spirit: The Use and Misuse of People's Religion* (New York: Simon and Schuster, 1973), 128.

176. *Sword and Shield*, May 1957: 1–2; *Sword and Shield*, June 1957: 2; *Sword and Shield*, Feb 1959: 2; *Sword and Shield*, June 1960: 1; Mimi Ayres Sanderson, Untitled Parishfield Memoir, n.p.

177. *Ann Arbor News*, July 5, 1957: 9.

178. *Sword and Shield*, Apr 1958: 1.

179. BHL, Box 2, Fol: Partners for Renewal (Parishfield Records): Roger Barney, "Partners for Renewal" (1958): 6, 8.

180. Sara C. Winter, Parishfield Oral Histories (1994–1995): Transcript of Jane Barney Interview—Tape One, 17–18.

181. Sanderson, Untitled Parishfield Memoir, n.p.

182. Winter, *Religious Journey*, qtd. 4.20.

183. Sara C. Winter, Parishfield Oral Histories (1994–1995): Transcript of Bob DeWitt Interview—Tape One, 21.

184. Mimi Ayres Sanderson, interview with author, London, Apr 14, 2015.

185. BHL, Box 1, Fol: Correspondence—Emrich, Bishop (Parishfield Records): Richard S. Emrich to Francis Ayres, Dec 24, 1962; Richard S. Emrich to Roger Barney, Oct 11, 1963.

186. Paul M. van Buren, *Theological Explorations* (New York: Macmillan, 1968), 19.

187. William A. Clebsch, "Founding of the Episcopal Theological Seminary," qtd. 252.

188. An example of this engagement was participation by ETSS students and faculty in the civil rights protests that took place in Austin in the spring of 1960: *LC*, May 8, 1960: 1–2.

189. Blandy and Brown, *Seminary of the Southwest*, 28, 41–3; Robert W. Tobin, interview with author, Deer Isle, ME, Aug 13, 2013.

278 NOTES

190. Hays H. Rockwell, "John B. Coburn: An Appreciation," *ATR* June 1976 [Suppl. Series no. 6]: 14.

191. Milton McC. Gatch, "John Bowen Coburn, 1914–2009," *AEH* 79.4 (Dec 2010): 341.

192. EDS, 2.36 (Coburn Papers): John B. Coburn to Theodore O. Wedel, Dec 6, 1958.

193. Nathan M. Pusey, "In the Depth of Mystery, A Face," *Presbyterian Life*, Jan 11, 1958: 10.

194. Glenn T. Miller, *Piety and Profession: American Protestant Theological Education, 1870–1970* (Grand Rapids, MI: Eerdmans, 2007), 726; Morton Keller and Phyllis Keller, *Making Harvard Modern: The Rise of America's University* (New York: Oxford UP, 2001), 174–5.

195. Gatch, "John Bowen Coburn,": 340, 343.

196. *NYT*, May 16, 1958: 19.

197. Syracuse, Box 79 (Pike Papers): John B. Coburn, "Bishops – Bound and Free" (1958), 4–5.

198. Syracuse, Box 53 (Pike Papers): George Hadley, "I Like Pike" (1961), 1.

Chapter 4

1. *LC*, Nov 2, 1958: 16.

2. *NYT*, May 13, 1980: D23.

3. Yale, 67.1.6.177 (Sherrill Papers): Massey H. Shepherd to Henry K. Sherrill, Nov 12, 1958.

4. Yale, 67.3.42 (Sherrill Papers): Sherrill Oral History Project: "Reminiscences of Henry W. Sherrill" (1982), 39.

5. Columbia (Oral History): "Reminiscences of Warren Turner" (1984), 1.12–13. Succeeding Lichtenberger as bishop of Missouri was George Cadigan, whom diocesan historiographer Charles Rehkopf characterized as "a prophet in the succession of Tuttle, Scarlett, and Lichtenberger." Charles F. Rehkopf, "Reactions to Events of the '60s and '70s," *HMPEC* 47.4 (Dec 1978): 453.

6. Columbia (Oral History): "Reminiscences of John E. Hines" (1986), 4.324.

7. AEC, 43.5.9 (Lichtenberger Papers): Arthur Lichtenberger, installation sermon (1959), 5–6; Unsigned, "Pageantry of Prayer and Praise Marks Installation of New Presiding Bishop," *CA* 34.1 (Spring 1959): 2–3.

8. *Episcopalian*, August 1961: 12.

9. AEC, 43.5.8 (Lichtenberger Papers): Arthur Lichtenberger, "The Social Implications of the Liturgical Revival" (1960), 17, 20.

10. Foster, *Role of the Presiding Bishop*, 104.

11. AEC, 43.5.8 (Lichtenberger Papers): Arthur Lichtenberger, untitled sermon (1960), 6–8.

12. *LC*, Dec 18, 1949: 5.

13. DioWMo, 1047-S (Welles Papers): Edward R. Welles, Bishop's Convention Address (1961), 1.

NOTES 279

14. For a discussion of the 1952 survey, see Chapter 2.

15. *Episcopalian* April 1960: 2. This claim to increasing socioeconomic diversity was corroborated by a statistical review published later in the year: see *Episcopalian*, Oct 1960: 13, 15–19.

16. *LC*, Aug 31, 1958: 7–8; AEC, 85.5.9 (CSR Records): Unsigned, "The Image of the Episcopal Church in Small Communities" (1964), 2.

17. *Witness*, Aug 10, 1961: 9.

18. *Witness*, Dec 10, 1959: 10.

19. Winter, *Suburban Captivity*, 144.

20. DioWMo, 1099 (Welles Papers): Edward R. Welles, Bishop's Convention Address (1963), 3–4, 6.

21. *NYT*, Apr 20, 1959: 28.

22. Booty, *American Apostle*, qtd. 196.

23. Jesse Zink, "Changing World, Changing Church: Stephen Bayne and 'Mutual Responsibility and Interdependence,'" *ATR* 93.2 (Spring 2011): 250–1.

24. AEC, 4.6.7 (Kitagawa Papers): Daisuke Kitagawa, "Problems of the U.S. Churches in the World Today" (1960), 2.

25. Douglas, *Fling Out the Banner!*, 253–4.

26. Columbia (Oral History): "Reminiscences of John E. Hines" (1986), 4.326.

27. *Christian Century*, Nov 27, 1963: 1461.

28. *LC*, July 20, 1958: 3.

29. Opinion Research Corporation, *Episcopal Church Today*, 22.

30. *Episcopalian*, July 1961: 24–5, 28.

31. *LC*, Mar 26, 1961: 7.

32. Despite the comparative wealth of its membership, in 1951 the Episcopal Church ranked fourth among major Protestant denominations in national spending on social education and community action, coming after the Presbyterians, Lutherans, and Congregationalists. Weston, *Episcopalians at Work*, 34–5.

33. Weston, *Social Policy*, 403, 413–14, 422.

34. *Episcopalian*, Oct 1960: 62.

35. Weston, *Social Policy*, 417. See also James Dator and Jan Nunley, *Many Parts, One Body: How the Episcopal Church Works* (New York: Church Publishing, 2010), 93–5.

36. AEC, 211.1.5 (JUP Records): Arthur Walmsley, "Policy and Procedures Concerning Social Issues" (1960), 3.

37. Daniel B. Stevick, "Christian Mission and Social Action," in *Christian Mission and Social Action: How Should the Church Be Involved in Controversial Social Questions?* (New York: National Council of PECUSA, 1962), 6.

38. *LC*, Nov 23, 1958: 7, 26.

39. AEC, 43.5.6 (Lichtenberger Papers): Arthur Lichtenberger, "The Church and Social Welfare" (1962), 2, 4.

40. *NYT*, Dec 29, 1959: 10.

41. AAEHC, A17, Series 3.6.40.10 (Dennis Diocesan Papers): Walter D. Dennis to Arthur Walmsley, Nov 9, 1959.

42. *Christian Century*, Mar 16, 1960: 309.

280 NOTES

43. *Witness*, Apr 14, 1960: 3–4.

44. Arthur E. Walmsley, interview with author, Concord, NH, Jan 6, 2014.

45. AEC, 211.1.5 (JUP Records): Arthur Walmsley and Kenneth B. Clark to the Presiding Bishop, June 19, 1961.

46. Shattuck, *Episcopalians and Race*, 111.

47. *NYT*, May 22, 1961: 34.

48. *NYT*, Sept 14, 1961: 32.

49. Raymond Arsenault, *Freedom Riders: 1961 and the Struggle for Racial Justice* (New York: Oxford UP, 2006), 434. The following year, William Stringfellow cited the Jackson incident when providing a theological rationale for acts of Christian disobedience against the state: see *Episcopalian*, Nov 1962: 31–4. See also Paul Ramsey, *Christian Ethics and the Sit-In* (New York: Association Press, 1961).

50. *NYT*, Sept 18, 1961: 43.

51. *Witness*, Sept 21, 1961: 8.

52. Schaller, "Appendix," A28.

53. *Witness*, Feb 8, 1962: 7.

54. *LC*, Feb 12, 1961: 16.

55. *Witness*, May 4, 1961: 10.

56. Sweet, "Modernization of Protestant Religion," 33–4.

57. John B. Gessell, "What the Church Might Learn from Sewanee," *St. Luke's Journal of Theology* 5.3 (Commencement 1962): 6–8, 10.

58. Michael B. Friedland, *Lift Up Your Voice like a Trumpet: White Clergy and the Civil Rights and Antiwar Movements, 1954–73* (Chapel Hill: University of North Carolina Press, 1998), 18–48; Shattuck, *Episcopalians and Race*, 74–8.

59. DioWash, 6.31.10 (Creighton Papers): Anne Braden to James Dombrowski, Oct 11, 1962. Braden knew whereof she spoke; both she and her husband Carl had been subjected to various forms of intimidation for championing civil rights:Anne Braden, *The Wall Between* (New York: Monthly Review Press, 1958). See also Fred Hobson, *But Now I See: The White Southern Racial Conversion Narrative* (Baton Rouge: Louisiana State UP, 1999), 86–7.

60. *LC*, Oct 14, 1962: 9.

61. Johnston, *One Was a Priest*, 189–92.

62. Duncan M. Gray, Jr., "The Days are Coming—A Sermon," in *On the Battle Lines: A Manifesto for Our Times by 27 Militant Clergymen*, ed. Malcolm Boyd (New York: Morehouse-Barlow, 1964), 113–14.

63. *WP*, May 27, 1957: B3.

64. *WP*, Oct 28, 1957: B1.

65. WNC, 18003.1.6 (Sayre Papers): Francis B. Sayre, Jr., "A Sermon Delivered Before a Special Session of the Church Assembly on Civil Rights" (1964), 2.

66. WNC, 18002.1.1 (Sayre Papers): Francis B. Sayre, Jr., "Faith, Religion and Ethics as Elements of National Power" (late 1950s/early 1960s), 12.

67. WNC, 18002.3.1–2 (Sayre Papers): Francis B. Sayre, Jr., "The Mission of the Church" (1961), 2–3, 5–7.

68. *NYT*, May 22, 1959: 9.

NOTES 281

69. Oral History Interview with Francis B. Sayre, Jr., June 25, 1964, Washington, DC. Interview conducted by Samuel E. Beck, for the John F. Kennedy Oral History Program of the John F. Kennedy Presidential Library, 2–9.

70. *Saturday Evening Post*, Sept 21, 1963: 70.

71. Shannon, "God's Emissary," 10.

72. *Episcopalian*, August 1960: 17–18.

73. Teresa F. Morales, "The Last Stone Is Just the Beginning: A Rhetorical Biography of Washington National Cathedral." Ph.D. diss., Georgia State University, 2013: 165–6.

74. WNC, 18004.6.6 (Sayre Papers): Francis B. Sayre, Jr., untitled sermon after assassination of John F. Kennedy (1963), 2. See also Unsigned, "The Cathedral Mourns John Fitzgerald Kennedy," *CA* 38.4 (Christmas 1963): 17; *Renewal*, Dec 9, 1963: 2.

75. Butler Private Papers: Butler, "My Life and Times," 14, 19; TCW, 109 (Heuss Papers): John V. Butler to Stephen F. Bayne, Sr., July 19, 1951.

76. *Newsweek*, Jan 4, 1960: 58; *NYT*, Mar 13, 1960: 80.

77. AAEHC, A19: Series 1 (Dennis Personal Papers): John V. Butler to Walter D. Dennis, July 15, 1960; *Episcopal New Yorker*, Nov 1965: 3.

78. Paul Moore, *Presences*, 149.

79. Michael Battle, *Black Battle, White Knight: The Authorized Biography of Malcolm Boyd* (New York: Seabury Press, 2011), 61, 147.

80. Malcolm Boyd, *As I Live and Breathe: Stages of an Autobiography* (New York: Random House, 1969), 123–8.

81. *LC*, Apr 23, 1961: 7–8; *Christian Century*, May 17, 1961: 614.

82. E.g., Malcolm Boyd, *If I Go Down to Hell: Man's Search for Meaning in Contemporary Life* (New York: Morehouse-Barlow, 1962), 58, 147–51, 208.

83. *NYT*, March 14, 1964: 26.

84. *Episcopalian*, June 1963: 5–6.

85. Malcolm Boyd, *Half Laughing/Half Crying* (New York: St Martin's Press, 1986), 95; *Jet*, Jan 16, 1964: 50.

86. *NYT*, Aug 21, 1964: 18; *Jet*, Sept 17, 1964: 15.

87. *Witness*, Sept 3, 1964: 5–6.

88. DioNY, 80.7 (Moore Papers): Philip J. Olin to Paul Moore, Jr., Nov 27, 1964; John B. Morris to Paul Moore, Jr., Dec 23, 1964; Arthur Walmsley to Paul Moore, Jr., June 28, 1965.

89. Allen, *This Time, This Place*, 45, 78–9.

90. Douglas Davis, "The Church in a New Bohemia," in *The Search for Community in Modern America*, ed. E. Digby Baltzell (New York: Harper and Row, 1968), 117, 121; Lawrence Estey, interview with author, Deer Isle, ME, July 28, 2015.

91. Allen, *This Time, This Place*, 81.

92. In 1964, the suffragan bishop of Albany, Charles Persell, reported to John Heuss that "Malcolm Boyd was in town some months ago, and he was whaling the daylights out of the middle-class. Finally I pointed out to him that he looked to me as if he were from the middle-class, I was from the middle-class, the people present were middle-class people, and they were the ones in Albany who were concerned for

282 NOTES

the plight of the Negro and wanting to do something about it." TCW, 107.7 (Heuss Papers): Charles B. Persell to John Heuss, July 18, 1964.

93. Robert Lee, "The Organizational Dilemma in American Protestantism," in *Cities and Churches: Readings on the Urban Church*, ed. Robert Lee (Philadelphia: Westminster Press, 1962), 222, 233.

94. Paul Moore, *Church Reclaims the City*, 211–13.

95. AEC, 211.1.30 (JUP Records): "Urban Strategy Conference, Holy Trinity Church, Brooklyn, NY" (1962), 1, 11.

96. Paradise, *Detroit Industrial Mission*, 127.

97. Paradise Private Papers: Interview with Scott Paradise by Charles Weiner: Session 2, Part 1, May 21, 1992: 25; Muffy Paradise, interview with author, Bedford, MA, Jan 6, 2015.

98. Paradise, *Detroit Industrial Mission*, 59, 66.

99. Paradise Private Papers: Scott I. Paradise, "The Real Religion of the Manager" (1962), 6–7.

100. WSU, 131.2.1.9.42 (DIM Records): Scott I. Paradise Journal Selections: "Toward a Social Philosophy"—"Industrialism and Christian Criticism" (late 1950s/early 1960s), 56.

101. WSU, 131.2.1.9.42 (DIM Records): Scott I. Paradise Journal Selections: "Toward a Christian Industrial Theology"—"Peculiarly Christian" (late 1950s/early 1960s), 38.

102. WSU, 131.2.1.9.42 (DIM Records): Scott I. Paradise Journal Selections: "Toward a Social Philosophy"—"Toward a Christian Industrial Philosophy" (late 1950s/early 1960s), 41.

103. Paradise, *Detroit Industrial Mission*, 130.

104. Robert S. Ellwood, *The Sixties Spiritual Awakening: American Religion Moving from Modern to Postmodern* (New Brunswick, NJ: Rutgers UP, 1994), 126, 137.

105. *LC*, Sep 17, 1961: 11.

106. Paul M. van Buren, *The Secular Meaning of the Gospel, Based on an Analysis of Its Language* (New York: Macmillan, 1963). For a cogent summary of the book's strengths and weaknesses, see Langdon B. Gilkey, untitled review of *The Secular Meaning of the Gospel* by Paul M. van Buren, *Journal of Religion* 44.3 (July 1964): 238–43.

107. WSU, 131.2.1.9.42 (DIM Records): Scott I. Paradise Journal Selections: "Toward a Christian Industrial Theology"—"What is Christianity?" (late 1950s/early 1960s): 35. Martin Marty made the same point, warning it was a serious misreading of Bonhoeffer "when his explorations are taken to mean a denial of Christian community, of the Word and the sacraments. Such a denial would have meant a denial of all his preceding theology." *Christian Century*, Apr 20, 1960: 469.

108. WSU, 131.2.1.9.42 (DIM Records): Scott I. Paradise Journal Selections: "Toward a Christian Industrial Theology"—"Offensive and Defensive Theology" (late 1950s/early 1960s), 2.

109. WSU, 131.2.1.9.42 (DIM Records): Scott I. Paradise Journal Selections: "Toward a Christian Industrial Theology"—"Theological Erosion" (late 1950s/early 1960s), 13. See also *Sword and Shield*, Sept 1963: 1.

NOTES 283

110. BHL, Box 1, Fol: Parishfield Histories (Parishfield Records): Roger Barney, "Parishfield 1964" (1964), 12.

111. WSU, 131.2.1.9.42 (DIM Records): Scott I. Paradise Journal Selections: "Toward a Christian Industrial Theology"—"Venturing Far Out" (late 1950s/early 1960s), 42–3.

112. WSU, 131.2.1.9.43 (DIM Records): Edward Wickham, "Appraisal of the Detroit Industrial Mission" ([1961]: 1–2; Paradise Private Papers: Interview with Scott Paradise by Charles Weiner: Session 2, Part 1, May 21, 1992, 8, 10.

113. *Witness*, Oct 12, 1961: 15–16.

114. WSU, 131.2.1.22.20 (DIM Records): Industrial Study Project of the Joint Commission on the Church in Human Affairs, 1961–1966, 20.

115. WNC, 18003.2.9 (Sayre Papers): Francis B. Sayre, Jr. to Daniel Corrigan, Nov 3, 1961; Daniel Corrigan to Francis B. Sayre, Jr., Nov 13, 1961.

116. Woodard, *Episcopal Church's Struggle*, 56–7, 63–5.

117. Steven M. Tipton, *Getting Saved from the Sixties: Moral Meaning in Conversion and Cultural Change* (Berkeley: University of California Press, 1982), 27.

118. Harvey G. Cox, "The 'New Breed' in American Churches: Sources of Social Activism in American Religion," *Daedalus* 96.1 (Winter 1967): 136ff.

119. Guy E. Swanson, *The Vocation of a Church in America: A Sociologist's View* (Detroit: Detroit Industrial Mission, 1962), 5–6.

120. Paul Moore, *Presences*, 154.

121. *Episcopalian*, Oct 1962: 24.

122. This name change was approved by the 1964 General Convention. Douglas, *Fling Out the Banner!*, 284–5.

123. Woodard, *Episcopal Church's Struggle*, 74, 79–80, 108–11.

124. Perry L. Norton, *Church and Metropolis* (New York: Seabury Press, 1964), 30.

125. James Parks Morton, "Day 4: Programs for the Urban Plunge in New York and Chicago" (c. 2014), 2–4. Courtesy of James Parks Morton.

126. James Morton et al., "Conference Assignment," in *Metabagdad: The Report of the Chicago and New York Conferences on Metropolitan Planning*, ed. James Morton (New York: PECUSA National Council, 1963), n.p.; Norton, *Church and Metropolis*, 44.

127. Columbia (Oral History): "Reminiscences of Paul Moore, Jr." (1985), 8.376.

128. *Witness*, Feb 20, 1964: 3–4; *Christian Century*, Mar 4, 1964: 302–3.

129. Chaired by the Archdeacon of Southern Ohio, David Thornberry, the advisory committee consisted of prominent activists and thinkers such as Julian Bartlett, John Burgess, Robert Castle, Robert DeWitt, Raymond Ferris, Calvin Hamilton, Paul Moore, Kim Myers, Charles Willie, and Gibson Winter, with Charles Lawrence consulting and James Morton, Perry Norton, and others attending as staff. AEC, 99.031.3 (Woodard Papers): JUAC Minutes, Nov 11–12, 1963, meeting at Episcopal Church Center; *Church in Metropolis* 1 (Spring 1964): 3–4.

130. AEC, 99.031.3 (Woodard Papers): JUAC Minutes, May 18, 1964, meeting at Thompson House, St. Louis.

131. AEC, 99.031.4 (Woodard Papers): Scott Field Bailey to Jack Woodard, Apr 23, 1962.

132. AEC, 99.031.4 (Woodard Papers): Jack Woodard, Report and Recommendations of the Metropolitan Division of the Diocese of Texas Department of Missions (1962), 1.

284 NOTES

133. See AEC, 99.031.4 (Woodard Papers): Jack Woodard (ed.), "Suggestions for a Creative Approach to the Establishment of the Episcopal Church in Clear Lake City" (1963).

134. *Church in Metropolis* 3 (Fall 1964): 3ff.

135. *Witness*, June 6, 1963: 5.

136. Woodard, *Episcopal Church's Struggle*, 82–8.

137. AEC, 99.031.5 (Woodard Papers): Ruel Tyson to Jack Woodard, Mar 29, 1963.

138. *Church in Metropolis* 3 (Fall 1964): 13.

139. *NYT*, June 3, 1963: 25.

140. See Saul D. Alinsky, *Reveille for Radicals* (Chicago: University of Chicago Press, 1946), 99–111. See also Aaron Schutz and Mike Miller, "Introduction," in *People Power: The Community Organizing Tradition of Saul Alinsky*, ed. Aaron Schutz and Mike Miller (Nashville: Vanderbilt UP, 2015), 4–5.

141. William G. McLoughlin, *Revivals, Awakenings, and Reform: An Essay on Religion and Social Change in America, 1607–1977* (Chicago: University of Chicago Press, 1977), 194.

142. Barry Menuez, interview with author, by telephone, July 23, 2015; Barry Menuez, email to author, June 17, 2016.

143. James and Pamela Morton, interview with author, New York, Dec 17, 2014.

144. WSU, 131.2.2.43.25 (DIM Records): C. Kilmer Myers, untitled address delivered to the Chicago City Missionary Society (1963), 1; *Witness*, Feb 6, 1964: 4; *Church in Metropolis* 1 (Spring 1964): 20–1.

145. Morton, "Day 4: Programs for the Urban Plunge," 6–8, 11–12.

146. DioWash, 6.29.8 (Creighton Papers): C. Kilmer Myers, sermon at consecration of Paul Moore as Suffragan Bishop of Washington (1964), 2.

147. *LC*, Aug 16, 1964: 4; Woodard, *Episcopal Church's Struggle*, 100.

148. BHL, Box 1, Fol: Correspondence–Advisory Committee (Parishfield Records): Gibson Winter to Roger Barney, May 26, 1964.

149. C. Kilmer Myers, "At the Core of the City," in *On the Battle Lines: A Manifesto for Our Times by 27 Militant Clergymen*, ed. Malcolm Boyd (New York: Morehouse-Barlow, 1964), 30–1, 35.

150. BHL, Box 18, Fol: Kilmer Myers (Diocese of Michigan Records): John Heuss to F. Plummer Whipple, Aug 22, 1964. Heuss preached at Myers's consecration in Detroit on Michaelmas Day. *LC*, Oct 18, 1964: 10.

151. *Christian Century*, Jan 2, 1963: 4–5. Edward T. Demby (1869–1957) and Henry B. Delany (1858–1928) became the first African American bishops in the Episcopal Church in 1918 when they were appointed suffragans "for colored work" in Arkansas and North Carolina, respectively. See Michael J. Beary, *Black Bishop: Edward T. Demby and the Struggle for Racial Equality in the Episcopal Church* (Urbana: University of Illinois Press, 2001); and Sarah L. Delany and A. Elizabeth Delany, *Having Our Say: The Delany Sisters' First Hundred Years* (New York: Dell, 1994). Other black bishops had likewise been appointed to serve overseas jurisdictions such as Liberia and Haiti prior to Burgess's election in Massachusetts.

152. *LC*, Dec 22, 1963: 5.

NOTES 285

153. *LC*, Sept 29, 1963: 7.

154. *Potomac Magazine*, Sept 20, 1970: 8.

155. Paul Moore, *Presences*, 164–6. Not long after moving to Washington, Moore was invited to become a fellow of the Yale Corporation by Kingman Brewster, an old classmate and the university's recently elected president. Paul Moore, Jr., "A Touch of Laughter," in *My Harvard, My Yale*, ed. Diana Dubois (New York: Random House, 1982), 207. See also Geoffrey Kabaservice, *The Guardians: Kingman Brewster, His Circle, and the Rise of the Liberal Establishment* (New York: Henry Holt, 2004), 183–4.

156. Friedland, *Lift Up Your Voice*, qtd. 240.

157. AEC, 2003.01.26 (Moore Papers): Paul Moore, Graduation Address at St. Paul's School, Concord, NH (1964), 6.

158. *LC*, Jan 5, 1964: 6.

159. Sheldon Hackney, "Social Justice, the Church, and the Counterculture, 1963–1979," in *This Far by Faith: Tradition and Change in the Episcopal Diocese of Pennsylvania*, ed. David R. Contosta (University Park: Pennsylvania State UP, 2013), 300, 303.

160. Paul M. Washington with David M. Gracie, *"Other Sheep I Have": The Autobiography of Father Paul M. Washington* (Philadelphia, PA: Temple UP, 1994), 33–5.

161. *Philadelphia Inquirer*, Apr 17, 1986: 6.

162. *LC*, Nov 15, 1964: 9; *Christian Century*, Sept 11, 1968: 1141.

163. Syracuse, Box 100 (Pike Papers): James A. Pike, sermon at "Church and Race Conference" (1963), 1–2; *NYT*, May 15, 1963: 36; *NYT*, July 8, 1963: 17.

164. Arthur Lichtenberger, *The Day Is at Hand* (New York: Seabury Press, 1964), 113. See also *NYT*, May 26, 1963: 59.

165. Schaller, "Appendix," A30–1. Bishop William Marmion of Southwestern Virginia later claimed that the Whitsuntide Message "galvanized our entire Church into action." AEC, 85.5.6 (CSR Records): "The Changing Role of Christian Social Relations in the Modern World" (1966), 14.

166. *NYT*, July 6, 1963: 4; *NYT*, July 8, 1963: 17.

167. Hein, *Noble Powell*, 91–3.

168. Carroll Greene, Jr., "'Rise Up and Make Her Great,'" *CA* 38.3 (Christmas 1963): 11, 30.

169. *NYT*, Aug 29, 1963: 1ff; *LC*, Sept 8, 1963: 1. See also Lucy Barber, *Marching on Washington: The Forging of an American Political Tradition* (Berkeley: University of California Press, 2004), 154–9.

170. Roger Blanchard, "A Statement on the Church and the Racial Crisis, Adopted by the Bishop and Chapter of the Diocese of Southern Ohio, October 12, 1963" (n.p: 1963), 3, 8–9.

171. James F. Findlay, Jr., *Church People in the Struggle: The National Council of Churches and the Black Freedom Movement, 1950–1970* (New York: Oxford UP, 1993), 89–91.

172. TCH, Series II: Fol: Mississippi (Weber Papers): William M. Weber, announcement about Civil Rights work (1964).

173. DioWash, 6.31.19 (Creighton Papers): Paul Moore to E. Felix Kloman, July 17, 1964.

174. *Witness*, Oct 8, 1964: 10.

175. TCH, Series IV: Fol: Mississippi (Weber Papers): Charles Granville Hamilton to William M. Weber, Aug 19, 1964.

286 NOTES

176. David L. Chappell, *Inside Agitators: White Southerners in the Civil Rights Movement* (Baltimore, MD: John Hopkins UP, 1994) xxii–xxiii, 231, n.1; David L. Chappell, *A Stone of Hope: Prophetic Religion and the Death of Jim Crow* (Chapel Hill: University of North Carolina Press, 2004), 176–8; and Carolyn Renée Dupont, *Mississippi Praying: Southern White Evangelicals and the Civil Rights Movement, 1945–1975* (New York: New York UP, 2013), 15–38, 86–92.

177. *Christian Century*, Sept 19, 1962: 1133.

178. Friedland, *Lift Up Your Voice*, qtd. 251; Paul Moore, *Take a Bishop like Me*, 18.

179. For an account of the remarkable life and career of W. Hodding Carter, Jr. (1907–1972), see Ann Waldron, *Hodding Carter: The Reconstruction of a Racist* (Chapel Hill, NC: Algonquin Books, 1993).

180. Columbia (Oral History): "Reminiscences of Paul Moore, Jr." (1985), 10.445–6.

181. Findlay, *Church People*, 111ff.

182. Joel L. Alvis, Jr., "Racial Turmoil and Religious Reaction: The Rt. Rev. John M. Allin," *HMPEC* 50.1 (Mar 1981): qtd. 89–90.

183. Civil Rights Hearings, "Religious Panel," in *Rhetoric, Religion, and the Civil Rights Movement, 1954–1965*, ed. Davis W. Houck and David E. Dixon (Waco, TX: Baylor UP, 2006), 826–51.

184. *Witness*, Feb 18, 1965: 3; *NYT*, March 8, 1998: 44.

185. Alvis, "Racial Turmoil and Religious Reaction," 90–5.

186. Columbia (Oral History): "Reminiscences of John M. Allin" (1991), 4.225–6.

187. Shattuck, *Episcopalians and Race*, 148–52.

188. DioMass (Coburn Papers): John Coburn, remarks introducing Joint Commission of Ecumenical Relations report to General Convention (1964), 1.

189. DioMass (Coburn Papers): "A Report to the General Convention from the Representatives of the Episcopal Church on the General Board of the National Council of Churches" (1964), 3.

190. Friedland, *Lift Up Your Voice*, 109.

191. *WP*, Sept 14, 1964: A1; *NYT*, Sept 16, 1964: 14.

192. WNC, 18002.8.1 (Sayre Papers): Francis B. Sayre, Jr., sermon delivered on Sept 13, 1964, 2–3.

193. *WP*, Sept 18, 1964: A1; *WP*, Sept 21, 1964: A18.

194. *Witness*, Oct 1, 1964: 3. Preaching again two weeks later, Sayre sought to nuance his position: "Just because, at this moment, we are all of us caught in a tide of pettiness and cynicism that is but the culmination of our long apathy and selfish fear, this does not mean that there is no choice to make in a national election, or in our own lives. There are arks to be built, new beginnings, sacrifices and decisions; no one can simply cry 'a plague on every house' and be dormant or inactive in his responsibility." WNC, 18002.8.1 (Sayre Papers): Francis B. Sayre, Jr., sermon delivered on Sept 27, 1964, 1–2.

195. WNC, 18002.8.1 (Sayre Papers): Scott Paradise to Francis B. Sayre, Jr., Sept 23, 1964.

196. WNC, 18002.8.1 (Sayre Papers): Francis B. Sayre, Jr., to T. A. Hart, Sept 30, 1964.

197. *Witness*, Oct 15, 1964: 8.

198. Opinion Research Corporation, *Episcopal Church Today*, 12, 20.

NOTES 287

199. Foster, *Role of the Presiding Bishop*, 107; Sumner, *Episcopal Church's History*, 9–11.
200. Weston, *Social Policy*, 26–7.
201. *Christian Century*, Nov 11, 1964: 1392.
202. DioMinn (McNairy Papers): Philip F. McNairy, "New Theatre of Controversy" (c. 1965), 4–5.
203. *NYT*, Oct 16, 1964: 43; *Witness*, Nov 5, 1964: 7.
204. Quinn, *A House of Prayer*, 101–2, 109–13.
205. Cynthia Wedel, "Women at the General Convention," *CA* 39.4 (Christmas 1964): 35.
206. *Christian Century*, Nov 11, 1964: 1392.
207. *Christianity Today*, Nov 6, 1964: 52.
208. *American Church News: General Convention Daily*, Oct 21, 1964: 2.
209. *Episcopalian*, Apr 1980: qtd. 15.
210. Cornell, 4438.8 (Stringfellow Papers): Wiliam Stringfellow et al., "A Statement of Conscience on Racism in the Presidential Campaign" (1964). See also Seymour P. Lachman, "Barry Goldwater and the 1964 Religious Issue," *Journal of Church and State* 10.3 (Autumn 1968): 400–1.
211. *LC*, Oct 25, 1964: 15.
212. *NYT*, Oct 14, 1964: 20.
213. *Witness*, Nov 5, 1964: 7.
214. Kesselus, *Granite on Fire*, 196–202.
215. DioMinn (McNairy Papers): McNairy, "New Theatre of Controversy," 6.
216. *Episcopalian*, Oct 1964: 28.
217. John E. Hines, "The Concluding Address at the New York Conference," in *Metabagdad: The Report of the Chicago and New York Conferences on Metropolitan Planning*, ed. James Morton (New York: PECUSA National Council, 1963), V7.

Chapter 5

1. WNC, 18001.1.7 (Sayre Papers): Francis B. Sayre, Jr., to John E. Hines, Nov 25, 1964.
2. William H. Swatos, Jr., "A Primacy of Systems: Confederation, Corporation, and Communion," in *Church, Identity, and Change: Theology and Denominational Structures in Unsettled Times*, ed. David A. Roozen and James R. Nieman (Grand Rapids, MI: Eerdmans, 2001), 204–7.
3. *Witness*, Feb 4, 1965: 8.
4. John E. Hines, *Thy Kingdom Come* (New York: Morehouse-Barlow, 1967), 119–20.
5. *LC*, Feb 14, 1965: 4.
6. Shattuck, *Episcopalians and Race*, 147, 175.
7. *LC*, Feb 12, 1961: 7ff. See also Caroline Booth Pinkston, "The Gospel of Justice: Community, Faith, and the Integration of St. Andrew's Episcopal School." Master's thesis, University of Texas at Austin, 2014.
8. *Episcopalian*, Nov 1966: 15.
9. Charlie Sumners, interview with author, Austin, TX, August 27, 2014.

288 NOTES

10. *Episcopalian*, Oct 1966: 8.

11. Foster, *Role of the Presiding Bishop*, 114–15.

12. *Episcopalian*, Oct 1966: 9.

13. Kesselus, *Granite on Fire*, 232.

14. *NYT*, Feb 7, 1965: 49; *NYT*, Feb 18, 1965: 26.

15. Cornell, 4438.10 (Stringfellow Papers): William Stringfellow to John Hines, Feb 11, 1965.

16. *Witness*, Mar 4, 1965: 3–4.

17. Brandt Leonard Montgomery, "Time's Prisoner: The Right Reverend Charles Colcock Jones Carpenter and the Civil Rights Movement in the Episcopal Diocese of Alabama." Master's thesis, General Theological Seminary, New York, 2012, 82–3.

18. Douglas M. Carpenter, *A Powerful Blessing: The Life of Charles Colcock Carpenter, Sr., 1889-1969, Bishop of Alabama, 1938-1968* (Birmingham, AL: TransAmerica Printing, 2012), 26ff.

19. Douglas Carpenter, email to author, Apr 3, 2014.

20. *Time*, Mar 19, 1965: 27.

21. DioWash, 6.31.10 (Creighton Papers): Charles C. J. Carpenter to William F. Creighton, Mar 9, 1965; *LC*, Mar 21, 1965: 8–9.

22. Friedland, *Lift Up Your Voice*, 131.

23. S. Jonathan Bass, *Blessed Are the Peacemakers: Martin Luther King Jr., Eight White Religious Leaders, and the "Letter from Birmingham Jail"* (Baton Rouge: Louisiana State UP, 2001), 28–30.

24. Curtis Flowers, email to author, Sept 22, 2014.

25. *LC*, Apr 4, 1965: 7.

26. *Newsweek*, Mar 29, 1965: 75–8; *Time*, Mar 26, 1965: 30.

27. AEC, 99.031.6 (Woodard Papers): Jack Woodard, "A Walk in Montgomery" (1965), 1, 5.

28. WNC, 18002.8.2 (Sayre Papers): Francis B. Sayre, Jr., untitled sermon (1965), 2.

29. Mary Nickerson, emails to author, Aug 21 and 22, 2013.

30. TCH, Series IV: Fol: Mississippi (Weber Papers): Unsigned, "Some Aspects of Black-White Problems as Seen by Field Staff" (1964), 1–2; Friedland, *Lift Up Your Voice*, 4.

31. Hale, *Nation of Outsiders*, 204–7, 224–36; Rossinow, *Politics of Authenticity*, 196–207.

32. William Stringfellow, "Through Dooms of Love," in *New Theology No. 2*, ed. Martin E. Marty and Dean G. Peerman (New York: Macmillan, 1965), 294–5.

33. Cornell, 4438.12 (Stringfellow Papers): William Stringfellow, "The Inner City Ministry: how the churches have failed" (1966), 3; Stringfellow, *Dissenter in a Great Society*, 5, 13.

34. Cornell, 4438.12 (Stringfellow Papers): William Stringfellow to "Friends," Oct 1, 1967.

35. Cornell, 4438.10 (Stringfellow Papers): Jonathan M. Daniels to William Stringfellow, May 21, 1965.

36. EDS, Binder I: Correspondence and Writings (Daniels Papers): Jonathan M. Daniels to Mary Elizabeth Macnaughton, Mar 29, 1965. See also Robert B. Slocum, "Faith, Freedom, and Sacrifice," in *AEH* 89.2 (June 2020): 121–2.

37. *NYT*, Aug 25, 1965: 24.

NOTES 289

38. Cornell, 4438.10 (Stringfellow Papers): William Stringfellow to Jonathan M. Daniels, May 18, 1965.

39. Charles W. Eagles, *Outside Agitator: Jon Daniels and the Civil Rights Movement in Alabama* (Chapel Hill: University of North Carolina Press, 1993), 213–49. See also *NYT*, June 22, 1997: 26.

40. EDS, 2.36 (Coburn Papers): John B. Coburn, address at ETS memorial for Jonathan M. Daniels (1965), 2.

41. Michael Coburn, interview with author, Cranston, RI, Dec 23, 2014.

42. John B. Coburn, "The Jonathan Daniels Story: A Personal Perspective," Daniels Memorial Lecture, Episcopal Divinity School, 1991, http://eds.edu/sites/default/files/danielslecture1991.pdf, accessed Apr 1, 2017 (site discontinued).

43. In 1991, the General Convention voted unanimously to commemorate Daniels each year in the church calendar on August 14, the day he had been arrested in Lowndes County. Eagles, *Outside Agitator*, 263–4.

44. Dean R. Hoge and David A. Roozen, "Some Sociological Conclusions about Church Trends," in *Understanding Church Growth and Decline, 1950–78*, ed. Dean R. Hoge and David A. Roozen (New York: Pilgrim Press, 1979), 328; Wade Clark Roof, "America's Voluntary Establishment: Mainline Religion in Transition," *Daedalus* 111.1 (Winter 1982): 173–7.

45. *Harvard Crimson*, May 15, 1963: 1. For an account of Pusey's attempts to reassert the role of religion at "Godless Harvard," see Keller and Keller, *Making Harvard Modern*, 176–7.

46. Peter Gomes, "A Minister Remembered: Charles Philip Price '41: The Harvard Years," in *Each of Us Will Never Be the Same: Memories of Charles Philip Price* (Cincinnati, OH: Forward Movement, 2003), 17–18.

47. VTS, M26.2000.0003 (Price Papers): Charles P. Price, "Things that are Caesar's—Things that are God's" (1964), 7.

48. VTS, M26.2000.0003 (Price Papers): Charles P. Price, "Success, Authority, and the Ground of Confidence" (1965), 2.

49. Richard Rorty, *Achieving Our Country: Leftist Thought in Twentieth-Century America* (Cambridge, MA: Harvard UP, 1998), 43.

50. Richard Lints, *Progressive and Conservative Religious Ideologies: The Tumultuous Decade of the 1960s* (Farnham, Surrey: Ashgate, 2010), 13–17; Tipton, *Getting Saved*, 27.

51. John L. Kater, Jr., "Dwelling Together in Unity: Church, Theology and Race 1950–1965," *ATR* 58.4 (Oct 1976): 449–51, 457.

52. Coburn, *Twentieth-Century Spiritual Letters*, 136.

53. Paul Moore, *Presences*, 210.

54. *WP*, Oct 9, 1966: A6.

55. *WP*, Apr 24, 1966: E1.

56. *Potomac Magazine*, Sept 20, 1970: 46.

57. *WP*, Mar 17, 1966: B1.

58. *NYT*, July 11, 1966: 18.

59. *WP*, July 15, 1967: D12.

290 NOTES

60. Reichley, *Religion in American Public Life*, 277.

61. *Witness*, June 10, 1965: 10–11.

62. *Church in Metropolis* 6 (Summer 1965): 5–8.

63. Reinhart B. Gutmann, "The Church and Social Welfare," *St. Luke's Journal of Theology* 10.4 (June 1967): 13–14, 16.

64. AEC, 211.1.6 (JUP Records): Arthur Walmsley to John E. Hines, May 9, 1966.

65. *NYT*, Oct 23, 1966: E5.

66. AEC, 211.1.6 (JUP Records): Arthur Walmsley, "What Place Do Social Action Staff Have in a Revolutionary World?" (1966), 1–2, 4, 8; Arthur Walmsley, "Social Action: Twentieth Century Evangelism" (1966), 3–4.

67. *Episcopalian*, August 1966, 11.

68. AEC, 211.1.30 (JUP Records): Jack Woodard to John E. Hines and Warren H. Turner, Jan 27, 1967.

69. *LC*, July 18, 1965: 9; *LC*, Sept 12, 1965: 35.

70. Anthony Morley, "The Inner-City," Kellogg Lectures, Episcopal Divinity School, 1966, http://research.eds.edu/c.php?g=358676&p=2421446, accessed Apr 1, 2016 (site discontinued).

71. Anthony Morley, emails to author, Sept 7, Dec 7, and Dec 9, 2016.

72. Woodard, *Episcopal Church's Struggle*, 91.

73. Lester W. McManis, *Handbook on Christian Education in the Inner City* (New York: Seabury Press, 1966), 7–9.

74. DioWash, 6.4.3 (Creighton Papers): House of Bishops, "Population, Poverty, and Peace: A Statement of the House of Bishops of the Episcopal Church, October 1966," 5–6.

75. *NYT*, Feb 24, 2005: B11. A prolific writer, Wright published widely on this topic: see, for example, *Black Power and Urban Unrest: The Creative Possibilities* (New York: Hawthorn, 1967); *Let's Work Together* (New York: Hawthorn, 1968); and *Ready to Riot* (New York: Holt, Rhinehart and Winston, 1968).

76. *Witness*, Apr 28, 1966: 13–14.

77. *Church in Metropolis* 12 (Spring 1967): 23.

78. *LC*, Aug 21, 1966: 5.

79. TCW, 143.1 (Butler Papers): Horace B. Donegan, untitled sermon (1966), 8.

80. Butler Private Papers: John V. Butler, "My Life and Times at Trinity and Before," 1b–2b, 3.

81. TCW, 1060.1 (Woodard Papers): Lewis B. Cuyler and G. H. Woodard, *Trinity Grants Program: Report and Recommendation by the Parochial Policy Committee and its Sub-Committee on Financial Resources Utilization, Sept 1971*; Clifford P. Morehouse, *Mother of Churches: An Informal History of Trinity Parish in the City of New York* (New York: Seabury Press, 1973), 323.

82. Bernard Eugene Meland, *The Secularization of Modern Cultures* (New York: Oxford UP, 1966), 145–6.

83. John A. T. Robinson, *Honest to God* (London: SCM Press, 1963). For an assessment of the book in its intellectual and cultural context, see Rowan Williams's essay on Robinson in *Anglican Identities* (London: Darton, Longman, Todd, 2004), 103–20.

NOTES 291

84. James A. Pike, *A Time for Christian Candor* (New York: Harper & Row, 1964). Robinson and Pike were frequently paired in the American media, such as when *Time* magazine referred to them as "the Tweedledum and Tweedledee of Anglican theology." *Time*, Apr 8, 1966: 98.

85. Robert Bruce Mullin, untitled review of *Honest to God* by John A. T. Robinson, *ATR* 86.4 (Fall 2004): 714.

86. Pike, *Time for Christian Candor*, 9.

87. VTS, M26.2000.0003 (Price Papers): Charles P. Price, "The Troubler of Israel?" (1965), 6, 13.

88. DioMinn (McNairy Papers): Philip F. McNairy, "New Theatre of Controversy," 3–4. See also Van A. Harvey, "On the Intellectual Marginality of American Theology," in *Religion and Twentieth-Century American Intellectual Life*, ed. Michael J. Lacey (New York: Cambridge UP, 1989), 176–7.

89. The term was borrowed from Gabriel Vahanian's 1961 volume *The Death of God: The Culture of our Post-Christian Era*. Van Buren always rejected it as sensationalist and a misrepresentation of his ideas. *NYT*, July 1, 1998: A21.

90. Van Buren, *Theological Explorations*, 23.

91. Thomas W. Ogletree, *The "Death of God" Controversy* (Nashville, TN: Abingdon Press, 1966), 85–6. See also Peter Berger, "A Sociological View of the Secularization of Theology," *Journal for the Scientific Study of Religion* 6.1 (Spring 1967): 6ff; and Sydney E. Ahlstrom, "The Radical Turn in Theology and Ethics: Why It Occurred in the 1960's," *Annals of the American Academy of Political and Social Science* 387 (Jan 1970): 1–13.

92. Harvey Cox, *The Secular City: Secularization and Urbanization in Theological Perspective* (New York: Macmillan, 1965).

93. Gibson Winter, *The New Creation as Metropolis* (New York: Macmillan, 1963), 85. See also Hudnut-Beumler, *Looking for God*, 194.

94. Joseph Fletcher, *Situation Ethics: The New Morality* (Philadelphia: Westminster Press, 1966), 151.

95. Edwin G. Wappler, "Anglicans and the New Morality," in *The Anglican Moral Choice*, ed. Paul Elmen (Wilton, CT: Morehouse-Barlow, 1983), 162–3.

96. Wilford Oakland Cross, "The Moral Revolution: An Analysis, Critique, and Appreciation," *ATR* 48.4 (Oct 1966): 369–70; Edwin G. Wappler, "Four Anglican Situationists and Their Tradition: A Study in Fletcher, Pike, Robinson, and Rhymes." Ph.D. diss., Duke University, 1972, 218–19.

97. VTS, M132.19 (Booty Papers): John Booty, "The New Theologians and the Utopian View of Man" (c. 1966), 2–3.

98. BHL, Box 2, Fol: Sermons–1963–1965 (Parishfield Records): Roger Barney, "Power to Those Who Receive Him" (1965), 1.

99. BHL, Box 2, Fol: Meetings: William Hamilton (Parishfield Records): Roger Barney to C. M. Judd, Jan 22, 1966.

100. Sanderson, Untitled Parishfield Memoir.

101. *Sword and Shield*, July–Aug 1965: 1–2.

102. BHL, Box 2, Fol: Advisory Committee–1962–1966 (Parishfield Records): "Parishfield Advisory Committee—Report of May 1966 Meeting," 2.

103. BHL, Box 2, Fol: Writings (Parishfield Records): Roger Barney, "Harvey Cox: An Unpublished and Unfinished Essay" (1965), 1.

104. BHL, Box 1, Fol: Staff–Roger Barney (Parishfield Records): Roger Barney, "Sidelights on City Life" (1965), 2; BHL, Box 6, Fol: Jane Barney Personal Files, J-Q (Barney Papers): Jane Barney to Kim Myers (1965).

105. BHL, Box 2, Fol: Home Dept Project (Parishfield Records): G. H. Jack Woodard to James B. Guinan, Aug 5, 1966.

106. BHL, Box 2, Fol: Home Dept Project (Parishfield Records): Roger Barney, "Estimate of Parishfield's Ability to Help Jack Woodard" (1966), 1; Home Dept Project (Parishfield Records): Jane Barney, "Notes" (1966), 1.

107. BHL, Box 1, Fol: Correspondence–Emrich, Bishop (Parishfield Records): Francis Ayres to Richard S. Emrich, Apr 5, 1966.

108. Scott Paradise, *Requiem for American Industrial Missions: Audenshaw Papers No. 41* (Richmond, Yorkshire: Audenshaw Foundation, 1974), 1.

109. Robert W. Terry, "Reflections on Paradise," *Life and Work* 11.1 (Jan 1969): 3–4.

110. Paradise Private Papers: Interview with Scott Paradise by Charles Weiner: Session 3, Part 2, Oct 6, 1992, 10–11.

111. *Boston Globe*, Nov 28, 1968: 58.

112. Paradise Private Papers: Interview with Scott Paradise by Charles Weiner: Session 3, Part 2, Oct 6, 1992, 12, 18.

113. For an account of this experience, see Daisuke Kitagawa, *Issei and Nisei: The Internment Years* (New York: Seabury Press, 1967).

114. AEC, 315.6.8 (Kitagawa Papers): Daisuke Kitagawa, "The Work of the Integrating Community" (1960s), 142.

115. AEC, 315.6.8 (Kitagawa Papers): Daisuke Kitagawa, "Problems of the U.S. Churches in the World Today" (1960), 2. See also Daisuke Kitagawa, *Race Relations and Christian Mission* (New York: Friendship Press, 1964).

116. AEC, 151.3.18 (CSR Records): International Peace Advisory Committee, "Peace in Viet Nam: The Christian Commitment" (1965), 1.

117. VTS, M26.2000.0003 (Price Papers): Charles P. Price, "Multitudes in the Valley of Decision" (1965), 9–10.

118. WNC, 18002.8.3 (Sayre Papers): Francis B. Sayre, Jr., "Thoughts on Viet Nam at the New Year" (1966), 2.

119. Handy, *Christian America*, 198–9.

120. TCW, Box 128, File: Episcopal elections (Butler Papers): Paul Moore, Jr., to John V. Butler, June 27, 1969; Columbia (Oral History): "Reminiscences of Paul Moore, Jr." (1985), 10.470–1.

121. For an account of the growing opposition to Vietnam among mainline clergy during the pivotal years of 1966–1967, see Friedland, *Lift Up Your Voice*, 164–88.

122. *Witness*, June 24, 1965: 8.

123. George M. Marsden, *The Soul of the American University: From Protestant Establishment to Established Nonbelief* (New York: Oxford UP, 1994), 418.

NOTES   293

124. Harvard, UAI 15.900.13 (Pusey Papers): Nathan M. Pusey, Baccalaureate Address to Harvard Class of 1965, 4–7.

125. Harvard, UAI 15.900.13 (Pusey Papers): Nathan M. Pusey, Baccalaureate Address to Harvard Class of 1967, 5–6, 15.

126. *NYT*, Sept 7, 1969: E16.

127. Frederick Houk Borsch, "Apt Teachers: Bishops as Teachers and Theologians," *ATR* 79.2 (Spring 1997): 205.

128. *Time*, Nov 11, 1966: 56.

129. Pike's chief antagonist by this time was the bishop of South Florida, Henry Louttit, but others, such as Bishop Albert Stuart of Georgia, had previously threatened to bring a presentment against him. By the time the Wheeling meeting took place, Pike had already resigned as diocesan of California, but doing so did not affect his episcopal status or his opponents' desire to see him disciplined. *NYT*, Jan 29, 1961: 31; Oct 1, 1966: 28.

130. Columbia (Oral History): "Reminiscences of John E. Hines" (1986), 5.354–5.

131. For an account of the Wheeling episode sympathetic to Pike, see William Stringfellow and Anthony Towne, *The Bishop Pike Affair: Scandals of Conscience and Heresy, Relevance and Solemnity in the Contemporary Church* (1967; Eugene, OR: Wipf and Stock, 2007), 75–92.

132. DioWash, 5.9.2 (Dun Papers): William J. Wolf to Angus Dun, Nov 16, 1966.

133. DioWash, 5.9.2 (Dun Papers): Angus Dun to William J. Wolf, Nov 20, 1966; *LC*, Oct 8, 1967, 12.

134. Columbia (Oral History): "Reminiscences of Paul Moore, Jr." (1985), 11.494.

135. DioWash, 6.4.3 (Creighton Papers): House of Bishops, working press release (1966). For a list of the bishops who signed the minority statement, see Stringfellow and Towne, *Bishop Pike Affair*, 223.

136. Robertson, *Passionate Pilgrim*, 182.

137. Stringfellow and Towne, *Death and Life of Bishop Pike*, qtd. 110–11.

138. Ephraim Radner and Philip Turner, *The Fate of Communion: The Agony of Anglicanism and the Future of a Global Church* (Grand Rapids, MI: Eerdmans, 2006), 17–18; Alan W. Jones, untitled review of *The Death and Life of Bishop Pike* by William Stringfellow and Anthony Towne, *HMPEC* 46.1 (March 1977), 108.

139. *NYT*, Sept 15, 1966: 30; *Pacific Churchman*, Dec 1979: 1ff.

140. *Christianity and Crisis*, July 10, 1967: 164.

141. *Witness*, Feb 2, 1967: 12.

142. John Rawlinson, emails to author, Sept 4 and 7, 2013.

143. *Christian Century*, May 17, 1967: 667–8.

144. BHL, Box 6, Fol: Jane Barney Personal Files, F-I (Barney Papers): Leon Harris to All Saints Parish, Mar 28, 1967.

145. BHL, Box 6, Fol: Jane Barney Personal Files, F-I (Barney Papers): Leon Harris to All Saints Parish, Mar 29, 1967. For a full account of the dispute over Harris's work with the hippies, see Laurence Holbein, *For All the Saints: The First Hundred Years of All Saints' Episcopal Church, San Francisco* (Philadelphia: Xlibris Corporation, 2010), 267–98. Similar tensions would arise at Christ Church in Cambridge, Massachusetts,

294 NOTES

during the summer of 1968, when rector Murray Kenney opened up the parish hall for use by the crowds of young people assembling in the city common across the street. Even in this self-consciously progressive community, some questioned how long the church should focus its resources on those with so little interest in its life and worship. Ann L. Austin, "A Community of Faith Moves through Change: The 1960s and 1970s," in *The Biography of a Church*, Volume II: *Voices from the Pews*, ed. Martha Jacoby et al. (Cambridge, MA: Christ Church Cambridge, 2012), 45–50.

146. E.g., *Time*, Mar 17, 1967: 23; *Life*, Mar 31, 1967: 15–16; *Episcopalian*, Oct 1967: 37.

147. Timothy Miller, *The Hippies and American Values* (2nd ed.; Knoxville: University of Tennessee Press, 2011), 87–103; W. J. Rorabaugh, *American Hippies* (New York: Cambridge UP, 2015), 132–66.

148. Allen, *This Time, This Place*, 59–60.

149. *NYT*, Oct 10, 1967: 36; *NYT*, Oct 16, 1967: 1ff.

150. *Washington Diocese*, Mar 1968: 6–7.

151. BHL, Box 6, Fol: Sermons, 1967–1969 (Emrich Papers): Richard S. Emrich, untitled sermon (1968), 2.

152. AAEHC, Oral History Interview with Arthur B. Williams, Jr. (2009): MZ000043; Lawrence Otis Graham, *Our Kind of People: Inside America's Black Upper Class* (New York: Harper Collins, 1999), 13, 287. See also Andrew Wiese, "'The House I Live In': Race, Class, and African American Suburban Dreams in the Postwar United States," in *The New Suburban History*, ed. Kevin M. Kruse and Thomas J. Sugrue (Chicago: University of Chicago Press, 2006), 116–19.

153. Among the statement's signatories were Episcopalians John Burgess, Quinland Gordon, Robert Hood, Kenneth Hughes, Leon Modeste, David Nickerson, Henri Stines, Paul Washington, and Nathan Wright. *NYT*, July 31, 1966: E5.

154. Shattuck, *Episcopalians and Race*, 171–2; Jeffrey O. G. Ogbar, *Black Power: Radical Politics and African American Identity* (Baltimore, MD: John Hopkins UP, 2004), 93–100; Jack M. Bloom *Class, Race, and the Civil Rights Movement* (Bloomington: Indiana UP, 1987), 218–21.

155. AAEHC, Oral History Interview with Arthur B. Williams, Jr. (2009), MZ000044.

156. Harold T. Lewis, "Racial Concerns in the Church since 1973," *AEH* 67.4 (Dec 1998): 470, n.11.

157. Findlay, *Church People*, 213; John L. Kater, Jr., "Experiment in Freedom: The Episcopal Church and the Black Power Movement," *HMPEC* 48.1 (Mar 1979): 71–2.

158. *NYT*, Nov 13, 1966: 84; *Witness*, Nov 24, 1966: 4; *LC*, Dec 4, 1966: 7.

159. Shattuck, *Episcopalians and Race*, qtd. 174; VTS, M24.Lit Com 1A (Price Papers): John Morris, "ESCRU: The Episcopal Society For Cultural and Racial Unity, 1959–1967" (1995), 25.

160. Daniel S. Lucks, *From Selma to Saigon: The Civil Rights Movement and the Vietnam War* (Lexington: University of Kentucky Press, 2014), 120–40.

161. Robert W. Tobin, interview with author, Deer Isle, ME, Aug 13, 2013.

162. *Witness*, Feb 23, 1967: 10–12; *Episcopalian*, Apr 1967: 44–5.

163. Accompanying Primo at the meeting were Jesse Anderson, James Breeden, Tollie Caution, Austin Cooper, Walter Dennis, Quinland Gordon, Robert Hood, John

Johnson, Irving Mayson, Harold Nicholson, St. Julian Simpkins, Henri Stines, John Walker, Frederick Williams, and Harold Wright. AAEHC, A57, Box 3 (Mayson Papers): H. Irving Mayson, "Meeting of the Ad Hoc Committee concerned with racial inequalities existing in the Protestant Episcopal Church with the Presiding Bishop, April 18, 1967," 1–3.

164. AAEHC, A39.01.03.4.2 (Hayden Papers): Quinland Gordon and Austin R. Cooper, "Second Meeting of Negro Clergy with Presiding Bishop and other Bishops and Priests, June 27, 1967," 1–2, 6.

165. VTS, M182.3 (Walker Papers): John T. Walker, untitled sermon (1967), 3.

166. DioWash, 7.1.1 (Walker Papers): Walker, "At the Bottom of the Well," 10.

167. *Church in Metropolis* 15 (Winter 1967): 32.

168. Charles V. Willie, *Oreo: On Race and Marginal Men and Women* (Wakefield, MA: Parameter Press, 1975), 11–22.

169. *NYT*, Feb 15, 1968: 42.

170. Syracuse, Box 52 (Pike Papers): Press conference by C. Kilmer Myers and John E. Hines (1967), 2–3. Hines continued to avoid taking a stand on Vietnam in the months to follow. Addressing the Executive Council in May 1968, he admitted that "while others appear to be painfully precise and clear about what Christians both ought to be doing and can be doing, . . . I am able to discern no clear Christian guidance as to what this country should do or, for that matter, just what this Church should do." AEC, 238.J.38 (Spong/Hines Papers): John E. Hines, Statement to the Executive Council (1968), 5.

171. VTS, M26.2000.0003 (Price Papers): Charles P. Price, "The Gantlet" (1967), 1, 4–5.

172. Jill K. Gill, *Embattled Ecumenism: The National Council of Churches, the Vietnam War, and the Trials of the Protestant Left* (DeKalb: North Illinois UP, 2011), 183–5.

173. AEC, 2003.095.2 (Barrett Papers): George W. Barrett, "Mission to Southeast Asia, June 13–July 6, 1967," 45–50. Something of Barrett's moderate tone is discernible in the introduction to the final report: see AEC 2003.095.1 (Barrett Papers): Robert S. Bilheimer et al., statement of NCCC Vietnam delegation (1967), 1–2.

174. AEC 2003.095.1 (Barrett Papers): George W. Barrett to W. C. Westmoreland, July 13, 1967.

175. AEC, 2003.095.1 (Barrett Papers): George W. Barrett, untitled sermon (1969), 2.

176. Tom Turney Edwards, "The Suburban Church," Kellogg Lectures, Episcopal Divinity School, 1966, http://research.eds.edu/c.php?g=358676&p=2421446, accessed Apr 1, 2017 (site discontinued).

177. *Christian Century*, Apr 5, 1967: 434–5.

178. *LC*, Apr 2, 1967: 9–10.

179. Hale, *Nation of Outsiders*, 207.

180. BHL, Box I, Fol: Closing of Parishfield–1967 (Parishfield Records): Parishfield Staff to "Friends," Jan 1, 1967.

181. Sanderson, Untitled Parishfield Memoir.

182. *Christian Century*, June 14, 1967: 776; BHL (Sara C. Winter Oral History Collection): Interview with Paul van Buren, conducted by Sara Winter (1994/1995).

183. Ayres Private Papers: Francis Ayres, "Revolution or Revolutionary Action?" (1968), 1–5. For a lively account of the counterculture in Boston and Cambridge during these

296 NOTES

years, see Ryan H. Walsh, *Astral Weeks: A Secret History of 1968* (New York: Penguin Press, 2018).

184. Kenneth L. Woodward, *Getting Religion: Faith, Culture, and Politics from the Age of Eisenhower to the Era of Obama* (New York: Convergent, 2016), 105.

Chapter 6

1. For a recent account of the events in Newark, see Max Arthur Herman, *Summer of Rage: An Oral History of the 1967 Newark and Detroit Riots* (New York: Peter Lang, 2013). For a critique of the liberal response to the crisis, see Malcolm McLaughlin, *The Long, Hot Summer of 1967: Urban Rebellion in America* (New York: Palgrave Macmillan, 2014).

2. AEC, 151.2.10 (CSR Records): Leland Stark to the Clergy of the Diocese of Newark, July 13, 1967.

3. *LC*, Aug 13, 1967: 4.

4. *NYT*, Feb 24, 2005: B11; AAEHC, Oral History Interview with Arthur B. Williams, Jr. (2009), MZ000038–43.

5. *LC*, Sept 3, 1967: 21.

6. *WP*, July 9, 2001: B6.

7. *Witness*, Aug 17, 1967: 3.

8. *LC*, Aug 20, 1967: 6.

9. *WP*, July 29, 1967: A10.

10. *LC*, Aug 13, 1967: 5.

11. Three years prior to Hines's urban tours, William Stringfellow had written: "If I were a bishop, I would first of all devote myself to walking the streets, trying to see the inner city for myself. . . . I would visit and try to listen to the voices that can be heard in the taverns and the tenements, on the street corners, and in the shops. First, I would try to hear the city, if, indeed, the city would tolerate my presence long enough to permit me to listen." Stringfellow, *Free in Obedience*, 41.

12. Kesselus, *Granite on Fire*, 246–9.

13. *Episcopalian*, Nov 1969: 24–6.

14. David L. Holmes, "Presiding Bishop John E. Hines and the General Convention Special Program," *AEH* 61.4 (Dec 1992): 399.

15. AEC, 31.5.5 (CSR Records): Jack Woodard et al. to John E. Hines, Aug 8, 1967, 2–3.

16. AEC, 31.5.5 (CSR Records): Statement by delegation of black community leaders (1967), 1–2.

17. Carter Donnan McDowell and Lucy Newton Boswell Negus, interview with William Booth, in John Shelby Spong (ed.), *Anniversary Booklet: A Tribute to John Elbridge Hines on the Fiftieth Anniversary of His Ordination to the Priesthood, October 1984* (1984), n.p.

18. Woodard, *Episcopal Church's Struggle*, 167–8.

19. DioMass (Coburn Papers): Executive Council Minutes, Sept 15, 1967: "The Crisis in American Society: A Call by the Presiding Bishop," A2, A4.

20. *LC*, Oct 1, 1967: 6; AEC, 211.1.10 (JUP Records): "Proposed Response to the Presiding Bishop by the Executive Council" (1967), 1.
21. Gardiner H. Shattuck, Jr., "'Contending from the Walls of Sion': The General Convention Special Program and the Crisis in American Society, 1967–73," *AEH* 67.4 (Dec 1998): 508.
22. Since the early 1870s, the Women's Auxiliary to the Board of Missions was founded to encourage Episcopal women in mission work. From 1889, this organization sponsored the United Thank Offering, which raised funds for a range of missionary activities. Renamed Episcopal Church Women in 1958, the group continued its practice of convening a Triennial Meeting in parallel with General Convention, from which its members were excluded. ECW and its antecedents provided crucial financial support for the national church throughout the twentieth century. See Frances M. Young, *Thankfulness Unites: The History of the United Thank Offering, 1889–1979* (Cincinnati, OH: Forward Movement, 1979).
23. *Summary of General Convention Actions 1967* (New York: Executive Council, 1967), 3–5.
24. Bishop Leland Stark of Newark convened the committee. He was joined by fellow bishops Richard Emrich of Michigan, Kim Myers of California, and Richard Martin of Long Island. *Episcopalian*, Nov 1967: 15.
25. *General Convention Actions 1967*, 6–9.
26. *Time*, Sept 29, 1967: 57.
27. *Episcopalian*, Nov 1967: 11, 14.
28. E.g., DioWash, 5.9.2 (Dun Papers): Paul Moore, Jr. to Angus Dun, Sept 29, 1967; *Episcopalian*, Nov 1967: 51.
29. *Witness*, Oct 5, 1967: 4–5.
30. No specific vote by orders was taken on GCSP, which was approved as part of the overall triennial program and budget. *LC*, Oct 8, 1967: 5, 7.
31. It is important to note that the much-touted figure of $9 million was never intended to go solely to grant giving. This total included $1.5 million per annum already in the national budget for programs not under the purview of GCSP. By the end of the 1968–1970 triennium, GCSP had thus allocated $4.424 million in grants, approximating $1.5 million per year. *General Convention Actions 1967*, 9; Sandy M. Pringle, *GCSP—The Episcopal Church's Program for the Empowerment of Minority Groups: A Case Study* (Washington, DC: Department of State, 1971), 13.
32. Charles V. Willie, *Church Action in the World: Studies in Sociology and Religion* (New York: Morehouse-Barlow, 1969), 137–8.
33. Shattuck, "Contending from the Walls of Sion," qtd. 515.
34. *LC*, Oct 15, 1967: 19.
35. Kater, "Experiment in Freedom," 74–5.
36. Douglas Carpenter, email to author, Apr 3, 2014.
37. Syracuse, Box 52 (Pike Papers): Frederick M. Morris, "What Happened at Seattle?" (1967), 2; DioWash, 5.9.2 (Dun Papers): Robert Curry to Angus Dun, Oct 3, 1967.
38. Michael Coburn, interview with author, Cranston, RI, Dec 23, 2014.
39. Harry F. Havemeyer, "An Introduction," in John Coburn, *Holiness and Community: John Coburn Preaches the Faith* (Harrisburg, PA: Morehouse, 2010), qtd. ix.

298 NOTES

40. Gatch, "John Bowen Coburn," 350.

41. *Witness*, Feb 2, 1967: 8.

42. Cynthia Wedel, "The Major Minority," *CA* 42.3 (Fall 1967): 10–11.

43. *Witness*, Sept 28, 1967: 4; *Episcopalian*, Nov 1967: 6.

44. *Church and Society in Crisis: Social Policy of the Episcopal Church 1964–1967* (New York: Executive Council of the Episcopal Church, 1968), 80–1.

45. *Witness*, Oct 12, 1967: 3; *LC*, Oct 15, 1967: 8.

46. Columbia (Oral History): "Reminiscences of John M. Allin" (1991), 4.220–1.

47. *Witness*, Sept 15, 1966: 10; *Episcopalian*, July 1967: 19–20.

48. DioMinn (McNairy Papers): Philip F. McNairy, Suffragan Bishop's Report to the Diocesan Convention (1966), 3.

49. Harvard, UAI 15.900.14 (Pusey Papers): Nathan M. Pusey, statement made to the House of Deputies of the General Convention concerning the Report of the Special Committee to Study Theological Education (1967), 1.

50. Nathan M. Pusey and Charles L. Taylor, *Ministry for Tomorrow: Report of the Special Committee on Theological Education* (New York: Seabury Press, 1967), 21, 59, 120. See also Booty, *Episcopal Church in Crisis*, 45–6.

51. Stephen F. Bayne, Jr., "Preface," in Stephen F. Bayne, Jr., et al., *Theological Freedom and Social Responsibility: Report of the Advisory Committee of the Episcopal Church* (New York: Seabury Press, 1967) ix.

52. Stephen F. Bayne, Jr., et al., "The Report," in *Theological Freedom and Social Responsibility: Report of the Advisory Committee of the Episcopal Church*, ed. Stephen F. Bayne, Jr., et al. (New York: Seabury Press, 1967), 5–7.

53. *NYT*, Aug 15, 1967: 1ff; *WP*, Aug 15, 1967: A11; *LC* Aug 27, 1967: 1.

54. Bayne et al., "The Report," 32–3.

55. John Knox, "The Identifiability of the Church," in *Theological Freedom and Social Responsibility: Report of the Advisory Committee of the Episcopal Church*, ed. Stephen F. Bayne, Jr., et al. (New York: Seabury Press, 1967), 67–71, 74–6.

56. James Pike, "Doctrine, Data, and Due Process," in *Theological Freedom and Social Responsibility: Report of the Advisory Committee of the Episcopal Church*, ed. Stephen F. Bayne, Jr., et al. (New York: Seabury Press, 1967), 120–2.

57. Syracuse, Box 31 (Pike Papers): William Stringfellow to James A. Pike, Aug 27, 1967.

58. DioWash, 5.9.2 (Dun Papers): Robert Curry to Angus Dun, Oct 3, 1967.

59. *Look Magazine*, Apr 29, 1969: 57.

60. *NYT*, Aug 1, 1976: 172.

61. *NYT*, July 22, 1997: A15.

62. *Witness*, Sept 21, 1967: 3; *Episcopalian*, Nov 1967: 9.

63. *Episcopalian*, Nov 1967: 51. See also Robert Wuthnow, *The Restructuring of American Religion: Society and Faith Since World War II* (Princeton, NJ: Princeton UP, 1988), 98.

64. Woodard, *Episcopal Church's Struggle*, 150.

65. DioWash, 6.3.2 (Creighton Papers): Department of Communication, Executive Council, "Questions and Answers about the Church's Program on the Crisis in American Life" (1967).

66. Holmes, "John E. Hines," 399.

NOTES 299

67. John E. Hines, "The Agonised Cry of a People Who Had No Place in American Society," in *All One Body*, ed. Timothy Wilson (London: Darton, Longman and Todd, 1969), 281; Carter Donnan McDowell and Lucy Newton Boswell Negus, interview with Richard B. Martin, in John Shelby Spong (ed.), *Anniversary Booklet: A Tribute to John Elbridge Hines on the Fiftieth Anniversary Of His Ordination to the Priesthood, October 1984* (1984), n.p.

68. Lewis, "Racial Concerns," 470.

69. GTS, C25.31.43 (Caution Papers): Tollie L. Caution to Philip Zabriskie and Daniel Corrigan, Nov 22, 1967.

70. Shattuck, *Episcopalians and Race*, 181.

71. GTS, C25.31.43 (Caution Papers): Tollie L. Caution to John E. Hines, Dec 7, 1967.

72. *LC*, Jan 14, 1968: 7; GTS, C25.31.43 (Caution Papers): "A List of Those Who Sent Letters Concerning Dr. Caution's Impending Retirement" (1968).

73. GTS, C25.31.43 (Caution Papers): H. Albion Farrell to Daniel Corrigan, Jan 8, 1968.

74. DioMass, 1.A.12:19, Fol: Correspondence (Burgess Papers): John M. Burgess to Daniel N. Corrigan, Jan 8, 1968.

75. Lawrence held this office until 1985, just one year before his death. *NYT*, Apr 5, 1986: 32.

76. GTS, C25.31.43 (Caution Papers): Charles R. Lawrence to Daniel Corrigan, Jan 18, 1968.

77. GTS, C25.31.43 (Caution Papers): Walter Dennis to Daniel Corrigan, Jan 16, 1968.

78. AAEHC, A39.01.03.4.2 (Hayden Papers): Austin R. Cooper, "Concerning an Association of Negro Priests" (1968), 4.

79. Besides Cooper, the committee formed to launch UBCL consisted of Tollie Caution, Moran Weston, St. Julian Simpkins, Jesse Anderson, Kenneth Hughes, and John Walker. AAEHC, A39.01.03.4.2 (Hayden Papers): Austin R. Cooper, "Meeting of the Ad Hoc Committee of Negro Clergy, St. Philip's Church, Harlem, February 7, 1968," 1; *NYT*, Feb 9, 1968: 57.

80. GTS, C25.30.43 (Caution Papers): Donald O. Wilson et al. to John E. Hines, Feb 19, 1968.

81. When the black priests meeting at St. Philip's confronted Modeste about his role in Caution's exclusion from GCSP, he denied responsibility, claiming the decision had come directly from the top. This, it was noted by the group, was in marked contrast to the version of events already provided by the presiding bishop. AAEHC, A39.01.03.4.2 (Hayden Papers): Cooper, "Meeting of the Ad Hoc Committee," 2.

82. David L. Holmes, "John E. Hines," 412–13.

83. GTS, C25.31.43 (Caution Papers): Daniel Corrigan to Austin R. Cooper, Jan 15, 1968; Daniel Corrigan to Kenneth Hughes, Jan 30, 1968; Vine Deloria, Jr., "GCSP: The Demons at Work," *HMPEC* 48.1 (Mar 1979): 87–8.

84. Edward Rodman, *Let There Be Peace among Us: A Story of the Union of Black Episcopalians* (Lawrenceville, VA: Brunswick Press, 1990), 4.

85. Richard B. Martin, *On the Wings of the Morning: Two Islands, One Church* (Garden City, NY: Diocese of Long Island, 2006), 105.

300 NOTES

86. Carter Donnan McDowell and Lucy Newton Boswell Negus, interview with Frederick Williams, in John Shelby Spong (ed.), *Anniversary Booklet: A Tribute to John Elbridge Hines on the Fiftieth Anniversary of His Ordination to the Priesthood, October 1984* (1984), n.p.; Woodard, *Episcopal Church's Struggle*, 194, 242.

87. *Episcopalian*, Nov 1969: 54; AEC, 87.5.50 (GCSP Records): Cecil C. F. Wagstaff to Leon E. Modeste, Mar 8, 1968.

88. AEC, 87.5.51 (GCSP Records): Leon E. Modeste Correspondence (1967–1968).

89. In 1970, Menuez moved to the role of assistant to the director for Communications and Budget as part of an effort to promote a better understanding of GCSP in the church at large. *GCSP Newsletter*, Oct 1970: 1–2; Barry Menuez, interview with author, by telephone, July 23, 2015.

90. Pringle, *GCSP*, 14.

91. Hood, *Social Teachings*, 123.

92. *LC*, Jan 7, 1968: 4; AEC, 87.1.6 (GCSP Records): Leon E. Modeste, "Mission: Empowerment" (1974), 47–8.

93. For an examination of this question in legal terms, see Dator and Nunley, *Many Parts, One Body*, 142–5.

94. John Woolverton, "Editorial," *AEH* 67.4 (Dec 1998): 446; Kenneth Kesselus, *Granite on Fire*, 285.

95. Columbia (Oral History): "Reminiscences of John M. Allin" (1991), 4.227–8, 4.242.

96. AEC 87.5.53 (GCSP Records): C. Kilmer Myers to Leon E. Modeste, July 1, 1969.

97. AEC, 87.1.1/2 (GCSP Records): GCSP, "The First Five Years: A History of the General Convention Special Program" (1972), 54.

98. AEC, 87.1.6 (GCSP Records): Modeste, "Mission: Empowerment," 1.

99. DioMass (Coburn Papers): Executive Council Minutes, Sept 24–26, 1968: "Report of Screen and Review Committee of GSCP": A21; GTS, B29.3.2.58c (Bayne Papers): Stephen F. Bayne to Carman Hunter, Nov 25, 1968.

100. *Episcopalian*, November 1969: 26; interview with Barry Menuez, July 23, 2015, by telephone.

101. AEC, 87.5.52 (GCSP Records): Charles V. Willie to Leon E. Modeste, Apr 18, 1969.

102. *LC*, July 8, 2001: 18.

103. Andrew W. Walsh, "The Mainline and the Soul of International Relations," in *The Future of Mainline Protestantism in America*, ed. James Hudnut-Beumler and Mark Silk (New York: Columbia UP, 2018), 151.

104. *Los Angeles Times*, Oct 17, 1967: 22; AEC, 299.1.4 (Corrigan Papers): Robert L. DeWitt to John E. Hines and Arthur Walmsley, Oct 30, 1967.

105. E.g., DioPenn, 1.15: 4.2-Vietnam (DeWitt Papers): P. Blair Lee to Robert L. DeWitt, Oct 17, 1967; Charles Woodward to Robert L. DeWitt, Oct 18, 1967.

106. DioPenn, 1.15: 4.5-Vietnam (DeWitt Papers): Edward L. Lee, "The Church and Peace" (1967), 2–3, 5.

107. WSU, 131.2.1.10.25 (DIM Records): Robert Morrison, "Sanctuary to Draft Resisters" (1967), 2–3; *LC*, Nov 5, 1967: 5.

108. See Mitchell K. Hall, *Because of Their Faith: CALCAV and Religious Opposition to the Vietnam War* (New York: Columbia UP, 1990), 1–25.

NOTES 301

109. *NYT*, Aug 3, 1968: 17.
110. BHL, Box 1, Fol: Pastoral Letters (Emrich Papers): Richard S. Emrich, Letter to the Diocese, Mar 18, 1969.
111. *NYT*, Nov 28, 1967: 10; *Witness*, Dec 7, 1967: 4.
112. BHL, Box 6, Fol: Jane Barney Personal Files, A-C (Barney Papers): John Pairman Brown, "The Liberated Church in America" (1968), 2; John Rawlinson, email to author, Sept 4, 2013.
113. DioPenn, 1.15.6.2-Tension (DeWitt Papers): Robert L. DeWitt to Clergy of the Diocese (1967), 1; *Witness*, Nov 9, 1967: 3–4.
114. *Evening Bulletin* [Philadelphia], Sept 2, 1969: 1.
115. *Christian Century*, Sept 11, 1968: 1140–1.
116. Donald Armentrout, *Episcopal Splinter Groups: A Study of Groups Which Have Left the Episcopal Church, 1873–1985* (Sewanee, TN: School of Theology, University of the South, 1985), 28.
117. *NYT*, Jan 1, 1968: 2; Deborah Mathias Gough, *Christ Church, Philadelphia: The Nation's Church in a Changing City* (Philadelphia: Christ Church Philadelphia, 1995), 367.
118. *LC*, Aug 20, 1967: 6; *Philadelphia Inquirer*, Feb 5, 2002: B11.
119. *Delaware County Daily Times*, Sept 13, 1967: 10.
120. *Today*, Apr 14, 1968: 9.
121. *Main Line Chronicle*, Feb 20, 1969: 4.
122. DioPenn, 1.15.6.2-Tension (DeWitt Papers): Stanhope S. Browne et al., "Report of the Committee on Ministry to Areas of Tension" (1968), 13–16, 22–30, 37. The other members of the committee were priests Frederick A. Breuninger, Wilfred F. Penny, and Paul M. Washington, as well as layman Sidney B. Dexter.
123. Lewis Baldwin, *The Voice of Conscience: The Church in the Mind of Martin Luther King, Jr.* (New York: Oxford UP, 2010), 181.
124. For an account of this episode, see Sylvie Laurent, *King and the Other America: The Poor People's Campaign and the Quest for Economic Equality* (Berkeley: University of California Press, 2018).
125. *Witness*, Apr 18, 1968: 3–4.
126. John Burgess, "I Was a Black Man before I Was a Christian," in *All One Body*, ed. Timothy Wilson (London: Darton, Longman and Todd, 1969), 168.
127. *WP*, Apr 6, 1968: E9. Von Hoffmann could not have known that the same day as the memorial service, Sayre had telegrammed Coretta Scott King, offering her "the privilege of sepulture" for her husband within the cathedral. Though this invitation was politely refused, Sayre believed he had been right to proffer it, since King "had outgrown his southern soil and become of the great Americans who should be buried in a place where all could honor his memory." WNC, 18004.6.7 (Sayre Papers): Francis B. Sayre, Jr., to Mrs. Martin Luther King, Apr 5, 1968; Francis B. Sayre, Jr., to John Baiz, May 21, 1968.
128. *Witness*, Apr 25, 1968: 4.
129. DioNY, 125.5 (Moore Papers): Paul Moore and Milton Zatinsky, *A Design for Interfaith Involvement in Economic Development in the Ghetto* (1968), 15–16; *WP*, Apr 17, 1968: C8; *Witness*, May 2, 1968: 4.

302 NOTES

130. *Washington Diocese*, Feb 1968: 1ff.
131. Paul Moore, *Presences*, 201–2.
132. *NYT*, Aug 22, 1988: D11.
133. Robert M. Pennoyer, *As It Was: A Memoir* (Westport, CT: Prospecta Press, 2015), 260–1.
134. For an examination of the interplay between race and class in the industrial towns during this period, see John Hinshaw, "Steel Communities and Memories of Race," *Pennsylvania History* 60.4 (Oct 1993): 510–18.
135. Bonner, *Called Out of Darkness*, 218, 226.
136. *NYT*, Mar 8, 1970: SM17ff. In 1969, Deloria published the first of over twenty books on the social, political, and religious experience of Native Americans, entitled *Custer Died for Your Sins: An Indian Manifesto* (New York: Macmillan, 1969). He spent the next thirty-five years teaching at universities across the American West, establishing the first master's degree program in American Indian Studies at the University of Arizona in 1990. See also Vine Deloria, Jr., *For This Land: Writings on Religion in America*, ed. James Treat (New York: Routledge, 1999).
137. Owanah Anderson, *400 Years: Anglican/Episcopal Mission among American Indians* (Cincinnati, OH: Forward Movement, 1997), 316–18.
138. Philip Deloria, email to author, July 17, 2015.
139. Deloria, "GCSP," 86–8.
140. DioMass (Coburn Papers): Vine Deloria, Jr., statement to Native American clergy (1968–1969); *LC*, Jan 12, 1969: 5–6.
141. Angela Tarango, *Choosing the Jesus Way: American Indian Pentecostals and the Fight for the Indigenous Principle* (Chapel Hill: University of North Carolina Press, 2014), 159–60.
142. DioWash, 6.3.2 (Creighton Papers): Virginia Miller to Charles L. Glenn, July 1, 1968.
143. GTS, B29.3.2.55c (Bayne Papers): Edward Winckley to Stephen F. Bayne, May 29, 1969.
144. *Witness*, Feb 27, 1969: 3–4. Throughout the program's existence, the national church provided regular reports on GCSP disbursements. E.g., AEC, 87.4.19 (GCSP Records): "Where did all that money go? Grants made by the General Convention Special Program of the Episcopal Church to June 1, 1968" (1968).
145. Kesselus, *Granite on Fire*, 305.
146. *WP*, Oct 7, 1968: A27.
147. DioMass (Coburn Papers): Executive Council Minutes, Dec 10–12, 1968: "Message from the President," A12.
148. Willie, *Church Action*, 12, 23.
149. *LC*, July 14, 1968: 3.
150. See also DioMinn (McNairy Papers): Philip F. McNairy, Suffragan Bishop's Report to the Convention (1968), 2; DioNY, 4.9 (Donegan Papers): Horace W. B. Donegan, "We Move Forward" (1969), 12–13.
151. *Witness*, Feb 27, 1969: 3.
152. DioMass (Coburn Papers): Executive Council Minutes, Feb 11–13, 69: "Message from the President," A11.

153. DioMass (Coburn Papers): David E. Richards, confidential memo (1969), 1. By 1970, the national church would be running a deficit of $3.5 million. Holmes, *Brief History*, 166.

154. DioMass (Coburn Papers): David E. Richards to John E. Hines et al., Mar 24, 1969.

155. *LC*, Mar 16, 1969: 19.

156. John Rawlinson, email to author, Sept 4, 2013.

157. *LC*, Sept 1, 1968: 10–12; *Jet*, Nov 9, 1967: 20.

158. Booty, *American Apostle*, 153.

159. GTS, B29.3.2.50c (Bayne Papers): Stephen F. Bayne to William Moore, Dec 13, 1968.

160. By 1980, the number of enrolled Episcopalians had fallen to 3.04 million, and by 1990, to 2.44 million. Prichard, *A History*, 320–1. This decline has continued without substantial reversal ever since.

161. E.g., Jeffrey K. Hadden, *The Gathering Storm in the Churches* (Garden City, NY: Doubleday, 1969), 71–99; Dean M. Kelley, *Why Conservative Churches Are Growing: A Study in Sociology of Religion* (New York: Harper and Row, 1972), 133–53.

162. Roozen, "Fifty Years," 68; James Hudnut-Beumler, "Conclusion," in *The Future of Mainline Protestantism in America*, ed. James Hudnut-Beumler and Mark Silk (New York: Columbia UP, 2018), 180.

163. Snow, *Gospel in a Broken World*, 17; C. Kirk Hadaway, "Denominational Defection: Recent Research on Religious Disaffiliation in America," in *The Protestant Mainstream "Decline": The Presbyterian Pattern*, ed. Milton J. Coalter et al. (Louisville, KY: Westminster/John Knox Press, 1990), 103–7.

164. *LC*, July 21, 1968: 2–3.

165. DioPenn, 1.15.3.4-Addresses (DeWitt Papers):Robert L. DeWitt, *The Church Wrestling with the World Today: Six Lenten Addresses* (1969), 33–4.

166. Snow, *Gospel in a Broken World*, 17.

167. William Stringfellow, *Imposters of God: Inquiries into Favorite Idols* (1969; Eugene, OR: Wipf and Stock, 2006), 35. See also William R. Coates, "A Prophet of the Biblical World," in *Prophet of Justice, Prophet of Life: Essays on William Stringfellow*, ed. Robert Boak Slocum (New York: Church Publishing, 1997), 170–1.

168. *Christian Century*, Apr 26, 1967: 527–8.

169. *NYT*, Jan 29, 1968: 62.

170. Glenn T. Miller, *Piety and Profession*, 759.

171. EDS, 2.34 (Coburn Papers): John Coburn et al., "A Statement by the Deans of the Seminaries of the Episcopal Church, February 24, 1968—Draft A," 1–3.

172. EDS, 2.35 (Coburn Papers): John B. Coburn to the Deans of the Seminaries, Nov 29, 1968.

173. EDS, 2.36 (Coburn Papers): John B. Coburn to the ETS community, June 7, 1968.

174. *Episcopalian*, June 1969: 24–6, 43.

175. *NYT*, Sept 29, 1969: 40.

176. Havemeyer, "Introduction," vii–viii.

177. Michael Coburn, interview with author, Cranston, RI, Dec 23, 2014. DioMass (Coburn Papers): John B. Coburn to Patricia Page, Feb 24, 1972; John B. Coburn to Robert Morrison, Jun 20, 1972.

304 NOTES

178. Cornell, 4438.13 (Stringfellow Papers): Arthur Walmsley to John E. Hines, June 10, 1968.
179. DioPitt, 1.51 (Pardue Papers): Pardue, "Where the danger is," 3.
180. Findlay, *Church People*, 189–90.
181. For an account of the Manifesto's origins and reception, see Elaine Allen Lechtreck, "'We Are Demanding $500 Million for Reparations': The Black Manifesto, Mainline Religious Denominations, and Black Economic Development," *Journal of African American History* 97.1–2 (Winter–Spring 2012): 39–71.
182. *NYT*, May 2, 1969: 46; *LC*, June 1, 1969: 5.
183. *LC*, June 15, 1969: 12.
184. *Summary of General Convention Actions 1967*, 20.
185. *Witness*, June 12, 1969: 3; Shattuck, *Episcopalians and Race*, 191–2.
186. AEC, 87.5.52 (GCSP Records): Stephen F. Bayne to Leon E. Modeste, Apr 24, 1969.
187. *LC*, June 29, 1969: 6.
188. *LC*, July 27, 1969: 12.
189. AAEHC, Oral History Interview with Arthur B. Williams, Jr. (2009), MZ000051–3.
190. Eg. BHL, Box 6, Fol: Sermons, 1967–1969 (Emrich Papers): Richard S. Emrich, "A Sermon of Thanksgiving for the Life and Work of Arthur Carl Lichtenberger" (1968), 2; Fol: Lectures and Addresses (Emrich Papers): Richard S. Emrich, "The Christian Woman and Politics" (1968): 4; Fol: Articles and Commentaries, 1950s/1960s (Emrich Papers): Richard S. Emrich, "Getting Back on Track" (1968), 3–5.
191. BHL, Box 21, Fol: Black Manifesto, 1968–1970 (Diocese of Michigan Records): Robert E. Morrison to Rector, Wardens and Vestry of Christ Church Cranbrook, June 18, 1969. See also Keith Dye, "The Black Manifesto for Reparations in Detroit: Challenge and Response, 1969," *Michigan Historical Review* 35.2 (Fall 2009): 58–9.
192. *Detroit News*, June 23, 1969: 1; *The Record*, July 1969: 1ff.
193. *Detroit News*, June 26, 1969: 14.
194. *Detroit News*, June 24, 1969: 3.
195. *LC*, July 27, 1969: 7.
196. Michael E. George, "The Black Manifesto and the Churches: The Struggle for Black Power and Reparations in Philadelphia." Master's thesis, Temple University, Philadelphia, 2013, 40–1.
197. *Witness*, Aug 1, 1969: 5; *LC*, Aug 17, 1969: 6.
198. AAEHC, A19: Series X.2 (Dennis Personal Papers): Walter D. Dennis, untitled sermon (1969), 5–6.
199. AAEHC, A19: Series X.1 (Dennis Personal Papers): Dennis, "Spiritual Pilgrimage," 9, 20.
200. DioPitt, 1.51 (Pardue Papers): Pardue, "Where the danger is," 3b–4; Paul Moore, *Presences*, 187.
201. Murray provides an account of her interracial antecedents in the 1956 book *Proud Shoes: The Story of an American Family* (New York: Harper, 1956).
202. Sarah Azaransky, *The Dream Is Freedom: Pauli Murray and American Democratic Faith* (New York: Oxford UP, 2011), 3–87. More recently, see also Rosalind Rosenberg, *Jane Crow: The Life of Pauli Murray* (New York: Oxford UP, 2017).

NOTES   305

203. Pauli Murray, *The Autobiography of a Black Activist, Feminist, Lawyer, Priest, and Poet* (Knoxville: University of Tennessee Press, 1989), 397–8.

204. Radcliffe, MC 412.62.1045 (Murray Papers): David Garcia to "Brothers and Sisters," Aug 12, 1969.

205. Radcliffe, MC 412.62.1045 (Murray Papers): Pauli Murray to David Garcia, Aug 26, 1969.

206. Pauli Murray, "The Dilemma of the Minority Christian," in *Daughters of Thunder: Black Women Preachers and Their Sermons, 1850–1979*, ed. Bettye Collier-Thomas (San Francisco: Jossey-Bass, 1998), 261.

207. John Crocker, Jr., *A Rebirth of Freedom: The Calling of an American Historian* (Philadelphia: Xlibris, 2005), 264–5.

208. The band first played at St. Mark's in November 1968. They did so again the following April, when ABC featured them in a national broadcast called the "Christian Rock and Roll Worship Service." *LC*, Dec 15, 1968: 5–6; "14th Mass First Nationally Televised Christian Rock Service," http://www.mindgarage.com/, accessed Jan 12, 2020.

209. Radcliffe, MC 412.62.1045 (Murray Papers): Michael Allen to Pauli Murray, Sept 8, 1969.

210. Radcliffe, MC 412.62.1045 (Murray Papers): Pauli Murray to Michael Allen, Sept 11, 1969.

211. DioMass (Coburn Papers): Report of the Committee for the Implementation of the Spirit of the (Executive Council) Response to the Manifesto (1969), 3–6, 11.

212. DioMass (Coburn Papers): Executive Council Minutes, Aug 29, 1969 Special Meeting in South Bend, A8.

213. *Episcopalian*, Sept 1969: 22–4.

214. Of the four minority members elected, it was also agreed that two would be chosen from a list of nominees supplied by UBCL. DioMass (Coburn Papers): Executive Council Minutes, Aug 29, 1969, Special Meeting, A5–6.

215. DioPenn, 1.15.4.2-GCSP (DeWitt Papers): Advisory Committee on Agenda, "Recommendations of Advisory Committee on Agenda" (1969), 1–2; DioMass (Coburn Papers): Advisory Committee on Agenda, "A Conception of the Theme of Special General Convention II, Second Draft" (1969), 3; *Witness*, Feb 27, 1969: 3–4.

216. Twelve dioceses situated abroad likewise failed to send representatives, but they cited financial constraints as the reason, rather than principled opposition. *NYT*, Sept 1, 1969: 8.

217. *NYT*, Sept 2, 1969: 27.

218. *Episcopalian*, Oct 1969: 41–2.

219. Kesselus, *Granite on Fire*, 321–2; Shattuck, "Contending from the Walls of Sion," 522.

220. *NYT*, Sept 1, 1969: 8.

221. Washington, *Other Sheep I Have*, 91–2.

222. *Witness*, Sept 1, 1969: 4. According to Edward Rodman, Kenyatta's supporters planned the whole intervention in advance. He himself had recommended that nothing be done while the "formidable" John Coburn was presiding, so that "the more affable and less combative John Hines would have to deal with our move"

306 NOTES

instead. Edward Rodman, *Let There Be Peace*, 15–16; Edward Rodman, "Before and after We Seized the Microphone," *The Rt. Rev. John B. Coburn, 1914–2009: Leader of the House*, https://johncoburnatdiomass.wordpress.com, accessed Jan 22, 2020.

223. *Boston Globe*, Sept 2, 1969: 11.

224. One black deputy criticized for not joining the walk-out was Charles Lawrence, who later described the episode as "a great process of catharsis and learning." *NYT*, Sept 2, 1969: 27; *Episcopalian*, June 1985: 14.

225. *Boston Globe*, Sept 2, 1969: 11.

226. *Christianity Today*, Sept 26, 1969: 42–4.

227. *New York Post*, Sept 3, 1969: 30.

228. DioPitt, 1.51 (Pardue Papers): Pardue, "Where the danger is," 4. See also Junius F. Carter, Jr., "God's Call to Unity, Love and Service," in *Black Gospel/White Church*, ed. John M. Burgess (New York: Seabury Press, 1982), 82–3.

229. *NYT*, Sept 4, 1969: 38.

230. AEC, 99.031.2 (Woodard Papers): Jack Woodard to Kenneth R. Clark, Sept 9, 1969; *Witness*, Sept 11, 1969: 7.

231. *NYT*, Sept 4, 1969: 1; *Episcopalian*, Oct 1969: 4.

232. DioMass (Coburn Papers): Stephen F. Bayne to Albert H. Palmer, Nov 14, 1969; DioWash, 6.25.12 (Creighton Papers): William F. Creighton, untitled sermon (1969), 2–3.

233. AEC, 2003.095.1 (Barrett Papers): George W. Barrett, Bishop's Convention Address (1969), 21.

234. *LC*, Oct 26, 1969: 16.

235. *Episcopalian*, Oct 1969: 43–4.

236. UML (Carr Papers): Oscar Carr, "The Stewardship of the Gospel" (1976), 3–4; Oscar Carr, Commencement Address at St. Andrew's School, Jackson, MS (1976), 9.

237. As part of this process, Carr had come to the aid of his friend Duncan Gray, whose civil rights activities had prompted some Episcopalians to withdraw their financial support from St. Peter's Church in Oxford. By publicly supporting Gray, Carr helped stave off insolvency and nailed his own colors to the mast of racial progress. John F. Kennedy Presidential Library and Museum, Boston, MA: Oral History Interview with Oscar Clark Carr, Jr., May 6 and 7, 1969, Clarksdale, Mississippi. Interview conducted by Dennis J. O'Brien, for the Robert F. Kennedy Oral History Program of the John F. Kennedy Presidential Library, 11, 20–4.

238. UML (Carr Papers): Carr, "Stewardship of the Gospel," 6–7.

239. *Episcopalian*, Oct 1969: 18–20.

240. *Witness*, Sept 11, 1969: 7–8.

241. UML (Carr Papers): Oscar Carr, Address at Convention of Diocese of Florida (1970), 5–6; Christopher Epting, *With Gladness and Singleness of Heart: A Bishop's Life in a Changing Church* (Bettendorf, IA: Ecubishop Publishing, 2016), n.p.

242. DioMass (Coburn Papers): Executive Council Minutes, Sept 23–25, 1969: "Message of the Presiding Bishop to Executive Council," A17–A20; Columbia (Oral History): "Reminiscences of John E. Hines" (1986), 6.448.

243. Lucila Woodard, interview with author, Alexandria, VA, Dec 20, 2013.

NOTES 307

244. *Episcopalian*, Oct 1969: 44.

245. Douglas Carpenter, emails to author, April 3, 2014, and Sept 20, 2014.

246. Pauli Murray, *Selected Sermons and Writings*, ed. Anthony B. Pinn (Maryknoll, NY: Orbis, 2006), 182, 186–7.

247. Radcliffe, MC 412.63.1078 (Murray Papers): Pauli Murray to Members of the Vestry, Mar 27, 1966.

248. Lawrence Estey, interview with author, Deer Isle, ME, July 28, 2015.

249. *Boston Globe*, Sept 2, 1969: 11.

250. Radcliffe, MC 412.62.1045 (Murray Papers): Pauli Murray to Anson Stokes, Oct 19, 1969.

251. Cornell, 4468.1 (Schiess Papers): Pauli Murray to Betty Bone Schiess, Oct 24, 1969.

252. Radcliffe, MC 412.62.1045 (Murray Papers): John M. Burgess to Pauli Murray, Oct 24, 1969.

253. *NYT*, Sept 6, 1969: 28.

254. *NYT*, Sept 11, 1969: 46.

255. *Minneapolis Tribune*, Apr 12, 1970: 3C.

256. *Episcopalian*, Oct 1969: 43.

257. BHL, Box 21, Fol: Black Manifesto, 1968–1970 ii (Diocese of Michigan Records): Thomas Frisby to Congregation of St. John's Church Detroit, Sept 26, 1969; *LC*, Oct 5, 1969: 9–10.

258. *Christian Century*, Oct 15, 1969: 1306.

259. Interview with Lawrence Estey, Deer Isle, ME, July 28, 2015; Radcliffe, MC 412.62.1045 (Murray Papers): Michael Allen to St. Mark's Parish, Oct 6, 1969. These changes to the "St. Mark's Liturgy" were soon implemented.

260. Allen, *This Time, This Place*, 147–53.

261. The goal of $100,000 was largely met by the summer of 1972. *Witness*, Feb 11, 1970: 8–9; *LC*, July 23, 1972: 7.

262. Roberta Star Hirshson, "A Committee of Blacks and a Committee of Whites," in *The Biography of a Church*, Volume II: *Voices from the Pews*, ed. Martha Jacoby et al. (Cambridge, MA: Christ Church Cambridge, 2012), 86–94.

263. *Chicago Sun-Times*, Sept 6, 1969: 3; Nathaniel W. Pierce and Paul L. Ward, *The Voice of Conscience: A Loud and Unusual Noise? The Episcopal Peace Fellowship, 1939–1989* (Charlestown, MA: Charles River, 1989), 47.

264. Fowler, *Unconventional Partners*, 85; Clarence E. Tygart, "Social Movement Participation: Clergy and the Anti-Vietnam War Movement," *Sociological Analysis* 34.3 (Autumn 1973): 202–11.

265. *WP*, Nov 15, 1969: A1ff.

266. WNC 18003.5.7 (Sayre Papers): Press release of sermon delivered by Francis B. Sayre, Jr., June 27, 1971.

267. *WP*, Nov 14, 1969: A18; Pierce and Ward, *Voice of Conscience*, 48–9.

268. Columbia (Oral History): "Reminiscences of Paul Moore, Jr." (1985), 11.485–6.

269. Paul Moore, "A Bishop Views the Underground Church," in *The Underground Church*, ed. Malcolm Boyd (London: Sheed and Ward, 1969), 222.

270. DioNY, 124.5 (Moore Papers): Paul Moore, sermon at GTS, New York (1969), 5–6.

308   NOTES

271. Paul Moore, *Presences*, 211.

272. Columbia (Oral History): "Reminiscences of Paul Moore, Jr." (1985), 12.508–9.

273. *Potomac Magazine*, Sept 20, 1970: 47.

274. *WP*, Dec 13, 1969: A4

275. *NYT*, Dec 14, 1969: 44.

Chapter 7

1. Leonard I. Sweet, "The 1960s: The Crises of Liberal Christianity and the Public Emergence of Evangelicalism," in *Evangelicalism and Modern America*, ed. George Marsden (Grand Rapids, MI: Eerdmans, 1984), 30; Peter Clecak, *America's Quest for the Ideal Self: Dissent and Fulfillment in the 60s and 70s* (New York: Oxford UP, 1983), 4–6.

2. DioMass (Coburn Papers): Executive Council Minutes, Feb 17–19, 1970: "Message of the Presiding Bishop to Executive Council," A13.

3. AEC, 99.031.7 (Woodard Papers): Jack Woodard, sermon at St Augustine's Chapel, New York (1971), 1–2.

4. *Christian Century*, Oct 27, 1971: 1258; E. Allen Kelley, "Editorial," in *The Episcopal Church Annual 1972* (New York: Morehouse-Barlow, 1972), 9; Sydney E. Ahlstrom, "National Trauma and Changing Religious Values," *Daedalus* 107.1 (Winter 1978): 28 [13–29].

5. *Christian Century*, Nov 11, 1970: 1347–8.

6. VTS, M26.2000.0003 (Price Papers): Charles P. Price, "A Priest in the Church of God" (1970), 8.

7. DioMass (Coburn Papers): John B. Coburn to John J. Bishop, Apr 5, 1971.

8. *Washington Daily News*, Nov 16, 1970: 19.

9. *Episcopalian*, Aug 1973: 15–16.

10. AEC, 238.2.37 (Spong/Hines Papers): John E. Hines, "The Role of the Parish in a Revolutionary World" (1970), 2. Whatever Hines was feeling at the time, his son Chris claimed that his father never allowed the stresses of office to interfere with family life. Chris Hines, interview with author, Austin, TX, August 28, 2014.

11. AEC 87.5.53 (GCSP Records): Kenneth D. Thompson to Leon E. Modeste, Feb 12, 1970.

12. Kesselus, *Granite on Fire*, 396–7.

13. Shattuck, "Contending from the Walls of Sion," 526–7.

14. AEC, 238.2.39 (Spong/Hines Papers): Transcript of "The Dick Cavett Show" (1970).

15. *LC*, Oct 31, 1971: 10; Pringle, *GCSP*, 1.

16. *NYT*, May 10, 1970: 57.

17. *NYT Magazine*, Dec 28, 2003: SM39; Honor Moore, *Bishop's Daughter*, 224.

18. DioNY, 39.11 (Donegan Papers): Horace W. B. Donegan, sermon at installation of Paul Moore (1970), 8.

19. *NYT*, May 9, 1970: 1.

NOTES   309

20. Michael B. Friedland, "Giving a Shout for Freedom: The Reverend Malcolm Boyd, the Right Reverend Paul Moore, Jr., and the Civil Right and Antiwar Movements of the 1960s and 1970s," *Viet Nam Generation Journal* 5.1–4 (Mar 1994), http://www2.iath.virginia.edu/sixties/HTML_docs/Texts/Scholarly/Friedland_Boyd_01.html, accessed Jan 12, 2020.

21. *NYT*, May 9, 1970: 1; TCW, 143.3 (Butler Papers): John C. Goodbody, "John V. Butler: An Appreciation" (1983), 2.

22. Snow, *Gospel in a Broken World*, 117–18; *New Republic*, Apr 3, 1971: 21.

23. Michael Novak, "The Volatile Counterculture," in *New Theology No. 8*, ed. Martin E. Marty and Dean G. Peerman (New York: Macmillan, 1971), 246.

24. Daniel K. Williams, *God's Own Party: The Making of the Christian Right* (New York: Oxford UP, 2010), 80–8; Seth E. Blumenthal, "Children of the 'Silent Majority': Richard Nixon's Young Voters for the President, 1972," *Journal of Policy History* 27.2 (2015): 348–9.

25. Austin Warren, "The Crisis of the Young," in *Search for the Sacred: The New Spiritual Quest*, ed. Myron B. Bloy, Jr. (New York: Seabury Press, 1972), 25–6.

26. *NYT*, Apr 10, 1969: 1.

27. *NYT*, Feb 17, 1970: 1.

28. Harvard, UAI 15.900.13 (Pusey Papers): Nathan M. Pusey, Baccalaureate Address (1971), 3.

29. BHL, Box 1, Fol: Correspondence (Emrich Papers): Richard S. Emrich to John E. Hines, Sept 22, 1972.

30. *NYT*, Apr 13, 1969: E14; *Sunday News Magazine*, June 7, 1970: 14ff.

31. Kesselus, *Granite on Fire*, 326–7.

32. Booty, *American Apostle*, qtd. 159, 164. While at GTS, Bayne was instrumental in developing the General Ordination Examination, which sought, among other things, to ensure academic standards were maintained across the seminaries. John Booty, "Stephen F. Bayne and the General Ordination Examination," *AEH* 67.3 (Sept 1998): 320–1.

33. Stephen F. Bayne, "PECUSA in the 70's," *Pan-Anglican* July 1970: 33–4. Cf. Bayne et al., *Theological Freedom*, 8–9.

34. Hadden, *Gathering Storm*, 26–7.

35. Yale, 67.1.5.133 (Sherrill Papers): Frederic C. Lawrence to Henry K. Sherrill, Nov 6, 1970; *Christian Century*, Jan 18, 1978: 45.

36. *Journal of the Ninety-Eighth Annual Convention of the Protestant Episcopal Church in Diocese of Arkansas, April 1970* (n.p., 1970), 37.

37. *Newsweek*, Dec 25, 1972: 55.

38. *Witness*, Oct 11, 1970: 8.

39. Kater, "Experiment in Freedom," 78.

40. *Witness*, Feb 11, 1970: 7–8.

41. *UBCL Newsletter*, Sept 1970: 2.

42. *Houston Post*, Oct 12, 1970: 1; *LC*, Nov 1, 1970: 7.

43. *Houston Chronicle*, Oct 12, 1970: 1.

44. *LC*, Nov 8, 1970: 5.

310   NOTES

45. *NYT*, Oct 16, 1970: 45.

46. *Christian Century*, Nov 18, 1970: 1390.

47. *Episcopalian*, Dec 1970: 23.

48. *Witness*, Nov 1, 1970: 7–8.

49. Woodard, *Episcopal Church's Struggle*, 191–2.

50. *Episcopalian*, Dec 1970: 46–7.

51. Holmes, "John E. Hines," 405.

52. *Witness*, Feb 1, 1970: 4–5.

53. *Christian Century*, Dec 23, 1970: 1530–1; *Witness*, Jan 1, 1971: 3.

54. DioMinn (McNairy Papers): Philip F. McNairy, Bishop's Address to the Diocesan Convention (1971), 8.

55. *LC*, Jan 3, 1971: 4.

56. UML (Carr Papers): Oscar Carr, Sermon at Grace Episcopal Church, Monroe, LA, Mar 15, 1972, 1.

57. Cornell, 4438.33 (Stringfellow Papers): William Stringfellow, "On Being a Reluctant Episcopalian" (1970s), 31–2.

58. *LC*, Jan 12, 1969: 5; AEC, 151.1.11/1–2 (PECUSA Dept of CSR, 1925–73): J. Brooke Mosley to Coleman McGhee, Sept 11, 1969.

59. *NYT*, Feb 2, 1971: 1.

60. DioMass (Coburn Papers): Jesse E. Christman and Hugh C. White, "General Motors and South Africa: A case describing a stockholder proposal to General Motors by the Executive Council of the Episcopal Church over G.M.'s manufacturing activities in South Africa, November 1970 to May 1971," 1; Hood, *Social Teachings*, 169–70.

61. *LC*, Jan 1, 1978: 5.

62. *Witness*, Nov 24, 1974: 8.

63. *WP Magazine*, Aug 20, 1989: 24.

64. *WP*, Feb 1, 1970: D5.

65. WNC, 18003.3.3 (Sayre Papers): John D. Van Wagoner, "A Minority Response by a Member of the Interracial Task Force" (1970), 4; *WP*, May 2, 1971: D1.

66. *LC*, Aug 1, 1971: 5.

67. *WP*, June 30, 1971: C4; Nancy S. Montgomery, "Oh Happy Day!" *Cathedral Age* 46.3 (Fall 1971): 3.

68. *WP*, May 13, 1974: B1, B3.

69. *WP*, Oct 2, 1989: A14.

70. Harrison, *Transformed by the Love of God*, qtd. 151.

71. Mary Sudman Donovan, *Women Priests in the Episcopal Church: The Experience of the First Decade* (Cincinnati, OH: Forward Movement, 1988), 5.

72. Joan R. Gunderson, "Women and the Parallel Church: A View from Congregations," in *Episcopal Women: Gender, Spirituality and Commitment in an American Mainline Denomination*, ed. Catherine M. Prelinger (New York: Oxford UP, 1992), 111–32.

73. Cordelia Moyse, "Gender Perspectives: Women and Anglicanism," in *The Oxford History of Anglicanism*, Volume IV: *Global Western Anglicanism, c. 1910-Present*, ed. Jeremy Morris (Oxford: Oxford UP, 2017), 82–3. See also Sandra Hughes

Boyd, "The History of Women in the Episcopal Church," *HMPEC* 50.4 (Dec 1981): 423–433.

74. Heather Huyck, "Indelible Change: Woman Priests in the Episcopal Church," *HMPEC* 51.4 (Dec 1982): 386–7.

75. Committee to Study the Proper Place of Women in the Ministry of the Church, "Progress Report to the House of Bishops, October 1966," in *Readings from the History of the Episcopal Church*, ed. Robert W. Prichard (Wilton, CT: Morehouse-Barlow, 1986), 170.

76. Gardiner H. Shattuck, Jr., *A Whole Priesthood: The Philadelphia Ordinations (1974) and the Continuing Dilemmas of Race in the Episcopal Church* (Cambridge, MA: Episcopal Divinity School, 2001), 5–6.

77. DioMass (Coburn Papers): Executive Council Minutes, May 19–21, 1970: "Report of the Special Committee on the Laity," A13; *NYT*, Oct 25, 1970: E11.

78. *Witness*, Nov 1, 1970: 8.

79. Carter Heyward, *She Flies On: A White Southern Christian Debutante Wakes Up* (New York: Church Publishing, 2017), 82.

80. *Journal of the General Convention of the Episcopal Church 1973* (New York: Seabury Press, 1973): 1064.

81. *LC*, Dec 5, 1971: 13.

82. Cornell, 4468.1 (Schiess Papers): Robert DeWitt to Ned Cole, Dec 17, 1971.

83. *Christianity and Crisis*, Dec 13, 1971: 275–6; *Episcopalian*, Feb 1972: 8–9.

84. Cornell, 4468.3 (Schiess Papers): Elizabeth Farians to John Burt, Feb 4, 1972; *Christianity and Crisis*, Mar 6, 1972: 49ff.

85. Radcliffe, MC 412.70.1210v (Murray Papers): William J. Wolf, "A Reply to Bishop Myers on the Ordination of Women" (1971), 2–4.

86. Howard Jones, *My Lai: Vietnam, 1968, and the Descent into Darkness* (New York: Oxford UP, 2017), 289ff.

87. *NYT*, Apr 5, 1971: 33.

88. *NYT*, Apr 17, 1971: 29.

89. Dotson Rader, "The Day the Movement Died," *Esquire*, Nov 1, 1972: 196–7. See also Nancy Zaroulis and Gerald Sullivan, *Who Spoke Up? American Protest against the War in Vietnam, 1963–1975* (Garden City, NY: Doubleday, 1984), 373.

90. *NYT*, Dec 7, 1971: 41; *LC*, Jan 9, 1972: 5.

91. *NYT*, May 2, 1972: 45.

92. AEC, 2003.01.17 (Moore Papers): Paul Moore, "Mission '72" (1972), 9–11.

93. Paul Moore, Jr., "The Witness of the Bishop in the Local Church," *Concilium* 1.8 (Jan 1972): 114.

94. *Newsweek*, Dec 25, 1972: 57.

95. Smyllie, "Church Growth and Decline," 77.

96. *Christian Century*, Jan 18, 1978: 43–4.

97. William Stringfellow, *A Keeper of the Word: Selected Writings*, ed. Bill Wylie Kellermann (Grand Rapids, MI: Eerdmans, 1994), 149; cf. 259–61.

98. *Newsweek*, June 8, 1970: 108.

312 NOTES

99. Stephen R. Lyne, *The Episcopal Church: Splits and Schism* (Washington, DC: Department of State, 1978), 1.

100. *Christian Century*, Jan 24, 1973: 96–7; John Hooper, interview with author, Blue Hill, ME, July 28, 2015.

101. Robert N. Bellah, *The Broken Covenant: American Civil Religion in a Time of Trial* (New York: Seabury, 1975), 106.

102. *LC*, Dec 4, 1977: 6.

103. *Christianity Today*, Nov 9, 1973: 65.

104. *Episcopalian*, Apr 1973: 28–33.

105. UML (Carr Papers): Oscar Carr, "A Renewed People: The Christian's Ministry in Shaping the 70's" (1972), 3.

106. UML (Carr Papers): Oscar Carr, Sermon at Grace Episcopal Church, Monroe, LA (1972), 5–6.

107. UML (Carr Papers): Oscar Carr, "On Christian Stewardship" (1977), 1.

108. UML (Carr Papers): Oscar Carr, Address to Episcopal Churchwomen of Diocese of New York (1972), 6.

109. UML (Carr Papers): Oscar Carr, "On Development and the Budget" (1974), 1.

110. *Newsweek*, Dec 25, 1972: 58; Kesselus, *Granite on Fire*, 376–7.

111. *Journal of the General Convention 1973*, 1082.

112. *WP*, Oct 25, 1972: C9; *Christian Century*, Oct 17, 1973: 1021.

113. *Journal of the General Convention 1973*, 1129–31.

114. *LC*, Feb 4, 1973: 10.

115. DioMinn (McNairy Papers): Philip F. McNairy, Bishop's Address to the Diocesan Convention (1973), 7.

116. Betty Bone Schiess, *Why Me, Lord?: One Women's Ordination to the Priesthood with Commentary and Complaint* (Syracuse, NY: Syracuse UP, 2003), 28, 37.

117. DioMass (Coburn Papers): Executive Council Minutes, Dec 12–14, 1972: unedited transcript of remarks by the Rt. Rev. Wilburn C. Campbell and the Rt. Rev. John E. Hines: EMP-3, 2–5, 11–13.

118. McDowell and Negus, interview with Frederick Williams, in *Anniversary Booklet*, n.p.

119. AEC, 87.4.18 (GCSP Records): John E. Hines, untitled memo, Feb 20, 1973, including "Staff Reply to Statement of Bishop Campbell," 4.

120. DioMass (Coburn Papers): Executive Council Minutes, Feb 20–23, 1973: "Message from the Chair to Executive Council": PB-1, 3; *LC*, March 18, 1973: 6.

121. Shattuck, "Contending from the Walls of Sion," 534, 537–8.

122. *Witness*, July 13, 1975: 6; John E. Hines, "Easter Sermon (22 April 1984)," in John Shelby Spong (ed.), *Anniversary Booklet: A Tribute to John Elbridge Hines*, n.p.

123. Faramelli et al., "Seeking to Hear," 107–8; Woodard, *Episcopal Church's Struggle*, 242.

124. *LC*, Nov 5, 1972: 6.

125. *LC*, Dec 3, 1972: 9.

126. BHL, Box 6, Fol: Jane Barney Personal Files, S (Barney Papers): Jane Barney, "Mother, to Granny—March 15, 1973," 1–2.

NOTES 313

127. BHL, Box 6, Fol: Jane Barney Personal Files, S (Barney Papers): Robert DeWitt to "Seabury Caucus," June 14, 1973.

128. DioMass, 1.B.4.4, Fol: Church and Society (Arnold Papers): Robert L. DeWitt, "A Proposal for a Project on the Church and Society" (1973), 1, 5.

129. DioMass, 1.B.4.4, Fol: Church and Society (Arnold Papers): Robert L. DeWitt, "An Initiating Plan for a 'Church and Society' Network in Cooperation with *The Witness Magazine*" (1974), 1.

130. AEC, 2004.037 (Records of the Conference on Church and City, 1959–1992): Form Letter from St. Julian Simpkins, Mar 31, 1971; Edward Rodman, *Let There Be Peace*, 64–5.

131. *LC*, Oct 28, 1973: 7.

132. *NYT*, Oct 7, 1973: 80.

133. *LC*, Oct 21, 1973: 10–12.

134. *Time*, Oct 15, 1973: 133; Columbia (Oral History): "Reminiscences of Roger Wilson Blanchard" (1982), 1.32.

135. Woodard, *Episcopal Church's Struggle*, 201–3.

136. After further consultation in 1974–1975, Community Action and Development was reconfigured as the Coalition for Human Needs. *LC*, Nov 18, 1973, 6; AEC, 87.1.6 (GCSP Records): Leon E. Modeste, "Mission: Empowerment" (1974), 67; Norman Faramelli et al., "Seeking to Hear," 109.

137. AEC, 322.5.2 (Allin Papers): John M. Allin to John S. Higgins, Feb 8, 1971; Columbia (Oral History): "Reminiscences of John M. Allin" (1991), 2–127, 610.

138. *Christianity and Crisis*, Nov 28, 1977: 282.

139. *LC*, Oct 21, 1973: 5.

140. *Episcopalian*, Nov 1973: 19–20; AEC, 322.4.8 (Allin Papers): Hugh R. Jones, "Report on Confirmation by the House of Deputies of the Election of Bishop Allin as Presiding Bishop" (1973), 2.

141. John M. Allin, "Acceptance Address," in *The Episcopal Church Annual 1974* (New York: Morehouse-Barlow, 1974), 10.

142. *Episcopalian*, Dec 1973: 21.

143. In fact, the measure would have passed by a simple majority among both clergy and lay orders, but the Constitution and Canons of the Episcopal Church dictate that where the votes of a diocesan delegation (in either order) are divided, these votes are counted as negative. So, even though the clergy delegations voted 50 yes, 43 no, and 20 divided, and the lay delegations voted 49 yes, 37 no, and 26 divided, the motion was nonetheless defeated. *Journal of the General Convention 1973*, 222–5.

144. Carter Heyward, *A Priest Forever: The Formation of a Woman and a Priest* (New York: Harper and Row, 1976), 20–30, 43–50.

145. *Christian Century*, Oct 24, 1973: 1046.

146. Donovan, *Women Priests*, 7.

147. *The Churchman*, Dec 1973: 7–8.

148. Edward Rodman, *Let There Be Peace*, 39–40. Derived from the name of the Kenyan insurgents who rebelled against British colonial power in the 1950s, the word

314   NOTES

"mau-mau" was first employed as a verb by Tom Wolfe in his book *Radical Chic and Mau-Mauing the Flak Catchers* (New York: Farrar, Straus, and Giroux, 1970).

149. VTS, M159, 2001.0082 (Spong Papers): John Shelby Spong, "And in Jesus Christ His Son, Our Lord" (1972). Cf. John Shelby Spong, *A New Christianity for a New World: Why Traditional Faith Is Dying and How a New Faith Is Being Born* (San Francisco: HarperCollins, 2001).

150. John Shelby Spong, *Here I Stand: My Struggle for a Christianity of Integrity, Love, and Equality* (San Francisco: HarperCollins, 2000), 225. See also Walter C. Righter, *A Pilgrim's Way* (New York: Knopf, 1998), 89.

151. Foster, *Presiding Bishop*, 121–2; Urban T. Holmes, III, *What is Anglicanism?* (Wilton, CT: Morehouse-Barlow, 1982), 90. See also Harold E. Quinley, *The Prophetic Clergy: Social Activism among Protestant Ministers* (New York: Wiley, 1974), 28.

152. Columbia (Oral History): "Reminiscences of John M. Allin" (1991), 3.166–7, 4.245, 5.297–8, 7.450; AEC, 322.3.2 (Allin Papers): John M. Allin, "Convention Address" (1976), 10.

153. John M. Allin, "The Inaugural Sermon," *New Life* July 1974: 14–15.

154. The deacons present at this meeting were Carol Anderson, Merrill Bittner, Emily Hewitt, Carter Heyward, Sue Hiatt, Marie Moorefield, Betty Bone Schiess, Barbara Schlachter, and Julia Sibley. They were joined by bishops Paul Moore, Robert Spears, Robert DeWitt, Lyman Ogilby, and William Mead, as well as Harvey Guthrie of ETS and Thomas Pike of Calvary Church, Manhattan. Pamela Darling, *New Wine: The Story of Women Transforming Leadership and Power in the Episcopal Church* (Cambridge, MA: Cowley Publications, 1994), 124–5.

155. Heyward, *Priest Forever*, 56–9. See also Mark Oppenheimer, *Knocking on Heaven's Door: American Religion in the Age of Counterculture* (New Haven, CT: Yale UP, 2003), 141–2.

156. Radcliffe, MC 412.67.1160 (Murray Papers): Pauli Murray to Paul Moore, Dec 16, 1973.

157. Judith Maltby, *Prayer Book and People in Elizabethan and Early Stuart England* (Cambridge: Cambridge UP, 1998), 228–37; Charles Hefling, "Anglicans and Common Prayer," in *The Oxford Guide to the Book of Common Prayer: A Worldwide Survey*, ed. Charles Hefling and Cynthia Shattuck (New York: Oxford UP, 2006), 1–6; Brian Cummings, "Introduction," in *The Book of Common Prayer: The Texts of 1549, 1559, and 1662*, ed. Brian Cummings (Oxford: Oxford UP, 2011) ix–lii.

158. For a brief account of the evolution of the American BCP, see Marion J. Hatchett, *Commentary on the American Prayer Book* (New York: Seabury Press, 1980), 9–13.

159. Charles P. Price, *Introducing the Proposed Book: A Study of the Significance of the Proposed Book of Common Prayer for the Doctrine, Discipline, and Worship of the Episcopal Church* (New York: Church Hymnal Corporation, 1976), 11–13. See also Louis Weil, "Liturgical Renewal and Modern Anglican Liturgy," in *The Oxford History of Anglicanism*, Volume IV: *Global Western Anglicanism, c. 1910–Present*, ed. Jeremy Morris (Oxford: Oxford UP, 2017), 50–67.

160. *Christian Century*, Jan 18, 1978: 44.

NOTES 315

161. E.g., DioMass, Correspondence (Coburn Papers): John B. Coburn to Ellen M. Johnson, Jan 25, 1972; DioMinn (McNairy Papers): Philip F. McNairy, Bishop's Address to the Diocesan Convention (1972), 8–9.

162. *Episcopalian*, Jan 1972: 7; William L. Sachs, *The Transformation of Anglicanism: From State Church to Global Communion* (Cambridge: Cambridge UP, 1993), 326–7.

163. *LC*, Oct 31, 1971: 13; Marllene Campbell, "An American Indian Viewpoint," in *Realities and Visions: The Church's Mission Today*, ed. Furman C. Stough and Urban T. Holmes, III (New York: Seabury, 1976), 140–1.

164. Frank Griswold, interview with author, by telephone, July 23, 2015.

165. Samuel T. Lloyd, "Grasped by God," in *Each of Us Will Never Be the Same: Memories of Charles Philip Price* (Cincinnati, OH: Forward Movement, 2003), 49–50; *Parkersburg Sentinel*, July 23, 1977: 13.

166. John Snow, *The Impossible Vocation: Ministry in the Mean Time* (Cambridge, MA: Cowley Publications, 1988), 63–4.

167. *LC*, Sept 2, 1979: 8.

168. BHL, Box 21, Fol: Bishops' Convention Addresses (Diocese of Michigan Records): Coleman McGhee, "Convention Address" (1975), 3–4.

169. Johnston, *And One Was a Priest*, 244.

170. Charles C. Hefling, Jr., "Non Nobis Domine," in *Each of Us Will Never Be the Same: Memories of Charles Philip Price* (Cincinnati, OH: Forward Movement, 2003), 104; Epting, *Gladness and Singleness of Heart*, n.p.

171. Lantzer, *Mainline Christianity*, 62; Frank Griswold, interview with author, by telephone, July 23, 2015.

172. DioMass, 1.A.12:18, Fol: Printed Sermons (Burgess Papers): John M. Burgess, *Cathedral Sermons: A Church in Turmoil* (1972), 7.

173. Harold Louis Wright, "The Test of Evangelism," in *Black Gospel/White Church*, ed. John M. Burgess (New York: Seabury Press, 1982), 107.

174. Charles P. Price, "Christ's Challenge to His Church," *St Luke's Journal of Theology* 20.1 (Dec 1976): 17–18.

175. *Forth*, July–Aug 1950: 7–8; *Witness*, May 24, 1951: 9; Gurdon Brewster, *Ministry on the Frontier: The Contribution of Episcopal Campus Ministry to the Present and Future of the Church* (New York: Episcopal Church Foundation, 2000), 1–2.

176. Marsden, *American University*, 419. See also Conrad Cherry, *Hurrying Toward Zion: Universities, Divinity Schools, and American Protestantism* (Bloomington: Indiana UP, 1995), 227–8.

177. Miller M. Cragon, Jr., "Church Education in the 70's," *ATR* 52.4 (Oct 1970): 240–1.

178. *Episcopal New Yorker*, Feb 1974: 1.

179. Hein, *Noble Powell*, 116–17; Sweet, "The 1960s," 42.

180. John H. Snow, "Christian Identity on Campus," in *Christian Identity on Campus*, ed. Myron Bloy (New York: Seabury Press, 1971), 103–4.

181. John F. Smith, "Context as Contradiction: Campus Ministry in the Diocese of Massachusetts," in *A History of College Work within the Episcopal Diocese of Massachusetts* (Boston: Diocese of Massachusetts, 1997), 7–8.

316 NOTES

182. Cornell, 4468.3 (Schiess Papers): Daniel Corrigan, Robert DeWitt, and Edward R. Welles, "An Open Letter" (1974).

183. *Christian Century*, Sept 4, 1974: 813.

184. Honor Moore, *Bishop's Daughter*, 264; AWTS, 1.2: After Philadelphia (Heyward Papers): Paul Moore to Carter Heyward, July 22, 1974.

185. Ned Cole, "Why I Will Not Ordain a Woman Until General Convention Authorizes Me," in *The Ordination of Women—Pro & Con*, ed. Michael Hamilton and Nancy S. Montgomery (New York: Morehouse-Barlow, 1975), 71–5.

186. DioWash, 6.12.6 (Creighton Papers): "A Statement of Protest by Clergy of the Diocese of Central Pennsylvania" (1974), 1–3; DioWash, 6.13.1 (Creighton Papers): Dean T. Stevenson to Robert L. DeWitt, July 22, 1974; AWTS, Box 1, Fol 2 (Barrett Papers): statement by Faculty of Nashotah House (1974), 1–2.

187. The bishop's father, Remsen Brinckerhoff Ogilby, was president of Trinity College Hartford, 1920–1943. He died aged 62 while saving one of his household servants from drowning. *NYT*, Aug 8, 1943: 36.

188. Hackney, "Social Justice," 321–2; *NYT*, Nov 7, 1990: D25.

189. DioMass, 1.A.12:13.3: Women (Burgess Papers): Lyman C. Ogilby to Members of the Diocese of Pennsylvania, July 19, 1974.

190. DioMass, 1.A.12:13.3: Women (Burgess Papers): John M. Burgess to Lyman C. Ogilby, July 26, 1974.

191. VTS, M182.4 (Walker Papers): John T. Walker, "The Episcopacy and the Philadelphia Four" (1974), 3.

192. Harrison, *Transformed by the Love of God*, qtd. 38–9; *WP Magazine*, Aug 20, 1989: 26–7.

193. Washington, *Other Sheep I Have*, 168; Shattuck, *Whole Priesthood*, 3–4.

194. Honor Moore, "Charles Willie," *Ms.*, Dec 1974: 48ff.

195. Charles Willie, interview with author, Concord, MA, Jan 6, 2015.

196. Edward Rodman, *Let There Be Peace*, 52–3.

197. Charles V. Willie, "Appendix: The Priesthood of All Believers," in Betty Bone Schiess, *Why Me, Lord?: One Women's Ordination to the Priesthood with Commentary and Complaint* (Syracuse, NY: Syracuse UP, 2003), 148–9.

198. The deacons who took part in the service on July 29, 1974, were Merrill Bittner, Alla Bozarth-Campbell, Alison Cheek, Emily Hewitt, Carter Heyward, Suzanne Hiatt, Marie Moorefield, Jeannette Picard, Betty Bone Schiess, Katrina Welles Swanson, and Nancy Constantine Hatch Wittig. *NYT*, July 30, 1974: 1ff.

199. *LC*, Aug 18, 1974: 5.

200. *LC*, Aug 25, 1974: 7. For an account of the individual deacons and their experiences, see Darlene O'Dell, *The Story of the Philadelphia Eleven* (New York: Seabury Books, 2014), 13–83.

201. AWTS, 2.9: Church/Religion (Heyward Papers): Carter Heyward, "Some Thoughts on 'Recognition and Acceptance'" (1976), 3–4.

202. Shattuck, *Whole Priesthood*, 5–6.

203. Radcliffe, MC 412.100.1786 (Murray Papers): Moran Weston to Pauli Murray, June 23, 1975; July 7, 1975; J. Carleton Hayden, "New Men, Strange Faces,

Other Minds: The Human Rights Revolution, 1954–1978," *HMPEC* 49.1 (Mar 1980): 73, 80–1.

204. *Witness*, May 1979: 5.

205. Paul Moore, *Take a Bishop like Me*, 17.

206. *Christian Century*, Sept 4, 1974: 812–13.

207. *NYT*, Aug 15, 1974: 68.

208. *Christian Century*, Sept 4, 1974: 813.

209. Stringfellow, *Instead of Death*, 12.

210. Darling, *New Wine*, qtd. 134; *LC*, Nov 10, 1974: 5–6.

211. Charles Willie, interview with author, Concord, MA, Jan 6, 2015. Willie had already written to John Allin prior to the meeting suggesting that the issues should be addressed in a more open forum. Willie Private Papers: Charles V. Willie to John M. Allin, Aug 6, 1974.

212. *WP*, Aug 16, 1974: A3.

213. *Episcopalian*, Apr 1980: qtd. 17.

214. Paul Moore, *Take a Bishop like Me*, 27.

215. Charles Willie, interview with author, Concord, MA, Jan 6, 2015.

216. *LC*, Sept 15, 1974: 11.

217. Willie Private Papers: Charles V. Willie, "1974—The Year the Episcopal Church Failed" (1975), 2.

218. *LC*, Sept 1, 1974: 7.

219. AWTS, 2.9: Church/Religion (Heyward Papers): Carter Heyward, "A Statement on the Philadelphia-Chicago Dilemma" (1974), 1.

220. *LC*, Nov 17, 1974: 10.

221. AEH, 2003.01.23 (Moore Papers): Paul Moore, Pastoral Letter to the Diocese of New York, Oct 30, 1974.

222. *NYT*, Nov 23, 1974: 31.

223. AWTS, 1.2: After Philadelphia (Heyward Papers): Jorge and Carolyn Gutierrez to Paul Moore, Feb 12, 1975; Paul Moore to Jorge and Carolyn Gutierrez, Feb 20, 1975; *Christianity and Crisis*, Aug 18, 1975: 188–9.

224. Carter Heyward, *Priest Forever*, 123–4; AWTS, 1.2: After Philadelphia (Heyward Papers): Paul Moore to Carter Heyward, Feb 20, 1975.

225. AWTS, 1.2: After Philadelphia (Heyward Papers): Carter Heyward to Paul Moore, Mar 10, 1975.

226. *Christianity and Crisis*, Sept 16, 1974: 197; Radcliffe, MC 412.68.1176 (Murray Papers): Patricia N. Page to Tom Tull, Feb 11, 1975.

227. AAEHC, A17, Series 9.130.9–10 (Dennis Diocesan Papers): Paul Moore to John Burgess, Feb 5, 1975.

228. DioMass, 1.A.12:22, Fol: Appointments (Burgess Papers): John M. Burgess to the Rector et al. of the Church of the Messiah, Woods Hole, Mar 3, 1975.

229. *LC*, Aug 24, 1975: 5.

230. DioMass, 1.A.12:13.7 (Burgess Papers): John M. Burgess to the Rector et al. of the Church of the Messiah, Woods Hole, July 21, 1975; AAEHC, Oral History Interview with Arthur B. Williams, Jr. (2009), MZ000104.

318 NOTES

231. *NYT*, Nov 11, 1974: 32. For a detailed account, see O'Dell, *The Philadelphia Eleven*, 137–74.
232. *NYT*, Apr 28, 1975: 35.
233. *NYT*, May 1, 1975: 31; May 3, 1975: 1; May 7, 1975: 1.
234. *NYT*, June 6, 1975: 52. Additional proceedings against Wendt carried on throughout 1975, as he continued to violate Bishop Creighton's instructions. Asked after receiving two formal reprimands whether he was now prepared to desist, Wendt admitted: "I could never promise." *LC*, Feb 1, 1976: 5.
235. Radcliffe, MC 412.68.1178 (Murray Papers): Pauli Murray to William Stringfellow and Edward C. Bou, June 6, 1975.
236. DioWash, 6.12.6 (Creighton Papers): William F. Creighton to Diocesan Bishops, Apr 1, 1975.
237. AWTS, Box 1, Fol 2 (Barrett Papers): George W. Barrett to William F. Creighton, July 28, 1975; William F. Creighton to George W. Barrett, July 31, 1975.
238. AEC 2003.095.1 (Barrett Papers): John M. Allin to George W. Barrett, Aug 25, 1975; *NYT*, Sept 8, 1975: 15.
239. *NYT*, Sept 24, 1975: 48.
240. Clecak, *America's Quest*, 6–7, 19–21; *Witness*, Oct 27, 1974: 6–7; *WP*, Aug 27, 1975: A14.
241. Radcliffe, MC 412.68.1173 (Murray Papers): Pauli Murray to Carter Heyward, June 25, 1975; *LC*, Oct 12, 1975: 10.
242. DioMass, 1.B.4.4. Fol: Office Files (Arnold Papers): Morris F. Arnold to John Burgess, Oct 24, 1973; Morris F. Arnold, "Ben Arnold's impressions of the meeting at Seabury House, Greenwich, January 7–8, 1974," 1.
243. DioMass, 1.B.4.4 (Arnold Papers): Robert L. DeWitt, "Report on Efforts to November 1, 1975," 1.
244. *Witness*, Mar 23, 1975: 3.
245. *Witness*, Aug 1976: 3.
246. Unsigned, "Introduction," in *Struggling with the System, Probing Alternatives: A Study/Action Guide*, ed. Robert L. DeWitt (Ambler, PA: Episcopal Church Publishing, 1976), 1–3.
247. Unsigned, "What Right Does the Church Have to Speak about These Things?" in *Struggling with the System, Probing Alternatives: A Study/Action Guide*, ed. Robert L. DeWitt (Ambler, PA: Episcopal Church Publishing, 1976), 35, 41.
248. EDS, 3.8 (BIM): "An Introduction to Boston Industrial Mission" (1970s), n.p.
249. Norman J. Faramelli, *Technethics: Christian Mission in an Age of Technology* (New York: Friendship Press, 1971), 75–6.
250. Paradise Private Papers: Scott Paradise, "Keynote Address for S.E.A.S." (1973), 1.
251. *Witness*, May 18, 1975: 4–5. Paradise left BIM in 1978 to become Episcopal chaplain of MIT, where he presided over the highly regarded Technology and Culture Seminar, begun by his predecessor Mike Bloy in the early 1960s. Paradise Private Papers: Interview with Scott Paradise by Charles Weiner: Session 4, Part 1, Nov 5, 1992, 2–5; EDS, 4.8 (BIM): Scott Paradise to Dave Dayton, Feb 13, 1978.

252. Paradise Private Papers: Interview with Scott Paradise by Charles Weiner: Session 3, Part 2, Oct 6, 1992, 12, 28.
253. *Worldview*, Apr 1975: 39–41.
254. *Witness*, June 22, 1975: 8–10; *Sojourners*, Feb 1976: 12.
255. DioMass, 1.B.4.1 (Arnold Papers): Norman J. Faramelli, "Origins and Purpose of the Boston Affirmations" (1976), 1.
256. *Worldview*, Mar 1976: 45–7.
257. DioMass, 1.B.4.1.Fol: Norman Faramelli (Arnold Papers): Norman J. Faramelli to Morris Arnold, Jan 14, 1976; Sweet, "Modernization of Protestant Religion," 40.
258. Paradise Private Papers: Scott I. Paradise, "Response to the Boston Affirmations" (1976), 1.
259. Richard John Neuhaus, "Calling a Halt to Retreat: Hartford and Social Justice," in *Against the World for the World: The Hartford Appeal and the Future of American Religion*, ed. Peter L. Berger and Richard John Neuhaus (New York: Seabury Press, 1976), 155–6.
260. Holmes, "Once Again," 177–9, 183.
261. AEC, 2003.01.23 (Moore Papers): Paul Moore, "What's Wrong with the World?" (1975), 2.
262. DioNY, 102.15 (Moore Papers): Paul Moore to Robert L. DeWitt, Jan 22, 1976; AEC, 2003.01.17 (Moore Papers): Paul Moore to Phyllis Ames Cox, Sept 21, 1977.
263. Jervis Anderson, "Standing Out There on the Issues," *New Yorker*, April 28, 1986: 82–3.
264. *LC*, July 9, 1972: 5; *NYT*, May 21, 1973: 1.
265. *WP*, Oct 4, 1973: C10; James and Pam Morton, interview with author, New York, Dec 17, 2014.
266. AAEHC, A19: Series X.1 (Dennis Personal Papers): Walter D. Dennis, "A Spiritual Pilgrimage," 12–13. Dennis's sentiments were later echoed privately by John Burgess, who, after a long ministry in the Episcopal Church, concluded that "when liberal whites come in, they tend to want to take over." AAEHC, A16.7.3.13 (Logan Papers): John Burgess to Thomas Logan, May 13, 1980.
267. *NYT*, Oct 28, 1984: 40.
268. NY Cathedral, ACC 2014: JPM.12.20 (Morton Papers): James Parks Morton, "The Revolution in the Cathedral: Moore and Morton 1972–1997: A Look Back" (2005), 3–4.
269. *New York*, May 26, 1980: 12–14; *NYT*, Sept 30, 1982: 1.
270. See Edward M. Gramlich, "The New York City Fiscal Crisis: What Happened and What Is to Be Done?" *American Economic Review* 66.2 (May 1976): 415–29.
271. AEH, 2003.01.23: Paul Moore, "Statement Regarding President Ford's Veto Message" (1975), 2.
272. Paul Moore, *Presences*, 303.
273. *LC*, July 18, 1976: 10–11.
274. *NYT*, Apr 19, 1976: 1.
275. *NYT*, July 12, 1976: A1; Mar 13, 1978: A11.

320 NOTES

276. Nancy S. Montgomery, "Washington Cathedral: A Brief History," *CA* 53.1 (Spring 1978): 21.

277. Francis B. Sayre, Jr., "Report of the Dean to the Washington Cathedral Chapter, 1974–1975: The Cathedral's Future over the Years," *CA* 50.4 (Winter 1975): 19–20.

278. DioWash, 7.3.5 (Walker Papers): Francis B. Sayre, Jr., to Katharine Graham, Apr 17, 1975.

279. *WP*, June 17, 1977: A1; *WP Magazine*, Apr 3, 1983: 14.

280. AWTS, 2.9: Church/Religion (Heyward Papers): Carter Heyward, "An Open Letter to Bishops of the Episcopal Church" (1976).

281. AEC, 299.1.5 (Corrigan Papers): George Barrett, Daniel N. Corrigan, Robert L. DeWitt, "Thoughts on Regularization" (1976), 3.

282. *NYT*, Sept 22, 1976: 19; Sept 23, 1976: 28.

283. Ronald T. C. Lau, "Editorial," in *The Episcopal Church Annual 1976* (New York: Morehouse-Barlow, 1976), 4.

284. Ruth Tiffany Barnhouse, "Is Patriarchy Obsolete?" in *Male and Female: Christian Approaches to Sexuality*, ed. Ruth Tiffany Barnhouse and Urban T. Holmes (New York: Seabury Press, 1976), 234; Urban T. Holmes, "Theology and Religious Renewal," *ATR* 62.1 (Jan 1980): 11–12.

285. *LC*, June 22, 1975: 5; Oct 31, 1976: 8.

286. George L. W. Werner, "From Minneapolis to Minneapolis," *The Rt. Rev. John B. Coburn, 1914–2009: Leader of the House*, Aug 17, 2009, https://johncoburnat diomass.wordpress.com/, accessed Jan 22, 2020.

287. *NYT*, Sept 17, 1976: A1; *LC*, Oct 10, 1976: 6–7.

288. Columbia (Oral History): "Reminiscences of Paul Moore, Jr." (1985), 13.560.

289. *Christianity Today*, Oct 8, 1976: 48–52. See also Don S. Armentrout, "Episcopal Splinter Groups: Schisms in the Episcopal Church, 1963–1985," *HMPEC* 55.4 (Dec 1986): 295–320.

290. Lyne, *Episcopal Church*, 17; Huyck, "Indelible Change," 394.

291. *WP*, Jan 9, 1977: A3; Pauli Murray, *Autobiography*, 434–5.

292. Radcliffe, MC 412.67.1148 (Murray Papers): Pauli Murray, "Healing and Reconciliation," Feb 13, 1977, 1.

293. Radcliffe, MC 412.100.1786 (Murray Papers): Pauli Murray to Moran Weston, June 16, 1975.

294. Pauli Murray, "Black Theology and Feminist Theology: A Comparative View," *ATR* 60.1 (Jan 1978): 3–4.

295. Edward W. Rodman, "Soul Sisters: The Emergence of Black Women's Leadership," in *Deeper Joy: Lay Women and Vocation in the 20th Century Episcopal Church*, ed. Fredrica Harris Thompsett and Sheryl Kujawa-Holbrook (New York: Church Publishing, 2005), 223–4.

296. *NYT*, Jan 11, 1977: 34.

297. *LC*, Aug 31, 1975: 6.

298. Brown, 2007.09.1.21 (Barrett Papers): Paul Moore to Ellen Barrett, Dec 2, 1975.

299. Paul Moore, *Take a Bishop like Me*, 65–6; *LC*, Mar 6, 1977: 9–10.

300. *Time*, Jan 24, 1977: 58.

NOTES 321

301. Brown, 2007.09.1.21 (Barrett Papers): Paul Moore to Ellen Barrett, Mar 3, 1977.

302. Five years after her father's death in 2003, Honor Moore published a memoir in which she revealed that besides being married twice and having fathered eight children, Bishop Moore had been sexually active as a gay man: Honor Moore, *Bishop's Daughter*, 314–40. Shortly after the book's publication, Bishop Mark Sisk of New York issued a pastoral letter in which he characterized Moore as "an exploiter of the vulnerable," about whom the diocese had received multiple complaints. More recently, in September 2018, Sisk's successor Andrew Dietsche issued another pastoral letter, in which he labeled Moore a "serial predator," who had engaged in "long-time" patterns of sexual exploitation and abuse. *Boston Globe*, Oct 15, 2018: A2.

303. *NYT*, Oct 4, 1977: A18.

304. Paul Moore, *Take a Bishop like Me*, 167–74.

305. *NYT*, Oct 4, 1977: A18; *LC*, Oct 30, 1977: 5.

306. Darling, *New Wine*, 143.

307. Stringfellow also pointed out that because the House of Deputies had not been consulted, the "conscience clause" had no formal standing in canon law. *Witness*, May 1979: 5–6.

308. *Witness*, Nov 1977: 4–5.

309. *Christianity and Crisis*, Nov 28, 1977: 281.

310. DioMass, 1.B.4.4. Fol: Church and City (Arnold Papers): Arthur Walmsley, presentation at Church and City Conference, Rehoboth (1977), 4.

311. *Christian Century*, Jan 18, 1978: 44–5.

312. Price, *Anglican Tradition*, 10–11.

313. *Witness*, Feb 1977: 3.

314. Gessell, *Grace and Obedience*, 37.

315. *NYT*, June 17, 1977: A13; *WP*, 16 Jan 1978: C5.

316. WNC, 18004.8.13 (Sayre Papers): John T. Walker, "Mission and Ministry of Diocese and Cathedral" (1977), 1–3.

317. *WP*, Sept 23, 1977: B10; *WP*, Sept 25, 1977: 1ff.

318. WNC, 18001.1.7 (Sayre Papers): Francis B. Sayre, Jr., "The Future Leadership of Washington Cathedral" (1977), 2.

319. DioWash, 7.3.5 (Walker Papers): John T. Walker to Francis B. Sayre, Jr., Nov 15, 1977.

320. *WP Magazine*, Aug 20, 1989: 23–4.

321. Columbia (Oral History): "Reminiscences of Henry S. Noble" (1983), 1.12; "Reminiscences of John Bowen Coburn" (1984), 1.6.

322. Columbia (Oral History): "Reminiscences of John M. Allin" (1991), 7.513, 8.551; Frank Griswold, interview with author, by telephone, July 23, 2015.

323. *Episcopalian*, June 1985: 16; Sachs and Holland, *Restoring the Ties*, 117.

324. DioMass, 1.B.4.4 (Arnold Papers): Arthur Walmsley, presentation at Church and City Conference, 8; *Record*, Oct 1978: 10; *Witness*, June 1979: 8.

325. Woodard, *Episcopal Church's Struggle*, 207.

326. DioMass, 1.B.4.4 (Arnold Papers): Hugh C. White and Brian R. McNaught, "Towards the Organizing of the Episcopal Urban Caucus: A Synopsis, March 1979," 2.

322 NOTES

327. *Christian Century*, May 17, 1978: 524. Signatories of the statement were bishops Mosely, Walker, Sims, Arnold, Speers, Spong, Moore, Krumm, McGhee, Rath, Ogilby, Jones, Ramos, Creighton, Primo, Robinson, DeWitt, and Belshaw. DioWash, 7.3.1 (Walker Papers): "Bishops' Call for a Mission to the City Focus of the Venture in Mission Program" (1976), 1–2.

328. *LC*, June 24, 1977: 5; Norman Faramelli et al., "Seeking to Hear," 110–11.

329. Urban Bishops Coalition (ed.), *To Hear and To Heed: The Episcopal Church Listens and Acts in the City* (Cincinnati, OH: Forward Movement, 1978), 4–6.

330. VTS, M182.4 (Walker Papers): John T. Walker, "The Church and Social Action" (1975), 5–6.

331. DioMass, 1.B.4.4. Fol: Episcopal Urban Coalition (Arnold Papers): Morris F. Arnold, "Public Hearings by the Urban Bishops" (1978), 7.

332. Joseph A. Pelham, "The Episcopal Church in the Urban Crisis: The Decade Ahead," in *To Hear and To Heed: The Episcopal Church Listens and Acts in the City*, ed. Urban Bishops Coalition (Cincinnati, OH: Forward Movement, 1978), 47–8, 51–2; *Witness*, May 1978: 15.

333. Earl H. Brill, *The Christian Moral Vision* (New York: Seabury Press, 1979), 135–6.

334. William A. Yon, "The Indigenization of Newark: Urban Mission Strategy in the Diocese of Newark," in *To Build the City—Too Long a Dream: Studies of Urban Churches*, ed. William A. Yon (Washington, DC: Alban Institute, 1982), 4–5.

335. R. E. Hood, "Christian Witness and Social Transformation," *St. Luke's Journal of Theology* 22.4 (Sept 1979): 310.

336. E. Don Taylor, "Tensions and Opportunities between West Indian and American Blacks in the Episcopal Church," *St. Luke's Journal of Theology* 22.4 (Sept 1979): 282.

337. AAEHC, A19, Items FIC, 2012 (Dennis Personal Papers): Walter D. Dennis, untitled sermon (c. 1980), 1–2; AAEHC, A16.7.3.13 (Logan Papers): John Burgess to Thomas Logan, May 13, 1980.

338. Pringle, *GCSP*, 2.

339. According to the *Episcopalian*, such a figure in composite was a white woman over 49 years old, residing in a town of under 50,000 in the Northeast. She did not generally work, but if she did, it was at the professional level. She had a slightly older husband, two grown children, and a family income of $20,000 a year. *Episcopalian*, Apr 1980: 19.

340. Grant Gallup, untitled sermon, May 29, 2005, http://rci.rutgers.edu/~lcrew/homil ygrits04_05/msg00052.html, accessed Apr 1, 2017 (site discontinued); *Pacific Churchman* 117.9 (Dec 1979): 1ff.

341. *LC*, Nov 10, 1974: 5–6.

342. VTS, M26 (Price Papers): C. Kilmer Myers, "Notes for the 9/77 House of Bishops Meeting" (1977), 3–4.

343. John Rawlinson, email to author, Sept 4, 2013.

344. John M. Krumm and Marian Kelleran, *Denver Crossroads: General Convention 1979* (Cincinnati, OH: Forward Movement, 1979), 13.

345. Alexander D. Stewart, "Guest Editorial," in *The Episcopal Church Annual 1979* (New York: Morehouse-Barlow, 1979), 5.

346. *LC*, Oct 21, 1979: 14.

NOTES   323

Chapter 8

1. *Witness*, Feb 1978: 12.
2. Hein and Shattuck, *The Episcopalians*, 147–50; Booty, *Episcopal Church in Crisis*, 126.
3. Paradise Private Papers: Scott I. Paradise, "Response to the Boston Affirmations" (1976), 1.
4. Joseph C. Hough, Jr., "The Loss of Optimism as a Problem for Liberal Christian Faith," in *Liberal Protestantism: Realities and Possibilities*, ed. Robert S. Michaelson and Wade Clark Roof (New York: Pilgrim Press, 1986), 155–7.
5. *NYT Magazine*, Sept 1, 1985: SM38.
6. William C. Morris, Jr., "Avoiding the Dangers of a Monumental Church," in *A New Conversation: Essays on the Future of Theology and the Episcopal Church*, ed. Robert Boak Slocum (New York, 1999), 194.
7. Gardiner H. Shattuck, Jr., "Should the Episcopal Church Disappear?: Reflections on the Decade of Evangelism," *ATR* 73.2 (Spring 1991): 184–5.
8. Graham Reside, "The Story of Contemporary Mainline Protestantism," in *The Future of Mainline Protestantism in America*, ed. James Hudnut-Beumler and Mark Silk (New York: Columbia UP, 2018), qtd. 54.
9. Audrey R. Chapman, *Faith, Power, and Politics: Political Ministry in Mainline Churches* (New York: Pilgrim Press, 1991), 122–4; Peter L. Berger, "Religion in Post-Protestant America," *Commentary* 81.5 (May 1986): 44.
10. Dwight J. Zscheile, *People of the Way*, 28–9.
11. Columbia (Oral History): "Reminiscences of John M. Allin" (1991), 4.244–5; David T. Gortner et al., *Around One Table: Exploring Episcopal Identity—Expanded Version* (New Bern, NC: College for Bishops/CREDO Institute, 2009), 90.
12. Lantzer, *Mainline Christianity*, 64.
13. Reeves, *Empty Church*, 159; Kew and White, *New Millennium*, 30–1.
14. Harmon L. Smith, "Decorum as Doctrine: Teachings on Human Sexuality," in *The Crisis of Moral Teaching in the Episcopal* Church, ed. Timothy Sedgwick and Philip Turner (Harrisburg, PA: Morehouse Barlow, 1992), 33; Gary Dorrien, *Soul in Society: The Making and Renewal of Social Christianity* (Minneapolis, MN, 1995), 366.
15. Peter W. Williams, *America's Religions: Traditions and Cultures* (New York: Macmillan, 1990), 341; N. J. Demerath, "Cultural Victory and Organizational Defeat in the Paradoxical Decline of Liberal Protestantism," *Journal for the Scientific Study of Religion* 34.4 (1995): 461–2; Hollinger, *After Cloven Tongues*, 46.
16. Stanley Hauerwas, *After Christendom? How the Church Is to Behave if Freedom, Justice, and a Christian Nation Are Bad Ideas* (Nashville, TN: Abingdon, 1991), 58.
17. Richard John Neuhaus, *The Naked Public Square: Religion and Democracy in America* (2nd ed.; Grand Rapids, MI: Eerdmans, 1997), 226–7.
18. Paradise, *To Speak with Power*, 41.
19. Episcopalians were not the only Anglican elites during the twentieth century to revise their establishmentarian narrative in the face of social and political change: see, for example, Robert Tobin, *The Minority Voice: Hubert Butler and Southern Irish Protestantism, 1900–1991* (Oxford: Oxford UP, 2012).

324 NOTES

20. John E. Hines, "Easter Sermon," n.p. See also Thomas W. Overholt, *Channels of Prophecy: The Social Dynamics of Prophetic Activity* (Minneapolis: Fortress Press, 1989), 165–6.

21. Laura R. Olson, "Clergy and American Politics," in *The Oxford Handbook of Religion and American Politics*, ed. Corwin E. Smidt et al. (New York: Oxford UP, 2009), 381.

22. *LC*, June 18, 1978: 12.

23. *NYT*, Apr 28, 1981: B17; *Time*, May 22, 1989: 95; Fowler, *Unconventional Partners*, 93–5.

24. Allan M. Parrent, "On War, Peace and the Use of Force," in *The Crisis of Moral Teaching in the Episcopal Church*, ed. Timothy F. Sedgwick and Philip Turner (Harrisburg, PA: Morehouse Barlow, 1992), 113.

25. Peter L. Berger, "American Religion: Conservative Upsurge, Liberal Prospects," in *Liberal Protestantism: Realities and Possibilities*, ed. Robert S. Michaelson and Wade Clark Roof (New York: Pilgrim Press, 1986), 34–5; Nigel Biggar, "Why the 'Establishment' of the Church of England Is Good for a Liberal Society," in *The Established Church: Past, Present and Future*, ed. Mark Chapman et al. (London: T&T Clark, 2011), 3.

26. C. Kirk Hadaway and David A. Roozen, *Rerouting the Protestant Mainstream: Sources of Growth and Opportunities for Change* (Nashville, TN: Abingdon Press, 1995), 63; James D. Davidson and Ralph E. Pyle, *Ranking Faiths: Religious Stratification in America* (Lanham, MD: Rowman & Littlefield, 2011), 21.

27. Reside, "Contemporary Mainline Protestantism," 31–2; Roof and McKinney, *American Mainline Religion*, 120–2.

28. Dwight J. Zscheile, *People of the Way*, 63.

29. David Steigerwald, *The Sixties and the End of Modern America* (New York: St. Martin's Press, 1995), 243; R. R. Reno, "Good Restaurants in Gomorrah," *First Things*, Feb 1998: 15.

30. Dwight J. Zscheile, "Beyond Benevolence: Toward a Reframing of Mission in the Episcopal Church," *JAS* 8.1 (May 2010): 93–4.

31. Harold T. Lewis, "Racial Concerns," 473–4; Nancy Carol James, *The Developing Schism within the Episcopal Church, 1960–2010* (Lewiston, NY: Edwin Mellen Press, 2010), qtd. 156–7.

32. Harold T. Lewis, *Christian Social Witness* (Cambridge, MA: Cowley Publications, 2001), 85. See also Karen E. Fields and Barbara J. Fields, *Racecraft: The Soul of Inequality in American Life* (London: Verso, 2012), 268.

33. *LC*, July 11, 1993: 10–11.

34. Malcolm Boyd, "To Bill Stringfellow, A Prophet Dying Young," *Journal of Law and Religion* 4.1 (1986): 2.

35. Mark Thiessen Nation, "The Vocation of the Church of Jesus the Criminal," in *William Stringfellow in Anglo-American Perspective*, ed. Anthony Dancer (Aldershot, Hants: Routledge, 2005), 121.

36. *NYT Magazine*, Dec 28, 2003: 39; Jordan Hylden, "The Contradictions of Paul Moore," *LC*, Nov 19, 2014, https://livingchurch.org/covenant/2014/11/19/bishop-paul-moore-of-new-york/, accessed Jan 2, 2020.

NOTES   325

37. WNC, Oral History Project: Interview with Dean Francis B. Sayre, Jr. (2000), 54–5; Mark Tooley, "Death of a Presidential Grandson," *American Spectator*, Oct 21, 2008, https://spectator.org/42788_death-presidential-grandson/, accessed Jan 2, 2020.

38. Walter Russell Mead, "Sunday Jeremiad: Petty Prophets of the Blue Beast," *American Interest*, Feb 21, 2010, https://www.the-american-interest.com/2010/02/21/sunday-jeremiad-petty-prophets-of-the-blue-beast/, accessed Jan 2, 2020.

39. E.g., Van S. Bird, "Christian Witness and Social Transformation—I," *St. Luke's Journal of Theology* 22.4 (Sept 1979): 294; Constance H. Buchanan, "The Anthropology of Vitality and Decline: The Episcopal Church in a Changing Society," in *Episcopal Women: Gender, Spirituality and Commitment in an American Mainline Denomination*, ed. Catherine Prelinger (New York: Oxford UP, 1992), 327; Bennett J. Sims, *Why Bush Must Go: A Bishop's Faith-Based Challenge* (New York: Continuum, 2004), 129–34.

40. David Paulsen, "Racial Audit of Church Leadership Seen as Step toward Ensuring Episcopal Culture of Welcome," *Episcopal News Service*, Sept 9, 2019, https://www.episcopalnewsservice.org/2019/09/09/racial-audit-of-church-leadership-seen-as-step-toward-ensuring-episcopal-culture-of-welcome/, accessed Jan 10, 2020; Gortner, *Around One Table*, 82.

41. Philip Turner, "How the Church Might Teach," in *The Crisis of Moral Teaching in the Episcopal Church*, ed. Timothy F. Sedgwick and Philip Turner (Harrisburg, PA: Morehouse Barlow, 1992), 156.

42. Radner, "Theological Accoutrements," 36; Dwight J. Zscheile, "From Establishment to Innovation: Rethinking Structure in a New Apostolic Age," in *What We Shall Become: The Future and Structure of the Episcopal Church*, ed. Winnie Varghese (New York: Church Publishing, 2013), 62–4.

43. Gardiner H. Shattuck, Jr., "Knowing the Tasks," in *A New Conversation: Essays on the Future of Theology and the Episcopal Church*, ed. Robert Boak Slocum (New York: Church Publishing, 1999), 38, 43–4.

44. Hood, *Social Teachings*, 183–4, 189; Kater, "Whose Church Is It Anyway?" *ATR* 76.1 (Winter 1994): 45–6.

Bibliography and Sources

Published Sources

A. Periodicals

The Akron Beacon Journal
The American Church News: General Convention Daily
American Economic Review
The American Historical Review
The American Interest [online]
The American Spectator [online]
Anglican and Episcopal History
Anglican Theological Review
Anglican World
Ann Arbor News
Annals of the American Academy of Political and Social Science
The Army and Navy Chaplain
The Atlanta Constitution
The Boston Globe
The Bulletin [Pittsburgh]
British Studies
Bulletin of the Missouri Historical Society
The Cathedral Age
The Chicago Daily Tribune
The Chicago Sun-Times
Christian Century
Christianity and Crisis
Christianity Today
Church History
Church in Metropolis
The Churchman
The Cleveland Plain Dealer
Commentary
Concilium
Daedalus
The Delaware County Daily Times
The Detroit News
Episcopal Churchnews
The Episcopalian
The Episcopal New Yorker
Episcopal News Service [online]

328 BIBLIOGRAPHY AND SOURCES

Esquire
The Evening Bulletin [Philadelphia]
First Things
Foreign Affairs
Forth
GCSP Newsletter
The Harvard Crimson
The Historian
Historical Magazine of the Protestant Episcopal Church
The Houston Chronicle
The Houston Post
Interpretation
Jet
Journal for the Scientific Study of Religion
Journal of African American History
Journal of Anglican Studies
Journal of Church and State
Journal of Law and Religion
Journal of Negro Education
Journal of Policy History
Journal of Religion
Journal of Religious History
Life
Life and Work
The Living Church
Look Magazine
The Los Angeles Times
The Main Line Chronicle [Ardmore, PA]
The Michigan Historical Review
The Minneapolis Tribune
Ms.
New Life
The New Republic
The Newark Evening News
New York
The New York Herald Tribune
The New York Post
The New York Times
The New York Times Magazine
The New Yorker
Newsweek
The Pacific Churchman
Pan-Anglican: A Review of the World-wide Episcopal Church
Parkersburg Sentinel [West Virginia]
Parsons: For the Clergy of the Episcopal Church
Pastoral Psychology
Pennsylvania History
The Philadelphia Inquirer

Potomac Magazine [*Washington Post*]
Presbyterian Life
Presidential Studies Quarterly
The Record [Diocese of Michigan]
Religion and American Culture
Renewal
St. Alban's Bulletin
St. Luke's Journal of Theology
Saturday Evening Post
Sewanee Theological Review
Sociological Analysis
Sojourners
Spirit of Jefferson Advocate [West Virginia]
Sunday News Magazine [Detroit]
The Sword and Shield [Brighton, MI]
Time
Today [*Philadelphia Inquirer*]
UBCL Newsletter
Union Now: Magazine of Union Theological Seminary
Viet Nam Generation Journal [online]
VTS Journal
The Washington Daily News
Washington Diocese
The Washingtonian
The Washington Post
The Washington Post Magazine
The Witness
Worldview: Journal of Religion and International Affairs

B. Printed Works

Abrams, Ray H. *Preachers Present Arms: The Role of the American Churches and Clergy in World War I and II, with Some Observations on the War in Vietnam.* 1969. Eugene, OR: Wipf and Stock, 2009.

Alinsky, Saul D. *Reveille for Radicals.* Chicago: University of Chicago Press, 1946.

Allen, Michael. *This Time, This Place.* Indianapolis: Bobbs-Merrill, 1971.

Allin, John M. "Acceptance Address." In *The Episcopal Church Annual 1974*, 9–11. New York: Morehouse-Barlow, 1974.

Anderson, Owanah. *400 Years: Anglican/Episcopal Mission among American Indians.* Cincinnati: Forward Movement, 1997.

Anglican Fellowship for Social Action. N.p.: 1948.

Armentrout, Donald, *Episcopal Splinter Groups: A Study of Groups Which Have Left the Episcopal Church, 1873–1985.* Sewanee, TN: School of Theology, University of the South, 1985.

Arsenault, Raymond. *Freedom Riders: 1961 and the Struggle for Racial Justice.* New York: Oxford UP, 2006.

Austin, Ann L. "A Community of Faith Moves through Change: The 1960s and 1970s." In *The Biography of a Church*, Volume II: *Voices from the Pews*, edited by Martha Jacoby et al., 34–69. Cambridge, MA: Christ Church Cambridge, 2012.

330 BIBLIOGRAPHY AND SOURCES

Ayres, Francis O. *The Ministry of the Laity: A Biblical Exposition*. Philadelphia: Westminster Press, 1962.

Azaransky, Sarah. *The Dream Is Freedom: Pauli Murray and American Democratic Faith*. New York: Oxford UP, 2011.

Bagshaw, Paul. *The Church beyond the Church: Sheffield Industrial Mission, 1944–1994*. Sheffield: Industrial Mission in South Yorkshire, 1994.

Baldwin, Lewis. *The Voice of Conscience: The Church in the Mind of Martin Luther King, Jr*. New York: Oxford UP, 2010.

Baltzell, E. Digby. *Judgment and Sensibility: Religion and Stratification*, edited by Howard G. Schneiderman. New Brunswick, NJ: Transaction Publishers, 1994.

Baltzell, E. Digby. *Philadelphia Gentlemen: The Making of a National Upper Class*. Glencoe, IL: Free Press, 1958.

Baltzell, E. Digby. *The Protestant Establishment: Aristocracy & Caste in America*. 1964. New Haven, CT: Yale UP, 1987.

Barber, Lucy. *Marching on Washington: The Forging of an American Political Tradition*. Berkeley: University of California Press, 2004.

Barnhouse, Ruth Tiffany. "Is Patriarchy Obsolete?" In *Male and Female: Christian Approaches to Sexuality*, edited by Ruth Tiffany Barnhouse and Urban T. Holmes, 223–35. New York: Seabury Press, 1976.

Bass, S. Jonathan. *Blessed Are the Peacemakers: Martin Luther King Jr., Eight White Religious Leaders, and the "Letter from Birmingham Jail."* Baton Rouge: Louisiana State UP, 2001.

Battle, Michael. *Black Battle, White Knight: The Authorized Biography of Malcolm Boyd*. New York: Seabury Press, 2011.

Bayne, Stephen F., Jr. *The Optional God*. 1953. Wilton, CT: Morehouse-Barlow, 1980.

Bayne, Stephen F., Jr. "Preface." In *Theological Freedom and Social Responsibility: Report of the Advisory Committee of the Episcopal Church*, edited by Stephen F. Bayne, Jr., et al., vii–xi. New York: Seabury Press, 1967.

Bayne, Stephen F., Jr., et al. "The Report." In *Theological Freedom and Social Responsibility: Report of the Advisory Committee of the Episcopal Church*, edited by Stephen F. Bayne, Jr., et al., 5–33. New York: Seabury Press, 1967.

Beary, Michael J. *Black Bishop: Edward T. Demby and the Struggle for Racial Equality in the Episcopal Church*. Urbana: University of Illinois Press, 2001.

Bellah, Robert N. *The Broken Covenant: American Civil Religion in a Time of Trial*. New York: Seabury Press, 1975.

Berger, Peter L. "American Religion: Conservative Upsurge, Liberal Prospects." In *Liberal Protestantism: Realities and Possibilities*, edited by Robert S. Michaelson and Wade Clark Roof, 19–36. New York: Pilgrim Press, 1986.

Berger, Peter L. *The Noise of Solemn Assemblies: Christian Commitment and the Religious Establishment in America*. Garden City, NY: Doubleday, 1961.

Bethge, Eberhard. *Dietrich Bonhoeffer: Theologian, Christian, Man for His Times: A Biography*. Rev. ed. Minneapolis: Fortress Press, 2000.

Biggar, Nigel. "Why the 'Establishment' of the Church of England Is Good for a Liberal Society." In *The Established Church: Past, Present and Future*, edited by Mark Chapman et al., 1–25. London: T&T Clark, 2011.

Blandy, Gray M., and Lawrence L. Brown. *The Story of the First Twenty-five Years of the Episcopal Seminary of the Southwest*. Austin, TX: Episcopal Seminary of the Southwest, 1976.

BIBLIOGRAPHY AND SOURCES   331

Bloom, Jack M. *Class, Race, and the Civil Rights Movement*. Bloomington: Indiana UP, 1987.

Bonner, Jeremy. *Called Out of Darkness into Marvelous Light: A History of the Episcopal Diocese of Pittsburgh, 1750–2006*. Eugene, OR: Wipf and Stock, 2009.

Bonhoeffer, Dietrich. *Christ the Center*. Translated by Edwin H. Robertson. New York: Harper and Row, 1978.

Bonhoeffer, Dietrich. *Letters and Papers from Prison*. Translated by Reginald H. Fuller. New ed. New York: Touchstone Books, 1997.

Bonhoeffer, Dietrich. *Life Together*. Translated by John W. Doberstein. New York: Harper, 1954.

Bonomi, Patricia U. *Under the Cope of Heaven: Religion, Society, and Politics in Colonial America*. New York: Oxford UP, 1986.

Booty, John. *An American Apostle: The Life of Stephen Fielding Bayne, Jr.* Valley Forge, PA: Trinity Press International, 1997.

Booty, John. *The Episcopal Church in Crisis*. Cambridge, MA: Cowley Publications, 1988.

Booty, John. *Mission and Ministry: A History of the Virginia Theological Seminary*. Harrisburg, PA: Morehouse, 1995.

Bourgeois, Michael. *All Things Human: Henry Codman Potter and the Social Gospel in the Episcopal Church*. Urbana: University of Illinois Press, 2004.

Boyd, Malcolm. *As I Live and Breathe: Stages of an Autobiography*. New York: Random House, 1969.

Boyd, Malcolm. *Half Laughing/Half Crying*. New York: St. Martin's Press, 1986.

Boyd, Malcolm. *If I Go Down to Hell: Man's Search for Meaning in Contemporary Life*. New York: Morehouse-Barlow, 1962.

Braden, Anne. *The Wall Between*. New York: Monthly Review Press, 1958.

Brands, H. W. *Traitor to His Class: The Privileged Life and Radical Presidency of Franklin Delano Roosevelt*. New York: Doubleday, 2008.

Brewster, Gurdon. *Ministry on the Frontier: The Contribution of Episcopal Campus Ministry to the Present and Future of the Church*. New York: Episcopal Church Foundation, 2000.

Brill, Earl H. *The Christian Moral Vision*. New York: Seabury Press, 1979.

Brueggemann, Walter. *The Prophetic Imagination*. 2nd ed. Minneapolis: Fortress Press, 2001.

Buchanan, Constance H. "The Anthropology of Vitality and Decline: The Episcopal Church in a Changing Society." In *Episcopal Women: Gender, Spirituality and Commitment in an American Mainline Denomination*, edited by Catherine Prelinger, 310–29. New York: Oxford UP, 1992.

Burgess, John. "I was a black man before I was a Christian." In *All One Body*, edited by Timothy Wilson, 167–73. London: Darton, Longman and Todd, 1969.

Butler, Jon. *Awash in a Sea of Faith: Christianizing the American People*. Cambridge, MA: Harvard UP, 1990.

Cadwell, Matthew Peter. *A History of Episcopal Divinity School: In Celebration of Its Twenty-fifth Anniversary*. Cambridge, MA: Episcopal Divinity School, 2000.

Campbell, Marllene. "An American Indian Viewpoint." In *Realities and Visions: The Church's Mission Today*, edited by Furman C. Stough and Urban T. Holmes, III, 137–43. New York: Seabury Press, 1976.

Campbell, Will D. *And Also with You: Duncan Gray and the American Dilemma*. Franklin, TN: Providence House, 1997.

332 BIBLIOGRAPHY AND SOURCES

Carpenter, Douglas M. *A Casserole for a Horse and Other Food for Thought*. Birmingham, AL: Mercy Seat Press, 2005.

Carpenter, Douglas M. *A Powerful Blessing: The Life of Charles Colcock Carpenter, Sr., 1889-1969, Bishop of Alabama, 1938-1968*. Birmingham, AL: TransAmerica Printing, 2012.

Carroll, Jackson W., and Wade Clark Roof. "Introduction." In *Beyond Establishment: Protestant Identity in a Post-Protestant Age*, edited by Jackson W. Carroll and Wade Clark Roof, 11-27. Louisville, KY: Westminster/John Knox Press, 1993.

Carter, Junius F., Jr. "God's Call to Unity, Love and Service." In *Black Gospel/White Church*, edited by John M. Burgess, 79-84. New York: Seabury Press, 1982.

Chapman, Audrey R. *Faith, Power, and Politics: Political Ministry in Mainline Churches*. New York: Pilgrim Press, 1991.

Chappell, David L. *Inside Agitators: White Southerners in the Civil Rights Movement*. Baltimore, MD: John Hopkins UP, 1994.

Chappell, David L. *A Stone of Hope: Prophetic Religion and the Death of Jim Crow*. Chapel Hill: University of North Carolina Press, 2004.

Charry, Ellen T. "Introduction." In Paul M. van Buren, *The Austin Dogmatics, 1957-1958*, edited by Ellen T. Charry, xvii-xxvii. Eugene, OR: Cascade Books, 2012.

Cherry, Conrad. *Hurrying Toward Zion: Universities, Divinity Schools, and American Protestantism*. Bloomington: Indiana UP, 1995.

Chidsey, Alan Lake. *The Bishop: A Portrait of the Right Reverend Clinton S. Quin*. Houston, TX: Gulf Publishing, 1966.

Childs, Brevard S. *Biblical Theology in Crisis*. Philadelphia: Westminster Press, 1970.

Church and Society in Crisis: Social Policy of the Episcopal Church 1964-1967. New York: Executive Council of the Episcopal Church, 1968.

Civil Rights Hearings. "Religious Panel." In *Rhetoric, Religion, and the Civil Rights Movement, 1954-1965*, edited by Davis W. Houck and David E. Dixon, 826-31. Waco, TX: Baylor UP, 2006.

Clecak, Peter. *America's Quest for the Ideal Self: Dissent and Fulfillment in the 60s and 70s*. New York: Oxford UP, 1983.

Clark, J. C. D. *English Society 1660-1832: Religion, Ideology and Politics during the Ancien Regime*. 2nd ed. Cambridge: Cambridge UP, 2000.

Coates, William R. "A Prophet of the Biblical World." In *Prophet of Justice, Prophet of Life: Essays on William Stringfellow*, edited by Robert Boak Slocum, 165-73. New York: Church Publishing, 1997.

Coburn, John B. *Twentieth-Century Spiritual Letters: An Introduction to Contemporary Prayer*. Philadelphia: Westminster, 1967.

Coffmann, Elesha J. *The Christian Century and the Rise of the Protestant Mainline*. New York: Oxford UP, 2013.

Cole, Ned. "Why I Will Not Ordain a Woman until General Convention Authorizes Me." In *The Ordination of Women—Pro & Con*, edited by Michael Hamilton and Nancy S. Montgomery, 70-81. New York: Morehouse-Barlow, 1975.

Committee to Study the Proper Place of Women in the Ministry of the Church. "Progress Report to the House of Bishops, October 1966." In *Readings from the History of the Episcopal Church*, edited by Robert W. Prichard, 168-74. Wilton, CT: Morehouse-Barlow, 1986.

Cox, Harvey G. *The Secular City: Secularization and Urbanization in Theological Perspective*. New York: Macmillan, 1965.

BIBLIOGRAPHY AND SOURCES   333

Cox, Harvey G. *The Seduction of the Spirit: The Use and Misuse of People's Religion*. New York: Simon and Schuster, 1973.

Crocker, John, Jr. *A Rebirth of Freedom: The Calling of an American Historian*. Philadelphia: Xlibris, 2005.

Cummings, Brian. "Introduction." In *The Book of Common Prayer: The Texts of 1549, 1559, and 1662*. Edited by Brian Cummings, ix–lii. Oxford: Oxford UP, 2011.

Darling, Pamela. *New Wine: The Story of Women Transforming Leadership and Power in the Episcopal Church*. Cambridge, MA: Cowley Publications, 1994.

Dator, James, and Jan Nunley. *Many Parts, One Body: How the Episcopal Church Works*. New York: Church Publishing, 2010.

Davidson, James D., and Ralph E. Pyle. *Ranking Faiths: Religious Stratification in America*. Lanham, MD: Rowman & Littlefield, 2011.

Davis, Douglas. "The Church in a New Bohemia." In *The Search for Community in Modern America*, edited by E. Digby Baltzell, 111–22. New York: Harper and Row, 1968.

Dawley, Powel Mills. *The Episcopal Church and Its Work*. Greenwich, CT: Seabury Press, 1955.

Dawley, Powel Mills. *The Story of the General Theological Seminary: A Sesquicentennial History, 1817–1967*. New York: Oxford UP, 1969.

Dean, Robert D. *Imperial Brotherhood: Gender and the Making of Cold War Foreign Policy*. Amherst: University of Massachusetts Press, 2001.

Delany, Sarah L., and A. Elizabeth Delany. *Having Our Say: The Delany Sisters' First Hundred Years*. New York: Dell, 1994.

Deloria, Vine, Jr. *Custer Died for Your Sins: An Indian Manifesto*. New York: Macmillan, 1969.

Deloria, Vine, Jr. *For This Land: Writings on Religion in America*, edited by James Treat. New York: Routledge, 1999.

DeMille, George E. *The Episcopal Church Since 1900: A Brief History*. New York: Morehouse-Gorham, 1955.

DeWitt, Robert L., ed. *Struggling with the System, Probing Alternatives: A Study/Action Guide*. Ambler, PA: Episcopal Church Publishing, 1976.

Diamond, Etan. *Souls of the City: Religion and the Search for Community in Postwar America*. Bloomington: Indiana UP, 2003.

Didion, Joan. *The White Album*. 1979. New York: Farrar, Straus, and Giroux, 1990.

Diocese of Mississippi Department of Christian Social Relations. *The Church Considers the Supreme Court Decision*. Jackson: Diocese of Mississippi, 1954.

Division of Urban Industrial Church Work. *Report of the Joint Commission to Survey the Missionary Problems in Industrial Areas*. New York: National Council of PECUSA, 1958.

Dominiak, Paul. "Moses the Magistrate: The Mosaic Theological Imaginaries of John Jewel and Richard Hooker in Elizabethan Apologetics." In *Defending the Faith: John Jewel and the Elizabethan Church*, edited by Angela Ranson et al., 161–82. University Park: Pennsylvania State UP, 2018.

Donovan, Mary Sudman. *Women Priests in the Episcopal Church: The Experience of the First Decade*. Cincinnati: Forward Movement, 1988.

Dorrien, Gary. *Social Ethics in the Making: Interpreting an American Tradition*. Malden, MA: Wiley-Blackwell, 2008.

Dorrien, Gary. *Soul in Society: The Making and Renewal of Social Christianity*. Minneapolis: Fortress Press, 1995.

Douglas, Ian T. *Fling Out the Banner!: The National Church Ideal and the Foreign Mission of the Episcopal Church*. New York: Church Hymnal Corporation, 1996.

334 BIBLIOGRAPHY AND SOURCES

Dozier, Verna. *Confronted by God: The Essential Verna Dozier*. Edited by Cynthia L. Shattuck and Fredrica Harris Thompsett. New York: Seabury Books, 2006.

Dudziak, Mary L. *Cold War Civil Rights: Race and Image of American Democracy*. New ed. Princeton, NJ: Princeton UP, 2011.

Dun, Angus. "The Social Responsibility of the Christian and of the Church." In *Christianity Takes a Stand: An Approach to the Issues of Today*, edited by William Scarlett, 9–23. New York: Penguin, 1946.

Dupont, Carolyn Renée. *Mississippi Praying: Southern White Evangelicals and the Civil Rights Movement, 1945–1975*. New York: New York UP, 2013.

Drury, Clifford M. *The History of the Chaplain Corps, United States Navy, 1939–49*. Washington, DC: Government Printing Office, 1984.

Eagles, Charles W. *Outside Agitator: Jon Daniels and the Civil Rights Movement in Alabama*. Chapel Hill: University of North Carolina Press, 1993.

Ehle, John. *Shepherd of the Streets: The Story of the Reverend James A. Gusweller and His Crusade on the New York West Side*. New York: William Sloane, 1960.

Ellul, Jacques. *The Presence of the Kingdom*. Translated by Olive Wyon. 1951. Colorado Springs, CO: Helmers and Howard, 1989.

Ellwood, Robert S. *The Fifties Spiritual Marketplace: American Religion in a Decade of Conflict*. New Brunswick, NJ: Rutgers UP, 1997.

Ellwood, Robert S. *The Sixties Spiritual Awakening: American Religion Moving from Modern to Postmodern*. New Brunswick, NJ: Rutgers UP, 1994.

Epting, Christopher. *With Gladness and Singleness of Heart: A Bishop's Life in a Changing Church*. Bettendorf, IA: Ecubishop Publishing, 2016.

Evans, Christopher H. *The Social Gospel in American Religion: A History*. New York: New York UP, 2017.

Faramelli, Norman J. *Technethics: Christian Mission in an Age of Technology*. New York: Friendship Press, 1971.

Faramelli, Norman, Edward Rodman, and Anne Scheibner. "Seeking to Hear and to Heed in the Cities: Urban Ministry in the Postwar Episcopal Church." In *Churches, Cities, and Human Community: Urban Ministry in the United States 1945–1985*, edited by Clifford J. Green, 97–122. Grand Rapids, MI: Eerdmans, 1996.

Ferguson, Ron. *George MacLeod: Founder of the Iona Community*. London: Collins, 1990.

Fields, Karen E., and Barbara J. Fields. *Racecraft: The Soul of Inequality in American Life*. London: Verso, 2012.

Findlay, James F., Jr. *Church People in the Struggle: The National Council of Churches and the Black Freedom Movement, 1950–1970*. New York: Oxford UP, 1993.

Fletcher, Joseph. *Situation Ethics: The New Morality*. Philadelphia: Westminster Press, 1966.

Foster, Roland. *The Role of the Presiding Bishop*. Cincinnati, OH: Forward Movement, 1982.

Fowler, Robert Booth. *Unconventional Partners: Religion and Liberal Culture in the United States*. Grand Rapids, MI: Eerdmans, 1989.

Fox, Richard Wrightman. *Reinhold Niebuhr: A Biography*. 1985. Ithaca, NY: Cornell UP, 1996.

Friedland, Michael B. *Lift Up Your Voice like a Trumpet: White Clergy and the Civil Rights and Antiwar Movements, 1954–1973*. Chapel Hill: University of North Carolina Press, 1998.

BIBLIOGRAPHY AND SOURCES   335

Gatehouse, Gordon. "The Church League for Industrial Democracy." In *Struggling with the System Probing Alternatives: A Study/Action Guide*, edited by Robert L. DeWitt, 38–43. Ambler, PA: Episcopal Church Publishing, 1976.

Gaustad, Edwin S. "The Pulpit and the Pews." In *Between the Times: The Travail of the Protestant Establishment in America, 1900–1960*, edited by William R. Hutchison, 21–47. Cambridge: Cambridge UP, 1989.

Gessell, John M. *Grace and Obedience: Theological Essays in Criticism.* Sewanee, TN: Proctor's Hall Press, 2002.

Gill, Jill K. *Embattled Ecumenism: The National Council of Churches, the Vietnam War, and the Trials of the Protestant Left.* DeKalb: North Illinois UP, 2011.

Glock, Charles Y., Benjamin B. Ringer, and Earl R. Babbie. *To Comfort and to Challenge: A Dilemma of the Contemporary Church.* Berkeley: University of California Press, 1967.

Gomes, Peter. "A Minister Remembered: Charles Philip Price '41: The Harvard Years." In *Each of Us Will Never Be the Same: Memories of Charles Philip Price*, 11–21. Cincinnati, OH: Forward Movement, 2003.

Gortner, David T., et al. *Around One Table: Exploring Episcopal Identity—Expanded Version* (New Bern, NC: College for Bishops/CREDO Institute, 2009).

Gough, Deborah Mathias. *Christ Church, Philadelphia: The Nation's Church in a Changing City.* Philadelphia: Christ Church Philadelphia, 1995.

Graham, Lawrence Otis. *Our Kind of People: Inside America's Black Upper Class.* New York: Harper Collins, 1999.

Gray, Duncan M., Jr. "The Days are Coming—A Sermon." In *On the Battle Lines: A Manifesto for Our Times by 27 Militant Clergymen*, edited by Malcolm Boyd, 109–14. New York: Morehouse-Barlow, 1964.

Griffiss, James E. *The Anglican Vision.* Cambridge, MA: Cowley Publications, 1997.

Griffiss, James E. "A Hope for Theology in the Episcopal Church." In *A New Conversation: Essays on the Future of Theology and the Episcopal Church*, edited by Robert Boak Slocum, 201–12. New York: Church Publishing, 1999.

Griffiss, James E. "A Reluctant Anglican Prophet." In *Prophet of Justice, Prophet of Life: Essays on William Stringfellow*, edited by Robert Boak Slocum, 40–57. New York: Church Publishing, 1997.

Grimley, Matthew. "The State, Nationalism, and Anglican Identities." In *The Oxford History of Anglicanism*, Volume IV: *Global Western Anglicanism, c. 1910–Present*, edited by Jeremy Morris, 117–36. Oxford: Oxford UP, 2017.

Gunderson, Joan R. "Women and the Parallel Church: A View from Congregations." In *Episcopal Women: Gender, Spirituality and Commitment in an American Mainline Denomination*, edited by Catherine M. Prelinger, 111–32. New York: Oxford UP, 1992.

Hackney, Sheldon. "Social Justice, the Church, and the Counterculture, 1963–1979." In *This Far by Faith: Tradition and Change in the Episcopal Diocese of Pennsylvania*, edited by David R. Contosta, 298–334. University Park: Pennsylvania State UP, 2013.

Hadaway, C. Kirk. "Denominational Defection: Recent Research on Religious Disaffiliation in America." In *The Protestant Mainstream "Decline": The Presbyterian Pattern*, edited by Milton J. Coalter et al., 102–21. Louisville, KY: Westminster/John Knox Press, 1990.

Hadaway, C. Kirk, and David A. Roozen. *Rerouting the Protestant Mainstream: Sources of Growth and Opportunities for Change.* Nashville, TN: Abingdon Press, 1995.

Hadden, Jeffrey K. *The Gathering Storm in the Churches.* Garden City, NY: Doubleday, 1969.

336 BIBLIOGRAPHY AND SOURCES

Hale, Grace Elizabeth. *A Nation of Outsiders: How the White Middle Class Fell in Love with Rebellion in Postwar America*. New York: Oxford UP, 2011.

Hall, Mitchell K. *Because of Their Faith: CALCAV and Religious Opposition to the Vietnam War*. New York: Columbia UP, 1990.

Handy, Robert T. *A Christian America: Protestant Hopes and Historical Realities*. 2nd ed. Oxford: Oxford UP, 1984.

Harrelson, Walter. "The Hebrew Bible and Modern Culture." In *The Hebrew Bible and Its Modern Interpreters*, edited by Douglas A. Knight and Gene M. Tucker, 489–505. Philadelphia: Fortress Press, 1985.

Harrison, Robert. *Transformed by the Love of God: John Walker, A Man for the 21st Century*. Cincinnati: Forward Movement, 2004.

Harvey, Van A. "On the Intellectual Marginality of American Theology." In *Religion and Twentieth-Century American Intellectual Life*, edited by Michael J. Lacey, 172–92. New York: Cambridge UP, 1989.

Hatch, Nathan O. *The Democratization of American Christianity*. New Haven, CT: Yale UP, 1989.

Hatchett, Marion J. *Commentary on the American Prayer Book*. New York: Seabury Press, 1980.

Hauerwas, Stanley. *After Christendom? How the Church Is to Behave if Freedom, Justice, and a Christian Nation Are Bad Ideas*. Nashville, TN: Abingdon, 1991.

Havemeyer, Harry F. "An Introduction." In John Coburn, *Holiness and Community: John Coburn Preaches the Faith*, vii–xiv. Harrisburg, PA: Morehouse, 2010.

Hefling, Charles. "Anglicans and Common Prayer." In *The Oxford Guide to the Book of Common Prayer: A Worldwide Survey*, edited by Charles Hefling and Cynthia Shattuck, 1–6. New York: Oxford UP, 2006.

Hefling, Charles. "Non Nobis Domine." In *Each of Us Will Never Be the Same: Memories of Charles Philip Price*, 101–7. Cincinnati: Forward Movement, 2003.

Hein, David. *Noble Powell and the Episcopal Establishment in Twentieth Century America*. Urbana: University of Illinois Press, 2001.

Hein, David, and Gardiner H. Shattuck, Jr. *The Episcopalians*. Westport, CT: Praeger, 2004.

Herberg, Will. *Protestant, Catholic, Jew: An Essay in American Religious Sociology*. 1955. Chicago: University of Chicago Press, 1983.

Herman, Max Arthur. *Summer of Rage: An Oral History of the 1967 Newark and Detroit Riots*. New York: Peter Lang, 2013.

Heyward, Carter. *A Priest Forever: The Formation of a Woman and a Priest*. New York: Harper and Row, 1976.

Heyward, Carter. *She Flies On: A White Southern Christian Debutante Wakes Up*. New York: Church Publishing, 2017.

Higley, Stephen R. *Privilege, Power, and Place: The Geography of the American Upper Class*. Lanham, MD: Rowman & Littlefield, 1995.

Hines, John E. "The Agonised Cry of a People Who Had No Place in American Society." In *All One Body*, edited by Timothy Wilson, 279–87. London: Darton, Longman and Todd, 1969.

Hines, John E. "The Concluding Address at the New York Conference." In *Metabagdad: The Report of the Chicago and New York Conferences on Metropolitan Planning*, edited by James Morton, V1–V8. New York: National Council of the Episcopal Church, 1963.

Hines, John E. *Thy Kingdom Come*. New York: Morehouse-Barlow, 1967.

BIBLIOGRAPHY AND SOURCES   337

Hirshson, Roberta Star. "A Committee of Blacks and a Committee of Whites." In *The Biography of a Church*, Volume II: *Voices from the Pews*, edited by Martha Jacoby et al., 70–94. Cambridge, MA: Christ Church Cambridge, 2012.

Hobson, Fred. *But Now I See: The White Southern Racial Conversion Narrative*. Baton Rouge: Louisiana State UP, 1999.

Hofstadter, Richard. *The Paranoid Style in American Politics*. 1965. New York: Vintage, 2008.

Hoge, Dean R., and David A. Roozen. "Some Sociological Conclusions about Church Trends." In *Understanding Church Growth and Decline, 1950–78*, edited by Dean R. Hoge and David A. Roozen, 315–33. New York: Pilgrim Press, 1979.

Holbein, Laurence. *For All the Saints: The First Hundred Years of All Saints' Episcopal Church, San Francisco*. Philadelphia: Xlibris, 2010.

Holifield, E. Brooks. *God's Ambassadors: A History of the Christian Clergy in America*. Grand Rapids, MI: Eerdmans, 2007.

Hollinger, David A. *After Cloven Tongues of Fire: Protestant Liberalism in Modern American History*. Princeton, NJ: Princeton UP, 2013.

Holmes, David L. "The Anglican Tradition in Colonial Virginia." In *Perspectives on American Religion and Culture*, edited by Peter W. Williams, 66–79. Malden, MA: Blackwell, 1999.

Holmes, David L. *A Brief History of the Episcopal Church*. Harrisburg, PA: Trinity Press International, 1993.

Holmes, Urban T., III. "Once Again: To Comfort or To Challenge?" In *Realities and Visions: The Church's Mission Today*, edited by Furman C. Stough and Urban T. Holmes, III, 177–84. New York: Seabury Press, 1976.

Holmes, Urban T., III. *What Is Anglicanism?* Wilton, CT: Morehouse-Barlow, 1982.

Honeywell, Roy John. *Chaplains of the United States Army*. Washington, DC: Department of the Army, 1958.

Hood, Robert E. *Social Teachings in the Episcopal Church: A Source Book*. Danbury, CT: Morehouse, 1990.

Hough, Joseph C., Jr. "The Loss of Optimism as a Problem for Liberal Christian Faith." In *Liberal Protestantism: Realities and Possibilities*, edited by Robert S. Michaelson and Wade Clark Roof, 145–66. New York: Pilgrim Press, 1986.

Howe, Daniel Walker. "Protestantism, Voluntarism, and Personal Identity in Antebellum America." In *New Directions in American Religious History*, edited by Harry S. Stout and D. G. Hart, 206–35. New York: Oxford UP, 1997.

Hudnut-Beumler, James. "Conclusion." In *The Future of Mainline Protestantism in America*, edited by James Hudnut-Beumler and Mark Silk, 175–97. New York: Columbia UP, 2018.

Hudnut-Beumler, James. *Looking for God in the Suburbs: The Religion of the American Dream and Its Critics, 1945–1965*. New Brunswick, NJ: Rutgers UP, 1994.

Huntington, William Reed. *The Church-Idea: An Essay Towards Unity*. 1870. Harrisburg, PA: Morehouse, 2002.

Hutchison, William R. "Discovering America." In *Between the Times: The Travail of the Protestant Establishment in America, 1900–1960*, edited by William R. Hutchison, 303–9. Cambridge: CUP, 1989.

Hutchison, William R. *Religious Pluralism in America: The Contentious History of a Founding Ideal*. New Haven, CT: Yale UP, 2003.

James, Nancy Carol. *The Developing Schism within the Episcopal Church, 1960–2010*. Lewiston, NY: Edwin Mellen Press, 2010.

338 BIBLIOGRAPHY AND SOURCES

Janowitz, Morris. *The Professional Soldier: A Social and Political Portrait*. Rev. ed. New York: Free Press, 1971.

Johnston, Araminta Stone. *And One Was a Priest: The Life and Times of Duncan M. Gray, Jr.* Jackson: UP of Mississippi, 2011.

Jones, Howard. *My Lai: Vietnam, 1968, and the Descent into Darkness*. New York: Oxford UP, 2017.

Journal of the General Convention of the Episcopal Church 1973. New York: Seabury Press, 1973.

Journal of the General Convention of the Protestant Episcopal Church in the United States of America. Held at Seattle, Washington, 1967. N.p., 1967.

Journal of the Ninety-Eighth Annual Convention of the Protestant Episcopal Church in Diocese of Arkansas, April 1970. N.p., 1970.

Kabaservice, Geoffrey. *The Guardians: Kingman Brewster, His Circle, and the Rise of the Liberal Establishment*. New York: Henry Holt, 2004.

Katerberg, William H. *Modernity and the Dilemma of North American Anglican Identities 1880–1950*. Montreal and Kingston: McGill-Queen's University Press, 2001.

Kaufmann, Eric P. *The Rise and Fall of Anglo America*. Cambridge, MA: Harvard UP, 2004.

Keller, Morton, and Phyllis Keller. *Making Harvard Modern: The Rise of America's University*. New York: Oxford UP, 2001.

Kelley, Dean M. *Why Conservative Churches Are Growing: A Study in Sociology of Religion*. New York: Harper and Row, 1972.

Kelley, E. Allen. "Editorial." In *The Episcopal Church Annual 1972*, 9ff. New York: Morehouse-Barlow, 1972.

Kenrick, Bruce. *Come Out the Wilderness*. New York: Harper and Row, 1962.

Kesselus, Kenneth. *John E. Hines: Granite on Fire*. Austin, TX: Episcopal Theological Seminary of the Southwest, 1995.

Kew, Richard, and Roger J. White. *New Millennium, New Church: Trends Shaping the Episcopal Church for the 21st Century*. Cambridge, MA: Cowley Publications, 1992.

King, William McGuire. "An Enthusiasm for Humanity: The Social Emphasis in Religion and Its Accommodation in Protestant Theology." In *Religion and Twentieth-Century American Intellectual Life*, edited by Michael J. Lacey, 49–77. Cambridge: CUP, 1989.

King, William McGuire. "The Reform Establishment and the Ambiguities of Influence." In *Between the Times: The Travail of the Protestant Establishment in America, 1900–1960*, edited by William R. Hutchison, 122–40. Cambridge: CUP, 1989.

Kitagawa, Daisuke. *Issei and Nisei: The Internment Years*. New York: Seabury Press, 1967.

Kitagawa, Daisuke. *Race Relations and Christian Mission*. New York: Friendship Press, 1964.

Knox, John. "The Identifiability of the Church." In *Theological Freedom and Social Responsibility: Report of the Advisory Committee of the Episcopal Church*, edited by Stephen F. Bayne, Jr., et al., 67–79. New York: Seabury Press, 1967.

Krumm, John M., and Marian Kelleran, *Denver Crossroads: General Convention 1979*. Cincinnati: Forward Movement, 1979.

Kruse, Kevin M., and Thomas J. Sugrue. "Introduction: The New Suburban History." In *The New Suburban History*, edited by Kevin M. Kruse and Thomas J. Sugrue, 1–10. Chicago: University of Chicago Press, 2006.

Lantzer, Jason S. *Mainline Christianity: The Past and Future of America's Majority Faith*. New York: New York UP, 2012.

BIBLIOGRAPHY AND SOURCES   339

Lau, Ronald T. C. "Editorial." In *The Episcopal Church Annual 1976*, 4–5. New York: Morehouse-Barlow, 1976.

Laurent, Sylvie. *King and the Other America: The Poor People's Campaign and the Quest for Economic Equality*. Berkeley: University of California Press, 2018.

Lee, Robert. "The Organizational Dilemma in American Protestantism." In *Cities and Churches: Readings on the Urban Church*, edited by Robert Lee, 221–35. Philadelphia: Westminster Press, 1962.

Lewis, Harold T. *Christian Social Witness*. Cambridge, MA: Cowley Publications, 2001.

Lichtenberger, Arthur. *The Day Is at Hand*. New York: Seabury Press, 1964.

Lindsley, James Elliott, et al. *An Anecdotal History of the General Theological Seminary, 1947–1957*. N.p., 1996.

Lints, Richard. *Progressive and Conservative Religious Ideologies: The Tumultuous Decade of the 1960s*. Farnham, Surrey: Ashgate, 2010.

Lloyd, Samuel T. "Grasped by God." In *Each of Us Will Never Be the Same: Memories of Charles Philip Price*, 45–50. Cincinnati: Forward Movement, 2003.

Lovin, Robin W. *Reinhold Niebuhr and Christian Realism*. Cambridge: Cambridge UP, 1995.

Lucks, Daniel S. *From Selma to Saigon: The Civil Rights Movement and the Vietnam War*. Lexington: University of Kentucky Press, 2014.

Lyne, Stephen R. *The Episcopal Church: Splits and Schism*. Washington, DC: Department of State, 1978.

MacKinnon, Donald. *The Stripping of the Altars*. London: Collins/Fontana, 1969.

McLaughlin, Malcolm. *The Long, Hot Summer of 1967: Urban Rebellion in America*. New York: Palgrave Macmillan, 2014.

McLoughlin, William G. *Revivals, Awakenings, and Reform: An Essay on Religion and Social Change in America, 1607–1977*. Chicago: University of Chicago Press, 1978.

McManis, Lester W. *Handbook on Christian Education in the Inner City*. New York: Seabury Press, 1966.

McThenia, Andrew W., Jr. "Introduction: How This Celebration Began." In *Radical Christian and Exemplary Lawyer: Honoring William Stringfellow*, edited by Andrew W. McThenia, 1–16. Grand Rapids, MI: Eerdmans, 1995.

Maltby, Judith. *Prayer Book and People in Elizabethan and Early Stuart England*. Cambridge: Cambridge UP, 1998.

Markwell, Bernard Kent. *The Anglican Left: Radical Social Reformers in the Church of England and the Protestant Episcopal Church, 1846–1954*. Brooklyn, NY: Carlson Publishing, 1991.

Marsden, George M. *The Soul of the American University: From Protestant Establishment to Established Nonbelief*. New York: Oxford UP, 1994.

Martin, Richard B. *On the Wings of the Morning: Two Islands, One Church*. Garden City, NY: Diocese of Long Island, 2006.

Marty, Martin E. *Righteous Empire: The Protestant Experience in America*. New York: Dial Press, 1970.

Mead, Sydney E. *The Lively Experiment: The Shaping of Christianity in America*. 1963. New York: Harper and Row, 1976.

Meland, Bernard Eugene. *The Secularization of Modern Cultures*. New York: Oxford UP, 1966.

Miller, Glenn T. *Piety and Profession: American Protestant Theological Education, 1870–1970*. Grand Rapids, MI: Eerdmans, 2007.

340 BIBLIOGRAPHY AND SOURCES

Miller, Timothy. *The Hippies and American Values*. 2nd ed. Knoxville: University of Tennessee Press, 2011.

Mills, Frederick V. *Bishops by Ballot: An Eighteenth-Century Ecclesiastical Revolution*. New York: Oxford UP, 1978.

Moore, Honor. *The Bishop's Daughter: A Memoir*. New York: W. W. Norton, 2008.

Moore, Jenny. *The People of Second Street*. New York: William Morrow, 1968.

Moore, Paul, Jr. "And Suddenly Nothing Happens." In *On the Battle Lines: A Manifesto for Our Times by 27 Militant Clergymen*, edited by Malcolm Boyd, 62–71. New York: Morehouse-Barlow, 1964.

Moore, Paul, Jr. "A Bishop Views the Underground Church." In *The Underground Church*, edited by Malcolm Boyd, 221–37. London: Sheed and Ward, 1969.

Moore, Paul, Jr. *The Church Reclaims the City*. New York: Seabury Press, 1964.

Moore, Paul, Jr. "The Church's Mission I." In *Viewpoints: Some Aspects of Anglican Thinking*, edited by John B. Coburn and W. Norman Pittenger, 226–43. Greenwich, CT: Seabury Press, 1959.

Moore, Paul, Jr. "The Making of a Marine on Guadalcanal." In *The Pacific War Remembered: An Oral History Collection*, edited by John T. Mason, Jr., 125–41. Annapolis: Naval Institute Press, 1986.

Moore, Paul, Jr. *Presences: A Bishop's Life in the City*. Cambridge, MA: Cowley Publications, 1997.

Moore, Paul, Jr. *Take a Bishop like Me*. New York: Harper and Row, 1979.

Moore, Paul, Jr. "A Touch of Laughter." In *My Harvard, My Yale*, edited by Diana Dubois, 196–208. New York: Random House, 1982.

Moorhead, James H. "Presbyterians and the Mystique of Organizational Efficiency, 1870–1936." In *Reimagining Denominationalism: Interpretive Essays*, edited by Robert Bruce Mullin and Russell E. Richey, 264–87. New York: Oxford UP, 1994.

Morehouse, Clifford P. *Mother of Churches: An Informal History of Trinity Parish in the City of New York*. New York: Seabury Press, 1973.

Morris, William C., Jr. "Avoiding the Dangers of a Monumental Church." In *A New Conversation: Essays on the Future of Theology and the Episcopal Church*, edited by Robert Boak Slocum, 190–200. New York: Church Publishing, 1999.

Morton, James, et al., "Conference Assignment." In *Metabagdad: The Report of the Chicago and New York Conferences on Metropolitan Planning*, edited by James Morton, n.p. New York: PECUSA National Council, 1963.

Moyse, Cordelia. "Gender Perspectives: Women and Anglicanism." In *The Oxford History of Anglicanism, Volume IV: Global Western Anglicanism, c. 1910–Present*, edited by Jeremy Morris, 68–92. Oxford: Oxford UP, 2017.

Mullin, Robert Bruce, *Episcopal Vision/American Reality: High Church Theology and Social Thought in Evangelical America*. New Haven, CT: Yale UP, 1986.

Murray, Pauli. *The Autobiography of a Black Activist, Feminist, Lawyer, Priest, and Poet*. Knoxville: University of Tennessee Press, 1989.

Murray, Pauli. "The Dilemma of the Minority Christian." In *Daughters of Thunder: Black Women Preachers and Their Sermons, 1850–1979*, edited by Bettye Collier-Thomas, 257–62. San Francisco: Jossey-Bass, 1998.

Murray, Pauli. *Proud Shoes: The Story of an American Family*. New York: Harper, 1956.

Murray, Pauli. *Selected Sermons and Writings*. Edited by Anthony B. Pinn. Maryknoll, NY: Orbis, 2006.

BIBLIOGRAPHY AND SOURCES 341

Musselman, G. Paul. *The Church on the Urban Frontier*. Greenwich, CT: Seabury Press, 1960.

Myers, C. Kilmer. "At the Core of the City." In *On the Battle Lines: A Manifesto for Our Times by 27 Militant Clergymen*, edited by Malcolm Boyd, 27–36. New York: Morehouse-Barlow, 1964.

Myers, C. Kilmer. *Baptized into the One Church*. New York: Seabury Press, 1958.

Myers, C. Kilmer. *Behold the Church*. New York: Seabury Press, 1958.

Myers, C. Kilmer. *Light the Dark Streets*. Greenwich, CT: Seabury Press, 1957.

Nation, Mark Thiessen. "The Vocation of the Church of Jesus the Criminal." In *William Stringfellow in Anglo-American Perspective*, edited by Anthony Dancer, 114–24. Aldershot, Hants: Routledge, 2005.

Neuhaus, Richard John. "Calling a Halt to Retreat: Hartford and Social Justice." In *Against the World for the World: The Hartford Appeal and the Future of American Religion*, edited by Peter L. Berger and Richard John Neuhaus, 138–64. New York: Seabury Press, 1976.

Neuhaus, Richard John. *The Naked Public Square: Religion and Democracy in America*. 2nd ed. Grand Rapids, MI: Eerdmans, 1997.

Niebuhr, H. Richard. *Christ and Culture*. 1951. New York: Harper and Row, 1975.

Niebuhr, H. Richard. *The Social Sources of Denominationalism*. 1929. New York: Meridian Books, 1957.

Norman, E. R. *The Conscience of the State in North America*. Cambridge: Cambridge UP, 1968.

Norton, Perry L. *Church and Metropolis*. New York: Seabury Press, 1964.

Novak, Michael. "The Volatile Counterculture." In *New Theology No. 8*, edited by Martin E. Marty and Dean G. Peerman, 243–56. New York: Macmillan, 1971.

O'Dell, Darlene. *The Story of the Philadelphia Eleven*. New York: Seabury Books, 2014.

Ogbar, O. G. *Black Power: Radical Politics and African American Identity*. Baltimore, MD: John Hopkins UP, 2004.

Ogletree, Thomas W. *The "Death of God" Controversy*. Nashville, TN: Abingdon Press, 1966.

Olson, Laura R. "Clergy and American Politics." In *The Oxford Handbook of Religion and American Politics*, edited by Corwin E. Smidt et al., 371–93. New York: Oxford UP, 2009.

Opinion Research Corporation. *The Episcopal Church Today as Seen by Clergymen and Laymen: A Survey for the Episcopal Church Foundation*. Princeton, NJ: Opinion Research Corporation, 1964.

Oppenheimer, Mark. *Knocking on Heaven's Door: American Religion in the Age of Counterculture*. New Haven, CT: Yale UP, 2003.

Overholt, Thomas W. *Channels of Prophecy: The Social Dynamics of Prophetic Activity*. Minneapolis: Fortress Press, 1989.

Packard, Vance. *The Status Seekers: An Exploration of Class Behavior in America*. New York: D. McKay, 1959.

Paradise, Scott I. "Christian Mission and the Technician Mentality in America." In *Christians in a Technological Era*, edited by Hugh C. White, 127–43. New York: Seabury Press, 1964.

Paradise, Scott I. *Detroit Industrial Mission: A Personal Narrative*. New York: Harper and Row, 1968.

Paradise, Scott I. *Requiem for American Industrial Missions: Audenshaw Papers No. 41*. Richmond, Yorkshire: Audenshaw Foundation, 1974.

342 BIBLIOGRAPHY AND SOURCES

Paradise, Scott I. *To Speak with Power: Sermons*, edited by Peter Paradise. N.p., 2003.

Parrent, Allan M. "On War, Peace and the Use of Force." In *The Crisis of Moral Teaching in the Episcopal Church*, edited by Timothy F. Sedgwick and Philip Turner, 94–118. Harrisburg, PA: Morehouse-Barlow, 1992.

Patterson, James T. *Brown v. Board of Education: A Civil Rights Milestone and Its Troubled Legacy*. New York: Oxford UP, 2001.

Pehl, Matthew. "Discovering Working-Class Religion in a 1950s Auto Plant." In *The Pew and the Picket Line: Christianity and the American Working Class*, edited by Christopher D. Cantwell et al., 96–114. Urbana: University of Illinois Press, 2016.

Pelham, Joseph A. "The Episcopal Church in the Urban Crisis: The Decade Ahead." In *To Hear and To Heed: The Episcopal Church Listens and Acts in the City*, edited by Urban Bishops Coalition, 23–63. Cincinnati, OH: Forward Movement, 1978.

Pennoyer, Robert M. *As It Was: A Memoir*. Westport, CT: Prospecta Press, 2015.

Phillips, Paul T. *A Kingdom on Earth: Anglo-American Social Christianity, 1880–1940*. University Park: Pennsylvania State UP, 1996.

Pierce, Nathaniel W., and Paul L. Ward. *The Voice of Conscience: A Loud and Unusual Noise? The Episcopal Peace Fellowship, 1939–1989*. Charlestown, MA: Charles River, 1989.

Pike, James A. "Doctrine, Data, and Due Process." In *Theological Freedom and Social Responsibility: Report of the Advisory Committee of the Episcopal Church*, edited by Stephen F. Bayne, Jr., et al., 117–37. New York: Seabury Press, 1967.

Pike, James A. *A Time for Christian Candor*. New York: Harper and Row, 1964.

Polenberg, Richard. *One Nation Divisible: Class, Race, and Ethnicity in the United States since 1938*. New York: Viking Press, 1980.

Preliminary Commission on Social Reconstruction. *A Better World for All Peoples*. Cincinnati, OH: Forward Movement, 1943.

Price, Charles P. *The Anglican Tradition: What Is it? Can It Last?* Cincinnati, OH: Forward Movement, 1980.

Price, Charles P. *Introducing the Proposed Book: A Study of the Significance of the Proposed Book of Common Prayer for the Doctrine, Discipline, and Worship of the Episcopal Church*. New York: Church Hymnal Corporation, 1976.

Prichard, Robert W. *A History of the Episcopal Church*. 3rd ed. Harrisburg, PA: Morehouse, 2014.

Pringle, Sandy M. *GCSP—The Episcopal Church's Program for the Empowerment of Minority Groups: A Case Study*. Washington, DC: Department of State, 1971.

Program of the Church League for Industrial Democracy. New York: Church League for Industrial Democracy, 1946.

Pusey, Nathan M., and Charles L. Taylor. *Ministry for Tomorrow: Report of the Special Committee on Theological Education*. New York: Seabury Press, 1967.

Quinley, Harold E. *The Prophetic Clergy: Social Activism among Protestant Ministers*. New York: Wiley, 1974.

Quinn, Frederick. *A House of Prayer for All People: A History of Washington National Cathedral*. New York: Morehouse, 2014.

Radner, Ephraim, and Philip Turner. *The Fate of Communion: The Agony of Anglicanism and the Future of a Global Church*. Grand Rapids, MI: Eerdmans 2006.

Ramsey, Paul. *Christian Ethics and the Sit-In*. New York: Association Press, 1961.

Rasmussen, Larry. "Morality and Power." In *Reinhold Niebuhr, Theologian of Public Life: Selected Writings*, edited by Larry Rasmussen, 45–46. London: Collins, 1988.

Reeves, Thomas C. *The Empty Church: The Suicide of Liberal Christianity*. New York: Free Press, 1996.

Reichley, A. James. *Religion in American Public Life*. Washington, DC: Brookings Institution, 1985.

Reside, Graham. "The Story of Contemporary Mainline Protestantism." In *The Future of Mainline Protestantism in America*, edited by James Hudnut-Beumler and Mark Silk, 17–58. New York: Columbia UP, 2018.

Rhoden, Nancy L. *Revolutionary Anglicanism: The Colonial Church of England Clergy during the American Revolution*. New York: New York UP, 1999.

Righter, Walter C. *A Pilgrim's Way*. New York: Knopf, 1998.

Robertson, David M. *A Passionate Pilgrim: A Biography of Bishop James A. Pike*. New York: Knopf, 2004.

Robinson, John A. T. *Honest to God*. London: SCM Press, 1963.

Rodman, Edward. *Let There Be Peace among Us: A Story of the Union of Black Episcopalians*. Lawrenceville, VA: Brunswick Press, 1990.

Rodman, Edward. "Soul Sisters: The Emergence of Black Women's Leadership." In *Deeper Joy: Lay Women and Vocation in the 20th Century Episcopal Church*, edited by Fredrica Harris Thompsett and Sheryl Kujawa-Holbrook, 219–33. New York: Church Publishing, 2005.

Roof, Wade Clark, and William McKinney. *American Mainline Religion: Its Changing Shape and Future*. New Brunswick, NJ: Rutgers UP, 1987.

Roozen, David A., Jackson W. Carroll, and Wade Clark Roof. "Fifty Years of Religious Change in the United States." In *The Post-War Generation and Establishment Religion: Cross-Cultural Perspectives*, edited by Wade Clark Roof et al., 59–86. Boulder, CO: Westview Press, 1995.

Rorty, Richard. *Achieving Our Country: Leftist Thought in Twentieth-Century America*. Cambridge, MA: Harvard UP, 1998.

Rorabaugh, W. J. *American Hippies*. New York: Cambridge UP, 2015.

Rosenberg, Rosalind. *Jane Crow: The Life of Pauli Murray*. New York: Oxford UP, 2017.

Rossinow, Doug. *The Politics of Authenticity: Liberalism, Christianity, and the New Left in America*. New York: Columbia UP, 1998.

Rupp, George. *Culture Protestantism: German Liberal Theology at the Turn of the Twentieth Century*. Missoula, MT: AAR Studies in Religion/Scholars Press, 1977.

Sachs, William L. *The Transformation of Anglicanism: From State Church to Global Communion*. Cambridge: Cambridge UP, 1993.

Sachs, William L., and Thomas Holland, *Restoring the Ties That Bind: The Grassroots Transformation of the Episcopal Church*. New York: Church Publishing, 2003.

Scarlett, William. "Introduction." In *Christianity Takes a Stand: An Approach to the Issues of Today*, edited by William Scarlett, 1–8. New York: Penguin, 1946.

Scarlett, William, ed. *The Christian Demand for Social Justice*. New York: New American Library, 1949.

Schaller, Warren A. "Appendix: Social Policy of the Episcopal Church, 1951–1963." In *Social Policy of the Episcopal Church in the Twentieth Century*, edited by M. Moran Weston, A1–A57. Rev. ed. New York: Seabury Press, 1964.

Schiess, Betty Bone. *Why Me, Lord?: One Women's Ordination to the Priesthood with Commentary and Complaint*. Syracuse, NY: Syracuse UP, 2003.

Schutz, Aaron, and Mike Miller. "Introduction." In *People Power: The Community Organizing Tradition of Saul Alinsky*, edited by Aaron Schutz and Mike Miller, 1–16. Nashville: Vanderbilt UP, 2015.

344 BIBLIOGRAPHY AND SOURCES

Schutz, Kevin M. *Tri-Faith America: How Catholics and Jews Held Postwar America to its Protestant Promise*. Oxford: Oxford UP, 2011.

Scudder, Vita Dutton, "Anglican Thought on Property." In *Christianity and Property*, edited by Joseph F. Fletcher, 124–50. Philadelphia: Westminster Press, 1947.

Shattuck, Gardiner H., Jr. *Episcopalians and Race: Civil War to Civil Rights*. Lexington: UP of Kentucky, 2000.

Shattuck, Gardiner H., Jr. "Knowing the Tasks." In *A New Conversation: Essays on the Future of Theology and the Episcopal Church*, edited by Robert Boak Slocum, 36–47. New York: Church Publishing, 1999.

Shattuck, Gardiner H., Jr. *A Whole Priesthood: The Philadelphia Ordinations (1974) and the Continuing Dilemmas of Race in the Episcopal Church*. Cambridge, MA: Episcopal Divinity School, 2001.

Sheep, Mathew L. "Meaning, Discourse, and Design Thinking: Organizational Becoming in the Episcopal Church." In *What We Shall Become: The Future and Structure of the Episcopal Church*, edited by Winnie Varghese, 47–58. New York: Church Publishing, 2013.

Sherrill, Henry Knox. *Among Friends: An Autobiography*. Boston: Little Brown, 1962.

Siefer, Gregor. *The Church and Industrial Society: A Survey of the Worker-Priest Movement and Its Implications for the Christian Mission*. London: Darton, Longman and Todd, 1964.

Silk, Mark. *Spiritual Politics: Religion and America since World War II*. New York: Simon and Schuster, 1988.

Sims, Bennett J. *The Time of My Life: A Spiritual Pilgrimage Grounded in Hope*. Hendersonville, NC: Institute for Servant Leadership, 2006.

Sims, Bennett J. *Why Bush Must Go: A Bishop's Faith-Based Challenge*. New York: Continuum, 2004.

Smith, Harmon L. "Decorum as Doctrine: Teachings on Human Sexuality." In *The Crisis of Moral Teaching in the Episcopal Church*, edited by Timothy Sedgwick and Philip Turner, 15–40. Harrisburg, PA: Morehouse-Barlow, 1992.

Smith, John F. "Context as Contradiction: Campus Ministry in the Diocese of Massachusetts." In *A History of College Work within the Episcopal Diocese of Massachusetts*, 2–23. Boston: Diocese of Massachusetts, 1997.

Smyllie, James H. "Church Growth and Decline in Historical Perspective: Protestant Quest for Identity, Leadership, and Meaning." In *Understanding Church Growth and Decline, 1950–78*, edited by Dean R. Hoge and David A Roozen, 69–93. New York: Pilgrim Press, 1979.

Snape, Michael. *God and Uncle Sam: Religion and America's Armed Forces in World War II*. Woodbridge, Suffolk: Boydell Press, 2015.

Snape, Michael. "War and Peace." In *The Oxford History of Anglicanism*, Volume IV: *Global Western Anglicanism, c. 1910–Present*, edited by Jeremy Morris, 214–42. Oxford: Oxford UP, 2017.

Snow, John H. "Christian Identity on Campus." In *Christian Identity on Campus*, edited by Myron B. Bloy, Jr., 99–111. New York: Seabury Press, 1971.

Snow, John H. *The Gospel in a Broken World*. Philadelphia: United Church Press, 1972.

Snow, John H. *The Impossible Vocation: Ministry in the Mean Time*. Cambridge, MA: Cowley Publications, 1988.

Spong, John Shelby. *Here I Stand: My Struggle for a Christianity of Integrity, Love, and Equality*. San Francisco: Harper Collins, 2000.

BIBLIOGRAPHY AND SOURCES 345

Spong, John Shelby. *A New Christianity for a New World: Why Traditional Faith Is Dying and How a New Faith Is Being Born*. San Francisco: Harper Collins, 2001.

Steigerwald, David. *The Sixties and the End of Modern America*. New York: St. Martin's Press, 1995.

Stevick, Daniel B. "Christian Mission and Social Action." In *Christian Mission and Social Action: How Should the Church Be Involved in Controversial Social Questions?* n.p. New York: National Council of PECUSA, 1962.

Stewart, Alexander D. "Guest Editorial." In *The Episcopal Church Annual 1979*, 4–5. New York: Morehouse-Barlow, 1979.

Stoneburner, Tony. *Making Waves: The Life and Work of Mike Bloy (The Rev. Myron B. Bloy, Jr.), 1926–1985*. Minneapolis, MN: Limekiln Press, 2015.

Stringfellow, William. *Dissenter in a Great Society: A Christian View of America in Crisis*. 1966. Eugene, OR: Wipf and Stock, 2005.

Stringfellow, William. *An Ethic for Christians and Other Aliens in a Strange Land*. 1973. Wipf and Stock, 2004.

Stringfellow, William. *Free in Obedience*. 1964. Eugene, OR: Wipf and Stock, 2006.

Stringfellow, William. *Imposters of God: Inquiries into Favorite Idols*. 1969. Eugene, OR: Wipf and Stock, 2006.

Stringfellow, William. *Instead of Death*. 2nd ed., 1976. Eugene, OR: Wipf and Stock, 2004.

Stringfellow, William. *A Keeper of the Word: Selected Writings*, edited by Bill Wylie Kellermann. Grand Rapids, MI: Eerdmans, 1994.

Stringfellow, William. *My People Is the Enemy: An Autobiographical Polemic*. 1964. Eugene, OR: Wipf and Stock, 2005.

Stringfellow, William. *A Private and Public Faith*. 1962. Eugene, OR: Wipf and Stock, 1999.

Stringfellow, William. "Through Dooms of Love." In *New Theology No. 2*, edited by Martin E. Marty and Dean G. Peerman, 288–96. New York: Macmillan, 1965.

Stringfellow, William, and Anthony Towne. *The Bishop Pike Affair: Scandals of Conscience and Heresy, Relevance and Solemnity in the Contemporary Church*. 1967. Eugene, OR: Wipf and Stock, 2007.

Stringfellow, William, and Anthony Towne. *The Death and Life of Bishop Pike: An Utterly Candid Biography of America's Most Controversial Clergyman*. 1976. Eugene, OR: Wipf and Stock, 2007.

Strong, Rowan. *Anglicanism and the British Empire, c. 1700–1850*. Oxford: Oxford UP, 2007.

Summary of General Convention Actions 1967. New York: Executive Council, 1967.

Sumner, David E. *The Episcopal Church's History, 1945–1985*. Wilton, CT: Morehouse, 1987.

Swanson, Guy E. *The Vocation of a Church in America: A Sociologist's View*. Detroit: Detroit Industrial Mission, 1962.

Swatos, William H., Jr. "A Primacy of Systems: Confederation, Corporation, and Communion." In *Church, Identity, and Change: Theology and Denominational Structures in Unsettled Times*, edited by David A. Roozen and James R. Nieman, 198–226. Grand Rapids, MI: Eerdmans, 2001.

Sweet, Leonard I. "The 1960s: The Crises of Liberal Christianity and the Public Emergence of Evangelicalism." In *Evangelicalism and Modern America*, edited by George Marsden, 29–45. Grand Rapids, MI: Eerdmans, 1984.

Sweet, Leonard I. "The Modernization of Protestant Religion in America." In *Altered Landscapes: Christianity in America, 1935–85*, edited by David W. Lotz et al., 19–41. Grand Rapids, MI: Eerdmans, 1989.

346 BIBLIOGRAPHY AND SOURCES

Tarango, Angela. *Choosing the Jesus Way: American Indian Pentecostals and the Fight for the Indigenous Principle*. Chapel Hill: University of North Carolina Press, 2014.

Temple, William, et al. *Malvern, 1941: The Life of the Church and the Order of Society, Being the Proceedings of the Archbishop of York's Conference*. London: Longmans, 1941.

Tipton, Steven M. *Getting Saved from the Sixties: Moral Meaning in Conversion and Cultural Change*. Berkeley: University of California Press, 1982.

Tobin, Robert. *The Minority Voice: Hubert Butler and Southern Irish Protestantism, 1900–91*. Oxford: Oxford UP, 2012.

Turner, Philip. "How the Church Might Teach." In *The Crisis of Moral Teaching in the Episcopal Church*, edited by Timothy F. Sedgwick and Philip Turner, 137–59. Harrisburg, PA: Morehouse-Barlow, 1992.

Urban Bishops Coalition, ed. *To Hear and to Heed: The Episcopal Church Listens and Acts in the City*. Cincinnati, OH: Forward Movement, 1978.

Van Buren, Paul M. *The Austin Dogmatics, 1957–1958*. Edited by Ellen T. Charry. Eugene, OR: Cascade Books, 2012.

Van Buren, Paul M. *The Secular Meaning of the Gospel, Based on an Analysis of Its Language*. New York: Macmillan, 1963.

Van Buren, Paul M. *Theological Explorations*. New York: Macmillan, 1968.

Waldron, Ann. *Hodding Carter: The Reconstruction of a Racist*. Chapel Hill: Algonquin Books, 1993.

Walmsley, Arthur E. "The Mission of the Church in the New Era." In *The Church in a Society of Abundance*, edited by Arthur E. Walmsley, 58–73. New York: Seabury Press, 1963.

Walsh, Andrew W. "The Mainline and the Soul of International Relations." In *The Future of Mainline Protestantism in America*, edited by James Hudnut-Beumler and Mark Silk, 139–74. New York: Columbia UP, 2018.

Walsh, John, and Stephen Taylor. "The Church and Anglicanism in the 'Long' Eighteenth Century." In *The Church of England c. 1689–c. 1833: From Toleration to Tractarianism*, edited by John Walsh et al., 1–64. Cambridge: Cambridge UP, 1993.

Walsh, Ryan H. *Astral Weeks: A Secret History of 1968*. New York: Penguin, 2018.

Wappler, Edwin G. "Anglicans and the New Morality." In *The Anglican Moral Choice*, edited by Paul Elmen, 161–77. Wilton, CT: Morehouse-Barlow, 1983.

Warren, Austin. "The Crisis of the Young." In *Search for the Sacred: The New Spiritual Quest*, edited by Myron B. Bloy, Jr., 21–30. New York: Seabury Press, 1972.

Washington, Paul M., with David M. Gracie. *"Other Sheep I Have": The Autobiography of Father Paul M. Washington*. Philadelphia, PA: Temple UP, 1994.

Weil, Louis. "Liturgical Renewal and Modern Anglican Liturgy." In *The Oxford History of Anglicanism*, Volume IV: *Global Western Anglicanism, c. 1910–Present*, edited by Jeremy Morris, 50–67. Oxford: Oxford OUP, 2017.

Wellman, James K., Jr. *The Gold Coast Church and Ghetto: Christ and Culture in Mainline Protestantism*. Urbana: University of Illinois Press, 1999.

Wentz, Richard E. *Religion in the New World: The Shaping of Religious Traditions in the United States*. Minneapolis: Fortress Press, 1990.

Weston, M. Moran, *Episcopalians at Work in the World: A Study of Social Education and Community Action in the Protestant Episcopal Church in the United States of America 1949–1951*. New York: National Council, 1952.

Weston, M. Moran. *Social Policy of the Episcopal Church in the Twentieth Century*. Rev. ed. New York: Seabury Press, 1964.

BIBLIOGRAPHY AND SOURCES   347

White, Ronald C., Jr., and C. Howard Hopkins. *The Social Gospel: Religion and Reform in Changing America*. Philadelphia: Temple UP, 1976.

Whyte, William H. *The Organization Man*. New York: Simon & Schuster, 1956.

Wickham, E. R. *Church and People in an Industrial City*. London: Lutterworth Press, 1957.

Wiese, Andrew. "'The House I Live In': Race, Class, and African American Suburban Dreams in the Postwar United States." In *The New Suburban History*, edited by Kevin M. Kruse and Thomas J. Sugrue, 99–119. Chicago: University of Chicago Press, 2006.

Williams, Daniel K. *God's Own Party: The Making of the Christian Right*. New York: Oxford UP, 2010.

Williams, Peter W. *America's Religions: Traditions and Cultures*. New York: Macmillan, 1990.

Williams, Peter W. *Religion, Art, and Money: Episcopalians and American Culture from the Civil War to the Great Depression*. Chapel Hill: University of North Carolina Press, 2016.

Williams, Rowan. *Anglican Identities*. London: Darton, Longman, Todd, 2004.

Willie, Charles V. "Appendix: The Priesthood of All Believers." In Betty Bone Schiess, *Why Me, Lord?: One Women's Ordination to the Priesthood with Commentary and Complaint*, 145–52. Syracuse, NY: Syracuse UP, 2003.

Willie, Charles V. *Church Action in the World: Studies in Sociology and Religion*. New York: Morehouse-Barlow, 1969.

Willie, Charles V. *Oreo: On Race and Marginal Men and Women*. Wakefield, MA: Parameter Press, 1975.

Winter, Gibson. *The New Creation as Metropolis*. New York: Macmillan, 1963.

Winter, Gibson. *The Suburban Captivity of the Churches: An Analysis of Protestant Responsibility in the Expanding Metropolis*. Garden City, NY: Doubleday, 1961.

Wittkofski, Joseph. "Joseph Wittkofski." In *Modern Canterbury Pilgrims*, edited by James Pike, 114–25. New York: Morehouse-Gorham, 1956.

Wolfe, Tom. *Radical Chic and Mau-Mauing the Flak Catchers*. New York: Farrar, Straus, and Giroux, 1970.

Woods, Jeff. *Black Struggle, Red Scare: Segregation and Anti-Communism in the South, 1948–1968*. Baton Rouge: Louisiana State UP, 2004.

Woodward, Kenneth L. *Getting Religion: Faith, Culture, and Politics from the Age of Eisenhower to the Era of Obama*. New York: Convergent, 2016.

Woolverton, John F. *Colonial Anglicanism in North America*. Detroit: Wayne State UP, 1984.

Woolverton, John F., with James D. Bratt. *A Christian and a Democrat: A Religious Biography of Franklin D. Roosevelt*. Grand Rapids, MI: Eerdmans, 2019.

Wright, Harold Louis. "The Test of Evangelism." In *Black Gospel/White Church*, edited by John M. Burgess, 106–8. New York: Seabury Press, 1982.

Wright, Nathan, Jr. *Black Power and Urban Unrest: The Creative Possibilities*. New York: Hawthorn, 1967.

Wright, Nathan, Jr. *Let's Work Together*. New York: Hawthorn, 1968.

Wright, Nathan, Jr. *Ready to Riot*. New York: Holt, Rhinehart and Winston, 1968.

Wuthnow, Robert. *The Restructuring of American Religion: Society and Faith since World War II*. Princeton, NJ: Princeton UP, 1988.

Yon, William A. "The Indigenization of Newark: Urban Mission Strategy in the Diocese of Newark." In *To Build the City—Too Long a Dream: Studies of Urban Churches*, edited by William A. Yon, 4–9. Washington, DC: Alban Institute, 1982.

Young, Frances M. *Thankfulness Unites: The History of the United Thank Offering, 1889–1979*. Cincinnati: Forward Movement, 1979.

348 BIBLIOGRAPHY AND SOURCES

Zaroulis, Nancy, and Gerald Sullivan. *Who Spoke Up? American Protest against the War in Vietnam, 1963–1975*. Garden City, NY: Doubleday, 1984.

Zscheile, Dwight J. "From Establishment to Innovation: Rethinking Structure in a New Apostolic Age." In *What We Shall Become: The Future and Structure of the Episcopal Church*, edited by Winnie Varghese, 59–67. New York: Church Publishing, 2013.

Zscheile, Dwight J. *People of the Way: Renewing Episcopal Identity*. Harrisburg, PA: Morehouse, 2012.

Unpublished Sources

A. Dissertations, Interviews, Memoirs

Gahan, Patrick. *An Interview with The Right Reverend John E. Hines*. 1993. Located at Booher Library, ETSS, Austin, TX.

George, Michael E. "The Black Manifesto and the Churches: The Struggle for Black Power and Reparations in Philadelphia." Master's thesis, Temple University, Philadelphia, 2013.

Montgomery, Brandt Leonard. "Time's Prisoner: The Right Reverend Charles Colcock Jones Carpenter and the Civil Rights Movement in the Episcopal Diocese of Alabama." Master's thesis, General Theological Seminary, New York, 2012.

Morales, Teresa F. "The Last Stone Is Just the Beginning: A Rhetorical Biography of Washington National Cathedral." Ph.D. diss., Georgia State University, 2013.

Pinkston, Caroline Booth. "The Gospel of Justice: Community, Faith, and the Integration of St. Andrew's Episcopal School." Master's thesis, University of Texas at Austin, 2014.

Sanderson, Mimi Ayres. Untitled Parishfield Memoir. Unpublished manuscript, 2002. Courtesy of Mimi Ayres Sanderson.

Spong, John Shelby, ed. *Anniversary Booklet: A Tribute to John Elbridge Hines on The Fiftieth Anniversary of His Ordination to the Priesthood, October 1984*. 1984. Located at Booher Library, ETSS, Austin, TX.

Wappler, Edwin G. "Four Anglican Situationists and Their Tradition: A Study in Fletcher, Pike, Robinson, and Rhymes." Ph.D. diss., Duke University, 1972.

Winter, Sara C. *Religious Journey, Secular Road: An Account of the Parishfield Community, 1949–1967*. Unpublished manuscript, c. 2002. Courtesy of Sara C. Winter.

Woodard, G. H. Jack. *The Episcopal Church's Struggle to Light the Dark Streets: Urban Ministry, 1948 to 1994*. 1994. Located at Booher Library, ETSS, Austin, TX.

B. Archives

Connecticut

Hartford: Trinity College, Watkinson Library, Special Collections.

William M. Weber Papers.
Series II: Fol: Arlington to Littleton.
Series II: Fol: Weber's trip to Mississippi.
Series III: Fol: AFSA [Anglican Fellowship for Social Action].
Series III: Fol: AFSA Correspondence.
Series III: Fol: ELSA [Episcopal League for Social Action].
Series IV: Fol: Mississippi: Current Material.

BIBLIOGRAPHY AND SOURCES   349

New Haven: Yale University, Yale Divinity School Library, Special Collections.

RG 67: Henry Knox Sherrill Family Papers.
Series 1: Correspondence.

Massachusetts

Boston: Episcopal Diocese of Massachusetts Archives.

RG 1.A.12: John M. Burgess Papers
1.A.12:1: Fol: Urban Strategy.
1.A.12: 13.3: Women in the Church.
1.A.12:13:7: Women in the Church.
1.A.12:18: Fol: Printed Sermons, 1965–1975.
1.A.12:19: Fol: Correspondence, 1934–1946, 1950–1984.
1.A.12:22: Fol: EDS—Appointment of 2 women as priests—1975.

RG 1.B.4: Morris Fairchild Arnold Papers.
1.B.4.1: Fol: The Revd Norman J. Faramelli.
1.B.4.4. Fol: Office Files, 1971–1981.
1.B.4.4: Fol: Church and City Conference—Report.
1.B.4.4: Fol: Episcopal Urban Coalition—Public Hearings Project 1978.
1.B.4.4: Fol: Episcopal Church Publishing Co—*Witness*—1973–1979.
1.B.4.4: Fol: Episcopal Church Publishing Co.— " Church and Society"—1974–1975.

John B. Coburn Papers.
(i) Personal Files.
Stephen F. Bayne to Albert H. Palmer, Nov 14, 1969.
John B. Coburn to John J. Bishop, Apr 5, 1971.
John B. Coburn to Ellen McA. Johnson, Jan 25, 1972.
John B. Coburn to Robert Morrison, Jun 20, 1972.
John B. Coburn to Patricia Page, Feb 24, 1972.
David E. Richards to John E. Hines et al., Mar 24, 1969.

(ii) PECUSA: Executive Council Records and Minutes.
Executive Council Minutes, Sept 15, 1967: "The Crisis in American Society: A Call by the Presiding Bishop": A2–A5.
Executive Council Minutes, Sept 24–26, 1968: during "Report of Screen and Review Committee of GSCP": A21.
Executive Council Minutes, Dec 10–12, 1968: "Message from the President": A10–A12.
Executive Council Records: Vine Deloria, Jr., statement to Native American Episcopal clergy, regarding "Indian work," [undated (1968–1969)].
Executive Council Minutes, Feb 11–13, 1969: "Message from the President": A9–A11.
David E. Richards, confidential memo [undated (March 1969)].
Executive Council Records, "Report of the Committee for the Implementation of the Spirit of the (Executive Council) Response to the Manifesto," Aug 29, 1969.
Executive Council Minutes, Aug 29, 1969, Special Meeting in South Bend, Indiana: A1–8.
Executive Council Minutes, Sept 23–25, 1969: "Message of the Presiding Bishop to

350 BIBLIOGRAPHY AND SOURCES

Executive Council": A15–A20.

Executive Council Minutes, Feb 17–19, 1970: "Message of the Presiding Bishop to Executive Council": A9–A18.

Executive Council Minutes, May 19–21, 1970: "Report of the Special Committee on the Laity": A13–A16.

Executive Council Records: Jesse E. Christman and Hugh C. White, Jr., "General Motors and South Africa: A case describing a stockholder proposal to General Motors by the Executive Council of the Episcopal Church over G.M.'s manufacturing activities in the Republic of South Africa, Nov 1970 to May 1971."

Executive Council Minutes, Dec 12–14, 1972: unedited transcript of extemporaneous remarks by the Rt. Rev. Wilburn C. Campbell and the Rt. Rev. John E. Hines: EMP-3: 1–13.

Executive Council Minutes, Feb 20–23, 1973: "Message from the Chair to Executive Council": PB-1: 1–6.

(iii) PECUSA: General Convention Documents.

Remarks introducing Joint Commission of Ecumenical Relations report to General Convention [1964].

"A Report to the General Convention from the Representatives of the Episcopal Church on the General Board of the National Council of Churches" [1964].

Advisory Committee on Agenda [A.T. Eastman with S.F. Bayne and J.A. Pelham], "A Conception of the Theme of Special General Convention II," Second Draft [1969].

Boston: John F. Kennedy Presidential Library and Museum.

John F. Kennedy Oral History Program.

Oral History Interview with Francis B. Sayre, Jr., June 25, 1964, Washington, DC. Interview conducted by Samuel E. Beck.

Robert F. Kennedy Oral History Program.

Oral History Interview with Oscar Clark Carr, Jr., May 6 and 7 1969, Clarksdale, Mississippi. Interview conducted by Dennis J. O'Brien.

Cambridge: Episcopal Divinity School, Sherril Library, Archives.
Now located at the Episcopal Archives, Austin, Texas.

Boston Industrial Mission Papers.

3/8: BIM Publications.

4/8: Scott I. Paradise Correspondence.

RG 2: John B. Coburn Papers.

2.34: "A Statement by the Deans of the Seminaries of the Episcopal Church, February 24, 1968: Draft A."

2.35: John B. Coburn to Deans of the Seminaries of the Episcopal Church, Nov 29, 1968.

2.36: Correspondence and Addresses.

Jonathan M. Daniels Papers.

Binder I: Correspondence and Writings.

Joseph M. Fletcher Papers.

FLE 1/4: Joseph F. Fletcher, anecdotes collection [undated (mid-1980s)].

BIBLIOGRAPHY AND SOURCES   351

Cambridge: Harvard University, Pusey Library, University Archives.

UAI 15.900: Nathan Marsh Pusey Papers.
15.900.13: Baccalaureate Addresses.
15.900.14: Statement made to the House of Deputies of the General Convention concerning the Report of the Special Committee to Study Theological Education [1967].

Cambridge: Radcliffe Institute (Harvard University), Schlesinger Library, Archives.

MC 412: Pauli Murray Papers.
412.62.1045: Black Manifesto & Correspondence, 1969.
412.63.1078: PM: Post-ordination, 1977.
412.67.1148: Scrapbook on the ordination of women.
412.67.1160: Ordination of Women, Diocese of New York.
412.68.1173: Ordination of Women, Correspondence, Summer 1975.
412.68.1176: Page, Patricia.
412.68.1178: Ordination of Women: Wendt Trial.
412.70.1210v: Women in the Church.
412.100.1786: St. Philip's Church NYC.

Michigan

Ann Arbor: University of Michigan, Bentley Historical Library, Michigan Historical Collections.

Roger Warren Barney and Jane Lockwood Barney Papers.
Box 3, Fol: Navy, Iwo Jima, Diary, Etc.—1945–1956.
Box 5, Fol: Sermons, 1968.
Box 6, Fol: Jane Barney Personal Files, A–C.
Box 6, Fol: Jane Barney Personal Files, F–I.
Box 6, Fol: Jane Barney Personal Files, J–Q.
Box 6, Fol: Jane Barney Personal Files, S.
Box 8, Fol: Parishfield, Hugh White Correspondence, 1963–1971.

Richard S. M. Emrich Papers.
Box 1, Fol: Correspondence.
Box 1, Fol: Pastoral Letters.
Box 6, Fol: Articles and Commentaries, 1950s and 1960s.
Box 6, Fol: Lectures and Addresses, undated.
Box 6, Fol: Sermons, 1967–1969.

Parishfield Records, 1948–1971.
Box 1, Fol: Background—Parishfield Histories.
Box 1, Fol: Background—Closing of Parishfield—1967.
Box 1, Fol: Staff—Roger Barney.
Box 1, Fol: Correspondence—Emrich, Bishop Joe—1966–1967.
Box 1, Fol: Correspondence—Advisory Committee—1958–1966.
Box 2, Fol: Advisory Committee—1962–1966.
Box 2, Fol: Partners for Renwal—Study Materials—1958.
Box 2, Fol: Meetings: William Hamilton—1966.

352 BIBLIOGRAPHY AND SOURCES

Box 2, Fol: Programs—DIM—Writings, minutes, misc.—1957–1966.
Box 2, Fol: Sermons—1963–1965.
Box 2, Fol: Writings.
Box 2, Fol: Home Dept Project.

Parishfield History, Sara C. Winter Oral History Collection, 1994–1995, 1998.
Interview with Gibson Winter, conducted by Sara Winter, 1994/1995.
Interview with Paul van Buren, conducted by Sara Winter, 1994/1995.

**Detroit: Wayne State University, Walter P. Reuther Library,
Archives of Labor and Urban Affairs.**

AR 131: Detroit Industrial Mission Records, Part 1.
131.1.1: Detroit Industrial Mission, 1957.
131.1.1: Christ Church, 1957.
131.1.1: Christ Church, 1958.
131.1.1: Annual Dinner, 1959.
131.1.2: The Very Reverend Francis B. Sayre, 1957–1958.
131.1.2: Miscellaneous T, 1957–1958.
131.1.3: Hugh C. White and Edward "Ted" Wickham, Correspondence, 1957–1958.

AR 131: Detroit Industrial Mission Records, Part 2.
131.2.1.9.42: Scott I. Paradise Journal Selections [undated (late 1950s/early 1960s)].
131.2.1.9.43: Studies and Reports on D.I.M., 1957–1961.
131.2.1.10.25: Peace in Vietnam, 1966–1968.
131.2.1.22.20: Industrial Study Project of the Joint Commission on the Church in Human Affairs, 1961–1966.
131.2.1.25.22: Washington National Cathedral, the Rev. Francis B. Sayre, Jr., 1958–1970.
131.2.1.25.43: Church and Industry Lecture, 1959.
131.2.2.29.11: Paul Van Buren, Correspondence, 1957–1965.
131.2.2.43.25: The Church in the Metropolis

Minnesota

Minneapolis: Minnesota Historical Society.

Episcopal Church. Diocese of Minnesota. Philip F. McNairy Papers.
"New Theatre of Controversy" [undated (c. 1965)].
Suffragan Bishop's Report to the Diocesan Convention [1966].
Suffragan Bishop's Report to the Diocesan Convention [1968].
Bishop's Address to the Diocesan Convention [1971].
Bishop's Address to the Diocesan Convention [1972].
Bishop's Address to the Diocesan Convention [1973].

Missouri

Kansas City: Episcopal Diocese of West Missouri Archives.

Edward R. Welles Papers.
1047-S: Bishop's Convention Address [1961]
1099: Bishop's Convention Address [1963].

BIBLIOGRAPHY AND SOURCES   353

New York

Ithaca: Cornell University, University Library, Division of Rare and Manuscript Collections.

MS 4438: William Stringfellow Papers.
4438, Box 1: Addresses and Writings, 1940s–1950s.
4438, Box 3: East Harlem Protestant Parish.
4438, Box 4: Writings and Correspondence, 1960.
4438, Box 6: Writings and Correspondence, 1962–1963.
4438, Box 8: Writings and Correspondence, 1964.
4438, Box 10: Writings and Correspondence, 1965.
4438, Box 12: Writings and Correspondence, 1966–1967.
4438, Box 13: Arthur Walmsley to John E. Hines, June 10, 1968.
4438, Box 33: Writings, 1960s–1970s.

MS 4468: Betty Bone Schiess Papers.
4468, Box 1: Correspondence, 1969–1971.
4468, Box 3: Women's Ordination.

New York: Cathedral Church of St. John the Divine Archives.

ACC 2014: James Parks Morton Papers.
ACC 2014: JPM-12-20: Moore-Morton Cathedral (2005).

New York: Columbia University, Butler Library, Columbia Oral History Research Office.

Henry Knox Sherrill Oral History Project.
(Interviews conducted by John T. Mason.)
"Reminiscences of Roger Wilson Blanchard" (1982).
"Reminiscences of John Bowen Coburn" (1984).
"Reminiscences of Frederic C. Lawrence" (1982).
"Reminiscences of Henry S. Noble" (1983).
"Reminiscences of Henry W. Sherrill" (1982).
"Reminiscences of Arthur E. Walmsley" (1984).

Arthur Carl Lichtenberger Oral History Project.
(Interview conducted by John T. Mason.)
"Reminiscences of Warren Turner" (1984).

Biographical Oral History Project.
(Interviews conducted by John T. Mason.)
"Reminiscences of John M. Allin" (1991).
"Reminiscences of John E. Hines" (1986).
"Reminiscences of Paul Moore, Jr." (1988).

New York: Columbia University, Butler Library, Rare Books and Manuscripts Library.

MS 1326: M. Moran Weston Papers.
1326.7, Fol 52: Personal Correspondence (1929–1982).

354 BIBLIOGRAPHY AND SOURCES

New York: Episcopal Diocese of New York Archives.

Horace W. B. Donegan Papers.
4.9: Donegan Addresses.
8.25: Sermon Excerpts.
39.11: Installation Sermon.
50: Fol: Moore, Paul, Jr.

Paul Moore, Jr. Papers.
80.7: Boyd, Malcolm.
100.23: Myers, C. Kilmer.
102.15: DeWitt, Robert L.
124.5: Sermons.
125.5: Printed Materials.

New York: General Theological Seminary, Keller Library, Special Collections.

MSS B29: Stephen F. Bayne, Jr. Papers.
B29.3.2.50c: Deputy for Program: Memoranda 1968.
B29.3.2.55c: Deputy for Program: GSCP 1969–1970.
B29.3.2.58c: Correspondence 1967–1968.

MSS. C25: Tollie LeRoy Caution, Sr. Papers.
C25.22.33: Negro Work.
C25.30.43: Retirement.
C25.31.43: Retirement.

New York: Trinity Church Wall Street Archives.

John Vernon Butler Papers.
Box 128: Episcopal elections: Bishop of New York.
Box 143.1: Installation.
Box 143.3: Articles about the Rev. J. V. Butler.

John Heuss Papers.
Box 44.20: East Side Work 1952.
Box 109: Correspondence.

George H. "Jack" Woodard Papers.
File 1060.1: Grants, 1971–2004.

New York: Union Theological Seminary, Burke Library,
Archive of Women in Theological Scholarship.

George W. Barrett Papers.
Box 1, Fol 2: Correspondence 1974.

Carter Heyward Papers.
Box 1, Fol 2: After Philadelphia.
Box 2, Fol 9: Church/Religion.

New York: Union Theological Seminary, Burke Library, Seminary Archives.

East Harlem Protestant Parish Papers.
Box 10: Group Ministry—1957.

Syracuse: Syracuse University, University Libraries, Special Collections Research Center.

James A. Pike Papers.
Box 1: Correspondence.
Box 31: Correspondence.
Box 52: Miscellaneous materials.
Box 53: Miscellaneous materials.
Box 79: Miscellaneous materials.
Box 100: Sermons.
Box 101: Addresses.
Box 102: Addresses.

Pennsylvania

Philadelphia: Episcopal Diocese of Pennsylvania Archives, Lutheran Theological Seminary.

RG 1.15: Robert L. DeWitt Papers.
1.15.3, Fol 4: Texts of Addresses.
1.15.4, Fol 2: GCSP.
1.15.5, Fol 2: Vietnam.
1.15.5, Fol 5: Vietnam.
1.15.6, Fol 2: Areas of Tension.

Pittsburgh: Episcopal Diocese of Pittsburgh Archives.

Austin Pardue Papers.
1.51: Austin Pardue with Timothy Wilson, "The Church has to go where the danger is . . . ," Oct 16, 1968.

Rhode Island

Providence: Brown University, John Hay Library, Special Collections.

MS 2007.09: Ellen M. Barrett Papers.
2007.09.1.21: Ordination: the Rt. Rev. Moore, Correspondence, 1975–1977.

Tennessee

Memphis: University of Memphis, University Library, Special Collections.

Oscar Clark Carr, Jr. Papers.
Address at Convention of Diocese of Florida, Jan 23–24, 1970.
"A Renewed People: The Christian's Ministry in Shaping the 70's" [1972].
Sermon at Grace Episcopal Church, Monroe, LA, Mar 15, 1972.

356   BIBLIOGRAPHY AND SOURCES

Address to the Episcopal Churchwomen of Diocese of New York, Oct 3, 1972.
"On Development and the Budget" [undated (1974)].
"The Stewardship of the Gospel," Apr 3, 1976.
Commencement address at St. Andrew's Episcopal School, Jackson, MS, May 26, 1976.
"On Christian Stewardship," Oct 2, 1977.

Texas

Austin: Archives of the Episcopal Church.

RG 31: PECUSA. Executive (National) Council. Department of Christian Social Relations. Files 1921–1969.
31.5.5: Race Relations—Riots—Church's Response 1967.

RG 32: PECUSA. Executive (National) Council, Home Department.
32.15.1: Urban Work—Beginning of Program, History.

RG 43: Arthur Lichtenberger Papers, 1958–1964.
43.5.6: Sermons/Addresses—1962.
43.5.8: Sermons/Addresses—1960.
43.5.9: Sermons/Addresses—1959.
43.6: Manuscripts, 1948–1963.

RG 85: PECUSA. Executive (National) Council. Department of Christian Social Relations. Records, 1893–1968.
85.5.6: Studies and Reports—Miscellaneous.
85.5.9: Studies and Reports—Miscellaneous.
85.12.1: Social Education and Community Action Survey—Committee Files.
85.13.40: Urban Industrial Church Work (CSR): Conferences, 1953–1957.

RG 87: PECUSA. General Convention. General Convention Special Program, 1965–1974.
87.1.1/2: GCSP, "The First Five Years, A History of the General Convention Special Program, 1972."
87.1.6: "Mission: Empowerment" [1974].
87.4.18: John E. Hines, untitled memo, including "Staff Reply to Statement of Bishop Campbell," Feb 20, 1973.
87.4.19: Pamphlets.
87.5.50: Correspondence.
87.5.51: Correspondence.
87.5.52: Correspondence.
87.5.53: Correspondence.

RG 107: William Scarlett Papers.
107.3.12: "The Christian Ministry" [undated (c. 1949)].
107.3.12: "The Church" [undated (c. 1947)].
107.3.13: "The New Crusade" [undated (c. 1945)].
107.5.4: "The Social Gospel" [undated (1962)].
107.5.6: "One World—Under God" [1952].
107.5.8: untitled sermon [1945].

BIBLIOGRAPHY AND SOURCES   357

107.7.1/2: Reinhold Niebuhr, "Foreword," in William Scarlett, "A Parson's Tale" [c. 1963].

107.7.1/2: William Scarlett, "A Parson's Tale" [c. 1963].

107.7.11: Miscellaneous correspondence, 1951–52.

107.9.12: Social Justice Commission, 1932–53.

107.10.24: Reinhold Niebuhr, untitled address [undated (1950)].

107.11.22: Cornelius C. Tarplee, "Report of the Intergroup Education Project to the Department of Christian Social Relations, April 22, 1958."

RG 151: PECUSA. Executive (National) Council. Department of Christian Social Relations. Files 1925–(1958–1968)–1973.

151.1.11: Investments, etc. 1965–1971.

151.2.10: Urban Crisis—Newark 1967.

151.3.18: Vietnam 1965–1967.

RG 211: PECUSA. Executive (National) Council. Home Department. Joint Urban Program Records, 1954–1968.

211.1.1: Urban-Industrial Church Work.

211.1.5: Arthur E. Walmsley, Division of Christian Citizenship, general records, 1959–1963.

211.1.6: Arthur E. Walmsley, Division of Christian Citizenship, general records, 1964–1966.

211.1.10: Urban Crisis: Presiding Bishop's Call and Response of the Executive Council, Sept 1967.

211.1.30: JUP Policy Statements, 1962–1965.

211.1.31: Presiding Bishop, material prepared for, 1965–1967.

RG 238: John Shelby Spong/ John E. Hines Biography Project Papers.

238.2.37: Sermons, Prayers, and Meditations, 1966–1973.

238.2.38: Statements to the Executive Council and House of Bishops, 1966–1973.

238.2.39: Public Speeches and Interviews, 1961, 1965–1974.

RG 299: Daniel Corrigan Papers.

299.1.4: Correspondence—Vietnam War/Peace Movement, 1966–1970, 1972.

299.1.5: Correspondence—Women's Ordination, 1975–1989.

RG 315: Daisuke Kitagawa Papers.

315.6.7: Essays and addresses, 1945–c. 1963.

315.6.8: Drafts, working papers and notes, 1959–1967.

RG 322: John Maury Allin Papers.

322.3.2: Sermons and Addresses.

322.4.8: Presiding Bishop Election and Installation, 1973–1974.

322.5.2: Correspondence, 1940–1998.

AR 99.031: George H. "Jack" Woodard Papers.

99.031.2: General Convention—Sept 1976.

99.031.3: Joint Urban Advisory Committee.

99.031.4: Urban Industrial File.

99.031.6: Sermons.

358 BIBLIOGRAPHY AND SOURCES

99.031.6: Race.
99.031.7: Sermons.

AR 2003.095: George W. Barrett Papers, 1963–2000.
2003.095.1: Sermons and Addresses.
2003.095.1: Vietnam.
2003.095.1: Women's Ordination.
2003.095.2: Vietnam Journal.

AR 2003.101: Paul Moore, Jr. Papers.
2003.01.8: "War Diary–Letters 1942" [undated (1940s)].
2003.01.17: "Mission '72" [1972].
2003.01.23: Addresses—Diocese of New York, 1970s.
2003.01.24: Addresses—Jersey City, 1950s.
2003.01.25: "A City Parish" [undated (c. 1966)].
2003.01.26: Unsigned, "Parishfield: Working Paper on Frontier Evangelism No. 1" [undated (early 1950s)].
2003.01.26: Unsigned, "Parishfield: Working Paper on Frontier Evangelism No. 2" [undated (early 1950s)].
2003.01.26: Graduation address at St. Paul's School, Concord, NH, June 8, 1964.
2003.01.28: G. Paul Musselman to Paul Moore, August 12, 1958.

AR 2004.037: Records of the Conference on Church and City, 1959–1992.
2004.037: Conference, 1970–75: Form Letter from St Julian Simpkins, Mar 31, 1971.

Virginia

Alexandria: Virginia Theological Seminary, Bishop Payne Library, African American Episcopal Historical Collection.

RG A16: Thomas W. S. Logan, Sr. Papers.
A16.7.3.13: John Burgess correspondence.

RG A17: Walter Decoster Dennis Diocesan Papers.
A17, Series 3: 6, Box 40, Fol 10: Walter D. Dennis to Arthur Walmsley, Nov 9, 1959.
A17, Series 9, Box 130, Fol 9–10: Paul Moore to John Burgess, Feb 5, 1975.

RG A19: Walter Decoster Dennis Personal Papers.
A19, Series 1: Correspondence.
A19, Series X, Subseries 1: Writings, 1983–1990 and undated.
A19, Series X, Subseries 2: Sermons, 1960–2002 and undated.
A19, Series X2: Boxes 1–4.
A19, Items FIC, 2012.

RG A25: David Harris Papers.
A25.1. Fol. 11: "Autobiography" [1947].

RG A39: J. Carlton Hayden Papers.
A39, Series 01.03, Fol. 2: UBE Formation 1967–1968.

RG A57: H. Irving Mayson Papers.
A57.3: H. Irving Mayson, "Meeting of the Ad Hoc Committee concerned with racial inequalities existing in the Protestant Episcopal Church with the Presiding Bishop, April 18, 1967."

BIBLIOGRAPHY AND SOURCES   359

Arthur B. Williams, Jr., Oral History.
Oral History Interview with Arthur B. Williams, Jr., Oct 19–21, 2009, VTS, Alexandria, VA.
Interview conducted by Melana Nelson-Amaker.

Alexandria: Virginia Theological Seminary, Bishop Payne Library, Seminary Archives.

RG M24, M26: Charles P. Price Papers.
M24.Lit Com 1A: John Morris, "ESCRU: The Episcopal Society for Cultural and Racial Unity, 1959–1967" [1995].
M26: C. Kilmer Myers, "Notes for the 9/77 House of Bishops Meeting, On Homosexuality," Aug 22, 1979.
M26.2000.0003: Sermons.

RG M132: John Booty Papers.
M132.19: "The New Theologians and the Utopian View of Man" [undated (1960s)].

RG M159: John Shelby Spong Papers.
M159, 2001.0082: "And in Jesus Christ His Son, Our Lord" [1972].

RG M182: John T. Walker Papers.
M182.3: Misc Sermons.
M182.4: Misc Sermons and Columns.
M182.11: Misc urban ministry documents.
M182.63.28: John T. Walker, untitled lecture at Virginia Seminary, Jan 20, 1984.

Washington, DC

Episcopal Diocese of Washington Archives.

RG 5: Angus Dun Papers.
5.9.2: Correspondence.

RG 6: William F. Creighton Papers.
6.3.2: Urban Crisis Fund.
6.4.2: House of Bishops.
6.4.3: House of Bishops.
6.12.6: Philadelphia Ordinations.
6.13.1: Philadelphia Ordinations.
6.25.12: Sermons.
6.29.8: Paul Moore.
6.31.10: Civil Rights.
6.31.19: Standing Committee: General Correspondence, 1961–1965.

RG 7: John T. Walker Papers.
7.1.1: Biographical Statements.
7.3.1: Addresses, Essays.
7.3.5: Dean Francis B. Sayre, Jr.

Washington National Cathedral Archives.

RG 180: Francis B. Sayre, Jr. Papers.
18001.1.7: Miscellaneous Documents.
18002.1.1: Addresses, 1950s.

360 BIBLIOGRAPHY AND SOURCES

18002.3.1–2: Writings, 1961–1962.

18002.5.1: Sermons, 1950.

18002.8.1: Sermons and Correspondence, 1964.

18002.8.2: Francis B. Sayre, untitled sermon, Mar 1965.

18002.8.3: Francis B. Sayre, "Thoughts on Viet Nam at the New Year" [1966].

18003.1.6: Civil Rights.

18003.2.7: Industrial Chaplaincy, 1940s.

18003.2.8: Industrial Chaplaincy, 1940s.

18003.2.9: Industrial Chaplaincy, 1950s/1960s.

18003.3.3: Interracial Task Force, 1970.

18003.5.7: Press release of sermon delivered by Francis B. Sayre, June 27, 1971.

18004.2.7: John Burgess Correspondence.

18004.6.6: Francis B. Sayre, sermon after assassination of John F. Kennedy, Nov 24, 1963.

18004.6.7: Martin Luther King, Jr., 1968.

18004.8.13: John Walker, "Mission and Ministry of Diocese and Cathedral," Sept 13, 1977.

18004.13.1: Henry Knox Sherrill to Francis B. Sayre, Dec 12, 1945.

National Cathedral Oral History Project.
Oral History Interview with Francis B. Sayre, Jr., Nov 10, 2000, Martha's Vineyard, MA. Interview conducted by Robert Becker.

C. Personal Papers

1. John V. Butler Papers.
(Courtesy of Janet B. Haugaard, St. Mary's City, MD, Dec 2014.)

John V. Butler, "My Life and Times at Trinity and Before" [undated (1972)].
Warren H. Turner to Ruth Butler, Sept 27, 1983.
Warren H. Turner to Janet B. Haugaard, Jan 17, 1984.

2. James Parks Morton Papers.
(Courtesy of the late James Parks Morton, New York, NY, Dec 2014.)

"The Third Day: Jersey City" [undated (c. 2014)].
"Day 4: Programs for the Urban Plunge in New York and Chicago" [undated (c. 2014)].

3. Scott I. Paradise Papers.
(Courtesy of Jeanne Paradise, Bedford, MA, Jan 2015.)

"The Real Religion of the Manager: The Logic of His Beliefs" [1962].
"Keynote Address at S.E.A.S" [1973].
"Response to the Boston Affirmations" [1976].
"Paradise Saga" [2007].

Interviews with Scott I. Paradise by Charles Weiner, Apr–Nov 1992.
Session 1: Apr 29, 1992.
Session 2, Part 1: May 21, 1992.

Session 3, Part 2: Oct 6, 1992.
Session 4, Part 1: Nov 5, 1992.

4. **Arthur E. Walmsley Papers.**
   (Courtesy of the late Arthur E. Walmsley, Concord, NH, Jan 2015.)

   "Second Meditation: Looking Ahead," delivered to the Diocese of Vermont [2012].

5. **Charles V. Willie Papers.**
   (Courtesy of Charles V. Willie, Concord, MA, Jan 2015.)

   Charles V. Willie to John M. Allin, Aug 6, 1974.
   "1974—The Year the Episcopal Church Failed" [1975].

6. **Francis O. Ayres Papers.**
   (Courtesy of Mimi Ayres Sanderson, London, Apr 2015.)

   Francis O. Ayres to parishioners on active service [undated (1944)].
   "Revolution or Revolutionary Action?" [1968].

7. **Sara C. Winter, Parishfield Oral Histories.**
   (Courtesy of Sara C. Winter, New York, Dec 2014.)

   Jane Barney Interview—Tape 1 [undated (1994/1995)].
   Tony Stoneburner Interview [undated (1994/1995)].
   Mary White Interview—Tape One [Mar 10, 1995].
   Mary White Interview—Tape Two [Mar 10, 1995].
   Robert DeWitt Interview—Tape One [undated (1994/1995)].

Index

For the benefit of digital users, indexed terms that span two pages (e.g., 52–53) may, on occasion, appear on only one of those pages.

African Americans, Episcopal
  bishops, 37–38, 111–12, 148–49, 168–69, 207–8, 225–26, 229–30, 241–42, 284n.151
  Black Manifesto, 185–88, 191–93
  discrimination against, 37–39, 50–52, 55–56, 75–76, 119–20, 146–49, 166–67, 211, 275n.126, 294–95n.163
  social standing, 37–39, 76–77, 146–47, 167, 186, 235–36, 244, 250–51, 319n.266
  women's ordination, 225–26, 229–30, 238–39
  See also Black Caucus movement; Black Power movement; National Committee of Negro (Black) Churchmen; Union of Black Clergy and Laymen (UBCL)
Alinsky, Saul, 109–10
Allen, Michael, 33–34, 102–3, 113–14, 145–46, 187–88, 197
Allin, John Maury, 116–17, 122–23, 169–70, 217–20, 222–23
  as presiding bishop, 223–24, 226–28, 230–31, 240–43
All Saints' Church, San Francisco, 144–45, 293–94n.145
Anglican Communion, 3–4, 91–92, 140, 254n.23
Anglo-Catholicism, 13–16, 41–42, 45–48, 71–72, 209–10, 222–23
anglophilia, 3–4, 6
anti-institutionalism, 7, 100–3, 111, 117–18, 131–32, 136–39, 143, 152–54, 181–82, 198–99, 214–15, 223–24

anti-war movement, 6–7, 140–42, 150–51, 170–73, 197–98, 202–3, 210–11, 292n.121
Arnold, Morris F., 75, 111–12
authority, episcopal, 26–29, 35–36, 89, 100, 143, 165, 202, 204–5, 214–15, 223–24, 231, 240–41, 251–52
  See also Episcopacy; "Episcopal Principle"; presiding bishop, office of
Ayres, Florence, 57–58, 60
Ayres, Francis O., Jr., 18–19, 57–62, 83–85, 138–39, 153–54

Barney, Jane (née Lockwood), 58–59, 83–85, 138–39, 153–54, 215–16
Barney, Roger, 83–85, 105–6, 138–39
Barrett, Ellen M., 239–40
Barrett, George W., 151–52, 192–93, 231, 237–38
Barth, Karl, 29, 62–64
Bayne, Stephen F., Jr., 13–14, 30–31, 56–57, 76–77, 89–92, 113–14, 120, 121–22, 163–64, 178–80, 183–84, 193–94, 204–5, 309n.32
  The Optional God (1953), 30–31
  Theological Freedom and Social Responsibility (1967), 163–65, 204–5
Benedict, Donald, 45–46, 109–10
Berger, Peter, 233–34, 247–48, 264n.122
  "An Appeal for Theological Affirmation" (1975), 233–35
Betts, Darby, 143
Black Caucus Movement, 147–50, 187–88, 197

364 INDEX

Black Economic Development Conference (BEDC), 183–86, 187–90
Black Manifesto (1969), 183–93, 196–97, 304n.181
Black Power movement, 39–40, 134–35, 146–48, 150–51, 155–57, 167, 173, 197–98, 225–26
Blanchard, Roger, 24–25, 26–27, 109, 114–15, 206–7
Block, Karl Morgan, 12–13
Bloy, Caroline *née* Kuhn, 61–62
Bloy, Myron B., Jr., 61–62, 271n.43, 318n.251
Bonhoeffer, Dietrich, 58–59, 62, 83–84, 104–6, 136–37, 277nn.172–73, 282n.107
Life Together (1939), 62, 271n.45
Book of Common Prayer, 59, 221–23, 314n.158
Booth, William H., 157–58
Booty, John, 137–38
Boston Industrial Mission (BIM), 139–40, 232–33, 234
"Boston Affirmations" (1976), 234–35
Boyd, Malcolm, 100–3, 197–98, 251, 281–82n.92
Braden, Anne, 97–98, 280n.59
Brill, Earl H., 152, 244
Brown, H. Rap, 155–56
Brown, Robert, 191–92, 204–5
Brown v. Board of Education (1954), 52–53, 98–99
Bundy, McGeorge, 111–12, 140–41
Burgess, John M., 37–39, 50, 111–12, 148–49, 167, 174–75, 178, 195–96, 207–8, 222–23, 224–26, 227–28, 229–30, 284n.151, 319n.266
Butler, John V., 13–14, 46–47, 89–90, 100, 124–26, 135–36, 199, 202–3, 235–36

Cadigan, George, 131–32, 278n.5
California, diocese of, 87–88, 143–44, 171–72, 244–45
Campbell, Wilburn C., 214–15
campus ministry, 24–25, 101–2, 133, 141–42, 206–7, 223
Carpenter, Charles C.J., 16, 123–25

Carr, Oscar C., Jr., 97–98, 193–94, 205–7, 212–13, 306n.237
Carter, Junius F., Jr., 191–92
Carter, W. Hodding, III, 116
Casserley, J.V. Langmead, 78–79, 164
catholicity, 1–2, 32–33, 55–56, 64–65, 71–72, 91–92, 140, 143–44, 251–52
Caution, Tollie L., Sr., 38, 94–95, 166–68, 265n.152, 299n.81
Chandler, Edward, 47–48
Chapman, William D., 133
Cheek, Alison, 228–29, 230–31
Christ Church, Cambridge, MA, 19, 197, 293–94n.145, 307n.261
Christ Church Cathedral, Indianapolis, 73–74
Christ Church Cranbrook, Bloomfield Hills, MI, 59, 66–67, 112–13, 184–85, 270n.30
Christian education, 24–25, 61–62, 71–72, 133–34, 212–13, 223
Christian realism, 10, 257n.4
Christian socialism, 4–5, 14–15, 34
Christian social relations, 13–14, 32, 48, 91, 93–94, 106–7, 131, 161, 233–35
Church and City Conference, 75, 106, 216–17, 274n.123
Church Association for the Advancement of the Interests of Labor (CAIL), 4
Church League for Industrial Democracy (CLID), 14–16, 34, 215–16
See also Episcopal League for Social Action (ELSA)
churchmanship, 2–3, 12, 13–14, 46–47, 161–62, 267n.202
Church of England, 1–2, 3–4, 13, 16, 98–99, 221
Church of the Advocate, Philadelphia, 112–13, 133–34, 225–26
Church of the Messiah, Woods Hole, MA, 229–30
Church's Teaching Series, 24–25, 48–49, 244
civil disobedience, 94–96, 119–20, 123–24, 128, 170–73, 280n.49
See also anti-war movement; civil rights movement

INDEX 365

civil rights movement
clergy involvement, 6–7, 77, 94–96, 97–
98, 113–16, 122–25, 127–28, 129
Episcopal policies, 50–51, 77–78, 95–97,
113–15, 116–17, 119–20, 122–23
Freedom Summer (1964), 115–
17, 125–26
Northern activists, 74–75, 77, 95–96,
97–98, 115–17, 124–26, 147–
48, 219–20
Selma marches (1965), 123–25
white Southerners, 26, 40, 50–52, 77,
97–98, 115–17, 120, 122–24, 193–
94, 213, 219–20
See also civil disobedience
class, social, 1–2, 5–7, 20, 29, 60–61, 69–
70, 73–75, 115–16, 129–30, 173–74
Episcopal identity, 31–33, 64–65, 90–91,
190, 211–12, 216–17, 264n.122
racial dynamics, 37–39, 76–77, 146–47,
167, 174–75, 176, 226, 235–36,
242–44, 302n.134
working class, 4–5, 22–24, 108–9, 202–
3, 250
See also elitism, Episcopal;
privilege, social
Clergy and Laymen Concerned About
Vietnam (CALCAV), 171–
72, 197–98
Clergy, Episcopal
post-war, 6–9, 28–29, 32–33, 38, 45–46,
53–56, 140–41, 182–83, 241, 247–
48, 249
training, 25–26, 85–87, 109–11,
162–63
vocation, 33–34, 55–56, 67–70, 109
wartime experience, 6–7, 18–21, 26–27,
140–41, 256n.48
Coalition E, 216–17
Coburn, John B., 43–44, 86–88, 116–17,
126–27, 128, 181–83, 200–2, 217,
220, 240–41
president of the House of Deputies,
161–62, 183–84, 188–90, 191, 193–
94, 196–97, 238
Cole, Ned C., Jr., 111–12, 223–24,
226–27
Coleman, Tom, 126–27

Committee of Concern,
Mississippi, 116–17
communism, 29, 34–37, 53, 83–84,
115–16, 205, 259–60n.41,
265n.146
Cook, Ralph, 102–3
Cooper, Austin R., 167–68
Corrigan, Daniel, 106, 107–9, 114,
143, 166–68, 197–98, 223–24,
226, 237–38
counterculture, 7, 100–1, 141–43, 144–47,
155, 180–81, 186, 188, 202–4, 212–
13, 293–94n.145
Cox, Harvey, 83–84, 136–37
The Secular City (1965), 136–37
Craine, John, 73–75
Creighton, William F., 111–12, 114, 117–
18, 123–24, 143, 230–31, 238–39,
318n.234
"Culture-Protestantism," 29–31

Daniels, Jonathan M., 126–27, 289n.43
Day, Peter M., 96–97, 152–53
De Diétrich, Suzanne, 59–62
Deloria, Vine, Jr., 176–77, 302n.136
Delta Ministry, Mississippi, 116–
17, 122–23
DeMille, George E., 32
demographics, Episcopal, 4–5, 32, 90–91,
244, 250, 251–52, 322n.339
numerical decline, 127–28, 180, 247–48,
303n.160
Dennis, Walter D., 38, 94–95, 100, 167–68,
186, 235–36
Detroit Industrial Mission (DIM), 64, 66–
69, 88, 103–6, 273n.88
Detroit News, 184–85
DeWitt, Robert L., 59, 66–68, 85, 241
bishop of Pennsylvania, 112–14, 143,
170–71, 172–74, 180–81, 185–86,
215–16, 224–25
Church and Society initiative, 215–
16, 231–32
*Struggling with the System, Probing
Alternatives* (1976), 231–32
women's ordination, 209, 223–24, 226–
27, 237–38
DeWolfe, James, 35–36, 265n.146

366 INDEX

Donegan, Horace, 18, 53, 64–65, 73, 100, 113–14, 135–36, 199, 202, 211, 235–36
Dozier, Verna, 38–39
Dun, Angus, 17–18, 26–27, 49–50, 111–12, 142–43, 259n.40

East Harlem Protestant Parish (EHPP), 45–46, 79–81, 82–83, 110–11, 275n.144
Ecumenism, 3–4, 29, 45–47, 68–69, 79–81, 109–11, 116–17, 133, 209–10, 221
Edwards, Tom Turney, 152
elitism, Episcopal, 2–3, 4–6, 31–33, 40, 64–65, 73–74, 90–92, 110–11, 146, 178, 211–12, 247–48, 250
See also class, social; privilege, social
Ellul, Jacques, 82–84
The Presence of the Kingdom (1948), 82–83
Ellwood, Robert S., 55–56
empowerment, 70–71, 115–16, 129–36, 146–48, 154, 157–61, 169–70, 173, 175–76, 177–78, 183–84, 188–89, 197, 215, 217, 241–42
Emrich, Richard, 39–40, 57–58, 63–64, 66–67, 85, 101–2, 138–39, 171–72, 184–86, 203–4, 214
episcopacy, 1–2, 35–36, 87–88, 111, 143–44, 171–73, 211
See also authority; "Episcopal Principle"; presiding bishop, office of
Episcopal Church Center, 106–7, 170, 176–77, 183, 206–7
Episcopal Church Foundation (ECF), 28–29, 242–43, 263n.107
Episcopal Church Women (ECW), 160, 217–18, 297n.22
Episcopal Covenant Parish, Houston, TX, 108–9
Episcopal Divinity School (EDS), 229–30
See also Episcopal Theological School (ETS)
Episcopal Fellowship of Urban Workers, 48
Episcopal League for Social Action (ELSA), 34
See also Church League for Industrial Democracy (CLID)

Episcopal Peace Fellowship (EPF), 197–98, 216–17
"Episcopal Principle," 114, 116–17, 122–24, 169–70
See also authority, episcopal; Episcopacy; presiding bishop, office of
Episcopal Society for Cultural and Racial Unity (ESCRU), 39–40, 94–95, 97, 146–48
"Prayer Pilgrimage" (1961), 95–96, 101–2
Episcopal Theological School (ETS), 10, 26, 86–87, 126–27, 142–43, 181–82, 208–9
See also Episcopal Divinity School (EDS)
Episcopal Theological Seminary of the Southwest (ETSS), 25–26, 63–64, 85–86, 208–9, 277n.188
Episcopal Women's Caucus (EWC), 209, 217–18
establishment, religious, 1–2, 3–4, 32–33, 98–99
establishmentarianism, 3–4, 9, 63–64, 78–79, 98–99, 128, 151–52, 158, 170–71, 211–12, 215, 231–32, 244, 247–48, 249, 251–52, 323n.19
Executive Council, 106–7, 157–58, 165–66, 178–79, 206–7, 212–13, 215, 216–17, 249
ethical investments, 207
race relations, 116–17, 122–23, 148–49, 166, 170, 176–77, 183–84, 188–90, 214–15
See also National Council

Faramelli, Norman, 232–33, 234
Technethics: Christian Mission in an Age of Technology (1971), 232–33
Farrell, Albion, 166
feminism, 186–87, 208–9, 214, 225–26, 238–39
Fletcher, Joseph, 14–15, 22–23, 34, 83–84, 137–38, 263n.117
Ford, Gerald, 236–37
Forman, James, 183, 186

INDEX   367

Gallup, Grant, 70
Garcia, David, 187–88, 215–16
General Convention
 1940, 16
 1943, 16, 27–28
 1946, 46–47
 1949, 29–30, 48, 50–51
 1952, 48, 55–56
 1955, 55–56, 123–24
 1958, 77–78, 89
 1961, 95–96, 106–7
 1964, 116–17, 118–20, 160
 1967, 158–64, 165–66, 221, 249
 1969 (Special GC II), 183–84, 189–98,
  204, 249, 305n.216
 1970, 205–7, 208–9
 1973, 214, 216–18, 313n.143
 1976, 217–18, 237–38, 242–43
 1979, 222–23, 245–46
General Convention Special Program
  (GCSP), 158–61, 166, 169–70,
  178, 183–84, 188–90, 201–2,
  205–7, 212–13, 214–15, 216–
  17, 297nn.30–31, 302n.144,
  313n.136
 "An Open Letter to the Presiding
  Bishop" (1967), 159–60
 local involvement, 165–66, 167–69,
  175–76, 177–78, 182, 183–84,
  188–89, 215
 Screening and Review Committee, 176–
  77, 205–6, 214–15
General Theological Seminary (GTS), 13,
  26, 40–41, 198–99, 204
Gessell, John M., 97
Gilbert, Charles K., 41–43, 64–65
Gladden, Washington, 10–11
Goldwater, Barry, 117–18, 119–20
Grace Church Van Vorst, Jersey City, 42–
  43, 44–46, 47–48, 73–74, 107–8,
  133–34, 244–45, 266n.182
Gracie, David M., 170–74, 215–16
Gray, Duncan M. Jr., 51–52, 97–99, 222–
  23, 306n.237
Great Depression, the, 12, 13–14, 18, 24–
  25, 26–27, 89–90, 145–46
Griffiss, James, 29
Griswold, Frank, 221–22

Guinan, James B., 138–39
Gusweller, James, 72–73, 132–33
Gutmann, Reinhart B., 130–31

Hamilton, William, 136–37, 138
Harris, David, 37–38
Harris, Leon, 144–45, 293–94n.145
Harvard University, 127–28, 141–42,
  203–4
Herberg, Will, 29–30, 83–84
Heuss, John, 47–48, 111
Heyward, Carter, 217–18, 220, 226, 228–
  31, 237–38
Hiatt, Suzanne R., 209, 217–18, 229–31
Hines, John E., 12–13, 89, 92–93, 120,
  249, 251
 bishop of Texas, 25–26, 31, 85–86, 108–
  9, 121–22
 GCSP, 158–60, 165–66, 167–68,
  169–70, 178–80, 201–2, 205, 214–
  15, 216–17
 presiding bishop, 121–24, 131–32, 142–
  43, 148–49, 154, 163–64, 176–77,
  200, 201–2, 204, 206–7, 214–17,
  219–20, 242–43, 308n.10
 race relations, 77–78, 121–22, 124, 156–
  58, 190–91, 196–97
 Vietnam, 150–51, 295n.170
Holmes, Urban T., 234–35
Hood, Robert, 244
House of Bishops, 16, 24–25, 53, 77–78,
  89, 118, 120, 133–34, 162, 181–82,
  192–93, 217, 228–29
 "A Call for Unity" (1970), 205
 "Committee of Nine," 46–47,
  267n.202
 meetings
  Chicago (1974), 226–29
  New Orleans (1972), 214
  Port St. Lucie, FL (1977), 240–41
  Wheeling, WV (1966), 142–43,
   293n.129, 293n.131, 293n.135
 "A Statement of Conscience" (1977),
  240–41, 321n.307
 "Toward Tomorrow" (1979), 245–46
 women's ordination, 208–10, 214,
  217–18, 226–28, 230–31, 237–
  38, 240–41

368 INDEX

House of Deputies, 16, 46–47, 118–20, 161–
62, 167, 191–92, 195–96, 205–6, 217
civil rights, 50–51, 77–78, 119–20
Vietnam, 162
women's ordination, 217–18, 238
Huntington, William Reed, 3–4

identity politics, 248–49, 250–51
Incarnation, the, 4, 80, 81–83, 98–99, 132–
33, 243–44
inclusivity, 32–33, 69–70, 91, 159–60, 248–
49, 250–52
Indianapolis Plan, 73–75
Industrial Areas Foundation
(IAF), 109–10
industrial mission, 20–25, 36–37, 48–49,
64–69, 88, 103–6, 176, 232–33
Integrity (organization), 239–40
Iona Community (Scotland), 57–
58, 65–66

Johnson, John Howard, 75–76
Johnson, Lyndon B., 117–18, 131,
201–2
Joint Urban Program (JUP), 106–11, 131–
32, 133–34, 138–39, 149–50, 167,
283n.129
Church in Metropolis (journal), 108–9
"Metabagdad" Conferences, 107–9,
120, 133
Urban Pilot Diocese Program,
109, 131–32

Kean, Charles, 46–47
Kennedy, John F., 99–100, 111–12
Kenney, W. Murray, 56–57, 197,
293–94n.145
Kent State University, 202
Kenyatta, Muhammad, 185–86, 191,
305–6n.222
King, Martin Luther, Jr., 123–24, 174–75,
301n.124, 301n.127
"Letter from Birmingham Jail"
(1963), 124
Kitagawa, Daisuke, 140
Knox, John, 164–65
Kraemer, Hendrick, 59–60, 83–84
Krumm, John, 194–95

laity, Episcopal
conservatism, 8, 32–34, 72–73, 77–78,
118–20, 129–30, 162, 178–79, 249
ministry, 24–25, 56–58, 88, 182–83, 241
social responsibility, 48–49, 91, 94, 193–
94, 213, 215
Lambeth Conference, 3–4, 91–92, 182–83,
254n.23
Lawrence, Charles R., 167, 299n.75,
306n.224
Lawrence, W. Appleton, 13–14, 26–
27, 79–80
Lea, William, 194–95, 206–7
Lee, Edward, 170–71
Lee, Robert, 103
Lichtenberger, Arthur, 43–44, 48, 53, 56–
57, 89–91, 92–93, 94, 95–96, 113–
14, 118, 119, 120, 122–23, 247
"Whitsuntide Message to the Church"
(1963), 113–14, 285n.165
Lilly, Eli, 74–75
Lindsay, John V., 111–12, 157–58, 202
liturgy, 188, 197, 221–23, 307n.259
Living Church, The, 15–16, 152–53

mainline Protestantism, 3, 6–7, 22–23, 29–
31, 56–57, 63–64, 69–70, 129–30,
202–3, 204–5, 223, 233–34, 247,
248–49, 256n.43
decline, 8, 127–28, 180–81, 200
post-war revival, 24–25, 28, 29
progressivism, 53, 96–97, 103, 106–7,
109–10, 113–14, 124–25, 131
See also "Culture-Protestantism";
Protestant establishment
March on Washington (1963), 114–15
Marshall, Thurgood, 76–77, 119–
20, 186–87
Martin, Richard B., 55–56, 168–69, 207–8
"Mass for Peace" (1969), 197–98
McAllister, Gerald, 191–92
McCarthy, Joseph, 53
McGhee, Coleman, 222–23
McManis, Lester, 133–34
*Handbook on Christian Education in the
Inner City* (1966), 133–34
Melish, William Howard, 36–37
Menuez, D. Barry, 109–10, 169, 300n.89

INDEX   369

Michigan, diocese of, 39–40, 57–58, 62–
    64, 84–85, 101–2, 171–72, 184–85,
    203–4, 222–23
Military, American, 5–7, 18–19, 30–31,
    150–52, 260n.47
Mind Garage (rock band), 188, 305n.208
Minnis, Joseph, 100–1
Modeste, Leon, 156–57, 165–66, 167–71,
    176–78, 183–84, 201–2, 206–7,
    299n.81
Moore, Jenny, 40–43, 44–45, 47–48, 73–
    75, 199, 235–36, 268n.209
Moore, Paul, Jr., 20–21, 40–45, 47–48, 73–
    75, 100–2, 103, 106–9, 164, 198–
    99, 219–20, 244–45, 251, 285n.155
  bishop of New York, 202, 211, 235–
    37, 242–43
  The Church Reclaims the City
    (1964), 103
  civil rights, 115–17, 122–23, 129,
    156, 175–76
  homosexuality, 239–41, 321n.302
  suffragan of Washington, 111–13, 119–
    20, 129, 143, 180–81
  Vietnam, 140–41, 197–98, 210–11
  women's ordination, 217–18, 220, 223–
    24, 226–29, 238
Morehouse, Clifford, 50–51, 119–
    20, 183–84
Morley, Anthony, 131–33, 152
Morris, John B., 39–40, 94–95, 147–48
Morrison, Robert, 171–72
Morton, James Parks, 47–48, 103, 107–9,
    110–11, 235–36, 237
Morton, Pamela, 47–48
Mosley, J. Brooke, 34, 183
Mullin, Robert Bruce, 136
Murray, George, 160, 177–78
Murray, Pauli, 186–88, 195–96, 197, 220,
    230–31, 238–40
Musselman, G. Paul, 23, 48–49, 64–
    65, 69–70
"Mutual Responsibility and
    Interdependence in the Body of
    Christ" (MRI), 91–92
Myers, C. Kilmer, 41–43, 45–48, 70–72,
    92–93, 103, 109–13, 132–33, 209–
    10, 244–45, 266n.182, 276n.151

Baptized into the One Church (1958), 71–72
Behold the Church (1958), 71–72
bishop of California, 143–45, 204–5,
    217, 234
civil rights, 94–96, 124–25, 146–47
GCSP, 160, 169–70
Light the Dark Streets (1957), 70–71
Vietnam, 150–51, 171–72, 197–98

National Cathedral, Washington, D.C.,
    5–6, 40, 49–50, 99–100, 121, 149,
    174–75, 197–98, 237, 238–39, 241–
    42, 301n.127
national church ideal, 3–4, 32–33, 247–48
National Committee of Negro (Black)
    Churchmen, 146, 192–93,
    294n.153
National Congress of American
    Indians, 176–77
National Council, 27–28, 48–49, 92–94,
    106–9, 279n.32
  race relations, 38, 77, 94–95
  social relations survey, 32–33
  See also Executive Council
National Council of Churches (NCC), 29,
    92–93, 115–17, 122–23, 151–52
National Society for the Parents of Flower
    Children, 145–46
Native Americans, Episcopal, 176–77
Neuhaus, Richard John, 233–35
  "An Appeal for Theological Affirmation"
    (1975), 233–35
New Deal, the, 6, 14
New York City, 73, 79–80, 156–57, 182–83,
    202–3, 235–37
New York, diocese of, 4, 64–65, 135–36,
    171–72, 199, 211, 213
New York Times, 190, 196–97, 202–
    3, 239–40
Niebuhr, H. Richard, 1, 29
  Christ and Culture (1951), 29
Niebuhr, Reinhold, 10, 12–13, 17–18,
    40, 43–44
  Moral Man and Immoral Society
    (1932), 10
Nixon, Richard, 202–3, 223–24
noblesse oblige, 4–5, 7, 41–42, 134–35
Norton, Perry L., 107–8

370 INDEX

Ogilby, Lyman, 224–25, 316n.187
Operation Connection (OC), 175–76

Paradise, Scott I., 65–70, 103–6, 117–18, 139–40, 232–33, 234–35, 247, 248–49, 282n.107, 318n.251
Pardue, Austin, 23–24, 48, 176, 182–83
Parishfield community (Michigan), 57–64, 83–85, 88, 105–6, 137–39, 153–54, 247, 270n.37
Parish Life Conferences, 24–25
parochial ministry, 13–14, 23–24, 33–34, 35–36, 52, 55–56, 67–68, 69–70, 85–86, 103, 109, 132–33, 152, 199
pastoral care, 1–2, 41–42, 52, 88, 98–99, 180, 221–22, 233–35
Pegram, Robert, 41–43, 47–48, 244–45
Pelham Joseph A., 191–92, 243–44
Pennsylvania, diocese of, 112–13, 170–71, 172–74, 185–86, 209, 215–16, 224–25
Pepper, Almon R., 48–49
Philadelphia ordinations (1974), 223–29, 316n.198, 316n.200
Pike, James A., 40, 51–52, 53, 56, 64–65, 87–88, 100, 102–3, 113–14, 119–20, 136, 142–44, 163–64, 165, 219–20, 247, 266n.166, 291n.84, 293n.129
    A Time for Christian Candor (1964), 136
Pittenger, Norman, 26, 31–32, 46–47, 181–82
Potter, Henry Codman, 4
Potter, Robert S., 175–76, 215–16
Powell, Noble, 114, 123–24
Presbyterian Church, 46–47, 68–69, 257n.62
presiding bishop, office of, 27–29, 55–56, 89, 121–24
    See also authority, episcopal; "Episcopal Principle"
Price, Charles P., 127–28, 136, 140–42, 150–51, 200–1, 221–23, 241
Primo, Quentin E., 148–49
privilege, social, 4–5, 7, 20, 38–39, 49–50, 60, 65–66, 73–74, 78–79, 81–82, 159, 178, 186–87, 202–3, 207, 211, 214–15, 219–20, 231–32, 237
    See also class, social; elitism, Episcopal

progressives, Episcopal, 7–9, 15–16, 32–33, 34, 77, 111–12, 124–25, 128, 129–30, 136, 152–53, 208–9, 215–17, 231–32, 247, 248–49
prophecy
    biblical precedents, 7–8, 130–31, 152–53, 219–20
    Christian servanthood, 129–31
    institutional, 7–8, 78–79, 88, 112–13, 120, 143, 152–53, 172–73, 219–20, 226, 249–50, 251–52
    social critique, 53–54, 56, 98–100, 117–18, 131–32, 170–71, 248–49
Protestant establishment, 3, 6–7, 8, 28–29, 128, 211–12, 251
    See also mainline Protestantism
Purnell, John, 96–97
Pusey, Nathan M., 86–87, 127–28, 141–43, 162–63, 203–4, 289n.45
    Ministry for Tomorrow (1967), 162–63

Quarterman, George, 92–93
Quin, Clinton, 55–56, 77–78

race riots (1967), 155–57
radical theology, 136–38, 164–65, 291n.89
Ramos, José Antonio, 207–8, 226
Rauschenbusch, Walter, 10–11
    Christianity and the Social Crisis (1907), 10–11
Reagan, Ronald, 247, 249
Red Scare, 36–37, 53, 269n.233
"religionless Christianity," 83–84, 104–6, 136–37, 138–39, 277n.172, 282n.107
    See also Bonhoeffer, Dietrich
Richards, David E., 178–79
Righter, Walter, 23–24
Robinson, John A.T., 136, 164, 218–19, 291n.84
    Honest to God (1963), 136
Rochester, diocese of, 192–93, 206–7
Rodman, Edward, 218–19, 243–44, 313–14n.148
Roosevelt, Franklin D., 6, 14, 19

INDEX   371

Sayre, Francis B., Jr., 18–20, 26–27, 36–37, 53
  civil rights, 49–50, 98–99, 124–25
  dean of National Cathedral, 98–100, 117–18, 121, 149, 174–75, 200–1, 237, 241–42, 251, 286n.194, 301n.127
  industrial chaplaincy, 20–23, 64, 65–67
  Vietnam, 140–41, 150–51, 197–98, 210–11
Sayre, Harriet, 49–50
Scarlett, William, 10–13, 16–18, 36–37, 53–54, 258n.12
  A Better World for All Peoples (1943), 16
  Christianity Takes a Stand (1946), 17–18
Scudder, Vida Dutton, 14–16, 53–54, 259n.35
Seabury Caucus, 215–16
Seabury Series (education program), 24–25, 61–62
secularity, 7–8, 30–31, 70–71, 83–84, 104–6, 136–37, 138–39, 164–65, 175–76, 188–89, 214, 231, 234–35, 248–49
seminarians, 14–15, 26, 51–52, 85–86, 142–43, 181–82, 198–99, 221–22, 277n.188
Sewanee (University of the South), 26, 50–52, 97
Sherrill, Henry Knox, 21–22, 26–30, 43–44, 46–47, 55–56, 89, 92–93, 123–24, 242–43
Simcox, Carroll E., 152–53, 161, 178–79
Sims, Bennett, 227–28
situationism, 137–38
slum priests, 41–42, 65–66, 132–33
Snow, John, 147–48, 180–81, 221–22
Social Gospel movement, 4–6, 10–11, 14–15, 16–17, 34, 258n.6
Society for the Promotion of Industrial Mission (SPIM), 23–24, 48
Spofford, William B., Jr., 34
Spofford, William B., Sr., 15–16, 28, 31, 34, 51–52, 95–96, 103, 119–20, 141–42, 215–16, 231–32, 264n.137
Spong, John Shelby, 218–19, 244, 314n.149
Stark, Leland, 155, 297n.24
St. James's Church, Manhattan, 18, 182–83

St. John's Church, Waterbury, CT, 18–19
St. John the Divine, Cathedral of, Manhattan, 100, 202, 210–11, 220, 235–37
St. Mark's Church in-the-Bowery, Manhattan, 33–34, 102–3, 145–46, 187–88, 195–96, 197, 307n.259
St. Matthew and St. Timothy, Church of, Manhattan, 72–73
St. Peter's Church, Manhattan, 41–42
St. Peter's Church, Oxford, MS, 97–98, 306n.237
St. Philip's Church, Manhattan, 76–77, 119–20, 133–34, 146, 167–69
St. Stephen and the Incarnation, Church of, Washington, 47–48, 133–34, 156, 175–76, 230–31
Stoneburner, Tony, 58–59
Stringfellow, William, 30–31, 73, 79–84, 103, 119–20, 122–23, 125–26, 180–81, 200, 207, 211–12, 215–16, 226–28, 230–31, 240–41, 247, 251, 275n.144, 296n.11, 321n.307
  My People Is the Enemy (1964), 82–83
  "Statement of Conscience" (1964), 119–20
Student Nonviolent Coordinating Committee (SNCC), 115–16, 129, 155, 183
suburbanism, 41–42, 53–54, 69–70, 75–76, 91, 273n.93, 273n.96
Sweet, Leonard, 96–97

Tarplee, Cornelius C., 77–78, 94–95
Taylor, Don, 244
Temple, William, 12, 16, 259n.35
Texas, diocese of, 31, 50–51, 55–56, 108–9, 121–22
To Comfort or to Challenge (1967), 234–35
Trinity Church, Arlington, NJ, 34–35
Trinity Church, St. Louis, 13, 56–57, 131–32
Trinity Parish, New York, 47–48, 70, 135–36, 202–3
two-martini lunch, 112–13
Tyson, Ruel, 109

372 INDEX

Union of Black Clergy and Laymen of the Episcopal Church (UBCL), 167–68, 185–86, 188–89, 191–92, 205, 216–17, 218–19, 299n.79, 299n.81

Urban Bishops Coalition (UBC), 242–44, 322n.327

urban mission, 4, 41–46, 47–49, 70–75, 91, 106, 132–35, 173–74, 242–45

Urban Mission Priests group, 45–46, 48, 70, 88, 247

Urban Training Center for Christian Mission (UTC), 109–11

Van Buren, Anne, 62–64

Van Buren, Paul M., 62–64, 67–68, 85–86, 104–6, 136–37, 138

  The Secular Meaning of the Gospel (1963), 104–5

Vance, Cyrus, 111–12, 140–41

Venture in Mission (VIM), 242–44

Vietnam War, 140–42, 150–52, 202–3, 210–11

  Episcopal divisions, 162, 170–73, 181–82, 197–98

Virginia Theological Seminary (VTS), 12, 39–40, 208–9

Vogel, Arthur, 164, 226–27

Von Hoffmann, Nicholas, 174–75

Walker, John T., 39–40, 149–50, 207–8, 225–26, 241–44

Walmsley, Arthur, 56–57, 77, 91, 93–95, 131–32, 152, 156–57, 182–83, 200–1, 240–41

War on Poverty, the, 131, 133–34

Warren, Austin, 203–4

Washburn, Benjamin, 34–36, 42–44

Washington, diocese of, 37–38, 47–48, 112–13, 123–24, 129, 145–46, 207–8, 231, 241–42

Washington, Paul M., 112–13, 185–86, 191, 193, 225–26

Washington Post, 129, 156, 237

Weber, William M., 34–36, 43–44, 115–16

Wedel, Cynthia, 119, 162

Welles, Edward R., 90–91, 160, 223–24, 226

Wendt, William A., 20–21, 47–48, 70, 156, 175–76, 230–31, 318n.234

Weston, M. Moran, 76–77, 118, 156, 168–69, 238–39

Wetmore, Stuart, 202, 227–28

White, Hugh C., Jr., 59, 60–61, 64–65, 66–68, 106, 215–16, 231–32, 243–44

White, Mary, 59, 60–61, 64

Wickham, E.R., 21–22, 65–67, 83–84, 106, 272n.70

Williams, Arthur B., 146–47

Willie, Charles V., 149–50, 161, 170, 178, 183–84, 189–90, 192–93, 201–2, 205–6, 225–26, 227–28, 317n.211

Winckley, Edward, 177–78

Winter, Blair, 57–58, 60

Winter, Gibson, 18–19, 57–62, 64, 66–67, 69–70, 91, 103, 109–11, 129–30, 136–37, 138

  Metropolis as the New Creation (1963), 136–37

  The Suburban Captivity of the Churches (1961), 69–70

Winter, Sara, 60

Witness, The, 15–16, 31, 215–16, 231–32

Witte, Walter, 179–80

Wittkofski, Joseph, 23–24, 176, 261n.75

Wolf, William, 142–43, 209–10

women, Episcopal

  experimental ministries, 47–48, 60, 268n.209, 270n.37

  marginalization, 89–90, 119, 162, 195–96, 208–9, 226–28, 250–51

  ordination struggle, 208–10, 214, 217–18, 220, 223–31, 237–39, 314n.154

Woodard, George H., 108–11, 124–25, 131–32, 138–39, 156–57, 200, 250–51

Woodard, Lucila, 194–95

Woodruff, James E.P., 173–74

worker-priest movement, 21–22, 41, 65–66, 83–84, 266n.171

Wright, Nathan, Jr., 134–35, 155, 161, 290n.75